THE
ENCYCLOPEDIA OF
ADOPTION

THE ENCYCLOPEDIA OF ADOPTION

Christine Adamec
William L. Pierce, Ph.D.

Facts On File
New York • Oxford

THE ENCYCLOPEDIA OF ADOPTION
Copyright © 1991 by Christine Adamec and William L. Pierce, Ph.D.

All rights reserved. No part of this book may be reproduced or utilized in any form or by any means, electronic or mechanical, including photocopying, recording, or by any information storage or retrieval systems, without permission in writing from the publisher. For information contact:

    Facts On File, Inc.   Facts On File Limited
    460 Park Avenue South   Collins Street
    New York NY 10016   Oxford OX4 1XJ
    USA   United Kingdom

Library of Congress Cataloging-in-Publication Data

Adamec, Christine A., 1949–
    The encyclopedia of adoption / by Christine Adamec, William L. Pierce.
      p. cm.
    Includes bibliographical references and index.
    ISBN 0-8160-2108-2 (alk. paper)
      1. Adoption—United States—Encyclopedias. I. Pierce, William L.
II. Title.
HV875.55.A28   1991
362.7'34'0973—dc20   91-4629

A British CIP catalogue record for this book is available from the British Library.

Facts On File books are available at special discounts when purchased in bulk quantities for businesses, associations, institutions or sales promotions. Please call our Special Sales Department in New York at 212/683-2244 (dial 800/322-8755 except in NY, AK or HI) or in Oxford at 865/728399.

Composition by the Maple-Vail Book Manufacturing Group
Manufactured by Hamilton Printing Company
Printed in the United States of America

10 9 8 7 6 5 4 3 2 1

This book is printed on acid-free paper.

CONTENTS

Preface by Christine Adamec vii
Preface by William L. Pierce, Ph.D. ix
Acknowledgments xiii
Introduction—A Brief History of Adoption xvii
Entries A–Z 1
Appendixes 309
Bibliography 361
Index 373

PREFACE
BY CHRISTINE ADAMEC

Adoption is a fascinating and complex social institution that directly affects the lives of millions of people in the United States, not only members of the adoption triad but also their extended families and the many helping professionals who facilitate adoptions.

Numerous factors directly affect adoption as an institution and as a practice, including abuse, the foster care system, infertility and teenage pregnancy.

Increasing problems of drug abuse and drug-affected newborn infants, abandoned in hospitals or later abused or neglected, are of great concern to the adoption community. The "nature-nurture" argument, over whether heredity or environment is more important, has continued to intrigue scientists and the general public. As a result, *The Encyclopedia of Adoption* offers essays on heredity topics and also explores the impact of environment on adopted children.

Although a small percentage of adoptions are adoptions of adults by other adults, adoption is primarily about children. It is the children who are the adults of tomorrow. It has been said that the child is the parent to the adult, in that childhood experiences directly affect the adult's later values, beliefs and behavior. If this is true, then how important it must be for those both directly and peripherally involved with adoption to learn as much as possible about the adoption experience and how it affects children and their development into adults. In addition, we must consider how the children might develop if they are not adopted: If the sexually abused four-year-old girl remains in the abusive family? Or if the unwed mother who desires to make an adoption plan is talked out of it? Or if the unwed mother wants to parent her child and is talked into an unwanted adoption? Such events profoundly affect and shape the lives of the birthmother, the child and, when the child is adopted, the adopting parents.

One fact we can be sure of: Hundreds of thousands of "waiting children" need adoptive families now. They don't know about rules and regulations or why they have to stay in a group home or a series of foster homes. They only know they want a family to love and care about them.

Dr. Pierce and I know of no other encyclopedic reference to adoption in print. There are directories and listings of adoption agencies, there are books for professionals on specific topics, and there are a variety of how-to books. But there is no reference book that attempts to bring together the interdisciplinary research and knowledge on adoption that has been amassed and analyzed by social scientists, social workers, lawyers, physicians and others.

viii Preface

We have attempted to seek out as much of the current and previous research we could identify and report on these findings to the readers. We could not hope to include every reference, every study and every aspect of adoption within one volume; however, we have provided an extensive bibliography. *The Encyclopedia of Adoption* also provides appendixes with listings of adoption agencies, both public and private, adoption support groups and other related agencies and organizations.

This book is meant for both the general reader and the adoption expert. As a result, jargon has been kept to a minimum, or, when the use of jargon has been necessary, clear explanations on what these terms really mean and what they imply are provided. In addition, we have also discussed the meaning and the value of terminology in adoption and how, too often, common terms and phrases that are thoughtlessly used convey an overly negative view of adoption.

Dr. Pierce and I hope this book will not only enlighten the reader but may also inspire him or her to look further into this subject, even to launch a study or investigation on some aspect of adoption that needs further exploration. In my view, adoption is a very complicated, imperfect and yet wonderful institution. Learning about adoption further advances the knowledge and understanding among those who are directly affected by adoption—adopted individuals, birthparents and adoptive parents—as well as those within our society who set the standards and the lawmakers who make the rules we live by. The children are worth every effort we can make.

PREFACE
BY WILLIAM L. PIERCE, PH.D.

Adoption. The word is used in so many contexts. This encyclopedia only begins to touch on the complex issues that have been, are and will be involved when adoption is necessary, contemplated or avoided.

Adoption touches so many people in the United States and uniquely so because it is so much an American practice. It has touched the life of my family: Nearly 30 years ago, confronting secondary infertility, my wife Paula and I explored adoption with an agency though we were ultimately successful in having additional pregnancies.

Adoption has touched people around me as well. I have dear friends who have made the difficult decision, the loving decision, to make an adoption plan for their children. Some made the decision against the recommendations of their friends and the fathers of their babies. Some were pressured by circumstances, economics and other factors to make the decision for adoption—just as all of us are pressured about decisions we would rather not make, decisions that are often painful. Some few were manipulated or coerced into that decision, just as today teenagers and women are being manipulated or coerced into decisions they will later regret. It is tragic that this does happen. It is very important to offer understanding and support to these women today, even if their treatment has, at times, made many people bitter enemies of all adoption—including adoptions chosen freely and with truly informed consent by the women and men involved.

There will be those who disagree with a discussion of the pain that is sometimes part of adoption because these realities play into the hands of those in the media and elsewhere that so often talk about adoption solely in negative terms. Yes, adoption is a wonderful and positive social invention. But so also, at times, adoption can be a painful experience—especially for the woman who is most central to making that decision, the woman who gave birth to the child.

Adoption, some of those in the field say, is a lifelong experience. This comment is used in various ways to justify a range of actions that are sometimes appropriate, legal and ethical—and sometimes not. It is true that adoption affects large numbers of persons for many years, but so do other life events, such as the region where one happens to grow up, the schools one happens to attend, the family into which one is born or adopted, the religious beliefs and values with which one is reared and a host of other developments. Adoption is a lifelong experience; life is a lifelong experience. Adoption should be neither alibi nor justification—adoption should instead be a factor in one's life.

Adoption, despite all the media coverage, still remains a relatively vague notion to many people in our society. Even for generally well-educated persons, people concerned about ways of coping with unintended pregnancies—for themselves or their friends—the option of adoption may not even come to mind. As one born in 1936 and raised in a context where adoption should have been one of the alternatives that came to mind in an unplanned or untimely pregnancy, I know that this was not the case for me. Friends had crisis pregnancies and asked me for advice, yet the option of adoption never entered the picture. It was not until my professional life focused on the subject of unwed pregnancy, particularly among teenagers, in the mid-1970s, that this option and this word began to have any reality for me. I suspect this is true for a substantial segment of the population that has never had a direct connection with adoption, regardless of their levels of education, sophistication and so forth.

Adoption, however, does affect a great many people in America. If we consider all adoptions, not merely those adoptions of a child by someone or some couple who is not related to the child, we have numbers in the millions. Estimates are that there were at least 100,000 adoptions by U.S. citizens—related and unrelated, formal and informal, within the United States and abroad—per year over the last 30 years. That's a total of three million adoptions. But more people are involved in adoptions than the persons who were adopted. There are also the biological or birthparents of those three million—another six million. And there are the biological grandparents of those three million—another twelve million. And there are adoptive parents of those three million adopted people, over three million adoptive parents presuming at least one adoptive parent per child. And there are the adoptive grandparents of those three million, at least another twelve million.

If your arithmetic has been keeping score, we are already at a conservative estimate of thirty million people who are directly affected by adoption—and given the ages of those affected, it is reasonable to state that most of them are still alive. So, without counting all the aunts and uncles and cousins and siblings, without factoring in all the doctors and nurses and lawyers and clergy and counselors who have been indirectly touched by adoption, more than 10% of the total U.S. population of under 250 million has been touched by adoption.

And what a wonderful, hopeful, loving touch this adoption has been for most of these persons! Stepchildren have been adopted by loving stepparents. The singer Patti LaBelle is an adoptive mother. Loving grandmothers, aunts and sisters have adopted children within the family because their parents were unable or unwilling to care for them. The actor Jack Nicholson, who was raised by his mother's mother, has spoken about this experience. And there are those millions of families, including single-parent households, who legally adopted children who were not related to them. They are of all races and creeds and from every corner of America. And the children are from every corner of the globe. These millions of families have been created or expanded or enhanced by the loving choice of adoption.

The essence of adoption—and this is true in some religions as well, where adoption is part of the tradition—is the unconditional love of a parent for a child who may not have asked to be adopted but who certainly benefited from that loving decision. Adoption is about love—and not in a sentimental sense. Adoption is about the kind of love that is reflected when people put their names on waiting lists to adopt children born with spina bifida or Down Syndrome or children who test positive for the HIV virus (AIDS) or who were affected in utero by a mother's use of alcohol or drugs. Adoption is about the kind of love that will try with a child who seems beyond loving, a child who has been so affected by what others have handed him or her, often in the form of sexual and physical abuse, that there is little real chance of a longterm positive adjustment. But there is some chance, and some children do make miraculous recoveries and adjustments, and that chance for a competent adulthood is what adoption is also all about.

For decades, adoption was seen as the answer for only a portion of the many children who needed permanent families. It was presumed that only infants and young children should be adopted, and consequently, many older children remained in foster care. That has changed, thanks to the efforts of those who, perhaps a bit too naively, made the phrase "there is no such thing as an unadoptable child" part of the American belief system. That phrase has resulted in some heartbreak and some unrealistic expectations, but it has produced so much more in terms of hope and effort and results for children.

Adoption is about children above all, but it is also about adults. Two large groups of adults in particular benefit from adoption. One group is made up of those women who have a pregnancy that is a crisis to them, for whatever reason or reasons, and for which, after good counseling and time to consider their options, adoption is a godsend. Adoption is the answer they need to be able to make the decision that is right for them—a decision to allow them to move on with their lives, their careers, their families, their spouses. The fact that others, including the child, also benefit is a happy bonus.

Adoption benefits those who want to be parents, whether because they are infertile (as the National Center for Health Statistics says an estimated one in twelve couples of childbearing age are), whether they simply would like to raise more children or whether they are unmarried and believe they have a great deal to offer—and to gain themselves—by adopting a child who has no one he or she can call Mom or Dad.

Adoption, in my view, is clearly something that, on balance, is extraordinarily beneficial. It is beneficial to American society and ought to be ranked far ahead of many of our other innovations as one of our crowning achievements. Would that other nations, other cultures had the same complex of services to offer their citizens. Would that the estimated 10 million children who are growing up on the streets of cities all around the world had this option readily available in their own societies. Would that there was a worldwide understanding of the necessity to free up the children, to overcome the boundaries of race and culture and ethnicity and creed so that all children on earth would have someone to parent them and care for them.

Adoption, for all its benefits, is far from perfect—even in the United States. There are many areas where more work needs to be done, many aspects of our own practices that need drastic change now. For instance, the United States, instead of criticizing the practices of other countries regarding their children who need families, ought to free its own children who are waiting for international adoption.

Adoption, however, is a fortunate social invention in that it is the subject of increasing attention. There are many of us, with often diametrically opposed views, who are concentrating our efforts on adoption. Through all this ferment that at times can degenerate into outright squabbling, there are real achievements, and real progress is being made.

A decade ago, there was an oversimplified view of adoption, especially in the minds of those of us who were operating from a context of agency adoption. We thought, in essence, that agencies could do no wrong and private adoption practitioners could do no right. The last decade has taught us something about that prejudiced view: There are good and bad agencies and good and bad private adoption practitioners. The task now is to try and sort out the better from the less good, to try and improve the practices of those who are good and ethical and to remove from the field those—agencies or others—who are not.

There are other changes as well, too numerous to discuss here. But perhaps the most important change is exemplified by this book. That change is in the area of information about adoption.

Americans are almost comical in their enthusiasm for information and facts. We often believe that, given the facts, eventually we will come to the right decision about things.

Adoption is no exception. So we have had an explosion of facts. The explosion has been, in context, rather modest since so little information existed for so long. But in terms of what is being written and said about adoption, there has been substantial growth.

It may be that the persons who were born in 1966 and 1976 and 1986 will not say, as I have said, that they were largely ignorant of the benefits and shortcomings of adoption. It may be that as we offer this initial encyclopedia, as students and professionals and ordinary citizens read its entries and follow up on the leads we provide, that there will be more understanding of adoption in all its manifestations. We certainly hope this book will stimulate others to study adoption and the services and systems related to it. We hope there will be more careful research and more targeted spending. We hope there will be more dialogue and less name-calling. We hope there will be, finally, more hope and less despair, more love and less hate, among all the individuals and groups, whether affected directly or peripherally.

As you read and use this book, I invite you to send me your comments, criticisms and suggestions at the following address.

National Committee For Adoption
1930 17th Street NW
Washington, D.C. 20009

ACKNOWLEDGMENTS

Without the assistance of many talented and knowledgeable professionals, this interdisciplinary compendium of sociological, psychological, psychiatric, legal and medical information would not have been possible. We owe a great debt of gratitude to many people.

First, we would like to thank the many dedicated researchers who have so carefully studied the numerous complex aspects of adoption and the topics related or important to the field of adoption. Some of them have spent years of their lives dedicated to uncovering information that has helped and will continue to help adopted individuals, adoptive parents, birthparents and the wide variety of adoption professionals who seek to assist the entire triad. We are convinced that their professional studies, doctoral dissertations, books and magazine features deserve to be read in their entirety by many people. We hope that readers of this volume will be encouraged to explore more freely many of the materials we have only begun to tap. We hope our book will encourage many readers in their further studies and analyses of the fascinating topic of adoption.

Although many people helped us with this book, we would like to acknowledge three adoption professionals in particular. They agreed to read the entire manuscript and offered us many constructive criticisms and suggestions: Marietta Spencer, M.S.W., adoption triad consultant and founder of Post Legal Services for the Children's Home Society of Minnesota in St. Paul and an adoption author; Richard Zeilinger, M.S.W., an adoption professional with extensive experience at the Children's Bureau of New Orleans, a Louisiana voluntary agency; and Jerome Smith, Ph.D., author of *You're Our Child: The Adoption Experience* and a therapist, adoption expert and faculty member of the School of Social Work at the University of Indiana at Indianapolis.

There are also many people we would like to thank individually for reviewing one or more of our essays and pointing out matters that needed to be clarified or expanded or that had been inadvertently omitted. Our thanks to the following people: Howard Altstein, Ph.D., associate dean, School of Social Work, University of Maryland at Baltimore; Christine A. Bachrach, Ph.D., statistician, National Institutes of Health; Michael P. Bentzen, Esq.; Kristi Boattenhamer, Concerned United Birthparents staff; Pamela Beere Briggs, congressional fellow/legislative aide to U.S. Congresswoman Patricia Schroeder; Susan Brite, director of publications for the Child Welfare League of America; Aaron Britvan, Esq.; the Congressional Coalition on Adoption staff; David M. Brodzinsky, Ph.D., adoption author and psychologist; Susan K. Coti, office of news and media production, National Association of Social Workers; Susan Cox, director of development, Holt International Children's Services; Douglas R. Donnelly, Esq.; Richard Ducote, Esq.; Nancy Erickson, Esq.; Gordon Evans, information and services office, National Association of Foster Parents; Florence Anna Fisher, founder and director of Adoptees' Liberty Movement Association (ALMA); Ruth Frank, editor of *Adoptalk,* North American Council on Adoptable Children (NACAC); Susan Freivalds, executive director, Adoptive Families of America; Mark Hardin, director, foster care project, American Bar Association; Gloria Hochman, director of communications and marketing, National Adoption Center; Joan H. Hollinger, Esq., professor of law, University of Detroit School of Law; U.S. Senator Gordon Humphrey and his staff; Claudia Jewett, author, therapist and international consultant on separation and loss issues; Patricia Johnston, author, adoption and infertility publisher and chair of the board, RESOLVE; David H. Kim, A.C.S.W., president, Holt International Children's Services; Steven M. Kirsch, Esq.; Betty Laning, board member, International Concerns Committee for Children; Lawrence B. Lennon, Ph.D., Lennon & Associates; Adele Liskov, associate staff for appropriations, office of Rep. William Lehman (FL); Neil Lombardi, M.D., director of medical services, St. Mary's Hospital for Children, Bayside, New York; Hope Marindin, director, Committee for Single Adoptive Parents; Penelope Maza, Ph.D., senior assistant to the assistant commissioner for the Children's Bureau, U.S. Department of Health and Human Services; Patricia O'Neal-Williams, national staff director, One Church, One Child; Marilyn Panichi, A.C.S.W., director, Adoption Information Center of Illinois; William D. Mosher, Ph.D., statistician, Family Growth Survey Branch, National Center for Health Statistics; Paul Placek, Ph.D., Chief Followback Survey Branch, National Center for Health Statistics; Ruby Lee Piester, executive director emeritus, Edna Gladney Center; Robyn Quinter, communications director, American Adoption Congress; Jeannie I. Rosoff, president, the Alan Guttmacher Institute; David Shover, executive director, Council on Accreditation of Services for Families and Children; Peggy Soule, director of the CAP Book; Beverly Stubbee, M.S.W., director, program operations division of the Children's Bureau, U.S. Department of Health and Human Services; and Joellen Williams, perinatal/pediatric social worker, Holmes Regional Medical Center.

We would both like to thank the staff of the National Committee For Adoption for their rapid responses to urgent questions and requests. Thanks to Mary Beth Seader, vice president, and Dawn Bes, administrative assistant.

Several important people have played a major role in helping with the research of this book. The entire staff of the Palm Bay Public Library in Palm Bay, Florida, from library director Karen Nelson to the women at the front desk, have been tremendously supportive and helpful to author Christine Adamec during this project. In particular, library assistant Ginny Pettit has prepared and submitted countless requests for the journal articles and books from within the United States and from faraway lands. She has also provided many practical suggestions.

Shirley Welch, librarian at the Brevard County Library Services in Cocoa, and the interlibrary loan staff at the Florida State Library in Tallahassee, Florida have filled requests for a broad array of journal articles and books, going the extra mile to locate the particularly hard-to-find items.

Debra Smith, A.C.S.W., assistant director of the National Adoption Information Clearinghouse, provided extensive assistance and information on adoption and made many helpful recommendations.

Special thanks to Tracy Lewis, congressional aide to Rep. Bill Nelson (FL), for her assistance in tracking down and obtaining a wide array of government articles and documents on adoption and related subjects.

Annette Melnicove, law librarian at the Brevard County Law Library in Melbourne, Florida provided assistance in identifying and locating a broad variety of legal articles.

Acknowledgments xv

We would also like to especially thank our editor, Neal Maillet, who is himself an adopted adult, for his great interest in this project and his thoroughness in offering critically important suggestions for improvement.

Although we deeply appreciate the assistance of these individuals, as well as the assistance of many others, we alone are responsible for any errors of fact or interpretation or for any inadvertent omissions.

Christine Adamec would like to thank, above all people, her husband and best friend, John M. Adamec Jr. His unflagging conviction of the importance of this topic and his total support has been immeasurable.

INTRODUCTION—A BRIEF HISTORY OF ADOPTION

Adoption, the lawful transfer of parental obligations and rights, is not solely a child of the 20th century but is a very old and constantly evolving institution. Societies have formally sanctioned the adoption of children, or closely similar arrangements, for more than 4,000 years, since the Babylonian Code of Hammurabi in 2285 B.C.—and probably before recorded history. Adoption is also mentioned in the Hindu Laws of Manu, written about 200 B.C. Perhaps the earliest known adoption is mentioned in the Bible, which describes the adoption of Moses by the Pharaoh's daughter.

The ancient Romans supported and codified adoption in their laws; in fact, Julius Caesar continued his dynasty by adopting his nephew Octavian, who became Caesar Augustus. The ancient Greeks, Egyptians, Assyrians, Germans, Japanese and many other societies all practiced some form of adoption.

Adoption satisfied religious requirements in some cases; for example, in the Shinto religion, ancestral worship and the performing of certain religious rituals were perceived as necessary and important reasons for the institution of adoption. Adopted individuals could still carry on the family lineage and rituals when the family did not have biological children.

Despite a disparity of motivations in cultures worldwide for institutionalizing adoption formally or informally, the common denominator among them all was that adoption functionally satisfied the needs of society or the family.

Although the adopted person usually benefited from the adoption, such benefit was peripheral and was generally a happy accident. This underlying societal view sharply contrasts with views toward adoption today, when the needs and interests of the child are usually considered the primary reason and purpose for adoption as an institution. This is not to say that the benefits of adoption to society are not important. For example, many individuals believe that orphanage-raised children may be less effective as adults than are adopted children.

Today, most cultures worldwide provide for children needing families, although they may not provide the legal family membership that is inherent in adoption. Some Islamic cultures have interpreted the Koran to ban adoption altogether; however, in all these societies, orphaned and abandoned children are cared for despite the lack of formal adoption. The legislation of several Islamic countries contains detailed rules on alternative solutions for family care, such as *kafalah*.

Notable exceptions in Islamic societies to the ban on formal adoptions are the predominantly Islamic countries of Tunisia and Indonesia, where Muslims may adopt. In addition, in Egypt and Syria, where the system of personal religious laws is followed, Christians may adopt.

Most Western societies (with the exception of England) base their adoption laws on the original Roman code or the later Napoleonic code. Most experts agree that U.S. adoption law has combined aspects of Roman law with its own U.S. adaptations.

Adoption is a very modern institution in Europe, which has followed the lead of the United States. The first adoption law in England was the Adoption of Children Act of 1926. The Swedes enacted their first Adoption Act in 1917, and in 1959 adopted children in Sweden became full-fledged family members by law. Modern adoption laws came into being in West Germany in 1977.

It is critically important to understand that adoption laws and practices should be evaluated based on their functionality and the existing conditions of the time rather than on our contemporary values only. How adoption was and is now perceived in society and how adoption was and is now actually practiced has depended on a myriad of factors: social, economic and political conditions; societal attitudes toward parentless and deprived children; out-of-wedlock births; minimum standards of parenting; views on parental rights and children's rights; views on the importance of property and inheritance as well as other issues in the social order; the perception of the overriding importance of blood ties; and religious and moral values. This essay will only be able to touch on key issues within several periods in past history and in modern times.

Historical Adoption Practices

Babylonian adoption laws stated, "If a man has taken a young child from his waters to sonship and has reared him up no one has any claim against the nursling."

There are also biblical references to adoption; for example, Moses' mother, in an attempt to save her child from death by the Pharaoh's decree, placed him in a reed basket at the edge of the Nile River. Found by the Pharaoh's daughter, Moses was later formally adopted by her. (His birthmother served as his nurse during Moses' infancy.)

The ancient Romans practiced two types of adoptions: "adrogatio" (or "adrogation") and "adoptio" (or "adoption"). Adrogation usually referred to the adoption of an adult male, who became the legal heir of the adopter.

Adrogation was fairly common in ancient Rome, according to author John Boswell. Its purpose was to enable a childless man to ensure the continuity of his family name and also to provide someone to carry out religious rituals and memorials after his death.

In contrast, adoption was the process by which a minor child became a legal heir and dependent of the adoptive parent, with the agreement of his or her biological father. According to the law at that time, and based on the Laws of the Twelve Tables (mid-500s B.C.) the birthfather would perhaps sell his son up to three times and his daughter or granddaughter once, after which he could not reclaim the children. Unquestioned family allegiance was expected whether the person was adopted as a child or an adult.

The "paterfamilias" (male family head) had great power and could literally condemn his children to death. He could also sell them or abandon them (apparently girl children were more likely to be abandoned) with no negative social or legal consequences accruing to such acts.

In Roman law only men were allowed to adopt until A.D. 291. Thereafter, women were allowed in special circumstances to adopt, for example, in the event of the loss of a biological child.

It is unclear whether the ancient Hebrews recognized adoption, although some experts have contended that St. Paul referred to adoptions among Hebrews in his writings, while other experts contend that his examples referred to adoptions among the Romans or Galatians.

Laws slowly changed and evolved. Under the reign of Byzantine emperor Justinian (A.D. 527–565), the adoptive parents, the person to be adopted and the head of the birth family all were required to formally appear before a magistrate in order for an adoption to be legally recognized (a precursor of the "consent" aspect of Western law).

Some societies attached military significance to the act of adoption; for example, in ancient Germany, military ceremonies occurred at the point of adoption, with weapons placed in the hands of the adopted person. In ancient France, the adopted person swore to defend the adoptive family.

The English law of inheritance, with its heavy emphasis on blood lines became prominent in the Western world, and little or no provisions were made for a family name to "live on" through adopted children.

The concept of primogeniture—a practice whereby the eldest son would inherit the family property and, in turn, his eldest son would inherit from him—was core to the English, Germans and other Europeans.

According to law professor C. M. A. McCauliff, "There could be no question of adoption in England so long as the heir at law held sway. The notion of any heir outside a natural orderly succession was repugnant to English society."

Legitimation, an issue of concern for centuries, was seen as a particularly important issue to the Christian church. In A.D. 335, the Emperor Constantine, a Christian, ordered that children born to unmarried parents who later married would automatically become legitimate children. This legitimation law was ultimately abolished in 1235 in England, after which legitimation was to be determined by a jury on a case by case basis.

Legitimation was especially important in England because it was bound up in inheritance and rights. Since there was no legal way to adopt a child, legitimation was the only route for a child born out of wedlock to be considered an heir.

Children who needed parents were cared for by relatives, friends or others who "took pity on them." Or they fended for themselves, living as thieves, prostitutes or beggars. Abandoned children were also at risk of being kidnapped by individuals who would put out their eyes or cut off their feet, mutilating them so they could be more effectively used as beggars.

It is also important to remember that the Black Death claimed the lives of many thousands of people in the 14th century. Thus survival was the primary goal at that time, and many people could only afford to care for children related to them. Consequently, many children who were orphaned quickly died.

The Elizabethan Poor Law of 1601 formally provided for poor people in England, requiring parents either to care for their children or indenture them to others. This law also was the basis for the local systems of public charity in the colonies that later became the United States. Local overseers of the poor provided local relief for orphans. Although there were people in Europe who wished to legally tie children to their families through adoption, there were no provisions for such status to be attained.

In some areas, the situation for unwed mothers and their infants became very desperate.

Law professor C. M. A. McCauliff described a horrifying practice of unscrupulous "baby farmers," partially quoting the *Report of the Select Committee on the Protection of Infant Life:*

"In Victorian England, unwed mothers were practically forced to give up their babies, who were then sent to baby-farming houses where they were fed 'a mixture of laudanum, lime, cornflour, water, milk and washing powder . . . with rare exceptions they all of them die in a very short time.'"

According to author Diana Dewar, baby farmers took out insurance policies on children's lives and ensured their rapid demise so they could collect payments. These people also reassured unsuspecting single mothers that their children would be placed with loving families; however, many baby farmers would subsequently sell the children to the highest bidders.

Not everyone was indifferent to the plight of the children, and some individuals decided to take action. Nineteenth century British social reformer Thomas Coram, horrified by the sight of abandoned dead babies in the streets, started a foundling hospital. Handel, the famous composer, donated all the royalties for his work *The Messiah* to the hospital.

Because people in Britain could not adopt children and have parental rights and obligations transferred to them (as adoptive parents), many children who were orphaned or whose parents could not care for them were placed in foster homes or almshouses.

The concept of *parens patriae,* wherein the government acts as a parent, enabled the government to take such actions. This aspect of British common law has been incorporated into U.S. law and is part of U.S. child protection statutes and of the Indian Child Welfare Act, allowing the state to remove children from abusive or neglectful families.

The concept of the dominance of parental rights prevailed prior to the establishment of adoption and child protection statutes. Many 19th century individuals in Britain (as well as in other countries) who were otherwise interested in fostering children were fearful of doing so because they could be subjected to blackmail threats from birthparents demanding money in exchange for allowing the foster parents to rear the child. (Recall, if you will, the attempt at blackmail by Eliza Doolittle's father present in the movie "My Fair Lady" for an example of practices common at the time or read *Oliver Twist* by Charles Dickens to gain a feel for the hopelessness and helplessness of children during this era.)

In addition, unscrupulous relatives could reclaim the child and literally sell him to tramps, prostitutes or anyone. It must be remembered that children were not revered or protected as they are now by statute and were often conceptualized as property rather than persons. Yet many kind individuals would have eagerly adopted children had that legal option been available and had they been assured that the integrity of their family would not be disrupted by birthparents or others.

It was not until 1851 that the first modern adoption statute worthy of the name was passed, and it was in the state of Massachusetts: "An Act to Provide for the Adoption of Children." Adoptions were, however, taking place with regularity in Texas, Louisiana and other localities long before 1851. Although most law in the United States is based on British common law, the United States was the pioneer in modern adoption. When the English passed their first adoption laws in 1926, they based them on U.S. adoption laws, specifically, New York adoption laws.

Prior to the Massachusetts adoption statute, no judicial review or court appearance was required to adopt a child. As a result, it was considered to be the first modern adoption law that formally (and, by today's standards, very minimally) took into account the interests of the child. It is interesting to note that the adoption statute in Massachusetts was barely noticed by the press and few, if any, people envisioned the impact of this statute on other states or noted that Massachusetts was a pacesetter in adoption law.

The institution of adoption cannot be fully discussed without also providing a brief historical overview of the institutions of foster care, or "placing out," as well as the institution of the group home, also known as the almshouse, "poor house" and orphanage.

To date, the argument continues, not just in the United States but worldwide, as to whether institutional care or foster care is preferable for children who cannot remain with their birthparents and who need temporary care. This essay will also include a brief overview of these institutions.

Orphaned Children and Adoption in the United States Informal adoptions were the norm in the colonial days of early America, long before the passage of the Massachusetts law.

Governor Sir William Phips of Massachusetts was allegedly the first recorded adoptive father in the original thirteen colonies. He adopted a child in 1693. The word "adoption" appeared in Governor Phips' will, as well as in the act of the colonial legislature that allowed for the legal name change of the son.

In fact, it was fairly common for colonial legislatures to pass special bills recognizing the adoption of a child. Some historians have hypothesized that legislators became weary of passing so many bills for individual cases, bills that increased to such a great extent they bottlenecked other legislation. As a result, the legislators may have eased their legislative load by legalizing what was already common.

Laws prior to the 1851 Massachusetts adoption law, for example, in Texas (1850) and Mississippi (1846), have not been considered adoption laws by experts because such laws simply enabled individuals to leave their estates to nonrelatives in a similar manner in which property deeds were registered.

The groundwork for a philosophy favoring adoption had been laid well ahead of this time by Thomas Jefferson, who detested the concept of primogeniture and dedicated time during his early political career as a member of the Virginia House of Delegates to eliminate primogeniture in Virginia, ultimately succeeding in 1783. It's interesting to note that some British parents, still shackled by the bonds of primogeniture, sent their second or later-born sons to Virginia subsequent to Virginia's lifting of primogeniture.

Another status granted to children during the colonial era of the United States was that of godchild, and often the godchild did assume the name of the godparent. In addition, godchildren frequently inherited from godparents, although such an inheritance had to be stipulated in the will of the godparent.

According to Kawashima, one man left his estate to his wife and ordered that after her death the property would be left to a goddaughter, "except for one cow, which was given to the other goddaughter."

In his 1694 will, New Yorker William Moncom bequeathed half his property to his godson and the other half was divided among his three children.

Some colonists informally fostered orphaned children, treating them as adopted children. These early "foster families" frequently developed great affection for the children, and in some cases, the children inherited property when the "master" died; for example, as early as 1769, William Russell of Georgia provided a dowry of 300 pounds to Anna Hunter, a child who resided with him, to be paid "on the day of her marriage or when she became of age."

Another key problem of the period was that illegitimacy was seen as evil and a shocking rip in the fabric of socially acceptable behavior and norms. Many people believed that if they solved the problem of the out-of-wedlock mother and child by arranging for another family to raise the child, they were condoning her "sin" and "making it easy" for her. Instead, it was believed she should be forced to raise her child, whether she wanted to or not, an opinion that continues to be held by some individuals today.

The effect on the child of pressuring the mother into parenting (or seeing the child reside in an orphanage and contributing money toward the child's support) was not of concern to society at large because the child was illegitimate and many people presumed the child was probably "bad," too. The severe shunning that Hester Prynne faced in the book *The Scarlet Letter* gives an idea of the prevalent view toward women who bore children out of wedlock and their children.

In later years, states began to create laws requiring investigations of the prospective adoptive parents. Michigan's 1891 statute was the first to order such an investigation (the precursor to today's home study) to further protect the child.

However, it should be noted that child protection laws were not passed until many years after the adoption statutes of Massachusetts and other states were legislated. It was not until an incident occurred in 1874 in New York City, in which Mary Ellen Wilson was severely beaten and abused by her parents, that any type of formal action was taken to protect children.

Outraged neighbors were unable to convince anyone to intervene to help Mary Ellen. Finally, the New York Society for the Prevention of Cruelty to Animals intervened to protect children, and the New York Society for the Prevention of Cruelty to Children, the first organization in the world to protect children from abuse, was subsequently formed in 1874.

The Rise and Fall of the Almshouse

In the 19th and early 20th century, not only unwed parents but poor people in general were often regarded with disdain and contempt. "Outdoor relief" was the early precursor to today's Aid to Families with Dependent Children (AFDC) and referred to cash or items such as food that were given to people who remained in their home rather than residing in an institution. Such relief was administered by the town or county in most cases; for example, the towns generally administered outdoor relief in New England, and the system of overseers was first introduced in Boston in 1691. In other areas of the country, the county managed outdoor relief.

In addition to almshouses or outdoor relief there were also two other methods of dealing with the poor: One was literally selling the poor, and the other was selling their labor. According to historian Michael B. Katz, the labor of the individual was literally auctioned off to the highest bidder in a form of slavery of the poor. Understandably, many people considered such practices to be unfair and inhumane. Children were also routinely apprenticed or indentured to families, some of whom were kind, some of whom were not.

There were also numerous problems of settlement (determining which town or city was financially responsible for poor individuals) in the 19th century and early 20th century. Sometimes overseers of the poor actually transported poverty-stricken individuals to other towns to avoid a financial liability.

Some social reformers believed outdoor relief was bad for the character of the individual and could ultimately encourage a class of individuals dependent on public welfare. In addition, outdoor relief was perceived as bad for children, the mentally ill and other categories of helpless individuals. Outdoor relief has always cost much less than institutionalization; however, social reformers believed that almshouses and later other institutions, such as orphanages, would be far better for the individuals as well as for society.

As a result, the rise of the almshouse (poorhouse) began in the mid-18th century. Yet although the almshouse was seen as the ultimate answer for indigent people by social reformers of the day, outdoor relief continued on throughout the almshouse era; for example, at the height of the almshouse era in 1880, there were an estimated 89,909 individuals residing in almshouses in New York, contrasted to 70,667 individuals receiving outdoor relief.

Supporters of almshouses stated that individuals would no longer be auctioned off nor would they receive outdoor relief and be allowed to be indolent. The settlement problem would be solved because the institutions would be county-run. It was also believed the almshouse would be a place where better character would be ingrained and where individuals would not wish to stay too long.

But the almshouse social experiment, initially running an almost parallel course in England, was not the ideal solution envisioned by early social reformers such as Josiah Quincy, author of the Quincy Report in 1821, or by Douglas Yates, author of the Yates Report of 1824. Many children suffered greatly, and too many died.

Infants were particularly at risk, primarily because they had to be breast-fed before the advent of safe formulas for infants. Wet nurses sometimes were used to breast-feed babies, although this solution was often unsatisfactory, due to unsanitary conditions and other problems.

According to author Homer Folks, 514 infants were nursed in a New York City almshouse in 1849, and of these, 280 died. "Boarding out" of infants with foster parents was begun again in 1871. (It had previously been a policy, then was discontinued.) Said Folks, "It was so successful in reducing the death rate that in 1900 and 1901 it was extended to include all foundlings coming directly under the care of New York."

When the child was weaned from the breast, he was usually returned to the almshouse, despite any affection and love that may have developed between the foster mother and the child.

Although the goal of those who recommended almshouses was the creation and maintenance of clean and safe facilities, almshouses were far more often crowded and disease-ridden institutions, rampant with such dangerous and then-fatal diseases as cholera or pneumonia as well as numerous chronic diseases. Nor were they safe: Some almshouses housed juvenile delinquents and seriously mentally ill individuals (and the indigent elderly) in the same facility that held the children of paupers.

The children were often not educated, nor were they sent to public schools because of the fear they would spread contagious diseases to the other children. As a result, they could neither read nor write nor were they trained for any trade, perpetuating the horrors of poverty into their adulthood.

Concerned citizens and child advocates became vocally opposed to almshouses in the mid-1800s when a variety of reports were written condemning almshouses. In 1856, a state Senate committee in New York issued a denunciation of the almshouse system. In 1857, commissioners of the poor in Charleston, South Carolina described dismal conditions at an almshouse, which was "swarming with vermin." In addition, although almshouses had been perceived as a means to encourage idle individuals to work, often people living in almshouses could not find employment, either because of youth or infirmity or because of a lack of available jobs.

As a result, although the almshouses had initially been created because of concerned citizens' strong convictions that they would be far preferable to outdoor relief, the reality did not resemble the dream.

Finally, by the end of the 1800s, many almshouses were no longer operating, and children who could not remain with their parents were instead housed in orphanages or placed with foster families. Institutions were created to care for the mentally ill, aged and juvenile offenders, thus separating the many categories of the poor that had formerly been housed together.

Several states led a movement away from almshouses and toward placing children in orphanages or with families; for example, in 1883, Ohio passed a law banning children over age three in almshouses, unless they were separated from indigent adults. Ohio dropped the age limit allowed in almshouses to one year in 1898.

According to the 1880 census, there were 7,770 children in almshouses throughout the United States. Author Homer Folks estimated the number to have declined to about 5,000 by 1890.

It's important to note that some prominent child welfare experts today are calling for a return to orphanages to care for the increasing numbers of abandoned, neglected or abused infants and children born to drug-addicted mothers. Proponents of modern-day orphanages insist that such facilities are not or would not be Dickensian scourges but instead would be clean and safe homes. Of course, it could also be argued that 19th century orphanage advocates clearly envisioned clean and safe facilities and did not wish for children to suffer from a lack of bonding to parental figures or from a failure to thrive.

In the 19th century and early 20th century, orphaned children or the children of poverty-stricken parents were often "put out" or apprenticed, often to childless couples.

If a family died and there were no living relatives or persons named in a will who would care for the child, then the court was required to bind them out to a responsible person.

Children who were indentured did not usually assume the name of the masters nor were they given any legal rights or inheritance rights. In addition, the responsibility of the master usually ended when the child reached adulthood and was given $50, a Bible and two suits of clothes. Children were not legally protected from abuse or overwork at the hands of the master, either.

Indenture was later decried by many as a form of slavery, although this practice persisted for some years even after the abolition of slavery.

The indenture system ultimately fell out of favor by the early 1900s, at about the same time that society decided against housing children and adults together in almshouses. Wrote Homer Folks, "The bound child has often been alluded to as typifying loneliness, neglect, overwork, and a consciousness of being held in low self-esteem."

Placing Out: The Orphan Train

Experts estimate over 10,000 homeless children roamed the streets of New York City in the mid-1800s, living on the ill-gotten gains from crimes they committed. Police reports in New York City in 1852 revealed that in 11 wards, 2,000 homeless girls ages 8 to 16 were arrested for theft. Things only got worse: According to author Francis Lane in his 1932 doctoral dissertation for the Catholic University of America in Washington, D.C., there were 5,880 commitments of female children for vagrancy in 1860.

Part of the problem was that there was almost no need for "honest labor" of children in the large cities, which was why the children had turned to dishonest labor. (This was prior to the child labor movement, and at this time, everyone worked.) Large numbers of immigrants streamed into the major cities of the Northeast, such as New York City, between 1847 and 1860.

There was insufficient demand for the labor of this huge influx of adults, let alone children. But at the same time, the midwestern and western farmers suffered a severe labor shortage.

Social reformers such as Charles Loring Brace, founder of the New York Children's Aid Society, saw almshouses and indenture as the problem, not the solution, and Brace initiated the Orphan Train movement in the mid-1850s. Brace believed that sending children to distant families would solve two problems: the family's desire for a child and the child's need for a family.

An estimated 150,000 children from the Northeast traveled to the Midwest, West and South to foster or adoptive homes from 1854 until the movement ended in about 1929, when the Great Depression hit the entire United States very hard, especially farmers. (Some of these children were not placed by the New York Children's Aid Society, Brace's organization, but were actually indentured by other agencies.)

From 1854 to 1929, these homeless children were placed on trains and taken to rural sites concentrated in the Midwest and West in search of rural homes where the children could live and work. The children ranged from as young as about one year old to age 16 or 17.

Limited follow-ups of the children revealed that then, as now, the children who adapted the most readily were usually the younger children, and the older teenagers faced the greatest difficulty in adjusting to a radically different environment.

Most of the children were poor, and some had been involved in minor or serious infractions of the law. Many also had siblings and were separated from them for life as a result of the move. Yet most of the children (including two later governors—Andrew Burke of North Dakota and John Brady of the Alaska Territory—and other prominent citizens) made successful new lives for themselves, leaving behind them severe poverty and desolation.

Brace was initially supported in his movement by organizations within the Catholic Church and other groups. The Sisters of Charity of St. Vincent de Paul and the New York Foundling Hospital, for example, were both actively involved in the Orphan Train movement. The movement was also known as the "Placing Out" program and preceded adoption as we know it today. (It is unknown how many of the children received de facto family membership.)

The children left the train at each stop and were chosen or not chosen by people who came to the station to see them. The children were "put up" on platforms for all to see, which is supposedly the source of the phrase "put up for adoption."

Critics questioned whether all the homeless children Brace sent off on the orphan trains were really without parents or relatives and challenged whether or not sufficient checking and safeguards were made of parental rights. Notice to birthparents was not required, and consequently, there were parents who might (and did) object to their children being "placed out."

In addition, most of the homeless children were from Jewish or Catholic immigrant parents, yet large numbers were placed by Brace in Protestant homes. Laws were subsequently created in many states, including New York, that mandated or strongly suggested religious matching, so that children of Catholic parents would be placed only with Catholic adoptive parents, Jews with Jews and so forth.

Critics also said Brace made insufficient investigations of the foster or adoptive homes and little follow-up or documentation. In Brace's defense, communications and transportation systems of his era had little resemblance to our society today: He could not just pick up the phone and contact someone in the Midwest nor could he send or receive fax messages.

Today one group that helps keep the history of the Orphan Train era alive is the Orphan Train Heritage Society of America, based in Springdale, Arkansas. Members, who were part of the Orphan Train or related to orphan train riders, assist each other in finding birth families and in reminiscing about their shared history.

Twentieth Century Adoption Adoption in the early 20th century was very different from adoption in the United States today. Most adoptions were still informal rather than legal, and adoption agencies did not become prominent until after World War II. Indeed, the first professional conference on adoption was held by the Child Welfare League of America in 1955. (The Child Welfare League of America was formed in 1921 and was first led by C.

C. Carstens, former director of the Massachusetts Society for the Prevention of Cruelty to Children.)

Many would-be adoptive parents could see no benefit to a legal adoption other than to provide for an inheritance, and there were no state or federal legal requirements to adopt or formally foster a child who they were rearing. Children needing parents were primarily cared for through orphanages ("orphan asylums") or by foster parents.

Confidentiality of the identities of the birthparents and adoptive parents was not commonly practiced, babies and children were bought and sold, and the whole concept of adoption was questioned by many as to whether or not it served a social good. Unwed mothers routinely advertised their children for sale in newspapers, and there was little or no protection for the children.

The economic climate of the early 1930s must also be taken into account: The Great Depression had forcibly ejected numerous people from their only means of livelihood, and poverty was rampant.

Society at large continued to view children born out of wedlock as liabilities, and the word "illegitimate" was often placed on birth certificates. The phrase "strangers of the blood" was used commonly to connote children raised by other than their biological parents or to connote the people who reared them. The word "bastard" was a value-laden insult against children born to unwed parents and was used with great effect.

Sometimes the birth certificate of a person born out of wedlock was a different color. Social reformers such as Edna Gladney of Texas believed labeling children from birth as "illegitimate" was a form of name-calling that was horrendously unfair to innocent children, often haunting them for life. She successfully fought to have references to illegitimacy removed from birth certificates in Texas in 1933. Said Edna Gladney in 1933, "There is no such thing as an illegitimate child. There are only illegitimate parents."

Unaware that moral values are received by children via parenting, child welfare experts and prospective parents worried a great deal about eugenics and genetics and whether or not the "illegitimate" child would or could ever turn out to be all right.

Still, lawful adoptions did occur and were sanctioned by the state in which the adoptive parents resided. Some states required a social investigation of the adopting parents, but many did not. Many adoptions were arranged by the parties themselves (birthparents and adopting parents); others were arranged by physicians, attorneys and other intermediaries.

According to a 1927 analysis by Boston researcher Ida Parker of 810 adoptions, about two-thirds of the adoptions in Massachusetts had not been arranged by agencies but were instead independent adoptions.

When adopted, infants were not placed immediately in adoptive homes but were held back for months, primarily because society at large believed it was important to ensure they were not "defective children." At this time, children born out of wedlock were still regarded as potentially abnormal and hence the great caution.

In addition, many individuals continued to believe that women should care for their infants, whether they wanted to or not. Five states, Maryland, Minnesota, North Carolina, Ohio and South Carolina, actually passed laws requiring birthmothers to parent their infants for a minimum of three to six months.

Another change was the institution of confidential adoptions. States began to pass laws requiring the sealing of the birth certificates of adopted children in the 1930s. The basis of the emphasis on confidentiality or anonymity and privacy was not only to protect the privacy rights of the adopted child, birthmother and adoptive family from the prying and curious eyes of outsiders but also to stress that the adoptive family would completely assume the parental rights and obligations in regard to the child.

An element of protection for the security of the family is inherent in these laws as well in that the birthparents might intrude or make later monetary or other demands on the adoptive parents or the adopted child if their identities were known.

The majority of states have retained confidentiality in adoptions today, although some groups actively seek to open all identifying adoption information. These groups, most notably the Adoptees' Liberty Movement Association (ALMA), state that the rights of the adopted adult should be of primary concern. This group believes an adopted adult's desire for information from the original birth record should take precedence over a birthparent's desire to withhold such information or to retain his or her privacy. They do not, however, believe a birthparent has a corresponding automatic right to the new amended birth record with identifying information about the adoptive parents and adopted child.

A variety of important social reforms occurred in the 1930s. By 1913, 20 states had passed laws authorizing pensions for indigent women, primarily widows. Historian Michael Katz says these laws were used as a basis for the Aid to Dependent Children portion of the 1935 Economic Security Act, itself a basis for today's Aid to Families with Dependent Children (AFDC).

Child labor laws were passed, limiting the use of children in the factories. Interestingly enough, the removal of children from the workplace, along with theories of child psychology by popular psychologists such as G. Stanley Hall, led to an even greater enhancement of the value of the child. According to Katz, "A seismic shift in the perceived value of children underlay the new child psychology." As a result, by the late 1930s, adopting a child for his or her labor was no longer seen as a valid or acceptable motive. The shift to wanting to adopt a child because of a desire to become a loving parent had begun.

Starting in about the 1950s, society began to accept and broadly sanction the idea of adopting infants, and infant adoptions flourished until the 1970s. In 1951, an estimated 70% of the children adopted in 21 states were under the age of one year. Unwed mothers were urged or pressured to choose adoption over single parenthood.

Prospective adoptive parents did not need to wait many years before being able to adopt infants, and the system appeared to be in approximate equilibrium insofar as the number of infants needing families and the number of couples desiring to adopt infants was roughly equivalent.

From about the 1950s to the 1970s, most adoption agencies and adoption intermediaries, such as attorneys or physicians, concentrated on placing healthy white infants with adoptive families. The number of nonrelative adoptions increased from about 33,800 nationwide in 1951 to 89,200 in 1970.

During this period, there still existed strong social disapproval of premarital or extramarital sex and out-of-wedlock pregnancies. Unmarried pregnant women were often expected to keep the impending birth a secret and either wait out their pregnancies at a maternity home or visit a "sick aunt" until the child was born. Illegitimacy was a stigma and a problem: There was even a National Council on Illegitimacy.

It should be mentioned that, in all these changes and activities, primary concern by society overall centered around white people, and few provisions were made for black orphans and orphans of other racial or ethnic minorities until the late 19th century. These minorities usually raised such children within the extended family or community, and children born out of wedlock were not as stigmatized in their social groups.

However, the Colonial Orphan Asylum, founded in 1836, was the first orphanage for black children and the predecessor of the Harlem-Dowling children's service agency in New York City, which still exists today.

Authors Patricia Turner Hogan and Sau Fong-Siu said some black children were placed in almshouses and were indentured; however, the social welfare available to poor black children was limited and often even more harshly administered than the dismal situation faced by the white children of the time.

Black children were generally excluded from the mainstream charities as part of a general pattern of racial discrimination, a pattern that persisted until the landmark U.S. Supreme Court decision of *Brown vs. Board of Education* in 1954. As a result, blacks began to develop their own child welfare. Not until the 1960s and the civil rights movement did blacks become prominent in child welfare services. To this date, black children are overrepresented in foster care, and they are often the last to be adopted.

Some blacks continue to believe the child welfare system is not sufficiently responsive to the needs of blacks and other minority children and adults.

There is also great controversy and debate today over whether or not whites should be allowed to adopt black or biracial children in transracial adoptions. The National Association of Black Social Workers is adamantly opposed to transracial adoptions, arguing that such adoptions are "racial genocide." Supporters of transracial adoptions contend that carefully screened white parents are far superior to long-term (and often a succession of several) foster care arrangements for black and biracial children.

In the 1970s, the emphasis on adoption began to shift again as social reformers became very alarmed at the burgeoning numbers of children living in private or group foster homes, usually for their entire childhoods. Policymakers became concerned about the rising costs of maintaining thousands of children in foster homes. Studies indicate as many as 500,000 children were living in publicly-supported foster homes in 1975.

Some studies revealed that many foster children went in and out of numerous placements, and researchers concluded this instability was very bad for children. There was also an apparent unwitting federal disincentive to place children in adoptive families. If the children remained in foster care, their foster families would receive monthly payments, the child would remain eligible for Medicaid, and the state would also receive federal funds. But if the child were adopted, the adoptive family would usually become fully responsible for all costs associated with the child, and Medicaid benefits would end. (Some states, such as New York, offered their own state subsidy to adoptive parents.)

Social workers, foster parents and others made a call for what came to be known in the 1980s as "permanency": to either return the children to their original families ("reunification") or, if that was not possible, to sever parental rights so the child could be adopted. (Other alternatives included placing the child in a group home or institution or allowing the child to remain in foster care.)

The culmination of this concern was the Adoption Assistance and Child Welfare Act of 1980, a federal law that mandates a judicial review of the status of a foster child after 18 months in foster care.

Today's child advocates charge that, because of indifference on the part of the Department of Health and Human Services and Congress, the law is not monitored adequately or properly enforced.

Still, the act did result in the adoption of many children who would not otherwise have been adopted, and it is hoped that many more families will be identified for the children who still wait for families and that such children can be pried loose from the bureaucratic quagmires where they are entrapped.

Another impetus to the adoption of children with special needs has been the continuance of Medicaid coverage in some cases. (Children placed through public agencies are the primary beneficiaries.) Adoption subsidies have also been created to provide monthly payments for some families who adopt some children with special needs, again, mostly children from public agencies. These legislative and legal actions were taken to encourage the adoption of foster children.

The concept that an older child could be successfully adopted and thrive in an adoptive family was a novel idea to many social workers and most of the general public in the late 1970s and early 1980s. (The emphasis and successful experience of child welfare experts in the early 20th century with the adoption of older children had been ignored or forgotten by most.)

It should be noted that, as more children are adopted at an older age, it is possible that increasing numbers of these children and their families will need some help with child or family adjustment. Whether the children will exhibit behavior problems because they were adopted or because of damage that occurred prior to the adoption is a matter of intense debate and a likely subject for further study.

Another major factor impacting adoption in the 1970s and to date was *Roe v. Wade,* the U.S. Supreme Court decision that legalized abortion nationwide in 1973. (Several years prior to that date, abortion had been legalized in such states as Hawaii and New York.)

Although it is unknown how many of the babies carried to term would have been adopted if abortion were still illegal today, it appears obvious that the abortion decision did decrease the number of babies needing adoptive parents. Nonrelative adoptions declined from a high of 89,200 in 1970 to 49,700 in 1974 and 47,700 in 1975.

Another development was the change in contraceptive use and effectiveness, particularly the variety of contraceptive choices and especially the increased use of the birth control pill, which enabled women to have more control in avoiding pregnancies.

Societal attitudes also changed radically. Because of the interplay of civil rights legislation and the feminist movement, as well as other social changes, such as the broad penetration of televisions and informational access into the majority of U.S. households, society began to change its collective mind about the formerly-perceived problems of illegitimacy. Other social changes were the availability of Aid to Families with Dependent Children, divorced women rearing children, thus making single parenthood by adolescents and never-married women more acceptable, the lowering of the age of majority to age 18 and other factors.

It became increasingly acceptable for single women and even young girls to engage in premarital sexual intercourse with the result that some number of them would become pregnant, bear and rear children.

This change in attitude became so prevasive in society that whereas adoption was earlier considered the presumed solution for a pregnant single woman, many individuals in the 1970s and to date began to believe that single parenting was a far preferable answer to adoption for both the mother and her child.

One important demographic trend affecting the "demand" for children to adopt was the huge bulge of the Baby Boom, children born in the years 1946–1964.

Because of various societal, economic, philosophical and legal changes, the previous emphasis by most of society on a woman's concentrating her life on her husband and children shifted. Now society saw it as increasingly important for women to prepare themselves for a paying career.

As a result, many Baby Boomer couples purposely delayed childbearing until their late twenties and mid-thirties. One end result was an increase in infertility problems. In addition, those individuals who responded to the "sexual freedom" espoused in the 1970s and early 1980s and practiced promiscuous sexual behavior found to their dismay that sexually transmitted diseases would and could inhibit fertility in later years.

Infertile couples desiring to adopt healthy infants found they faced the "baby shortage" that apparently resulted from more adults in relation to the number of babies born in later decades, in addition to all other factors enumerated previously.

As a result, affluent Baby Boomers, dismayed by long waiting lists to adopt healthy infants, have been motivated by a combination of altruism and impatience to adopt thousands of children born abroad. Families in the United States have adopted over 80,000 children from other countries in the relatively short time frame since 1970, while many others have sought to adopt older children in the United States.

Most of the children adopted from out of the United States are adopted as infants or very young children from lesser-developed countries. These countries have found it difficult to deal with large numbers of orphaned or abandoned children and generally house them in orphanages.

About half of the children adopted from other countries to date were adopted from Korea; however, increasing numbers of the children come from Latin America and other Asian countries.

It has also been postulated that appropriate citizens living in foreign countries should be allowed or encouraged to adopt U.S. children in need of family membership, such as black and biracial infants and older children of all races, when suitable parents are not readily found in the United States.

It must also be stressed that the child protection movement has continued to date with such compelling concepts as the "best interests of the child," based in part on the 1973 publication of the book, *Beyond the Best Interests of the Child* by Goldstein, Freud and Solnit. This ground-breaking book provided the primary impetus to child welfare professionals to concentrate the emphasis in an adoption on what is needed by the child rather than what is needed by the birthparents and adopting parents, although those needs are also considered.

In 1980, the National Committee For Adoption (NCFA) was formed to promote adoption as a positive option, provide and disseminate information on adoption, review and perform adoption research and promote excellence in adoption standards. In concert with adoption agencies, child welfare organizations and state and federal legislators, the NCFA has strived to improve adoption standards and practices for all children.

Most adoption agencies today pride themselves on seeking families for children more than on finding children for prospective parents. It must also be noted, however, that adoption agencies arrange an estimated half of all infant adoptions in the United States today while the remaining 50% of infant adoptions are arranged or facilitated by private intermediaries.

Home studies (also known as parent preparation or preadoptive counseling) of adopting parents are always required by licensed agencies prior to any adoptive placement, while home studies may not be initiated until after placement of the child in an independent arrangement. States license agencies to make adoptive placements, and agencies in turn are responsible to society for their work.

In addition, counseling of the adopting parents and birthparents occurs with far more frequency in agency adoptions than in independent adoptions, which leads to the primary criticism leveled by agency practitioners against independent adoptions. There appear to be an increasing number of independent intermediaries today who require or urge counseling prior to an adoptive placement, both in response to this criticism and also out of a desire to do better adoption work.

One change that has taken place over the past decade is that pockets of professionals have begun to argue that "open adoptions" (disclosure of the identities of birthparents and adoptive parents to each other) should be standard practice. Supporters of open adoptions frequently cite adoptions that occurred in the early 20th century and prior to the institution of confidentiality, sealing of birth records, and so forth. (Supporters of open adoptions apparently believe that the problem areas of the open adoptions of the early 20th century—social, financial and emotional pressures on adoptive parents, birthparents and even adopted children—would be avoided by today's more enlightened society.)

Some professionals believe open adoptions are more "humane" for adoption triad members, arguing, for example, that adults who seek to locate their birthparents will not have difficulty when the adoptions are open because they will know the identity of their birthparents.

Other professionals have responded to competitive pressures from lawyers and other adoption intermediaries who offer open adoptions and have begun to offer open adoptions or "semi-open" adoptions. Most adoption agencies and intermediaries continue to arrange adoptions with choices, such as the birthmother choosing the religion of the adopting couple, with the vast majority retaining the confidentiality aspect. (Open adoption is discussed at greater length within the text of this book.)

In addition, most agencies seek genetic and medical information from birthparents so this information can be provided to adopting parents who need this information to provide optimal appropriate care for the child and to help the child attain his or her full potential. Upon reaching adulthood, the adoptive parents will pass on the information to the adopted person, who can then plan for necessary preventive and other medical care for himself or herself and any offspring.

Another change that has taken place is in the area of birthfathers' rights. Prior to *Stanley v. Illinois* in 1972, no consideration was given to the desires of a birthfather not married to a child's birthmother. If the birthmother chose adoption for "her" child, then the adoption could go forth.

After the *Stanley* decision and several other subsequent U.S. Supreme Court decisions, states passed a variety of laws designed to protect the paternal rights of the birthfather. Today, a crazy quilt of laws nationwide provide for what actions, if any, must be taken by the state to obtain consent from the birthfather. In some states, the burden is on the birthfather to prove he would be a fit parent and to pursue that avenue legally. In other states, he is presumed to be on an equal footing with the birthmother.

Some states also provide grandparents with certain rights; for example, in Florida, if the child has lived with the grandparents for at least six months, the grandparents may block the child's adoptive placement with another family.

The sometimes overlapping and conflicting rights of the adoptive parents, birthparents, adopted person and relatives will undoubtedly continue to be debated, legislated and fought in court battles nationwide as states and the federal government struggle to achieve an equitable balance for all parties.

Conclusion If it is true, as American philosopher George Santayana once said, that "those who cannot remember the past are condemned to repeat it," then it is imperative that not only child welfare professionals but also legislators, therapists and the general public understand what has gone before, reviewing the successes and the failures of the formal and informal adoption systems and child welfare systems that preceded ours.

The "blood tie" argument still rages in courts throughout the country, as foster parents seek to adopt their foster children. Birthparents and some judges often resist such adoptions because of a lack of a blood tie, presuming that children should be reared by their biological parents even when those parents have proven extremely abusive or neglectful.

The argument has even been extended to the prebirth period, when fetuses in increasing numbers are exposed to harmful drugs. One group would terminate the rights of many of these mothers and immediately move to find adoptive families for the infants; the other group would first try treatment and other interventions. (And, as mentioned, a third group espouses a return to orphanages and long-term care for children.)

It is still hard for some people to accept or believe that a child can be raised better by someone who is not of "his own flesh and blood," despite the horrendous abuse many birthparents inflict on their children. In addition, in most cases, if a 14-year-old incompetent, pregnant teenager decides she wants to parent her baby, it is considered to be her right to do so. Only until and unless she actually abuses, neglects or abandons the child—sometimes repeatedly—can the state step in to protect the child.

Such injurious public attitudes may also provide a negative environment that subtly harms the child in the messages conveyed about adoption.

The United States continues to face many severe social problems that directly impact on the field of adoption: teenage pregnancy; drug abuse, especially the abuse of cocaine and alcohol; AIDS; child abuse; and more. Children are entering the foster care system at much younger ages than in past years: Some children are entering as newborns, abandoned by their drug-addicted mothers. Although the problem of AIDS seems unprecedented, past generations have also suffered diseases from which there was no cure and no apparent hope. Yet as the problems change, we can draw some parallels to the past and use solutions that have been implemented in the past to assist children.

We should never arrogantly assume today's solutions are brand-new and clearly superior to what has gone before. Nor can we ignore the challenges we face in resolving the problems of our children who need parents.

It is our belief that we are now seeing an increased acceptance that adoption indeed offers a very good solution for children who need families. The problems we face today are serious, and adoption cannot solve them all. But for many of the hundreds of thousands of children in foster care or destined for foster care, adoption may well be the answer.

For the increasing numbers of infants born testing positive for HIV or addicted to cocaine, adoption may be the most humane answer. And for the many thousands of infants born to single or married birthmothers in a crisis pregnancy, adoption may be the answer.

Adoption is by no means a rigid social institution. It continues to evolve according to the ideals and the prevalent political and economic forces of society. Adoption must be viewed from a systems perspective, studying and analyzing the social trends that have affected this institution and will continue to affect it.

Today, adoption is seen as a gateway, each year enabling thousands of children of all ages, races and ethnicity to enter permanent and loving families. We believe the emphasis in most cases now lies where it should be—on the child's needs and interests.

We have only touched briefly on some of the major themes in history in this brief essay on the history of adoption. We encourage readers to learn as much as possible about the changing world of adoption and hope this essay on history as well as this entire book will encourage thoughtful reflection and further study. The children are worth it.

Joseph Ben-Or, "The Law of Adoption in the United States: Its Massachusetts Origins and the Statute of 1851," *New England History & Genealogical Registry* 130 (1976): 259–272.

Michael Bohman and Soren Sigvardsson, "Outcome in Adoption: Lessons from Longitudinal Studies," in *The Psychology of Adoption* (New York: Oxford University Press, 1990).

John Boswell, *The Kindness of Strangers: The Abandonment of Children in Western Europe from Late Antiquity to the Renaissance* (New York: Pantheon Books, 1988).

C. L. Brace, *The Best Method of Disposing of Our Pauper and Vagrant Children* (New York: Wynkoop, Hallenbeck & Thomas, 1859).

John Francis Brosnan, "The Law of Adoption," *Columbia Law Review*, 22 (1922): 322–335.

Elizabeth S. Cole and Kathryn S. Donley, "History, Values, and Placement Policy Issues in Adoption," in *The Psychology of Adoption* (New York: Oxford University Press, 1990).

Lela B. Costin, "The Historical Context of Child Welfare," in *A Handbook of Child Welfare: Context, Knowledge, and Practice* (New York: Free Press, 1985).

Diana Dewar, *Orphans of the Living: A Study of Bastardy* (London: Hutchinson, 1968).

Homer Folks, *The Care of Destitute, Neglected, and Delinquent Children* (New York: Macmillan, 1902).

Joan H. Hollinger, editor-in-chief, *Adoption Law and Practice* (New York: Matthew Bender, 1988).

Ruth-Arlene W. Howe, "Adoption Practice, Issues, and Laws," *Family Law Quarterly*, 17 (Summer 1983): 173–197.

Leo Albert Huard, "The Law of Adoption: Ancient and Modern," *Vanderbilt Law Review*, 9(1956): 743–763.

Michael B. Katz, *In the Shadow of the Poorhouse: A Social History of Welfare in America* (New York: Basic Books, 1986).

Yasuhide Kawashima, "Adoption in Early America," *Journal of Family Law*, 20:4(August 1982): 677–696.

Francis E. Lane, *American Charities and the Child of the Immigrant* (New York: Arno Press, 1974).

C. M. A. McCauliff, "The First English Adoption Law and Its American Precursors," *Seton Hall Law Review*, 16(Summer/Fall 1986): 656–677.

National Committee For Adoption, *Adoption Factbook* (Washington, DC: National Committee For Adoption, 1989).

Ida R. Parker, *"Fit and Proper"?: A Study of Legal Adoption in Massachusetts* (Boston: Church Home Society, 1927).

Leroy Pelton, "The Institution of Adoption: Its Sources and Perpetuation," in *Infertility and Adoption: A Guide for Social Work Practice* (New York: Haworth Press, 1988).

Ruby Lee Piester, *For The Love of a Child* (Austin, Texas: Eakin Press, 1987).

David J. Rothman and Sheila M. Rothman, eds., *The Origins of Adoption* (New York: Garland Publishing, 1987).

Patricia Turner-Hogan and Sau-Fong Siu, "Minority Children and the Child Welfare System: An Historical Perspective," *Social Work*, 33(November–December 1988): 493–498.

J. H. A. van Loon, *Report on Intercountry Adoption*, paper presented at Hague Conference on Private International Law Intercountry, Hague, Netherlands, April 1990, 26.

Leslie Wheeler, "The Orphan Trains," *American History Illustrated*, 18(December 1983): 12–23.

Jamil S. Zainaldin, "The Emergence of a Modern American Family Law: Child Custody, Adoption, and the Courts, 1796–1851," *Northwestern University Law Review*, 73:6(1979): 1038–1045.

A

abandonment The desertion of a child by a parent or adult caretaker with no provisions for reasonable child care or apparent intention to return. A child may be considered abandoned if left alone or with siblings or nonrelated and unsuitable individuals. Abandonment is considered a form of physical neglect by the National Center on Child Abuse and Neglect, which estimates about 17,100 children were abandoned in the United States in 1986 *(Study Findings: Study of National Incidence and Prevalence of Child Abuse and Neglect: 1988)*. This figure increased by 10,700 from 1980 statistics.

If the deserting parent does not return or contact the child or does not provide any support for an extended period, the state ultimately may seek to terminate parental rights and place the child with an adoptive family. A social worker must prove to the court of appropriate jurisdiction that abandonment has occurred. States vary on their adoption laws and what proof is required before parental rights may be terminated. Before such action is taken, the child is usually placed in foster care while the state or county social worker attempts to find the parent or relatives of the child. (See TERMINATION OF PARENTAL RIGHTS.)

The parent(s) who abandoned the child usually do not provide information on their own whereabouts, although social workers and police officers will seek to find them, using various investigative means.

Every year a number of infants are abandoned in trash cans, outside homes and in a variety of settings. The mother may have been a teenager who sought to conceal her pregnancy or who couldn't take care of a child. She may have been convinced she would be rejected by her parents, peers and others who could never accept her pregnancy or the infant itself. Also, she may not have obtained an abortion because she was denying the reality of her pregnancy, because she felt abortion was immoral or she was unaware of available abortion facilities and was afraid to ask anyone for information.

Although outsiders may find it difficult to believe a teenager's parents could fail to notice her progressing pregnancy, parents often assume the girl is merely gaining weight. Pregnancy can be particularly hard to recognize if the girl is overweight to start. In some cases parents even encourage the pregnant girl to exercise and diet, based on this mistaken assumption.

Sometimes the deserting mother has a romantic image of a happy couple finding a baby on the doorstep. Consequently, when she abandons the child in a safe place, the mother may falsely conclude the child will be reared by the people who find it; however, abandoned infants and children are almost always placed under the legal control of the state social services department and in a state-approved foster home. Efforts are made to locate the biological parents or any relatives before placing the child in a permanent foster home.

Increasing numbers of infants are abandoned in the hospital due to AIDS and maternal DRUG ABUSE. Because the birthmothers of such infants feel incapable of caring for their children, they may leave the hospital with no notice and presume the hospital staff will care for the babies. These children are classified as BOARDER BABIES, and such children represent a serious social problem today.

Infants are not the only children who are abandoned: children of all ages are abandoned by their parents. Very often today the problem of the biological parent is alcohol or drug abuse-related.

If neither parent and no relatives make a claim on the child within the course of at least 18 months after placement into a foster home, the court may opt to terminate the birthparents' parental rights so the child may be adopted by other parents.

In the event the birthparents are found, they may be given terms and conditions by the court with which they must comply in order for the child to be returned, for example, supervision by a social worker or intensive counseling by a trained therapist. Or if the problem was leaving the child alone for extended periods while the parent worked, a suitable babysitter may be arranged.

Older children are sometimes abandoned when the parent believes he or she cannot care for the child or if the parent is overcome by personal problems, alcoholism, drug abuse, financial difficulties or a combination of these.

Homeless families may attempt to live out of their cars or makeshift shelters. Such living arrangements may be considered NEGLECT or, if the parent leaves the child alone in such circumstances for an extended period, abandonment. If a child abuse worker is notified, the children may be taken from the parents by a state or county social worker and placed in a certified state foster home until and unless the parents provide adequate shelter.

Thousands of children in countries outside the United States are abandoned every year by their mothers, and some of them are placed in orphanages. People from the United States and abroad adopt some children who need families, but many of these children spend their entire childhoods in institutions until they are turned out to make room for younger homeless children.

Birthmothers from other countries who abandon their children do so primarily because of cultural factors or because they are destitute, powerless or are lacking in support and options and see no hope for their abilities to parent their children. They may or may not have other children. They may have been rejected by their parents or by the birthfathers.

In some cases, the birthmother from another country may be legally prohibited from voluntarily signing a consent to adoption. Abandoning her child at an orphanage or hospital may be the only route she can find that could ultimately lead her child to be placed in an orphanage and hopefully later in an adoptive home. (See also ABUSE.)

John Boswell, *The Kindness of Strangers: The Abandonment of Children in Western Europe from Late Antiquity to the Renaissance* (New York: Pantheon Books, 1989).

U.S. Department of Health and Human Services, Office of Human Development Services, Administration for Children, Youth and Families, Children's Bureau, National Center on Child Abuse and Neglect, *Study findings: Study of National Incidence and Prevalence of Child Abuse and Neglect: 1988.*

abortion The termination of a pregnancy. The method of termination is dependent on how advanced the pregnancy is. It may be an outpatient procedure in the early stages of pregnancy, or may require inpatient care if the pregnancy is advanced.

Terminations of pregnancies have been recorded since ancient times. In the United States, abortions were permitted by common law until about the 1870s, when laws were created to restrict abortions. By the year 1900, abortions were illegal in all states.

By the 1950s, some states had created laws that permitted abortions only in the circumstance where an abortion was considered necessary to save the life of the mother (therapeutic abortion).

In the late 1960s some states (17 in all) changed their laws to allow for abortions in other instances. Thirteen of these states restricted access to abortions to when a woman's life was endangered by pregnancy, or the pregnancy was the result of rape or incest, or the fetus was determined to be severely handicapped. Four states (Alaska, Hawaii, New York, Washington) repealed their antiabortion laws altogether prior to the *Roe v. Wade* Supreme Court decision.

Abortion became essentially legal nationwide with the U.S. Supreme Court decision of *Roe v. Wade* in 1973.

The *Roe v. Wade* decision did allow states to create laws against abortions during the third trimester of pregnancy or after viability of the fetus, unless the life or health of the pregnant woman were at stake. "Viability" refers to the potential of the fetus to survive outside the womb. The Court determined at that time that the fetus must be at least 20 weeks old for viability to be considered; consequently, states may not ban abortions prior to the 20-week point.

Since the *Roe v. Wade* decision, the number of abortions has increased to the current level of about 1,600,000 per year, according to the Alan Guttmacher Institute.

One possible result of the legalization of abortion was a decrease in the number of infants needing adoptive parents.

Although it is not clear how many aborted fetuses would have resulted in adopted children had the pregnancies all been carried full-term, many experts believe abortion has contributed to a lower number of babies in need of adoptive families.

Yet another important factor to consider has been an increased acceptance of single parenthood; many more women are opting to raise their children today than in previous years, when adoption was chosen. In addition, more effective contraception is available today than prior to the *Roe v. Wade* decision.

The July 1989 decision of *Webster vs. Reproductive Services* indicates states may have rights to further restrict abortion policies. The ultimate effect of this Supreme Court decision will continue to evolve over the next several years.

Women obtaining abortions are of all childbearing ages and socioeconomic statuses. Most women terminate their pregnancies at an abortion facility rather than in their doctors' offices. Some abortion facilities operate as for-profit businesses, while others are non-profit organizations.

Some states require parental permission or a court order before a minor may obtain an abortion, and numerous court cases discuss this issue and the fairness or unfairness of requiring parental or court permission. In June of 1990, the U.S. Supreme Court upheld the right of states to require parental notification of at least one parent before allowing abortions of most minors. However, in some cases, a judicial bypass is offered. According to the booklet, *Abortion and Women's Health: A Turning Point for America?* (published by the Alan Guttmacher Institute in 1990), nine states required parental consent in 1990: Alabama, Indiana, Kentucky, Louisiana, Maine, Massachusetts, Missouri, North Dakota and Rhode Island. In addition, three states require parental notification: Arkansas, West Virginia and Wyoming. Maryland and Utah required parental consent "if possible."

Supporters of parental consent argue that a child must have parental permission to go on a school field trip, pierce her ears and so forth. Since the decision to abort a fetus is a major decision, they believe parents should have a say in this decision. Pro-choice individuals who are opposed to parental consent limitations argue that girls who are forced to seek parental consent may not tell their parents about the pregnancy and so delay obtaining an abortion until it is too late or too dangerous. In addition, they say the girl who has not told her parents about the pregnancy is unlikely to have obtained any prenatal care. They also argue that a parent may unreasonably withhold consent. In addition, even if a girl may obtain court permission in lieu of parental consent, many girls may be fearful of the court system or have no idea how to approach a judge.

It is also important to note that courts have decided that Medicaid funds may be withheld from women seeking abortions. Thirty-seven states refuse to fund abortions for women receiving public assistance. The states that do fund abortions for Medicaid recipients are: Alaska, California, Connecticut, Hawaii, Maryland, Massachusetts, New York, New Jersey, North Carolina, Oregon, Vermont, Washington and West Virginia. Some states may provide public funds in the case of rape, incest or other conditions.

Most women seeking to terminate their pregnancies do so within the first trimester. According to the Alan Guttmacher Institute, over 50% of all abortions occur in the first eight weeks of pregnancy, 91% during the first 12 weeks and 96% within the first 15 weeks.

It is also true that some number of women who want abortions delay seeking the abortion until it is not legally permissible and the fetus is considered "viable." If a woman seeking an abortion is unable to obtain one legally because she is too advanced in her pregnancy, most abortion facilities will counsel the woman on her options, including parenting and adoption. Many will also provide the names of adoption agencies or attorneys who provide adoption services. A small number of abortion providers will both perform abortions and also arrange adoptions, offering counseling for each option.

The abortion rights issue remains a hotly debated topic. Numerous vocal groups actively seek to make abortions illegal, with most making an exception to save the life of the mother.

Supporters of legalized abortion fear that if most abortions were again made illegal, women would attempt to abort their own fetuses and risk their lives doing so, or they might contact unqualified persons to abort the fetuses, again risking their health. "Prochoice" advocates also believe that a woman has the right to determine the fate of her own body, and they do not perceive the fetus as a "person" in its own right—only as an extension of her body.

"Pro-life" advocates believe life begins at conception, and they regard abortion as the killing of a child. They may argue that, given the long waiting lists of willing adoptive parents, even "unwanted" babies can be adopted and reared by loving families if pregnancies are not discontinued.

"Pro-life" advocates tend to believe abortion is acceptable only in the cases of a pregnancy resulting from rape or incest or when the mother's health is endangered, and few believe abortion is never acceptable, although some do hold to this view.

If *Roe v. Wade* were overturned, states would then decide for themselves whether or not abortions would be lawful, and under what conditions. Experts say some states would allow abortions while others would ban them. Some argue that wealthy women could easily travel to a state or nation where abortion is legal, while poor women would be condemned to carry the pregnancy to term or obtain an illegal abortion.

Whether or not the overturning of *Roe v. Wade* would cause a sudden "baby surplus" of adoptable infants remains to be seen; however, some experts speculate this scenario could become a reality and insist that the number of infants needing families to adopt them would far exceed the demand.

They argue that a sudden overturning of *Roe v. Wade* would be disastrous, because it would not allow sufficient time to educate the public and set massive birth control education programs in place. Nor would it be possible to change overnight the attitudes of unwed teenagers toward sex and birth control, and unwed teenage pregnancy is a critical problem. If the estimated one million teenagers who became pregnant each year all actually gave birth, the ensuing social problem would be great in terms of dollars and personal hardships.

Proponents of adoption insist there are adequate numbers of people who would adopt the infants not aborted and in need of adoptive families. They point to categories of people who currently are often prevented from adopting, although they would potentially make good parents: parents with children who have become infertile, fertile couples, couples over age 40 and affluent single parents.

Judicial decisions on abortion issues may well have monumental social consequences and repercussions.

Rachel Benson Gold, *Abortion and Women's Health: A Turning Point for America?* (New York: Alan Guttmacher Institute, 1990).

David Shribman, "High Court Says Minors Can Be Required to Tell a Parent Before Getting Abortion," *The Wall Street Journal*, June 26, 1990, p. A3.

Dr. and Mrs. J. C. Wilke, *Abortion Questions & Answers* (Cincinnati: Hayes Publishing Co., 1988).

abuse Physical, sexual or long-lasting emotional damage to a child, most often perpetrated by parents, stepparents, a mother's male friend or a relative. (Adults and elderly people are also abused; however, the emphasis of this article is on abuse of children.) NEGLECT is also a form of child abuse.

According to the National Committee for Prevention of Child Abuse, 2.4 million cases of child abuse were reported to child welfare agencies in 1989, about 27% of which involved physical abuse.

Information from the American Association for Protecting Children (a division of the American Humane Association) gives the average age for the perpetrator of abuse as 31.7 years. When considering all forms of abuse and neglect, females commit 53.5% of all abuse, and males commit 46.5%. When considering sexual abuse only, males are responsible for the majority of cases: 82.4%. When considering cases of physical abuse, males are responsible for 50.5% of the cases.

Physical abuse is the most frequently occurring form of abuse, followed by emotional abuse and then sexual abuse. Moderate injuries occurred in 60% of the abused children's cases; serious injuries accounted for 15%. (One must remember, however, that of all the various forms of child abuse, physical abuse is the easiest to prove in court.)

In 1986, 1,100 children died of abuse in the United States, according to the report *Study Findings: Study of National Incidence and Prevalence of Child Abuse and Neglect: 1988*, published by the U.S. Department of Health and Human Services.

Physical abuse incidents increased by 58% from 1980 to 1986, and sexual abuse tripled. Females are more likely to be abused than are males. Fatalities are more prevalent among young children, and moderate injuries are more common among older children.

Some prevalent or predictive Factors in child abuse include:

Family income. Low income is correlated to abuse. Children in families whose 1986 income was less than $15,000 experienced abuse at a higher rate than families with greater incomes; however, it is important to note that individuals from all socioeconomic strata can be guilty of child abuse.

Family size. Children in families with four or more children in the home show higher rates of abuse, particularly physical abuse and neglect.

Race and ethnicity. No significant differences were found among racial and ethnic groups.

Abusive parents are typically reported to police officers or to the state social service department, and a social worker is generally assigned to investigate. The abuse may have occurred only one time, but it is far more likely that it has been recurrent over a period of months or years. Often, abuse is not detected until a child enters kindergarten or first grade.

If a social worker or investigator determines that abuse has occurred to a child and that abuse was caused by a parent or relative with whom the child lives, the child is usually removed from the home and placed with relatives or in a state-approved foster home or group home.

The child will not be returned to the home until it is determined by social workers that the parent has been rehabilitated from the problem leading to the abuse, whether it was alcohol or drug use, emotional or mental problems in the abuser or some other cause.

Most social workers are increasingly striving to assist abusive parents in resolving their problems. For instance, the Minnesota Department of Human Services revealed in 1989 that workers in several areas of the state planned to spend up to 20 hours per week in counseling individuals accused of abuse. In support of such a trend, Peter Forsythe, vice president of the Edna McConnell Clark Foundation in New York was quoted in an article, "When faced with risk to a child, we should do more to remove the risk instead of so quickly removing the child." Contrasting these two alternatives, the Foundation has determined that an "emergency in-home program" costs from $2,600 to $3,500 per family versus the high cost of foster care, which is an estimated $8,000 to $12,000 a year. The article also stated that after an in-home program in Iowa was launched in 1987, 85% of the children who were at "immediate risk" remained safely at home.

Traditionally, however, a child can be removed from the home before the innocence or guilt of the alleged abuser is determined, for the sake of the child's safety. If the allegations of abuse prove to be false or their veracity cannot be determined, the child is returned to the home.

It may be extremely difficult for investigators to determine whether or not abuse has actually occurred, especially if injuries have healed or theoretically could have been caused by an accident. Investigators look for a pattern of "accidents" and also the type of injury that results from the alleged accident; for example, an injury incurred from a fall may be very different from an injury incurred by a parent violently jerking a child's arm. If the child has periodically "fallen" into scalding water or has wounds or lacerations that probably would not be the natural results of childhood mishaps, this is another indication of possible abuse. Witnesses to the abuse are extremely helpful, although many people may be reluctant or fearful of testifying against a violent person.

Abuse may be overtly violent and readily apparent, or it may be more covert and difficult to verify. In some cases, abuse is so extreme or so prolonged that it leads to the child's death. One mother force-fed her child large quantities of salt because the child stole a few cookies. The toddler died of sodium overdose. Other parents have shaken an infant so violently that brain hemorrhage and death have resulted.

In cases of severe abuse or when the social worker determines that it is unlikely the abusive parent can successfully raise the child in a healthy nonabusive atmosphere, the child will be permanently removed from the home, and parental rights will be terminated in a court of law. The child will then be in need of an adoptive family if authorities believe it is in the best interest of the child to be adopted.

Sometimes children are so damaged physically and/or psychologically by abuse that it would difficult, if not impossible, for most adopting parents to meet the child's needs. Consequently the child may be better off living in a group home or even in a psychiatric treatment setting. It has been speculated that many adults who are currently in prison were once abused children.

Sexual abuse can range from touching the child in the genital areas or requiring the child to touch another's genitals to forcing a child into full sexual intercourse. Adults have attempted intercourse with children as young as tiny infants with dire results. (See entry on SEXUAL ABUSE for further information.)

NEGLECT is also considered a form of child abuse. Neglectful parents may fail to feed their children or may feed them a grossly inadequate diet, may leave them alone for extended periods when they are very young or may otherwise fail to meet the normal needs of the child. For instance, a young child may be expected to watch an infant—

social workers report that children as young as two or three have been left alone to watch an infant sibling.

ABANDONMENT refers to a parent or caretaker leaving a child alone for an extended period and with no apparent intention to ever return.

Psychologists often use dolls, puppets and other toys to try to draw very young children out and determine whether physical or sexual abuse has occurred or not. Some allegations of abuse are false, yet even when vindicated, a person once charged with child abuse is haunted by this charge for life. As a result, it is extremely important to make an accurate determination of whether or not child abuse did take place.

When adoption is being planned for an abused child, some ethical social workers brief adopting parents completely in a nonidentifying way about the child's abusive treatment or the conditions of neglect under which the child has lived. However, social workers are often not fully aware of the extent of the abuse and in some cases may not even know abuse has indeed occurred. (The child may have been removed from the home for the reasons of overt abandonment or neglect.)

In some instances, social workers have failed to alert adopting parents to known severe problems that children faced in their past, and adoptive parents have successfully sued the state or agency for the withholding of information and the subsequent WRONGFUL ADOPTION. Adopting parents have generally argued in such cases that they would not have adopted the child had they known about problems or that they would have obtained therapy and treatment for the child had they been informed.

Abused children may also suffer physical handicaps resulting from their abuse. Consequently, it may be more difficult to locate a suitable adoptive family.

The effects of abuse are long-term, even when the abused child was only an infant or toddler at the time of abuse. Psychologists have found that love cannot always overcome the emotional and psychological effects of severe abuse and the internalized feelings of anger and guilt experienced even by very young children.

Abused children may "act out" their anger and aggression on adoptive parents and siblings. They may also behave in sexually precocious ways, based on what they have learned as "normal" behavior from their parents or the persons who sexually abused them. They may masturbate in public or display their genitals or behave in a seductive manner, unaware that this is not normally acceptable behavior.

Adoptive Parents of Abused Children
Adults who adopt sexually abused children must be very sensitive to this problem and comfortable with their own sexuality. Social workers report that children who are sexually abused are the hardest children to fit successfully into adoptive families.

When parents adopt abused children, they must realize the child may need therapy immediately or in 10 years. It is also possible that he or she could blossom in the adoptive home and never require counseling; however, adoptive parents should be open to the need for treatment.

Many parents and adoption professionals agree that adoptive parent support groups can be very helpful to parents adopting older children if other members of the group have themselves adopted older children or children with SPECIAL NEEDS.

Predicting Child Abuse Some social scientists, believing that a propensity to child abuse can be predicted, have actually developed a method to identify individuals who are at risk of abusing their children.

Researchers Solbritt Murphy, Bonnie Orkow and Ray Nicola reported on their findings in an article in *Child Abuse and Neglect*, entitled, "Prenatal Prediction of Child Abuse and Neglect: A Prospective Study."

Five-hundred-eighty-seven pregnant women were interviewed, and a "Family Stress Checklist" was administered. Seven percent of the women scored as "high risk" for becoming child abusers.

Two years later, the researchers studied the charts of 100 children whose mothers had been considered "at risk" and compared those children's charts to the charts of mothers who had been labeled "no risk" and "low risk" and mothers with a "mid-score."

Some checklist items that would indicate a person had a high risk potential for child abuse were "severe beatings; repeated foster homes . . . (no positive role) model in childhood," "current psychosis; chronic pattern of psychiatric problems," "severely depressed," "chaotic life style, severe environmental and/or marital problems," and "intolerance of normal behavior; very strict parent."

Some items indicating no risk were "infrequent spankings" of the pregnant woman during childhood and "consistent parenting."

According to the researchers, "Twenty-five children had experienced failure to thrive, neglect or abuse. Twenty of these were from the original high risk mothers, giving an incidence of neglect/abuse in that group of 52%. The no risk control group of 100 mothers showed a 2% incidence of abuse/neglect; a low risk group showed a 4% incidence of abuse/neglect; and a mid-score group has an abuse/neglect rate of 5%."

Other researchers have compared and contrasted the "social network characteristics" of abusers with nonabusers. Researchers Sara J. Corse, Kathleen Schmid and Penelope K. Trickett compared and contrasted these characteristics, and their study was reported in the January 1990 issue of the *Journal of Community Psychology*. Studying 52 mothers, half of whom had been identified as abusers, the researchers discovered that community involvement was "positively related to enjoyment of the child." They also reported that in abusive families, "The nuclear family is perceived as nonsupportive and conflicted, while few opportunities exist outside the family to balance limited inner resources."

The researchers hypothesized that the abusing mothers might be more likely to offend individuals who could offer needed assistance. In addition, they also found abusing mothers were unaware of potential sources of help.

Abuse and Neglect and Adolescent Parents Findings are mixed on whether adolescent single parents are more abusive or neglectful than other single parents, and some researchers say that it cannot and should not be presumed that a child is at greater risk from an adolescent mother than an older mother; however, there are factors that could theoretically predispose an adolescent to abuse her child.

For example, according to the *Encyclopedia of Child Abuse*, infants who are born prematurely and are of low birth weight may be at risk for abuse. Such infants are "more restless, distractible, unresponsive and demanding than the average child. Child-specific factors when combined with a parent who is inexperienced or easily frustrated greatly increase the risk of abuse." (Teenagers have a high rate of low birth weight infants. See TEENAGE PARENTS.)

Jerry S. Bigner, in *Parent-Child Relations: An Introduction to Parenting*, states that teenage parents have a very inaccurate idea of developmental norms. As a result, adolescent parents will often presume their children will achieve such goals as taking their first steps, attaining bladder control and understanding wrongdoing well before the children could be expected to achieve these developmental milestones. For example, teenage mothers in one study estimated their children would be able to achieve bowel control at 24 weeks, when the norm for this behavior is actually from 96 to 144 weeks.

Researchers hypothesize that when children fail to achieve these milestones, their teenage parents could become angry or frustrated as well as neglectful or even abusive.

It is also possible that adolescent motherhood itself could predispose a parent to abuse or neglect at some point in a child's life. According to research by Susan J. Zuravin, Ph.D., at the School of Social Work and Community Planning, University of Maryland, Baltimore, "chronic stress" combined with teenage motherhood may lead to higher than normal rates of abuse.

Zuravin collected data from 237 abusive single women on public assistance in Maryland and with at least one child age 12 or under. About half had abused their children, and half had neglected them; 281 nonabusive single women on public assistance served as controls.

The researcher hypothesized that many births, a long history of unemployment and lack of education were measurable stressors that impacted on child maltreatment. Her hypothesis was proven by the research, and Zuravin also found that the number of births was the most critical factor in both abuse and neglect.

She also found that abusive or neglectful mothers were younger when their child was born than were the control mothers. The averages ages at the first birth were 17.9 years for the neglectful mother and 18.3 years for the abusive mother. The control mother's average age at the time of her first child's birth was 19.5 years.

Also, both neglectful and abusive mothers had more children, less education and less history of employment than did the control mothers. For example, the average number of live births for the neglectful mothers was 3.9, and the average education was 9.8 grades. For the abusive mother, the average number of live births was 3.0, and the average education was 10.4 grades. The average control mother had 1.9 live births and had completed 11.1 grades in school.

Abuse and Adoptive Parents The much-publicized child abuse trial of attorney Joel Steinberg in 1989 misled some people into believing that child abuse is a prevalent problem among adoptive parents.

This conclusion is grossly unfair to adoptive parents nationwide, because abuse is extremely uncommon among adoptive parents.

According to the American Association for Protecting Children (a division of The American Humane Association), statistics for 1986 reveal less than 1% (.67%, to be exact) of the perpetrators of child abuse are adoptive parents. Biological parents are the abusers in 63.7% of the cases.

It would be highly inappropriate to generalize from the Steinberg case, which was unique. Steinberg had been given the child at infancy by the birthmother with the expectation that he would place the baby for adoption. The birthmother paid Steinberg for this service, which in itself was unusual. (Generally birthmothers who place their children for adoption pay no fee: all fees are paid by adoptive parents.)

Although labeled an "illegal adoption" by the media, in actuality there was no formal adoption. Steinberg never filed any adoption papers nor was he studied by any social workers in a home study.

In 1989, Steinberg was convicted of the abuse and death of 7-year-old Lisa Steinberg. His lover, Hedda Nussbaum, was given immunity from prosecution because she testified against Steinberg. Another younger child whom she and Steinberg had been rearing, also with no adoption or court permission, was subsequently returned to his birthmother's custody.

Abuse is probably rare among adoptive parents because most of them undergo HOME STUDY investigations by social workers and consequently must openly confront their feelings about infertility, raising an adopted child and a myriad of other issues that could affect their fitness as parents.

In addition, the home study process almost invariably includes a complete physical examination. A habitual drug abuser would likely be detected and denied the opportunity to adopt a child. (Steinberg was allegedly a cocaine abuser.)

The social worker's home study report on the prospective adoptive parents is usually presented to a judge after supervisory visits ranging over a period of anywhere from several months to a year, depending on the state, and the judge makes a final decision as to the parental fitness of the adopting parents. With the judge's approval, an adoption is finalized.

It is very unlikely that Joel Steinberg or his lover would have been approved as adoptive parents by social workers or a judge, had he approached adoption in a normal, legal manner.

Adoptive parents are subject to the same pressures and stresses as are all other parents; however, they have willingly chosen parenthood, and most are well prepared to handle the financial, emotional and psychological challenges of raising a child. (See also CHILDREN'S RIGHTS; FOSTER CARE; SEXUAL ABUSE.)

Jerry J. Bigner, *Parent-Child Relations: An Introduction to Parenting* (New York: Macmillan, 1989).
F. G. Bolton Jr., Ph.D., Roy H. Laner, Ed.D., and Sandra P. Kane, B.S., "Child Maltreatment Risk Among Adolescent Mothers," *American Journal of Orthopsychiatry,* 50(July 1980): 489–504.
Robin E. Clark and Judith Freeman Clark, *The Encyclopedia of Child Abuse* (New York: Facts On File, 1989).
Sara J. Corse, Kathleen Schmid, and Penelope K. Trickett, "Social Network Characteristics of Mothers in Abusing and Nonabusing Families and Their Relationships to Parenting Beliefs," *Journal of Community Psychology* 18(January 1990): 44–58.
Solbritt Murphy, M.D., M.P.H., Bonnie Orkow, M.S.W., Ray M. Nicola, M.D., M.H.S.A., "Prenatal Prediction of Child Abuse and Neglect: A Prospective Study," *Child Abuse and Neglect,* 9(1985): 225–235.
Sam Newlund, "State Plan is to Remove Risk, Not Child, in Cases of Abuse and Neglect," *Minneapolis Tribune,* February 7, 1990.
Susan J. Zuravin, Ph.D., "Child Maltreatment and Teenage First Births: A Relationship Mediated by Chronic Sociodemographic Stress?", *American Journal of Orthopsychiatry,* 58(January 1988): 91–103.
U.S Department of Health and Human Services, Office of Human Development Services, Administration for Children, Youth and Families, Children's Bureau, National Center on Child Abuse and Neglect, n.d. *Study Findings: Study of National Incidence and Prevalence of Child Abuse and Neglect: 1988.*

abuse and adolescent parents See ABUSE.

abuse and adoptive parents See ABUSE.

abuse and biological parents See ABUSE.

academic progress When used in references to adopted children, this term generally refers to school achievements of children under age 18.

Children who were adopted as infants can expect to achieve at a normal rate commensurate with their intelligence, although the adolescent years may be particularly tumultuous for an adopted teenager, as they are for many adolescents, adopted or not (see ADOLESCENT ADOPTED PERSONS).

Children who are adopted as older children, especially children who have already begun school and were foster children, will often struggle with academic achievement, primarily because much energy is spent adjusting to the new family and learning the daily ways of this family as well as what is acceptable and what is unacceptable behavior.

It is also possible that a newly adopted child's grades may rapidly improve if he or she feels very positive about the adoption; however, this should not be expected, and poor grades should not be considered by the family as an indication they have failed.

If the older child enters the adoptive family after the school year has already begun and must change schools, this adds to the adjustments the child must make.

Adoptive parents need to understand that teachers, like other members of society, may have negative and outdated views about adoption; consequently, a behavioral problem could be magnified in the teacher's eyes because it is blamed on adoption. In turn, the child perceives the teacher has a negative attitude, although she or he probably doesn't know the reason why, and may misbehave even more, resulting in a continuing cycle of problems. Parents must be very active and work hard to identify the details, not always assuming the teacher is right and the child is wrong or vice versa. (See also ADJUSTMENT; SPECIAL NEEDS ADOPTIONS; TEACHERS AND ADOPTED CHILDREN.)

acting out Negative behavior such as stealing, lying, constant whining and other behavioral problems. If the child was adopted, often these disciplinary problems can be directly or indirectly tied to unhappy experiences that occurred while the child lived in an abusive or neglectful home, faced many foster care placements or endured other psychological hardships.

Even children as young as two years old who are adopted into a new family can be expected to exhibit behavioral problems because it is difficult for them to adjust to new routines, loss of former security figures and new parents.

Social workers expect most older children will act out to some extent, and parents must learn how to gain the child's trust while at the same time setting appropriate disciplinary limits. Often, spanking and harsh words are the least effective forms of discipline because severe physical or verbal abuse may have been the reason for the initial development of negative behavior. If children receive a response only when they misbehave, they will learn that negative behavior is a good way to gain attention.

Adoptive parents can learn techniques of positive reinforcement, "time out" (sending the child to his or her room) and other methods of discipline from social workers and also from other adoptive parents; for example, one adoptive mother of an older child was dismayed that her daughter kept stealing items from her jewelry box. Other adoptive parents with similar experiences advised the mother to put a lock on her bedroom door. Although she considered this solution to be very radical, everything else she'd tried had failed, so the mother tried this technique, and the stealing stopped. Years later, her daughter thanked her for removing the temptation and making it impossible to steal.

Adopted children born in other countries may initially gorge themselves or hoard food, dismaying the rest of the family, but such behavior is understandably based on previous circumstances. The child may have experienced starvation or extreme hunger and consequently must gradually learn that food will always be provided and he or she need not stockpile food for hard times ahead.

Many newly adopted children are not grateful they have been adopted and may evince resentment, anger or distrust of adoptive parents until it becomes clear that the adoption is regarded as permanent by the parents. Until the adopted child feels confident and secure, he or she will test parents. (In fact, even after the child is secure, the normal testing that all children exhibit will continue.)

Acting out may be a temporary serious problem, although all children, adopted or born into their families, have times when they misbehave, especially when they are tired, ill or upset.

If acting out continues and the parents feel unable to cope with the child, they may need to seek professional help. Researchers have discovered that adoptions may actually disrupt if adoptive parents believe the older child's behavior is not improving and the acting out continues without abeyance. (See also DISRUPTION; OLDER CHILD.)

adjustment The process by which adopted children and adoptive parents learn to relate to and accept each other in their respective child-parent roles. (Readers should refer to ADULT ADOPTED PERSONS for questions relating to the lifelong psychological adjustment of adopted persons.)

Several parenting books have been written for adoptive parents, for example, *How to Raise an Adopted Child* (Crown), *Parenting the Adopted Child* (Prentice Hall Press), *Raising Adopted Children: A Manual for Adoptive Parents* (Harper & Row) and *After the Adoption* (Fleming Revell). *Adopting the Older Child* (Harvard Common Press) was specifically written for parents choosing to adopt older children rather than infants. *You're Our Child: The Adoption Experience* (Madison Books) is a helpful book for all members of the ADOPTION CIRCLE.

The time needed for all parties to begin to feel comfortable with one another and accepting of each other varies greatly depending on circumstances.

Experts agree that adjustment is generally the easiest and most rapid when a child is an infant and when the prospective parents are well prepared for the child and have seriously considered adoption issues, such as their own infertility and their feelings about the birthparents. They should also realize there will be a need to communicate about adoption issues with the child they hope to adopt. This communication, at the child's level of understanding, is vital once the child is old enough to understand and the parents must be willing to be candid about adoption as the child grows up. (See EXPLAINING ADOPTION).

One reason why all states do not instantly "finalize" an adoption is to ensure a time period has passed that has enabled the adoptive parents and the child to adjust to each other. As a result, most adoptions are not finalized for at least six months.

When older children are adopted, and even when the child is as young as a toddler, child development experts say there are usually stages of adjustment the child and parents must go through; an example of such a stage is the "honeymoon period," which may last for days, weeks or even months. During this time, the older child strives mightily to behave in a perfect way and please the adoptive parents.

A testing phase may come next, when the child misbehaves on purpose to see if the adopting parents will continue to parent him anyway despite his behavior. Although it may strain their patience, most adoptive parents do survive this period. Finally, the child will assimilate into the family and seem like a regular member, not overstressing the family but making reasonable demands on it.

Adopting parents also go through an adjustment period, whether they are adopting a newborn infant or an older child.

They may first shower the child with gifts and wish to throw away a toddler's tattered blanket or well-worn stuffed animal. This would be a serious mistake, because the item may be the only element of continuity the child knows, and it is very important for him to retain it until he feels ready to discard it.

The parents may feel unsure and insecure about disciplining an older child, and some children are adept at turning on the tears to manipulate their new mom and dad. Most parents and children must feel their way along until they feel truly comfortable with each other. To reach that point may take months or as long as a year or more, depending on the family.

An adoptive parent support group composed of other families who have each adopted a child of about the same age can be a tremendous help to a new adoptive family.

If the child is an older child from another country or a child with serious handicaps, both the child and the adoptive parents will need to give themselves extra time to adjust. The parents cannot expect the child to learn English overnight nor expect themselves to know automatically and immediately how to cope with a blind or deaf child.

The parents of children with SPECIAL NEEDS must also learn about resources available in the community so they can assist their children with specific conditions or problems.

Older children appear to fare much better in families with more than one child, and studies reveal they adjust the most rapidly in large families. Although on the surface this may seem contradictory, in that it would appear difficult for parents of large families to provide much attention to an additional child, what often happens is the children already in the home assist the adopting parents in welcoming the child and helping the child fit in.

Studies also reveal that people who already have children are favored by social service agencies as prospective parents for older children. The theory is that families with existing children understand child rearing and are not seeking a perfect child.

Another factor in adjustment is the attitudes of the family's support groups. Studies of new adoptive mothers indicate that many feel adoption is not accepted, at least initially, by family and peers; thus, it would appear that much more work needs to be done to educate the general public about adoption.

Adjustment is an ongoing process for parents as children grow older and become more independent: it is not a one-time achievement. (See also ADOLESCENT ADOPTED PERSONS; ATTITUDES ABOUT ADOPTION; MIXED FAMILIES; PREPARING A CHILD FOR ADOPTION; EXPLAINING ABOUT ADOPTION; SIBLINGS.)

Claudia Jewett, *Adopting the Older Child* (Boston: Harvard Common Press, 1978).
Lois Rusaki Melina, *Raising Adopted Children: A Manual for Adoptive Parents*, (New York: Harper & Row Publishers, 1985).
Cheri Register, *"Are Those Kids Yours?": American Families with Children Adopted From Other Countries* (New York: Free Press, 1990).
Stephanie E. Siegel, Ph.D., *Parenting Your Adopted Child* (New York: Prentice Hall Press, 1989).

adolescent adopted persons Adopted children ranging in age from the onset of puberty through about age 17 or 18.

It has been said that adolescence is the period of "normal psychosis," and clearly biological children as well as adopted children may face many conflicts during this turbulent period of physical and emotional changes.

Research on adopted adolescents offers very mixed findings on the level of adjustment or lack of adjustment within this group. Some researchers who have studied populations of psychiatric patients have reported a disproportionate number of adopted teenagers. Other researchers insist such samples are biased and contend that studies of adopted adolescents should be drawn from the general population and compared with nonadopted adolescents who are also drawn from the population at large.

Some researchers agree that the teen years can be stressful for any child but contend they may be particularly stressful for an adopted child because of the identity issues that must be faced during this period. Many adolescents are tempted to believe that they *must* be adopted, otherwise how could they have come from such "hopeless" parents? When children know they were adopted, they argue, this information may intensify fantasies about birthparents.

However, researchers Janet Hoopes and Leslie Stein found no evidence indicating that adopted adolescents have a more difficult adolescence than do non-adopted adolescents. (See IDENTITY.)

Sexual Identity Issues Dr. William Easson authored an influential paper on the "Special Sexual Problems of the Adopted Adolescent" in the July 1973 issue of *Medical Aspects of Human Sexuality*. According to Easson, "Most adopted children develop to be mature, comfortable adults, a source of continued pleasure and pride to their parents, but these adopted youngsters must reach appropriate sexual independence with greater effort than children in the natural, blood-related family."

Easson indicated the adopted adolescent faces three unique problems that must be overcome: the process of emancipation from adoptive parents, the overcoming of incestuous feelings and the ultimate identification with the parent of the same sex.

According to Easson, most children fantasize that they were actually adopted and their "real" parents were rich and famous. The problem is the adopted adolescent knows adoption was a reality, which may exaggerate the normal fantasies of teenagers. In addition, adoptive parents may sometimes tend to identify negative traits as genetic defects inherited from the birthparents.

Easson also felt adoption could slow down the emancipation process because of the likely age difference between the adopted child and the adoptive parents; in many cases, the adoptive parents may be closer to the age of the grandparents of the child's friends. (This difference is decreasing with today's demographics and the tendency of many Americans to delay childbearing until their late twenties or thirties.)

Says Easson, "When people adopt late in life, they may often act more like grandparents to their adopted child than parents so it makes it even more difficult when the youngster reaches adulthood for the parents and child to accept each other as adults."

One researcher hypothesized that adults who were adopted when their adopting parents were over age 35 would exhibit more depression than adopted persons with younger parents.

The age differential question was part of a 1987 doctoral dissertation by Judy M. Sobczak. She found no significant differences in depression between adopted adults with older parents and those with younger parents. She also found her study sample to be well adjusted and enjoying normal relationships with people. (See ADULT ADOPTED PERSONS for further information.)

Societal Attitudes Sometime it is very difficult for a teenager to admit that he or she was adopted because peers feel it is heartless to "give away" a baby and some express the opinion that abortion is more humane than adoption if the subject of a pregnant peer is brought up.

As a result, the child may be ashamed or embarrassed about the fact of having been adopted. Sometimes the family's attendance in an adoptive parent support group can help, particularly if the adolescent can meet other adopted teenagers.

Some researchers have identified special problems within subgroups of adopted persons, for example, Jewish adolescents who must resolve special identity issues or children who are raised in transracial adoptions.

A child's age at the time of adoption should be considered. In the past, nearly all adopted persons were adopted as infants; however, increasing numbers of children with SPECIAL NEEDS today are adopted over the age of eight.

The overwhelming majority of older adopted children were abused or neglected by their birthparents or stepparents and subsequently placed in FOSTER CARE for at least a year. As a result, they bring to the adoptive home many emotional and psychological problems they must resolve.

Studies by Barth, Festinger and others have also revealed that the older the child was at the time of adoption, the greater the probability the adoption will be at least initially troubled or even disrupted; however, children adopted as adolescents may also develop a strong rapport with their adoptive parents and resolve the earlier conflicts life placed on their young shoulders. (See DISRUPTION.)

As a result, when considering adopted adolescents, it is critically important to determine both the age of the adopted child at the time of adoption and the quality of nurturing care prior to the placement. It would be unreasonable to include adolescents adopted at birth in a study with adolescents adopted at age 14 and presume any valid conclusions could be drawn.

Unrealistic Societal Attitudes Adopted adolescents must also contend with a variety of unrealistic, negative and often erroneous ideas that society at large holds about adoption, for example, that the child should be grateful about the adoption, particularly if he or she was adopted from outside the United States.

It is usually presumed by society that the child's birthparents were poverty-stricken and of a lower socioeconomic status than the adoptive parents and, consequently, the adopted person should be thankful he or she was "saved" from a less positive situation. This idea can cause conflict in the adopted adolescent, because few teenagers feel a constant gratitude for their parents—adoptive or biological.

According to an article by G. A. Rickarby and Pauline Egan in the May 17, 1980, issue of *The Medical Journal of Australia,* it is a common societal fable that the adopted child should be grateful to adoptive parents for adopting him when birthparents were rejecting. The authors believe this fable has a negative for adopted adolescents who need to understand the reality of adoption.

The authors note another problem issue—the presumption of genetic inferiority or the presumed sense of failure that adoptive parents may feel when a child misbehaves. (See also ADOPTIVE PARENTS.) "This may mitigate the family's own guilt and inadequacy when they cannot activate behavior to meet often rigid requirements from the adolescent, or fit their own idea of 'proper parents' . . . ."

Jewish Adopted Adolescents A paper by Deborah N. Silverstein entitled "Identity Issues in the Jewish Adopted Adolescent" discussed problems unique to this group.

According to Silverstein, many issues become paramount when a Jewish adopted child reaches adolescence. Says Silverstein, "At this time three factors intersect: (1) an acute awareness of the significance of being adopted; (2) the profound meaning of being a Jew in history; and (3) a bio-psychosocial striving toward the development of a whole identity."

A key source of tension, according to Silverstein, is that many Jews adopt children who are not descended from Jews. Silverstein believes Jewish laws and attitudes make it difficult for adopted adolescents to regard themselves as Jews; for example, she says a civil adoption of a child by Jewish adoptive parents does not automatically make a child a Jew. Instead, the child must be formally converted to Judaism. (The conversion practice varies according to the particular branch of Judaism.) She adds that the child can be converted as young as age one.

The author concludes,

Jewish agencies which directly provide adoption services need also to offer more education and more post-adoption services. Jewish families need to be encouraged to adopt through Jewish agencies, so that they can benefit from inclusion in the community and can be permitted to view adoption as part of the Jewish experience. Adoption by Jewish parents in Jewish agencies can foster the family's integration into the Jewish community, thereby strengthening the adoptee, the family, and the community.

Transracially Adopted Adolescents Adolescents whose appearance is greatly different from the adoptive parents may experience a crisis during adolescence; for example, black children adopted by white parents may experience particular questions of identity. However, studies to date indicate that transracial adoption generally works very well.

A study by Ruth G. McRoy and Louis Zurcher on transracially and "inracially" adopted teenagers was described in their book, *Transracial and Inracial Adoptees: The Adolescent Years.*

According to the authors, it was primarily the "quality of parenting" that was critical to the child's adjustment rather than whether the adoption was transracial or inracial. Most of the adoptive parents studied by the researchers were able to successfully handle the challenges of transracial adoption; however, they conceded that some parents do not succeed as well.

They also noted that adopted adolescents in transracial adoptions who were raised in integrated neighborhoods had a more flexible racial perception than those who were raised in all-white neighborhoods.

Said the authors, "Adoptees in those contexts seemed to acknowledge their black background not only on a cognitive level but also on an affective level. Their parents instilled in these adoptees positive feelings about their racial background. They tended to desire contact with other black children and their families."

It is also clear from studies of children adopted transracially, most of whom are of different racial or ethnic backgrounds from their parents, that these adoptions have good results.

Juvenile Crime Although a few studies claim some linkage has been shown between criminality in adopted adults and similar behavior in birthparents, a similar relationship has yet to be established for adopted adolescents. In addition, experts disagree on whether adopted children are over- or underrepresented in the population of juvenile delinquents. Research has also indicated that, in the case of adopted persons, most juvenile criminal behavior does not continue into adulthood. (See DELINQUENCY.)

(See also ADULT ADOPTED PERSONS; FANTASIES OF ADOPTED CHILDREN; "CHOSEN CHILD"; IDENTITY; PSYCHIATRIC PROBLEMS OF ADOPTED PERSONS; TRANSRACIAL ADOPTION.)

William M. Easson, "Special Sexual Problems of the Adopted Adolescent," *Medical Aspects of Human Sexuality*, 28(July 1973): 92–103.

William Feigelman and Arnold Silverman, *Chosen Children: New Patterns in Adoptive Relationships* (New York: Praeger, 1983).

Jill Krementz, *How It Feels To Be Adopted* (New York: Knopf, 1988).

Ruth G. McRoy and Louis Z. Zurcher Jr., *Transracial and Inracial Adoptees: The Adolescent Years* (Springfield, Ill. 1983).

Deborah N. Silverstein, "Identity Issues in the Jewish Adopted Adolescent," *Journal of Jewish Communal Service*, Summer 1985: 321–329.

Judy M. Sobczak, "A Comparison of Adult Adoptees and Nonadoptees on Level of Depression and Quality of Relationships with Parents," Ph.D. diss., The University of Toledo, 1987.

adolescent birthmothers See BIRTHMOTHERS; TEENAGE PARENTS.

Adolescent Family Life Program A federal research and demonstration program enacted in 1981, authorized under Title XX of the Public Health Service Act and administered by the Office of Population Affairs within the Department of Health and Human Services.

The Adolescent Family Life Program supports research projects centering around adolescent pregnancy and includes studies on adoption and pregnant teenagers and teen parenting.

For further information, contact

Public Information Officer
U.S. Department of Health and Human Services
Office of Population Affairs
200 Independence Ave. SW, Room 736E
Washington, DC 20201
(202) 245-6335

adopted-away/adopted-in Two terms often used to identify adopted persons in legal matters, usually in regard to *inheritance* questions. "Adopted-away" refers to a child in reference to the family of the birthmother; an "adopted-in" child is one who has entered a family via adoption. Adoption practitioners find these terms to be negative and prefer to avoid them altogether.

"adoptee" v. "adopted person" "Adoptee" is now generally considered to be the less acceptable substitute label for the words "adopted person," "adopted adult," "adopted child" or "adopted teenager." (In many cases, the word "adopted" is an unnecessary descriptive adjunct, as in a newspaper article describing a public figure and his two daughters and "adopted son.")

The word "adoptee" is considered negative by many adoption professionals because it defines a person's entire existence around the issue of adoption, which is only one among many factors affecting an individual. It may also create the impression of a great degree of differentiation between "adoptees" and "nonadoptees," even though an adopted person is the lawful child of adoptive parents with the same rights and privileges as any child born to them. (See also ATTITUDES ABOUT ADOPTION; TERMINOLOGY.)

Adoptees' Liberty Movement Association (ALMA)

A search organization, which primarily provides information to adopted adults or birthparents seeking each other.

Founded in 1971 by an adult adopted person, Florence Fisher, ALMA membership today includes adopted persons over age 18, birthparents of adopted persons over age 18, birthparents of adopted minor children (ALMA will not provide assistance to birthparents searching for minor children), foster children, and adoptive parents. Other birth relatives are also eligible for membership, for example, birth grandparents and birth siblings.

The organization is based in New York and has chapters nationwide; ALMA assists adopted persons, adoptive parents and birthparents when the child is over age 18.

The association is also active in lobbying for OPEN RECORDS (availability of the original unamended birth certificate) and is opposed to sealed records.

A "reunion registry," a databank of information on adopted persons and birthparents, is operated by ALMA. The databank includes such information as the sex of the child, birth date and birthplace and can be used to assist ALMA members who are searching for their genetic antecedents.

The organization also publishes *The ALMA Searchlight*, the organizational newsletter. As of this writing, new members also receive a copy of *The Official ALMA Searchers' Guide*.

For more information contact

Adoptees' Liberty Movement Association
P.O. Box 154
Washington Bridge Station
New York, NY 10033
(212) 581-1568

adoption The act of lawfully assuming the parental rights and responsibilities of another person, usually a child under the age of 18. A legal adoption imposes the same rights and responsibilities on an adoptive parent as are imposed on and assumed by a parent when the child is born to the family. Adoption grants social, emotional and legal family membership to the person who is adopted.

An old and inappropriate definition of adoption is "to raise someone else's child," and in some minds, this definition may still prevail. Yet it mistakenly implies the concept of ownership, and people cannot own other people, including children. Instead, parents are responsible for their children, unless they choose to end that responsibility or the state decides to end the responsibility.

The birthparent cannot sever the genetic inheritance; however, she or he can terminate parental rights by transferring them to another family, or the court may opt to terminate parental rights and transfer them to another family when the family adopts the child.

The act of adoption generally includes a HOME STUDY, or family study, evaluation and counseling of the prospective adoptive parents, either before or after placement. The study is usually performed by a licensed social worker or individual serving in a caseworker capacity. This home study and the recommendations of the social worker are provided to the JUDGE at the time of FINALIZATION of the legal completion of the adoption.

The judge will then approve or disapprove the request for adoption. If approved, the adoption is valid thenceforth. The adopted child has all the rights of children born to a family, and the birthparents' parental rights and obligations are permanently severed by law.

The original birth certificate is usually "sealed" (see SEALED RECORDS), and a new birth certificate is prepared with the adoptive parents listed as parents.

If the birthparents wish to revoke their consent to the adoption, they must petition the court for a legal hearing and provide compelling reasons why the adoption should be invalidated. Very few adoptions are invalidated after finalization. (See also ADOPTIVE PARENTS; BIRTHMOTHER; BIRTHFATHER; INHERITANCE).

Adoption Assistance and Child Welfare Act of 1980 Public law 96-272, passed by Congress in 1980. This act was passed to correct or alleviate problems in the foster care system and to promote permanency rather than multiple foster placements. Another goal of the act was to encourage social workers to work toward reunification of the family and to avoid long-term foster care for the children if possible. If the child could not be returned to the family, another plan was to be sought: adoption, long-term foster care or some other resolution. The act also established the ADOPTION ASSISTANCE PROGRAM through which SPECIAL NEEDS adoptions are partially subsidized by the federal government.

Reasons for removing a child from a home are generally ABUSE, NEGLECT or ABANDONMENT. The act requires a review of each case every six months and a judicial review when the child has been in foster care for 18 months. Most states have great difficulty complying with the 18 month requirement; however, the act has been successful in bringing about the adoption of many children who were once considered UNADOPTABLE. (See also FOSTER CARE.)

Implementation of the act has apparently been very haphazard throughout the United States. According to a report released by the NORTH AMERICAN COUNCIL ON ADOPTABLE CHILDREN (NACAC) in 1990, with contributions from former Vice President Walter Mondale and key people in the child welfare field, there are still serious problems with implementation; for example, there is insufficient data on the numbers of children in foster care, and good information is critically needed. There is also an uneven enforcement of the law by states, and in some areas, judges are still not fully complying with the law because of lack of training, heavy court calendars and other reasons.

According to Representative George Miller (D, Calif.), the status of foster children in many cases is as problematic as it was in 1980, although the reasons why children are entering the foster care system have changed greatly. (Many more cocaine babies and infants afflicted with pediatric AIDS or orphaned by families with AIDS are entering and will enter the system.)

Unfortunately, a recent General Accounting Office (GAO) report supports such conclusions by revealing that no states are fully complying with this law. According to the 1989 report, "Federal reviews have revealed problems in the case review system, most frequently involving the lack of timeliness in conducting reviews, that are often traced to inadequacies in state court performance."

Even so, the length of time children remain in foster care has decreased since 1977, according to the report, from a median length of time of 31 months in 1977 to 17 months in 1985. (A significant number of children reenter the system.) (Also, according to the GAO, several projects and studies have revealed a higher success rate with adoptions than with REUNIFICATION of children with their parents or caretakers.)

Also, on the positive side, the NACAC report indicated that many more older children are entering adoptive families than in past years and more adoptive parents are receiving adoption subsidies, enabling them to afford to adopt children with special needs.

According to attorney Mark Hardin, director of the Foster Care Project at the American Bar Association's Center on Children and the Law, one problem has been crowded court calendars that make it difficult to comply with the 18-month judicial hearing. Another problem has been a misinterpretation of the 18-month judicial hearing requirement. Some states consider the 18-month hearing to be a routine review of the case when, in fact, it is supposed to be a rigorous review.

Writes Hardin of the 18-month review, "Within 18 months after placement the court is to decide whether to return the child home, to legally free the child for adoption or to authorize some other permanent arrangement. Extensions of regular foster care are permitted only in special circumstances."

Sometimes legal counsel to public agencies is spread too thinly, and an attorney may only meet a social worker just prior to the hearing, allowing insufficient time to understand the case and the goals for the child. Social workers may find themselves acting in an inappropriate role as legal counsel.

In some cases, judges have apparently purposely subverted the goals of the act, for example, by assigning a completely different case number to each sibling, even when siblings have been placed in foster homes together. There are many other problems not addressed here.

Some states, however, have not only met but actually exceeded the provisions of the act. Hardin cites the example of Ohio, which requires a hearing within 12 months of foster care placement, a special advance motion on the child's status and also a written explanation from the court if foster care is extended.

The act also provided federal funds and required states to create adoption subsidy programs. In past years, many children with SPECIAL NEEDS were not adopted because adoptive parents could not afford the extensive medical bills. This problem has increased in recent years with the entry into the foster care system of children with AIDS and COCAINE AND CRACK BABIES (see DRUG ABUSE), as well as children who need continuing psychotherapy. (See also ADOPTION ASSISTANCE PROGRAM; WAITING CHILDREN.)

General Accounting Office, *Foster Care: Incomplete Implementation of the Reforms and Unknown Effectiveness,* GAO/PEMD-89-17, August 1989.

Mark Hardin, "Ten Years Later: Implementation of Public Law 96-272 by the Courts," in *The Adoption Assistance and Child Welfare Act of 1980: The First Ten Years* (St. Paul, Minn.: NACAC, 1990).

North American Council on Adoptable Children, eds., *The Adoption Assistance and Child Welfare Act of 1980: The First Ten years* (St. Paul, Minn.: NACAC, 1990).

Adoption Assistance Program The ADOPTION ASSISTANCE AND CHILD WELFARE ACT OF 1980 was the enabling legislation that authorized federal subsidies to adoptive parents. It has become even more meaningful since Congressional actions in 1986. Monthly payments are made to the adoptive parents of children with SPECIAL NEEDS who were adopted through a public agency or through a private agency that coordinated the adoption with the public agency.

These subsidies are part of the federal Adoption Assistance Program. Payment amounts may be changed, depending on circumstances. Federal subsidies end when the child is 18 unless he or she is physically or mentally handicapped, in which case, at state option, payments may continue until the child is 21. They also end if the parents are no longer supporting or are no longer legally responsible to support the child or if the parents (or the child) die.

A determination is made of the child's eligibility prior to the time of adoption, and an adoption assistance agreement is drawn up between the adopting parents and the state or other public agency.

The federal definition of a child with special needs is a child (1) who cannot or should not be returned to the home of his or her parents, (2) for whom there is a special factor or condition (such as ethnic background, age, membership in a minority or sibling group or a physical, mental or emotional handicap, because of which the state has concluded that the child cannot be adopted without a subsidy) and (3) an effort has been made to place the child with appropriate adoptive parents without providing adoption assistance.

Because factors related to children who are considered to have special needs vary from state to state, a child who is over age eight in one state may be considered to have special needs by virtue of age, while in another state the cutoff age may be older or younger.

Some families who are interested in adopting a particular child or children may feel inhibited about requesting a subsidy from the state, assuming that the social worker may pass them by for a family who does not need a subsidy and the paperwork it entails. An open discussion of the needs of the child and the circumstances of the parents is an important part of the negotiation of the adoption assistance agreement.

Subsidies may also be paid to foster parents who adopt their foster children if the children are determined to have special needs and it is determined that the foster parents and children have strong emotional ties that would make it detrimental for the state agency to seek a family that would adopt without a subsidy.

The Adoption Assistance Program may provide monthly payments to adoptive parents, based on the adoption agreement signed between the adopting parents and the public agency. The states and the federal government share the cost of these subsidies.

Payment amounts are determined through the agreement, which takes into consideration the needs of the child and the circumstances of the adoptive family. The subsidy may not exceed the amount the child would have received under Aid to Families with Dependent Children (AFDC) foster care.

One-time payments of up to $2,000 are also authorized to adopters of children with special needs for expenses related to adopting the child or children. This payment may be authorized whether or not the child is eligible for a continuous subsidy and includes reimbursement for court costs and lawyer fees, home study fees, transportation and food and lodging expenses directly incurred in the adoption process.

Before January 1, 1987, adoptive parents were allowed to claim a $1,500 tax deduction related to expenses incurred in adopting a child with special needs. This tax deduction was repealed by Congress.

According to the Committee on Ways and Means in the U.S. House of Representatives report, "Background Material and Data on Programs Within the Jurisdiction of the Committee on Ways and Means," six states participated in the subsidy program in the 1981 fiscal year. By the 1988 fiscal year, all 50 states were participating in the program, and an estimated 33,000 children were being provided for.

Children with special needs who are adopted under the federal program are also eligible for MEDICAID. The Medicaid card is issued by the state in which the child resides with the adoptive parents. (In the past, when children were adopted from other states or moved with their adoptive families to other states, the "sending" state issued the Medicaid card; however, many providers refused to accept an out-of-state card. As a result, the rules were changed.)

The Adoption Assistance Program may also include social services to adoptive families, and some states provide additional payments and services, using both federal and state funds; for example, according to the book *Adoption Law and Practice*, the program in Virginia can offer special payments for dental needs, speech therapy, psychiatric treatment, agency and legal fees for adoption and other expenses.

Often the existence of a subsidy means the difference between children being adopted or remaining in foster care. (This is why Congress, responding to child advocacy groups, created legislation enabling subsidies.)

Researcher Richard Barth found the receipt of adoption subsidies was a positive element in the success of the adoption of a child with SPECIAL NEEDS, although actual subsidies received by adoptive parents occurred far less frequently than expected by researchers.

Families with high risk placements disrupted less often when the family received a subsidy. Perhaps the subsidy eased the financial burden for the family that succeeded, and the lack of one added to the problems of the families who were denied subsidies or who received inadequate subsidies.

Deborah Hage, a parent of nine children, wrote about her personal experience with subsidies in a March/April 1987 issue of *OURS* magazine:

> "One thing is certain: without the prospects of a subsidy, we would not have considered adopting . . . The expense would have been too much of a burden. We would have had to change the standards of living of the children we already had in order to meet the expenses of three more children with problems. And we simply would not have done it. We would have lived comfortably with six children instead of extending our resources to cover nine. In all likelihood, Jamie, Jesse, and Amber would have been split up."

She concluded, "That is the bottom line on adoption subsidies: they enable children to be adopted who otherwise might not be."

U.S. Congress, House, Committee on Ways and Means, *Background Material and Data on Programs Within the Jurisdiction of the Committee on Ways and Means,* 1989 edition, March 15, 1989.

Richard P. Barth and Marianne Berry, *Adoption & Disruption: Rates, Risks, and Responses* (New York: Aldine De Gruyter, 1988).

Deborah Hage, "Love Those Subsidies!" *OURS*, March/April 1987, 18–19.

Joan H. Hollinger, editor-in-chief, *Adoption Law and Practice* (New York: Bender, 1989).

Sharon House and Sharon Stephan, "Federal Programs Affecting Children," Congressional Research Service (CRS) Report for Congress, March 1, 1987.

adoption benefits See EMPLOYMENT BENEFITS; INSURANCE; PARENTAL LEAVE.

adoption circle Refers to the key parties involved in an adoption: the adopted individual, the birthparents and the adoptive parents, as well as birthgrandparents, adoptive grandparents, siblings and others. A similar concept is more frequently expressed as an ADOPTION TRIAD or ADOPTION TRIANGLE.

Adoption Defense Fund An incorporated and charitable fund created to lobby for improvements in state and federal adoption laws and to force compliance with existing laws created to protect children and families; an organization independent of the NATIONAL COMMITTEE FOR ADOPTION, although committee members also serve on the Adoption Defense Fund's board of directors.

Some legislative improvements sought by the Adoption Defense Fund are

changes in insurance laws (so adopted children will receive coverage as do children born to the family)

tax breaks for adoptive parents

changes and improvements to immigration laws in order to improve international adoptions requirements to take more rapid action on children who are stuck in the foster care system for years

protection of confidentiality for the members of the adoption triad

In addition, the Adoption Defense Fund works for important changes to the judicial treatment of triad members, for example, by filing friend of the court (amicus curiae) briefs in major cases, filing lawsuits to force public agencies to fulfill their responsibilities and becoming involved in other legal battles as needed.

For more information, contact

Adoption Defense Fund
1930 17th St. NW, Suite B
Washington, DC 20009
(202) 332-5728

Adoption Hall of Fame Annual award proffered by the National Committee For Adoption since 1987 to the persons or organizations who have contributed the most to the field of adoption during the preceding year. Recipients of the award include President Gerald Ford, the Rev. George Clements, and Dorothy and Robert DeBolt. For more information, contact

Adoption Hall of Fame
c/o National Committee For Adoption
1930 17th St., NW
Washington, DC 20009

adoption triad Concept describing the genetic and/or legal relationship of the birthparents, adoptive parents and adopted child to each other. Those who support the concept of a "triad" rather than a "triangle" or a "circle" believe that the triad concept is more clear because it does not connote a tightly knit relationship.

Rather than being at opposite ends, as in a triangle, or facing each other, as in a circle, the triad describes the major parties to the adoption but does not presume there will be a continuing relationship between the birthparents and the adopted person (although such a relationship could theoretically develop as in the case of an OPEN ADOPTION).

adoption triangle Similar concept to the ADOPTION CIRCLE; refers to the adopted person, birthparents and adoptive parents as three points on the triangle and the three parties most involved in an adoption. It is considered a negative phrase by many adoption professionals (See also ADOPTION TRIAD.)

Adoptive Families of America Inc. (AFA) Formerly known as OURS Inc. (Organization for a United Response), Adoptive Families of America, a national nonprofit organization, is the largest organization of adoptive parents in the United States, with a membership of over 15,000 adoptive and prospective adoptive families and individuals and 220 adoptive parent support groups, all committed to building families through adoption. (The name change occurred in 1989 because members believed the new name would be clearer and more accurate than the former name.)

According to an April 1989 release from AFA, "AFA seeks to create opportunities for successful adoptive placements and promotes the health and welfare of children without permanent families."

The original organization of OURS was formed in 1967 by 10 families gathering together at the Minneapolis/St. Paul, Minnesota airport to meet the children arriving from Korea they planned to adopt. Today, members include parents who have adopted their children from the United States and abroad or who plan to adopt a child.

Adoptive Families of America publishes a bimonthly award-winning magazine, *OURS: The Magazine of Adoptive Families,* which members receive; AFA also sells adoption books oriented to both children and adults and products for multiethnic families.

The organization provides a free adoption information packet explaining the adoption process and listing agencies for potential placement, and its staff responds to questions and assists with referrals.

A 24-hour hotline—"Helpline"—is available for families in a crisis situation. In addition, AFA refers callers to support groups and adoptive families in their communities. A grant program provides financial aid to organizations serving children without permanent families.

The organization also assists local support group members by offering financial grants and a videotape lending library of tapes as well as technical assistance on questions related to operating a support group. Support group leaders receive a quarterly newsletter, *Adoptive Parent Support Group Leader.*

The organization works in the federal and state legislatures for equitable laws and regulations affecting adoptive and prospective adoptive families; AFA provides accurate, nonsensationalized adoption information to the media.

For more information, contact

Adoptive Families of America Inc.
3333 Highway 100 North
Minneapolis, MN 55422
(612) 535-4829

adoptive parents People who lawfully adopt children. (This entry concentrates on nonrelative adoptions. See GRANDPARENT ADOPTIONS or RELATIVE ADOPTION for information on those topics.)

Most adoptive parents are married couples; however, single people may also adopt children. Some states prohibit homosexuals from adopting children. (See GAY AND LESBIAN ADOPTION.)

According to a national estimate of step-, biological and adopted children by Jeanne Moorman and Donald Hernandez based on 1980 U.S. Census statistics and published in *Demography,* 4% of U.S. married couples have adopted at least one child. Adoptions were deduced by using the marital and birth history data of the family. If a child was not a birth child of either member, then the child was presumed to be an adopted child. Stepchildren who were adopted by stepparents were still considered stepchildren for the purposes of the study; consequently, all the children considered adopted were not genetically related to either the husband or wife.

About half of the families had both adopted and biological or stepchildren, and half had adopted children only. (Those with adopted children only were called "purely adoptive" families.)

Age of Adoptive Parents Most infertile couples who seek to adopt infants range in age from their twenties to late thirties. Many adoption agencies will not accept applications for an infant from prospective adoptive parents under age 25 or over age 40 or 45.

It is also interesting to note that in the general population, many more older mothers bore children in 1988, according to the National Center for Health Statistics, as compared to earlier years; for example, the birth rate for women ages 30–34 increased by 3% in 1988 to 73.7 per 1,000, the highest rate in 20 years. The largest increase was seen in the birth rate for women ages 40–44, which increased by 9% over 1987 rates. (See also FERTILITY RATES.) As a result, adoptive parents and many biological parents in the general population will be much closer in age than in past years.

Moorman and Hernandez found adoptive parents with no children born to them and no stepchildren to be older parents; for example, "purely adoptive" parents in the 1980 Census statistics were more likely to be at least 45 years old as compared to the ages of parents in other types of families.

Adoptive parents who adopt internationally may be older than those who adopt domestically because guidelines on age may be less strict: Some Latin American countries will accept adoptive parents up to age 55 or 60; other countries, however, have age guidelines as strict or even stricter than U.S. adoption agencies have for children born in the United States.

There are several reasons for this less restrictive policy, but probably the paramount reason is the fact that in some countries numerous babies and toddlers are residing in orphanages and need parents. As a result, their need for families overrides considerations such as age and marital status of the adoptive parents.

There are also political reasons for international adoption policies, and some extremely poor countries severely restrict adoptions by individuals in other countries or ban them altogether.

Couples or singles who seek to adopt so-called "hard to place" children, also known as children with SPECIAL NEEDS, or WAITING CHILDREN, range in age from about 25 to late forties or even fifties. As with other limiting criteria, age limits are relaxed when a child is considered to fall into a special needs category by virtue of race or ethnicity, age, sibling group membership, handicap or other category.

Age of Child Adopted According to a 1990 report by the National Center for Health Statistics, most adoptive parents adopted children under age one: 81% adopted infants and children under age one; 5% adopted children under 2; 3% adopted two-year-old children; and about 11% adopted children over age two.

Marital Status Most agencies limit applications for healthy infants to couples and may require the couple to have been married at least two or three years. Singles are often referred to "waiting children"; however, many singles adopt infants from other countries and some succeed in adopting U.S. babies.

Race The overwhelming percentage of adoptive parents identified by the National Center for Health Statistics in their 1990 report were white. According to their study, 93.2% of the adoptive mothers were white, and 4.5% were black. (The number of adopted children was 1,081.)

In 92.4% of the cases, the adoptive mother and child were of the same race; consequently, transracial adoptions represented 7.6% of the adoptions. Of this 7.6%, in 1.2% of the cases, the mother was white, and the child was black. In 1.6% of the cases, the mother was another race, and the child was white. In 4.8% of the cases, the mother was white, and the child was a race other than black. (See TRANSRACIAL ADOPTION.)

Moorman and Hernandez found black and white families were both equally likely to have an adopted family member; however, the black families were more likely to adopt relatives' children and stepchildren (31% stepchildren for black families versus 15% for white families). In addition, INFORMAL ADOPTION, which is not legally supported, is apparently more common among black families. This finding is also supported by the 1990 data from the National Center for Health Statistics.

Education According to data from the National Center for Health Statistics reported in 1990, 54% of the adoptive mothers studied in 1987 had 13 or more years of education. Only 6.6% had less than 12 years of education.

Foster Parent Status Some adoptive parents were previously foster parents to the children they subsequently adopted, and in some states, 50% or more of the children adopted through the state social services department were adopted by their foster parents. (See FOSTER PARENT ADOPTIONS.) When parental rights were terminated by the court, the foster parents requested permission to adopt the child in these cases.

Foster parents are by no means guaranteed the right to adopt the child they are fostering. Social workers first strive to reunite a child with the birth family or family of origin. As a result, a child could live with a foster family for a year or longer and then leave it; however, there appears to be a movement toward allowing or even encouraging foster parents to adopt. In addition, experts urge social workers to place children with families who would be appropriate to adopt them should reunification with the birth family not be possible.

Studies by Richard Barth and other researchers have revealed foster parent adoptions disrupt at a lower rate than "new" adoptions, and various states have begun instituting programs to train people who wish to become foster parents about adoption as well, sometimes combining classes for adoptive parents and foster parents. (See DISRUPTION.)

A possible reason for this success is that foster parents have had ongoing in-service training opportunities and also ongoing social work postplacement support. Adoptive parents who were not foster parents receive counseling and assistance to the point of finalization, when services stop. (See POSTLEGAL ADOPTIVE SERVICES.)

Infertility Infertility is a prerequisite to apply to most adoption agencies placing babies, and the applicant may be required to provide medical proof of infertility.

Most adoptive parents have a primary infertility, which means they are childless and have never borne a child. Others face secondary infertility, which means they have had one or more children but are now infertile.

The agency social worker seeks to determine if the couple has successfully resolved most of their conflicts and anxieties about their infertility so they will be able to fully accept an adopted child.

Fertility or infertility is generally not an issue when a special needs adoption is being contemplated, and infertility is often not an issue in international adoption. As a result, optional adopters or preferential adopters are individuals who are fertile but prefer to adopt rather than reproduce.

In a study to determine the "propensity" to adopt among white women, Dudley L. Poston Jr. and Ruth Cullen analyzed data from women who were surveyed in 1973, 1976 and 1982. The researchers found that "parity" (whether or not the women already had children and how many children they had) was the most significant factor, and childless women were the most interested in adoption.

Good Character Most agencies require at least three written references of the applicants' good character; hence, presumably most adoptive parents have good characters. In addition, in the case of an independent adoption, there is usually a HOME STUDY made of the adoptive family. Part of that home study is to determine if the prospective family is of good character. In addition, police checks may be run to ensure the applicant has no criminal record. Agencies operated under religious auspices may require a reference from a member of the clergy of the applicants' faith group.

Citizenship United States citizenship may be required by agencies or attorneys arranging the adoption of children in the United States; hence, most adoptive parents are U.S. citizens. If a couple in the United States wishes to adopt a child from another country, at least one of them must be a U.S. citizen, based on U.S. Immigration and Naturalization Service requirements. If a single person wishes to adopt a child from another country, she or he must be a U.S. citizen.

Socioeconomic Status There are indications adoptive parents of newborn infants tend to be middle class and upper middle class in income and overall socioeconomic status. In a 1990 study of adoptive mothers by the National Center for Health Statistics, researchers found more than one-third of the adoptive mothers had a family income of $35,000 or more.

Adoptive parents who have adopted their foster children generally are blue collar or working class, primarily because most foster parents tend to fall into this category. Fees involved in adopting a former foster child are low, and subsidies may be available to parents who adopt children with special needs.

Number of Children in the Home Agencies that place infants may restrict applications to childless couples or couples with one child. Some agencies will accept an application from a family with one adopted child only if that adopted child was adopted through their agency. As a result, many families adopt only one or no more than two children (unless they adopt a sibling group, which is considered one category of "special needs").

When agencies place children with special needs, the number of children already in the home is not usually seen as a barrier, but the ages of the children in the home may be a determining factor in the age(s) of the child or children placed in the home by the social worker. For example, the social worker may not wish to place teenagers with a family who has preschoolers.

According to Moorman and Hernandez, joint biological-adoptive families averaged the greatest number of children, with 3.8 per family, including 2.4 biological and 1.4 adopted children. Purely adoptive families averages 1.3 adopted children; purely biological families averaged 1.9 biological children. Consequently, families composed of only adopted children are usually smaller than other types of families.

Psychological Adjustment to Children
Infertile couples may have undergone years of physically and psychologically painful fertility tests and procedures. When a couple decides to adopt a child, they must then undergo a home study, which is generally perceived as threatening no matter how positive and supportive the social worker is.

As a result of this insecurity, some researchers have hypothesized that adoptive parents are far more insecure than biological parents. This view is based on anecdotal literature rather than studies. A doctoral dissertation by Thomas Cook in 1988 revealed that adoptive parents can be well-adjusted and even more well-adjusted than first-time biological parents.

According to Cook's data, biological parents faced more difficulty than their "adoptive counterparts." Cook compared first-time biological parents with adoptive parents who adopted children of the same race and adoptive parents who adopted transracially.

He found biological parents experienced the most adjustment difficulties, followed by the transracial adopters. The adoptive parents of children of the same race experienced the least difficulty. Parenthood was not perceived as a crisis event for parents in the three groups. Adoptive parents were married almost twice as long as biological parents, which probably contributed to their stability.

Cook stated, "Another consideration is that adoptive parenthood is a highly desired and voluntary status for those choosing to be adoptive parents." He speculated some of the biological parents may have had unplanned pregnancies.

In another study, adoption experts compared the attachment levels of adoptive parents and biological parents to their infants, finding no significant differences. (See IN-FANT ADOPTION.)

A comparison study of first-time adoptive and biological families was made by Kathryn Goettl for her master's thesis in nursing at the University of Wisconsin in 1989. Studying 60 couples, Goettl found the adoptive mothers tended to take more time off from work after the arrival of the infant than did the biological mothers. She speculated that perhaps the reason for this finding was that the adoptive mothers were older and possibly more secure in their jobs. In addition, the adoption agency may have required the adoptive mother to stay home with the child. Finally, the decision to take an extended leave may have been a personal one, prompted by the usually long wait to adopt the child.

A similarity she found in her study was that both prospective adoptive parents and biological parents fantasized equally about the child, which seems to contradict other studies that indicate adoptive parents suppress fantasizing.

She hypothesized that although adoptive parents apparently do fantasize about their future children, their fantasies and daydreams may "lack specificity as far as features, coloring, or the degree that the imagined baby looks like someone." Interestingly, she found that when preadoptive parents and birth parents did visually fantasize, they later reported that the actual baby looked very different from the fantasy child. Hypothesized Goettl, "This finding suggests that perhaps not only adoptive parents, but birth parents as well, must mourn the idealized child in order to bond more effectively with the child who is theirs."

Attitudes of Others Studies have also revealed that support or the lack of support for an adoption is important to adoptive parents. Charlene Miall reported on the "stigma" some adoptive parents feel and the impression they have that adoption is perceived as "second class." (See ATTITUDES ABOUT ADOPTION.)

Working Mothers Some adoption agencies require adoptive mothers to take an extended maternity leave. But the number of all mothers working outside the home has increased in the past 10 years along with the number of adoptive mothers working outside the home.

According to an article by Christine Bachrach in a 1986 issue of the *Journal of Marriage and the Family,* only 35% of the adopted children in 1976 had mothers who worked outside the home. By 1982, 51% of the adopted children had mothers who worked outside the home. That figure is probably greater today.

As a result, agencies that require one parent to leave work may find some resistance from adoptive parents. Each state has its own laws on PARENTAL LEAVE, and some states require parental or maternal leave for adoptive parents while others limit leave rules to biological parents. In addition, EMPLOYMENT BENEFITS, including leave, adoption reimbursements and other benefits, vary by employer. Generally, larger employers are more generous with adoption benefits than are small employers.

Reasons for Adoption Most childless people report they wish to adopt a child because they love children and feel something is missing in their lives without a child. Families who already have children place a greater emphasis on what they can give a child, for example, a stable and happy family life.

A dissertation by Barbara Moulden Reid at the University of Texas at Austin in 1983 revealed a difference between how adopters of children with special needs and adopters of healthy infants perceived themselves and traits important to adoptive parents.

Both groups wished to create families or enlarge their families. But the healthy white infant adopters stressed spousal relationship, love of children and desire for parenthood as most important parental traits, while the adopters of children with special needs stressed flexibility and patience.

Adoptive Parents Evaluating Adoption A British study of adult adopted persons and their adoptive parents by Lois Raynor yielded valuable information. Raynor reported her findings in *The Adopted Child Comes of Age.*

Of the adoptive parents who were interviewed, 85 percent reported their overall experience with their child had been "very satisfactory" or "reasonably satisfactory." Of the families who had been disappointed in the adoption experience and their child, several were unhappy because of severe health problems experienced by the child.

One family was very negative about ILLEGITIMACY, considering it a "curse." Raynor believed their child ultimately disappointing them was a self-fulfilling prophecy.

She also found molding the child was important to adoptive parents. Those who were most dissatisfied felt they had failed to "mold" the child.

According to Raynor's study, the adoptive parents' perception of similarities between themselves and the child was critically important to parental satisfaction: 97% who thought the child was like them in appearance, interests, intelligence or personality were happy with the adoption, while about 62% were satisfied when the child was perceived as different.

The child didn't necessarily resemble adoptive parents nor was he or she very similar to them when observed by an outsider—it was the adoptive parents' perception of the similarity that was key.

Overall Impact on Their Children: Nature vs. Nurture Numerous studies have been performed both on twins separated at birth and on adopted children and adults to determine the effects of genetics and the environment. (See ENVIRONMENT; GENETIC PREDISPOSITIONS; INTELLIGENCE.) A wide array of effects have been observed by researchers, who have noted disparities and similarities in personalities, physical abilities and many other aspects of life. Most researchers believe both heredity and environment play important roles in a child's life.

A study by T. W. Teasdale and T. I. A. Sorensen found a tendency for male adopted persons to enter the same career field or trade as their adoptive fathers.

Other researchers have noted personality differences between adoptive parents and their children; however, the authors of one study made an important and highly perceptive point. In their study, authors Sandra Scarr, Patricia L. Webber, Richard A. Weinberg and Michele A. Wittig stated, "Adoptive parents, knowing that there is no genetic link between them and their children, may expect less similarity and thus not pressure their children to become like the parents." (The researchers did find a "modest degree of personality resemblance among biological relatives," which "exceeded the minimal similarities of adopted relatives.")

Adoptive Parents of Large Sibling Groups Social workers are often reluctant to place sibling groups with families who have never parented and are inexperienced at rearing children.

Said Margaret Ward, an instructor at Cambrian College in Ontario, Canada,

"Adoptive parents who eagerly anticipate an intimate parent-child relationship could be bitterly disappointed. A couple with no children or only one or two may also find it difficult just to manage the number of newly placed children. In addition, if the parents have little experience with groups of children, they may have problems understanding and thus dealing with the existing patterns of interaction among the siblings." (See also ADULT ADOPTED PERSONS; EMPLOYMENT BENEFITS; ENTITLEMENT; LARGE FAMILIES; PARENTAL LEAVE; SIBLINGS; SPECIAL NEEDS.)

Christine A. Bachrach, "Adoption Plans, Adopted Children, and Adoptive Mothers," *Journal of Marriage and the Family,* 48(May 1986): 243–253.

Christine A. Bachrach, Ph.D., Patricia F. Adams, Soledad Sambrano, Ph.D. and Kathryn A. London, Ph.D., "Adoption in the 1980's," *Advance Data from Vital and Health Statistics of the National Center for Health Statistics,* January 5, 1990.

Thomas F. Cook, "Transition to Parenthood: A Study of First-time Adoptive and Biological Parents," Ph.D. diss., University of Alabama, 1988.

"Family Types Vary in Education, Income," *The Wall Street Journal,* July 26, 1989, B1.

Kathryn Goettl, "Transition to Parenthood: A Comparison of Adoptive and Birth Parents," M.S.N. thesis, University of Wisconsin-Madison, 1989.

Jeanne E. Moorman and Donald J. Hernandez, "Married-Couple Families with Step, Adopted, and Biological Children," *Demography,* 26(May 1989): 267–277.

Katherine A. Nelson, *On the Frontier of Adoption: A Study of Special Needs Adoptive Families* (New York: Child Welfare League of America, 1985).

Dudley L. Poston Jr. and Ruth Cullen, "Propensity of White Women in the United States to Adopt Children," *Social Biology,* 36(Fall–Winter 1989): 167–185.

Lois Raynor, *The Adopted Child Comes of Age* (London: George Allen & Unwin, 1980).

Barbara Moulden Reid, "Characteristics of Families Who Adopt Children with Special Needs,"

Ph.D. diss., University of Texas at Austin, 1983.

Sandra Scarr, Patricia L. Webber, Richard A. Weinberg and Michele A. Wittig, "Personality Resemblance Among Adolescents and Their Parents in Biologically Related and Adoptive Families," *Journal of Personality and Social Psychology*, 40(1981): 885–898.

T. W. Teasdale and T. I. A. Sorensen, "Educational Attainment and Social Class in Adoptees: Genetic and Environmental Contributions," *Journal of Biosocial Science*, 15(1983): 509–518.

U.S. Department of Health and Human Services, National Center for Health Statistics, "Advance Report of Final Natality Statistics, 1988," *Monthly Vital Statistics Report*, 39, no. 4, supplement (August 15, 1990).

Margaret Ward, "Choosing Adoptive Families for Large Sibling Groups," *Child Welfare*, 66(May–June 1987).

adult adoptee The less acceptable substitute for the phrase "adult adopted person" or "adopted adult." (See ADULT ADOPTED PERSONS).

adults, adoption of Refers to the adoption of a person who is over age 18 by another adult, usually for reasons of inheritance or to make official a long-standing informal parent-child relationship. The adopted adult voluntarily consents to the adoption, as does the adopter. In some states, notice of the adoption to birthparents may be required despite the adult status of the adopted person, and in other states, permission from the adopted person's spouse is required.

The overwhelming majority of all adoptions are of adults adopting children; however, it is legally permissable in all states for adults to adopt other adults if no fraud is intended. The laws governing the adopting of adults vary from state to state, as do restrictions. In many cases, the adopting party must be older than the person adopted.

According to Irving J. Sloan, author of *The Law of Adoption and Surrogate Parenting*, an adult may not adopt another adult in Illinois unless the person to be adopted has lived with the prospective adopter for at least two years.

Also, Sloan says only those who are permanently disabled or retarded or those who established a foster child relationship or stepchild relationship while the person to be adopted was still a child may be adopted in Ohio.

In some cases, an adult homosexual may have attempted to adopt another adult homosexual as a way to create a legal relationship since they may not legally marry. However, some courts have denied such petitions on the grounds that such an adoption is not in the best interests of society in general; for example, in 1984 an adoption was denied in New York because of a lack of a "genuine" parent-child relationship.

At least one state, Louisiana, allows the adoption of adults by creating and registering a private agreement between the two parties.

Gay couples who are interested in protecting each other's right of inheritance would be better served by contacting an attorney to draw up wills. In addition, several courts have held that homosexual individuals who have been involved in long-term relationships may inherit on the principle of an implied trust.

Adult adoption does not usually involve any HOME STUDY, since presumably the adult to be adopted can manage his or her own affairs and does not need the protection of a social worker's analysis of the adopter; however, some states may require a social worker's report for all adoptions.

Joan H. Hollinger, editor-in-chief, *Adoption Law and Practice* (New York: Matthew Bender, 1988).

Irving J. Sloan, *The Law of Adoption and Surrogate Parenting* (New York: Oceana Publications, 1988).

adult adopted persons A person over age 18 who was adopted as a child or, in some cases, (usually for reasons of inheritance) as an adult. Most adopted adults were adopted as infants or children.

Some adopted adults have stated they resent the label of "adopted child" that society often places on all adopted persons, regardless of age. They believe this phrase connotes an aura of immaturity and diminishes the adopted person's responsible adult status.

In the recent past, adopted adults were expected to behave similarly to all adults. If they were well-adjusted, adopted adults would presumably face no problems related to their adoption and would, in general, merge seamlessly with the overall population of all adults.

Psychological Adjustment of Adopted Persons Most adults who were adopted as children appear to have successfully resolved conflicts stemming from their adoption.

Studies of adopted adults reveal those who are the most well-adjusted and confident have known of their adoptive status for a long time; however, some who learned of their adoption later in life are able to accept this information constructively. Most, however, have difficulty accepting their adoption when they find out accidentally; they often feel betrayed and wonder what else their parents did not tell them.

As a result, most psychologists and social workers strongly recommend adoptive parents share with their child that he or she was adopted by them. This information must be provided at a level of understanding appropriate to the child's age and discussed more than once. (See EXPLAINING ADOPTION.)

A paper published in 1960 by Marshall Schecter concluded that adopted children were overrepresented in his caseload of psychiatric patients, based on a sample of 16 psychiatric patients who were adopted persons.

As a result, many people involved in the field of adoption (as well as people opposing the concept of adoption) concluded that adoption could contribute to instability and even mental illness in people. This argument has been used to promote OPEN ADOPTION and also to condemn all adoption as inhumane and unworkable.

A study of both children and adult adopted persons receiving psychiatric services was reported by Paul and Evelin Brinich in 1982, and the authors came to a very different conclusion in their article, "Adoption and Adaptation."

According to researchers, the percentage of adopted persons among Children's Service patients was somewhat higher than expected (5% as against an expected 2.2%), and the percentage among adult patients (1.6%) was actually below the expected rate of 2.2% in the population at large.

The authors also stated that adoptive parents are generally middle class people and may be more sensitized to psychological or psychiatric problems and more willing to take their children to therapists when needed.

Other researchers have stated their opinion that it is unfair to study only adopted persons who have been institutionalized or those identified as suffering from psychoses. These researchers believe a valid comparison between adopted persons and nonadopted persons should be made by drawing from the general population.

A 1980 Ph.D. dissertation by Susan Marie Raffloer contrasted 30 adopted and 30 nonadopted women drawn from the general population and evaluated their levels of adjustment. The author concluded, "The results of this investigation do not indicate adoption to be a significant determinant in adult adjustment/maladjustment."

A 1987 doctoral dissertation study by Judy H. Sobczak at the University of Toledo analyzed adopted adults who joined their families as infants and found that their sample was well-adjusted and enjoyed normal relationships with people. Again, this finding is in contrast with anecdotal literature that describes feelings of negativism, anxiety and depression in adopted adults.

The study also found a significant correlation between "maternal control issues" in the group of adopted persons raised without siblings. "Only children" adopted adults perceived their adoptive mothers as more controlling than did adopted adults who had been raised with siblings.

The researcher also studied whether children whose adoptive parents were over 35 years old when they were adopted exhibited greater symptoms of depression than adopted persons whose adoptive parents were younger at the time of adoption.

The hypothesis was that adopted persons would exhibit more depression when adopted by older parents. The data did not, however, reveal any significant difference between adopted adults whose parents were over or under 35 when they were adopted; consequently, it was concluded older parents generate no more depression in adopted offspring than did the younger parents.

Katherine A. Kowal and Karen Maitland Schilling reported on adult adopted persons in the *American Journal of Orthopsychiatry*. They studied 110 adopted adults, ages 17 to 77, recruited through adoption agencies and a "search" group; 75% were female, and 108 were white.

The adopted adults were asked for their perceptions of their adoptions and could agree or disagree with one or more of the suggested statements. 35.45% reported they felt "chosen or special"; 21.82% reported they felt "no different from anybody else"; 20.91% reported "feeling different, but neither better nor worse than others"; 25.45% were "worried or insecure about being adopted"; and 17.27% were "embarrassed or uncomfortable with the fact of their adoption."

When asked what information they wish adoption agencies would provide to adoptive parents, presumably to be passed on to them later, the adults reported medical information as the most desired data—75% of the subjects wanted information on the birthparents' medical history.

Seventy-one percent said they wanted information on personality characteristics of the birthparents. (This information was actually given to only about 4% of the adopted persons.)

It's unclear whether adoption agencies had provided such information to the adoptive parents, but it seems likely that a personality appraisal probably was not given. In addition, the researchers stated that other studies had revealed that adoptive parents tend to present a very positive and euphemistic view of the birthparent. They wrote,

> Many subjects had been given a reason why they were placed for adoption, yet this information still ranked high on their list of things they wanted to know . . .

Some other information desired by adopted adults included a physical description of birthparents; the ethnic background of the birthparents; information on the adopted person's early medical history; the names of the birthparents (in most cases, unknown to the adoptive parents); interests of the birthparents; the reasons why an adoption decision was made for the adopted person; the education and occupation of the birthparents; where they resided as young children before the adoption took place, (in a foster home, with a relative, etc.); and other factors.

At least one study has found adopted persons to be better-adjusted than those who were not adopted. Kathlyn Marquis and Richard Detweiler reported on their findings.

Wrote the authors, "Contrary to expectations, adopted persons are significantly more confident and view others more positively than do nonadopted persons."

In addition, the attitudes of adopted adults toward their parents was compared to the attitudes of nonadopted persons toward their parents. The researchers found that "adoptive parents are experienced as significantly more nurturant, comforting, predictable, protectively concerned and helpful than nonadoptive parents." (See also ADJUSTMENT.)

Adopted adults were also found to have a stronger sense of control over their lives, and demonstrated more self-assurance of their own judgement.

The authors concluded,

> The adopted may be different but, in contrast to the literature, may be different by being more positive rather than more negative than their nonadopted peers . . . If, as the earlier literature implies, there were large numbers of mentally ill adopted adults, one would expect to find some indication of this in the community population when compared with a similar community population of nonadopted peers . . .

It is important to note the overwhelming majority of adult adopted persons studied by Marquis and Detweiler were adopted as infants: 89% were adopted within three months of birth, and 95% were adopted within one year of birth.

The social and psychological adjustment of adopted persons who were adopted at an older age could yield very different results, particularly if they had been victims of child abuse or were placed in one or more foster care settings prior to the adoption. (See DISRUPTION for further information.)

Lois Raynor studied adopted adults among adopted Britons and reported her findings in her book *The Adopted Child Comes of Age*.

Out of 104 adopted adults interviewed, 80% reported their adoption experience was "very satisfactory" or "reasonably satisfactory" (58% reported very satisfactory and 22% reported reasonably satisfactory).

Reported Raynor, "Of the three who were very unhappy in their adoption, one was a young woman who had been placed in a very busy and incredibly class-conscious family, who attributed everything, good or bad, to heredity." In another case, a very intelligent boy was placed in an "unsophisticated" family, and the parents were unable to control the child.

The third very unhappy adopted person had been placed shortly after his adoptive parents had lost a beloved infant because his birthmother had reclaimed him. "Apparently the adoptive mother had not been able to work through her grief at the time, as nearly 25 years later at the research interview she wept bitterly for her lost baby. The son said he had always been compared unfavourably with the reclaimed child."

It's readily apparent this family was in no way ready to accept a child at the time they were placed with one. Most social workers today would refuse to place a child in a home where the adoptive parents were grieving such a loss.

Adopted persons were also far happier about their adoption when they perceived some common grounds with their adoptive parents in interests, appearance or other factors. Of the adopted adults who felt "very much like" their adoptive parents, 97% rated their adoption experience as satisfactory. Conversely, 52% who perceived themselves as "unlike or uncertain" rated the experience as satisfactory.

Individual satisfaction with information provided the adopted person about the adoption was related to the perception of the adoption experience. It was not the amount of information provided but whether or not the individual felt it was a sufficient amount that was the critical element.

Raynor noted, "Some were content with very little while others wanted much more. No apparent relationship was found between satisfaction and how *often* the adoption was discussed within the family—this seemed to be a highly individual matter—but there *was* a clear relationship with the degree of ease and comfort people felt in being able to ask their adoptive parents for further information if they wanted it."

The adopted persons were also rated by Raynor on current levels of adjustment: 70% were rated as "excellent" or "good," 25% were "marginal," and 5% were "poor".

Among the 5% who were poorly adjusted, Raynor interviewed one man who was in prison and very depressed and had been delinquent since age eight. "The adoptive mother had died before he went to school, his uninterested father somewhat later, and he was brought up by an adoptive relative who felt it was her Christian duty but who had no enthusiasm for the task," reported Raynor.

Raynor also observed that biological parents are rarely contrasted with adoptive parents, nor are biological children asked later in life if they were and are happy.

> No one knows what proportion of parents are satisfied with the children born to them, or vice versa. No one can say what proportion of young adults would be considered well-adjusted by the rather stringent criteria which we used in this project . . . the cost and technical problems in finding a properly matched sample of adopted adults have defeated all researchers so far.

(See also ADOLESCENT ADOPTED PERSONS; ADOPTIVE PARENTS; PSYCHIATRIC PROBLEMS OF ADOPTED PERSONS; REUNION; SEARCH; SPECIAL NEEDS; TRANSRACIAL ADOPTION.)

Paul M. Brinich, Ph.D., and Evelin B. Brinich, M.A., "Adoption and Adaptation," *The Journal of Nervous and Mental Disease*, 170:8, 489–493.

Katherine A. Kowal, Ph.D., and Karen Maitland Schilling, Ph.D., "Adoption Through the Eyes of Adult Adoptees," *American Journal of Orthopsychiatry*, 55(July 1985) 354–362.

Susan Marie Raffloer, "A Comparative Study of Adjustment Variables Among Adopted and Nonadopted Adults," Ph.D. diss., Ohio University, 1980.

Jerome Smith, Ph.D., and Franklin I. Miroff, *You're Our Child: The Adoption Experience* (Lanham, Mo.: Madison Books, 1987).

Kathlyn S. Marquis and Richard A. Detweiler, "Does Adopted Mean Different? An Attributional Analysis," *Journal of Personality and Social Psychology*, 48:4(1985): 1054–1066.

Lois Raynor, *The Adopted Child Comes of Age* (London: George Allen & Unwin, 1980).

Marshall D. Schecter, M.D., "Observations on Adopted Children," *Archives of General Psychiatry*, 3(July 1960): 21–32.

Judy M. Sobczak, "A Comparison of Adult Adoptees and Nonadoptees on Level of Depression and Quality of Relationships with Parents," Ph.D. diss., University of Toledo, 1987.

advertising and promotion Print or electronic media are sometimes used to recruit adoptive parents or parents considering placing their children for adoption. Paid advertising is also used by some adoption agencies, attorneys or prospective parents who are seeking to adopt infants, while agencies that seek to recruit adoptive parents for WAITING CHILDREN are generally not charged by the media.

Promoting the Adoption of "Waiting Children" A popular form of advertising used by state social services departments nationwide is the "Wednesday's Child" type of program (or Thursday, Friday or whatever day the feature runs). Usually showing an older or minority child available for adoption, the print media offer a photograph of the child and a brief description along with a telephone number interested parties can call for further information. The television media usually show a videotape of the child, stating his or her first name, basic information about the child's age and other very general information.

The goal is to interest people reading the article or viewing the program and inspire them to investigate adoption, either of this particular child or in general.

Most state adoption offices maintain a photolisting of available adoptable children, and this book is shown to couples and individuals interested in adopting children with SPECIAL NEEDS.

In addition to social service agencies successfully using this advertising/public relations approach, adoptive parent support groups also assist adoption agencies by publishing photos and descriptions of WAITING CHILDREN in their newsletters.

The largest adoptive parent support group in the United States is Minneapolis-based ADOPTIVE FAMILIES OF AMERICA INC. (formerly known as OURS). This organization prints photolistings of waiting children in the United States and overseas in each issue with phone numbers of the agencies responsible for placement.

Often, listed children have physical disabilities, although otherwise healthy children may also be included for whom it is hard to find families because of the "special need," such as being black or of mixed race or part of a sibling group.

There are also several national nonprofit groups that sell photolistings of waiting children. One is Children Awaiting Placement (CAP), located in Rochester, New York, which publishes a two-volume listing of children with special needs nationwide and issues biweekly updates. The organization charges $75 for its listing.

The International Concerns Committee for Children in Boulder, Colorado offers a photolisting of about 500 waiting children overseas. A 12-month subscription with monthly updates costs $25.

Some tabloids have also run adoption listings of waiting children.

Couples Advertising for Babies In addition to advertisements or promotions run by adoption agencies, people hoping to adopt infants sometimes use advertising to identify a pregnant woman interested in placing her child. This is the most controversial type of advertising.

Although today it is primarily prospective adoptive parents who advertise their desire to adopt, in the early 1900s parents wishing to place their infants and children with adoptive parents frequently advertised *for* adoptive parents. A probable reason for the advertising of one's children at that time was the fact that the number of available infants and children exceeded the demand for adoptable children, particularly during the Depression years.

A 1927 monograph by the Church Home Society in Boston condemned such advertising of one's own children, and advertising one's children was a practice ultimately banned in every state. Today such a practice would be considered "baby selling," unlawful in every state in the United States.

Ads placed by prospective parents today usually refer to a couple's infertile status and state in emotional language that they "long for" a child and will provide a good home.

Advertising by private parties seeking to adopt babies is legal in some states, not addressed and therefore considered legal in other states and illegal in others. Some states require a special wording or phraseology to the advertising. In other states, only child-placing agencies may advertise.

In some cases, ads that appear to have been placed by people desperately seeking a baby are actually placed by an attorney or agency trying to identify pregnant women for adoptive parents. (There is no way to know the prevalence of misleading advertising, but it does exist.)

Those who oppose advertising for babies do not approve of a direct contact between a pregnant woman and prospective parents and prefer initial contact be made through a social worker or attorney. They also believe advertising demeans adoption and treats babies as commodities rather than human beings.

Some attorneys approve of placing advertisements themselves but discourage prospective parents from advertising; they believe an attorney is more adept at screening pregnant women. There are also risks involved for pregnant women responding to advertisements, including the risk of contacting an unscrupulous person who plans to sell the baby and defraud the woman. Most pregnant women considering adoption are in a crisis situation and unable to judge the sincerity or reputation of a person through a phone call. They are likely to be completely unaware of adoption laws and are highly vulnerable.

Proponents of advertising insist that it works for both adoptive parents and pregnant women, helping facilitate a match that would not otherwise occur.

Agency Outreach Ads In recent years some adoption agencies have begun aggressive advertising campaigns, primarily to attract pregnant women considering adoption for their babies. In addition to an ad in the telephone book's yellow pages, larger agencies often offer a toll-free hotline, and some agencies use billboards, brochures and other marketing techniques.

When contacted by a pregnant woman, such aggressive agencies respond immediately rather than waiting until office hours, while more traditional agencies are not staffed or prepared to handle cases except during business hours. Larger agencies will often meet the woman at her home or in a designated site, such as the local fast food hamburger chain, so she need not go to the agency office.

A new method of adoption is the practice of DESIGNATED ADOPTION or TARGETED ADOPTION, wherein prospective parents find a pregnant woman on their own and ask an adoption agency to perform the home study.

Some agencies actually encourage prospective parents to advertise for a child and offer to screen pregnant women for the adopting parents. If a caller appears right for the adopting parents, as determined by the agency social worker, then the adoption will take place. (See also AGENCIES; ADOPTIVE PARENTS; BIRTHMOTHER; CAP BOOK; PHOTO LISTINGS.)

agencies Organizations that screen prospective adoptive parents and place children in adoptive homes.

Agencies vary according to the types of children they place. Some agencies concentrate on newborns, while others primarily place older children or hard-to-place children. Some agencies concentrate on U.S.-born children while others specialize in international adoption. There are an estimated 3,000 adoption agencies in the United States.

Agencies that make adoptive placements must be licensed by the state in which they practice, although some agencies are also licensed to place children in other states. Agencies that place children in other states usually work with another agency in that state and through the INTERSTATE COMPACT ON THE PLACEMENT OF CHILDREN, which is a sort of treaty between the states and governs interstate adoption. A small number of agencies are licensed by more than one state to make direct adoptive placements in a state other than the one in which they are based.

Sometimes adopting parents deal with two adoption agencies; for example, an agency in their state who approved them and an agency in another state where the child to be placed resides.

The size of agencies varies greatly, ranging from agencies with a staff of one director and one social worker placing 10 children a year to facilities that include a large complex with housing, a hospital and other facilities and place hundreds of children per year.

Agencies under the auspices of a particular religious faith are called sectarian agencies. Such agencies may concentrate on serving individuals of a particular faith or group of faiths. Some sectarian agencies serve persons of all faiths and even allow adoptive parents of other faiths to apply to adopt a child.

Agencies operated under nonreligiously affiliated auspices that do not restrict applications from prospective adoptive parents based on their religious preference are called nonsectarian agencies. Although questions may be and probably are asked about the applicants' background and current religious participation, membership in a specific religious group is not required as a criteria for adopting.

Nonsectarian agencies generally do not have denominational or religious labels, such as "Baptist," "Catholic," "Lutheran,"

"Jewish" and so forth, as part of the agency's name.

Public adoption agencies are nonsectarian, as are many private adoption agencies. Persons who are strongly religious as well as persons who are moderately religious or not religious may apply to nonsectarian adoption agencies.

Agencies are usually staffed by social workers who have a degree in social work or a degree in a helping profession, such as psychology or counseling. They are usually supervised by a person with a master's degree in social work or psychology.

Most adoption agencies believe strongly that their mission is to find good families for "their" children, rather than to find babies and children for families. They may, however, have criteria limiting the applications for healthy infants to only infertile couples.

Most agencies engaged in adoption work provide counseling to pregnant women and mothers considering placing their infants or older children for adoption. Their goal is to ensure that the birthparents make a good parenting plan for their child and for themselves and that, if adoption is chosen, they be as comfortable as possible with it.

Agencies also offer counseling and assistance to birthfathers and the parents of birthmothers and birthfathers to help them deal with their feelings of grief and loss.

The birthparents considering adoption are almost always in a period of crisis. The pregnant woman may have been abandoned by a man she thought loved her, or she may have been shunned by her own parents. In addition, she may have difficulty meeting her basic needs of survival, including food and shelter. The birthfather may feel that he and the birthmother are too young and immature to marry and raise a child. (Some birthparents are married. See MARRIED BIRTHPARENTS.)

The agency will assist by helping the pregnant woman find a place to live, showing her how to apply for public assistance and providing extensive supportive services so desperately needed. In addition, they will help her find a physician who can provide her much-needed prenatal care.

Such agencies also provide counseling to prospective adoptive parents and perform an evaluation of their potential parental fitness in a process called the HOME STUDY or family study.

When prospective parents are applying for an infant, social workers also want to ensure that the family has worked through all or most of their feelings of grief related to infertility. They want parents who consider adoption their first choice and not a poor "second-best" option.

Most adoptive parents have been through extensive infertility testing, which was painful physically and emotionally. By the time they come to the adoption agency, they may still be distraught and the social worker helps them work through any remaining sense of trauma connected with their infertility. Prospective adoptive parents and also pregnant women considering adoption are often very fearful of the social worker and the power invested in her or him to make decisions of lifelong impact.

Some agencies have introduced more candor into their process and encourage the adopting parents to write a nonidentifying RESUME, which describes why the family wants to adopt, what the family's hobbies and interests are and other facts. A pregnant woman or a birthmother considering adoption will review these resumes and select the family she wants for her child.

OPEN ADOPTION is another option offered by some agencies, wherein a total disclosure of identities is directly or tacitly given by the adoption agency social worker.

Agencies placing older children and children with SPECIAL NEEDS must also provide counseling to the child(ren), preparing the child for adoption, explaining adoption, introducing the prospective parents to the child and serving as a child advocate if there are any questions or problems subsequent to placement.

One purpose of the home study is to help in preparation for parenting and explanation of many adoption issues, for example, how and when to talk to the child about adoption and how to deal with the reactions of friends and family to adoption. The average person is very unaware and uneducated about adoption issues, and social workers do not want adoptive parents to be as ignorant; therefore, an educational component has become a popular addition to the adoptive parent preparation process.

CLASSES with other prospective adoptive parents are increasingly popular among adoption agencies. These classes cover a variety of adoption issues and also enable adopting parents to meet others in the same situation. Often friendships are formed that last for years.

Agencies may not discriminate against minority pregnant women or adoptive parents, although some agencies may have difficulty identifying appropriate parents for a minority child, particularly a black or biracial infant or child.

Some agencies place only American-born children, while other agencies concentrate on international adoptions. Most of the international adoption agencies also place a small number of children from the United States.

Most adoption agencies are nonprofit, but their funding varies depending on whether they are public or private and several other factors.

Public agencies are state, county or local social services adoption units, and these are funded through state, county and federal funds. The primary focus and activity of public adoption agencies is to find families for children with SPECIAL NEEDS who are awaiting adoption.

Private agencies include sectarian agencies—those with religious auspices, such as Bethany Christian Services, Catholic Social Services, Jewish Family Services, LDS (Latter-day Saints) Social Services and similar agencies. These agencies may receive partial funding from members of their respective religious groups and are usually able to charge less than agencies that receive no outside funding.

Other agencies are nonsectarian but receive a portion of their funding from charitable, fundraising organizations, such as the United Way. The balance of their funding comes from the money paid by adoption applicants.

Many adoption agencies rely solely on fees paid by prospective adoptive parents. These fees must cover expenses related to the pregnant women themselves (for example, shelter provided to them or money paid for food or medical bills), counseling services to adoptive parents, salaries of social workers and office expenses, such as rent, heat, lights, phone.

Agencies vary greatly in what they charge adopting parents. They may charge a flat rate or a percentage of gross income or have some other means of computing the adoption fee; for example, they may charge a flat rate for the home study and add on the cost of the prenatal care and hospital bill.

The key advantage to the pregnant woman, the prospective adoptive parents and the child in dealing with an adoption agency is the counseling provided by an adoption agency before an adoption as well as the counseling available after the adoption has been finalized.

The disadvantages of agency adoptions are that the waiting period may be longer than the adoptive parents desire and that a newborn child is usually placed in a temporary foster home rather than directly from the hospital into the adoptive home. (Some agencies do strive to place infants as quickly as possible to promote early bonding and will even place an infant in a LEGAL RISK adoptive home. See AT RISK PLACEMENT; HIGH RISK PLACEMENTS.)

Agencies use their own foster homes rather than the state foster homes. Birthmothers sometimes confuse the term "foster home" with the shelter homes provided by the state when an abused child is removed from the home. The reason many agencies insist on temporary foster care for infants is that they want the birthmother to have time to fully rethink the decision and plan she embarked upon before the child's birth.

They believe she may be too emotional to think rationally right after the baby is born and needs to go home without the child to think the whole idea of adoption through thoroughly. Then, if she still wants the child adopted in a few days or weeks, depending on the agency and the situation, she signs the appropriate papers, and the child is placed.

Some mothers voluntarily make an adoption plan for toddlers and older children, and agencies also place these children. Many young women think they can parent a child successfully but find the burden of single parenthood intolerable. After a period of months or even a year or more, they turn to the agency for assistance.

Virtually all agencies place children with SPECIAL NEEDS, and the definition of special needs varies drastically from agency to agency. One agency may consider any child over the age of two as a child with special needs because that agency rarely receives children over that age. Another agency may consider only children over age eight as falling under the category of special needs. In addition, newborn infants and older children with birth defects and/or correctable or noncorrectable problems are also considered to have special needs.

Children who are black and biracial are almost always considered to have special needs, even when they are healthy and of normal intelligence, because their number exceeds the number of homes available to adopt them. The reason for this apparent "surplus" is complex and much-disputed. The National Association of Black Social Workers has alleged that insufficient numbers of black parents have been recruited and contends that many more black adoptive parents could be identified. Others contend that the problem is in public or private agencies that discourage TRANSRACIAL ADOPTION.

Agency criteria for individuals wishing to adopt a child with special needs are usually relaxed in the sense of age limits, number of children already in the home and other criteria in effect for people who want to adopt healthy white infants. As a result, a person over age 40 who is single and already has three children may often be considered as a prospective parent.

Some agencies charge a much lower rate for children with special needs while other small agencies cannot afford to charge substantially less because of their own expenses.

Agencies may also assist the state social services office by placing children with special needs for adoption, primarily children who have been abused, neglected and abandoned and subsequently lived in foster homes.

Postplacement services are provided by many agencies, who will counsel adopted persons, adoptive parents and birthparents years after the adoption. If the adopted adult wishes information about birthparents, the agency will usually provide assistance within the limits of their agency policies and the laws of the state.

Although agencies are usually licensed, mere licensure of an agency does not necessarily ensure that good, ethical practices will be provided by an agency. Agencies should be investigated by various means, including an examination of accreditation, to ensure as much as possible that services and fees will be appropriate. Similarly, nonagency adoption arrangements should also be checked out. Professional licensure of an attorney, member of the clergy, physician or social worker is no guarantee of competence in adoption practice. (See also AUTOBIOGRAPHY; CONFIDENTIALITY; INFANT ADOPTION; INTERSTATE COMPACT ON THE PLACEMENT OF CHILDREN; OPENNESS; POSTPLACEMENT SERVICES; SOCIAL WORKERS; TRADITIONAL ADOPTION.)

AIDS Acquired Immune Deficiency Syndrome, caused by the Human Immunodeficiency Virus (HIV). This disease is almost always fatal and is apparently even more virulent in afflicted children. An estimated 2% of all AIDS cases in the United States are found in infants and children.

AIDS will have an increasingly devastating effect on children until a cure is found. Children can contract AIDS in utero from an infected mother and can also contract the disease from an infected breast-feeding mother.

According to the Centers for Disease Control in Atlanta, about 30% of the infants who test positive for AIDs at birth will continue to test positive after about age 20 months. This indicates that the majority of the newborn infants who test positive for the virus are testing positive because of their mother's antibodies but do not actually have the disease. Whether one child develops AIDS or not has no effect on subsequent children: Each birth is an independent event.

Children have also contracted AIDS through contaminated blood transfusions. In addition, many healthy children are orphaned when their parents die of the disease. It may be difficult to find foster parents or adoptive parents for children who test positive for AIDS, and many such children languish in hospitals.

In 1988, scientists developed an AIDS test for newborns called "HIV DNA by PCR," a test by Specialty Laboratories, Inc. in Santa Monica, California. (PCR stands for "polymerase chain reaction.") This test allegedly can determine if the child is actually infected with HIV to differentiate from the child testing positive because he or she has maternal antibodies to the disease.

According to company officials, the test costs about $175 as of this writing and is still being researched. They note that they have tested newborn twins and found one twin infected and one twin not infected. Since their test, the infected twin died, and the other child is thriving.

One agency in New York has been very successful in finding foster families for children testing positive for the human immunodeficiency virus. The Leake & Watts Children's Home in Yonkers, New York found foster families for 90 infants testing positive for HIV from 1986 to 1989, and over 50% of the children were adopted by their foster parents (30% who originally tested positive continued to test positive as toddlers). The agency has not seen seropositivity (continuing to test positive for HIV) as a factor affecting whether or not the child has been adopted by foster parents.

The agency believed its success rate was due to active recruitment, strong support to foster parents and also the relatively high rate of foster care stipend paid in New York (in 1990, $1,231 per month). The agency actively networked with existing foster parents, asking them to bring interested prospective foster parents to meetings. In addition, the agency solicited help from the gay community.

Virulence of Pediatric AIDS The HIV virus is particularly virulent in young children. In a study reported in the *New England Journal of Medicine,* 17% of the children studied died in their first year of life, and the median survival for the 172 children studied was 38 months from diagnosis.

According to the authors, "There is only a short period during which antiviral treatment or other prophylactic measures can be initiated before the onset of clinical disease." The problem is that infants who are infected at birth are "asymptomatic." As a result, it would seem prudent to test all high-risk newborns, if not all newborns. (High-risk newborns would include newborns born to drug addicts and prostitutes.)

Societal Costs Physicians at Harlem Hospital Center in New York analyzed the financial cost of boarder babies who tested positive for AIDS. The total care cost for these children over the period of 1981–1986 was over $3 million, and the average lifetime costs of the infants who were born and died in the hospital were about $90,000 per child. (The children who died lived about 129 days.)

These boarder babies remained in the hospital about four times longer than the AIDS babies for whom there were homes: 339 days for the boarder babies compared to 89 days for children with homes. The two key predictors for an extended hospital stay were intravenous drug abuse by the mother and boarder baby status.

After the child is released from the hospital, societal costs may still be high. The Leake & Watts Children's Home in Yonkers, New York, estimates that institutionalization costs about double what it costs the state to place a child with a foster family.

Societal Shunning Children who carry the AIDS virus are shunned by many. Often many parents do not want their children to attend school alongside a child with AIDS, fearful their own child could contract this dread disease.

Experts insist that AIDS may only be contracted by sexual intercourse, by an exchange of body fluids, by using contaminated needles, or by the transfusion of contaminated blood. Since these activities are unlikely among children under the age of 12, most parents need not fear the child with AIDS; however, the fear is very real and very pervasive.

Guarded Hope One optimistic note was reported in *Science News*. Researchers treating AIDS-afflicted children with zidovudine (AZT) discovered that this drug increases the intelligence level of the treated children. Children over age 6 improved dramatically in perception and motor skills.

In addition, although infants born with the virus suffered lower IQs than children who were later infected through blood transfusions, AZT enabled the IQs of both groups to increase about the same percentage.

Unfortunately, AZT does not cure the disease altogether, and much more work must be done to find that elusive cure.

Finding Foster Families and Adoptive Families The problem with finding adoptive or foster families for children with pediatric AIDS is complicated by many states' requirement to keep the AIDS condition confidential. As a result, some placing agencies have found themselves unable to tell prospective parents about the ailment, while at the same time fearing that withholding such information could lead to legal liability.

Some workers have "gotten around" confidentiality restrictions by stating that the child is MEDICALLY FRAGILE or severely disabled or by using other code words. Unfortunately, adopting parents don't always comprehend social worker jargon.

Despite various problems with finding an appropriate family, agencies are locating adoptive families. Such families should be aware of the problems they'll face, including psychological and financial burdens; for example, if the general community discovers the child has AIDS, the family is likely to be shunned. It's also extremely difficult or even impossible to locate a babysitter who will care for a child with pediatric AIDS.

Phyllis Tourse and Luanne Gundersen of the Massachusetts Adoption Resource Exchange (MARE) have said, "Respite care for children with AIDS is largely unavailable. It may also be difficult to get babysitters even for a few hours."

Financial burdens in adopting a child who tests positive for HIV can be great, and parents need to know this fact. If MEDICAID and adoption subsidies are made available, some of the financial strain can be alleviated.

Many adoption agencies have no formal policy on when to test a birthmother for AIDS; however, if the pregnant woman is a drug abuser or has had numerous sexual partners, it is likely she will be tested. (It would seem good policy for the agency to request such testing to protect itself legally in the event the mother is infected and has passed on the virus to the child.)

Adopting parents who are concerned should ask the agency what its AIDS policy is;

however, it is unlikely (as of this writing) the agency caseworker will require information on every sexual partner the pregnant woman has known.

Screening of ADOPTIVE PARENTS for AIDS is not a mandatory requirement of any state as of this writing; however, Idaho's policy says foster parents and prospective adoptive parents in high risk groups should be tested. (It's unlikely the state would approve foster or adoptive parents who are drug abusers or child molesters because these activities are undesirable in and of themselves, whether the person carries HIV or not.)

Probably the only category of foster parent or adoptive parent who might potentially be approved yet need to be tested is the person who suffers from hemophilia.

HIV Among Adolescents The HIV virus is also a problem among teenagers. Researchers evaluated the tests of 1,141,164 individuals who applied for admission into the U.S. military service, finding 393 who tested positive, and concluded, "Infections with the human immunodeficiency virus are not rare among teenaged Americans." Males and females were about equally alike in numbers testing positive. Black teenagers had the highest rate (1.06 per 1,000), followed by Hispanics (0.31 per 1,000) and whites (0.18 per 1,000).

Geographically, the researchers found a wide variation, with the highest incidences seen in individuals from the states of Maryland, New York, South Carolina, California, Texas and Florida. (States are listed in order from greatest prevalence to least of individuals from the six states with the highest incidences, for example, a prevalence of .90 per 1,000 in Maryland to a prevalence of .40 per thousand tested in Florida.) (See also DRUG ABUSE; SPECIAL NEEDS.)

Col. Donald S. Burke, M.C., U.S.A.; Lt. Col. John F. Brundage, M.C., U.S.A.; Mary Goldenbaum, M.S.; Lytt I. Garnder, Ph.D.; Lt. Col. Michael Peterson, V.C., U.S.A.F.; Col. Robert Visintine, M.C., U.S.A.; Lt. Col. Robert R. Redfield, M.C., U.S.A.; and the Walter Reed Retrovirus Research Group, "Human Immunodeficiency Virus Infections in Teenagers: Seroprevalence Among Applicants for US Military Service," *Journal of the American Medical Association (JAMA)*, 263(April 18, 1990): pp. 2074–2077.

Centers for Disease Control, "Adoption/Fostering Best Option for Orphans with HIV," *CDC AIDS Weekly*, August 13, 1990.

James D. Hegarty, M.P.H., Elaine J. Abrams, M.D., Vincent E. Hutchinson, M.D., Stephen W. Nicholas, M.D., Maria S. Auarez, M.D., Margaret C. Heagarty, M.D., "The Medical Care Costs of Human Immunodeficiency Virus—Infected Children in Harlem," *Journal of the American Medical Association*, 260 (October 7, 1988): 1901–1905.

"Promising Drug for Children with AIDS," *Science News*, February 11, 1989, p. 88.

Phyllis Tourse and Luanne Gundersen, "Adopting and Fostering Children with AIDS," *Children Today*, May–June 1988, pp. 15–19.

Gwendolyn B. Scott, M.D., Cecelia Hutto, M.D., Robert W. Makuch, Ph.D., Mary T. Mastrucci, M.D., Theresa O'Connor, M.P.H., Charles D. Mitchell, M.D., Edward J. Trapido, Sc.D. and Wade P. Parks, M.D., "Survival in Children with Perinatally Acquired Human Immunodeficiency Virus Type 1 Infection," *New England Journal of Medicine*, 321 (December 28, 1989): 1791–1796.

alcohol abuse and adopted persons

Alcoholism is the excessive and chronic consumption of alcohol over time. The American Medical Association and other influential groups recognize and treat alcohol dependence as a disease. Alcoholism among pregnant women is a serious social problem today. Alcohol abuse during pregnancy can cause severe and irreversible mental and physical problems in children. If an alcoholic woman with a CRISIS PREGNANCY is considering adoption for her child, physicians should carefully monitor the pregnancy and assist her in entering a detoxification program as soon as possible. (See FETAL ALCOHOL SYNDROME.)

Certain subcultures and ethnic groups appear to have a greater problem with alcoholism than others; for example, many Native American tribes have a documented problem with alcoholism, a problem many are working to prevent. (Because of the great diversity in drinking practices among various tribal groups, however, it is impossible to generalize about the drinking problems of Indians as a whole.)

A Genetic Predisposition Studies of adopted persons, adoptive parents and birthparents have revealed that alcoholism is at least partially an inherited trait; consequently, adopted persons with alcoholic birthparents may have a genetic predisposition to the disease. However, the majority of adopted persons do not exhibit alcoholic behavior, even when birthparents are alcoholics. Currently, most scientists agree that alcoholism is based on a complex mix of genetic, cultural and social factors. Much of the current evidence for a genetic contribution to alcoholism is derived from Scandinavian studies of the incidence and patterns of the disease among adopted adults, as well as of adopted twins who were separated at birth. However, scientists continue to find evidence for a genetic role in a number of studies along many different lines, including selective breeding experiments of animals, analyses of similarities between certain brain wave phenomena of alcoholic fathers and their sons, examination of hereditary psychological deficits and studies of biochemical markers of a predisposition to alcoholism.

In April of 1990, it was reported in the *Journal of the American Medical Association* that a research team headed by Dr. Ernest P. Noble of the University of California at Los Angeles and Dr. Kenneth Blum of the University of Texas Health Science Center in San Antonio had identified a gene that is believed to be linked to a higher risk of alcoholism. The gene, located on chromosome 11, is the "D2" receptor gene for dopamine, a chemical tied to pleasure seeking behavior, and was found in the brains of 77% of the 35 people studied who had died of alcoholism. The gene was present in the brains of only 28% of the nonalcoholics studied. The finding will need to be repeated on a larger number of alcoholics before it can be considered certain.

The most frequently cited studies supporting a genetic role in alcoholism are the Scandinavian adoption studies, which consistently show that the biological susceptibility for alcoholism is active even when children are separated from their biological families. These studies have become increasingly sophisticated since the landmark Swedish finding in 1960 that, of identical twins separated at birth, the chance that one twin would become alcoholic if the other did as well was 74%. (In contrast, the concordance of alcoholism between fraternal twins was found to be 26%.) Given their number and variety, it is possible to report on these studies in only a cursory way here, and readers are referred to sources at the end of this entry for more information. Among the most compelling findings of these adoption studies, it was found that the biological sons of alcoholics, as well as the biological daughters of alcoholic mothers, were three times as likely as other adopted persons to develop alcoholism. The most recent research in this area has focused on heritability of specific drinking behaviors, such as frequency, quantity and regularity of drinking at particular times. Interestingly, the heritability estimates for these behaviors have been found to range from 36 to 40%.

Among the most important of adoption studies was the analysis of Swedish research that has revealed the existence of two types of genetic predispositions to alcoholism (Cloninger et al, 1981). Type I, or milieu-limited, alcoholism fit most closely into existing causal patterns for alcoholism. This type was found to occur in both sexes (it could be transmitted by either biological parent and could be passed to children of either sex) and was implicated in most cases of alcoholism. It was associated with low-level, late-onset drinking behavior in either biological parent and little parental criminal behavior (a further indicator of a lower severity of drinking behavior). Adopted persons with this type of predisposition were reported to be heavily influenced in their drinking behavior by factors in their postnatal environment—or milieu—rather than exclusively by the genes they inherited from their biological parents.

Type II alcoholism was said to be male-limited, as it was transmitted exclusively from father to son and accounted for approximately 25% of male alcoholics. This type of susceptibility was found to be unaffected by environment. In cases of severe alcoholism in the biological father, for example, as evidenced by early-onset drinking as well as increased criminal behavior and extensive treatment, adopted sons, regardless of their postnatal environment, were nine times more likely than controls to abuse alcohol. Despite the strong heritability of this type of alcoholism, some environmental influence was suspected in the severity of alcohol abuse, as the sons tended to be less alcoholic than their biological fathers.

Interestingly, in milieu-limited alcoholism, the type of postnatal environmental provocation that was likely to act as a factor in alcohol abuse was *not* alcoholism in the adoptive parents. Instead, the only significant factor that was found necessary to activate susceptibility was a low socioeconomic status of the adoptive parents.

Recently, Dr. Cloninger has suggested other traits that can be associated with these types of alcohol heritability—novelty seeking, harm avoidance and reward dependence. Type I behaviors will tend to represent low levels of novelty seeking and exhibit traits of a "passive dependent personality," as well as high harm avoidance and concern for others' feelings (high reward dependence). Type II behaviors, in contrast, are more strongly antisocial and exhibit high levels of novelty seeking and impulsivity, uninhibited behavior (low harm avoidance) and little reward dependence (weak development of social relations) (Cloninger, 1987).

Perhaps if adoptive parents or social workers could identify such personality traits in an individual during childhood—those that apparently predispose to alcoholism—then psychiatric treatment could help prevent alcoholic behavior in the future.

Michael Bohman's work in adoption studies of alcoholism has revealed that when alcoholic adopted persons also displayed criminal behavior, this behavior was generally related to the alcoholism; for example, violent and repetitive behavior was tied to alcoholism. When adopted persons who were not alcoholics committed crimes, these crimes were generally of a nonviolent nature, for example, minor property crimes.

Bohman also concluded that although criminality may appear to be hereditary, when it is combined with alcoholism, it is far more likely that the alcoholism is the inherited trait rather than the criminality. "Criminality may only appear to be inherited because it is often a *consequence* of alcohol abuse."

Because such social problems as alcoholism and criminality can destroy an individual and his or her family and waste millions of dollars as well as lives, it is hoped that scientists will continue to analyze this problem, its genetic basis and any identified environmental causal factors. (See also CRIMINAL BEHAVIOR IN ADOPTED ADULTS; FETAL ALCOHOL SYNDROME; GENETIC PREDISPOSITIONS; PSYCHIATRIC PROBLEMS OF ADOPTED PERSONS.)

Kenneth Blum, Ph.D., Ernest P. Noble, Ph.D., M.D., Peter J. Sheridan, Ph.D., Anne Montgomery, M.Sc., Terry Ritchie, Ph.D., Pudur Jagadeeswaran, Ph.D., Harou Nogami, Ph.D., Arthur H. Briggs, M.D. and Jay B. Cohn, M.D., Ph.D., "Allelic Association of Human Dopamine D2 Receptor Gene in Alcoholism," *Journal of the American Medical Association*, 263 (April 18, 1990): 2055–2077.

Michael Bohman, M.D., "Alcoholism and Crime: Studies of Adoptees," *Substance and Alcohol Actions/Misuse,* 4(1983): 137–147.

Remi J. Cadoret, M.D., Colleen A. Cain and William M. Grove, M.S., "Development of Alcoholism in Adoptees Raised Apart from Alcoholic Biologic Relatives," *Archives of General Psychiatry,* 37(May 1980): 561–563.

C. Robert Cloninger, "Neurogenetic Adaptive Mechanisms in Alcoholism," *Science,* 236(1987): 410–416.

C. Robert Cloninger, M. Bohman and S. Sigvardsson, "Inheritance of alcohol abuse," *Archives of General Psychiatry,* 38(1981): 861–868.

Kathleen Whalen Fitzgerald, Ph.D., *Alcoholism: The Genetic Inheritance* (New York: Doubleday, 1988).

Enoch Gordis, M.D., ed., *Seventh Special Report to the U.S. Congress on Alcohol and Health* (Rockville, MD.: NIAAA, 1990), chapter III.

Robert O'Brien and Morris Chafetz, M.D., *The Encyclopedia of Alcoholism* (Editor of the 2nd Edition: Glen Evans) (New York: Facts On File, 1991).

John S. Searles, "The Role of Genetics in the Pathogenesis of Alcoholism," *Journal of Abnormal Psychology,* 97(May 1988): 153–167.

alcohol abuse and birthmothers See (FETAL ALCOHOL SYNDROME.)

almshouses Institutions designed in the 1800s to house poor children, adults, the elderly and the mentally ill, generally with no distinctions made between these groups in terms of services; also known as "poorhouses."

Because of reports condemning such facilities as unsafe and unclean, almshouses fell out of favor with the public by the late 1800s and no longer exist today. An alternative to alsmhouses at that time was "outdoor relief," which was financial aid to the poor in their own homes, usually provided by a town "overseer of the poor" and in later years by the county or state public agencies. (See "A Brief History of Adoption" (Introduction) at the beginning of this book.)

According to author Homer Folks in his book, *The Care of Destitute, Neglected and Delinquent Children,* published in 1902, the first American almshouses were built in the latter part of the 1700s in such large cities as Philadelphia, New York City, Baltimore and Boston.

Almshouses were later created in other states as one means of caring for the poor. In some cases, parents actually lived with the children in the almshouse. Orphans were also housed together with the indigent elderly and the mentally ill, as well as with juvenile delinquents. The percentages of families, orphans and elderly varied with the facility, the state and the conditions at the time. Later reformers decided it would be far preferable to separate children in orphanages, and separate institutions were created for different groups, such as children, the mentally ill and the indigent elderly. (*In the Shadow of the Poorhouse: A Social History of Welfare in America* provides a depiction of almshouses and institutions.)

A Michigan report in 1870 revealed there were over 200 children under age 16 in Michigan almshouses. Subsequent to the report, the state legislature created a state public school for dependent children in 1874.

Massachusetts began separating poor children from poor adults in 1872. Then in 1879, legislation required overseers of the poor to place the children of paupers in either families or orphan asylums.

The state of New York passed legislation in 1875 requiring the removal of all healthy children over age three from almshouses and placement of them into orphanages, families or other institutions. (The age of the children to be removed was dropped to age two in 1878 and no longer exempted children who were not healthy.)

In 1878, Wisconsin followed suit with legislation ordering the removal of all children from almshouses. A state school housing the children was built in 1885.

The trend continued among states until the early 20th century, when orphaned, abandoned and indigent children were cared for apart from almshouses with funds for outdoor relief, orphanages and such social experiments as the ORPHAN TRAIN.

Homer Folks, *The Care of Destitute, Neglected and Delinquent Children* (New York: Macmillan, 1902).

Michael B. Katz, *In the Shadow of the Poorhouse: A Social History of Welfare in America* (New York: Basic Books, 1986).

ambivalence The existence of two conflicting desires. When children over age 10 are offered an opportunity to be adopted, they often experience ambivalent feelings, for example, the desire to be loved in an adoptive home versus the fear of leaving the familiar foster home or group home.

The wishes of older children are almost always taken into account when an adoptive placement is considered, and many daylong or weekend visits may occur before the child feels ready to make a change and ultimately be adopted.

When sibling groups are involved, some siblings may wish to be adopted while others do not, causing feelings of ambivalence among all the children. A sibling who wants to be adopted may feel guilty about leaving behind the child who is unready or unwilling to be adopted, and conversely, a sibling who does not wish to be adopted may believe she or he is holding back the other children.

In addition, being adopted may signify to an older child a painful renouncement of the birthparents. Even though a child may have been abused severely enough for the state to have terminated parental rights, he or she may fear the final severing of psychological ties to the birthparents.

Trained social workers understand the ambivalence felt by older children who are to be adopted and can assist both foster parents and adopting parents with suggestions to ease the transition.

The American Academy of Adoption Attorneys (AAAA) Formed in early 1990, the organization held its first national conference in Scottsdale, Arizona in May of 1990. Its membership (200 members, as of this writing) is composed of attorneys throughout the United States who specialize in adoption-related matters, such as assistance in independent placements, representation of adoptive and biological parents in court and preparation and filing of adoption-related pleadings.

While most members are attorneys in private practice, some serve as officers or staff of licensed child-placing agencies. The vast majority of AAAA members represent parties in INDEPENDENT ADOPTION.

The stated goal of the organization is to improve adoption laws and practices, especially in the area of independent adoption. The organization provides referrals for adoption attorneys who are members. The current president is Mark McDermott and the president-elect is Stephen Kirsh.

Prospective members must apply for membership acceptance and are screened by current members.

For more information, contact

American Academy of Adoption Attorneys
P.O. Box 33053
Washington, DC 20033-0053

American Adoption Congress (AAC)
Formed in 1978, the American Adoption Congress is a nonprofit national organization of search groups and individuals interested in changing legislation, attitudes and policies in order to guarantee access to identifying information to all adopted individuals and their birthparents and adoptive families.

The organization comprises 11 regions, and according to the AAC, its 1,500 members include agencies, search/support groups and individuals, such as adopted adults, birthparents, adoptive parents, siblings, and adoption mental health, medical and legal professionals, throughout the United States,

Canada, Europe, Mexico, Australia and New Zealand. Membership is $40 per year.

The AAC holds one national conference each year; regional and local conferences are also held. It offers members a quarterly newsletter, *The Decree,* as well as the *AAC Annual Report;* an extensive adoption bibliography is offered for sale.

The organization initiated a National "Open My Records" Day in 1990, and it is planned to be an annual event each May 1.

The AAC offers a "Search Referral Hotline" to provide information and assistance; the telephone number is (505) 296-2198.

For more information, contact

American Adoption Congress
1000 Connecticut Ave., NW, Suite 9
Washington, DC 20036
(800) 274-OPEN

American Bar Association National professional organization of attorneys with over 350,000 members (an estimated 50% of all U.S. attorneys); founded in 1878.

Members are attorneys, law professors, judges and others. The ABA is divided into committees, or categories, ranging from administrative law and regulatory practice to the young lawyers division. Generally, attorneys handling independent adoptions fall under the family law or general practice categories.

The American Bar Foundation is an affiliate of the American Bar Association. Created in 1952, this organization performs studies and research on legal matters.

The ABA offers books, pamphlets, audiotapes and videotapes on a wide variety of topics. *The Rights of Foster Parents,* a pamphlet produced by the ABA in 1989, describes legal issues concerning the adoption of foster children by foster parents.

For more information, contact

American Bar Association
750 N. Lake Shore Dr.
Chicago, IL 60611
(312) 988-5000

The American Fertility Society Founded in 1944 by 100 original members, the Society has grown to over 10,000 doctors and scientists in the United States and over 75 countries abroad.

The goal of the American Fertility Society is to provide the latest information on infertility, reproductive endocrinology and conception. The organization offers ethical guidelines on new reproductive technologies, a position paper on insurance coverage of infertility services and other papers.

In addition, the American Fertility Society also offers pamphlets on a variety of topics, reading lists, resource lists and regional postgraduate courses. *Fertility and Sterility* is the monthly medical journal published by the organization.

Annual scientific meetings are held.

For more information, contact

The American Fertility Society
2140 Eleventh Ave. South, Suite 200
Birmingham, AL 35205-2800
(205) 933-8494

American Public Welfare Association (APWA) Founded in 1930 at the time of the Great Depression, the American Public Welfare Association is a nonprofit professional organization that represents the interests of 50 state human services departments and Washington, D.C. as well as local public welfare agencies and caseworkers.

The association first rose to prominence in 1930 when it aided President Hoover's Emergency Committee for Employment in the creation of public relief and welfare programs; APWA was also involved in the Social Security Act and has been involved in numerous other social welfare programs from the Depression Era to the present.

In addition to a strong commitment to poor children and their families, APWA is also actively concerned with such issues as teenage pregnancy, immigration reform, abuse of the elderly and other major issues facing Americans today.

It serves as the secretariat for two interstate compacts involved with the placement of children for adoption across state lines: the INTERSTATE COMPACT ON THE PLACEMENT OF CHILDREN and the INTERSTATE COMPACT ON ADOPTION AND MEDICAL ASSISTANCE.

Two councils and nine affiliates are included within APWA. The National Council of State Human Service Administrators and the National Council of Local Public Welfare Administrators are the two councils. The nine affiliates include American Association of Food Stamp Directors, American Association of Public Welfare Attorneys, American Association of Public Welfare Information Systems Management, Association of Administrators of the Interstate Compact on the Placement of Children, National Association of Hearing Officials, National Association of Human Service Quality Control Directors, National Association of Public Child Welfare Administrators, National Staff Development and Training Association and the State Medicaid Directors' Association.

The association also performs or assists with research on public welfare issues and offers training and seminars to members. Publications include *Public Welfare,* the quarterly professional journal of the organization; *APWA News,* a quarterly membership newsletter; *Public Welfare Directory,* an annual directory; *This Week in Washington,* a weekly newsletter; and *W-Memo,* a monthly review of current federal policy changes, legislation, and similar issues.

For further information or to obtain copies of the interstate compacts, contact APWA directly:

American Public Welfare Association
810 First St. NE, Suite 500
Washington, DC 20002-4205
(202) 682-0100

Asians See INDIA; INTERNATIONAL ADOPTION, KOREAN ADOPTED CHILDREN.

Association of Jewish Family & Children's Agencies An organization of 145 adoption agencies that serve Jewish families and children; founded in 1973.

The organization works to coordinate national programs and issues affecting Jewish families and children. It works with local agencies and their communities and speaks out on key issues. In addition, the association works with national Jewish organizations to promote their goals.

The association meets three times a year and produces a bimonthly bulletin.

For more information, contact

Association of Jewish Family & Children's
  Agencies
3084 State Hwy. 27, Suite 1
P.O. Box 248
Kendall Park, NJ 08824-0248
(800) 634-7346
(201) 821-0909

at risk placement Also known as legal risk placement or fost-adopt placement. It refers to the placement of a child into an adoptive family when the birthparents' rights have not yet been legally severed by a court or when birthparents have not yet signed a voluntary relinquishment of their parental rights.

Such placements are made only when the social worker is reasonably confident that a termination of the biological parents' rights is imminent.

attachment disorders see BONDING AND ATTACHMENT.

attitudes about adoption Societal attitudes about adoption affect how adopted persons, adoptive parents and birthparents feel about adoption.

If members of the ADOPTION TRIAD are given the impression that adoption is not considered acceptable by society, negative consequences may result: A pregnant woman may feel it would be wrong to consider adoption even though she may feel unwilling or unready to become a parent. An adopted person may have identity problems and feel "second-best" when societal attitudes make this belief appear true. The adoptive parent, particularly the infertile adoptive parent, may perceive adoptive parenthood as second-rate and vastly inferior to biological parenthood.

Although societal attitudes appear to be changing, it is also true that adoption TERMINOLOGY has not kept pace with this change; for example, when a birthmother decides adoption is the right answer for herself and her child, she is said to "give up" or even "give away" her baby, rather than to "plan" or "choose" or "decide on" adoption for her child, indicating both a lack of control and a negative act.

A prevailing negative attitude about adoption can actually pressure a woman into an unwanted abortion or undesired single parenthood.

A study by Charlene E. Miall in the January 1987 issue of *Family Relations* reported on the feelings of adoptive parents about their status in the community and the stigma of infertility faced by many adoptive parents.

Miall wrote, "Although an adoptive couple may approach adoption as a means of obtaining children of 'their own' to raise, society conveys the message that adoptive parents are not, in fact, real parents."

Miall studied 58 infertile women who either had adopted or imminently planned to adopt children (82% had adopted, and the rest were in the process of adopting). The women were white, ages 25 to 45, well-educated and middle- to upper-class.

Attitudes of the extended family, neighbors and close friends were very important to the women interviewed; however, half of the women reported that adoptive parenthood was viewed as different from biological parenthood by family and friends. The women did report, however, that they felt attitudes changed with actual knowledge of an adoption and with time, and more than two-thirds of the adoptive parents' friends and family members ultimately did accept adoption as comparable to parenting children born to the family.

Yet nearly two-thirds of the women also reported societal beliefs that continued to bother them. Said Miall, "An analysis of open-ended responses revealed three general themes: (a) The biological tie is important for bonding and love and therefore bonding and love in adoption are second best; (b) adopted children are second rate because of their unknown genetic past; and (c) adoptive parents are not real parents."

The women were asked if they talked about adoption differently with other adoptive parents than with friends or relatives, and 70% said they did.

As a result, this research, along with research performed by numerous other adoption experts, reveals the importance of adoptive parent support groups in which adoptive parents and prospective adoptive parents have an opportunity to freely discuss the subject of adoption as well as parenting in general in an atmosphere of acceptance.

Miall reported several respondents spoke of comments that not only indicated a failure to accept adoption but also an indication of a failure to accept an adopted child as well. She quoted one mother as saying, "There is one comment that really annoys me because it is so insensitive when you think about it and our lives. 'Oh I could never love someone else's child.' That really bothers me as if the children are so unlovable because they are someone else's."

Although the women studied believed society at large is negative about adoption, nearly 87% were themselves happy with their decision to adopt. Of the 58 women, 50 said adoption had fulfilled their desire to have children, 5 said it had not, and 3 said their feelings were mixed.

Miall concluded, "It may be that the success or failure of adoption depends more on the ability of family members to resist devaluing societal attitudes and behaviors than on psychological adjustment per se."

In any discussion of attitudes toward adoption, it is important to note the works of H. David Kirk, adoptive parent and author of *Shared Fate, Adoptive Kinship* and *Explaining Adoptive Family Life.*

Kirk's key contribution is the concept of the need for parents to lovingly acknowledge the fact that adoption and adoptive family relationships are different from birth relationships where adoption is not a factor.

Other studies have cautioned, however, against an overemphasis on differences, contending that too much focus on differences can be as serious a problem as too little.

Blood ties Most state adoption laws recognize the importance of "blood ties," and blood ties are presumed to be very important, even mystical, by some members of society. Some infertile individuals refuse to adopt children, reasoning that if they cannot have a genetic child, they do not wish to parent any child.

Unfortunately, even when individuals decide they can and will parent an adopted child, there are individuals who see the non-blood tie as problematic.

Some authors have spoken eloquently on the meaning of blood ties, both to birthparents and to children. The psychiatrists and authors of *Beyond the Best Interests of the Child* said, "Unlike adults, children have no psychological conception of relationship by blood-tie until quite late in their development . . . What registers in their minds are the day-to-day interchanges with the adults who take care of them and who, on the strength of these, become the parent figures to whom they are attached." (See also MEDIA.)

Joseph Goldstein, Anna Freud, Albert Solnit, *Beyond the Best Interests of the Child* (New York: Free Press, 1979).

Charlene E. Miall, "The Stigma of Adoptive Parent Status: Perceptions of Community Attitudes Toward Adoption and the Experience of Informal Social Sanctioning," *Family Relations* vol. 36(January 1987): 34–39.

attorneys Lawyers are almost invariably involved in adoptions, although the extent of typical legal involvement varies from state to state.

Lawyers may be involved in an agency adoption by preparing and filing the appropriate court papers to finalize an adoption. Attorneys may also be heavily involved in an adoption by overseeing all phases of an INDEPENDENT ADOPTION—from offering advice to prospective parents or birthparents to preparing finalization papers.

In the case of an independent adoption, in those states that do not allow attorneys to advertise their adoption services or to seek out pregnant women considering adoption for their babies, attorneys may advise prospective adoptive parents on how they might search for a birthmother and what legal and practical matters they should consider, for example, what expenses of the birthmother may be paid by the adoptive parents and what risks are involved in an independent adoption. In addition, the attorney will also advise the prospective adoptive parents of their options if the birthfather refuses to consent to the adoption or if there are other concerns or problems.

In some cases, the attorney will also represent the birthparents while in others the attorney will represent only the birthparents or the adopting parents. If the lawyer works with the birthparents, legal advice will be provided and information, such as medical and ethnic background, will be collected on the birthparents.

In the case of an INTERSTATE ADOPTION, attorneys from each state work with interstate compact offices to ensure state laws are complied with.

Attorneys may also be appointed when state or county social workers attempt to terminate parental rights so a child can be placed for adoption. In some cases, there may be an attorney assigned for the birthparents, another attorney for the child and a third attorney for the social services agency as well.

The primary role of the attorney in a SPECIAL NEEDS adoption is to finalize the adoption in court. Lawyers may also represent the state, when social workers are attempting to terminate the parental rights of abusive or neglectful parents. In addition, some states require that minor children be represented by counsel in court hearings on adoption.

Lawyers may also be involved in lawsuits. An example is WRONGFUL ADOPTION suits in which the adoptive parents allege they were not provided with sufficient information about a child when they were considering whether or not to adopt.

Attorneys involved in adoption may belong to the AMERICAN ACADEMY OF ADOPTION ATTORNEYS as well as the AMERICAN BAR ASSOCIATION.

autobiography Often requested by adoption agencies, the autobiography is a written history of the adoptive parent, including educational background, career and a variety of other information; also called a profile or a RESUME.

Often guided by the agency on the type of information to include, the prospective adoptive parent prepares the autobiography for review by agency staff.

The agency staff may use the autobiography to help them evaluate the family in the HOME STUDY or family study process. Some agencies also provide nonidentifying autobiographies to pregnant women or birthmothers considering adoption and ask them to select which adoptive parents they would like for their child.

auxiliaries Another name for self-help SUPPORT GROUPS for adoptive parents and prospective adoptive parents. Such groups provide information and support to parents, arrange speakers from agencies or other organizations in the community, promote adoption, engage in outreach, and make fundraising appeals.

B

baby selling Refers to the selling of an infant to adoptive parents or other persons by the birthparent and/or an intermediary. Baby selling is unlawful in every state in the United States; however, desperate couples and unscrupulous individuals apparently continue to risk the legal penalties.

It is extremely risky for a couple to try to buy a baby because of the distinct possibility of that adoption being overturned at a later date. In addition, the fear that state or federal authorities may eventually "catch up" with them can generate intense anxiety in the adopting parents or persons who buy the infants; however, unscrupulous individuals involved in baby selling will continue to operate as long as there is a profit to be made.

Some individuals may try to buy a baby to avoid a HOME STUDY investigation of the family because they believe they would not be approved after such a study. This is a morally reprehensible reason for buying a child and failing to protect a child's legal rights.

It is unclear how many babies are actually "sold" in the United States, although it is clear from people who are identified in baby selling rings that such practices do occur.

It is also evident that some forms of adoption, especially those involving direct, unsupervised contact between birthparents and prospective adoptive parents, offer ample opportunity for undetected soliciting or offering of cash or other things of value in exchange for the decision to place a child with a particular family.

Periodically there are rumors of baby selling among INTERNATIONAL ADOPTION agencies. It is often extremely difficult to determine where the truth lies and how many of these reports are generated by groups opposed to Americans adopting children from abroad.

Some mistakenly equate INDEPENDENT ADOPTION with baby selling. Independent adoption is lawful in most states, and if the adoptive parents and their attorneys comply with state laws, then no baby selling has occurred.

Every state has its own laws on adoption

and the lawful expenses related to adoption. Payments that would be considered excessive and perhaps baby selling in some states are acceptable in others; however, in no state is a birthmother allowed to accept a direct payment solely in exchange for her baby.

States that allow pregnant women to receive any sums of money consider the money to be for her support and maintenance during the latter part of her pregnancy and directly thereafter. Some states ban any payments of money at all to the pregnant woman.

In some cases, it is clear when a mother or father attempts to sell their baby, for example, if they request enough money for a worldwide cruise, car or other significant expenditure unrelated to the maintenance during pregnancy of if they request other similar payment.

In other cases, it is less clear where to draw the line between legitimate support payments and unreasonably excessive payments. It is always best to identify and rely on a reputable adoption agency or attorney's judgement on what constitutes an acceptable sum of support.

It is usually through independent adoption that attorneys or other intermediaries provide support money to indigent pregnant women planning to place their babies for adoption; however, increasing numbers of adoption agencies will also provide a limited amount of support to pregnant women needing financial assistance.

Some attorneys and social workers require an exact accounting of how the money will be spent before they will approve any payment to a pregnant women making an adoption plan for her child.

They may insist on making vendor payments directly, for example, paying the woman's landlord for her rent, the phone company and electric company for her utilities and the doctor for her obstetrician bill. Other attorneys will give the woman a lump sum or a weekly payment, and she will take responsibility for paying her own bills.

Because of a large gray area between what is and is not considered baby selling, some states have set strict payment rules; for example, Connecticut law will only allow an amount equal to what the pregnant woman would have received had she applied for welfare benefits.

Although attorneys are blamed for most of the baby selling that occurs in the United States, it is also true some agencies charge unusually high fees for their adoptions. They claim these fees are necessary to cover advertising costs and salary expenses.

baby shortage Because the number of people interested in adopting infants exceeds the number of infants in need of adoption, experts have called this problem a "baby shortage."

An estimated one million childless couples under age 44 actively seek to create a pregnancy by visiting infertility specialists; however, it is unknown how many infertile couples are actively interested in and pursuing adoption. It is known, however, that some number will only be satisfied with a biological child and if they cannot have a biological child, will remain childless.

Many single women and girls are opting to parent their children rather than place them for adoption. Another important factor to consider is that the "Baby Boomers" who are infertile are attempting to adopt infants from a population of "Baby Busters" or those women now bearing children who were born from 1966–1977. (These terms are used in such publications as *American Demographics* as well as in the book *100 Predictions for the Baby Boom: The Next 50 Years* by Cheryl Russell.)

Because there is a "Baby Boomlet" just behind the "Baby Busters," it appears likely that by the time the Busters reach the age at which they decide to adopt (generally in the early to late thirties), the number of infants needing adoptive families and the number of families desiring to adopt will be more in equilibrium than in the early and mid-1990s;

however, many other factors could also intervene in that period as well.

background information Data provided to prospective adoptive parents on the child they are considering adopting and also on the child's biological family.

In the case of an infant adoption, background information generally includes such nonidentifying information as the pregnant woman or birthmother's age, a physical description, her racial and ethnic background, religion, education and medical history. Information on the birthfather is gathered by caseworkers as well, and caseworkers may also obtain data on birth grandparents.

Some workers also include information on personality or hobbies, for example, the birthmother's good sense of humor or the birthfather's musical talent.

If the adoption is an OPEN ADOPTION, then the adopting parents and birthmother (and birthfather, if possible) usually meet and may exchange extensive identifying information beyond that provided by the social worker.

Particular attention is paid to recent illnesses the pregnant woman or birthfather may have suffered, and social workers attempt to determine if there has been any drug or alcohol abuse before or during the pregnancy. Whether or not the birthmother has obtained any prenatal care is also determined.

In the case of an older child's adoption, workers will try to obtain the same information on biological parents as they do in an infant adoption as well as data on the child since birth. (Most older children have been in foster care for several years, and the information should be in their case files.)

Background information on an older child will include a medical history, previous foster and/or adoptive placements, behavioral problems, any siblings and other information that could be valuable to the child in the future or to his or her adoptive parents.

If the child has been abused and the social worker knows this, that information should be shared with adopting parents. This knowledge will help the adopting parents with their own adjustment to the child; for example, if a child shrinks from her adoptive father's hugs, it helps to know that she is fearful of men because of attacks she suffered from her biological father or her biological mother's boyfriend.

Sometimes the adopting parents will meet foster parents and discuss the child's likes and dislikes and information that could aid the parents in helping the child with the adjustment.

Studies have revealed that parents who are well-informed are far less likely to disrupt an adoption, and workers should make every effort to ensure that the adopting parents feel they have as much information as caseworkers can give them.

Several organizations, including the NATIONAL COMMITTEE FOR ADOPTION, publish and distribute model background information forms.

GENETIC DATA is also important to all members of the adoption triad. Authors Julia B. Rauch, Ph.D., an assistant professor of the School of Social Work and Community Planning at the University of Maryland, and Nancy Rike, M.S., M.S.W., a genetic counselor, have prepared a paper entitled *Adoption Worker's Guide to Genetic Services* that includes much helpful information and is available through the National Resource Center for Special Needs Adoption in Chelsea, Michigan.

P. O. Box 337
Chelsea, MI 48118
Tel (313) 475-8693

bibliography A listing of references (sometimes annotated) related to a particular subject or subjects. Although there are many different adoption bibliographies, the most comprehensive bibliography to date has been prepared by Paul Brinich, M.D.

His bibliography, entitled "A Bibliography on Some Social and Psychological Aspects of Adoption," is approximately 100 pages in length. The bibliography is available for $10 to cover the cost of photocopying. Brinich also has a smaller bibliography that is a subset of his larger bibliography. It is entitled "Psychoanalytic and Psychodynamic Views of Adoption: A Bibliography." Dr. Brinich's address is

Dr. Paul Brinich
Division of Child Psychiatry
Hanna Pavilion
University Hospitals of Cleveland
2040 Abington Rd.
Cleveland, OH 44106-5099

bioethics   Also known as biomedical ethics; the evolving study of moral responsibilities created by recent advances in reproductive medicine.

Such conflicts have developed because public values and laws have not kept pace with rapid developments in high technology medicine. On the heels of "test tube" babies and new "cures" of infertility have also come such innovations as frozen embryos, genetic testing and a host of options undreamed of in past years.

In addition, although artificial insemination has been a technique used for many years, new information on genetics provides new dilemmas: How much screening should a donor for artificial insemination undergo? Is it ethical to inseminate a woman with donated sperm mixed with her husband's sperm? And what should be done with frozen embryos when, for example, a couple is killed in a plane crash? In a recent case, one couple began divorce proceedings, with "custody" of the frozen embryos a hotly-disputed issue. (This husband fought implantation of the embryos, while the wife sought implantation.)

SURROGATE MOTHERHOOD, an option available since biblical times, has undergone ethical scrutiny as a result of the intense publicity surrounding the "Baby M" case. Mary Beth Whitehead, the so-called surrogate mother, agreed to bear a child for the Stern couple. The child was biologically the child of Whitehead and Stern. After the birth of the baby girl, Whitehead sought to rear the child herself.

The high court in New Jersey ruled that surrogate motherhood was tantamount to BABY SELLING; however, custody was awarded to the Sterns. The adoption by Mrs. Stern was invalidated, and Whitehead was given visitation rights.

Organizations such as the NATIONAL COMMITTEE FOR ADOPTION and others believe surrogate motherhood is planned baby selling. Proponents of surrogate motherhood believe couples should have the right to create a biological child by another woman who consents.

In a 1990 California case, a gestational mother sought to obtain custody of a newborn infant. The child was the biological child of another couple, whose embryo was implanted in the gestational mother. (The biological mother was able to create ova but unable to carry a child.) Lawyers for the gestational mother argued that she was the birthmother and thus was entitled to raise the child if she so wished. The child was placed with the biological parents, who ultimately won sole custody.

Also in 1990, new techniques have made it possible to withdraw an egg from one woman who is unable to carry a child, fertilize the egg with sperm donated by her husband, and implant the fertilized egg into a surrogate mother who is postmenopausal but has a healthy uterus.

Many moral dilemmas center around aborted fetuses, fertilized eggs and frozen embryos. For example, should aborted fetal tissue be used to treat patients with Alzheimer's disease, diabetes or other ailments, or would such a use encourage women to become pregnant and then abort for profit? If a test reveals a fetus is a healthy female and the parents wanted a boy, is it morally acceptable for the physician to abort? Would it be acceptable to abort a fetus that would result in a handicapped child? These are only a few of the moral and legal quandries facing physicians and average Americans today.

In addition, part of the problem revolves around the intense disagreement among various groups as to whether or not abortion itself is morally acceptable. Although abortion has been a legal procedure since the U.S. Supreme Court decision of *Roe v. Wade* in 1973, there are segments of the population who are adamantly opposed to abortion. Those who support abortion rights are equally committed to their position.

Pro-life (antiabortion) groups are more likely to oppose any use of fetal tissue, whereas pro-choice (pro-abortion rights) groups are more likely to believe it would be acceptable to use discarded fetal tissue from abortions in an effort to save or enhance lives. Neither group would support pregnancies for profit or women becoming pregnant in order to sell fetal tissue.

Even if fetal tissue were used on a wide basis to cure diseases, the 1984 National Organ Transplant Act would apparently prevent women from selling the tissue: This act bans people from selling human organs. (There is always a possibility of a black market for fetal tissue as with other outlawed but wanted substances, such as illegal drugs.)

Religious constraints are also a factor in ethics, and various religious groups have spoken out against a variety of new REPRODUCTIVE TECHNOLOGIES. Probably the most vocal religious organization opposing many new reproductive options is the Roman Catholic church. In 1987, the Vatican published *Instruction on Respect for Human Life in its Origin and on the Dignity of Procreation*. This document, among other stances, opposed the donation of sperm in artificial insemination. The Catholic Church and other religions have also consistently opposed abortion, despite its legalization after *Roe v. Wade*.

As a result, both the physician and the average layman receive many conflicting views on what is and is not ethical, and it is likely these biomedical dilemmas will only increase with evolving technologies.

Congress created the Biomedical Ethics Board in 1985 in an attempt to resolve and, in some cases, anticipate problems that may occur as a result of increasing scientific knowledge.

Other organizations grapple with biomedical quandaries. The American Fertility Society created an ethics committee, which explores legal, moral and medical responsibilities of physicians. The Center for Biomedical Ethics at the University of Minnesota also tackles numerous ethical dilemmas, such as the ethics of using tissue or organs from aborted fetuses for transplants into patients with debilitating diseases and issues. (See also ETHICAL ISSUES.)

For more information, contact

American Fertility Society
2140-Eleventh Ave. South, Suite 200
Birmingham, AL 35205-2800

Center for Biomedical Ethics
3-110 Owre Hall, UMHC Box 33
Harvard St. at East River Rd.
Minneapolis, MN 55455
(612) 625-4917

Hastings Center
225 Elm Rd.
Briarcliff Manor, NY 10510
(914) 762-8500

Roger D. Kempers, M.D., editor-in-chief, "Ethical Considerations of the New Reproductive Technologies," *Fertility and Sterility* supplement 1, 46(September 1986).

Emmanuel Thorne, "Regulating Commerce in Fetal Tissue," *Society,* 25(November/December 1988): 61–63.

biographical information Usually refers to information on prospective adoptive parents, including age, interests, reasons why they wish to adopt, hobbies and other information needed by the caseworker and/or the birthparents.

Some agencies ask prospective adoptive parents to write a special RESUME or profile that will be seen by birthparents considering adoption. Such a resume will usually include nonidentifying information, such as the individual's profession (if this information is nonidentifying), hobbies and so forth. (See also BACKGROUND INFORMATION.)

biological parents Also known as genetic parents, birthparents or natural parents, the man and woman who conceive a child. (See BIRTHFATHER, BIRTHMOTHER.)

biracial A child of mixed race; usually refers to a child born to a black parent and a white parent.

Some agencies place biracial children with white families, while others are opposed to such placements believing biracial children should be placed with black families. The presumption is that society identifies biracial children as black. (See also TRANSRACIAL ADOPTION.)

birth certificate See SEALED RECORDS; OPEN RECORDS.

birthday An adopted child's birthday is important and should be celebrated with cake, presents and the usual birthday accoutrements. A child who is adopted as an older child may be unfamiliar with birthday celebrations, and if he or she appears bewildered, parents should explain what will happen and what the child should do.

Some adoptive parents celebrate both "adoption day"—the day the child arrived in the home—and the child's birthday as well. Experts have mixed views on celebrating two holidays each year. Therapist and adoptive parent Stephanie Siegel, author of PARENTING YOUR ADOPTED CHILD, advises against celebrating both days and instead urges concentrating on the child's birthday.

She says that "adoption is a memorable occasion and should be treated as such. A birthday, however, is the day to be celebrated each year. Do not confuse your children by celebrating their adoption day as well."

Therapists Judith Schaffer and Christina Lindstrom, authors of *How to Raise an Adopted Child,* believe it is acceptable to celebrate the anniversary of the child's entry into the family. "It should never take the place of a birthday, but it's a special day your whole family can enjoy and be part of. In fact, some adoptive family support groups hold very moving candlelight celebrations each month to honor kids whose adoption anniversaries fall within that month."

A birthday may also be a time when questions about birthparents arise, particularly as the child reaches adolescence and adulthood. Say Schaffer and Lindstrom, "For some adopted children, this is a day of intensely ambivalent feelings . . . We do not mean to suggest that birthdays are melancholy affairs for all adopted kids. But it would certainly fall within the range of normal behavior if your adopted child has some mixed feelings about his day."

Judith Schaffer and Christina Lindstrom, *How to Raise an Adopted Child* (New York: Crown Publishers, 1989).
Stephanie E. Siegel, Ph.D., *Parenting Your Adopted Child* (New York: Prentice Hall Press, 1989).

birthfather Popular, if somewhat inaccurate, term for the biological father of a child; usually a term applied to the biological father of an adopted child.

Whenever possible, social workers and/or attorneys obtain information about and from the birthfather, not only to protect his legal rights but also to ensure that important medical and genetic background information is provided to adoptive parents.

In recent years, unwed birthfathers have made legal gains in their custodial rights to a child, although they are generally not perceived in the same legal manner as a birthmother; for example, a birthmother need not usually prove to a court she would make a suitable parent or has provided support for the child financially. And the court is more likely to assume a woman can go on public assistance as a single parent if she wishes.

The rights of birthfathers vary greatly from state to state, although every state has addressed the issue. If the birthparents are married, the birthfather must usually consent to an adoption along with the birthmother. In almost all cases, the married man is presumed to be the biological father and is also the LEGAL FATHER.

Studies on birthfathers are very rare. In one of the few reports on birthfathers, Eva Y. Deykin, Patricia Patti, and Jon Ryan interviewed 125 birthfathers who volunteered to be studied. The birthfathers studied were reported to be about the same age as the respective birthmothers, within a year or two, and the majority of birthfathers studied were in their late teens or early twenties at the time of their children's births. It is not at all clear whether this study is representative of the typical birthfather but is described because of the overall dearth of information on birthfathers.

The birthfathers were mostly Catholic or Protestant men between the ages of 21 and 57 years old, and the average age of the birthfather at the time of the child's birth was 21.

Most were middle-class at the time they were contacted by the researchers; 28% were in professional or managerial careers, 32% were white collar workers, and the remaining 40% were skilled or semi-skilled. Most were or had been married, and 10% had been married at the time the child was placed. Twenty-five percent were currently married to the birthmother.

One very big difference researchers found for birthfathers in their study compared to birthmothers was that birthfathers who search for their children often actively seek to take the child back. In contrast, studies of birthmothers have revealed that birthmothers who search for their children do so to reassure themselves the child is all right and are not generally seeking to take the child away from the adoptive parents.

Birthfathers' Rights Prior to 1972, unwed birthfathers rights were rarely recognized, and a birthmother could decide to place her child for adoption or parent the child as she chose. It was generally presumed unwed fathers had no interest in parenting an illegitimate child or, if they did, would make unfit parents.

Married men whose wives desired to place their children for adoption were (and remain) in a different category. They must consent to an adoption of their child unless parental rights are lawfully terminated or special circumstances are met.

Supreme Court decisions about the rights of birthfathers point to a trend indicating the court is clearly interested in whether or not the birthfather has or had a parental relationship with the child and the nature of that relationship. (Supreme Court cases are summarized at the end of this essay.)

Individuals and groups who are concerned about an overemphasis on birthfathers and their rights strongly argue against giving a birthfather who does not reside with the birthmother "veto power" over an adoption.

Such groups as the Committee for Mother and Child Rights argue that birthmothers considering adoption may feel compelled to parent a child if the birthfather says he will contest the adoption. Rather than allow the birthfather to rear the child and fearing the court would allow him to parent the child if the birthmother sought adoption but the birthfather protested, the birthmother might feel unable to make an adoption plan.

In addition, although the birthmother considering adoption for her child usually no longer has a relationship with the birthfather, if she elects to rear the child herself rather than have the birthfather rear the child, she may face the prospect of maintaining an unwanted relationship with the birthfather for the next 18 to 21 years as the child grows up. The birthfather could press for visitation rights and other parental rights. In addition, if the birthfather parented the child, he could sue the birthmother for child support.

The birthmother may suffer severe economic stress. There is no guarantee that the birthfather who presses the birthmother to parent the child (or who alleges he would like to parent the child) is in a financial position to provide the necessary economic support. The birthmother may be compelled to apply for public assistance.

Those who argue for birthfathers' rights stress that a birthfather may be ready and able to parent a child, despite the lack of readiness or willingness of some birthmothers to provide parenting. In addition, they argue that the right of a woman to abort a fetus should not also give her the sole right to determine the fate of a newborn infant.

Finally, birthfathers' advocates argue that a birthfather may be forced to seek legal counsel to assert his parental rights, while a birthmother generally need only state her desire to parent a child.

Some states are very precise as to which notices must be filed and what steps should be taken to ensure a birthfather's rights are protected, while other states presume that he does not wish to pursue paternity rights if he doesn't initiate any legal action. In some states, birthfathers must register with PUTATIVE FATHER REGISTRIES.

In some cases, the birthfather may be difficult to find or the birthmother may refuse to identify him. Attorney Martha Atwater wrote about terminating paternal rights without written consent in her 1989 *University of Detroit Law Review* article on birthfathers. She said, "There can be no denying that one of the policy reasons behind many state termination statutes is the difficulty in finding or determining who the biological father is."

She recommended the court be required to ask the birthmother for the birthfather's name, and compel her, if necessary, to provide this information.

Susan Sapp has written recommended statutes on the issue, combining various existing statutes, in her article for the *Nebraska Law Review*. These set forth the duties of the person who notifies the biological father about the child, the appointment of a guardian *ad litem* for the child, the formal notice of termination of parental rights by publishing information (usually in a newspaper) and the termination of the rights of the unknown father or known father who fails to appear at a paternity hearing.

Important U.S. Supreme Court Cases
In 1972, the landmark case of *Stanley v. Illinois* was heard by the U.S. Supreme Court. Stanley was an unwed father who had lived with the birthmother periodically for 18 years and who had a parental relationship to their three children.

When the birthmother died, the state sought to remove the children from Stanley's custody and denied him a hearing based on his nonmarital relationship with the deceased and the out-of-wedlock status of the children.

Stanley ultimately won his case and custody of the children because the court believed he had been denied due process. The court was sympathetic to Stanley's case because he had maintained a relationship with his children and had acted in a paternal manner. In this case, the court apparently strove to maintain existing family units.

The next landmark birthfather case was *Quillon v. Walcott,* which the Supreme Court heard in 1978. Quillon was an unmarried father whose lover later married. Their child lived with her mother and stepfather as a family unit, and Mrs. Walcott's husband sought to adopt her.

Quillon attempted to block the adoption of the 11-year-old child. He had never taken responsibility for the child, nor did he seek custody. He lost his case.

The next major case was *Caban v. Mohammed* in 1979. The unmarried couple had lived together for five years and parented two children. Ms. Mohammed later moved away and married, and her husband petitioned to adopt the children. New York law held that a birthmother could block an adoption but not a birthfather, so there was no bar to this stepparent adoption.

The Supreme Court rejected the distinction between birthmothers and birthfathers; however, very important to the court was the fact that the children were older and were known to and by the father. In addition, Caban had established "a substantial relationship" with his children and had admitted paternity. (He was listed on the birth certificates as the father.) As a result, Caban was successful in blocking the adoption of his children.

The case of *Lehr v. Robertson* was another case of birthfather's rights and was heard by the U.S. Supreme Court in 1982. Mr. Lehr had never provided financial support to Ms. Robertson or the baby, nor did they live together after the child's birth. His name was not listed on the birth certificate, and he never registered with New York's Putative Father Registry.

Robertson later married and her husband sought to adopt the child. Lehr tried to block the adoption and asked for visitation rights. The court rejected Lehr's claims and held that "the mere existence of a biological link" does not guarantee due process unless the unwed father "demonstrates a full commitment to the responsibilities of parenthood" and is involved in the rearing of his child.

These cases were all interesting to birthfather rights advocates, but not until 1988 was an adoption case involving unrelated adoptive parents scheduled. Edward McNamara was a birthfather who had conceived a child as the result of a casual affair. When he learned the birthmother had placed the child for adoption in 1981 through a San Diego, California county agency, he began his fight to stop the adoption. *(In re Baby Girl M.)*

While he began his legal battle, the agency placed the baby with Robert and Pamela Moses, an adoptive family selected by the birthmother.

When his case was heard initially, the court decided it would be in the "best interests" of the child for the child to remain with the adoptive parents. McNamara continued to fight until his case was heard in 1988, seven years after the child's birth. He sought to have himself declared the legal father and to obtain visitation rights with the child. A California court denied his claim, contending that the parental rights of a fit parent could be terminated in the best interests of a child.

The Supreme Court dismissed the case and said that no federal question had been raised.

The most recent Supreme Court case involving birthfathers as of this writing was *Michael H., and Victoria D., Appellants v. Gerald D.* (June 13, 1989), wherein an alleged birthfather and the child's legal father were in conflict.

The mother had had a relationship with an unmarried man and had a child. Because she was married, the LEGAL FATHER was presumed to be her husband. The alleged father did have a relationship with the child; however, the mother elected to return to her husband. The alleged father sued for visitation rights.

The Supreme Court found the presumption of the legal father's paternity in this case as irrebuttable, and the requests for visitation and a continuing relationship was denied. (However, in many states the contention of paternity based on marriage to the child's mother may be rebutted and may also require proof, such as genetic testing.) The court also stated that had the husband or wife wished to challenge the law, that request would have been considered; however, the unmarried man who alleged paternity had no standing.

Numerous state cases have been tried. One that was an apparent attempt to model the Supreme Court's reasoning was *Doe v. Roe* in Florida in 1988. In this case, a woman became pregnant, and the birthfather urged her to abort. She refused, bore the child and placed it for adoption.

The birthfather then urged the birthmother to marry him, and they jointly sought to overturn the adoption. The Florida Supreme Court denied the birthparents on the basis that the birthfather provided no financial or emotional support to the birthmother during her pregnancy, despite his affluent status. Thus his "pre-birth abandonment" was used as a basis on which to decide the case. (See also BIRTHMOTHER; TEENAGE PARENTS.)

Martha W. Atwater, "A Modern-Day Solomon's Dilemma: What of the Unwed Father's Rights?," *University of Detroit Law Review*, 66(1989): 267–296.

Eva Y. Deykin, Dr. P.H., Patricia Patti, M.S., and Jon Ryan, B.S., "Fathers of Adopted Children: A Study of the Impact of Child Surrender on Birthfathers," *American Journal of Orthopsychiatry*, 58(April 1988): 240–248.

John Hamilton, "The Unwed Father and the Right to Know of His Child's Existence," *Kentucky Law Journal*, 76(1987–88): 949–1009.

Joan H. Hollinger, editor-in-chief, *Adoption Law and Practice* (New York: Matthew Bender, 1989).

"Michael H. and Victoria D., Appellants v. Gerald D.," *United States Law Week*, June 13, 1989, 4691–4705.

Susan Kubert Sapp, "Notice of Relinquishment: The Key to Protecting the Rights of Unwed Fathers and Adoptive Parents," *Nebraska Law Review*, Vol. 67, 383–407.

Jo Lynn Slama, "Adoption and the Putative Father's Rights: Shoecraft v. Catholic Social Services Bureau," *Oklahoma City University Law Review*, 13(Spring 1988): 231–255.

Sue Wimmershoff-Caplan, attorney for proposed *Amici Curiae*, "In the Matter of the Adoption of A Child Whose First Name is Raquel Marie," Court of Appeals, State of New York, March 5, 1990.

birthgrandparent The biological or genetic grandparent of an adopted child. It would be more clear to use the phrase "the birthmother's parents" or "the birthfather's parents."

Studies have revealed the tremendous impact the birthgrandparent, particularly a birthgrandmother, has on a birthmother's decision to parent a child or place it for adoption.

Author Leroy H. Pelton found the attitude of birthgrandparents to be very critical in the adoption decision of birthmothers. The birthgrandparents' unwillingness to accept the child into the family was the strongest factor that decided a birthmother to choose adoption rather than parenting.

Birthgrandparents also face tremendous societal pressure. Those who encourage their daughter or son to choose adoption for the child rather than to parent often incur societal disapproval from friends, relatives and others, who cannot understand how they can "give up their own flesh and blood."

If the birthmother is a teenager, her parents will often end up parenting the child themselves if the birthmother decides against adoption, particularly if the birthmother is a young teenager living at home.

Some birthgrandparents-to-be don't wish to raise another child or don't feel they can provide an adequate environment for an infant and consequently encourage adoption as the better solution, while others may still believe the proper solution is for the birthmother to parent the baby.

It is often difficult for birthgrandparents-to-be to understand that they cannot forbid their child to choose either parenthood or adoption, although they can exert tremendous moral and economic influence. Individuals whose daughters or sons are expecting a child should take care that they are well aware of all the options available to them so regret and resentment will not overwhelm them in later years.

Jeanne Warren Lindsay addressed the emotional issues of helping your daughter make an adoption plan in her book *Parents, Pregnant Teens and the Adoption Option: Help for Families*.

Lindsay reports that birthgrandparents are unlikely to receive or seek out support from their peers and may not want to discuss their daughter's pregnancy at all. "Their friends may not know how to approach them for fear of offending them," Lindsay writes. "Many birthgrandparents feel terribly alone during this time."

Grandparents' Rights Grandparents' rights vary, but most states allow the birthparents to decide for or against adoption. In some states, grandparents have limited rights; for example, in the state of Florida, if the child has lived with a grandparent continuously for six months and the birthparents decide to place the child for adoption, the grandparent must be notified by the agency or intermediary before the petition for adoption is filed. If the grandparent wishes to adopt the child, he or she will be given first priority over nonrelatives (excluding stepparents).

Virtually every adoption agency is eager to involve birthgrandparents in the counseling process, particularly the parents of the birthmother, in order to help them work through the issues of grief and loss. (See also BIRTHFATHER; BIRTHMOTHER; GRANDPARENT RIGHTS.)

Gay Lewis, "Adoption is an Option," *Today's Christian Woman*, September/October 1988, 11.

Jeanne Warren Lindsay, *Parents, Pregnant Teens and the Adoption Option: Help for Families* (Buena Park, Calif.: Morning Glory Press, 1989).

Leroy H. Pelton, "The Institution of Adoption: Its Sources and Perpetuation," *Infertility and Adoption: A Guide for Social Work Practice* (New York: Haworth Press, 1988).

Phyllis Robinson, "Adoption—Simply Hiding a Mistake?" *Today's Christian Woman*, September/October 1988, 12.

birth kin The biological relatives of an adopted person, including birthparents, birthgrandparents, siblings by birth, aunts and uncles by birth, and so forth.

birthmother or birth mother The biological or genetic mother of an adopted child; the woman who, with the birthfather, conceived the child and who carried the pregnancy to term and delivered, then subsequently placed the child for adoption.

The term is sometimes also used to refer to all biological mothers, whether their parental rights are transferred to adoptive parents or they choose to parent their children, but usually the terms is used to refer solely to a woman who chose adoption for her child.

It is not clear how many birthmothers voluntarily select adoption today; however, data from the 1988 National Survey of Family Growth indicate that less than 4% of the infants born to single white mothers over the period 1982–1988 had been placed for adoption compared to 8% for the period 1973–1981 and 20% for infants born to single white women before 1973.

It is unknown if this percentage still holds or has increased or decreased since 1988. (No other research of this nature has been performed since then.)

According to studies by the National Center for Health Statistics on births (as of this writing, the most recent data is for the year 1988), most single births were to women over age 18. The highest incidence of nonmarital births were to women ages 18–19 and ages 20–24. The rate for teenagers ages 15–17 also increased 6% in 1988 and was the highest rate since 1977.

Age of Birthmothers The National Survey of Family Growth researchers also studied women ages 15–44 who had ever placed a child for adoption. (Thus, the birthmothers studied in the 1988 survey could have placed children for adoption anytime from the 1950s to 1988.) Among this broad sampling of women from young teens to middle-aged women, researchers found the greatest percentages of birthmothers choosing adoption to be under age 17 at the time of the child's birth. It is unclear, however, if young single women under age 17 of the 1980s and 1990s are still more likely to place a child for adoption than are women over age 17, as in the past. Trends have changed radically since the 1950s with the legalization of abortion, changes in societal attitudes and so forth.

Some authors and researchers believe older birthmothers are more likely to choose adoption today than younger birthmothers under age 17. Author Leroy Pelton has stated that in past years, birthmothers tended to be younger women living at home, but he hypothesized that this pattern began to reverse in the 1970s when older mothers became more likely to choose adoption than younger women.

It should also be noted that there has been an increasing trend for older single women to have children, which may mean that there are greater numbers of women ages 18 and over who choose adoption.

In addition, according to Pelton, the women choosing adoption for their infants were "more likely to be living independently, less likely to report that the baby's father was supportive of her during pregnancy, and less likely to receive help during pregnancy from family and friends than the nonrelinquishing mother."

Pelton also points out that many more unwed TEENAGE PARENTS today are parenting their children than in past years, some living with their parents and some living apart.

Pelton's contention was backed up by researcher Lucille J. Grow in her 1979 study of 210 unmarried mothers. The mothers were ages 14–24 at the time of the child's birth. Of the group, 182 chose to parent their children, and 28 made an adoption plan.

Although unmarried mothers who chose adoption for their children prior to the early 1970s were often young students living at home with their parents (based on various studies, including one by Trudy Festinger in 1971), Grow found a reversal and a trend for older mothers rather than younger mothers to choose adoption. Said Grow, "In contrast to earlier findings, it was found that younger women—that is, those under age 21—were more likely to keep than surrender their children."

In addition, she also found the birthmother choosing adoption was more likely to be living away from home and was less likely to receive assistance from family and friends. The young mother who chose parenting was more likely to have parents who were divorced or separated. Grow hypothesized that the women who had lived in a one-parent household were less likely to consider single parenthood in a negative light and more likely to consider parenting their child.

A study by Cynthia Leynes of teenage parents in a Salvation Army Home, reported in a 1980 issue of *Child Psychiatry and Human Development*, revealed her findings that older teenagers were more likely to make an adoption plan. They were also less influenced by the birthfathers than were the mothers who decided to parent the child.

In a 1985 "working paper" for the National Center for Health Statistics, Christine Bachrach indicated that younger teenagers (ages 15–17) and Protestant mothers were more likely to place their children for adoption than older and non-Protestant teenagers; however, the difference was not statistically significant. It is hoped that more research will be accomplished on this critical factor of age to enable human services agencies, including adoption and other social services agencies, to better tailor their services to the woman in a crisis pregnancy, whether she is very young or a more mature woman.

Birth Order According to the report by Bachrach for the National Center for Health Statistics, a birthmother choosing adoption is usually placing her first child for adoption. An estimated 75% of all infant adoptions are firstborns, 12% are second children, and 13% are the third, fourth (fifth, etc.) child.

Race Women choosing adoption are overwhelmingly white, and infants born to white single mothers are much more likely to be placed for adoption with nonrelatives (12%) than are the newborns of black mothers (less than 1%), according to studies by the National Center for Health Statistics.

This does not mean, however, that black and other nonwhite birthmothers are invariably disinterested in learning about adoption. A study by Margaret Klein Misak in 1981 of 387 women of all races (217 white, 111 black, 50 Latina and 9 racially designated as "other") revealed that as many as 51% of the black "clients" were considering adoption, compared to 53% of white women in crisis pregnancies. An apparent factor affecting the number of black women choosing adoption for their babies was the insufficient number of families interested in adopting black infants. Today, public and private agencies continue to find it difficult to recruit enough adoptive families for minority infants and children. (See BLACK ADOPTIVE PARENT RECRUITMENT PROGRAMS.)

Attitudes Affecting the Choice of Adoption It has been hypothesized by some that birthmothers who plan for their babies' adoptions have a lower self-esteem than those who choose to parent. Dr. Steven McLaughlin of the Battelle Human Affairs Research Centers in Seattle, Washington compared adolescent "relinquishers" (adolescents who chose adoption) to "parenters" (adolescents who chose parenting) in his 1987 study. "The Consequences of the Adoption Decision," and found both groups had about the same levels of self-esteem.

A 1984 dissertation by Elizabeth Lindner at the University of Wisconsin found no significant differences in the self-esteem of women who chose adoption for their children and women who opted to parent.

Others have speculated that women who elected adoption for their babies may quickly become pregnant again to replace the child they lost, but McLaughlin found this was not the case. Instead, the teenagers who chose parenting were more likely to become pregnant again shortly after the first child's birth, and many of these pregnancies ended in abortion.

Another important factor is the woman's own parents' attitude toward adoption, particularly her mother. (See BIRTHGRANDPARENT.)

A 1986 doctoral dissertation by Kathleen Herr at Brandeis University revealed if a pregnant woman's mother supports an adoption plan for the baby, the pregnant woman is more likely to choose adoption. Herr also found teenagers whose infants had been adopted knew few peers who chose single parenthood.

External pressure on a birthmother is another major factor in her choice and can lead to dissatisfaction with the adoption decision in later years. Peer pressure is particularly strong among teenagers, who frequently presume that if a pregnant teen decides against abortion, than she should parent her child. Peers sometimes express horror at the idea of adoption and "giving up your own flesh and blood."

Gayle Geber and Michael Resnick studied adolescents who planned adoption for their babies and adolescents who chose parenting and found both groups were satisfied with their decision.

According to an article in *Adolescence*, Resnick studied 93 women, including 67 who chose parenting, 24 who chose adoption, 1 who had an abortion and 1 whose child was in foster care. Resnick stated that 85% of the "placers" (those who chose adoption for their infants) and 94% of those who chose parenting were satisfied with their decision.

When both placers and parenters were asked for the most crucial factor in their decisionmaking, 80% of the parents stated they were ready to be parents. Other reasons were that they felt they could not carry a child for nine months and then make an adoption plan or that the birthfather wanted them to parent the baby.

Of the placers, 75% said they were unable to parent a child and offer the type of environment they believed was important. Other reasons were that they believed adoption was in the child's best interest. Some cited their plans to continue their education.

A 1986 master's thesis by Anna Marie Courtney revealed that the birthmothers' "level of regret" increased if she felt she was pressured into relinquishing the child, and a variety of other studies have revealed that the level of self-acceptance of the adoption or parenting decision is directly tied to whether the pregnant woman feels the decision was truly her own.

According to the *Adoption Factbook,* family and societal pressure to parent a child rather than place the child for adoption is a problem whether the birthmother is a teenager or a more mature mother. (See TEENAGE PARENTS.)

Say the authors, "Teens are encouraged by friends to 'keep' the cute little baby with promises of babysitting, etc. Parents of teens receive pressure from their friends to stand by their daughter and support her in raising their grandchild. Some teens also fantasize about having a child of their own to provide them with love or see motherhood as a transition to adulthood."

"Older" mothers are not exempt from social pressure, and in fact, may be more vulnerable. According to the *Adoption Factbook,* "Because they may be in a better position to parent than a teen because of age, job, etc. they may be judged more harshly at 'not accepting responsibility for their actions' . . . Women in this age range also have more difficulty in finding appropriate services because most maternity programs focus on the needs of pregnant teenagers."

The Nurturing Network, set up by Mary Cunningham Agee, is a resource for women in their twenties or thirties in crisis pregnancies. (See MATURE WOMEN PLANNING ADOPTION.)

Marital Status Although most birthmothers are single (or divorced), birthmothers may also be married, and the National Center for Health Statistics estimates at least 5% to 6% of all infant adoptions are infants placed by a married couple. The couple may be in the process of divorcing or may be very poor and financially unable to support an additional child.

In some cases, the child may be the result of an extramarital affair, and although the husband would be the legal father if he opted to raise the child, he and his wife choose to place the baby for adoption.

Married couples who elect adoption for their children may also face mental or physical problems, drug addiction or alcoholism and a wide variety of social problems. They decide placing the child with a stable two-parent couple is in the best interests of the child. (See MARRIED BIRTHPARENTS.)

Single birthmothers represent the overwhelming majority of birthmothers. They too choose adoption as in the best interest of the child. The birthparents usually have ended their relationship and do not feel emotionally or financially capable or ready to raise a child.

Socioeconomic Status A 1986 article by Christine Bachrach for the National Center for Health Statistics contrasted women who chose adoption for their infants to women who chose parenting. Her raw statistics revealed that women who made an adoption plan were less likely to receive public assistance than women who chose parenting (51%

versus 21%). In addition, the women who chose adoption were more likely to complete high school than the women who chose parenting (77% versus 60%)

Researcher Carmelo Cocozzelli found a correlation between socioeconomic status and the decision to rear or place the baby. Women who are receiving welfare are more likely to decide to parent the baby than women who are not on public assistance. (This finding has been reported in study after study—women who choose adoption are usually of a higher socioeconomic level than women who choose parenting.)

Women whose fathers are employed or whose fathers are professionals were more likely to make an adoption plan. The socioeconomic finding was backed up by a study in 1987 by Jane Bose and Michael Resnick, who found a higher socioeconomic status among adolescents who chose adoption than among adolescents who chose parenting for their children. Similar findings were also reported by researchers Debra Kalmuss and associates in a 1991 issue of *Family Perspectives*.

Other Factors Grow found that women who spent their childhoods in cities with 500,000 or more people were more likely to choose parenting than adoption. In addition, she found that those who chose parenting were apparently less religious: 14% of the women who chose parenting reported regular church attendance versus 46% of the mothers who made an adoption plan.

Grow's findings were confirmed in the later study by Jane Bose and Michael Resnick on placers and parenters. Bose and Resnick found that placers tended to come from suburban areas rather than rural or urban areas. In addition, the placers were more religious than were teenagers who chose to parent.

The researchers also found that both placers and parenters came from a "high proportion" of families who had already faced a teenage pregnancy. In addition, placers were more likely than parenters to have a family member who was adopted or to have been adopted themselves. If a placer's sister became pregnant, the sister was more likely to choose adoption than the sisters of birthmothers who chose parenting.

According to Bachrach's raw data, women who chose adoption were also more likely to marry than the women who chose parenting (73% versus 51%).

Researcher Lindner studied maternal-fetal attachment in pregnant adolescents as well as self-esteem, the birthmother's relationship with her own mother and other issues.

Lindner found that adolescents who planned to rear their babies scored higher on maternal-fetal attachment than did adolescents who planned to transfer parental rights.

Lindner also found a strong factor in the decision to parent the baby was an ongoing relationship with the baby's father. In addition, she found that the decision to parent or transfer parental rights to adoptive parents was strongly tied to the wishes of the pregnant adolescent's mother.

Concluded Lindner, "The results support the idea that the environment in which the pregnancy is sustained and relationships with significant others are important factors in facilitating maternal-fetal attachment in pregnant adolescents."

The Adoption vs. Parenting Choice Several researchers have studied why birthmothers choose adoption for their children. A study on birthmothers and factors influencing their decision to choose adoption for their babies or to parent them was described in an 1989 issue of *Child Welfare*.

Carmelo Cocozzelli studied 190 biological mothers in Hawaii. She found three variables with which the decision could be predicted with 77% accuracy.

These variables included whether or not the birthmother had career or life plans that would be interrupted or delayed by parenthood (individuals with future plans were more likely to choose adoption); the number of interviews the birthmother had with a social worker, with a greater number of interviews correlating with a higher probability of choosing adoption; and whether or not the birthmother planned to view her newborn child, with those who expressed a plan to see the child being less likely to place.

The study also revealed mothers who choose single parenthood were more likely to have had a difficult delivery and also to have been born themselves to single mothers.

Birthmothers of Past Years Birthmothers who are today 40 and over and who placed their infants 20 or more years ago found a cultural climate that was vastly different from today's.

Adoption was what one was expected to do when one was a young unwed mother before 1970. Pressure was common from parents to place the baby for adoption, and women really did not have much of a choice at that time.

To understand these times, consider the factors today that have been discussed by the modern equivalent of the birthmothers of that time: women who say they have been pressured by others to choose parenting or abortion. In 1961, a parent frequently said, "You're pregnant, and you're not ready to be a parent. Either have the baby adopted or get out of the house."

In 1991, a parent frequently says, "You're pregnant, and you're not ready to be a parent. Either have an abortion or get out of the house." Conversely, some parents urge birthmothers to parent their babies and say, "Don't come home from the hospital without the baby."

Thousands of young women before 1970 went or were sent to maternity homes, but many more were quietly kept at home or taken to relatives, where they received no counseling or emotional support and little or no information about pregnancy and childbearing.

Very few agencies provided resumes of prospective adoptive parents to choose from, and the women retained little or no control.

Some women report that they were not even informed on what labor and delivery would be like. Alone and terrified in a strange hospital, they experienced childbirth.

The women were urged to then go home and forget. The problem was, not many of the others who knew about the pregnancy forgot about it. Adoption was never discussed, but everybody remembered and many wondered about the child who was, most literally, "given up." Even though she had been told she had done the "right thing," people who knew about the baby looked down on the birthmother. In essence, she was in a no-win situation. She would be condemned if she tried to raise the child as a single parent, and she was also condemned when she made an adoption plan.

Many of these birthmothers who suffered such conditions are intensely bitter today. Others have coped by denial. Few have forgotten the experience. They marvel at the real choices young women considering adoption are offered today, especially in terms of counseling, and they can barely believe the pendulum has swung so radically the other way. These birthmothers who have suffered should be treated, belatedly, with the compassion they were denied in their time of need. Their desire for confidentiality, or a chance to speak their minds, should be equally honored.

Birthmothers and Trends in Adoption Up until about 1980, the majority of adoption agencies and intermediaries arranging adoptions did not offer a birthmother a substantial role in the selection of adoptive parents. In addition, the birthmother who placed in 1960 or 1970 sometimes did not see her newborn infant. Social workers assured the birthmother that the child would be placed in a loving home, and that was that.

One indication of the social stigma of unwed parenthood was found in a study by Bachrach of birthmothers and adoptive mothers. According to Bachrach, white mothers "were more likely to place their premarital birth for adoption if it occurred before 1973 (20 percent) than if it occurred in 1973–1982 (8 percent)."

Over time, adoption practices evolved, and more and more agencies began to question prohibiting birthmothers from having any input in the adoption process. Today, nearly all agencies and increasing numbers of intermediaries provide extensive nonidentifying background information about the adopting couple, for example, their age, religion, why they want to adopt a child and many other factors.

In addition, many agencies show the birthmother resumes that describe approved prospective adoptive parents, and the birthmother chooses which family she feels would be the best.

Some agencies arrange one or more face-to-face meetings between birthmothers and prospective adopters on a first-name basis. There are also some agencies that allow continuing contact between birthparents and adoptive parents subsequent to the adoption.

The agency may arrange for photographs and letters to be sent back and forth with the agency maintaining confidentiality. In some cases, the identities of the birthparents and adoptive parents are known to each other, and they correspond or communicate over the phone directly (the last case describes a situation of an OPEN ADOPTION.)

Today, many social workers encourage birthmothers to see their babies at least once, believing the birthmother needs to view the child for several reasons, including to ensure for herself that the baby is healthy and normal. Most birthmothers do not choose rooming-in, an option whereby the baby is placed in the hospital room with the birthmother; however, birthmothers may wish to visit the child in the nursery to say goodbye.

Birthmothers in Intercountry Adoptions
Although researchers have not yet studied birthmothers in countries outside the United States whose children are adopted, most agencies and attorneys who handle INTERNATIONAL ADOPTIONS believe these birthmothers are young and/or poor. They may have other children and be unable to support additional children. In addition, the stigma of unwed parenthood is still very powerful in some countries of the world.

Children from other countries who are adopted by Americans usually live in orphanages (although, in some cases, the child may reside in a private foster home) and must be officially "abandoned" according to U.S. IMMIGRATION AND NATURALIZATION SERVICE rules. As a result, few American adoptive parents have the opportunity to gain much, if any, information on the birthmother. (See also ADOLESCENT BIRTHMOTHERS; ATTITUDES ABOUT ADOPTION; INTERNATIONAL ADOPTIONS).

Christine Adamec, *There ARE Babies to Adopt: A Resource Guide for Prospective Parents* (Lexington, MA: Mills & Sanderson, 1987).

"Advance Report of Final Natality Statistics, 1987," *Monthly Vital Statistics Report, Final Data from the National Center for Health Statistics*, 38, no. 3, supplement (June 29, 1989).

Christine A. Bachrach, "Adoption Plans, Adopted Children, and Adoptive Mothers," *Journal of Marriage and the Family* 48(May 1986): 243–253.

Christine A. Bachrach, "Adoption Plans, Adopted Children, and Adoptive Mothers: United States, 1982," Working paper no. 22 for the Family Growth Survey Branch/Division of Vital Statistics, March 1985.

Christine A. Bachrach, Kathryn A. London and Kathy S. Stolley, "The Relinquishment of Premarital Births for Adoption" (Poster prepared for presentation at the annual meeting of the National Council on Family Relations, November 11, 1990, Seattle, Washington).

Terril L. Blanton and Jeanne Deschner, "Biological Mothers' Grief: The Postadoptive Experience in Open Versus Confidential Adoption," *Child Welfare*, 69(November–December 1990): 525–535.

Jane Bose, M.S.S.S., A.C.S.W., principal investigator, Michael D. Resnick, Ph.D., study director and report author, and Martha Smith, M.A., research assistant and coauthor, *Final Report: Adoption and Parenting Decisionmaking Among Adolescent Females*, (University of Minnesota, July 1987).

Carmelo Cocozzelli, "Predicting the Decision of Biological Mothers to Retain or Relinquish their Babies for Adoption," *Child Welfare,* 63(January–February 1989): 33–44.

Anna Marie Courtney, "Birth Mothers Voluntarily Relinquishing a Child for Adoption: Variables Influencing Their Level of Regret About the Decision," (Master's thesis, The University of Texas at Arlington, 1986).

Diana Selsor Edwards, "Betrayal: A Birth Mother's View of Adoption," *Jacksonville Today,* May 1989.

Gayle Geber and Michael D. Resnick, "Family Functioning of Adolescents Who Parent and Place for Adoption," *Adolescence,* 23(Summer 1988): 417–428.

Lucille J. Grow, "Today's Unmarried Mothers: The Choices Have Changed," *Child Welfare,* 58(1979): 363–371.

Kathleen Mary Herr, "What Am I Going to Do About My Baby? An Analysis of the Cost Effectiveness of Decision-Making Groups for Pregnant Adolescents," Ph.D. diss., Brandeis University, 1986.

Debra Kalmuss, Pearila Brickner Namerow and Linda F. Cushman, "Adoption Versus Parenting Among Young Pregnant Women," *Family Planning Perspectives*, 23, (January-February 1991): 17–23.

Cynthia Leynes, "Keep or Adopt: A Study of Factors Influencing Pregnant Adolescents' Plans for Their Babies," *Child Psychiatry and Human Development,* 10(Winter 1980): 105–112.

Steven D. McLaughlin, principal investigator, Diane L. Manninen and Linda D. Winges, *Final Report: The Consequences of the Adoption Decision* (Seattle: Battelle Human Affairs Research Centers, April 1987).

Steven D. McLaughlin, Susan E. Pearce, Diane L. Manninen and Linda D. Winges, "To Parent or Relinquish: Consequences for Adolescent Mothers," *Social Work,* 33(July–August 1988) 320–324.

Edmund V. Mech, *Orientations of Pregnancy Counselors Toward Adoption,* Department of Health and Human Services, Office of Population Affairs, 1984.

Margaret Klein Misak, *Experience of Multiple Unwed Pregnancies: A Report from Selected Catholic Agencies* (Chicago: Catholic Charities of Chicago, 1982).

National Committee For Adoption, *Adoption Factbook* (Washington, D.C.: National Committee For Adoption, 1989).

———, "New Study Shows Black Unwed Mothers Want Adoption Counseling from Agencies," *Unmarried Parents Today,* February 12, 1982.

Leroy H. Pelton, "The Institution of Adoption: Its Sources and Perpetuation," *Infertility and Adoption: A Guide for Social Work Practice* (New York: Haworth, 1988).

Michael D. Resnick, "Studying Adolescent Mothers' Decision Making About Adoption and Parenting," *Social Work,* 29(January–February 1984): 5–10.

Kathleen Silber and Phylis Speedlin, *Dear Birthmother: Thank You for Our Baby* (San Antonio: Corona, 1982).

Jerome Smith, Ph.D., and Franklin I. Miroff, *You're Our Child: The Adoption Experience* (Lanham, MD: Madison, 1987).

birth order Refers to the child's ordinal position among children in the family. According to psychologists, whether a child is the class clown or a serious striving person is strongly related to whether the child is the oldest or youngest in the family or somewhere in the middle.

Because adoptive families may be composed of both biological and adopted children, perhaps "family order" is a more appropriate term when considering their relative age.

Most social workers seriously consider the ages of children already in the family when they are considering a placement; for example, they may not wish to place a child who is older than the oldest child already in the home.

Often the oldest child already in the home occupies a position with some privileges, and this role is very important to the child. To bring a new child in who is older and probably worthy of even greater privileges could be disturbing to the formerly oldest child.

The much-cherished baby of the family may find her or his nose out of joint when a newly-adopted baby or younger child receives a great deal of attention and seemingly everything done by the new child is perceived as amazing by the adoptive parents. Being bumped from the privileged status of the baby of the family to the role of the middle child requires a considerable adjustment, whether the new baby is born to the family or is adopted into the family.

Of course, bringing any child into the family will change the family order. A new child will become either the baby, be in the middle or be the oldest. Anyone who formerly occupied those positions—with the possible exception of the middle child—may evince resentment until adjustments have been made.

Author, therapist and adoptive parent Claudia Jewett disputes the common practice of placing only children younger than the children already in her home and says many families can successfully adopt a child who is older than children already in the home. Jewett says the practice of placing only younger children is unfair to older children who may need to behave younger than their chronological age would permit.

The authors of *Report on Foreign Adoption, 1989* point out that children adopted from other countries may be smaller than American children and may also lag behind in school because of language barriers and cultural norms to which the child must adjust. As a result, such factors should be considered in placements, sometimes ahead of the child's actual age. The authors write, "Birth order need not be interrupted even if you would then have two children the same age. The seven-year-old you already have in your family would still be older in U.S. terms than your new '7-year-old,' and it's very unlikely that you would have a pair of twins". (See also ONLY CHILD ADOPTIVE FAMILIES.)

International Concerns Committee for Children, *Report on Foreign Adoption, 1989*, (Boulder, Colo.: International Concerns Committee for Children, 1989).

Claudia L. Jewett, *Adopting the Older Child* (Boston: Harvard Common Press, 1978).

Dr. Kevin Leman, *The Birth Order Book: Why You Are the Way You Are* (New York: Dell, 1985).

birthparent Biological or genetic mother or father of a child; usually refers to a biological parent who places the child for adoption. (See BIRTHFATHER; BIRTHMOTHER; MARRIED BIRTHPARENTS.)

black adoptive parent recruitment programs Programs designed to encourage black couples and singles to adopt children of all ages, from infancy through adolescence. Although black adoptive parents adopt at about the same rate as white adoptive parents, there are greater numbers of black children in need of families.

Some social workers believe the social work system is dominated by whites who do not provide sufficient assistance to blacks interested in adoption. According to an article in *Ebony* magazine, blacks face numerous obstacles in their attempts to adopt, and as a result, "many begin the adoption process, become exasperated and then just forget about the whole idea."

ONE CHURCH, ONE CHILD is a program that recruits adoptive parents through black churches, with the goal of each church recruiting at least one adoptive family. This program was founded by Rev. George Clements, a Catholic priest who later adopted as a single parent. As of this writing, the president of the national organization and also president of One Church, One Child of Florida Inc. is Rev. R. B. Holmes Jr., pastor of the Bethel Baptist Missionary Church in Tallahassee, Florida. Patricia O'Neal-Williams is both director of One Church, One Child of Florida Inc. and the national executive director. O'Neal-Williams is employed by the Florida Department of Health and Rehabilitative Services in Tallahassee, Florida.

Black children are disproportionately represented in foster care nationally and remain in foster care for a longer period of time than do children of other races. Florida is no exception, but the One Church, One Child initiative in Florida has made a tremendous impact on black children in Florida's child welfare system. According to O'Neal-Williams, the Florida One Church, One Child program successfully placed 805 black children in families over the March 1, 1988, to September 30, 1990, period. Thirty-two states have implemented One Church, One Child programs, but Florida is the only state in the nation placing it into law. O'Neal-Williams says the success of the Florida program is a result of "a successful partnership between church and state."

Some adoption agencies concentrate on recruitment of black children. One example is Homes for Black Children, an adoption agency with affiliates in several cities. Some black organizations, such as the National Association of Black Social Workers and the National Urban League, have supported these recruitment efforts.

Despite outstanding efforts on the part of many black social workers, there are still large numbers of black children of all ages waiting to be adopted. Even though there are numerous black children awaiting adoption, there are some black social workers (and social workers of other races) who are adamantly opposed to TRANSRACIAL ADOPTION, while others believe it may be one solution to finding permanent homes for black children.

In their essay, "Recruiting and Preparing Adoptive Families for Black Children with Developmental Disabilities" published within the book *Mostly I Can Do More Things Than I Can't*, Gary T. Morgan and Drenda Lakin indicate that there is a great deal of mistrust of child welfare agencies among the black community, and this mistrust must be overcome.

They write, "Attitudes of staff as they work with churches and families who have been recruited are essential . . . If agencies make an all-out effort to churches and in the media to recruit families but remain bureaucratic, rigid, and insensitive in procedure, families will simply drop out of the process."

Rapid responsiveness to inquiries from prospective families is urged. The authors also say that instead of sending the prospective adoptive parents a sheaf of papers to fill out, they should receive a personal response.

They contend that agency flexibility and responsiveness are even more critical in the placement of black children with developmental disabilities, who usually wait for adoptive parents longer than healthy black children.

Some agencies and programs for black adoptions include the following:

Harlem-Dowling Children's Service
2090 Adam Clayton Powell, Jr. Blvd.
3rd floor
NY, NY 10027
(212) 749-3656

Homes for Black Children
2340 Calvert St.
Detroit, MI 48206
(313) 869-2316

The Institute for Black Parenting
7100 South Western Ave.
Los Angeles, CA 90046
(213) 565-2888

One Church, One Child
1317 Winewood Blvd., Bldg. 8
Tallahassee, FL 32301
(904) 488-8251

Author interview with Patricia O'Neal Williams, October 8, 1990.
Illinois Department of Children and Family Services, *Mostly I Can Do More Things Than I Can't* (Chelsea, MI: National Resource Center for Special Needs Adoption, 1987).

black families Because at least half of all the "WAITING CHILDREN" available through public welfare agencies are black, black children of all ages are often considered children with SPECIAL NEEDS.

Census studies indicate that blacks adopt at about the same rate as whites, but to successfully place all the black children available for adoption, experts estimate blacks would need to adopt children at three times the rate of white families.

A cultural/racial bias against adoption is blamed as one reason why black birthmothers often choose not to place babies for adoption and other blacks choose not to adopt, but the reasons are much more complex than this. For example, some blacks have alleged that adoption agencies are dominated by whites who unreasonably impose the same criteria on black families as they do on white prospective parents.

Whites have also adopted some of the available black children, and TRANSRACIAL ADOPTION has been one of the most hotly-debated topics of the past 20 years. Those who disapprove of whites adopting blacks, notably the National Association of Black Social Workers, believe that whites cannot truly understand blacks, that children will be deprived of their heritage and that their development will be harmed. They also worry that black children will feel inferior, particularly if raised in a predominantly white neighborhood.

Supporters of transracial adoption when suitable black adoptive families cannot be identified, such as the National Committee for Adoption, cite longitudinal studies, especially by researchers Rita Simon and Howard Altstein, that indicate black children raised by whites are generally well-adjusted. In addition, they state that permanence is the real issue and that loving, appropriate white parents are better than continuous foster care or other less suitable arrangements.

Research has revealed that black adoptive parents adopt for essentially the same reasons stated by Caucasian adoptive families.

A study by Gwendolyn Prater and Lula T. King discussed the motivations of black adoptive parents.

According to their article, the primary reasons given for adopting by the 12 families who participated in the study were "unable to have children biologically," the desire to "share their love with a child" and a desire to "give a child without a home, a home and a family." Three couples wanted to adopt a girl because they already had boys.

All the couples but one said they were glad they had adopted a child. One couple had adopted a five-year-old child, and Prater and King reported one of the adoptive parents stated, "I felt good when he told us he didn't ever want to leave me, his daddy, or brother."

The researchers concluded that black adoptive parents would make a valuable resource in recruiting other black adoptive parents. They warned, however, that families were reticent about discussing adoption with strangers, and thus adoption workers should be sure to maintain confidentiality unless the parents indicated their willingness to talk about adoption with prospective parents. (See also BLACK ADOPTIVE PARENT RECRUITMENT PROGRAMS; NATIONAL COALITION TO END RACISM IN AMERICA'S CHILD CARE SYSTEM.)

Gwendolyn Prater and Lula T. King, "Experiences of Black Families as Adoptive Parents," *Social Work*, 33(November–December 1988): 543–545.

Illinois Department of Children and Family Services, *Mostly I Can Do More Things Than I Can't* (Chelsea, MI: National Resource Center for Special Needs Adoption, 1987).

blended families Families with both biological and adopted children and/or families with children of different races. The term "blended family" is more commonly used to refer to stepparenting relationships resulting from remarriage when the parents already have children from a previous marriage or relationship. (See also MIXED FAMILIES.)

blood ties See ATTITUDES.

boarder babies See AIDS; DRUG ABUSE.

bonding and attachment Refers to the mutual affectionate connection that is cemented between a child and a parent, whether the child is a biological child or an adopted child. The process of establishing this connection includes a growing feeling of ENTITLEMENT to family life, love, responsibility and a variety of other emotions normally experienced by a parent and child.

A few adoption experts differentiate "bonding" from "attachment" and believe bonding can only be achieved between a biological parent and child while attachment can occur between a child and an important person in his or her life, such as an adoptive parent. Many adoptive parents would argue this point, and it's impossible to prove who is right.

Most adoptive parents and adoption experts are concerned about the timing of bonding in relation to the age of the child who is adopted, whether the child is six months old or six years old.

Psychiatrist Michael Rutter provides some information on this point. Rutter found that the idea that there are "sensitive periods" when environmental factors are critical does have some soundness, although the upper age limits of the sensitive periods may be at an older age than originally postulated by scientists. His study showed that children who were adopted before the age of four bonded well with their parents while children who were over age four experienced many of the same problems as children who remained in an institution.

Yet Rutter also supported the idea that even children adopted after the age of four years could bond with adoptive parents. He concluded that the "sensitive period" was either wrong or the timing occurred at a later age than previously thought.

Nurses Dorothy Smith and Laurie Sherwen studied the bonding process between mothers and their older adopted children. They confirmed mothers do indeed "bond" to their adopted children and discussed many of the aspects involved in the process.

One key aspect of bonding that they identified is the fantasizing parents experience about the child that occurs before the child's arrival and that is a normal process preceding parenthood.

Pregnant women and their husbands have nine months to think about the child and imagine what he or she will look like, sound like and so forth. But many adoptive parents, although they may have waited years for their child, often receive only a day or two of notice to pick up their child or to meet their child for the first time.

Hopefully, during the waiting process the prospective mothers (and fathers) will have spent time fantasizing about their future child, activities they'll perform together and other dreams common to all parents.

The First Meeting The first meeting with the child is a very dramatic moment for most parents, be they biological parents or adoptive parents. If they are adopting an older child, the parents usually will have seen photographs or a VIDEOTAPE of the child and will also have received information about the child as well.

Many adoptive parents have reported that they bonded to the child based on his or her picture alone, especially in the case of an INTERNATIONAL ADOPTION, when the decision to adopt was based solely on the photo and a sketchy description. In fact, when such an adoption has fallen through for some reason, adoptive parents actually experience a grieving process, even though they have never met the child.

If the child is an infant, the adoptive parents will have virtually no idea what the child will look like until they first see her or him, although they will know his or her racial and ethnic background and have general information about the birthparents' appearance.

The time when they first view the baby or older child is very important and unforgettable to most adoptive parents, as if it were imprinted in their brains along with other important scenes of their lives. Both adopting parents should be present at the first meeting along with older children and, if possible, the rest of the family.

The Bonding Process Part of bonding is physical touch, and because infants require much touching in the course of their care, most adoptive parents bond more rapidly to infants than to older children. Some research indicates that when parents are adopting siblings, they appear to bond more rapidly with the younger child, probably because of the greater amount of care needed by that child.

Parents bond to older children by teaching them how to cook, taking them shopping and performing other similar activities with them as a parent and a child.

Some older children do not respond to affection at first and, if they have been abused, may shrink from hugs and kisses. Adopting parents learn to "go slow" until the child is ready to accept love.

Studies indicate that parents seem to bond the most quickly and with the most lasting bond when they perceive the adopted child is similar to them in physical appearance, intelligence, temperament or some other aspect. As a result, adoptive parents will see "Uncle Bob's nose" and "Mom's smile" in an infant, even though they realize the child is completely unrelated to them.

Strangers may point out apparent similarities, and the adoptive parent may respond with embarrassment, confusion, pride or a mix of all of these emotions.

Bonding is not always instantaneous, even when the child is a newborn baby (nor is bonding always instantaneous between a biological mother and her child) and rarely occurs immediately when a child is an older child.

Often the bonding process is a slow evolution of a myriad of tiny events in the course of days, weeks or months, for example, the older child's first visit, the time when he comes to stay, registering him for school, taking him to the doctor.

Many parents of older adopted children report the first time they really knew they were parents was when they felt someone had threatened their child by speaking harshly to him or pushing him. The rush of parental anger and protectiveness is a clearcut sign that this parent has bonded to this child.

The support of the extended family is very important to the bonding process and helps legitimize the feeling of closeness the adoptive parents are developing with their child.

Unfortunately, sometimes extended families are distant or negative about the adoption, which causes considerable anxiety and may affect the bonding process. Adoptive parent support group members can help such families with their need for a feeling of importance and belonging.

Negative societal attitudes about bonding can sometimes make adoptive parents feel inferior. Author Patricia Johnston writes, "A romantic mysticism has developed around the physical process of motherhood and the mother/child relationship that has confused and upset many people . . . [who] are allowed and encouraged to feel guilty, disappointed and painfully second rate."

Others agree that the inability to parent a child in the first days of infancy (because the child is in the hospital, a foster home or someplace other than where the adoptive parents are) should not make adoptive parents feel they are less valid parents. Certainly professionals hardly claim that early contact at birth is essential to attachment.

Author Ellen Galinksy points out, "The idea that early contact is important for bonding has been incorporated into the mainstream of images of parenthood. And those parents who have a less than ecstatic first meeting or who have to miss that early time with their child because of the circumstances of their birth usually feel as if they have failed, feel that they are already remiss in their relationship with the baby."

Galinsky further states that fears and concerns about bonding can contribute more to a problem with bonding than does the actual timing of the placement.

Johnston identifies certain "claiming" behaviors common to both biological and adoptive parents that lead to bonding with the child, such as stroking the body of the infant, kissing the child, counting toes and others.

In a study of infant bonding that compared adoptive mothers to nonadoptive mothers, researchers Leslie M. Singer, David M. Brodzinsky, Douglas Ramsay, Mary Steir and Everett Waters studied infants ages 13 to 18 months. Some of the parents had adopted children of another race.

According to the researchers, they found "no differences in mother-infant attachment between nonadopted and intraracial adopted subjects or between intraracial and interracial adopted subjects." They did, however, find a greater incidence of "insecure attachment" in the interracial mother-infant groups compared to the nonadoptive groups. In addition, they reported that mothers who had adopted transracially were less willing to allow other people to care for their children.

The researchers also said they found no relationship between "quality of mother-infant attachment and either perceived social support, infant development quotient, infant temperament, number of foster homes experienced by the infant, or infant's age at the time of placement."

Researchers Leon J. Yarrow and Robert P. Klein studied the effect of moving an infant from a foster home to an adoptive home. They reported that "change *per se* in the environment is less important than change associated with less adequate care. Infants who experience a marked deterioration in quality of the environment following adoptive placement show disturbances in adaptation, whereas infants who are moved to an environment where there is a significant improvement in maternal care are less likely to show significant disturbances following the move."

The researchers compared and contrasted foster and adoptive mothers and found several major differences. Adoptive mothers were quicker to respond to infants and were more likely to hold the baby during feeding times then were foster mothers. In addition, adoptive parents expressed more concern about the children's feelings.

The researchers concluded that if the move from a foster family to an adoptive family also meant improved care, then a child's negative reaction to change would be mitigated by the improvement.

One aspect that can seriously impair the bonding process is if the adopted child is very different from the type of child the parent dreamed of, for example, if behavioral problems far exceed what the parent is ready to cope with or physical problems are more severe than what the parent said she or he could handle.

Consequently, it is very important for social workers to share as much nonidentifying information as possible about a child with prospective parents before a placement occurs.

Attachment Disorders Some infants and older children have difficulty relating to or accepting a parental figure. This problem is more common in older children and in foster children who are adopted than in children who were adopted as infants.

According to clinical social worker Mary-Lynn Harrison, certain traits are seen in unattached children, such as unresponsiveness to affection, serious problems with hoarding or stealing food, abnormal eye contact problems, a preoccupation with thinking about blood or fire or an overly friendly attitude toward strangers. (It should be noted that such problems could also indicate psychiatric problems unrelated to attachment disorders.)

Author and physician Vera Fahlberg says the most apparent trait of a child with an attachment disorder is the psychological and physical distancing from adults. In addition, the child may see himself or herself as an unworthy person. In most cases, the child is either overly dependent or greatly independent. Learning problems are common.

A related problem could be that instead of never having developed an attachment, the child may have suffered an "interrupted attachment" or experienced "unresolved separation issues."

A foster child with an attachment disorder may have been placed in many different homes or may not have received affection or love from any person at an early age. Severely neglected children are at the most risk for suffering an attachment disorder. Children who have been less severely neglected or emotionally or physically abused are more likely to have a damaged sense of attachment.

The "unattached" child could act out because of the lack of love and sociability in their own lives. They may appear manipulative, insincere and without a conscience. They may be distrustful and do their best to keep others at a distance, by either aggressive actions or withdrawal. The child may also be nondiscriminating in showing affection.

Indiscriminate affection probably deserves some explanation since it is not intuitively obvious why this could be a problem, especially in a young child. But when a child runs up to a total stranger and hugs him and says such things as "I love you," that is indiscriminate affection and may indicate an attachment problem, particularly if the child would normally be in the developmental stage where he or she would evince a fear of strangers. Although strangers may respond to such behavior in a very positive way and consider it charming, it is symptomatic of a problem.

Says Fahlberg, "It is difficult for foster or adoptive parents to feel close to a child who is acting close to everyone else. In addition, children who are willing to go with strangers pose real supervision problems for their parents."

Sometimes therapists can be "fooled" into thinking the problem is the family, not the child.

Foster Cline, one of the authors of *Working with Older Adoptees,* says if the parents have several children who are doing well at home and at school but one child has serious problems, then therapists should be careful not to quickly scapegoat the parents or the entire family.

Cline also says when children have problems with bonding and attachment, they are more likely to exhibit their negative behavior towards females rather than males. In addition, children adopted as older children may display very negative behavior toward their adoptive mothers and act normally with their adoptive fathers.

On the plus side, Cline says if a child gets along well with parents before puberty, "it does not matter how badly adolescence proceeds, the child will probably grow up to be an adult, loving the parents and modeling them."

Codependent Parents Christopher Waldmann of Evergreen Consultants in Human Behavior in Boulder, Colorado says parents of unattached children must be careful not to become codependent, which refers to a tendency of concentrating too heavily on others' needs while ignoring one's own needs.

He wrote, "The unattached child's disturbance will thrive with co-dependent parents . . . the more responsible the other (or father) is for the way the child behaves, thinks, and feels, the more disturbed the child becomes."

A parent could be having a codependency problem, according to Waldmann, when the parent exhibits some of the following symptoms: "feeling responsible for the way he [the child] feels, behaves and thinks," "working hard to protect the child from himself or trying to protect the world from this child," " 'walking on eggshells' for fear that the child will be out of control" or "experiencing general anxiety and anger."

Waldmann says many therapists convey the impression that if only the parent loved the child more or better, then the child would be fine. Such advice can only serve to make the problem worse.

If parents think they may have a codependency problem with an unattached child, they should identify a support group that can help and a therapist who understands the problem.

Help for Attachment Attachment can be encouraged, for example, a child's temper tantrums could be used to encourage attachment. After a tantrum, a child is usually exhausted, relaxes and is open to bonding with the parent.

Some positive interactions include such behaviors as telling the child "I love you," teaching the child a family sport such as skiing, reading to the child, helping the child understand family jokes and other activities.

Special trips or teaching the child skills such as cooking can create a favorable environment for creating an attachment between the parent and the child.

Initiating "claiming behaviors" is another technique. This encourages a child to claim a family as his own. For example, the family might send out adoption announcements, hold a religious or other ceremony that welcomes the child into the family, add a middle name of family significance or take the child to visit relatives. All such activities encourage a child to feel he belongs to the new family.

Organizations that assist parents whose children face attachment problems include the following:

Attachment Center at Evergreen
P.O. Box 2764
Evergreen, CO 80439

Attachment Disorder Parents Network
c/o Gail Trenberth
P.O. Box 12127
Boulder, CO 80303

National Resource Center for Special
 Needs Adoption
P.O. Box 337
Chelsea, MI 48118

Loren Coleman, Karen Tilbor, Helaine Hornby and Carol Boggis, ed., *Working with Older Adoptees: A Sourcebook of Innovative Models* (Portland, Me: University of Southern Maine, Human Services Development Institute, 1988).

Vera Fahlberg, M.D., *Attachment and Separation: Putting the Pieces Together* (Chelsea, MI: National Resource Center for Special Needs Adoption, 1979).

———, ed., *Residential Treatment: A Tapestry of Many Therapies* (Indianapolis: Perspectives Press, 1990).

Ellen Galinsky, *The Six Stages of Parenthood* (Reading, Mass.: Addison-Wesley, 1987).

Carol Hallenbeck, "Magical Mystical Bonding," *OURS*, 20(March/April 1987): 25–26.

Mary-Lynn Harrison, "Bonding and Attachment: The Glue that Binds," *OURS*, 23(July/August 1990), 10–13.

Patricia Irwin Johnston, *An Adoptor's Advocate* (Indianapolis: Perspectives Press, 1984).

Ken Magid and Carole A. McKelvey, *High Risk* (New York: Bantam Books, 1988).

Michael Rutter, "Family and School Influences on Behavioural Development," *Journal of Child Psychology and Psychiatry*, 26:3(1985), 349–368.

Leslie M. Singer, David M. Brodzinsky, Douglas Ramsay, Mary Steir and Everett Waters, "Mother-Infant Attachment in Adoptive Families," *Child Development*, 56(1985): 1543–1551.

Dorothy W. Smith and Laurie Nehls Sherwen, *Mothers and their Adopted Children—the Bonding Process* (New York: Teresias Press, 1983).

Christopher Waldmann, "The Good Mom," *Family Ties*, August 1989; published by Attachment Disorder Parents Network, P.O. Box 12127, Boulder, CO 80303.

Leon J. Yarrow and Robert P. Klein, "Environmental Discontinuity Associated with Transition from Foster to Adoptive Homes," *International Journal of Behavioral Development*, 3(1980): 311–322.

breast-feeding an adopted infant A small number of adoptive mothers choose to nurse their infants, and it is possible to induce lactation in a woman who has never borne children or never been pregnant. Even if an adoptive mother produces a tiny amount of milk or no milk at all, the tactile closeness to her infant is a very positive experience for many mothers.

Induced lactation, as defined by Kathryn Anderson in her La Leche League International pamphlet, *Nursing Your Adopted Baby,* is "the process of convincing the body to produce milk even though there has been no recent birth or even a previous pregnancy."

Stimulation of the glands in the breast by using a breast pump may result in ultimate stimulation of the pituitary gland and the production of breast milk in the adoptive mother.

The baby's sucking at the breast will further stimulate the production of milk; however, the lack of milk production or the production of only a small amount of milk should in no way cause an adoptive mother to feel she is unsuccessful. Instead, experts say the adoptive mother should concentrate on the closeness of the experience rather than worrying about producing large quantities of breast milk.

According to Anderson, it is unlikely an adoptive mother will be able to produce sufficient milk to fulfill all her baby's nutritional needs; however, she supports nursing as a positive experience that enhances mother/child bonding.

In some cases, the adoptive mother may have breast-fed biological or adopted children previously. She will need to "relactate." Anderson says mothers who have previously breast-fed must also begin the process to stimulate the production of breast milk, and there is little evidence that a mother who has previously breast-fed will have greater success than a mother who has never breast-fed or never been pregnant.

According to author Elizabeth Hormann, who has written about nursing adopted infants, "Women who have never been pregnant or who have not been pregnant or nursing within six months before their adopted baby arrives are just about equivalent, biologically speaking . . . A study of these women showed that they reach their peak nursing time within three to four months after they begin, and by that time, they are producing, on an average, about half of what their babies need."

If the adopting mother knows weeks or months ahead of time that the baby will be arriving, she may opt to use a breast pump to begin stimulating the breasts to induce a milk supply.

Breast milk may be supplemented by bottle-feeding or by special devices designed for adoptive mothers who are nursing. If the bottle is used, Anderson recommends using larger than usual nipple holes on the bottle, because the baby will quickly receive what she needs yet will still have a natural desire to suck and can then be breast-fed.

Devices that simulate nursing are commercially available. Such devices include an external bag of formula that is placed atop the mother's nipple while the child nurses. The baby can simultaneously nurse at the breast and the supplemental device or the device may be slipped into the infant's mouth after nursing has begun.

Breast fullness or a change in the menstrual cycle (for example, a reduced menstrual flow) are indications the body is undergoing hormonal changes in the endocrine system as the adoptive mother begins (or increases) her production of breast milk; however, these changes are not always present in an adoptive mother who is nursing.

Experts say newborn infants are the best candidates for nursing; however, adoptive mothers may also nurse older infants as well, and adoptive mothers have been successful with infants as old as six to nine months.

It is important for the adoptive mother who nurses to obtain moral support from others. Relatives and friends may not understand the value of the experience to the adoptive mother and may try to discourage her from nursing or find her efforts humorous or bizarre.

As a result, finding other adoptive parents who have successfully nursed can be a major boon to a new mother. The La Leche League may be able to recommend adoptive mothers or support groups who can help.

Kathryn Anderson, *Nursing Your Adopted Baby* (Franklin Park, IL: La Leche League International, 1986).

Elizabeth Hormann, *After the Adoption* (Old Tappan, NJ: Fleming Revell, 1987).

C

"Calling out" An annual event held by adoptive parent support groups nationwide during NATIONAL ADOPTION WEEK (Thanksgiving week).

Calling out refers to a ceremony in which the first names of children with SPECIAL NEEDS awaiting adoption in the state and in the custody of the state social service department are simultaneously read aloud nationwide.

The purpose of the ceremony is to generate interest in adoption and to recruit prospective adoptive parents for WAITING CHILDREN.

Groups vary in how they manage the ceremony. Some release balloons, while others orchestrate more elaborate ceremonies. Groups who use calling out also actively solicit media attention in order to promote the adoption of children with special needs in general and waiting children in particular.

Organizations such as the NORTH AMERICAN COUNCIL ON ADOPTABLE CHILDREN (NACAC) or ADOPTIVE FAMILIES OF AMERICA, INC. provide information and assistance to many groups on planning such an event.

CAP Book The more popular, shortened title of *The National Photo Listing of Children Waiting for Adoptive Parents*. The two-volume book features pictures and descriptions of children from throughout the United States who are available to be adopted.

The CAP Book was founded in 1972 by an adoptive parent group, the Council of Adoptive Parents. This group was one of the first adoptive parent groups to provide PHOTOLISTINGS of adoptable children.

Five children from the Rochester, New York area were listed in the first edition. The photolisting book was so successful that the organization expanded into a regional, and ultimately a national, photolisting, and today lists over 400 children from around the country.

About 450 subscribers around the United States receive the photolisting book, including individuals, parent groups, adoption agencies, physicians, libraries and others. The *National Enquirer* also photolists waiting children, using information provided by the CAP Book.

Callers are given the name of the child's social worker and other information. CAP Book workers record all inquiries and track the status of the child. In 1989, 68 children were adopted as a direct result of the CAP Book. CAP Book director Peggy Soule estimates that 6,000 children have been listed through the years, and about half were ultimately placed for adoption.

A one-year subscription to the CAP Book includes a two-volume book and biweekly updated information as well as listings of newly registered children with SPECIAL NEEDS. (See also ADVERTISING AND PROMOTION; WAITING CHILDREN.)

For further information, contact

The CAP Book
700 Exchange St.
Rochester, NY 14608
(716) 232-5110

case records The file maintained by the adoption agency on the child to be adopted, the biological parents or the prospective adoptive parents. In some cases, records may be very voluminous, particularly if the child has been in foster care for several years or more.

Case records include confidential and personal information about individuals and families that is generally not shared outside the agency, for example, information obtained during professional counseling, allegations of child abuse and results of investigations.

Prospective adoptive parents of children with SPECIAL NEEDS should request as much nonidentifying information as possible about the child they are planning to adopt, including permission to review appropriate portions of the case records when legally permissible. (See also OPEN RECORDS; SEALED RECORDS.)

case study HOME STUDY or family study of prospective ADOPTIVE PARENTS, also involving counseling and the preparation for adoption.

Catholic Adoptive Parents Association (CAPA) Formed in the 1970s to provide an opportunity for adoptive parents to meet and discuss shared interests.

Today, CAPA's primary goal is to educate members and others about adoption. To this end, the organization released a brochure entitled *Media Guidelines on Adoption Language*. It has dedicated a good deal of effort to the analysis of interaction of media and adoption and has commissioned a major study of media representations of the adoption experience, including a preliminary survey by George Gerbner of the Annenberg School of Communications at the University of Pennsylvania. Further media studies even broader in scope are planned for the future. The leaders of CAPA hope to educate media representatives about adoption as well as those in the entertainment industry.

The organization has over 400 family members, primarily in the New York metropolitan area. Members are adoptive parents or prospective adoptive parents who have completed their home study. Honorary members include social workers and clergy.

Members receive a bimonthly newsletter entitled *The CAPA Newsletter*. Officers meet monthly, the general membership meets semiannually, and the organization holds a Christmas party and picnic. Regional meetings are also held in Westchester County and Long Island, both in New York. (See also MEDIA; SUPPORT GROUPS.)

For more information, contact

Catholic Adoptive Parents Association Inc.
Box 893
Harrison, NY 10528

child abuse See ABUSE.

children, adopted See ADOLESCENT ADOPTED PERSONS; INFANT ADOPTION; SPECIAL NEEDS.

Children's Aid Society of New York The oldest formal child-placing agency in the United States, founded in 1853 by the Reverend Charles Brace; still in existence today in New York City.

Brace formed the organization to help the thousands of homeless children who roamed the streets of New York. He initiated the ORPHAN TRAIN program, which sent an estimated 150,000 children to families in the West, Midwest and other areas outside New York.

Leslie Wheeler, "The Orphan Trains," *American History Illustrated*, vol. 18 December 1983.

childrens' rights Although children do not have many of the civil rights of adults, they do have limited rights that were not afforded them in the earlier part of this century. At that time, children were considered "chattel" or possessions and were expected to work and earn their keep.

Today children are protected from exploitation by labor laws. They are also entitled to a free public education and in fact are required by law to attend school until reaching an age determined by the state (usually age 16), at which time they may choose to drop out.

Children are also protected by law from abuse, even when that abuse occurs at the hands of their parents. State social service workers are empowered with the authority to remove children from abusive homes and place them in foster homes or institutional shelters until a court decides what disposition to make of the children and whether or not abuse did occur.

Children are not automatically entitled to a permanent home and may wait in a series of foster homes for years to be adopted. In addition, PARENTAL RIGHTS may never be terminated if parents continue to appeal attempts by caseworkers to end them. (See also TERMINATION OF PARENTAL RIGHTS.)

Child Welfare League of America Inc.
National nonsectarian professional child advocacy organization of more than 600 public and private children's agencies; founded in 1920. It publishes standards of practice for a variety of child welfare services, including adoption services. Dues vary depending on the size of the agency.

The organization offers training conferences, publications, newsletters and journals to members; for example, *Child Welfare* is a professional journal it publishes that includes problem-solving techniques and ideas for social workers and other professionals involved in child welfare. The league also publishes a bibliography of adoption-related materials. The complete publications catalog is available at no cost. For a free catalog, write to

Child Welfare League of America Inc.
440 First St. NW, Suite 310
Washington, DC 20001
(202) 638-2952

"chosen child" A concept derived from a formerly popular book *(The Chosen Baby)* that social workers in past years encouraged adoptive parents to read to their adopted children and that told how the child had been "chosen" by them. This story was urged because it was believed the child would feel special and unique, and this feeling would overcome any anxiety or negativism about being adopted.

A problem with the "chosen child" story is that it was not always accurate in the past and is less likely to be so now, except in some international adoptions.

Very few adoptive parents now actually select the child they wish to adopt. Instead, a social worker, agency team, attorney or other individual decides a particular couple or single person would be most likely to meet the needs of a particular infant.

As a result, when an older child starts asking for details on *how* or *why* she was chosen, the whole "chosen child" story falls apart.

Parents can instead explain that they chose to adopt as a way of building their family and that, once the child was placed, they chose to follow through and legally finalize the adoption in a court of law.

Today it is more often birthmothers who do the choosing—in such cases, adoptive parents are selected by a birthmother from a number of nonidentifying resumes or profiles written by prospective adoptive parents who were selected by professional staff as all being appropriate parents for a particular child.

Another problem with the "chosen child" story is that sometimes adoptive parents have biological children, either before or after they adopt a child. Given current technology, biological children are not hand-picked and come out however nature decrees. The parents are not "stuck with" the biological child, although the "chosen child" story does imply that they are when a child is born into a family.

The "chosen child" story also has an underlying implication that the child should feel grateful he was chosen when, in fact, most adoptive parents feel very grateful themselves that they have had an opportunity to adopt this child.

Most social workers and adoption experts urge adoptive parents to tell the child about adoption in a positive yet honest way, such as they wanted a child to love and the birthparents who were not ready or able to be parents themselves wanted the child to be placed in a loving home. (See also EXPLAINING ADOPTION.)

Lillian G. Katz, "Adopted Children," *Parents*, January 1987, 116.
Valentina P. Wasson, *Chosen Baby* (Philadelphia: Lippincott, 1977).

citizenship Agencies may require adopting parents to be U.S. citizens. In the case of an international adoption, one member of a couple in the United States must be a U.S. citizen, and a prospective single adoptive parent must be a U.S. citizen.

Children adopted from other countries do not automatically become U.S. citizens. A formal application for U.S. citizenship must be made before the child's 16th birthday. (See also ADOPTIVE PARENTS; INTERNATIONAL ADOPTION.)

U.S. Department of Justice, Immigration and Naturalization Service, *The Immigration of Adopted and Prospective Adoptive Children*, rev. ed., M-249Y, 1990, Government Printing Office.

classes for adoptive parents See EDUCATION OF ADOPTIVE PARENTS.

cocaine and "crack" babies See DRUG ABUSE.

Committee for Single Adoptive Parents National organization for singles interested in adopting or who have adopted children.

The Washington, D.C.-based organization was formed in 1973 by the current chairman, Hope Marindin. It seeks to provide information and assistance to singles, to gather and disseminate legislation and research findings on single parent adoption and to promote the adoption of children despite their race, creed, national origin or any handicapping conditions.

Membership varies from year to year but averages about 350 members. A 1990 survey of its members revealed that nearly half were in the "helping" professions, such as teaching, social work, nursing. Businesspeople represented 37% of the total members. Other members included writers, engineers, musicians, artists and other professions.

A very large number of the members are well educated: The survey revealed that 86% of the prospective single adoptive parents were college graduates, and 14% had earned doctorate degrees.

Most of the members were in their thirties with 10% under age 30 and 23% older than 39.

Members receive a source list and updates of information on agencies placing children with single parents, including estimates of the waiting time and costs involved. The committee publishes the *Handbook for Single Adoptive Parents*, which covers the how-to aspects of adopting as well as information on bringing up the adopted child and includes single parent adoption accounts. The committee also provides information on local single adoptive parent support groups and books to read and upon request will provide names of single adoptive parents in the requester's area. (See also SINGLE ADOPTIVE PARENTS; SINGLE PARENTS ADOPTING CHILDREN EVERYWHERE (SPACE).)

For more information, contact

Committee for Single Adoptive Parents
P.O. Box 15084
Chevy Chase, MD 20825

computers Increasing numbers of social workers are using computers to match prospective adoptive parents with children who have SPECIAL NEEDS. All state adoption offices in the United States have computers that link them to the NATIONAL ADOPTION CENTER and its telecommunications system, allowing social workers to communicate with each other about the availability of families for their WAITING CHILDREN and giving them access to adoption information quickly and efficiently.

Initial reservations about the use of computers focused primarily on the lack of understanding about how they could be used in adoption, as well as some apprehension about technology. Today, however, an increased number of social workers are using computers, relying on their speed and efficiency to aid in the placement of children with special needs. Those who use computers testify that they have eased their caseloads and have increased their ability to find families for their waiting children. The use of computers has also proven to be cost-effective. (See also NATIONAL ADOPTION NETWORK; SUPPORT GROUPS.)

Concerned United Birthparents Inc. (CUB) A nonprofit organization composed primarily of birthparents and based in Des Moines, IA. Members are people from the United States, Canada and abroad who are interested in adoption issues.

Created in 1976 as a vehicle to provide support to birthparents who placed their children for adoption, CUB has since expanded to include adopted persons, adoptive parents and others.

It is actively interested in SEARCH-related issues, and new members may insert free ads in the organization's newsletter. The organization has a reunion registry for members searching for an adopted person, birthparent or birth sibling. Letter and phone call support is provided to searchers who are not near a branch. (Branches are in California, Colorado, Connecticut, Iowa, Kentucky, Massachusetts, Minnesota and Ohio.) Search workshops are provided for members who have attended at least three support group meetings.

Adoption "prevention" is another goal of CUB members, who believe adoption is not always necessary, especially when the birthparent's problem is a temporary one, such as inadequate finances or lack of emotional support. The members can provide assistance to birthparents for whom adoption is not the first choice yet who see no other answer.

The organization also works for changes in adoption policy and supports OPEN ADOPTION for those cases when members feel adoption is the appropriate choice for their children. The organization also promotes their views through talks to community groups and distribution of literature on search and other issues.

Members receive *CUB Communicator,* a monthly newsletter. Meetings are held monthly at branch locations.

For more information, contact

Concerned United Birthparents Inc.
2000 Walker St.
Des Moines, IA 50317
(515) 263-9588

confidentiality In adoption, the practice of preserving privacy or anonymity and refraining from providing information on the identities of birthparents and adoptive parents, either to each other or to the adopted children or adult adopted persons.

An adoption agency social worker, attorney or other intermediary is aware of the identities of all concerned and retains this information in confidence. Original birth certificates become SEALED RECORDS upon finalization of the adoption, and a new amended birth certificate is issued with the names of the adopting parents as parents.

Confidentiality in adoptions has been the standard in the United States since infant adoptions became widespread in the 1930s.

Today confidentiality is under attack by a variety of groups and individuals who seek to open all records and insist OPEN ADOPTION is in the best interests of all concerned. They are greatly opposed to confidentiality in adoptions. (See CONCERNED UNITED BIRTH-PARENTS INC.)

Critics of confidentiality believe "secrecy" in adoption is wrong and also argue that, should the adopted person need to contact his birthparents for whatever reason, no SEARCH would be necessary—the adopted person would know who his birthparents are and probably could learn exactly where they are. These critics believe it is wrong to deprive a birthparent or an adopted child of identifying information.

Advocates of continued confidentiality assert that all parties in an adoption, including the adopted person, birthparents and adoptive parents, are protected by confidentiality. They believe these groups could be negatively affected if identities were revealed. They also insist that some birthparents might choose ABORTION over adoption if confidentiality and privacy were banned in all cases.

In addition, advocates state that the child benefits when only NONIDENTIFYING INFORMATION is provided and the child can be raised by parents who are allowed a stronger sense of ENTITLEMENT.

Two-thirds of the U.S. population lives in one of the states with an adoption registry. Registries will provide identifying information to adopted persons, siblings or birthparents if the parties involved have registered their interest in such information. Some states also require the approval of adoptive parents as well, regardless of the age of the adopted person.

Information is generally not provided unless the adopted adult is at least 18, and some states have a higher age limit (usually 21 years). (See also TRADITIONAL ADOPTION.)

Congressional Coalition on Adoption

An informal bicameral caucus of 87 members of Congress who actively support adoption.

Members of the coalition are interested in children who would benefit from adoption and in adoptive parents and prospective adoptive parents. The coalition seeks to remove barriers to adoption, both domestic and international, promote understanding of infant adoption and support the adoption of children in foster care awaiting adoption.

As of this writing, there are four cochairmen, all of whom are adoptive parents. Staff coordination is provided by the office of Sen. Larry Craig of Idaho, as of this writing.

The other three cochairmen are Sen. Lloyd Bentsen (TX), Rep. Thomas Bliley (VA), and Rep. James Oberstar (MN).

Staff members of these four Congressmen collaborate in tracking key adoption legislation that is moving through Congress and regularly inform members and the general public of the status of a variety of bills related to adoption and foster care. For example, in the 1989 Congress the coalition tracked the Family Leave Benefits Act of 1989, the Fairness for Adopting Families Act and The Childless Veterans Assistance Act, among other legislative initiatives. The coalition was created through the efforts of former senator from New Hampshire Gordon Humphrey.

consent (to an adoption) Voluntary agreement of those with PARENTAL RIGHTS to make an adoption plan. Who may give legal consent for an adoption varies from state to state.

If the birthmother was married at the time of the conception or birth of the child, both she and her husband must consent to any adoption, even if the husband is not the biological father. If the mother is unmarried, her consent is necessary. In most states, consent of the PUTATIVE FATHER is also necessary if he fulfills certain statutory criteria. Often these criteria are modeled after the *Stanley v. Illinois* case. (See BIRTH-FATHER.)

An adoption agency that was asked to help arrange the adoption may also consent to the adoption by writing a report to the court.

In many states, the child must also consent to the adoption. According to the "Matrix of State Adoption Laws" published by the NATIONAL ADOPTION INFORMATION CLEARINGHOUSE, the minimum age of consent varies and is 14 in Alabama, 12 in Florida and 14 in Minnesota. (Most states that set an age of consent for the child was either 12 or 14 years.)

Consent may be waived if the state has terminated parental rights of the person whose consent would otherwise be required. In most states, parental rights may be terminated only on "fault" grounds (such as abuse, neglect, abandonment) or for serious incapacity (such as severe mental retardation or serious and incurable mental illness). (See also TERMINATION OF PARENTAL RIGHTS.)

The timing of when consent may be taken also varies from state to state; for example, Arizona sets a timeframe of 72 hours or more after the child's birth, as does Illinois. Kentucky and Louisiana set a period of 5 days following the child's birth. Many states set no time limit.

Some states allow for a withdrawal of consent after its execution; for example, consent may be revoked within 10 days in Georgia. Consent is irrevocable in other states unless there is a finding of fraud or duress.

In some states, revocability depends on whether the consent was given in court; for example, if consent is given in court in New York, consent is immediately irrevocable unless the consenting parent proves fraud or duress. If given out of court, the consent is revocable for 45 days. If the consent is revoked within that time period, however, the parent does not automatically receive the child but must prove it would be in the child's best interests to be returned to the parent. (See also REVOCATION.)

In 1991, Alabama passed a law allowing for "pre-birth" relinquishment, wherein birthparents could consent to an adoption prior to the childs birth. (The birthparents may revoke consent for a limited period after the birth of the child.)

contract Voluntary agreement between two or more parties. An attorney may require a contract with adopting parents before the adoption can proceed.

COURT-MANDATED CONTRACTS are created by the state and are between the state social services caseworker and the parent or parents. Generally, court-mandated contracts are required when children are removed from abusive or neglectful homes, and the children may not be returned unless or until the parent(s) fulfill the terms of the contract.

Although pregnant women may sign contracts with attorneys or other parties prior to the birth of their children, women in every state may change their mind about adoption subsequent to the child's birth. The length of time allowed after consent is signed and the timing of when consent may be signed vary from state to state. (See also CONSENT (TO AN ADOPTION); NOTICE; REVOCATION.)

cooperative adoption™ A trademarked term used in the book of the same name by Mary Jo Rillera and Sharon Kaplan to describe an adoption in which the birthparents, adoptive parents and adopted child have a continuing relationship with each other throughout the course of the child's life.

The birthparents may opt to visit regularly or during major holidays, such as Thanksgiving, and they also stay in phone or letter contact with the adoptive parents. Major decisions about the child are discussed with the birthparents. At a later point in life, but before age 18, the child may leave the adoptive family to live with one or both of the birthparents.

Such adoptions are of necessity OPEN ADOPTIONS and actually extend beyond most open adoptions in the active participation that birthparents play in a child's life.

The birthparents and adoptive parents may together decide on a birth name for the child, and the child will be aware of the identity of his birthparents and their relationship to him.

Proponents of cooperative adoption feel it is the most humane and compassionate form of adoption, and they are very opposed to traditional confidential adoptions, which they deem a form of "child abuse" because of the confidentiality aspect.

Cooperative adoption advocates believe a child can only benefit by knowing his birthparents as well as his adoptive parents. This knowledge also means the child will never need to SEARCH for his birthparents because they will be known and accessible.

In addition, cooperative adoption advocates argue that any conflicts between the birthparents and the adoptive parents can be worked out as disputes are worked out in all families. They view the birthfamily as a form of the extended family of the adoptive family and the child.

Those who disapprove of cooperative adoptions believe that birthparents placing the child under such an arrangement are not really ready for adoption and possibly should opt to parent instead of placing the child for adoption. In addition, they argue that the sense of ENTITLEMENT felt by the adoptive parents and the BONDING AND ATTACHMENT to the child could be hampered by continuous contact with the birthparents. They also believe such an arrangement would be very confusing to a child, who would have, at the least, two sets of parents, four sets of grandparents and a variety of other siblings, aunts, uncles, cousins and so forth.

If the birthparents should discontinue their relationship or divorce and then remarry, even more relatives would be introduced into the whole family, potentially causing greater confusion. Those who support cooperative adoption scoff at these contentions and insist that such problems can be worked out by intelligent adults. They believe additional relatives would be positive for the child, not negative.

Proponents of cooperative adoption also believe that more infant adoptions would occur if this option were more readily available. The total percentage of cooperative adoptions in the United States is small and is probably less than 1% of all infant adoptions.

Mary Jo Rillera and Sharon Kaplan, *Cooperative Adoption: A Handbook* (Westminister, CA: Triadoption, 1985).

co-parenting Sharing the responsibilities of parenthood with another person or family.

The term "co-parenting" is often used as a disparaging and negative term by people who dislike COOPERATIVE ADOPTION and OPEN ADOPTION and who believe the child should be parented by one mother and one father only, despite the biological tie with the parents who conceived the child.

corporate benefits See EMPLOYMENT BENEFITS.

costs to adopt There are always costs involved in adopting a child, but because of SUBSIDIES (see ADOPTION ASSISTANCE PROGRAM) and taxpayer underwriting for some adoptions, the term usually applies to the fees for adoptions that are paid by adoptive families.

The fee to the adopting parent varies greatly depending on the type of child adopted and on whether it is an agency or nonagency adoption, a public agency or private agency adoption, an international or U.S. adoption and on many other factors. There are usually no fees charged to birthparents: All fees are charged to adopting parents only, whether the adoption is through an agency or through an intermediary, such as an attorney.

Adoptive parents who adopt children through the state public social services adoption system usually incur the least expenses of any adoptive parents. The state social services department usually charges nothing for the family assessment or HOME STUDY, and the only other expense the adoptive parent may have is the attorney fee to finalize the adoption, which may be several hundred dollars.

In addition, many children with SPECIAL NEEDS are also eligible for continuing MEDICAID coverage after finalization of the adoption, and adoption SUBSIDIES may also be available to adoptive parents. The primary reason subsidies are offered is to help cover the cost of continuing medical care and counseling the child may need.

The definition of "special needs" is determined by individual states; however, in most cases, children with special needs include handicapped infants and older children, black and biracial infants and children, children over age eight and sibling groups. Many private agencies charge a lower fee for the children with special needs who are in their custody because it is far more difficult to find adoptive families for them.

When adopting through private agencies, the fee to adopt may vary according to the age and race of the child, and fees for healthy CAUCASIAN infants are usually the highest. Because of the very strong demand for healthy white infants, agencies are able to charge their full cost in placing a child. Some agencies amortize the expenses of children with special needs by charging fees for healthy children in excess of costs incurred for those particular children.

The average collected fee for a private agency placement was about $8,000 in 1989, according to a survey of agencies that belong to the NATIONAL COMMITTEE FOR ADOPTION.

When a private agency receives charitable donations or subsidies from a church, the United Way or some other source, the average fee for a healthy white infant may be less. A few agencies rely only on donations for their support and charge no fees. However, it is critically important to remember that fees vary dramatically depending on agency auspices (sectarian agencies usually charge less), the area of the country, agency funding and a variety of factors. Prospective adoptive parents should fully understand an agency's fees prior to deciding to work with a particular agency.

Some agencies charge a SLIDING SCALE FEE: The fee is dependent on the income of the adopting parents, with a floor and a ceiling fee.

If the child is adopted from another state, there will usually be additional fees and costs associated with complying with the INTERSTATE COMPACT ON THE PLACEMENT OF CHILDREN. This is an agreement between the states that governs interstate adoption and is administered by the public agency in each state.

If the adopting parents are adopting a child from another state, they will pay an agency in their own state to study them, and they will pay the agency or attorney in the other state to administer the paperwork involved with that state.

The expenses involved in an INDEPENDENT ADOPTION through an attorney, physician or other nonagency INTERMEDIARY vary greatly from state to state; for example, the state of Florida limits attorney fees to $1,500 (unless the court allows more), while other states do not set such a limit.

Some states allow payments for medical fees and reasonable living expenses while others do not. As a result, an independent adoption may cost $3,000 to $4,000 or as much as $15,000 or more.

If the birthmother was on MEDICAID prior to her delivery, the adoption fee should be a great deal less, because Medicaid will cover her prenatal care and the delivery and hospital bill of the infant. The medical expenses related to an independent adoption are usually at least half of all the expenses, especially when the birthmother has a caesarean section (about 15% of all births are caesarean sections).

INTERNATIONAL ADOPTION expenses also vary, depending on the child's native country. The adoption fee may be about the same as for a domestic adoption, but frequently the adoptive parents are required to travel to that country and stay for a week or longer.

As a result, total costs of an international adoption usually are as much or more than for a U.S. adoption. An estimated average fee for international adoption is $8,000 to $10,000, including travel expenses; however, there are tremendous variations, and it is wise to look at each country as a special case.

In some instances of international adoption, such as adoption of children from Korea or El Salvador, escorts can bring the children back to the United States. The escort's travel expenses are included in fees paid by adopting parents.

In the adoption process, the first cost incurred by prospective adoptive parents is usually the agency application fee, which may range from $25 to $100 or more. Application fees in excess of $200 should be questioned.

When the agency accepts the adoptive parents for a home study, the home study fee is then due. Other fees may be payable to the agency during the course of the family study, with the remainder of the payment usually due when a child is placed in the home.

Some agencies will allow a family to make payments for the adoption on a regular basis or even finance the fee, rather than requiring that the entire fee be paid initially or by the time of placement. The willingness to make such an arrangement varies according to the agency and is probably more likely when the family is adopting a child with special needs.

Attorneys usually also require some initial payment and would probably expect at least $100 for a one-hour consultation fee. When an attorney matches prospective adoptive parents to a pregnant woman, the adopting parents generally give the attorney money for expenses, and that money is usually placed in a special restricted bank account.

If an adopting parent is unsure where his money is going, he should ask the attorney for an accounting: Most ethical attorneys will be willing to provide such information within a reasonable time.

Some agencies oversee adoptions that are independently arranged, wherein the adopting couple finds the pregnant woman or birthmother on their own and asks the agency to do the home study (also known as DESIGNATED ADOPTION.)

Expenses for a designated adoption may parallel the expenses involved in an independent adoption if the agency (or attorney) provides private medical care and support money, including wage replacement payments, to the pregnant woman. (Many attorneys also handle designated adoptions.)

Other additional expenses incurred by adopting parents include physicals for themselves and sometimes for children already in the home, phone calls to out-of-state agencies, photographs (sometimes required by the agency) and postage.

Many prospective adoptive parents save the money needed for an adoption, and some parents work two jobs to earn the required amount. Others take a second mortgage on their homes or borrow money from relatives. The image of adoptive parents as all affluent people is inaccurate. It is true, however, that few parents adopting healthy infants are poor or on WELFARE. (See also AGENCIES; ATTORNEYS; EMPLOYMENT BENEFITS; INFANT ADOPTION.)

court-mandated contracts In many cases, when a child is removed from the parental home because of abuse, neglect or abandonment, a social worker or a judge will create a contract or "performance" agreement that the parent must meet before the child may be returned to the home.

Such a contract may require the parent to hold a job continuously for a period of time (six months, a year, etc.), to avoid problems with the police, to avoid alcohol and drugs, to attend individual and/or group counseling sessions. Presumably, if the parent fulfills the terms of the contract, then the child will be returned to the home. And if the parent fails to meet the terms of the contract, the child will remain in the custody of the state or county, usually in foster care.

According to author Brett A. Seabury, there are four primary characteristics of a responsibly drawn contract: "explicitness, mutuality, flexibility, and realism . . . A service contract is explicit and clear so that both family and worker understand all terms and nothing is taken for granted. Professional jargon and legalese are avoided; the family's own words are preferred."

In some cases, the contract may be verbal as well as written, for example, if the parents are illiterate, retarded or have some other problem that would make it difficult for them to understand a written contract.

In addition there can sometimes be primary and secondary contracts. The primary contract is the agreement between the family and their caseworker. Secondary contracts set down service agreements or other arrangements with relevant professionals, training programs or other sources of support, such as self-help groups.

Federal law requires a judicial review of a foster child's case after 18 months to determine what future action should be taken—a return to the child's parents, long-term foster care, the recommendation to terminate parental rights or some other course of action. The court may also decide to delay the decision on what actions should be taken until a later date.

An extremely high turnover rate of social workers nationwide, court systems that renegotiate contracts when parents fail to abide by the terms, large caseloads of foster children and numerous other factors often mitigate the judicial review at the 18-month point. As a result, many children remain in foster care for four or five years or more before parental rights are terminated.

As the children grow older, it becomes increasingly difficult for even the most dedicated social workers to find good families for the children.

In addition, the strong value attached to BLOOD TIES by many judges and legislators cause children to remain in foster care, as a biological parent repeatedly fails to live up to the terms of the court-mandated contract.

Understandably, the state has an aversion to depriving children and their biological parents of a relationship with each other; however, in some cases, the biological parents are unwilling or incapable of providing a suitable home for the child.

Brett A. Seabury, "The Beginning Phase: Engagement, Initial Assessment, and Contracting," in *A Handbook of Child Welfare: Context, Knowledge, and Practice* (New York: Free Press, 1985).

Council on Accreditation of Services for Families and Children Inc.

Founded in 1977 by the CHILD WELFARE LEAGUE OF AMERICA INC. and Family Service America and funded by many sources, including grants from the Department of Health and Human Services and foundations, the council provides national accreditation for social services agencies, a credential agencies may cite. This accreditation does not replace the licensing process of state, county or local governments.

According to executive director David Shover, accreditation is a voluntary and private activity that has been created and implemented to optimize professionalism. Shover envisions the council's primary purpose as encouraging high-quality service through a stringent review process as well as the building of confidence in the effectiveness of the accreditation process.

The council currently accredits 550 agencies in the United States and Canada. Its board of directors meets twice a year, and the executive committee also meets twice a year. The council publishes accreditation requirements in its *Provisions for Accreditation*, which includes sections on adoption and pregnancy counseling. The *COA Update* is published twice per year.

Social services agencies are evaluated by a broad array of criteria, for example, the council sets "generic organizational requirements," such as "The Agency in the Community" and "Fiscal Management." "Specialized service requirements" include such evaluation criteria as "emergency shelter for abused and neglected children," "pregnancy counseling and supportive services," "resettlement service" and critically important functions.

The council charges accreditation fees every four years and an annual maintenance fee.

The seven council sponsors are the ASSOCIATION OF JEWISH FAMILY & CHILDREN'S AGENCIES, Catholic Charities USA, Child Welfare League of America, Family Service America, Lutheran Social Ministry System, National Association of Services and Homes for Children and the NATIONAL COMMITTEE FOR ADOPTION.

For more information, contact

Council on Accreditation of Services for
 Families and Children Inc.
520 Eighth Ave., Suite 2202B
New York, NY 10018
(212) 714-9399

counseling Advice and discussion provided to adopting parents, birthparents or adopted persons.

One of the primary advantages of an adoption arranged by a good, ethical agency is the counseling services offered. Caseworkers assist both birthparents and prospective adoptive parents in working through a variety of issues, for example, the grief and pain associated with infertility and felt by most adopting parents. The grief associated with placing a child for adoption is another issue that the birthparents and particularly the birthmother must face.

Although nonagency adoptions traditionally did not include any form of counseling and adoptive parents and birthparents were often not ready or able to cope with the myriad of feelings associated with an adoption, counseling of some sort is being increasingly provided. (See also PREGNANCY COUNSELING.)

criminal behavior in adopted adults
Social scientists have performed a variety of studies to determine whether or not a predisposition to criminal behavior can be inherited by adopted children or if a genetic link appears likely.

Although a few studies have found apparent links between the criminal activity of a birthparent and adopted-out children, it must be stressed that the overwhelming majority of adopted persons are law-abiding citizens, even when born to a birthparent convicted of crimes.

The largest studies on crime and adopted persons have been done on populations of thousands of adopted adults and their biological parents in Denmark and Sweden. These countries were selected because they offer a broad array of research data; for example, the Danish Adoption Cohort Register, established by American and Danish investigators at the Psykologisk Institut in Copenhagen, contains information on all nonrelative adoptions between 1924 and 1947 (14,427 adoptions). Many researchers have used this population to study a variety of factors.

Smaller studies on adopted persons in the United States have been done. Studies performed in 1975 and 1978 on Iowa adopted adults revealed that antisocial behavior and criminality in adopted adults appear to be related to criminality in birthparents.

Sarnoff Mednick has done extensive studies on adult adopted persons and their biological parents, comparing and contrasting criminal behavior and using the Danish population described above. Researchers have found a correlation between the criminality of a birthparent and criminal behavior of a son who was adopted. As a result, the risk of an adopted male being convicted of a crime is increased if the birthparent had also been convicted of a criminal act. (These and other expert findings are reported in *The Causes of Crime: New Biological Approaches,* which Mednick co-edited with Terrie E. Moffitt and Susan A. Stack in 1987.)

Studies by Cloninger and associates revealed this relationship between the criminality of a birthparent and the petty criminality of an adopted person. (Using the large Swedish population of 1,775 adopted individuals.)

If neither the birthparent nor the adoptive parent had committed crimes, then 2.9% of the adopted men committed criminal acts. If the birthparent did have a criminal record, but the adoptive parent did not, then 12% of the adopted males had committed crimes and the majority were non-criminals.

Yet the highest rate of criminality occurred when both the birthparents and adoptive parents were criminals: 40% of the adopted sons in this category had committed crimes, thus demonstrating the importance of both heredity and environment.

A much weaker relationship was seen for adopted females. If neither birthparent nor adoptive parent had committed crimes, then only .5% of the adopted females committed petty crimes. If the birthparent had committed crimes but the adoptive parent had not, only 2.2% of the adopted females committed crimes. The highest risk occurred when both birthparent and adoptive parent were criminals: in that case, 11.1% of the adopted females committed petty crimes.

In addition to the criminal behavior of the parent social class is an important indicator of the potential criminality of an adopted child, based on research reported in *The Journal of Criminal Law & Criminology*.

The percentage of criminality rose inversely with the social class of both the birthparent and the adoptive parent: the lower the socioeconomic status of the adoptive parent and the birthparent, the higher the rate of criminal convictions.

The same relationship with social class held true for adopted women, although females committed crimes at a much lower rate.

Social class was measured by occupation and "prestige ratings"; for example a "low" social class worker would include individuals who were maids, low-level factory workers, taxidrivers, waiters and shop assistants. "Medium" professions include such occupations as police officers, factory foremen, semiprofessionals and business owners of moderate-sized businesses. "High" class individuals held such positions as engineers, physicians, army colonels, directors of large businesses and other career fields.

About 71% of the adoptive families were "high" or "middle" social class members, while about 58% of the biological families fit these criteria.

When male adopted persons were compared against both their birthparents' social status and their adoptive parents' status, researchers found the greatest percentage of criminal convictions occurred when both the biological parents and the adoptive parents were at the lowest socioeconomic strata.

The impact of a middle income or upper income home may lessen the chance of a child committing crimes. Some researchers have also suggested that such parents may also protect their children against prosecution, in the event they do commit crimes (by reimbursement, therapy, personal influence and so forth). This is pure speculation, and there is no evidence supporting or disproving this possibility.

Researchers Mednick and Gabrielli also studied chronic offenders among a population of adopted adults. Adopted persons who had been convicted of three or more criminal law offenses represented about 4% of the adopted adults studied, yet these individuals were responsible for 69% of all the convictions in the entire group of adopted persons.

Mednick and Gabrielli then compared the chronic offenders to their birthparents' crime offenses and found that the sons of biological parents who were chronic offenders were much more likely to be chronic offenders themselves.

One possible reason for this apparent genetic tie-in could be an inherited neurological tendency; for example, Mednick and Gabrielli found that the people in their study who were neurologically left-side dominant had a significantly higher rate of delinquency.

Most social scientists believe that rather than a predisposition to criminality being inherited, it is far more likely a predisposition to alcoholism could be inherited.

Michael Bohman described his study of crime and alcoholism among a population of Swedish adult adopted persons in "Alcoholism and Crime: Studies of Adoptees" in *Substance and Alcohol Abuse/Misuse*.

Bohman found most crimes by adopted men were a consequence of alcohol abuse and hypothesized that reducing alcohol abuse would reduce crime rates among adopted persons. He did, however, indicate there appeared to be a certain congenital predisposition to crime that was unrelated to alcoholism.

Alcoholism may then be the social problem that drives the person to crime, and if so, a tendency towards criminality is possibly only indirectly inherited.

It's also interesting to note that adopted sons who do turn to crime are far more likely to commit property offenses rather than violent offenses such as murder, rape, assault or other violent crimes.

Researchers also have found a connection between the admission of an adopted person's biological parents to a psychiatric hospital and an increased risk of the adopted person later being convicted of a crime.

About 15% of the adopted persons studied by Terrie Moffitt had been convicted of a crime. According to Moffitt, if the biological parents had never been hospitalized in a psychiatric facility, the risk of conviction dropped to 14.2%. But if at least one birthparent had been hospitalized in a psychiatric facility, the risk that the adopted person had been convicted increased to a significant level of 19.25%.

Trends were also seen in the reason for the birthparents' hospital admissions and criminal recidivism in adopted children. If the birthparents were admitted to the hospital because of a personality disorder or drug or alcohol abuse, their adopted-out sons were at a higher risk for later committing crimes than if the birthparents were admitted for other reasons.

Studies have also been performed to determine if "labeling" a child as potentially delinquent could affect his subsequent behavior; for example, if the adoptive parents are told the child's birthparent(s) are criminal, could there be a tendency for the child to fulfill this negative expectation, in an unhappy self-fulfilling prophecy? Fortunately, no indication was found that parental fears or expectations impacted on a child's later criminality.

Researchers have also hypothesized, but cannot always prove, that the fetal environment could ultimately affect the child's behavior as an adult, for example, if the pregnant woman did not receive prenatal care or proper nutrition, drank or smoked heavily.

It is clear that some actions taken by the pregnant woman can have a direct effect on the fetus and later the child; for example, excessive and continued use of alcohol during pregnancy may cause the fetus to develop FETAL ALCOHOL SYNDROME. Many physical and psychological problems have been seen in children with fetal alcohol syndrome. Children with fetal alcohol syndrome have been reported to sometimes have difficulty in developing values and a conscience; hence, they may perform criminal acts out of a lack of understanding that the acts are, in fact, criminal.

Authors of an overview on the effect of genetic predispositions to psychiatric disorders in *The Journal of Child Psychology and Psychiatry* reported that environmental effects are also important. The authors stated, "Indeed, some studies have suggested that the genetic risk is unlikely to result in adult crime unless there is also exposure to environmental risk factors."

In addition, they cited a study by Rutter, Quinton and Hill in 1990 that indicated a "much increased risk for criminality and personality disorder in institution-reared adults." This high risk could not be isolated only to disorders in the birthparents. (See also ALCOHOL ABUSE AND ADOPTED PERSONS; DELINQUENCY; GENETIC PREDISPOSITIONS; PSYCHIATRIC PROBLEMS OF ADOPTED PERSONS.)

Michael Bohman, M.D., "Alcoholism and Crime: Studies of Adoptees," *Substance and Alcohol Actions/Misuse,* 4(1983): 137–147.
C. R. Cloninger and I. I. Goltesman, "Genetic and Environmental Factors in Antisocial Behavior Disorders" in *The Causes of Crime: New Biological Approaches* (Cambridge: Cambridge University Press, 1987).
C. R. Cloninger, S. Sigvardsson and M. Bohman, "Pre-disposition to Petty Criminality in Swedish Adoptees," *Archives of General Psychiatry,* 39(1982): 1242–1247.
William F. Gabrielli Jr. and Sarnoff A. Mednick, "Genetic Correlates of Criminal Behavior," *American Behavioral Scientist,* 27(September–October 1983): 59–74.
Sarnoff A. Mednick and William F. Gabrielli Jr., "Genetic Influences in Criminal Convictions: Evidence from an Adoption Cohort," *Science,* May 25, 1984, 891–894.
Sarnoff A. Mednick, Terrie E. Moffitt and Susan A. Stack, eds., *The Causes of Crime: New Biological Approaches* (Cambridge, England: Cambridge University Press, 1987).
Terrie E. Moffitt, "Parental Mental Disorder and Offspring Criminal Behavior: An Adoption Study," *Psychiatry,* November 1987, 346–358.
Michael Rutter, Hope Macdonald, Ann Le Couteur, Richard Harrington, Patrick Bolton and Anthony Bailey, "Genetic Factors in Child Psychiatric Disorders—II. Empirical Findings," *Journal of Child Psychology and Psychiatry,* 31(January 1990): 39–83.
Katherine Teilmann Van Dusen, Sarnoff A. Mednick, William F. Gabrielli Jr. and Barry Hutchings, "Social Class and Crime in an Adoption Cohort," *The Journal of Criminal Law and Criminology,* 74(Spring 1983): 249–269.

crisis pregnancy An unplanned pregnancy or a planned pregnancy that becomes a serious problem to the pregnant woman because of the desertion by the birthfather, the lack of support from her own parents, financial problems or other factors.

A woman in a crisis pregnancy may need shelter and certainly also needs PREGNANCY COUNSELING. Many women in crisis pregnancies choose to abort, while others carry their pregnancies to term and either parent the child or place it for adoption.

MATERNITY HOMES provide shelter to pregnant women, usually young and unmarried but not necessarily indigent. Adoption agencies can advise women with crisis pregnancies who need a home.

cultural differences See CULTURE SHOCK; INTERNATIONAL ADOPTION.

culture camps Summer camps, either day camps or weeklong camps, for Korean or Latin American adopted children.

The goal of the culture camp is to promote the adopted child's awareness of and pride in his native origins and also enable him or her to meet other children of the same racial and ethnic background.

Culture camps cover history, music, dance and other aspects of the child's native culture, and campers eat foods prepared as they are in the country where the campers were born.

Korean culture camps are probably the most prominent, because the largest population of foreign-born adopted children have come from Korea.

Extracurricular activities such as arts and crafts and recreation are usually also provided.

Interested families should contact their local adoptive parent support group to locate the nearest culture camp, or they may contact the adoption agency from which their child was adopted or ADOPTIVE FAMILIES OF AMERICA INC., a national adoptive parents support group based in Minneapolis, Minnesota.

culture shock A feeling of disorientation and confusion experienced by a person visiting or relocating to a culture different from his nor her own.

Adults Adoptive families who adopt children internationally often must travel to the country and stay for days or several weeks until legal procedures are completed and they may leave with their children and return home.

Many families report a feeling of dismay at being strangers who don't speak the common language. It's very important for adoptive parents of children born abroad, whether they travel to the child's birth country or not, to learn some basics of the child's native language. Even if the child is an infant, he or she is used to the sounds of the language. And if the child is older than an infant, it is really considered a must by adoption experts for parents to learn some basics: "I love you." "Do you need to use the toilet?" "Come here." "What do you want?" "I am your mother (father)."

If parents have already traveled abroad, they will probably understand that attitudes and the overall atmosphere of another country may be very different from what the adopting parents consider "normal"; for example, the host country's prevailing attitude may be to "take things easy," whereas Americans like punctuality and high-tech order to things: They are not used to waiting until tomorrow or next week.

To alleviate culture shock, preparation well ahead of time is the best defense. Prior to traveling to a foreign land, it is advisable to read about the country and talk to other North Americans who have traveled there recently. Often an adoptive parents support group can advise how to find a fellow traveler or one who could provide good advance information.

Another aspect of culture shock can be fear. One American reported feeling a sick feeling in his stomach as he viewed armed soldiers on every street corner of a Latin American city: The local residents appeared not to notice.

Concentrating on the objective of legally adopting the child and relaxing as much as possible by taking deep breaths and reassuring oneself aloud and silently are several helpful steps. If possible, Americans should travel with fellow Americans and stay in the same hotel as well.

Children If adults who are well aware of their goals in traveling abroad to adopt a child experience culture shock, how much greater a shock must be felt by a small child who is adopted from overseas. Children adopted in intercountry adoptions must often contend with a complete language change as well as new parents and a totally different lifestyle.

Video cassette recorders, microwave ovens, fast foods, television and computers are all unknown in an overseas orphanage. The way Americans dress, think, behave, even how they beckon people or wave to them is different from the behavior and gestures of people from other countries.

As a result, the culture shock to an adopted child who is not an infant can be profound, and new parents should take this into account. Experts advise limiting parties and visits for at least a few days after the child's arrival to give the child an opportunity to begin the cultural assimilation process.

Even children adopted from within the United States can sometimes face a form of culture shock, although there are usually a shared language and many commonalities. For example, one adoptive parent was amazed when her child asked what an ocean was and drove the child to the ocean to see for herself.

Children raised in small towns or big cities need time to adapt to a radically different environment. Social workers generally try to place older children with families in environments similar to what they are accustomed, such as placing a child from a rural area with a family living in the country. But sometimes this is not possible.

Whether children are adopted from abroad or within the United States, most children are flexible and will, given the chance, adapt to their new families and their new homes. (See also INTERNATIONAL ADOPTION.)

custody Legal control of a child, usually of one who resides with the custodial parent. Foster parents are not considered to have legal custody: State social services departments retain control over major decisions about a child. Adoptive parents obtain complete custody of a child upon finalization of an adoption in a court of law.

Custody battles abound in the courtrooms, and most suits are between divorcing parents, although single parents have also argued over custody. In addition, relatives have argued for custody, including grandparents versus birthparents, aunts versus stepparents and many other variations. The court usually considers such factors as the "best interests of the child" as well as blood relationships, where the child has resided in the past and other issues, depending on state laws.

It is important for attorneys and judges to avoid making judgements about child psychology when psychologists, social workers and psychiatrists are more suitable at providing such information. Conversely mental health workers should avoid making legal decisions and should instead rely on legal counsel. For example, according to the authors of *In the Best Interests of the Child*, in one case a judge stated reasons why he decided to award custody to a mother: He found the father to be a "demeaning person" and made other psychological judgements about the father. This action was inappropriate because he was, in effect, acting as a child development professional or psychologist but one who could not be cross-examined.

In 1989, two separate lawsuits were filed over the custody of frozen embryos. In one case, divorcing spouses fought over custody, and in another case, a married couple sought custody of a frozen embryo from an in vitro fertilization clinic.

In recent years, birthfathers have begun to attempt to gain custody of their out-of-wedlock children. In some cases they have prevailed, while in others they have not. (See BIRTHFATHER; BIRTHMOTHER.)

There have also been custody battles between adoptive parents seeking to retain custody of an infant or toddler and birthparents who wished to revoke their consent to an adoption. Judges must decide the custody issue based on state law, legal precedents, the "best interests of the child" and a variety of factors.

Often the custody battles and appeals take years and cause serious emotional anguish to both sides—and probably to the child as well. (See also CONSENT [TO AN ADOPTION]; GRANDPARENTS RIGHTS; TERMINATION OF PARENTAL RIGHTS.)

Joseph Goldstein, Anna Freud, Albert J. Solnit and Sonja Goldstein, *In the Best Interests of the Child* (New York: Free Press, 1986).

D

delinquency Juvenile crime. Experts disagree on whether adopted children are over- or underrepresented in the population of juvenile delinquents.

A 1988 study published in the *Journal of the American Academy of Child and Adolescent Psychiatry* reported an overrepresentation of adopted youths in psychiatric inpatient units but an underrepresentation of adopted youths referred to juvenile court.

The authors expected to find an overrepresentation of adopted children in juvenile court but instead found an underrepresentation. The researchers also found an overrepresentation of nonadopted children from low socioeconomic status. The juvenile delinquents who had been adopted were generally from a higher socioeconomic status than the nonadopted children. The authors concluded that this result may have occurred because many adoptive parents are of a middle to high socioeconomic status. In addition, the researchers postulated that the higher socioeconomic status of the adoptive parents may have had a protective effect on their children, either in inhibiting delinquency itself or in mitigating the legal actions of delinquent behavior.

Other studies have also indicated a weak genetic relationship (if any) between juvenile delinquency in adopted children and antisocial behavior in their birthparents. In an overview of genetic factors in psychiatric disorders of childhood published in the *Journal of Child Psychology and Child Psychiatry,* the authors discussed the findings of Cadoret in 1978, who determined no differences in the juvenile delinquency of adopted children born to antisocial birthparents and the delinquent behavior of children born to normal birthparents.

Although there has been shown to be a linkage between criminality in an adopted adult and criminality in the birthparent, the authors stated that most juvenile criminality does not continue into adult life.

Older adopted children may sometimes exhibit delinquent behavior as part of acting out and previous traumas they have suffered. For example, if a child has suffered sexual abuse at the hands of parents, the child may exhibit precocious sexual behavior. If a child had been previously physically abused, the child may need to learn physical violence is unnecessary and discouraged. (See also ADOLESCENT ADOPTED PERSONS; CRIMINAL BEHAVIOR IN ADOPTED ADULTS; PSYCHIATRIC PROBLEMS OF ADOPTED PERSONS.)

Shari McCloud, "Seeing It Through," in *Adopting Children with Special Needs: A Sequel,* Linda Dunn, ed. (Washington D.C.: North American Council on Adoptable Children, 1983).
Wun Jung Kim, M.D., M.P.H., Charles Davenport, M.D., Jill Joseph, Ph.D., Joel Zrull, M.D., and Elizabeth Woolford, B.A., "Psychiatric Disorder and Juvenile Delinquency in Adopted Children and Adolescents," *Journal of the American Academy of Child and Adolescent Psychiatry,* 27(January 1988): 111–115.
Michael Rutter, Hope Macdonald, Ann Le Couteur, Richard Harrington, Patrick Bolton and Anthony Bailey, "Genetic Factors in Child Psychiatric Disorders—II. Empirical Findings," *Journal of Child Psychology and Psychiatry,* 31(January 1990): 39–83.

demographics See BIRTHMOTHERS; SOCIOECONOMIC STATUS; STATISTICS; TEENAGE PARENTS

designated adoption An adoption, usually of an infant, in which adopting parents locate a pregnant woman considering adoption for her child; also known as TARGETED ADOPTION or IDENTIFIED ADOPTION. After identifying the birthmother, the adopting parents request an adoption agency or attorney to oversee the adoption of the woman's child. Designated adoptions may or may not be open adoptions because the individuals do not always disclose their full names to each other. Instead, an intermediary agency or other third party may know the full names of the birthparents and adopting parents but keep this information in confidence.

In some cases, the pregnant woman herself finds a family who she would like as the adoptive parents to her child and then requests the assistance of an agency or attorney.

In the states that do not ban INDEPENDENT ADOPTION, designated adoptions may be offered as an option by agencies or attorneys; however, in the states that do ban nonagency adoption, the only form of designated adoption allowed is through an adoption agency. For example, the state of Delaware has banned independent adoption for many years, but in 1989, new adoption legislation provided for identified adoption through adoption agencies. In addition, the states of Colorado, Connecticut, Massachusetts, Minnesota and

North Dakota allow identified or designated adoptions within certain constraints. As of this writing, Michigan allows only agency adoptions and not designated adoptions.

The state of Colorado provides for designated adoption specifically in its statutes. Birthmothers are required to receive counseling from an agency social worker, and adopting parents must be approved by an adoption agency.

A designated adoption may be an OPEN ADOPTION or may be a confidential, anonymous adoption, depending on state laws and the wishes of the parties involved. According to authors Susan Price and Jody McElhinny, anonymity is waived in a designated adoption in the state of Colorado. In other states, such as Indiana, where confidentiality is maintained, birthmothers and adoptive parents communicate through letters, telephone conversations and sometimes meetings that are on a first-name basis.

The advantage of a designated adoption to the adopting parents is that the normal "waiting list" process is avoided altogether. If they find a pregnant woman interested in placing her child for adoption, the prospective parents may be able to adopt very rapidly because many pregnant women don't seriously consider adoption until the late second or third trimester of pregnancy.

The primary advantage of an identified adoption is that the birthmother may feel she is empowered because she has personally selected the adoptive parents or they have been located by a person she trusts. The adoptive parents may feel a sense of ENTITLEMENT because they were specifically chosen. They may avoid a waiting list of several years if they can quickly find a pregnant woman who believes they would make suitable parents.

When an adoption agency oversees the designated adoption, a key advantage to the pregnant woman as well as to the adopting couple is that they will all receive professional counseling and the full range of agency services. If, for some reason, the adopting couple is deemed unsuitable or they drop out of the adoption, the agency can recommend other approved couples to the birthmother. Also, increasing numbers of attorneys are requiring counseling or preplacement home studies of prospective adoptive parents and are also giving birthmothers the opportunity to receive professional counseling as well.

The disadvantage of a designated adoption for most couples is the difficulty in locating a pregnant woman considering adoption. When an agency becomes involved it is also possible that an agency social worker could veto an adoption for any number of reasons, even though a couple may have invested heavily of their emotions, time and money. Another disadvantage of an identified adoption is that the birthmother may have difficulty in choosing appropriate parents, particularly if she is close to delivering and feels desperately eager to resolve her situation.

Some also point out that adoptive parents might be tempted to agree to virtually any request or demand by the birthmother because they are so intent on adopting a child. This is one of the same disadvantages of OPEN ADOPTION. Later on, they may not wish to carry out the birthmother's requests, such as providing photographs or continuing contact, and may be reluctant or refuse to do so. Even if they have formally contracted with the birthmother to perform such acts, it's not at all certain such a contract would hold up in court once the adoption is finalized. There are reported cases on both sides of the issue.

Furthermore, although most couples are very eager to adopt an infant once they've decided on this course, they may not be psychologically or emotionally ready to succeed right away; for example, they may not have fully resolved anxiety over infertility and may not have faced adoption issues that need to be considered.

It is not clear how many designated adoptions are occurring nationwide; however, there does seem to be a slight upward trend in the number of adoptive parents who aggressively seek birthparents for the purpose of adopting infants. Most adoptive parents who do locate a pregnant woman proceed with a designated adoption through an attorney in an INDEPENDENT ADOPTION, instead of an agency adoption, rather than risk losing control of the situation.

Adoption agencies have only recently and rather reluctantly entered the field of identified adoption.

Social workers who administer identified adoptions generally believe that people who wish to have identified adoptions can usually find an attorney to perform an INDEPENDENT ADOPTION. But they believe that the counseling provided by an agency will at least ensure that the birthmother understands her options and the adopting parents learn some basics about adoption.

Agencies that administer designated adoptions reserve the right to disapprove the adoption if the match is clearly inappropriate or there is some valid reason to disapprove the adoptive parents' home study. It is tacitly understood, however, that if the adoptive parents complete a home study and are approved, then they will adopt the child of the pregnant woman they have identified to the agency.

Susan B. Price and Jody McElhinny, "Substantive Changes in Adoption and Relinquishment Law in Colorado," *Family Law Newsletter*, December 1987, 2183–2185.

developmental disabilities Chronic severe disabilities such as mental retardation, cerebral palsy, autism and other handicapping conditions.

The Federal Disabilities Act of 1984, P.L. 98–527, Sec. 102(7), further defines a developmental disability as a condition that occurs before age 22, can be attributed to a physical and/or mental impairment and is likely to continue. In addition, the individual experiences limits in three or more of the following areas: self care, language, learning, mobility, self-direction, potential for independent living and potential for economic self-sufficiency as an adult.

According to the NATIONAL ADOPTION INFORMATION CLEARINGHOUSE, an estimated half of the children with SPECIAL NEEDS who are available for adoption in the United States are developmentally disabled.

Within the many categories of developmental disabilities, children may face mild to severe problems; for example, within the category of retardation, some children are educable, other children are trainable, while other children are extremely retarded and function at the most basic level.

Children with epilepsy may be categorized as "developmentally delayed," although most children with epilepsy are of normal intelligence, and epilepsy can often be controlled with medication.

Some developmentally delayed children suffer from spina bifida, a birth defect causing incomplete development of the spinal cord. These children may be unable to walk, although some may walk unaided or with crutches or braces. Most victims of spina bifida are of normal intelligence.

Although children develop at very different rates, if a child does not use words at all by the age of 15 months or does not use short sentences or phrases by 24 months, then there may be a problem with language development.

An indication of an emotional problem is a lack of eye contact with the parent or others, lack of smiling when spoken to by family and friends and a cringing reaction to being held. (Some of these reactions may also be seen in cocaine babies.)

Developmental disabilities are not always detectable in infancy and may not show up until the child enters school.

Medications are often used in the treatment of developmental disabilities, including antispastic medications for children with cerebral palsy, psychostimulant medications for children with hyperactivty (Ritalin is the most commonly known drug for this disorder) and psychotropic medications for children with emotional and psychiatric problems.

A number of legal issues affect developmentally delayed or disabled individuals. Some of these issues are the right to a free public education (a right denied to many handicapped children until recently), the right to live in a community and the right to marry and have children.

Because only limited care was available at many institutions, many mentally retarded individuals were committed for life, usually to state hospitals. Their low level of functioning was seen as proof that they would be unable to function outside the institution. Consequency, retarded individuals were placed in a Catch-22 situation: They were not taught necessary skills and behaviors, yet because they didn't exhibit "normal" behavior, they were never taught. Many people believed this proved retarded children couldn't learn or be socialized.

Adoptive parents of developmentally delayed children should be flexible people who love children and can be positive about small improvements and changes in a child. In addition, it's very helpful if they have a support group of other adoptive parents or parents of disabled children. Support groups can also assist adoptive parents in learning about community resources for their children.

Although the federal government has defined the term developmentally delayed, it is still important for individuals considering adopting a child to obtain specific information from state and private agencies on their definitions of a disability. Some agencies consider a child born as a result of rape or incest to be a special needs child, although the child could suffer no physical or mental abnormalities at birth.

Children from other countries may also have developmental disabilities that could be greatly helped by technological advances in medicine.

Individuals considering adopting a developmentally delayed child should obtain as much information as possible on the particular medical ailments of the child and should also have appropriate specialists carefully review the medical records of the child before assuming parental responsibility.

Although it may be difficult to find families for children with developmental delays, many social workers believe it is possible and well worth the effort.

Individuals who adopt developmentally delayed children may also be eligible for adoption subsidies, which will help cover the costs of needed medical and/or psychological treatment. (See also ADOPTION ASSISTANCE PROGRAM; DISABILITIES OF ADOPTIVE PARENTS; DOWN SYNDROME; LEARNING DISABILITIES.)

Eva Brown, "Recruiting Adoptive Parents for Children with Developmental Disabilities," *Child Welfare,* 67(March–April 1988). 123–135.

National Adoption Information Clearinghouse, "Adopting Children with Developmental Disabilities," paper, Washington, D.C.

Siegfried M. Pueschel, M.D., Ph.D., M.P.H., James C. Bernier, M.S.W., and Leslie E. Weidenman, Ph.D., *The Special Child: A Source Book for Parents of Children with Developmental Disabilities* (Baltimore: Paul H. Brookes, 1988).

diagnostic home Temporary home in which a child is placed pending determination of whether he should reside in a foster home, which will help the social worker reunite the child with the birthparents, or a legal risk home (see AT RISK PLACEMENT), which is likely to adopt the child if and when parental rights are terminated.

According to author Ann Hartman, there are certain problems involved in placing a child in a diagnostic home. "A temporary placement in a 'diagnostic home' entails an additional move for the child. Moreover, such a plan suggests that the worker can make a determination in the space of sixty days or less concerning whether the goal is adoption or return home. However, some believe that such a prejudgment, early in a situation and before a legal determination is made, may have the effect of a self-fulfilling prophecy."

Ann Hartman, "Practice in Adoption," in *A Handbook of Child Welfare: Context, Knowledge and Practice* (New York: Free Press, 1985).

direct placement An adoption arranged by the birthparents and adoptive parents with only peripheral involvement of an agency or attorney. Some states mandate that an INDEPENDENT ADOPTION is only lawful if the adopting parents or birthparents themselves plan the adoption.

Infants in a direct placement are usually placed immediately from the hospital. (See also DESIGNATED ADOPTION; IMMEDIATE PLACEMENTS.)

disabilities of adoptive parents Adults who have physical or mental handicaps and wish to adopt may find themselves helped or hampered by state laws, although most states do not address disability criteria in their adoption laws.

The state of Florida bans discrimination of handicapped people wishing to adopt unless it can be proven the handicap would prevent the individual from raising a child.

According to the "Matrix of State Adoption Laws," provided by the NATIONAL ADOPTION INFORMATION CLEARINGHOUSE, Wisconsin's law says deaf, blind and physically handicapped individuals may not be denied the opportunity to adopt if they are otherwise capable of parenting a child.

Georgia's law requires adopting parents to be physically, mentally and financially able. Illinois does not allow the adopting person to be under a legal disability.

It should be noted that state laws are continually revised and rewritten, and handicapped people considering adoption should check current statutes in their state. (See also DEVELOPMENTAL DISABILITIES; SPECIAL NEEDS.)

disabilities, developmental See DEVELOPMENTAL DISABILITIES.

discipline The method used by a parent or a caretaker to correct a child's misbehavior.

Although many parents still use mild spankings to punish children subsequent to misdeeds (severe spankings may be considered a form of child abuse), most child developmental experts agree that positive reinforcement, such as deprivation of a toy or withholding of privileges (playing on the computer, watching TV and so forth), are more effective deterrents to future misbehavior.

It's particularly important to consider disciplinary means before adopting a child with SPECIAL NEEDS because the child may have been previously subject to severe physical abuse and thus be unresponsive to even mild spankings.

Most social workers ask prospective adoptive parents about how they would discipline a child. This is to ensure the discipline they envision is appropriate to children or to the particular type of child they are seeking to adopt.

disinformation See INTERNATIONAL ADOPTION.

disruption An adoptive placement that fails before the adoption is finalized. The child is removed from the home and returned to the placing agency or, if an independent adoption, to the attorney or other person who arranged it. An adoption that fails after finalization is called a DISSOLUTION, although it is important to understand that sometimes the term "disruption" is used interchangeably by researchers to describe an adoption that fails after finalization as well as an adoption that does not continue to the point of finalization.

Prior to the 1970s, most adoptions were of infants, and very few were disrupted adoptions. Even today, infant adoption disruptions are probably less than 1%. Disruptions of older children are estimated at about 10% by such experts as Richard Barth. (The disruption rates vary according to the child's age and other factors.)

The highest disruption rate is for children who are adopted as teenagers. According to an article by Barth and Marianne Berry, the researchers found a disruption rate of 24% for children adopted as adolescents. (Conversely, the remaining 76% of these placements were successful.)

In the 1970s and the 1980s, agencies began placing increasing numbers of older children in adoptive homes with the goal of providing children with permanent families rather than series of foster homes.

Many were very troubled children who had been physically or sexually abused, neglected or abandoned and faced great difficulty in their attempts to assimilate successfully in their adoptive homes. As a result, the number of adoption disruptions understandably increased.

A study by Trudy Festinger on disrupted adoptions among 1,500 adoptive placements in New York City yielded valuable information. Festinger reported her findings in *Necessary Risk: A Study of Adoptions and Disrupted Adoptive Placements*.

The children studied were all over six years old, and the average age was 10.2 years. Her research revealed that the disruption rate over the course of two years was about 8% for the adopted children ages 6 to 10, whereas the disruption rate for children 11 and up was 16% over the same period of time.

A study by Susan Partridge, Helaine Hornby and Thomas McDonald at the University of Southern Maine found less than 10% disruptions among children who had been placed with families for less than three years.

These researchers concentrated on comparing characteristics of children in adoptions that failed with the children in successful adoptions, based on 171 successful adoptions and 64 adoptions that disrupted or were dissolved.

Their findings also supported the idea that age is an important factor in disruptions: The average age at placement for the disrupted children in their study was 11 years old, while the nondisrupted group's average age was 6.6 years. (It should also be noted that the researchers studied adoptions that failed within the first three years of placement, including placements that had been legally finalized and were subsequently dissolved. These failed adoptions were all categorized as disruptions.)

Children in the disrupted group waited significantly longer for an adoptive home than did the successful placements: 978 days after becoming available for adoption for the disrupted children compared to 288 days for the children whose placements succeeded.

The Festinger study revealed a significant success rate when children were placed with their own siblings. Children placed with siblings disrupted at a lower rate than children placed alone: She found a 5.6% disruption rate for children placed with siblings contrasted to a 10.7% disruption rate for children placed alone. Children who were placed alone and who had siblings living elsewhere disrupted at a very high rate: 20.6%.

The separation may have been the source of the problem, or the reason for the separation may have caused problems; for example, siblings are separated when one is sexually or physically abusive to the other child.

If there are both biological children and adopted children in the home, one might conclude there would be greater anxiety for the adopted child than if he were placed with other adopted children. The reverse has been shown in a study by Marilyn R. Ternay, Bobbie Wilborn and H. D. Day.

The researchers contrasted homes that included both biological children and adopted children with homes of adopted siblings only.

The researchers found that the children from the mixed homes scored significantly higher on social adjustment tests. They also found that the adjustment of both the biological children and the adopted children in the mixed homes was equivalent to the adjustment of biological children with no adopted children; as a result, adoption did not produce a negative effect on either the adopted or biological child.

It was not clear to researchers why the mixed families fared better and whether the primary factor was interaction with siblings or a parental factor.

A study by Richard P. Barth and Marianne Berry did not find a significant level of disruptions among homes with nonadopted biological children already in the home. But if the adopted child is having severe conflicts with children already in the home, other researchers have found this can lead to a disruption.

A University of Southern Maine study found disruptions in over half the cases involving serious conflicts between adopted children and other nonrelated children in the home. (Normal sibling rivalries did not appear to lead to problems.)

Another indicator of a potentially disrupted adoption is if the child has been adopted before and that adoption failed. According to the Maine study, 34% of the disrupted children had previous disruptions compared to 12% for the successful placements.

Abused children are more likely to experience disruption than are children who have not been abused; for example, in the University of Southern Maine study, 86% of the disrupted adoptions involved children who had suffered physical abuse compared to 58% of the nondisrupted adoptions.

Overall, 90% of the disrupted adoptions were of children who had been abandoned, neglected or emotionally abused; 74% of the nondisrupted children had been abandoned or neglected, and 64% had suffered emotional abuse.

A 1987 master's thesis by Freddie Lee Denney at the University of Texas at Arlington found a majority of disrupted adoptions occurred in cases in which older children came from birth families with a history of alcohol or drug abuse. Presumably, families with members who are drug or alcohol abusers are also more likely to abuse or neglect their children.

Many children in disrupted adoptions continue to display disturbing behavioral characteristics that their adoptive parents find very difficult to cope with. For example, in the Maine study, 30% of the children in the disrupted adoptions had stolen, compared to 8% in the nondisrupted group; 25% of the children in the disrupted group exhibited some type of eating disorder contrasted to 4% for the successful placements.

The Barth study identified other behavioral problems especially linked with disruptions: cruelty, fighting, disobedience and vandalism. According to Barth, the adopted child's behavior did not necessarily get worse, it just didn't get better.

The race of the child and his or her adoptive parents did not show up as a significant factor in studies of disrupted adoptions. Transracial adoptions were apparently as likely to succeed as adoptions of same-race children.

Foster Parents Versus New Parents
Adopted children were adopted by either foster parents (nearly 70% of the children) or by "new" parents in the Festinger study. Among disrupted placements, 52.6% of the disrupted adoptions were with new parents even though the majority of adoptions were by foster parents. Barth also found a much higher success rate with foster parent adoptions.

This is understandable: A foster parent may have parented a child for years before adopting the child and is very familiar with the child's behavior. It should also be noted that the children placed with new parents had a higher number of previous placements. (3.4 vs. 1.2 for the children adopted by foster parents.)

Importance of the Extended Family The Barth study found families who disrupted had less contacts with extended families than those families whose adoptions succeeded, indicating the strong importance of the support of grandparents, siblings of adoptive parents, friends and relatives. Sometimes adoptive parent support groups can help fill part of the emotional gap; however, the support of family members is very important to adoptive parents.

Higher Education Several studies have indicated a relationship between the adoptive parent's education and the disruption rate. Adoptive mothers with higher educations were more prone to disrupt than adoptive mothers who were less educated, particularly when the children involved were between the ages of three and nine. Interestingly enough, educated mothers did not disrupt at a greater rate when they adopted teenagers unless the teenagers were emotionally disturbed.

Educated mothers are also less likely to have been foster parents, because foster parenting is perceived by them as a blue-collar working class activity. Since foster parent adopters were more successful, this could be a factor in the disruption rate of educated mothers.

Adoptive parents who were found to have very high expectations of their children with special needs were often disappointed and did disrupt, which may tie in with the findings on mothers with higher education.

Knowing Other Adoptive Families Another key factor in the success or disruption of a special needs adoption appears to be the adoptive family's interaction with other adoptive parents. Adoptive parents who receive support and understanding from other adoptive parents are more likely to persevere when they face problems.

As a result, classes with other adoptive parents and adoptive parent support groups appears to be crucial to the success of a special needs adoption.

Candor of Social Workers The Barth study found that providing realistic information to the special needs adoptive parents was critically important and could affect the outcome of an adoption.

Parents who were prepared and understood a child's previous sexual or physical abuse were less likely to disrupt than parents who had no information. The families with the greatest potential for disruption received the least information or information they later perceived as overly positive or not realistic.

Of course, social workers themselves do not always have complete information on a child, but when it is available, indications are clear that such information should be shared with adopting parents.

Adoption Subsidies Barth also found the receipt of adoption subsidies as a positive element in adoption, although actual subsidies received by adoptive parents occurred far less frequently than expected by researchers.

Families with HIGH RISK PLACEMENTS disrupted less often when the family received a subsidy. Perhaps the subsidy eased the financial burden for the family that succeeded and the lack of one added to the problems of the families who were denied subsidies or who received inadequate subsidies.

Counseling a Family at Risk for Disruption Psychotherapy is often recommended for adoptive families in turmoil; however, Barth did not find that therapy helped the family avoid the disruption. The therapy may have come too late, or therapists may not be attuned to the unique problems of adopting children with special needs.

Therapists may not have scheduled family therapy, instead concentrating on individual therapy for the child. In addition, a behavioral problem the child had prior to the adoption is sometimes mistakenly identified as an "adoption issue" rather than a problem that could be corrected by behavioral modification.

Stages of Disruption There appear to be basic stages leading to a disruption, and caseworkers should be particularly sensitive to these stages in order to save an adoption, if at all possible, that looks like it may disrupt. These stages were named by the University of Southern Maine research study.

The first stage of a disruption is the stage of "diminishing pleasures," when the parent starts to see the hardships of raising the child as overtaking the joys of parenthood.

Many adoptive parents have moments when they wonder "why in the world" they ever adopted this child, but when that attitude becomes foremost and prominent, it has become a problem.

A second stage occurs when the child is perceived as a major problem—one the adoptive parents aren't sure how to cope with. The parents want the child to change his behavior, but the child cannot or will not.

The next stage occurs when adoptive parents begin to complain freely to other people about problems they face with this child. Invariably, they will receive some feedback from people who urge them to give up. An adoptive parent support group can possibly provide the positive reinforcement needed by parents in this stage to stop them from proceeding to a more advanced stage of disruption.

The fourth stage is a turning point: A critical event occurs that leads the adoptive parents to believe they can no longer accept the child's behavior. The child may be extremely cruel to other family members, and this behavior could frighten the parents. Or he may run away again, after numerous warnings, counseling and other attempts to help him resolve this behavior. The adoptive parents begin to envision life without the child and no longer actively strive to assimilate him into their everyday life.

The fifth stage is a deadline stage. Either the child is given an ultimatum or the parents decide if the negative behavior occurs just one more time, they will return the child to the agency.

The final stage occurs when the adoptive parents give up and decide they will return the child to the agency. They feel they've done everything they can, and they just cannot cope with this child any further.

This stage is extremely painful for the child and for the parents and is also difficult for the caseworker. It is easy for the worker to blame the parents at this point or for the parents to blame the agency, even when blame cannot reasonably be conferred.

The child's self-image is especially fragile at this point. Even if the child realized his behavior was disturbing the parents and deliberately continued his actions, he will experience a profound feeling of rejection and failure himself. He may not have believed the parents would give up on him, despite what they said, and be genuinely shocked by the disruption.

Adoptive parents should strive to educate themselves as thoroughly as possible about adoption in general and the child they plan to adopt in particular before making the serious commitment of adoption, particularly when they plan to adopt an older child. (See also ACTING OUT; OLDER CHILD.)

Richard P. Barth and Marianne Berry, *Adoption & Disruption: Rates, Risks, and Responses* (New York: Aldine De Gruyter, 1988).

Marianne Berry and Richard P. Barth, "A Study of Disrupted Adoptive Placements of Adolescents," *Child Welfare*, 69(May/June 1990): 209–225.

Freddie Lee Denney, "Characteristics Descriptive of Maltreated Children Whose Adoptions Disrupt (Texas)," Master's thesis, University of Texas at Arlington, 1987.

Trudy Festinger, *Necessary Risk: A Study of Adoptions and Disrupted Adoptive Placements* (Washington, D.C.: Child Welfare League of America, 1986).

Susan Partridge, Helaine Hornby and Thomas McDonald, *Learning from Adoption Disruption: Insights for Practice* (Portland, ME.: Human Services Development Institute, 1986).

dissolution An adoptive placement that fails after the adoption has been finalized. If an adoptive placement fails before finalization, it is referred to as an adoption DISRUPTION. In most cases, a failure of an adoption occurs before finalization rather than afterwards, although there are no reliable statistics available on the percentage of adoptions that are dissolved. It should be noted that some adoption professionals and even researchers use the word "disruption" for any adoption that fails at any time, and such lack of precision and uniformity contributes to confusion. (See also OLDER CHILD; SPECIAL NEEDS.)

divorce of adoptive parents It is unknown how many adoptive parents ultimately divorce their spouses or how many single divorced parents adopt children, but with the high divorce rate nationwide, it is virtually certain that some number of adopted persons' parents will divorce.

Divorce is a traumatic event and process for any child, biological or adopted. In some cases, divorce may be even more painful for an adopted child, especially when that child was adopted at an older age. In addition, even children adopted as infants may feel acutely rejected, both because of loss and separation issues related to adoption and because of the normal losses all children suffer. (The child's age at the time of the divorce is significant in how the child copes with this radical change.)

In a 1989 doctoral dissertation study of how divorce affects adopted individuals, Matthew Sanford Seidman interviewed adopted adults ages 15–52 whose parents divorced when they were between ages 3 and 20. The subjects who experienced the least negative effects of the divorce of their adoptive parents were those who had "continuing, positive relationships with both parents." Some of the adopted adults expressed feelings of abandonment. However, according to Seidman, "No subject connected their having been adopted to the separation for divorce of their adoptive parents."

Researchers Dorothy Le Pere and Carolyne B. Rodriguez explored and wrote about how divorce affects adopted children at various stages of life. According to the two experts, the impact on the child depends in part on the age of the child when the parents divorce. For example, during infancy, the loss of an adoptive parent could be a serious "first loss." During toddlerhood, a child whose parents have just divorced may become unduly clingy and have difficulty striving for autonomy, an important aspect of this stage of life.

Preschoolers may blame themselves for the divorce, presuming some action or inaction on their part was the cause. The egocentrism of this stage of development causes such reasoning on the part of the child. The child may reason that because he had angry thoughts about his father, the father is now leaving, a form of "magical thinking" common to preschoolers.

School-age children may tend to see divorce as a personal rejection of themselves rather than of the other parent.

Adolescence is the rockiest point for many children. A severe reaction to divorce could be abuse of drugs or alcohol or promiscuous sexual behavior. The adolescent may also become concerned or confused by his or her own relationships.

In addition, adopted children may have more emotional baggage with which to struggle, especially if they were adopted at an older age. They need to understand that their place in the family is still secure. Most adopted children, however, can resolve difficulties with the help of the parents and, as needed, professional assistance.

Dorothy Le Pere, A.C.S.W., C.S.W.-A.C.P., Carolyne B. Rodriguez, A.C.S.W., C.S.W., "Adoption and Divorce: The Double Life Crisis," in *Adoption Resources for Mental Health Professionals* (Butler, PA.: Mental Health/Adoption Therapy, September 1986), 270–281.

Matthew Sanford Seidman, "Effects of Separation for Divorce of Adoptive Parents on the Adopted Child." Ph.D. diss., University of Southern California, 1989.

doctors See PHYSICIANS.

Down syndrome A chromosomal defect that causes mild, moderate or severe retardation in a child, also known as Down's syndrome. A Down syndrome child is developmentally disabled and considered a child with SPECIAL NEEDS when available for adoption. The syndrome is named after British physician Langdon Down, who identified many features of this syndrome.

An estimated one in 1,000 children has Down syndrome. A child with Down syndrome usually has a somewhat oriental appearance about the eyes, with smaller than usual folds at eye corners, and also has small hands, feet, ears and nose. About 40% of these children have heart ailments, and another 10% have defects in their gastrointestinal systems. Many of these birth defects are now correctable by surgery.

A prenatal diagnosis of Down syndrome may be obtained through the "chorionic villus biopsy," which can be performed at an earlier stage of fetal development than amniocentesis and provides more rapid results than amniocentesis.

What expectant parents do with this information depends on the individual. Some expectant parents will choose abortion, others will continue the pregnancy and elect to parent the child or place the infant for adoption.

It is probably not the appearance of the child that causes biological parents to choose adoption as much as the retardation, particularly if the child will apparently need lifelong care. The degree of retardation varies greatly from individual to individual.

In the past, many parents were urged to institutionalize their children under the assumption this was the best course. Today, parents of a Down syndrome child may choose other courses as well, opting to parent the child or place the child for adoption.

One source of information and assistance is the Up with Down Syndrome Foundation in Miami, Florida. Founded by a physician and his wife who adopted seven Down syndrome children, the organization provides free advice to parents as well as to adults with Down syndrome. Local parents may also receive day care services. (See also DEVELOPMENTAL DISABILITIES.)

For further information on adopting or placing a Down Syndrome child, contact

National Down's Syndrome Adoption Exchange
56 Midchester Ave.
White Plains, NY 10606
(914) 428-1236

Another organization with information is

Up with Down Syndrome Foundation Inc.
9270 Hammocks Blvd., Suite 301
Miami, FL 33196
(305) 386-9115

Siegfried M. Pueschel, M.D., Ph.D., M.P.H., James C. Bernier, M.S.W., and Leslie E. Weidenman, Ph.D., *The Special Child: A Source Book for Parents of Children with Developmental Disabilities* (Baltimore: Paul H. Brookes, 1988).

"They Give Love, Support to Down's Syndrome Kids," Associated Press story, Miami Herald, October 17, 1989.

Randy Wooldridge, as told to Sarah Hunter, "I Couldn't Keep My Baby," *Working Mother*, September 1989, 20–24.

drug abuse When pregnant women abuse drugs, there is a much greater probability the infant will suffer birth defects. Drugs such as cocaine, "crack," heroin and other drugs, including prescription drugs that are not normally dangerous, can be highly perilous for the developing fetus and can cause lifelong problems to the child after birth. Senator Christopher Dodd, chairman of the Senate Subcommittee on Children, Families, Drugs and Alcoholism, has estimated that by the year 2000, four million children will have been born with cocaine or crack cocaine in their systems, thus costing society billions of dollars in medical, educational and other costs (see LEARNING DISABILITIES).

Alcohol abuse is also a problem to the fetus, and children born to alcoholic mothers may suffer FETAL ALCOHOL SYNDROME and other effects.

Cocaine and Crack Babies Also known as "snow babies," cocaine and crack babies are infants born to mothers addicted to cocaine and/or crack cocaine. (Crack cocaine is an inexpensive street form of cocaine, almost instantly addictive.)

Even if cocaine-exposed infants are themselves not physically addicted at birth, they may suffer profound and lifelong physiological and psychological effects because of the woman's abuse of cocaine during her pregnancy. Cocaine affects the central nervous systems of the pregnant woman and the developing fetus.

However, it is still too soon to know exactly what the effects of the drug will be on growing children. The oldest children in controlled studies were only three years old in 1990. At Northwestern University, where up to 280 cocaine babies are being followed, Dr. Dan Griffith, the development psychologist, says most of the children are testing within the normal range; however, their tolerance for stimulation is below normal, and they are easily distractible with a low tolerance for frustration. It is still unknown whether the children will suffer learning disabilities and other problems, such as attention deficit disorder.

According to the National Association for Perinatal Addiction Research in Education (NAPARE), as many as 375,000 newborns per year are born to mothers who abused drugs prenatally, and the drug of choice for many of them was cocaine or crack cocaine.

Contrary to popular perception, the problem is not seen only among poor people. Dr. Ira Chasnoff, an associate professor of pediatrics and psychiatry at Northwestern University, president of NAPARE and a noted researcher on the problem of drug babies, studied the rate of drug use among pregnant women in Florida and found almost no difference in the prenatal drug problem of poor women at public health departments and the problem among middle-class and upper-class women paying for private medical care. Nor did he find significant statistical difference when comparing drug abuse among pregnant women of different races, although black women are about 10 times more likely to be charged with drug abuse. Hospitals are seeing drug abusers of all socioeconomic statuses abandoning their infants, uncommon from all statuses in previous years.

Short Term Effects on Infants Infants born to drug-addicted mothers may themselves be forced to undergo withdrawal, a struggle for survival that the baby may not win. Crack babies sometimes actually suffer strokes while still in utero.

Cocaine affects a fetus or newborn much longer than it affects the adult user. Although cocaine leaves an adult user's urine in about 24 hours, the drug and its metabolites can remain in the system of a fetus for as long as four to six days.

Crack babies are generally much smaller than healthy newborns and are also frequently premature births. They may be born feverish and tremulous and suffer vomiting and hyperactivity. They also suffer a risk of five to ten times the average risk for Sudden Infant Death Syndrome.

Some common symptoms of cocaine babies are hyperactivity, poor feeding, rapid heart rate, excessive sudden movements and poor sleep patterns. Other typical traits are a low birth weight, low Apgar score and smaller than normal head circumference.

In addition, studies have revealed that cocaine can be transmitted to infants by breast-feeding mothers who have ingested cocaine up to 60 hours before breast-feeding the infant.

A study by the Centers for Disease Control in Atlanta found that woman who abuse cocaine in the early stages of pregnancy are also almost five times more likely to bear children with urinary tract defects. Other studies have revealed that cocaine abuse can lead to spontaneous abortion or stillborn infants.

Some indications of cocaine abuse in a pregnant women include early contractions, a hyperactive or inactive fetus, premature labor and "abruptio placenta," a premature separation of the placenta from the uterus that endangers the fetus.

In addition, many of these MEDICALLY FRAGILE infants may also suffer from AIDS because their mothers were sexually promiscuous and/or took the cocaine by using a contaminated needle. Many agencies routinely test newborn infants for both the HIV virus and drug presence.

Infants born with cocaine in their systems should also be tested for hepatitis, since this disease is passed through needle use by drug abusers and may be transmitted prenatally.

The extent of the cocaine abuse and when it was used during the pregnancy are also factors in the severity of the symptoms and problems evinced by a newborn infant. Physician Ira Chasnoff and his colleagues investigated the impact of cocaine abuse during only the first trimester of pregnancy compared to abuse throughout pregnancy.

According to the researchers, the continuous abusers had a higher rate of premature and low birthweight babies than those women who abused in the first trimester only; however, "both groups of cocaine-exposed infants demonstrated significant impairment of orientation, motor, and state regulation behaviors on the Neonatal Behavioral Assessment Scale."

Adoptive and biological parents need to understand that cocaine babies may have particular difficulty in responding to a parent. According to the authors of "The Care of Infants Menaced by Cocaine Abuse" in *Maternal Child Nursing,* "many are difficult to engage visually and exhibit jerky eye movements when they attempt to track. They may continue to be irritable and difficult to handle and may have limited interaction with people and objects in their environment."

If parents understand responses may be delayed, they are more likely to avoid the loop of frustration, trying less, increased frustration, and so on. For example, the cocaine baby may appear to dislike being picked up, so the parent will pick the child up less. Parents who realize less responsiveness is normal for a cocaine baby can more patiently continue to care for the child with love and affection.

Boarder Babies: Human and Societal Costs Cocaine and crack seem to destroy the maternal instinct, and as many as half of all addicted mothers, mothers from all socioeconomic statuses, abandon their infants in the hospital. As a result, many children remain in hospitals as BOARDER BABIES (babies who have been abandoned or are homeless or whose mothers have died), far beyond the time when they need hospital care, because they await foster home placement. The growing population of boarder babies is dominated by infants who are born addicted to crack cocaine and/or test positive for AIDS. Many of these children are also born addicted to cocaine, heroin or other drugs.

The societal cost of caring for cocaine and crack babies is staggering. At Howard University Hospital, in Washington, D.C., one infant in 1989 had a bill of $250,000. The cost to care for one boarder baby at D.C. General in Washington, D.C., is estimated at $367 per day, as of this writing. Intensive care can reach nearly $2,000 per day. According to a 1990 report on drug-exposed infants, the median intensive care charge per day for a nonexposed infant was $1,400, while the median charge for a drug-exposed infant was $5,500.

The hospital costs are not the only financial cost of cocaine babies. Many cocaine-addicted women are indigent, and the state and federal government pay the medical bill under the MEDICAID program. In addition, addicted mothers who parent their babies are often eligible for public assistance programs, such as Aid to Families with Dependent Children (AFDC) and food stamps. Often, the relatives of these mothers are the true caretakers of the children.

If the children are abandoned in the hospital, foster care payments must be made as well. According to a General Accounting Office report, 1,200 of 4,000 drug-exposed infants born in 10 hospitals in 1989 were placed in foster care. The estimated cost of foster care for these children is over $7 million per year.

It is impossible to quantify the personal pain of the children themselves and fearsome to speculate how they will behave as adults. One child was terrified of fires. His cocaine-addicted mother had frequently left him alone in abandoned buildings, and on one occasion, he was inside a burning building and could have easily died if someone had not saved him.

Even if children are not physically threatened by abuse or abandonment, many of the children are neglected and must learn to fend for themselves at an early age. Passersby have discovered toddlers attempting to cross busy highways, the situation unknown to their mother who is on a "high" and oblivious to reality.

Some cocaine babies have been placed in shelters, modern-day ORPHANAGES, whose caretakers attempt to deal with the children's basic needs. Children as old as one year may continue to live in the hospital because of overcrowded shelters.

Psychiatric experts have wondered out loud what ultimate effect this environment may have had on children.

One concern is a possible "failure to thrive," first documented in war orphans who were fed, bathed and cared for but did not receive the personalized affection of a parent or other caregiver. Another concern is whether such children will be able to meet developmental milestones they might have met if raised by a family.

Abusive or Neglectful Parents If the parents abuse or neglect their children, the state will remove the children from the home and place them in foster care (See ABUSE.) If the mother is able to recover from her cocaine addiction, she may be able to parent her child effectively; however, there is also a high recidivism rate of cocaine abuse among mothers who bear children born with cocaine in their systems. At Northwestern University, 56% of the mothers studies are back on the drug within a month of the child's birth. Apparently there is also an association between when (and if) a mother requests help for her addiction—the later in her pregnancy a woman obtains formal treatment, the higher the probability she will use drugs again.

It's also not clear how much the prenatal environment and how much the postnatal environment affect learning and behavioral problems of children who were cocaine babies.

Children remaining in their biological homes with drug-abusing parents generally have very unfavorable environments, and some aspect of learning difficulties could theoretically be attributed to environment, while some aspects could be a result of actual neurological damage.

It would be enlightening to review a longitudinal study that compared and contrasted cocaine babies who are adopted as well as cocaine babies who remain in their biological homes.

Long-Term Effects Although physicians have not been able to observe a long history of crack abuse and its effects on children (particularly since the problem of crack cocaine abuse is relatively new), doctors as well as educators already say they are recognizing problems of children who were born addicted to drugs, including possible problems with memory and learning disabilities. (Researcher Richard Barth contends, however, that special education is "not routinely necessary" for drug-exposed children. See below).

The severity of a child's problem is not always immediately evident, and clear neurological signs as well as gross problems of motor functions may not show up until the child is one year old or older.

Researchers are only beginning to identify the medical and other problems—including difficulties with attachment and bonding, extreme apathy and extreme aggression—caused by cocaine use by pregnant women.

Cocaine Babies Who Develop Normally Some researchers believe there has been an overreaction to the degree of serious effects on cocaine-affected infants and children. Author Richard Barth, Ph.D., challenges the doomed thinking of many physicians and educators in his article for *Social Work in Education*.

Said Barth, "One kindergarten teacher reported to me that she has never had such a difficult year and there were at least 5 crack kids who were constantly clinging to her. Yet clinging is not often reported as an outcome of crack exposure. Further discussion found no particular evidence that these children had been perinatally drug exposed, although they had all clearly been in home environments which caused them significant stress."

According to Barth, many cocaine babies develop within the normal ranges of intelligence and appear to have "good learning ability in structured situations." Those infants with less exposure to cocaine have a brighter prognosis still.

Barth says children who have been exposed to cocaine should not be lumped together under one category by researchers or by society because they are a very diverse group. "Some will show few symptoms after the drugs leave their system and some continue to show neurological symptoms throughout life."

Advice to Adoptive and Biological Parents of Cocaine Babies Judith Schaffer of the New York State Citizen's Coalition for Children recommends parents try to avoid overexciting the cocaine baby. "Don't allow the infant to become frantic," she says. Indications of overexcitement include color changes, eye aversions, sneezes and other clues.

She also strongly recommends the use of swaddling blankets and pacifiers and gentle rocking. "Up and down rocking, as opposed to the more usual side to side, appears to be more comforting," Schaffer says.

Stimulation should be gentle, and babies should be played with when the baby appears ready to respond. The infants are far more stiff than a healthy baby and may need to be propped on their sides.

Schaffer recommends that the child be discouraged from standing until he or she can stand alone. She also actively discourages the use of jumpers or walkers for cocaine babies.

Finding Foster and Adoptive Homes It is becoming increasingly difficult to identify enough foster homes or adoptive homes for cocaine babies because they are very hard to care for. Social workers are struggling to deal with cocaine babies returned by foster parents who cannot cope with the extra care and attention the children need.

Yet it should be noted that children are affected in different ways by the drug and by such factors as when and how much of the drug was ingested. As a result, some children who test positive for cocaine in their urine at birth appear normal and behave normally. It is unknown what long-term effects may occur, but some adoptive parents believe the risk is well worth their efforts.

According to researcher Laura Feig, as many as 80% of infants who were exposed to drugs (including other drugs in addition to cocaine) are foster children. Because many have serious medical problems, it has been difficult for social service agencies to find enough foster or adoptive families. (When the infant has only "traces" of cocaine, the infant is much easier to place.) Many prospective foster parents fear taking care of these babies because they fear the infants may also be AIDS-infected, and children with AIDS suffer a broad array of ailments. (There are also people who fear they will contract AIDS from taking care of the infant.)

Individuals who are considering adopting cocaine-exposed infants should request copies of the child's medical record. An in-office review is inadequate, and the couple (or single person) should be able to take the copy of the medical record to their own physician, whether the child is still an infant or is an older child who was exposed to cocaine in utero. (The agency will almost always delete the identities of the birthparents for purposes of confidentiality.)

If the adopting couple are not the child's foster parents, they should also ask to speak to the child's foster parents to learn as much as possible about the child. The prospective parents should also ask the agency for names of local physicians and psychiatrists or psychologists who are knowledgeable in this area.

Help for Cocaine Addicts Two national organizations maintain toll-free telephone numbers for cocaine addicts to use if they decide to seek help for their addiction. One is the National Cocaine Hotline (1-800-CO-CAINE), which refers callers to drug treatment programs in their areas. The other is the National Institute on Drug Abuse, Drug Information Service (1-800-662-HELP), which also refers callers to drug treatment programs.

Richard P. Barth, Ph.D., "Educational Implications of Prenatally Drug Exposed Children," *Social Work in Education,* 13 (1990): 130–136.

Nancy E. Chaney, M.D., Jenny Franke, M.D., and W.B. Wadlington, M.D., "Cocaine Convulsions in a Breast-Feeding Baby," *The Journal of Pediatrics,* 112(January 1988): 134–135.

Ira J. Chasnoff, M.D., Dan R. Griffith, Ph.D., Scott MacGregor, D.O., Kathryn Dirkes, B.M.E. and Kaytreen A. Burns, Ph.D., "Temporal Patterns of Cocaine Use in Pregnancy," *Journal of the American Medical Association,* 261(March 24/31, 1989), 1741–1744.

"Crack Babies Overwhelm Child Welfare System, Senate Says," *Brown University Child Behavior and Development Letter,* 6(April 1990), 6.

Karen Dukess, "Cocaine's Most Innocent Victims: Couple Reaches Out to Care for Kids When All Others Fail," *St. Petersburg Times,* September 10, 1989, 9A.

Laura Feig, *Drug Exposed Infants and Children: Service Needs and Policy Questions,* U.S. Dept. of Health and Human Services, OASPE, January 29, 1990.

General Accounting Office, *Drug-Exposed Infants: A Generation at Risk,* GAO/HRD-90-138, June 1990.

Susan Jenks, "Drug Babies: An Ethical Quagmire for Doctors," *Medical World News,* February 12, 1990.

Keeta DeStafano Lewis, Barbara Bennett and Nadya Hellinger Schmeder, "The Care of Infants Menaced by Cocaine Abuse," *Maternal Child Nursing,* September/October 1989, 324–328.

Judith Schaffer, M.A., *Cocaine Use During Pregnancy: Its Effects on Infant Development and Implications for Adoptive Parents* (Ithaca, NY: New York State Citizens' Coalition for Children, 1988).

Jane Schneider, M.S., P.T., Dan R. Griffith, Ph.D., and Ira J. Chasnoff, M.D., "Infants Exposed to Cocaine in Utero: Implications for

Developmental Assessment and Intervention," *Infants and Young Children*, 2(July 1989): 25–36.

Cathy Trost, "Born to Lose: Babies of Crack Users Crowd Hospitals, Break Everybody's Heart," *Wall Street Journal*, July 18, 1989, A1.

———, "As Drug Babies Grow Older, Schools Strive to Meet Their Needs," *The Wall Street Journal*, December 27, 1989, A1.

E

economics of adoption See COSTS TO ADOPT.

Edna Gladney Center, The The largest maternity home and adoption agency in the United States. The facility is nonsectarian and is located in Fort Worth, Texas.

The agency was renamed the Edna Gladney Home in 1950 and then the Gladney Center in 1990.

It includes its own private 19-bed, 26-bassinet maternity hospital (the Duncan Memorial Hospital), dormitory or apartment living for pregnant women, a middle/senior high school, chapel, swimming pool and other facilities.

The Gladney Center was founded in 1887 by Rev. I. Z. T. Morris and was known at that time as the Texas Children's Home Aid Society. From 1887 to 1914, over 1,000 abandoned or orphaned children were placed by the Texas Children's Home and Aid Society.

Edna Gladney succeeded Rev. Morris in 1927. Mrs. Gladney was instrumental in removing the word "illegitimate" from Texas birth certificates as well as in the enactment of a law that provided that adopted children would inherit in the same manner as biological children born to a family. Mrs. Gladney's lifework was depicted in the film "Blossoms in the Dust" in 1941.

The center offers confidential adoptions to birthparents and adoptive parents. Nonidentifying information may be shared. Adoptive parents must be between the ages of 24 and 39 and infertile. According to information provided by the Gladney Center, the average waiting period for prospective adoptive parents accepted into the program is one to two years. (Nonresidents of Texas may be eligible to apply. Contact the agency for further information.)

The Gladney Center also provides a toll-free hotline that operates 24 hours a day, 365 days a year, to provide information and assistance to women with crisis pregnancies. The Texas toll-free number is (800) 772-2740. The national toll-free number is (800) 433-2922.

The agency also places SPECIAL NEEDS newborns as well as older children available for adoption through the Texas Department of Human Resources.

For more information, contact

The Gladney Center
2300 Hemphill St.
Fort Worth, TX 76110
(817) 926-3304

education of adoptive parents Numerous adoption agencies nationwide hold adoption classes for prospective adoptive parents as part of the family assessment process or HOME STUDY.

Policies of the agency are fully explained during the course of the classes, such as why a particular agency wishes one parent to stay home and be the primary caregiver for the child for the first three months of the child's placement (or some other timeframe) or why the agency places a child in a foster home after release from a hospital rather than directly with adopting parents.

Adoption issues are usually covered, such as when and how to talk to a child about adoption, how to deal with relatives and acquaintances and problems the child may have if the child does not resemble the parents in racial or ethnic background.

Parents adopting children with SPECIAL NEEDS will usually learn about physical and sexual abuse along with suggestions on how to handle problems that may occur as a result of previous abuse. Social workers usually encourage parents to ask for help and not fear that they will be unable to finalize their adoption if they let the social worker know about a problem.

The classes are primarily held to help prospective parents prepare for parenthood and to educate them as much as possible about adoption. Classes are usually small groups of up to 20 couples, and the couples often develop a strong camaraderie that may last for years after they've adopted their children.

In some cases, social workers bring in birthmothers, adult adopted persons and adoptive parents as speakers, either singly or on a panel. Social workers encourage prospective parents to ask many questions.

A doctoral dissertation by Marlene Ross revealed adoption classes can have a long-term positive effect. In her 1985 study, Ross studied 30 families with adopted adolescents. One-third of the families had attended adoption classes prior to adopting their children or when the children were young.

Her results: The parents who had had "early adoptive education activities" were more open to discussing adoption with their children and more willing to acknowledge differences between adoptive and birth families. They were more receptive to learning about adoption and more positive about adoption classes.

She also found that parents of adopted children only were more interested in adoptive education than were families of adoptive and birth children. Self-esteem scores were similar for adolescents in adopted-only families and adoptive/birth families.

Specifics of Childcare Because of the anxiety associated with the adoption process, even when adoption agencies offer classes, the prospective parents may not fully listen and take advantage of the information offered. In addition, they usually concentrate on adoption issues rather than basic child care issues, such as how to change a baby, give it a bath and so forth.

As a result, some educators offer child care classes to prospective parents or individuals who have recently become adoptive parents, combining information about adoption with basic child care information. Adoptive parent and professional nurse and childbirth educator Carol A. Hallenbeck describes many issues that should be covered by educators, including issues rarely covered by agency classes; for example, some adoptive parents may actually feel a postpartum depression after their infant arrives home.

Confused by this feeling and fearful about such feelings, they can be tremendously relieved to learn other adoptive parents often feel an initial overwhelming tiredness, especially during the first six weeks after adoption.

Says Hallenbeck, "No matter how perfectly this all too longed for child fits into your plan, he will most likely bring you down to earth with a *thud*."

According to Hallenbeck, parents must learn "parenting is hard work and fantasies about parenthood can almost never be lived up to." She described one father in a class who, before he became a parent, insisted he would never become frustrated if his son screamed through dinner every night. One week after becoming a parent, he said, "I really love my son, but I sure get tired of trying to eat dinner while he's screaming!" When such feelings are brought out and shared, they may be amusing. When bottled up, the parent may feel he or she is inadequate or not as good as a parent to whom a child is born.

Community education Adoption education is also sometimes provided to the community at large, either by local adoption agencies in a forum setting or by adoptive parent support groups. Some groups visit local schools and explain their views on adoption to adolescents. Others offer seminars to anyone in the public who is interested.

Large organizations, such as the ADOPTIVE FAMILIES OF AMERICA INC., NATIONAL COMMITTEE FOR ADOPTION, OPEN DOOR SOCIETIES and NORTH AMERICAN COUNCIL ON ADOPTABLE CHILDREN (NACAC), provide an annual meeting for both adoptive parents and professionals to discuss and learn about the most salient issues in adoption.

Carol A. Hallenbeck, *Our Child: Preparation for Parenting in Adoption—Instructor's Guide* (Wayne, Pa.: Our Child Press, 1988).

Marlene Ross, "The Educational Needs of Adoptive Parents," Ph.D. diss., The American University, 1985.

Diane Scovil, "Adoptive Parents Need Our Support," *RN*, 52(December 1989): 19.

emotional problems See ACADEMIC PROGRESS; ACTING OUT; BONDING AND ATTACHMENT; CULTURE SHOCK; OLDER CHILD; PSYCHIATRIC PROBLEMS OF ADOPTED PERSONS; SPECIAL NEEDS.

employment benefits Companies vary widely on adoption benefits provided to employees. According to the Bureau of National Affairs, "An adoption benefits plan is a company-sponsored program that financially assists or reimburses employees for expenses related to the adoption of a child and/or provides for paid or unpaid leave for the adoptive parent employee."

Financial Reimbursement Some companies offer financial reimbursement for adoption, reasoning that health insurance coverage pays for much of the cost of the hospital bill for the birth of a biological child and adoptive parents should receive a related benefit. Other companies will pay for part or all of the actual hospital expenses of a birthmother if the child is adopted by an employee.

Reimbursable fees are usually agency and attorney fees. Numerous companies who provide reimbursement will also cover medical expenses for the newborn child and/or the birthmother, physical examinations and the cost of short-term foster care for the child.

Corporations who do provide adoption benefits usually provide a cash payment to help cover adoption expenses; for example, some companies pay adoption expenses up to a ceiling of $2,000 to $3,000.

Payment may be on placement of the child or finalization of the adoption, depending on company policy. In addition, payment may be based on documented expenses, or the company may elect to give the employee a flat sum.

Survey on Corporate Adoption Benefits A survey of 77 companies that provide some form of adoption benefit was reported by the U.S. General Accounting Office in December of 1989. The purpose of the survey was to determine if the benefits offered to civilians were comparable to the adoption reimbursement benefits being offered on a test basis to military members through September 30, 1990.

The employers surveyed included 67 companies, 7 government agencies at the federal, state and local levels and 3 nonprofit organizations.

The size of the organization varied from 25 to over 400,000 employees; 61% of the employers were "Fortune 500" corporations.

Direct financial assistance to the adoptive parent, either in the form of a reimbursement or as a flat sum, were provided by 56 of the 77 employers. Of these 56, 49 provided reimbursement for adoption expenses, and 7 offered a flat payment.

A ceiling on the amount paid to the adoptive parent of from $1,000 to $4,000 was set by 53 of the 56. Most set a ceiling of $1,000 to $2,000. Most of the employers make the reimbursements after the adoption is final, but 22 out of 56 pay for expenses earlier.

The earlier payments are usually made either at the time the child is placed in the home or when the parents initially request reimbursement.

Some of the companies surveyed had an age limit on the adopted child as to whether or not benefits should be paid. Most of those with age limits specify the child must be under either 16 or 18.

Leave/Vacation Benefits Leave policies vary widely as well. Some companies provide adopting parents with the same parental leave that would be given to biological parents.

If an adoption agency requires an extended leave of absence from work on the part of one of the adopting parents (three to six months or more), most companies will not provide paid leave but may allow the employee to take leave without pay; however, some other companies will terminate the employment of an employee after a given period of time. (See PARENTAL LEAVE for a further discussion.)

Some employers will provide adoptive parents with the same leave they provide parents with a newborn/biological child, while others provide very limited leave to everyone.

In addition, if the parent is adopting an older child, it may be difficult for an employer to understand why someone who is not adopting a baby needs time off. (The adopted child may or may not need the adoptive parent full-time in the short-term, depending on the situation.) As a result, the employee may be forced to take leave without pay.

Adoption benefits provided by corporations are optional unless dictated by state law. Less than a dozen states require mandatory parental leave for adoptive parents who wish to take such a leave.

Some corporations allow for unpaid leave even when state law does not mandate such leave. According to a 1984 Catalyst Corporation survey of 384 companies, about 28% provided adoption benefits in 1984, up from 10.3% in 1980. Other companies were seriously looking at the benefits.

Insurance Benefits Insurance benefits for an adopted child depend both on corporate policy and state laws. States such as New Mexico and Florida require that adopted children be covered from the moment of placement into the home and that pre-existing medical conditions may not be precluded from coverage. In 1990, Kansas passed a law requiring insurance companies to cover the delivery and hospitalization of a baby who is adopted. (Florida has a similar law.) Some corporations are more generous than required by state law and provide such coverage even when not decreed by the state.

Whether or not INSURANCE covers the adopted child immediately depends on company policy, unless state law dictates such coverage. In some states, the adopted child may not be covered by the adoptive parents' health insurance until after finalization because medical problems she or he may have are considered pre-existing conditions.

Reasons for Providing Adoption Benefits According to the National Committee For Adoption, employers provide adoption benefits for three key reasons: (1) as an equalizer for adoptive parents to parents who are covered by and receive pregnancy benefits, (2) as a way to build a favorable image of the company among employees and (3) as a public relations tool to enhance the company's public image. It should also be noted that adoption benefits do not generally cost a company a great expense since far fewer employees adopt children than those who "birth" children.

Prospective adoptive parents should check with the personnel or benefits office of their companies before adopting a child to learn what is and is not covered in the areas of reimbursement, leave and insurance coverage.

They should not rely on what a clerk says are their entitlements because often lower-ranking individuals may not realize that adoption benefits are provided by the company. It's not an everyday occurrence for people to apply for such benefits; hence, they may be forgotten. (See also MATERNITY LEAVE.)

In 1991, in response to a request from President George Bush that he promote adoption of children with special needs, adopted adult and Wendy's International CEO R. David Thomas launched a business-to-business letter-writing campaign to encourage corporations to provide adoption benefits to employees. (The *R. David Thomas Platform*, Wendy's International, Inc., P.O. Box 256, Dublin, OH 43017.)

Adoption: Assistance Provided by Selected Employers to Adopting Parents, General Accounting Office GAO/HRD-47FS, December 1989.

Adoption Assistance: Joining the Family of Employee Benefits (Rockville, Md.: Bureau of National Affairs, 1988.

Adoption Benefits Plans: *Corporate Response to a Changing Society* (Philadelphia, PA: National Adoption Exchange, n.d.).

Corporate Support for Adoption Grows, National Adoption Reports, May–June 1986, 2.

National Committee For Adoption, *Adoption Factbook: United State Data, Issues, Regulations and Resources*, (Washington, D.C.: National Committee For Adoption, 1989).

Work & Family: A Changing Dynamic, A BNA Special Report, The Bureau of National Affairs, 1986.

entitlement   The term is usually used to describe the feeling of the adoptive parents that they deserve their adopted child and can truly bond to him or her. But this term can also be used to describe such feelings of anyone in the adoptive family.

Authors Jerome Smith and Franklin Miroff write in their book, *You're Our Child,*

> The sense of entitlement of the parents to child, of child to parents, and siblings to each other is a task unique to adoption. This is a relatively easy procedure in having a biological child and usually occurs at an unconscious level. For adoptive parents, however, there is this extra psychological step involved.

Author Patricia Johnston maintains that entitlement is not always an immediate feeling. "Developing a sense of entitlement is an ongoing process of growth rather than a single task identifiably completable, and the success of an adoption is related to the degree to which this sense of entitlement has been acquired by each family member rather than to its being seen as achieved or not achieved."

Some adoption experts believe infertile couples continually struggle over feelings of entitlement to their adopted child. Other researchers believe societal attitudes inhibit or enhance the feeling of entitlement. Charlene Miall studied how adoptive parents perceived community attitudes and found those she interviewed were dismayed by the attitudes and behavior of people they knew.

Miall observed that the absence of entitlement in some infertile adoptive parents was probably caused more by a knowledge of the attitudes of the surrounding society than by a failure to adequately deal with the infertility. She said the focus on bloodties in much social work literature relegates adoption to a second-rate position. (See also ATTITUDES ABOUT ADOPTION.)

Critics of OPEN ADOPTION state that when an adoptive family and the birthfamily know each other's identity and periodically exchange information, it may be difficult for the adoptive family to feel an entitlement to the child. (And visits with the child are becoming increasingly more common in open adoptions.) As a result, they will feel the child is really the birthfamily's child and not their own.

Proponents of open adoption as well as proponents of meetings between birthfamilies and adopting families hypothesize that when adoptive families believe they were actually selected by the birthfamily, they feel more of an entitlement than when they were simply selected from an adoption agency waiting list.

Patricia Irwin Johnston, *An Adoptor's Advocate* (Indianapolis: Perspectives Press, 1984).

Charlene E. Miall, "The Stigma of Adoptive Parent Status: Perceptions of Community Attitudes Toward Adoption and the Experience of Informal Social Sanctioning," *Family Relations*, 36(January 1987): 34–39.

Jerome Smith, Ph.D., and Franklin I. Miroff, *You're Our Child: The Adoption Experience* (Lanham, Md.: Madison Books, 1987).

environment Scientists have argued the "nature-nurture" controversy for years and will probably continue to disagree on whether heredity or environment is more important; however, most experts agree that both the child's genetic heritage and the environment are critical factors to a child's personality and development.

There are some indications that INTELLIGENCE levels can be positively affected by adoption. There are also indications that both heredity and environment play a role in an adopted person's contracting cancer.

ethical issues A variety of ethical issues exist concerning the adoption of children and are described in detail throughout this volume.

The idea that it is acceptable to do anything in order to adopt a child, particularly an infant, is a disturbing issue and a problem in contemporary society.

Desperate prospective adoptive parents will sometimes resort to baby buying, and unscrupulous attorneys will make it possible through BABY SELLING. In addition, some pregnant young women see an opportunity to make a large amount of money from an unwanted pregnancy and either actively pursue unethical attorneys or eagerly agree to a baby selling plan.

The issue of baby selling is complicated by the fact that what is legal in adoption in some states is considered baby selling in other states. An example of this is that some states allow pregnant women to receive support money while others place a ban on such payments.

The issue of SURROGATE MOTHERHOOD is another ethical problem in our society, and several states have moved to ban surrogate motherhood or limit such practices to a no-profit status.

Organizations such as the NATIONAL COMMITTEE FOR ADOPTION among others believe surrogate motherhood is planned baby selling. Proponents of surrogate motherhood, including RESOLVE Inc., believe couples should have the right to create a biological child by another woman who consents.

REPRODUCTIVE TECHNOLOGIES have enabled physicians to fertilize eggs outside the womb, which has created a host of ethical dilemmas when there are disagreements among the parties involved. (See BIOETHICS) In 1990, a California woman gave birth to the genetic child of another couple and sued for custody. She did not win her suit, but many related ethical issues were considered in light of this suit. It is now possible for physicians to use a donated ova, fertilize it and then implant the fertilized egg in another woman, even a woman past menopause. Concerned individuals wonder about the morality of buying and selling ova, as well as the ultimate effects on the child. (See ZYGOTE ADOPTION.)

Even artificial insemination by donor, a process that has existed for many years and wherein semen is either injected into the woman or an egg is fertilized outside the woman and later implanted, has come under attack by prominent individuals.

TRANSRACIAL ADOPTION is another major issue of our times. Proponents of transracial adoption believe that while it is the best plan to arrange adoptions for children in same-race families, it is not possible to find enough families for all the black and biracial children needing to be adopted; consequently, they believe a loving permanent home is preferable to foster care.

Opponents of transracial adoption, chiefly the National Association of Black Social Workers, believe transracial adoptions rob the children of their racial identity. They also believe social services agencies do not recruit black adoptive parents in sufficient numbers and state that more active recruitment would solve all or most of the problem of black WAITING CHILDREN.

The COSTS TO ADOPT are frequently debated as ethical issues; for example, SLIDING SCALE FEES are now banned in the state of Pennsylvania. A sliding scale ties the adopting parents' fee directly to their income, and less affluent people pay a lower adoption rate than more affluent people.

Critics charge that this is a form of baby selling, while proponents, including most professional standard-setting and accrediting organizations, believe it is fair to charge less affluent adopting parents a lower rate than wealthier parents, making adoption affordable to them.

There are also positive aspects of costs that are often ignored; for example, the cost to the state and federal government to maintain a child in foster care is greatly or totally diminished when that child is adopted. (Some adoptive parents receive subsidies for adopted children, so state and federal costs are still paid, albeit at far lower rates than when the child is a foster child. See ADOPTION ASSISTANCE PROGRAM.)

Additionally, when a pregnant woman chooses to place her child for adoption, the adoptive parents incur the expenses of raising the child. Should she desire to parent the child and receive Aid to Families with Dependent Children, food stamps and Medicaid for at least 18 years, the costs to society are hundreds of thousands of dollars.

For-profit adoption agencies disturb numerous adoption experts and create another ethical dilemma for state legislators. Although only about 5% of all adoption agencies are for-profit according to the National Committee for Adoption, experts worry that this percentage may be on the rise and fear that children will suffer as a result of the profit motive.

Dissenters of this view argue that even nonprofit adoption agencies can be greedy and hide large revenues in huge salaries for the director and staff, thus zeroing-out the "bottom line."

Some people believe INTERNATIONAL ADOPTION presents many ethical issues; for example, they wonder aloud why it costs $10,000 or more to adopt an infant from a South American orphanage (where costs are far lower than in the United States) when fees to adopt a healthy white baby in the United States may be less.

Critics also wonder why it is extremely difficult for a white couple to adopt a black or biracial child in the United States but comparatively easy to adopt a child of another race from another country.

State laws on INSURANCE vary greatly, and in some states an adopted child is covered from birth while in other states the child is covered on placement. There are also state laws that specifically release insurance companies from covering preexisting conditions; consequently, individuals in such states are often afraid to adopt children with medical problems.

Critics of such insurance laws believe adopted children should be considered in the same way as all children, while proponents believe such coverage would be an unfair burden on the insurance companies.

OPEN ADOPTION also presents numerous ethical issues to adoption agencies and others involved in adoption. Whether to introduce prospective adoptive parents to a pregnant woman, when to introduce them (before or after the child is born), whether to allow the adopting parents in the delivery room and other dilemmas face those who believe in open adoptions.

A key issue is whether meeting adopting parents provides too much pressure on the pregnant woman to choose adoption rather than parenting. Another key issue is the extent of her involvement in the child's life after he is adopted. Experts disagree widely on whether contact is good for the child and how much contact is advisable.

The OPEN RECORDS issue has generated considerable controversy, as proponents argue that adopted adults are unfairly deprived of their biological heritage by SEALED RECORDS.

Advocates of TRADITIONAL ADOPTION believe most pregnant women and adopting parents prefer confidentiality. They argue that if birthparents and adopted adults desire to find each other later in life, MUTUAL CONSENT REGISTRIES can afford them such an opportunity as long as both wish this confidential information to be released.

Adopting parents are demanding more information on children before they adopt them today. Adoptive parents who were deprived of critical information have filed WRONGFUL ADOPTION lawsuits. As a result, caseworkers are more sensitized than in past years to providing nonidentifying information about the child and the birthparents and information about any abuse or neglect that may have occurred.

Whether or not adopting parents should have access to confidential records, when they should have such access and how much information should be withheld are continuing controversies. (See also GENETIC PREDISPOSITIONS; INTELLIGENCE.)

etiquette In adoption, refers to the polite way to discuss or mention adoption-related issues or to refrain from mentioning them.

Most adoptive parents, adopted children and adults and birthparents would probably appreciate some generally accepted basic rules of etiquette regarding adoption. The following list is a set of several rules the authors have drawn up, based on their knowledge of adoption, for the friends and relatives of individuals whose lives are somehow affected by adoption:

1. If a woman says she is considering placing her child for adoption, it is impolite to react with extreme horror and exclaim, "How could you give up your own flesh and blood? I could never do that!" A woman who is thinking about adoption would prefer to hear empathetic comments, such as, "That must be a hard decision to make."
2. If a couple is considering adopting a child, it is impolite to say, "You mean you can't have kids of your own? How sad!" It is also not polite to tell about your cousin who waited nine years on a waiting list or ask how much money the adoption will cost. Instead, it is preferable to say something like, "That sounds very exciting."
3. If a family member or friend discovers someone has just adopted, it is inappropriate to ask if the "real mother" is known, what she looks like, how old she is and whether or not she is married. It is even less acceptable for the mailman or supermarket checkout clerk to ask these questions. It is appropriate to say, "Congratulations! How wonderful!"
4. If a family has adopted an infant from another country, it is inappropriate—and silly—to say, "How wonderful! She will be bilingual!" (Yes, people do say such things.)
5. In the case of an intercountry adoption, it is impolite to ask if the child was abandoned or had many unusual diseases or if the mother was starving to death.
6. It is always impolite to refer to a child's adoption in front of the child over age two as if she or he did not exist.

7. If a family has a biological child after adopting, it is unacceptable to tell them it is too bad they did not wait a little longer before adopting.
8. When a family adopts an older child, it is impolite to ask them if the child had been abused. If they wish to discuss the abuse (*if* it happened), they will bring it up.
9. It is impolite to ask an adopted adult if he plans to "search" for his birthparents. Adults who do not wish to search will feel embarrassed and may think they have to explain why they do not wish to search. Adopted adults who wish to discuss a planned or past search will talk about it if they wish.
10. It is equally impolite to ask a birthmother if she plans to search for her birth child or if she is worried he or she will someday search for her.

These are basic rules of etiquette for individuals who have not adopted. Hopefully, individuals who have adopted, placed or were adopted will also follow them. As Miss Manners stated in response to a question from an irate adoptive parent about prying questions from others, "Telling people pleasantly that there are things you refuse to discuss with them sets an excellent example for your baby." (See also TERMINOLOGY.)

Judith Martin, *Miss Manners' Guide to Excruciatingly Correct Behavior* (New York: Atheneum, 1982).

eugenics A science that is concerned with the improvement of hereditary characteristics of a race or breed. In some instances, as in Nazi Germany, eugenics has been taken to extremes, serving as the rationale for genocide and for breeding a so-called "master race." In recent times, the term has been somewhat loosely applied to the decisions parents may make as the result of increases in REPRODUCTIVE TECHNOLOGIES.

Genetic testing of the fetus helps a woman or enables a couple to know whether or not a child will have a genetic defect. If the fetus carries a condition that is unacceptable to the parent(s), there may be an election to abort it.

It is also possible to test for nondisabling conditions, such as the sex of a child. In some countries, it is common for a couple who wants a boy and learns the woman is pregnant with a girl to abort a healthy female.

Advocates of eugenics and genetic testing insist that much agony can be avoided by mothers and fathers knowing what they're up against. Advocates argue that if parents are sure they cannot possibly cope with a severely deformed or mentally deficient child, abortion would be more humane for all concerned. Others argue that testing actually prevents some abortions by reassuring prospective parents that the fetus is healthy. (See also BIOETHICS.)

expenses to adopt See COSTS TO ADOPT.

explaining adoption Whether children are adopted as newborn infants or as older children who are well aware of the adoption, it is important for adoptive parents to explain adoption and clarify what adoption is and is not.

Many parents who adopt children presume that if a child is curious about adoption, he or she will ask a question. However, adoption experts and researchers have learned that children are often afraid to bring up the subject of adoption because they fear their parents will become angry, offended or hurt. Even adopted adults are often fearful of asking questions.

As a result, although adoptive parents should not continually talk about adoption, it is a subject that should be brought up periodically to show the child that the parents are willing to discuss it and to offer information as needed. The child will then learn and remember that parents are comfortable with being asked questions and will retain this information for the future when he or she may have questions.

In the past, some parents were advised against sharing the fact of adoption with the child. They were urged to treat and raise the child in every way as if born to the family. The problem with this advice was that adopted persons usually found out they were adopted, often at a difficult time in life, such as adolescence or upon the death of their adoptive parents. When parents withhold true facts, the trust level in the ongoing parent-child relationships suffers seriously.

Also, this approach deprived adopted individuals of appropriate health and genetic information.

Until recently, many social workers encouraged parents to tell a version of the "CHOSEN CHILD" story, wherein it was maintained that the adopted child was "special" because he or she was chosen by the parents. Because very few adopted children are specifically selected, this tale has been found to have a ring of inaccuracy, and few now encourage its use. In any case, telling the truth about the child's adoptive status is the most ethical thing to do.

Experts ultimately agreed that it is important for a child to know he was adopted, although they still disagree on when to explain and discuss adoption and how to handle the discussion.

Some researchers insist that the child should hear the word "adoption" from infancy onward, whereas others say a child cannot possibly begin to understand such a complex subject as adoption until at least age five or six.

A study of 200 adopted and nonadopted children by David Brodzinsky, Leslie Singer and Anne Braff revealed that children under age six did not have a very good understanding of adoption, and few of them "differentiated between adoption and birth as alternative paths to parenthood or understood anything about the adoption process, or the motives underlying adoption."

The researchers found that children from about age six to eight understand that there is a difference between adoption and birth but are apparently unaware of the reasons for adoption. Between the ages of eight and eleven, the children's understanding increases. Preadolescent and adolescent children had the best understanding of adoption.

Many adoption experts agree that the child should know about the adoption prior to entering kindergarten or first grade. One very practical reason is that children constantly tease each other about a variety of real or imagined traits—wearing glasses, chubbiness and so forth.

A child's status as an adopted person could also be a subject used by another child as a taunting gesture, and the hurt would be compounded if the adopted child had no knowledge whatsoever about the adoption. As a result, adoptive parents can attempt to minimize the damage caused by teasing or cruelty by telling the child about adoption before entry into the school system.

Parents should also realize that adoption is not a subject that can be explained once and then forgotten. Instead, most experts believe explanations should be targeted to a child's developmental level of understanding. As a result, responses to an adolescent's questions will be more sophisticated than explanations given to an eight-year-old child. It should also be noted that of all the age groups, adolescence is likely to be the time when children question their identities; consequently, it is equally likely the child will have questions about his or her adoption during that period. (See also ADOLESCENT ADOPTED PERSONS.)

It is also advisable for adoptive parents to use positive adoption TERMINOLOGY when explaining any aspect of adoption. Even when said by the most loving parent, such phrases as "given away," "real parents" and other words and phrases almost invariably evoke a very negative image of both the birthparents and adoption itself. Far more preferable are such phrases as "made an adoption plan" or "chose adoption"—if the adoption was in fact a voluntary choice of the birthparent. "Transferred parental rights" could be used in the case of involuntary or voluntary termination of parental rights.

Parents should also realize the MEDIA may present distorted and negative views of adoption, and stereotypical or unfair depictions should be challenged aloud by parents, whether the child asks a question or not.

In addition, parents should note that the word "adopt" is sometimes used in an unusual context; for example, pet shelters may solicit new pet owners by advertising that they want people to "adopt" a pet.

Sharing Information About Birthparents
In the past, many adoptive parents were counseled to tell their child he was placed for adoption because "his mother loved him so much."

One problem with this explanation, true as it usually is, is that a child could logically conclude that if his adoptive parents also love him very much, then they may ultimately decide the child should be adopted by others, for example, if the adoptive family suffers from financial problems.

In addition, the adoptive family may not know how the birthparents felt about the child. They presume it was a difficult decision but can only guess about the birthparents' emotions about the adoption.

An intermediate approach is for the adoptive parents to explain to the child that while they don't know if the birthmother (or birthparents) loved the child, what they do know is that she (or they) cared about the child's happiness and made a request to find a mother and father who could care and love the child. This approach sidesteps the issue of whether the birthparent loved the child while, at the same time, it is not a cold rejection of the child or the birthparent.

Explaining adoption to family members and friends Often relatives, future grandparents and friends may have a very limited knowledge or no knowledge of adoption. (See also ATTITUDES ABOUT ADOPTION.)

General information can be much appreciated by such individuals, but specific information about an individual child (whether or not the birthparents were married, why they chose adoption and so on) should be left to the discretion of the adoptive parents, who need not feel compelled to answer questions.

If the child is of another nationality or race from the adoptive parents, it is more likely the parents will be asked questions by family as well as total strangers. (See also ETIQUETTE). Families adopting internationally or transracially should be prepared to deal with the intense curiosity of the general public, which is generally positive, and negative comments should be politely deflected.

Sometimes children's understanding of adoption and their insights are more comprehensive and accepting than parents realize. For example, Adele Liskov, associate staff for Appropriations (and on the staff of Rep. William Lehman, FL), has always been very open in discussing adoption with her child.

Ms. Liskov's daughter Alana was only six years old when she and her mother were discussing adoption and the child suddenly said (of her birthmother and mother), "She gave me starting life. You gave me growing life."

Ann Angel, *Real for Sure Sister* (Indianapolis, IN: Perspectives Press, 1988).
Linda Bothun, *When Friends Ask About Adoption* (Chevy Chase, Md.: Swan Publications, 1987).
Anne B. Brodzinsky, *The Mulberry Bird: An Adoption Story* (Indianapolis, IN: Perspectives Press, 1986).
David M. Brodzinsky, Leslie M. Singer and Anne M. Braff, "Children's Understanding of Adoption," *Child Development,* 55(1984): 869–878.
Jack Freudberg and Tony Geiss, *Susan & Gordon Adopt a Baby* (New York: Sesame Street Books, 1986).
Carol Livingston, *"Why Was I Adopted?"* (Secaucus, N.J.: Carol Publishing Group, 1978).
Fred Powledge, *So You're Adopted* (New York: Scribner, 1982).

Franz Rohr, *How Parents Tell Their Children They Are Adopted* (New York: New York State Adoptive Parents Committee, reprinted 1988).

F

failed adoptions See DISRUPTION.

family tree A genealogical chart denoting parents, grandparents and other relatives in the family as far back in history as information allows. The chart has many branches and consequently resembles a tree in appearance.

Family trees are often assigned as a project to schoolchildren and can be used to advantage in helping adopted children straighten out identity issues over belonging to their adoptive families.

The child will not be disturbed by the exercise when adults explain why he belongs on the family tree, namely via adoption. Each family member's genetic ancestry tree is another reality that may merit discussion; for example, the genetic ancestry of the mother and her parents and relatives is completely different from the genetic ancestry of the father and his parents and extended family. When they married, they formed a new legal entity and together they create their own family tree with their children.

Older children will need caring clarification, pointing out that with adoption, there was a transfer of family membership from one family to another family system. Their birth families still comprise their genetic ancestry trees.

If a family-tree exercise is assigned as a means of teaching genetic inheritance, e.g., eye color, haircolor, etc., such an exercise could be problematic for the adopted child.

fantasies of adopted children Many children, both adopted and nonadopted, fantasize about ideal parents somewhere who would always smile upon their every action and never punish them. It's common for adopted children to fantasize about birthparents, particularly during preadolescence and/or adolescence.

According to psychiatrist Dr. Barbara Stilwell, "Many children have fantasies that they have another set of parents somewhere who are superhuman beings . . . These fantasies arise when a child becomes angry at his parents. They dissipate when a child learns that he can love and hate the same person."

If the adopted child doesn't fantasize birthparents are handsome and wealthy people, the opposite may be imagined. The birthparent may be thought to be a prostitute, a drug addict or a highly undesirable and thoroughly evil person.

The adoptive parents need to present a view of the birthparent as a real person, with virtues and flaws; however, there are some indications that adoptive parents may be overly positive when they speak of birthparents, particularly the birthmother, to the adopted child.

In *You're Our Child,* authors Jerome Smith and Franklin I. Miroff said adoptive parents should thoroughly explore their own motives in adopting a child.

For example, if a parent associates undesirable behavior on the part of the child with the "bad seed" notion, such a parent is vulnerable and may make verbal attacks and innuendoes about the child's "real" parentage, which will cause further breakdown to the parent-child relationship.

Researchers Katherine A. Kowal and Karen Maitland Schilling, who studied adult adopted persons, revealed that adopted youth reported their fantasies about birthparents increased during adolescence and subsided subsequent to this turbulent period.

Parents should be able to express understanding of this wish for more certainty from their child. Adoptive parents also might wish to know more about the birthparents than was originally shared with them. They might both "wonder" together.

According to Kowal and Schilling, increased fantasizing during adolescence was also accompanied by a worsening quality in the relationship between the adoptive parents and adopted adolescent. The researchers were unsure whether a decline in the quality of relationships as perceived in their study could be generalized to other adopted adolescents or was limited to adopted adolescents who later sought to locate their birthparents.

It's also important to note that the fantasies of a child adopted as an infant differ from the fantasies of a child adopted as an older child, even though when a child remembers his birthparents in retrospect, he may tend to romanticize or idealize them. Often, however, because the older child remembers them, he may show less curiosity and need to locate them as an adult than adults who were adopted as infants. (See also ADOPTIVE PARENTS for information on adoptive parents and their fantasies about their future child.)

Katherine A. Kowal, Ph.D., and Karen Maitland Schilling, Ph.D., "Adoption Through the Eyes of Adult Adoptees," *American Journal of Orthopsychiatry,* 55 (July 1985): 357–358.

Jerome Smith, Ph.D., and Franklin I. Miroff, *You're Our Child: The Adoption Experience* (Lanham, Md.: Madison Books, 1987).

father, legal See LEGAL FATHER.

federal government Although states set their own adoption laws, the federal government also plays a role in adoption, particularly in the area of SPECIAL NEEDS. In order for states to receive federal funds, they are supposed to comply with federal regulations on the length of time children may spend in FOSTER CARE before returning to their parents or being placed for adoption. The federal government also provides funds for adoption SUBSIDIES, MEDICAID and numerous other entitlements. (See also ADOPTION ASSISTANCE AND FAMILY WELFARE ACT OF 1980; ADOPTION ASSISTANCE PROGRAM; INCOME TAX DEDUCTIONS; INDIAN CHILD WELFARE ACT OF 1978.; U.S. IMMIGRATION AND NATURALIZATION SERVICE.)

fertile adoptive parents Also known as OPTIONAL ADOPTERS and preferential adopters; individuals who could conceive a child if they wished, but for a variety of reasons, choose to adopt instead in order to introduce or expand the number of children in their family. They may believe in ZERO POPULATION GROWTH and believe it is better to care for already WAITING CHILDREN or children with SPECIAL NEEDS rather than to bring another child into the world.

fertility rates The fertility rate is a measure of the number of live births to women of childbearing age. According to the *Advance Report of Final Natality Statistics, 1988,* the latest information as of this writing, fertility rose slightly from previous years to 67.2 live births per 1,000 for women ages 15–44 years.

The birth rate for teenagers ages 15–17 years increased 6% to a rate of 33.8, the highest rate for young teens since 1977. The rate for older teens ages 18–19 increased 2% to a rate of 81.7. The rate for women ages 30–34 years increased 3% to 73.7 per 1,000, the highest rate since 1968. The greatest annual increase in birth rates was seen among women ages 40–44. Although this group represents a small percentage of total births, the rate increased 9% over 1987 to a rate of 4.8 in 1988 compared to a rate of 4.4 per 1,000 in 1987.

According to the National Center for Health Statistics, which also studies infertility, in 1988 there were approximately four million women ages 15–44 with an impaired ability to bear a child. This figure represents about 1 in 12 of the 57.9 million in this age group. Of this number, 2.2 million had had no births, and 2.7 million had had one or more births. (See tables.)

The AMERICAN FERTILITY SOCIETY says about 40% of infertility can be traced to the male as the "sole or a contributing cause."

Contrary to popular belief, the rate of infertility has not increased significantly since 1982: What has increased since that time is the number of couples delaying childbearing until their late twenties or even late thirties. This large number has resulted from individuals born during the "Baby Boom" (1946–1964). Many of the people in this group are delaying childbearing into older ages, where they are more likely to suffer fertility problems.

Fertility declines with age, and women over age 30 are twice as likely to have fertility problems as younger women. Because fertility declines from the early twenties to the late thirties, it is difficult or even impossible for a significant percentage of women aged 39 (or older) to successfully become pregnant and bear a child.

As a result of this delayed childbearing and subsequent fertility declines, the number of couples seeking to adopt an infant has increased out of proportion to the number of babies who need adoptive families. In addition, single parenthood has over the same period of time become socially preferable to the many young woman who would have considered placing their baby for adoption in earlier years.

Although women in their mid to late thirties who are physically able to bear children may ultimately become pregnant, the timeframe to achieve a conception may be longer than the timeframe for a woman aged 25. Many women in their mid to late thirties believe they can't afford to wait for years to become pregnant, and as a result, they visit infertility specialists, hoping to find a rapid answer to their problem.

About 20% of infertility cases are diagnosed as "unexplained infertility" and never respond to drug treatment, surgery, in vitro fertilization or any other methods tried by infertility specialists. However, physicians are constantly researching new techniques, and dramatic breakthroughs are expected over the next decade.

One problem infertile people often face is the lack of insurance coverage for expensive infertility treatments. Many insurance carriers refuse to cover such treatments as in vitro fertilization or other techniques, primarily because of the cost involved, although some states mandate such coverage.

Members of RESOLVE INC., a mutual aid support group, believe fertility treatments would be far less expensive than generally believed. According to RESOLVE leaders, less than 33% of infertile couples seek treatment for fertility problems. Of these, at most 15% seek expensive treatments such as in vitro fertilization.

According to officials at Blue Cross and Blue Shield of Massachusetts, after the state passed a bill requiring coverage for infertility treatments, the cost associated with that change was an estimated $2 million, which was 59 cents a month per policy holder.

As the Baby Boomer generation is replaced by the smaller Baby Bust generation (born 1965–1979), it is likely that demands for infertility treatment will decrease in number because of the decline in sheer numbers, according to demographer Cheryl Russell, the author of *100 Predictions for the Baby Boom: The Next 50 Years.* (see also INFERTILITY; REPRODUCTIVE TECHNOLOGIES.)

Judith N. Lasker and Susan Borg, *In Search of Parenthood: Coping with Infertility and High Tech Conception* (Boston: Beacon Press, 1987).
Male Infertility: A Guide for Patients (Birmingham, Ala.: American Fertility Society, 1989).
William D. Mosher, Ph.D., and William F. Pratt, Ph.D., *Fecundity and Infertility in the United States, 1965–88,* National Center for Health Statistics, Division of Vital Statistics, no. 192, December 4, 1990.
National Center for Health Statistics, *Advance Report of Final Natality Statistics, 1988,* 39: no. 4, supplement (August 15, 1990).
Sonia L. Nazario, "Infertility Insurance Gains Backing," *The Wall Street Journal,* December 5, 1989, B1, B4.
Cheryl Russell, *100 Predictions for the Baby Boom: The Next 50 Years* (New York: Plenum Press, 1987).

fetal alcohol syndrome (FAS) Brain damage and other severe birth defects in a child whose mother abused alcohol during pregnancy. The extent of the damage depends on the severity of the abuse, when the abuse occurred during the development of the fetus and many other factors. About 50,000 newborn infants per year are born with fetal alcohol syndrome or related symptoms, and FAS is a leading cause of mental retardation.

Physicians from ancient Greece through the present day recognized that the alcoholism of a pregnant woman was harmful to children born to her, yet it was not until 1973 that Kenneth Jones and David Smith of the University of Washington in Seattle identified the characteristics of fetal alcohol syndrome and perceived it as an actual syndrome.

Some infants and children also suffer from fetal alcohol effect (FAE), which may occur when the pregnant woman is a moderate drinker throughout her pregnancy and which causes less severe (but potentially serious) birth defects and less readily identifiable problems during infancy.

According to Patricia Mutch, Ph.D. and director of the Institute of Alcoholism and Drug Dependency at Andrews University in Michigan, even one drink per day by the pregnant woman can be harmful to the developing fetus. She cites studies revealing that children born to moderate drinkers evince problems with memory and may suffer attention deficits or other problems.

Information on both FAS and FAE suggest that any pregnant woman should consider avoiding alcohol altogether throughout her pregnancy. Alcoholic women who are pregnant and plan to continue their pregnancies should definitely seek prenatal care and treatment so they can recover from alcoholism and avoid the possibility of birth defects in their children. Indeed, any woman who normally drinks alcohol in any quantity whatsoever, including as little as one drink per day, should consult her physician to obtain information and advice about alcohol consumption during pregnancy. Women who suspect they are pregnant should immediately find out whether they are indeed pregnant so they can determine the appropriate course of action.

Families who adopt children with FAS or FAE should obtain as much information and assistance as possible from social workers, physicians and parent groups. They must understand that tender, loving care, although extremely important, cannot entirely alleviate the damage that occurred in utero to the child. Families should also learn about adoption subsidies and the child's eligibility for Medicaid.

In many cases, an adoptive family will adopt their FAS child through the state social services system, although they may also adopt through a private adoption agency.

Children with fetal alcohol syndrome are often premature and underweight with small heads and are likely to remain unusually small and thin. Many are mentally retarded: The average IQ of the FAS child is 68. They may also experience seizures and a host of other medical and psychological problems that are not outgrown as the child ages. Hyperactivity and a poor attention span are common problems.

Identifiable facial features of children with fetal alcohol syndrome include folds in the eyelids, short noses, thin upper lips, small chins and an overall "flattened" appearance. An estimated 30% of the children also suffer heart defects. Another characteristic of children with FAS is poor muscle coordination, and one-quarter to one-half of the children have heart murmurs. Other problems sometimes seen are cleft palates, hernias, hydrocephalus, kidney problems and defective teeth.

In a 1990 study of 461 infants whose mothers abused alcohol during pregnancy, researchers found a specific association between alcohol consumption and prenatal development during the last trimester of pregnancy: a five millimeter decrease in the infant head circumference for every daily drink. Alcohol abuse during the second trimester was also associated with a smaller infant head circumference, and there are risks of abnormalities during any trimester.

Follow-up research of this study revealed the infants were harder to feed than were infants born to nonalcoholic mothers. They also had a slower rate of growth than normal infants.

It is possible that Fetal Alcohol Syndrome may be more of a problem for groups that have a high rate of alcohol consumption. Dartmouth professor and adoptive father Michael Dorris, who is also an American Indian, writes sensitively of his own experiences in adopting a son with fetal alcohol syndrome in his book, *The Broken Cord*. Dorris believes the rate of fetal alcohol syndrome is a serious problem among some tribes and is also an often unrecognized problem among all races in the United States. (American Indians do have a higher rate of alcoholism than other ethnic or racial groups.)

Dorris also discusses what should or could be done to help pregnant women who continue to abuse alcohol and describes the relative merits of incarceration, enforced sterilization when a mother bears more than one child with fetal alcohol syndrome and other possible solutions. Dorris, who is a supporter of legal abortion, argues that the child is unfairly damaged for life by the alcohol consumption of his or her birthmother.

Groups such as the American Civil Liberties Union fight against constraints on drug or alcohol-abusing pregnant women, fearing that the number of constraints could greatly increase and inhibit the pregnant woman's freedoms and also fearing that pregnant women with such problems will be less likely to seek treatment if they fear imprisonment or other actions. (See also ALCOHOL ABUSE AND ADOPTED PERSONS; DRUG ABUSE; GENETIC PREDISPOSITIONS.)

Nancy L. Day, Gale Richardson, Nadine Robles, Usha Sambamoorthi, Paul Taylor, Mark Scher, David Stoffer, Dorcie Jasperse and Marie Cornelius, "Effect of Prenatal Alcohol Exposure on Growth and Morphology of Offspring at 8 Months of Age," *Pediatrics*, vol. 85, May 1990, 748–752.

Michael Dorris, *The Broken Cord* (New York: Harper & Row, 1987).

Melvin D. Levine, M.D., William B. Carey, M.D., Allen C. Crocker, M.D., and Ruth T. Gross, M.D., editors, *Developmental-Behavioral Pediatrics* (Philadelphia: Saunders, 1983).

Patricia B. Mutch, "Infant Addicts: A Preventable Rage," *Vibrant Life*, May–June 1990.

Robert O'Brien and Morris Chafetz, M.D., *The Encyclopedia of Alcoholism* (New York: Facts On File, 1991).

Robert O'Brien and Sidney Cohen, M.D., *The Encyclopedia of Drug Abuse* (New York: Facts On File, 1984).

finalization The process in a court of law by which an adoption is decreed to be permanent and binding by a judge. After this point, it is extremely difficult to overturn an adoption unless fraud, duress, baby-selling or other allegations can be proven.

The day of finalization is an exciting day for the adoptive parents and for the adopted child as well (if the adopted child is old enough to understand what's going on).

The JUDGE reviews appropriate papers, recommendations from the social worker and other documents and approves the adoption in writing.

Subsequent to the court hearing, most states require the original birth certificate to become (SEALED RECORDS) and a new amended birth certificate will be issued with the adoptive parents' names as the parents.

foreign adoption See INTERNATIONAL ADOPTION.

forever family Term used by adoptive parents to describe themselves and their tie with their children and to emphasize the permanency aspect; often used by families who adopt children from countries outside the United States although also used by families who adopt older children and children with SPECIAL NEEDS.

foster care Generally refers to the system set up to protect children who are abused, neglected or abandoned or whose parents or primary caretakers are unable to fulfill their parenting obligations because of illness, emotional problems or a host of other reasons. In such latter cases, the placement into foster care by parents may have been voluntary.

Children who are involuntarily removed from their families are placed in the state's custody by the court and reside with foster parents or in GROUP HOMES or RESIDENTIAL TREATMENT CENTERS.

It should be noted that there is still much confusion in the general public about the difference between an adoptive home and a foster home. An adoptive family has the same parental rights and obligations as a birth family does when the child is born to them. A foster family must defer many decisions about a child's welfare to a state or county social worker. Although a child may remain in a foster home for years as a foster child, the state can (and has) removed foster children for a variety of reasons. An adopted child, however, can only be removed for the same reasons as a birth child.

It is also true that some private adoption agencies place children into their own approved "foster care" homes for a period of days, weeks or months, allowing birthparents to make final decisions about adoption and to sign consent forms prior to the time judges sign permanent termination of parental rights. Such families are generally not the families meant when the media discusses foster care, foster children and foster families, and private agency foster care is usually funded by the agency rather than by the state. The remainder of this essay refers solely to foster children in state care.

According to Toshio Tatara, Director of Research and Demonstration for the American Public Welfare Association (APWA), there were an estimated 360,000 children in the public welfare foster care system in the United States in 1989.

The Child Welfare League of America estimates about 25,175 children in foster care are waiting to be adopted. Of the children who enter foster care each year, the APWA estimates about 24% are "re-entrants" or "recidivists," which means children who have previously been in the foster care system, been reunited with their families or permanent caretakers and then returned to the foster care system.

According to a 1989 report from the Select Committee on Children, Youth, and Families in the U.S. House of Representatives, one recent change has been the younger age of children entering care; for example, in 1985, 37% of the children needing foster parents were under age six, but by 1988, 42% of the children entering foster care were under six years of age. In the state of Missouri, nearly half of the children entering foster care are under age six.

There are important implications to the age of the child in the foster care system. Studies have indicated that children who enter the foster care system as very young children are much more likely to become attached to their foster parents than are children who enter as older children. As a result, some social workers have urged that policy makers and judges also consider the child's own feelings of permanence and attachment to foster parents when making placement decisions.

The goal of virtually all foster care workers is to "reunite" the children with their birthparents or permanent caretakers, and that goal is achieved in an estimated 59% of the cases (although some of the children later re-enter the system).

Approximately 50% of all foster children in the United States are white, 33% are black, 7% are Hispanic, and the remaining children are of other racial backgrounds. The average age of foster children in care is about six years.

Based on data compiled by the National Committee for Adoption, about 55% of the

Est. No. of Foster Children

1985	276,000
1986	280,000
1987	293,000
1988	330,000
1989	360,000

Source: American Public Welfare Association, 1990.

foster children who are ultimately adopted are adopted by their foster parents.

Generally, healthy young white children are the most readily and rapidly placed in adoptive homes, while black children remain in the foster care system longer.

According to a study of factors that affect the length of a child's stay in foster care, predictors for a longer time in foster care were the following variables: The child had been abandoned; the child was black; the child was male; the child was physically or mentally impaired; or adoption was being planned. (One possible reason why children with pending adoptions remain longer is the length of time required to terminate parental rights in the court.)

Children tended to spend a shorter than normal time in foster care if the child was in care because of abuse or other problems in the parent-child relationship, the goal of the social services department was reunification, parental contact with the child continued or the social worker had a degree in social work.

The number of children in foster care increases each year. In fiscal year 1985, there were about 276,000 children in foster care, but the APWA estimates that the number grew to 360,000 by 1989.

Foster care is theoretically a temporary solution, and social workers should seek PERMANENCY PLANNING for a child. According to the ADOPTION ASSISTANCE AND CHILD WELFARE ACT OF 1980, a review by some administrative body should be conducted each six months, which determines whether the problem causing the child's removal from the home has been resolved and when the child could be expected to return home or be placed with guardians or adoptive parents. In addition, a court hearing regarding the child's status must be held after a child has been in foster care for 18 months. At this time, the court may decide to return the child to his or her home, retain the child in foster care, recommend the process of terminating parental rights be started or decide to delay action altogether.

States may have considerable difficulty complying with this 18 month timeframe. A recent General Accounting Office report revealed that no state has yet fully complied with this law (see previous reference). Nonetheless, the outdated philosophy of allowing foster children to remain in foster care until adulthood is no longer accepted.

It should be noted, however, that older children who probably could be placed with adoptive families may decide against adoption for themselves. (If a child is over a certain age, for example, 12 years in some states, he has the option of declining adoption.) In such a case, a legal guardianship or extended foster care may be feasible.

Although the length of time children spend in foster care has declined in recent years, most children still spend much longer than 18 months in a foster home or group home.

Foster care providers must be licensed, and a limit is set on the number of children that may be placed in a home; however, practicality often rules (see FOSTER PARENTS). If there are not enough licensed foster homes for the children coming into care, state social services workers may be forced to place additional children in a foster home on an emergency basis (a problem that may contribute to abuse or neglect by an overwhelmed foster parent).

The Process The child is removed from the parental or permanent caretaker on an emergency basis after abuse, neglect or abandonment has been substantiated and/or the child is perceived as at risk for being abused. (The process may be different when a parent voluntarily requests the child be placed in foster care, depending on state laws.)

The social worker will then request a court date, at which time the court will decide the conditions under which the child should return home or stay in foster care.

Rules on foster care vary from state to state, but federal regulations also apply; for example, the federal government requires that "reasonable efforts" be made to prevent a removal from the home.

Expenses of Caring for Foster Children
Foster parents receive a monthly stipend to cover the child's expenses, and this amount varies from state to state. Amounts also vary depending on the age of the child. According to the National Foster Parent Association, the national average for young children is $268; for "middle" children (about ages 9–12), it is $291; and for teenagers, it is $338.

Most foster parents consider this amount highly inadequate to cover all the child's expenses and often spend their own money to cover basic expenses for food and clothes.

In many cases, the child may arrive in a foster home with the clothes on her back and nothing else because of the hurried nature of the move. Foster parents often are not equipped with the child's family medical/genetic history. This can be a serious problem, and physicians such as Burton Sokoloff urge that adequate medical records, including immunizations, be maintained. According to Sokoloff, good records are essential, especially in medical emergency situations (such as, is the scar on a child with a "suspicious abdomen" from a previous appendectomy). He also urges that two medical records be kept: one by the foster parents and one by the social worker.

Foster children are usually on MEDICAID, and foster parents may use the Medicaid card to obtain health care for the child.

Behavior and Development Problems in Foster Care Very often ungrateful about being "saved" and resentful of the social worker, foster children will sometimes act out: ACADEMIC PROGRESS may plummet, the child may over- or under-eat, behave aggressively, withdraw and so forth. If at all possible, siblings are placed together in a foster home to reduce the stress of the move as much as possible. If there are many children in the family, the probability they will stay together in the same foster home is low.

Children from newborns to age 18 are foster children, and increasing numbers of infants are entering the system because of drug and crack cocaine use, AIDS in the birthparent and sometimes in the foster child and abandonment or neglect of infants. (See ABUSE; DRUG ABUSE)

Visitations with parents are usually arranged by social workers. REUNIFICATION attempts are mandated whenever possible by the federal government as well as by state governments. In addition, social workers also recognize from current research that children separated from their parents are at greater risk of developing weaker or delayed conscience development, problems with cause and effect reasoning, an inability to delay gratification, a lack of control of impulses, an inability to form lasting relationships and a host of other problems that could stem from removal from the family.

As a result, the child's social worker will attempt to arrange visits between the child and parents on a weekly basis or as frequently as is feasible. The child is likely to act out in the foster home after visits, but social workers generally believe that visits with parents are in the child's best interests.

Visits may be supervised visits in the social services office or visits with the child at the foster home, depending on the individual case.

Adoption of Foster Children If all attempts at reunification with the parents fail, adoption may be considered as the plan for the child. Parental rights will be legally terminated, and the child can then be adopted. In some cases, an AT RISK ADOPTION will occur: this means the child is placed in an adoptive home before parental rights are terminated, in the belief that such an action is in the child's best interests and that the rights will be severed by the court.

In an increasing number of cases, foster children are adopted by their foster parents or placed in a legal risk situation with a family interested in adoption at the beginning of foster care or placed with extended family, and thus there is no need to relocate the child to another home, another school, new parents or new friends.

If the foster parents do not wish to adopt the child or are inappropriate for some reason, the caseworker will seek an adoptive home for the child.

Recruitment for adoptive parents is achieved through MEDIA advertising, photolisting books and listings on state and national computer databanks. Many state social service agencies also offer picnics, bringing WAITING CHILDREN to the picnic in the hope the child and prospective parents may meet. In addition, the caseworker may already know a family who appears a good match for the child.

Most social workers seek to find a same-race match for a child and use TRANSRACIAL ADOPTION as a last resort, if at all.

Increasingly, older children and children with SPECIAL NEEDS are successfully placed with adoptive parents who may be older parents, single parents or parents with children in the home already. (See also DISRUPTION; FOSTER PARENTS; FOSTER PARENT ADOPTIONS; OLDER CHILD; SIBLINGS).

Alice Bussiere, "Children in Foster Care," *Youth Law News,* 1988 (special issue), 5–9.

Mark Hardin, editor, *Foster Children in the Courts* (Boston: Butterworth Legal Publishers, 1983).

House Select Committee on Children, Youth, and Families, *No Place to Call Home: Discarded Children in America,* 101st Cong., 1st sess., November 1989.

Florence Lieberman, D.S.W., Thomas K. Kenemore, Ph.D., and Diane Yost, M.S.W., *The Foster Care Dilemma* (New York: Human Sciences Press, 1987).

National Committee For Adoption, *Adoption Factbook,* (Washington, DC: National Committee For Adoption, 1985).

J. R. Seaberg and E. S. Tolley, "Predictors of the Length of Stay in Foster Care," *Social Work Research and Abstracts,* 22:3(1986): 11–17.

Burton Z. Sokoloff, "Adoption and Foster Care," in *Developmental-Behavioral Pediatrics* (Philadelphia: Saunders, 1983).

Wladyslaw Sluckin and Martin Herbert, eds., "Substitute Parenting" in *Parental Behaviour,* (United Kingdom and New York: Basil Blackwell, 1986).

foster parent An individual who cares for children on a temporary basis, which may mean days, weeks or months. In some cases, the child remains in the home for years, and the foster parents adopt him or her subsequent to termination of parental rights. Increasingly, for teenagers, legal guardianships may be used rather than adoption.

Most foster parents are under the jurisdiction of the state public welfare department; however, many private adoption agencies that arrange infant adoptions place the babies in temporary foster care until the birthparents are certain adoption is the best plan for them and the child. This type of foster care generally lasts only a few weeks or months at most.

Foster parents undergo some type of licensing and/or certification process and sometimes attend classes prior to receiving their first foster child. The home will also be inspected for cleanliness and safety.

In addition, foster parents for the state will have an ongoing relationship with the public welfare social worker in regards to the child's progress, future plans for the child and so forth. The foster parents may in fact wish to have more contact with the social worker than the worker can provide due to heavy caseloads.

According to British author M. Shaw, studies have revealed two primary motivations among people who become foster parents. Foster mothers who choose to become foster parents to infants and young children are primarily motivated by the personal satisfaction they obtain through mothering the children. Foster mothers who concentrate on fostering older children achieve more satisfaction from a feeling of performing a socially responsible and important job.

Yet there can be severe frustrations with fostering. Foster parents may feel disturbed by what they consider unfair intrusions into decisions affecting the child by social workers or the child's parents. Conversely, some foster parents complain that they receive inadequate support from social workers and the constant turnover of social workers makes it difficult to create a relationship with one social worker.

According to a 1989 report by the U.S. House of Representatives Select Committee on Children, Youth, and Families, the number of available foster parents is inadequate and rapidly shrinking. One problem is a lack of women remaining in the home and available to be foster mothers. Other serious problems are low reimbursements that do not cover the cost of the child's care, low status attributed to foster parents by much of society, difficulty in identifying medical care of the child, deficiencies in channels of communication with social workers and other problems (such as lack of respite or babysitting care so the foster parents can obtain some time to themselves).

The authors of *The Rights of Foster Parents* believe the foster care system is undergoing a "metamorphosis," as increasing responsibilities are shifted to foster parents. They believe that foster parents must be able to be part of the "casework team" and should be able to visit with the child's parents and help in monitoring the child's progress. Rather than foster parents being perceived by social workers as "clients" and part of the overall "problem," foster parents would prefer to be perceived as part of the solution and treated as such.

Foster parents receive a monthly payment for the foster child, ranging from about $145 to $508, with an average payment of $250. Most foster parents do not believe this amount covers all the expenses involved in caring for a child.

In recent years, foster parents were required to document their expenses on the child to avoid foster payments being considered as income, according to *The National Advocate,* a publication of the National Foster Parent Association.

The tax code was changed in 1986 to make payment to foster parents of children from a public agency or private nonprofit agency exempt from taxes. (The National Foster Parent Association recommends IRS Publication 920 as a reference for further information.)

The National Foster Parent Association Inc. is a support group for foster parents that provides legislative updates, a resource center, news from various regions and information on key issues. For further information, contact

National Foster Parent Association
226 Kilts Drive
Houston, TX 77024
713-467-1850

(See also FOSTER CARE; FOSTER PARENT ADOPTION.)

Robert Horowitz, Mark Hardin and Josephine Bulkley, *The Rights of Foster Parents* (Washington, D.C.: American Bar Association, 1989).
House Select Committee on Children, Youth, and Families, *No Place to Call Home: Discarded Children in America,* 101st Cong., 1st sess., November 1989.
National Foster Parent Association Inc., "Foster Families and Federal Income Tax," *The National Advocate,* February/March 1990.
M. Shaw, "Substitute Parenting," in *Parental Behavior* (United Kingdom and New York: Basil Blackwell, 1986).

foster parent adoption The adoption of a child by his or her foster parent. Based on statistics compiled by the National Committee For Adoption, about 55% of foster children who are adopted are adopted by their foster parents. In many cases, the children have been living with the foster parents for years, and the foster parents are also the PSYCHOLOGICAL PARENTS.

It is probable this percentage will continue to increase, based on an attitude by social work professionals that moving a child is usually not in the best interest of a child.

In the recent past, social workers have begun attempting to place children with foster parents who would probably be suitable adoptive parents in the event that reunification efforts with the birth family fail.

Studies have also revealed that adoption disruptions are less likely in foster parent adoptions than in "new" parent adoptions. As a result, foster parents are more frequently considered as possible adoptive parent candidates than in past years.

Some states mandate foster parent consideration should the child become free for adoption; for example, according to the "Matrix of Adoption Laws" provided by the NATIONAL ADOPTION INFORMATION CLEARINGHOUSE, a licensed foster parent in South Dakota who has fostered a child for two or more years has first priority for adopting the child.

The state of Missouri gives foster parents who have fostered for more than 18 months first preference if the child becomes available for adoption. New Jersey gives foster parents first priority of they've been foster parents to the child for two or more years, and Tennessee gives foster parents priority to adopt if they've fostered the child for at least one year.

In Alaska, foster parents who have fostered a child for more than one year and who adopt the child are entitled by statute to an adoption subsidy. (See also FOSTER CARE; FOSTER PARENTS; SPECIAL NEEDS.)

foundations Endowed institutions that usually award project or study grants on a wide variety of social problems. Unfortunately, very few foundations have been formed to study or relate to the subject of adoption, and when adoption is addressed, SPECIAL NEEDS ADOPTIONS are almost invariably the only subject covered. This is very unfortunate because many social problems are related to and could be ameloriated by adoption, for example, teenage pregnancy, welfare dependency and infertility.

Some foundations are actually adoption agencies that prefer to use the word "foundation" in the name of their agency.

William Pierce, "Taking Adoption Seriously," *Philanthropy*, May–June 1989 9–10.

full disclosure adoption See OPEN ADOPTION.

G

gay and lesbian adoption Whether or not a person who is gay or lesbian is allowed to adopt depends on laws of the state where she or he lives, and such adoptions are at the center of much controversy. The recent WHITE HOUSE TASK FORCE ON ADOPTION declined to recommend adoption by gays and lesbians, and many religious groups oppose such adoptions.

New Hampshire and Florida ban adoption by homosexuals altogether as not in "the best interests of the child," while other states do not mention sexual preference criteria for eligibility to adopt. Consequently, a homosexual person may theoretically adopt. The state's "public policy" may decree against it, however; for example, a court decided in a 1988 case in Ohio that such a placement of a seven-year-old boy was not in concert with public policy. In 1991, Florida law was challenged by a South Florida man, and a circuit court declared the law to be discriminatory. This case did not overturn state law, although it could be cited in other cases. Only if the Florida Supreme Court or the state legislature overturned the law would it be removed, according to Linda Harris, acting counsel to the Florida Department of

Health and Rehabilitative Services (HRS). As of this writing, neither has occurred.

In a 1986 Arizona case, a bisexual man was denied the certification needed to adopt, primarily because of his sexual orientation. The court in that case indicated that a homosexual person would automatically be denied a preplacement certificate, although apparently a bisexual could be considered.

Even if the state court has not ruled on the issue of gay and lesbian adoptions, it is likely that some individual social workers who disapprove of gays because of their sexual orientation will find other reasons to reject their applications to adopt.

The issue of gay and lesbian adoptions became a very major issue in Massachusetts in 1985 after a story appeared in the *Boston Globe* about a gay couple who wished to adopt their foster children. The Department of Social Services withdrew the children and created a policy that foster parents should be chosen in the following order: (1) married heterosexual couples experienced in raising children, (2) married heterosexual couples without parenting experience (3) single parents or unmarried couples and (4) gay or lesbian singles or couples.

In addition, the Massachusetts legislature enacted an amendment to the state budget that banned the Department of Social Services from placing a child for adoption with a homosexual person other than the biological parent. The legislature said that "a homosexual preference shall be considered a threat to the psychological and physical well-being of a child."

When the partner of a homosexual or bisexual person wishes to adopt a biological child of one of them or they both wish together to adopt an unrelated child, they will often encounter difficulties. For example, some states require a biological mother to relinquish her parental rights before another woman can adopt her child; however, a lesbian mother would not wish to sign consent but would prefer to share parenting with her partner.

In a few cases cited by attorney Emily C. Patt, the biological parent retained parental rights while at the same time an unrelated person was allowed to adopt the child. As a result, a child can have a biological parent and a "psychological parent" as well.

In a 1985 Alaska case, *Adoption of a Minor Child,* a minor child's GUARDIAN AD LITEM recommended that a lesbian couple be allowed to adopt a child they had both parented since birth. The adoption was allowed because the court determined the mother's lesbian relationship was not a factor in whether she would be a good parent. Same-sex couples have also been allowed to adopt in California and Oregon.

Increasingly, both gay and lesbian parents are permitted to become adoptive parents, although in the vast majority of cases, it is one of the partners who adopts rather than both.

Attorney Shaista-Parveen Ali believes adoption law has lagged behind child custody law, and many states are still making it difficult for gays and lesbians to adopt, even when it is legal for them to do so. "Adoption agencies and courts still give undue weight to sexual orientation, and some absolutely bar homosexuals from adopting children," Ali said.

Ali lists five major categories of preconceptions about homosexuals that make it difficult or impossible for them to adopt:

1. Courts may believe homosexuals are mentally ill and unstable.
2. Courts may believe homosexuals will molest their children.
3. Courts may believe homosexuals will raise their children to be homosexual.
4. Courts may believe the child will be exposed to AIDS.
5. Courts may believe the child will be subjected to criticism from peers and others as a direct result of the parent being homosexual.

Ali says the first four preconceptions are based on wrong ideas and stereotypes and should be ignored. Ali then discusses studies and some basic common sense to refute the stereotypes; for example, most homosexuals were raised by heterosexual parents and were not somehow converted to homosexuality by their parents. In addition, child molestation appears to be more prevalent among heterosexuals than homosexuals. The social stigma argument is the only valid factor to consider, according to Ali.

There are three other major obstacles to gays or lesbians wishing to adopt: the marriage requirement for many adoptive parents, state antisodomy laws and the stereotypical, in the case of gays, idea that men cannot be nurturing.

Because gays and lesbians cannot legally marry, they are precluded from meeting that criteria. Ali cites the Massachusetts law, which prohibits marriage between homosexuals and has a direct preference for married couples as adoptive parents.

In addition, antisodomy laws are on the books in almost half of the states in the United States. Even when homosexuals are not currently involved in a sexual relationship, it is often presumed that they will at some time in the future resume sexual activities that are illegal according to state statutes.

The stereotype that men cannot be nurturing has also affected heterosexual men. (See SINGLE ADOPTIVE PARENTS.) In one case, an adoption agency turned down a married couple because the husband wished to stay home while the wife worked.

Shaista-Parveen Ali, "Homosexual Parenting: Child Custody and Adoption," *University of California, Davis,* 22 (1989): 1009–1038.

Joan H. Hollinger, editor-in-chief, *Adoption Law and Practice* (New York: Matthew Bender, 1989).

Emily C. Patt, "Second Parent Adoption: When Crossing the Marital Barrier Is in a Child's Best Interests," *Berkeley Women's Law Journal,* 3(1987–88): 96–132.

gender preference International and domestic adoption agencies report a very strong preference of adopting parents in the United States to adopt girls, whether they are childless couples or individuals or whether they already have children. This sex preference is seen in adopting parents of all races, socioeconomic statuses and ages.

Many domestic adoption agencies, however, refuse to allow adoptive parents to make a sex preference on their first child. If the parents wish to adopt again at a later date, the agency may sometimes allow the parents to express a sex preference then. If a family already has three boys or three girls and the agency allows them to adopt again, the agency will usually be far more amenable to the family adopting a child of the opposite sex than they now parent. Thus, the manifestation of this preference can be most clearly charted in INTERNATIONAL ADOPTIONS.

In her 1988 doctoral dissertation, which drew on the Korean-American adoption studies of Dr. Dong Soo Kim, Lois Lydens explained why her longitudinal data included 73% females: "Kim (1976) attributed this gender imbalance to the Korean cultural preference toward male children and the corresponding preference of many American parents to adopt girls."

Cosette Dahlstrom, points out in the 1990 Report on Foreign Adoption that the adoption agency Adoption Services of WACAP (Western Association of Concerned Adoptive Parents) receives far more requests from individuals seeking to adopt girls than for people wishing to adopt boys, whether the family wants to adopt a baby or older child. According to Dahlstrom, in one program there was one family wanting to adopt a boy for every five families wanting to adopt a girl. In a program for black families, there were several families seeking to adopt girls and none seeking to adopt boys.

The reverse is generally true when people have biological children: Most want a boy to be their first child. According to the article by Dahlstrom, Dr. Nancy Williamson of the Population Council reviewed preferences of biological parents in 1976 and concluded:

1. For an only child, 90% of men and 67% of women would choose a boy.
2. 80% of both parents prefer to have a boy as their first born child.
3. For a three-child family, most prefer two boys and one girl.

There are many theories on why adoptive parents tend to prefer to adopt girls. One theory is that girls are perceived as easier to raise than boys, and adoptive parents prefer that things go smoothly. They may have an unrealistic image of a cute little girl in a frilly dress, beaming at them and obeying every command.

Males, however, are perceived as more aggressive, getting into fights as boys, and are viewed as far less passive and submissive. Apparently, these are positive traits in a biological child but less positive to those who prefer to adopt a female child.

Female children may also appeal to the protective and altruistic side of people, and it is possible that adoptive parents have a higher level of such feelings than the average person, particularly, in the case of INTERNATIONAL ADOPTIONS. Male children don't fulfill this protective instinct as effectively as female children, at least in the abstract and the perception of many people planning to adopt.

Some families have stated that the clothes are much more attractive for girls than for boys. Needless to say, such a petty reason for adopting should not be the only reason to want to parent.

Carrying on the family name is an important reason for many biological families wishing to bear male children; however, sometimes the family is opposed to adoption and opposed to an adopted male child with no genetic connectedness to the family carrying on the family name.

Other reasons include the expectation that a girl will stay closer to the family even after marriage and the fact that society permits a more open show of affection toward female children.

Extended family support may be much stronger when the family adopts a girl for many of the reasons described here, and the adopting family may realize, consciously or unconsciously, that an adopted female would be more accepted than an adopted male.

The gender preference of adoptive parents in international adoption may also derive from the expectation of parents who believe females from other parts of the world can blend in with American society easier than a male.

Adoptive parents may think that boys adopted from abroad tend to be shorter and thinner than American boys and would be teased about their appearance by other schoolchildren, especially the boys. Petite and dainty girls, however, are seen in a positive light.

This sexist preference, when it exists, presents a particular problem to international adoption agencies and children abroad, because many people in other lands have an even more pronounced protective and positive preference for females than for male children.

Females are to be protected, while males are expected to fend for themselves. Females are economically more valuable: They can ultimately serve as maids and perform other menial tasks, whereas boys are often seen as a burden on their societies. As a result, at many international agencies male infants and older children are more readily available for adoption, and prospective adoptive parents who want to adopt females face a longer waiting period.

In the case of an independent or an open adoption, a particular family is usually matched to a particular pregnant woman, so it is very seldom that a family is offered a sex preference. However, many obstetricians routinely perform ultrasound examinations, which often detect the sex of a child. Ultrasound examinations are not, however, totally reliable in this regard: Many "girls" turn out to be boys at birth.

Christine Adamec, "Adopt a Boy," *OURS*, July/August 1988, 30–31.

Mary Ann Curran and Sue Eipert, "Wanted: An E.R.A. for Boys," *OURS*, September/October: 1983.

Cosette Dahlstrom, "Being a Boy Means Hard to Place," *Report on Foreign Adoption, 1990* (Boulder, Co.: International Concerns Committee for Children, 1990).

Lois Lydens, "A Longitudinal Study of Crosscultural Adoption: Identity Development Among Asian Adoptees at Adolescence and Early Adulthood," Ph.D diss., Northwestern University, 1988.

genetic data Information given to adopting parents so they may provide appropriate care for the child. When the child is an adult, they may give him or her the information to assist with future plans, offspring which may be born and so forth.

Researchers asked social workers at public agencies in all 50 states if systematically collected genetic data should be shared with an adoptive family or with an adopted adult. Their results were reported in the January 1990 issue of the *American Journal of Human Genetics*. They also sought to define problems associated with collecting genetic data.

Follow-up data included there was an interest among the majority of the state agencies in developing a standard of genetic data. Many agency personnel indicated a strong need to receive information on genetics: 80% of the respondents expressed an "intermediate to great" need for education. The authors pointed to several existing programs. For example, a 1984 Wisconsin program was a one and one-half day program covering "Genetic Family History: An Aid to Better Health in Adoptive Children." A University of Colorado program created for public health nurses, "Genetic Applications: A Health Perspective," is considered appropriate for other "health professionals."

Many states have already addressed the issue of collecting genetic data. For example, in Wisconsin, the law mandates the collection of genetic information. In Arizona, California, Hawaii, Idaho, Iowa, Kansas, Louisiana, Maine, Minnesota, New Jersey, New York, Ohio, Oregon, South Carolina and Texas, state law requires that genetic information be requested by social workers.

Two potential problems in gathering and disseminating data were identified as maintaining confidentiality and gathering data for adoptive parents when the child was a foster child with an inadequate family history.

In their paper for adoption workers, Julia B. Rauch, Ph.D. and assistant professor at the School of Social Work and Community Planning at the University of Maryland, and Nancy Rike, M.S., M.S.W., and genetic counselor at the Greater Baltimore Medical Center, discuss why genetic services are important. They list primary reasons for collecting data and providing such data: to reply to adopting parents and answer their questions; to assist the social worker and the adopting parent in determining whether they can parent a child; to make adopting parents aware of potential health problems, such as cancer or diabetes, so they can provide good health care; to meet the information needs of children who are handicapped or ill; and finally to try to avoid WRONGFUL ADOPTION situations.

Information should be gathered from the birthmother on herself and as many other family members as possible, including both birthparents, grandparents, full and half-siblings and other family members. The authors recommend specific questions be asked and offer a "Family Genetic History" questionnaire.

Adopting parents should be told if the child has a genetic disorder or has a probability of developing a disorder, whether the disorder is medical, psychiatric, behavioral or another problem that could be inherited.

The authors also recommend that after the adoption, if birthparents discover genetic information that could impact the adopted child, they should provide such information to the agency. Conversely, if the adoptive parents discover the child has a disease or problem with a possible genetic link, they too should inform the agency so the birthparents can be notified. (See also GENETIC PREDISPOSITIONS; MEDICAL HISTORY.)

Organizations that may assist with information on genetic disorders are

National Center for Education in Maternal and Child Health (NC EMCH)
38th and R Sts. NW
Washington, DC 20057

Diane Plumridge, Joan Burns and Nancy L. Fisher, "ASHG Activities Relative to Education. Heredity and Adoption: A Survey of State Adoption Agencies," *American Journal of Human Genetics,* 46 (January 1990): 208–214.

Julia B. Rauch, Ph.D., and Nancy Rike, M.S., M.S.W., *Adoption Workers' Guide to Genetic Services,* (Chelsea, Mich: National Resource Center for Special Needs Adoption, n.d.).

genetic fingerprinting A technique that analyzes genetic material (DNA) for a variety of purposes, including paternity, evidence of rape by a particular person and other uses.

The technique, developed by Dr. Alec Jeffreys, a genetics professor at the University of Leicester in England, was created in 1984. Prior to that time, it was possible to determine who might have fathered a child and who could not have fathered a child, but no overwhelming paternal evidence existed. Genetic fingerprinting provides a certainty of paternity in an estimated 99% of the cases in which the biological father has been tested and has successfully been used in many paternity lawsuits nationwide.

The relevance of genetic fingerprinting to adoption is that if a birthmother wishes to plan adoption for her child but a man who alleges he is the father tries to block the adoption, genetic testing can prove whether or not the man is actually the biological father.

If she is not married to the man and he is not the biological father, his claims are generally considered less valid than if he is the biological father. (In some cases, the law takes into account an existing relationship a minor has with a parent figure.)

If the birthmother is married, the law generally presumes her husband is the father of her child, although genetic testing may refute this presumption.

Genetic testing can also be used to determine custody when various men contend they are the father of the child. A current television program that depicts two fathers raising a girl because it is unknown who is her "real" father and her mother has died is unrealistic. Few judges would allow custody of a minor to two unrelated males, nor would they forego genetic testing to determine biological fatherhood.

If a woman alleges she has been raped, the perpetrator of the rape may be identified through genetic fingerprinting. If the woman becomes pregnant and bears a child and then chooses adoption for her child, the identities of the birthmother and rapist birthfather will be sealed in the overwhelming majority of cases.

genetic parents The individuals who together conceive a child; this term is generally used to refer to the genetic parents of an adopted child. More popularly used descriptive terms are "birthparents" or "biological parents" of a child. Sometimes the term "genetic parents" is contrasted to the term "psychological parents." The psychological parents are the individuals the child mentally and emotionally identifies as parents. (See also BIRTHPARENT; PSYCHOLOGICAL PARENT.)

genetic predispositions Children inherit many traits from their birthparents, including eye color, hair color, potential physical build, potential talents and others. In addition, children may also inherit propensities to certain genetically transmitted diseases, such as diabetes or Huntington's disease.

Not all predispositions are clearcut, and researchers believe genetics cause or may impact on such areas as personality and behavior. Studies of twins separated at birth and studies of adopted children and their birth and adoptive families have revealed a variety of possible inherited predispositions.

Some predispositions are far more apparent than others, and it is often difficult to tell where heredity ends and environment begins: The nature-nurture argument is likely to continue for many years. Also, in many cases, information on the birthfather has been unavailable, which is a limitation on the research.

Researchers have found some evidence of linkages in both medical/behavioral problems of the birthparent and adopted child. (See also ALCOHOL ABUSE AND ADOPTED PERSONS; CRIMINAL BEHAVIOR IN ADOPTED ADULTS.)

In addition, the tendency to develop some psychiatric ailments, such as schizophrenia, may be genetically transmitted; however, studies that have analyzed noninstitutionalized adopted individuals in the general population reveal no significant differences in the psychological adjustment levels of the adopted individuals and nonadopted individuals.

In a comprehensive article on the genetic factors related to psychiatric disorders reported in the *Journal of Child Psychology and Psychiatry,* the authors reported on a study that found a correlation between schizophrenia in siblings. The study by Kety, Rosenthal, Wender, Schulsinger and Jacobsen in 1975 found "13% of paternal half-siblings of adopted schizophrenics, compared with only 2% of control half-siblings, were diagnosed as being schizophrenic."

Yet later studies revealed environment was important, and a dysfunctional family influence could also be tied to the development of schizophrenia.

Other genetic predispositions have been demonstrated; for example, indications of a predisposition to obesity has been shown to exist among full and half-siblings raised apart.

Researchers P. Costanzo and S. Schiffman disagreed in their 1989 article for *Neuroscience Biobehavior Review* and argue that it is thin stature that is inherited rather than a predisposition to be obese.

Premature death of birthparents has also been correlated to premature death in their offspring. Researchers studied 960 families that included nonrelated children who had been adopted and who were born between 1924 and 1926 and computed the risk of the adopted persons' early deaths. (The researchers used data available from adopted Danes, predominantly Caucasians.)

According to their report in the *New England Journal of Medicine,* the researchers concluded that death from such diseases as cancer appears to be affected by the environment of the family. Premature deaths caused by infection or vascular causes, however, showed clear genetic links.

Early deaths of adoptive parents were also found to be significant to the longevity of adopted persons. If an adoptive parent died of cancer before age 50, the risk of the adopted person also dying from cancer increased by five times. This information indicates a strong environmental and lifestyle element at work in the case of cancer, for example, whether or not the adoptive parents are smokers.

Conversely, it would seem to be significant to the health of the children if the adoptive parents themselves lead a healthful life, for example, do not smoke, exercise regularly and eat a nutritious diet.

Some researchers also have identified a strong heritability of general mental ability and intelligence. (See also INTELLIGENCE.)

The Colorado Adoption Project is a longitudinal study of 245 adopted children, their adoptive parents and birthparents. The children were studied at ages one, two, three, four and seven years of age.

At ages one and two, the children were given the Bayley Scales of Infant Development. At ages three and four, the Stanford-Binet Intelligence Scale-Form was administered. At age seven, the researchers used the

Wechsler Intelligence Scale for Children-Revised.

The researchers reported on their findings in *Nature*, stating there were strong indicators of a relationship of intelligence to the birthparents, which increased as the child grew older. Apparently, adoptive parents have a strong impact on a child's intellectual level in the early years, and genetics "kick in" at a later date.

Researchers on the Texas Adoption Project, a study of children measured twice at ten year intervals, also found an increased heritability of intelligence, a relationship that strengthened until adolescence or even adulthood.

In a longitudinal study of 100 identical twins raised apart, the Minnesota Study, the researchers found a strong correlation for intelligence and other traits; however, they do not denigrate the value of environment and good parenting skills.

It will be interesting to note if this increasing relationship of mental ability between the adopted child and birthparent will continue, level off or increase as the children mature, and it is hoped that longitudinal studies will continue.

There have also been studies comparing the IQ levels of children who have been adopted to their half-siblings who were raised by birthparents. A study by Schiff and Lewontin in 1986 compared the IQ levels of adopted children whose birthmothers were "socially disadvantaged" to the IQ levels of half-siblings raised by the birthmother. They found the adopted children scored as much as 16 points higher in IQ levels than did the siblings who remained with the birthmother.

The physical activity level of the adopted person appears to be at least partially affected by genetics. One study revealed the type of exercise was dependent on the environment; however, the overall level of the adopted person's physical activity was significantly related to the physical activity level of the birthparent.

One might conclude that instead of choosing bowling or football, an adopted child might opt for swimming or tennis or whatever sport fits in best with the socioeconomic status of the adoptive parents.

A study by Cunningham, Cadoret, Loftus and Edwards in 1975 determined that hyperactivity was more common in adopted children with mentally ill birthparents than in adopted children whose parents suffered no psychosis (14% versus 2%). The percentage of hyperactivity was also increased (based on other studies) when a sibling was severely hyperactive.

It is important to note that scientists who have studied adopted persons and genetic predispositions have concentrated their efforts in studying problem areas, such as alcoholism, criminality and psychiatric problems.

Scientists have not dedicated much research to the study of physical attractiveness, sense of humor, artistic or musical ability or athletic prowess among adopted individuals. Creativity and other positive predispositions that could possibly be inherited by many adopted children have not yet been researched to a significant degree.

It must also be stressed that an alcoholic birthmother, criminal birthfather or schizophrenic birthparent does not automatically doom an adopted child to a future life as an alcoholic, criminal or mentally ill person.

Most scientists agree that both heredity and environment are important to a child's development. In addition, even when heredity is significant, the genetic markers cannot always be identified nor can the interaction of heredity and environment be clearly delineated.

Because some genetic predispositions can be very important to a child's future, it should be mandated that child-placing agencies and adoption attorneys learn as much as possible about birthparents so both nonidentifying medical and social information can be provided to the adoptive parents.

In addition, adopted adults in numerous studies have stated their desire for medical information, hobbies and interests of birthparents, so obviously the information would be valuable to them. Whether the adoption is a traditional confidential adoption or an open adoption, such information should be obtained from the birthparents.

It is important, however, to remember that many children who were adopted in the past, as now, did not come with this genetic and other information as part of their "passports." Orphaned children and foundlings can make excellent adjustments despite the lack of this information.

Also, most qualified medical practitioners realize the skills of testing and diagnosis, rather than a heavy reliance on detailed medical background information, are what is needed to provide sound medical care for their patients. Parents should be cautious if confronted by medical or other professionals who claim they can't help or treat the parents' child without such genetic and background information. (See also ADOLESCENT ADOPTED PERSONS; ADULT ADOPTED PERSONS; GENETIC DATA; PATHOLOGY AND ADOPTIVE STATUS; PSYCHIATRIC PROBLEMS OF ADOPTED PERSONS.)

Thomas J. Bouchard Jr., David T. Lykken, Matthew McGue, Nancy J. Segal and Auke Tellegen, "Sources of Human Psychological Differences: The Minnesota Study of Twins Reared Apart," *Science,* 250(October 12, 1990).

P. R. Costanzo and S. Schiffman, "Thinness—Not Obesity—Has a Genetic Component," *Neuroscience Biobehavior Review,* Spring 1989, 55–58.

D. W. Fulker, J. C. DeFries, and Robert Plomin, "Genetic Influence on General Mental Ability Increases Between Infancy and Middle Childhood," *Nature,* 336(December 1988): 767–769.

H. H. Goldsmith, "Genetic Influences on Personality from Infancy to Adulthood," *Child Development,* 54(1983): 331–355.

Joseph M. Horn, "The Texas Adoption Project: Adopted Children and Their Intellectual Resemblance to Biological and Adoptive Parents," *Child Development,* 54(1983): 268–275.

John C. Loehlin, Joseph M. Horn and Lee Willerman, "Modeling IQ Change: Evidence from the Texas Adoption Project," *Child Development,* 60(1989): 993–1004.

Harry Munsinger, "The Adopted Child's IQ: A Critical Review," *Psychological Bulletin* 82(September 1975), 623–659.

Herbert Pardes, M.D., Charles A. Kaufmann, M.D., Harold Alan Pincus, M.D., and Anne West, "Genetics and Psychiatry: Past Discoveries, Current Dilemmas, and Future Directions," *The American Journal of Psychiatry,* April 1989, 434–443.

L. Pérusse, A. Tremblay, C. Leblanc and C. Bouchard, "Genetic and Environmental Influences on Level of Habitual Physical Activity and Exercise Participation," *American Journal of Epidemiology,* 129(May 1989): 1012–1022.

Robert Plomin and J. C. DeFries, "The Colorado Adoption Project," *Child Development,* 54(1983): 276–289.

Michael Rutter, Patrick Bolton, Richard Harrington, Ann Le Couteur, Hope Macdonald and Emily Simonoff, "Genetic Factors in Child Psychiatric Disorders—I. A Review of Research Strategies," *The Journal of Child Psychology and Psychiatry and Allied Disciplines,* 31(January 1990) 3–37.

Michael Rutter, Hope Macdonald, Ann Le Couteur, Richard Harrington, Patrick Bolton and Anthony Bailey, "Genetic Factors in Child Psychiatric Disorders—II. Empirical Findings," *The Journal of Child Psychology and Psychiatry and Allied Disciplines,* 31(January 1990) 39–83.

Sandra Scarr, Patricia L. Webber, Richard A. Weinberg and Michele A. Wittig, "Personality Resemblance Among Adolescents and Their Parents in Biologically Related and Adoptive Families," *Journal of Personality and Social Psychology,* 40(1981): 885–898.

Sandra Scarr and Richard Weinberg, "The Minnesota Adoption Studies: Genetic Differences and Malleability," *Child Development,* 54(1983), 260–267.

M. Schiff and R. Lewontin, *Education and Class: The Irrelevance of IQ Genetic Studies* (Oxford: Clarendon Press, 1986).

Thoorkild I. A. Sørensen, R. Arlen Price, Albert J. Stunkard and Fini Schulsinger, "Genetics of Obesity in Adult Adoptees and Their Biological Siblings," *British Medical Journal,* 298(January 14): 1989, 87–90.

T. I. Sørensen, G. G. Nielsen, P. K. Andersen and T. W. Teasdale, "Genetic and Environmental Influences on Premature Death in Adult Adoptees," *New England Journal of Medicine,* 318(March 24, 1988): 727–732.

T. W. Teasdale and T. I. A. Sorenson, "Educational Attainment and Social Class in Adoptees: Genetic and Environmental Contributions," *Journal of Biosocial Science,* 15(1983): 509–518.

girls, adoptive parents' preference for
See GENDER PREFERENCES.

Gladney Center, The   See EDNA GLADNEY CENTER, THE.

grandparent   In adoption, refers to parents of adoptive parents, who become grandparents after the adoption occurs, just as children already in the home (or children who come later, either by birth or by adoption) become siblings of the adopted child. (Grandparents of children who are placed for adoption are called "birthgrandparents.") Some biological grandparents adopt their grandchildren. (See GRANDPARENT ADOPTIONS and RELATIVE ADOPTIONS).

The most famous grandparents in the United States are the "First Grandparents": President and Mrs. Bush, who are grandparents to two adopted children.

The grandparent relationship is very important to the child, and most grandparents are fully loving and accepting; however, there are still some individuals who believe only a genetic relationship is significant or valid.

A minority of adoptive parents find examples of discrimination; for example, their parents give gifts only to children born to the family, ignoring adopted children.

Grandparents may express reservations about illegitimacy, having been raised to think of children born out of wedlock in a negative way. Experts advise parents to speak to their parents about any inequities in treatment of the child. In fact, it is preferable if adopting parents discuss grandparenthood with their parents before the child is actually adopted.

If grandparents continue to exhibit negative behavior, parents may need to restrict the number of visits unless or until the grandparents realize their behavior is unfair.

Grandparents may have mixed feelings about an adopted child, and parents must also cope with this problem. Authors and therapists Judith Schaffer and Christina Lindstrom, in their book *How to Raise an Adopted Child,* advise parents to plan family outings that include grandparents, such as trips to the zoo.

The authors also recommend introducing the grandparents to other adoptive grandparents or asking the spouse's parents to speak to them.

Author and therapist Stephanie Siegel devotes a chapter of her book *Parenting Your Adopted Child* to adoptive grandparents. Siegel encourages grandparents to realize that families with adopted children have similarities and differences from families with children born to them, but this should not affect the grandparenting role.

To help grandparents adjust to grandparenthood, author Jamie Calvin has recommended that adoptive parents take them to an adoptive parent support group meeting, give them a subscription to an adoptive parent magazine, such as *OURS,* and provide them with at least one book or other informational resource on adoption.

In most cases, grandparents who expressed serious reservations about adoption are ultimately won over, once they have had a chance to interact with the child and sufficient time to adjust. (See also BIRTHGRANDPARENT.)

Jamie Calvin, "Help Grandma Prepare for Adoption," *OURS,* March/April 1990, 14–16.

Judith Schaffer and Christina Lindstrom, *How to Raise an Adopted Child* (New York: Crown 1989).

Stephanie E. Siegel, Ph.D. *Parenting Your Adopted Child* (New York: Prentice Hall Press, 1989).

grandparent adoptions It is not known how many grandparents have adopted their biological grandchildren, but laws in many states ease the way for RELATIVE ADOPTIONS. Most states waive the requirements for a HOME STUDY and also waive age criteria and other requirements used for nonrelative adoptions.

Grandparents may adopt for a variety of reasons. The birthmother may be a teenager and unready or unwilling to parent her child, while the grandparent is young enough to handle the task. Some grandparents who adopt their grandchildren are probably about the same age as adoptive parents who adopt nonrelatives—in their late thirties or early forties.

The birthmother may have abandoned a child or children to the custody of grandparents, and such situations are increasingly more common with the rise of cocaine and crack cocaine abuse. (See DRUG ABUSE.)

Grandparents in some states are given special adoption rights; for example, in Florida, grandparents have first preference to adopt a grandchild if the child has lived with them for at least six months. In Maryland, the consent of the birthparents to adoption may not be required if the child has lived with relatives for at least a year. And in Georgia, a blood relative may file an objection to an adoption if both biological parents have died.

If the birthmother remains in the home with the grandparents and adopted child, the situation may be different or awkward. In the past, some grandparents who raised an adopted child as their own biological child did not tell the child he or she was adopted, and the child grew up thinking his birthmother was his sister. The actor Jack Nicholson has talked about such a situation in his own case.

Experts today urge candor with adopted persons and believe it is better for an adopted man or woman to know as much as possible about his or her heritage (especially that he or she was adopted) rather than learning the information from a third party outside the family.

Because single parenthood is far more socially acceptable now than 20 or 30 years ago, many a young woman who becomes pregnant chooses to raise the child herself or place the child for adoption rather than pretend the child is actually her parents' child.

The difficulties of a RELATIVE ADOPTION exist when a grandparent adopts a child. Most of the family is aware of the adoption and may approve or disapprove very actively.

In addition, the family may consider the child to be "really" the birthmother's child rather than the child of the adoptive parents, although this situation is less likely than when the child is adopted by an aunt or a cousin, probably because of the closeness of the relationship.

grandparent rights In a few states, grandparents and relatives are given special rights and may adopt their grandchildren without the consent of the birthparents. (See GRANDPARENT ADOPTIONS.)

According to attorney Jody George in an article published in *Children Today,* 19 states require continuation of visitation rights despite adoption by a STEPPARENT; however, when the child is adopted by a nonrelative, in most cases it is presumed there will be no further contact between birthgrandparent and child, and courts have upheld this termination of grandparental rights.

Jody George, Esq., "Children and Grandparents: The Right to Visit," *Children Today,* November–December 1988, 14–18.

grief See LOSS.

group homes Residential facilities for children. Group homes may receive funding from state or federal sources, or they may be privately funded by religious organizations or donations from various groups. Some group homes receive a mixture of federal, state and private funding. The children may be foster children, or they may be children who have been placed in the group home voluntarily by parents.

Group homes usually house children over age five and provide temporary shelter for emergency situations or long-term shelter for hard to place children, such as teenagers or large sibling groups. Some children may have experienced adoption disruptions and need a group environment rather than a foster home environment because of the pain of loss and the acting out behavior of the child.

Once a popular solution for all children removed from the home or orphaned or abandoned, group homes have been heavily displaced by individual foster homes; however, the entry of increasing numbers of children into the foster care system has made social worker experts reconsider the group home as an appropriate answer for housing children. (See also FOSTER CARE.)

Children who have been severely physically or sexually abused may not be able to fit into the family environment of a foster home and may instead need the facilities of a group home and readily available psychiatric counseling.

One national group that works to improve services to children in group homes or other institutions is the National Association of Homes for Children (NAHC). The NAHC can be reached at

National Association of Homes and Services for Children
1701 K St. NW, Suite 200,
Washington, DC 20006
(202) 223-3447

guardian ad litem An individual, usually an attorney, appointed by the court to represent a child's best interests, often in relation to CUSTODY. Social workers will present the state's view of who should be given custody, and parents may also retain attorneys to represent their rights.

The guardian ad litem may also be a lay person who is dedicated to helping children. The guardian is given information from social workers and other authorities and may perform additional investigations as needed before making a recommendation to the court.

According to Richard Podell, chairman of the American Bar Association family law section, the guardian ad litem "examines the child's long-term goals, emotional state, and preferences and presents an independent opinion to the court."

Podell says the guardian ad litem should contact attorneys to gather additional information from them and determine the status of the case and what problems exist. In addition, the guardian should also ask for copies of affidavits and pleadings related to the case.

The guardian should meet with the parents, making it clear that the guardian is not their attorney and information they provide will not be held in confidence. Other actions the guardian should take, according to Podell, are to determine and discuss parental views on custody and to gather background information on the child's education, activities, religion and other relevant factors.

The guardian ad litem should also investigate any possible problems that could harm the child, such as drug or alcohol abuse or the battering of a spouse, if the child were placed with the family. (See also FOSTER CARE; FOSTER PARENT.)

Richard J. Podell, "The Role of the Guardian Ad Litem: Advocating the Best Interests of the Child," *Trial*, April 1989, 31–34.

H

handicapped children See DEVELOPMENTAL DISABILITIES.

hard to place children This phrase, now out of favor among adoption professionals, has been replaced by "children who have SPECIAL NEEDS." Depending on the definition—and the definition varies from state to state and adoption program to adoption program—the category may include black and biracial children of all ages, sibling groups, healthy and intellectually normal children over age eight and physically or mentally handicapped children of all ages.

Many families are eager to adopt children with a variety of special needs, and children who were once considered UNADOPTABLE are now being placed in good families. (See also DEVELOPMENTAL DISABILITIES).

health insurance See INSURANCE.

heredity See GENETIC DATA; GENETIC PREDISPOSITIONS.

high risk placements Adoptive placements that have a high probability of DISRUPTION; almost exclusively refers to the placement of children with SPECIAL NEEDS who are older or who suffer medical or mental disabilities; not to be confused with AT RISK PLACEMENT.

The age at which a child is considered a high risk placement varies from state to state, but most states consider the placement of a teenager to have a high level of risk.

However, studies have revealed that children who are older when adopted can often successfully adjust to their new families, despite a troubled past that might include abuse and neglect. Also, there is a positive relationship between large family size and the success of the placement.

Hispanics/Latinos Many U.S. adoptive parents adopt children from Latin America; in addition, Hispanic and Latino children are also available to be adopted in such states as Texas, New York, Florida, California and other states with large Hispanic populations. Most adoptive parents are probably not of Hispanic or Latino ancestry.

Most agencies are willing to place Hispanic children with non-Hispanic families, although some agencies make a concerted effort to place Hispanic children only in Hispanic homes of a similar culture, race and physical appearance.

A study of transethnically adopted Hispanic children was undertaken by Estela Andujo. Andujo studied 30 Anglo families who adopted Mexican-American children and 30 Mexican-American families who adopted Mexican-American children, both groups in the Los Angeles, California area. She found no differences in the self-esteem levels of the children in either group; however, she did find differences in how the children perceived themselves, with the children raised in Anglo families identifying more with their white parents and identifying less with the Mexican-American community. (See also INTERNATIONAL ADOPTION.) Resources for Hispanic children include

Hispanic Adoption Program
New York Council on Adoptable Children
666 Broadway, Suite 820
New York, NY 10012
(212) 475-0222

National Coalition of Hispanic Mental
  Health and Human Services Organization
1015 15th St. NW, Suite 402
Washington, DC 20005
(202) 638-0505

Puerto Rican Association for Family Affairs Inc.
853 Broadway, 5th Floor
New York, NY 10003
(212) 673-7320

Estela Andujo, "Ethnic Identity of Transethnically Adopted Hispanic Adolescents," *Social Work*, 33(November/December 1988): 531–535.

homeless children The increasing problem of homelessness has received much media attention. Some experts accuse the social service system of increasing the burden on the state by taking custody of children away from parents living in places such as in cars or on the streets and placing the children in FOSTER CARE.

Such an action theoretically ensures the children's safety; however, critics argue it would be far better to keep the family together by helping the family find shelter.

According to a 1989 report by the Congressional Select Committee on Children, Youth, and Families entitled *No Place to Call Home: Discarded Children in America,* an estimated one-third of the homeless population are part of families with children. In addition, many of the children entering the foster care system are homeless; for example, in New Jersey, homelessness is the sole reason for placement into foster care in an estimated 18% of placements and a contributing cause in 40% of all cases.

It is unknown how many homeless women opt to place their children for adoption, but it is certain that such adoptions do occur. Homeless women may feel their lives are very precarious and hopeless and believe that adoption will enable their children to have a far better opportunity than they can offer.

In some instances, adoptive parents have taken in a homeless pregnant woman and subsequently adopted the woman's child in an OPEN ADOPTION. There are numerous pros and cons involved in such a step, and many adoption experts prefer that pregnant women reside in a home with a family that does not intend to adopt her child.

Homeless women considering adoption usually have received no prenatal care and may be undernourished or malnourished. They may also face considerable difficulty with the welfare system should they opt to apply for welfare or food stamps, since they have no permanent or even temporary residence.

Some homeless women are homeless because they are pregnant. Despite a broad acceptance of single parenthood and unwed pregnancy by much of society, there are still some parents who will turn out a daughter because she is pregnant. The woman must depend on the charity of relatives, church members or total strangers. Some of the women enter maternity homes for the duration of their pregnancy.

Parents who already have children may become homeless due to loss of a job, unsuccessful relocations, problems with alcohol and drug abuse and a variety of problems.

Homeless children have a greatly increased risk of disease, according to an article in *Youth Law News,* which reported a study of thousands of homeless people. According to the article, the researcher James Wright found that homeless children suffered from such pests as lice at 35 times the national average. They were also 4 times more likely to have skin ailments and 10 times more likely to suffer dental problems than the average child nationwide. Chronic diseases such as anemia were seen twice as often in the homeless children,.

A study by Ellen Bassuk, M.D., and Lenore Rubin, Ph.D., of the department of psychiatry at Harvard University Medical School, also found psychological problems with homeless children.

In reporting on their findings, the authors said, "Developmental delays, severe depression and anxiety, and learning difficulties were common among the children."

In addition, of the 156 children in 82 families studied, the researchers found nearly 90% were headed by single mothers. The majority (60%) were receiving Aid to Families with Dependent Children (AFDC), and "more than 24% viewed their child as their major emotional support."

The researchers stated that one-third of the mothers had been abused during childhood and two-thirds had experienced a major family disruption in the course of their lives. Forty percent had lost a parent before their fifth birthday.

Most of the homeless women had moved approximately four times in the previous year.

The researchers tested the children and found 47% had at least one developmental disability. The greatest area of difficulty was language skills, followed closely by personal/social development. Other problems were with gross motor skills and fine motor coordination.

Comparing the homeless children to emotionally disturbed (and nonhomeless) children, the researchers found the homeless children "scored equal to or higher than the mean on the following factor scales: sleep problems, shyness, withdrawal, and aggression."

Ellen Bassuk, M.D., and Lenore Rubin, Ph.D., "Homeless Children: A Neglected Population," *American Journal of Orthopsychiatry,* 57(April 1987): 279–285.

"Homeless Children Face Increased Risk of Disease," *Youth Law News,* 9(March–April 1988): 22.

House Select Committee on Children, Youth, and Families, *No Place to Call Home: Discarded Children in America,* 101st Cong., 1st sess., November 1989.

home study The assessment and preparation process a prospective adoptive family undergoes to determine, among other things, whether they should adopt and what type of child would best fit the family. Some agencies refer to this process as the "family study" or "preadoptive counseling" or other phrases that are considered more accurate and descriptive.

The home study includes the entire process of evaluation and instruction about adoptive parenting and is not limited to visits to the residence of the family. (See EDUCATION OF ADOPTIVE PARENTS.)

Prospective parents initially fill out application forms for agency adoption, and agency criteria are applied to determine whether the parents fit the primary criteria, for example, age, length of marriage, number of children in home, religious affiliation (if it is a sectarian agency), infertility and other factors.

Many adoption agencies accept applications to adopt healthy infants only from couples who have been married at least three years, are childless or have only one child, are medically infertile and are under 40 years of age.

The criteria and application process vary from agency to agency. Some agencies may accept applications from couples who are in their mid-forties or older or who have been previously divorced. In addition, single applicants may also be accepted, although married couples are much preferred by most agencies.

The criteria to adopt a child with SPECIAL NEEDS are usually different from those for a healthy infant, and often agencies will accept applications from prospective adoptive parents who are well over age 40, already have children, are still fertile and so forth. This does *not* necessarily mean the home study will be easier.

Because children with special needs themselves need adoptive parents who can cope with whatever their special needs are, the social worker will carefully evaluate the family to ensure it is within their realm of coping to raise a child with special needs.

After initial screening, the couple or single person's name may be placed on a WAITING LIST until the agency decides it is ready to begin the HOME STUDY process with the individual(s).

If the prospective parents are adopting a child through INDEPENDENT ADOPTION, the home study may be performed by a state or county social worker or by a licensed adoption agency or private social worker, depending on the laws of the state where the adopting parents reside.

The home study process often includes one or more group orientation classes in which prospective parents learn about the agency and its policies. These classes may occur prior to the application process to provide general information or after initial acceptance of the applicants by the agency as a beginning step to the home study process.

Agencies may rely on individual conferences with prospective parents, or they may offer classes or a combination of the two in the assessment process.

If classes are offered, the subjects covered will depend on whether the prospective parents are interested in INFANT ADOPTION or SPECIAL NEEDS ADOPTION.

For those seeking to adopt healthy infants, many agencies will discuss subjects such as coming to terms with infertility, birthmothers and their feelings and reasons for placing the child for adoption, when and how to tell the child he or she was adopted and a variety of other topics that will improve the parent's ability to successfully rear the child.

The social worker may bring in a panel of adoptive parents, adopted persons or birthmothers to share their feelings with the group. An interchange of questions and an ongoing dialogue between the adopting parents and the social worker is usually encouraged.

Parents who plan to adopt children with special needs will often learn about physical and sexual abuse and neglect, developmental delays, problems that may be exhibited by newly adopted children and other topics.

Whether the group or individual home study approach is used, the adopting parents are always interviewed privately to obtain certain personal information from them.

The social worker will ask them together and individually why they want to adopt, what their expectations are in adopting, the type of child they hope to adopt, how their extended family feels about the adoption, whether the mother intends to work outside the home after the placement of a child and many other questions, including sensitive questions about their marital relationship, drug and alcohol use and philosophies about discipline for a child.

These questions are asked not only to help the social worker with the assessment of the family but also to help the family explore issues they may not have fully examined or understood.

If the prospective adoptive family already has children in the home, the children may be interviewed on their feelings about the introduction of a new sibling to ensure they are emotionally prepared for such a change.

A background investigation is also conducted to determine if the prospective adoptive parent has a criminal record or has ever been charged with child abuse or neglect. References are almost invariably requested by the social worker, and these may be written or verbal, depending on the agency, although most are written.

The agency will discuss management of the family finances, including a verification of the applicants' wages and income, to verify there will be sufficient income in the family to support the child. The social worker may also request copies of the previous year's income tax returns and request banks or other financial institutions to provide written verification of current balances.

A home study for an INTERNATIONAL ADOPTION will also include the requirement for the applicant to be fingerprinted, often by local police. Additional paperwork is usually required in an international adoption, and the international adoption agency or adoption lawyer should be able to assist the applicants if they have difficulty completing forms.

International adopters will often need visas to travel abroad, particularly if the child to be adopted resides in South America. They should obtain their visas well ahead of the time they need to travel to the country where their child awaits them.

A social worker's visit to the home of the prospective parents is also an essential aspect of any home study. Despite the fears of nearly every adopting parent, the social worker is rarely seeking to perform a "white gloves" study of the home, despite the term "home study." The house simply should be normally clean.

The home may be the site for many personal questions asked of the adopting parents regarding how they plan to discipline the child, religious beliefs and so forth. The social worker will usually want a tour of the home and will ask to see where the child would sleep.

The adopting family should have a plan for how they will accommodate the child. They need not have the nursery or room completely set up and decorated, but they should have a room or a plan to create a room or plan to have the child share a room with another child.

Safety is another issue the caseworker will be checking: Is the area free of safety hazards? Do the adopting parents seem sensitized to the needs of the type of children they wish to adopt? (For example, if they have a swimming pool, do they have a plan to protect a young child from wandering into that area?)

The interaction between a married couple is also observed, and the social worker will attempt to determine if both parties are committed to adopting or if the adoption is primarily the idea of one person with the other reluctantly agreeing. Although often one person is the instigator of the idea to adopt, both parties should be enthusiastic about adopting a child.

After completion of the home visit and gathering information from references, police check and so on, the caseworker will write up preliminary findings about the couple. The social worker will then write a formal evaluation of the couple with a recommendation to approve or disapprove the couple for adoption.

In some cases, especially cases of an INDEPENDENT ADOPTION in which a lawyer, doctor or other nonagency person is involved in facilitating the placement of the child, the child may actually already reside in the home before the home study commences.

Ideally, however, the home study is completed prior to placement of the child so the family will be prepared for the adoption and any problems can be determined well ahead of the child's entry into the home. Such a step would markedly reduce the probability of a child being in the custody of inappropriate people.

At least one or two other visits to the home (or with the parents and child elsewhere) will ordinarily occur after placement to ensure the child and adoptive parents are happy and adjusting to each other.

After a waiting period ranging from weeks to months to as long a a year (six months on average), depending in which state the adopting parents live, the adoption will be finalized in a court. A new amended birth certificate will be issued to the adopting parents, with their names on the birth certificate as parents. The original birth certificate is "sealed" in most states, which means it cannot be reviewed by anyone without a court order.

Reasons for rejecting couples or singles who are studied vary. Although most people who pass the initial criteria set by agencies will ultimately be approved in the home study process, a small number of people will be disapproved.

The couple or single may be disapproved for adopting an infant if it is apparent they have not at all come to terms with their infertility and it is very unlikely they could accept an adopted child as "their own." (This does not mean that infertility must be completely accepted or never cause the adoptive parents pain again. See INFERTILITY.)

If their marriage appears to be in jeopardy, this marital discord would be another reason to deny a couple the opportunity to adopt a child of any age.

The couple may be disapproved for adoption if the home study reveals the couple has provided the caseworker with false or misleading information, for example, if the investigation reveals a felony was committed in the past, perhaps a drug abuse or alcohol conviction.

Most home studies take at least 30 days to complete and may take several months before all steps can be accomplished. Frequently prospective adoptive parents are placed on a waiting list to obtain a home study. Some adoptive parents call this "a waiting list to get on a waiting list."

After a couple or single has been approved, their names may be placed on a WAITING LIST until they are matched with a child. A couple may receive a child the day after their home study is approved or may not receive a child for several years.

If the parents feel able to adopt a child with special needs, this may also shorten the wait; for example, if white adopting parents are interested in adopting a biracial baby or child, they may receive their child more rapidly than if they stipulate they will only adopt a racially matching child.

Although the home study process may be perceived as nerve-wracking to prospective adoptive parents, studies have revealed parents who are being studied or have been studied are significantly less anxious than couples who have not yet begun the home study process, probably because those who have begun or completed the process believe they will ultimately succeed at adopting their child.

Leah Vorhes Pendarvis studied anxiety levels of infertile couple who planned to adopt for her Ph.D. dissertation. According to Pendarvis, "The data showed that undergoing the adoption procedure results in lower but more fluctuating anxiety levels while waiting for the procedure results in higher but more consistent levels."

Leah Vorhes Pendarvis, "Anxiety Levels of Involuntarily Infertile Couples Choosing Adoption," Ph.D. diss., Ohio State University, 1985.

homosexual adoption See GAY OR LESBIAN ADOPTION.

hospitals' treatment of birthmothers
Hospitals play a critical role in dealing with birthmothers who are considering an adoption plan, far beyond assisting the birthmother with the delivery of her child and providing immediate postpartum care. The attitude of hospital staff, particularly nurses, may mean the difference between a woman deciding to parent her baby or to proceed with her previous plan of adoption, despite counseling beforehand by experienced social workers.

In addition, although she may follow through with her original plan, whether it was adoption or parenthood, the reactions and behavior of the hospital staff can affect the birthmother's own self-image, both during her stay and after she leaves; for example, if she felt the hospital staff were understanding and positive, she could begin the process of reorienting herself to her own individual goals. Conversely, if she perceived the hospital staff as very negative, the birthmother could have many lingering doubts about her decision.

Most hospitals have an adoption policy, and some hospitals even have separate policies for agency adoptions, independent adoptions and special needs adoptions. Because of turnover in nursing staff, it is possible new staff members may not have received in-service training on adoption policies. One way to avert potential errors is to involve the hospital social worker from the point of admission until the birthmother's discharge.

Some hospitals also offer birthmothers the opportunity to visit the hospital before the delivery, meet with the hospital social worker and be introduced to the head nurses of labor, delivery, obstetrics and the nursery. This advance visit can alleviate much of the anxiety of the pregnant woman, including both the fear of a first-time mother as well as a dread about later telling hospital staff about her adoption plan.

Ideally, the agency social worker or the attorney who is initially contacted by the pregnant woman about adoption will formally notify the hospital social work department by letter of a woman considering adoption who will deliver in their hospital. As much time as possible should be allowed so the hospital social worker can notify key people in labor and delivery, the nursery and, of course, the obstetrician.

The role of the hospital social worker will vary, depending on whether the pregnant woman has an established relationship with another counselor (usually a social worker) and whether that worker is on the staff of an adoption agency or retained through private adoption intermediaries.

The hospital social worker's role should be very minimal in relation to the pregnant woman when the woman already has a counseling relationship with a professional who specializes in working with pregnant women considering adoption.

Upon admission of a pregnant woman without a counselor, however, the hospital social worker begins the evaluation and support process. The social worker interacts with medical personnel, the patient's family, agency social workers attorneys and adoptive couples.

Although the pregnant woman should have already received counseling about her options, the hospital social worker is another checkpoint to ensure adoption really is what the birthmother wants for herself and her child. The hospital social worker can discuss what plans the birthmother has made for after her recovery, for example, if she will return to work or school and what her long-term goals are.

Many issues are involved during a hospital stay, for example, the birthmother may wish to see her baby after its birth or may even opt for "rooming in" (wherein the baby stays in the room with the mother throughout her hospital stay). Policy decisions regarding birthmothers should be carefully considered by hospital staff.

The choice to have the child "room-in" may not always be advisable for women considering an adoption plan. It is the view of Jerome Smith and Franklin Miroff, authors of *You're Our Child,* that at some point in such a process, the bond between the birthmother and child becomes so strong that to continue with the adoption plan could cause emotional trauma, including clinical depression over the experienced loss.

In addition, Smith advised against the birthmother nursing her child unless she plans to parent the baby. His general advice for the birthmother planning an adoption is to see the infant and hold it if she wishes but not to have constant close contact with the baby while in the hospital.

Smith also recommends that the birthmother be allowed to grieve her loss and be counseled about the feelings she will probably experience after she leaves the hospital.

Most hospital staffs know a birthmother has the right to see her child unless and until she signs consent papers for adoption (or even after signing consent, depending on state law and circumstances). But birthmothers may sometimes not realize this entitlement and wrongfully believe they have no rights.

Nurses and other well-meaning people sometimes mistakenly believe a woman "giving up" her child could not possibly want to see or hold it. They may also think it would be easier for a mother to follow through with an adoption decision if she does not risk bonding to the infant, a logical conclusion supported by some research.

Nonetheless, most social workers and other adoption practitioners today believe it is important for the birthmother to see for herself that the child is physically well and to observe the appearance of the child. (The birthmother should not, however, be overly pressured to see the child if she does not wish to.)

Some birthmothers wish to say goodbye to the child before signing the agreement to adoption. Although, as far as we know, the farewell will be meaningless to the newborn infant, the saying of goodbyes may be profoundly important to the birthmother as she explains to the child (and herself) why she has made this adoption decision and what she hopes the future will hold for the child. If the birthmother is deprived of the opportunity to say goodbye, such a deprivation could make the resolution of her loss even more difficult.

Jeanne Lindsay and Catherine Monserrat wrote in *Adoption Awareness: A Guide for Teachers, Counselors, Nurses and Caring Others:*

> Hospital staff need to be reminded how vulnerable a woman is during labor and delivery and immediately afterward. She is likely to take seriously everything said by the doctor and nurses. "I don't know how you could do this" or "Adoption must be really hard. I could never do that. . ."

The authors believe such comments, combined with the guilt and emotional pain the mother may be feeling, could lead her to decide impulsively that she should parent the baby.

One author was concerned about an apparent lack of confidentiality when nurses knew new mothers were considering adoption, and she stated that one nurse examined a baby who was not supposed to be shown to the public because the nurse was considering adopting a child herself. Nurse Susan Malestic has stated that sometimes nurses providing prenatal care tell friends about single pregnant women in an attempt to arrange an adoption. She cautioned that it is better to remain neutral about adoption and to refer the woman to adoption agencies where she can obtain counseling and assistance.

Hospital social workers may wish to bring adoption up if the birthmother has not made any plans for her child and seems unsure of the immediate future.

Many birthmothers are afraid to broach such a subject, thinking they will be judged as unfeeling, but if a nurse mentions it, they may be interested. (Again, the nurse should not promote adoption or parenting at this very vulnerable time; however, the patient may be afraid to verbalize her unspoken need for assistance.) In such a case, the hospital social worker should be contacted and can then follow up the case and provide referrals and counseling as needed.

Older single mothers are also sometimes interested in adoption for their babies. The average person can understand why a teenager would want to place her child for adoption (although most teenagers choose to parent) but might wrongfully presume that a 35-year-old single woman would invariably choose to parent.

Despite her age, the older single mother should also be advised of the option of adoption, to consider or reject according to her own desires.

In addition, married birthparents sometimes opt to place their baby for adoption. The family may be divorcing or may already have several children and feel unwilling or unable to parent an additional child. Although it may be difficult to withhold judgment in such a case, it's imperative to understand adoption or parenting is their decision to make. If the birthparents felt unwilling to abort and yet believed adoption would be a positive answer for the child, they should be supported in this decision.

Sometimes when nurses and other staff members are unsure of how they should treat a new mother planning to place her baby for adoption, they may avoid the woman altogether, not wishing to make a mistake and not really knowing what to say. As a result, they may leave her alone, bringing in trays and medication and keeping the door shut otherwise.

Experts such as Lindsay and Monserrat say just listening to a birthmother can help her considerably. Rather than conveying his or her own views for or against adoption, the nurse can listen to the birthmother in a compassionate manner. If the birthmother feels the staff is trying to avoid her, she may believe she is an object of shame and what she is doing is wrong and bad. If staff members are willing to talk with her, her psychological pain can be eased, although not erased.

It may be difficult for a nurse to merely listen to the birthmother when a nurse's role is generally to offer exact advice on actions a patient should take; however, listening is often what the birthmother needs as much or more than the physical care the nurse can provide. Most hospitals are short-staffed but even five minutes could help the birthmother.

Where the birthmother stays in the hospital is also important. Most women planning to place their child for adoption do not wish to be in the same area with other women who are joyous about the child they will bring home and are nursing or feeding their infants, nor do they wish to discuss their decision with other women who, particularly at this point in their lives, would have tremendous difficulty understanding why a woman would choose not to parent.

As a result, whenever possible, birthmothers are placed in rooms by themselves or in a surgical ward.

Hospital staff may understandably be confused by the array of options offered to birthmothers today. Although most adoptions are confidential, some birthmothers know the identity of the adoptive parents. Nurses who try to keep adoptive parents and the birthmother apart are looked at askance by both parties in an OPEN ADOPTION.

Yet if the adoption is confidential, the parties involved do wish to remain apart. If an attorney has arranged for a couple to see the baby, there is a risk that they may encounter the birthmother, and hospital staff should be alerted by the attorney if he wishes to avoid a possible meeting of the couple and the birthmother in the hallway.

Even when an adoption is planned as an open adoption, the birthmother may wish to be alone and not want to see the adoptive parents. The hospital social worker and her own social worker should ensure the birthmother's desires for privacy are met.

Increasing numbers of hospitals are now offering seminars to their staff on adoption and are enhancing staff awareness of why women choose adoption for their babies.

Seminars may include panels of adoptive parents, birthmothers and adopted persons as well as talks by trained social workers. Staff members may ask questions and enhance their understanding of the adoption process. Seminars also provide the opportunity to bring issues and problems out in the open and help nurses and other staff members offer the compassionate care they strive to give all patients. (See also PHYSICIANS.)

Susan L. Malestic, "Don't These Patients Have a Right to Privacy? (Pregnant Women Planning to Give Baby Up for Adoption)," *RN*, March 1989, 21.

Jeanne Lindsay and Catherine Monserrat, *Adoption Awareness: A Guide for Teachers, Counselors, Nurses and Caring Others* (Buena Park, Calif.: Morning Glory Press, 1989).

Jerome Smith, Ph.D., and Franklin I. Miroff, *You're Our Child: The Adoption Experience* (Lanham, Md.: Madison Books, 1987).

hotlines Toll-free telephone numbers oriented to a particular group; for example, adoption agency hotlines are oriented to pregnant women considering adoption for their children while hotlines for adoptive parents concentrate on placing special needs children

Hotlines are sometimes staffed 24 hours per day, or they may be operated during office hours with an answering machine available to take urgent calls. Hotlines are also available to take abuse allegations, and social workers may be given a certain amount of time by state law to respond to an allegation of child abuse.

identity Developing a clear sense of one's individuality, including one's distinct personality, talents, abilities and flaws, is difficult for the average person, and many people seriously question their values, beliefs and identity during adolescence.

For 25 years researchers Jane Hoopes and Leslie Stein studied adoptive families that had adopted young children. Concluded the authors in their 1985 report: "Evidence suggesting that the adoptee has greater or more sustained difficulty with the tasks of adolescence was not found, indicating that adoptive status in and of itself, is not predictive of heightened stress among adolescents . . . as a group, the adolescent adoptees were doing quite well."

Most children with SPECIAL NEEDS who were adopted were separated from their parents because of abuse, neglect or abandonment and may have internalized a negative sense of self. In addition, as foster children, they have experienced at least one foster home and probably several more.

Each move requires an adjustment to a new family, new school and different values and requirements. The child may never have realized what his or her innate talents and strengths are, and consequently the adopting parents' task is to help the child identify his or her best points and build self-esteem and self-knowledge.

The parent of the same sex as the child serves as a role model. Single parents who parent an opposite-sex child need to find appropriate role models among their families or friends. The child may also identify with a much loved teacher, neighbor or other person in his or her life.

Some individuals reach a point in their adult lives when they feel compelled to learn more about their birthparents or even to SEARCH for them. Adopted adults who are interested in locating birthparents are not only curious about their origins and the motivations of their birthparents in choosing adoption but are almost driven to search in their quest for "identity" and their own origins. Most searchers are females, usually in their early child-bearing years. (See also ADOLESCENT ADOPTED PERSONS; ADULT ADOPTED PERSONS.)

Leslie M. Stein and Janet L. Hoopes, *Identity Formation in the Adopted Adolescent: The Delaware Family Study* (Washington, D.C.: Child Welfare League of America, 1985).

identified adoption See DESIGNATED ADOPTION.

illegitimacy The legal status of a child born to unwed parents, now more properly described as "out-of-wedlock" or "nonmarital."

In the United States, illegitimacy, or "bastardy," was formerly a great stigma on a person, and people born out of wedlock were presumed to be "bad." Until recent years, BIRTH CERTIFICATES of those born out of wedlock were often a different color from those born legitimately and were separated and locked in a special vaults.

With the increase in the divorce rate and the resulting trend toward acceptability of single parenthood, the negative connotations associated with out-of-wedlock births have radically declined; however, there are still many people who harbor negative views toward persons born out of wedlock.

There are cases today, even in our "enlightened" age, of parents casting out their unmarried daughters who are pregnant. Although out-of-wedlock births are far more common today than 10 or 20 years ago, pregnant girls are sometimes tainted with the image of being "fast" or "cheap," and their child (or children) is also looked down upon.

immediate placements Usually refers to placements of infants who are newborns and have not been placed in temporary homes.

Such an adoption may be an AT RISK PLACEMENT and is usually done to facilitate bonding between the adoptive parents and the child. The birthmother may not have signed formal consents, or appropriate court actions may not yet have taken place. However, the social worker or attorney believes the adoption will go forth, and the birthmother has expressed the wish that the child be placed immediately from the hospital.

Immediate placement differs from DESIGNATED ADOPTION in which the birthparents select the adopting parents. The placement of the child with the adoptive family may or may not follow the infant's discharge from the hospital, depending on state laws, the wishes of the individuals involved, the advice of the social worker and other factors. (See also BONDING AND ATTACHMENT.)

immigration and naturalization In adoption, refers to the entry of children from other countries for the purpose of being adopted by U.S. citizens.

According to the U.S. Immigration and Naturalization Service (INS), 7,092 children were admitted as orphans to the United States in fiscal year 1990. A large number of the children—2,620—were born in Korea.

Adopted children may become citizens based on their adoptive parents' U.S.-born status. (This action is **not** automatic and must be applied for by the adoptive parents before the child's 16th birthday.) Adoption agencies or the INS can advise adoptive parents as to which documents are needed to naturalize the child after finalization. Adopted children from other countries enter the United States with visas based on their adoptive parents' citizenship.

The naturalization process was streamlined by Congress in 1989 to one interview with INS officials. Prior to that time, the naturalization process was more complex.

For further information, contact the Immigration and Naturalization Service to request the pamphlet *The Immigration of Adopted and Prospective Adoptive Children,* newly updated in 1990, 425 Eye St NW Washington DC 20536 (See also INTERNATIONAL ADOPTION; KOREAN ADOPTED CHILDREN; LATIN-AMERICAN ADOPTIONS; INDIA.)

incest See SEXUAL ABUSE.

income tax deductions Congress formerly allowed a $1,500 income tax deduction for adoptive parents who adopted children with SPECIAL NEEDS. This deduction was repealed in 1986 and all efforts to reinstate a new income tax deduction have not succeeded as of this writing.

The NATIONAL COMMITTEE FOR ADOPTION supports a tax credit for all adoptive parents.

It should be noted that although the federal income tax deduction was repealed, states that levy income taxes may have continued adoption exemptions, and individuals should verify whether or not their states will allow adoption expenses as an exemption.

independent adoption Nonagency adoption, usually handled through attorneys, physicians or other intermediaries, in which adoptive parents are not genetically related to the child. (Laws for RELATIVE ADOPTIONS differ from laws for nonrelative adopters.) At least half of all healthy infant adoptions nationwide are independent adoptions.

State Laws Governing Independent Adoption Independent adoption is legal in most states but not in Connecticut, Delaware, Massachusetts, Michigan and North Dakota.

It is important to note, however, that birthparents in every state except Michigan may choose nonrelative adoptive parents for their children and plan an adoption. (It is unclear whether or not Michigan citizens may choose direct placements; apparently, courts have interpreted the statutes differently, allowing DESIGNATED ADOPTION in some cases and disallowing it in others.) Presuming the laws of the states have been followed, the adoptive parents selected by the birthparents will be approved by the court.

154 independent adoption

In those states that prohibit nonagency adoptions (with the exception of Michigan), the assistance and approval of an adoption agency is required if birthparents and prospective adoptive parents wish to arrange an adoption between themselves, and an agency must counsel the birthparents and adopting parents and conduct a HOME STUDY of the prospective adoptive parents before they may adopt. As a result, the adoption agency could disapprove the prospective adoptive parents. These states call such adoptions "identified adoptions" or "designated adoptions."

As a result, in those states where independent adoption is banned (with the exception of Michigan), prospective adoptive parents and birthparents may seek each other out and then come to an adoption agency and ask the agency to arrange the adoption. Adoptive parents in such cases are not put on any "waiting lists" and are approved (or disapproved) for only the particular child they have requested to adopt. It is probable that most prospective adoptive parents chosen by the birthparents will be approved by the agency.

Studies and Opinions Although independent adoption may be lawful in some states, judges in particular areas sometimes frown on it and refuse to finalize such an adoption. In addition, some states strictly regulate independent adoptions, while others do not.

An example is the state of Colorado, where attorneys may arrange adoptions but may not charge "locator" or "placement" fees and may only charge their "normal reasonable fees" for those services they customarily perform. A licensed adoption agency must perform a home study of the prospective parents. In addition, counseling for the birthparent is mandated. Colorado calls such placements "designated adoptions," and they are arranged by both attorneys and agencies.

In Ohio, independent adoption is lawful under state laws, but county judges may choose to allow or disallow an adoption and to determine which conditions for adoption are acceptable and which are not.

New York requires that all adopting parents be certified and approved before the court before children may be placed in their homes. A home study by a licensed social worker or the court's probation department is part of this process. In addition, the prospective parents must also be cleared through a child abuse registry in New York.

A preliminary home study must be performed before placement in Florida, and an abuse registry check and police check is also made. The Department of Health and Rehabilitative Services, which is the public social services agency, performs the home study in the case of an independent adoption.

Some states require a preliminary home study prior to the placement of a child in an independent adoption, but most state laws do not mandate a home study until after placement or when ordered by the court. (However, a preliminary home study is always required in an interstate or international adoption.)

As a result, adoptive parents are not always fully evaluated or prepared by social workers before they receive their child. This lack of assessment and preparation is the key objection against independent adoption; however, a growing percentage of independent adoption practitioners recognize the importance of a preplacement home study and require all their clients to have an approved home study by a licensed agency or licensed social worker prior to placement of a child.

Nonagency adoptions are sometimes called "gray market" adoptions, which connotes unsavory, unethical or questionable practices; however, this is unfair since these adoptions are legal in most states. There are many ethical attorneys or intermediaries who handle adoption, and the legal rights of the birthparents and adoptive parents are protected. ("Black market" adoptions, also known as BABY SELLING, are illegal adoptions.)

Several studies of the outcome of independent adoptions have been performed in the past. In 1963, the findings of a study of 484 children placed with 477 families in

Florida was reported by Helen L. Witmer, Elizabeth Herzog, Eugene A. Weinstein and Mary E. Sullivan in their book *Independent Adoptions*. About two-thirds of the adoptions were rated "excellent" to "fair," while one-third were rated "poor."

A study by William Meezan, S. Katz and E. Manoff-Russo published by the Child Welfare League in 1978 found most independent adoptions had a good outcome; however, concern was expressed about the lack of background information provided on the birthmother. In addition, some adoptive parents reported extremely high amounts paid to adopt the child.

Most adoption agency social workers today still have a low opinion of the practice of independent adoption, just as most who handle independent adoptions believe agency adoptions are inferior. Many workers see independent adoption as a form of competition, a method to "beat the system" and an approach that often avoids important aspects of sound adoption practice.

Agency workers often feel the nondirective counseling they provide women contemplating adoption for their infants is especially important.

Independent adoption facilitators may see agencies as their competition. They may view agencies as antiquated, judgmental bureaucracies and perceive agency social workers as intrusive, cold busybodies who ask far too many irrelevant or personal questions.

Reasons for the Choice People who adopt independently usually adopt infants, and those who wish to adopt older children usually contact the state public agency or a private, nonprofit agency for assistance. Occasionally, people adopt toddlers through attorneys when mothers voluntarily place them.

The primary reason people choose independent adoption over agency adoption is that independent adoption offers them more of a sense of control. For instance, they can actively try to find a child, and independent adoption is often a much faster process than if they had adopted through an agency.

Individuals who choose to adopt independently may fit most adoption agency's criteria for their own applicants: under age 40, married for at least three years, infertile and other criteria a large percentage of agencies apply. On the other hand, independent adopters may be over 40, already have several children and be married for a short period.

Pregnant women choose independent adoption over agency adoption for several major reasons. Many prefer private medical care over Medicaid, and in most states, the law allows adoptive parents to pay for prenatal care and delivery.

The pregnant women may also receive support money (including wage replacement) from the adoptive parents or through the attorney or intermediary. Many agencies cannot afford such support money or refuse, on principle, to provide such money.

Another reason pregnant women choose independent adoption over agency adoption is a very strong aversion to the idea of temporary foster care for the newborn baby, which some agencies insist on for a few days. (Increasing numbers of agencies will place newborn infants with adoptive families right away, if they feel confident the birthmother is secure in her adoption decision.)

The birthmother frequently has an intense desire for her child to experience an immediate bonding with the adoptive parents, and she sees a foster home as a form of psychological deprivation.

One reason birthmothers are so adamant about the importance of bonding is because of impressions they have received from the media. (Bonding is one of the few child development concepts to be widely understood.) In addition, positive marketing by nonagency adoption intermediaries stress the importance of bonding. Yet studies indicate children need not necessarily bond within the first few days of life, and bonding can and does occur with older infants and toddlers. (See BONDING AND ATTACHMENT).

If a birthmother is very adamant about avoiding a foster home and appears very convinced that adoption is the right option for her child, some agency social workers will do an immediate AT RISK PLACEMENT; however, the majority still prefer to use temporary foster homes before the formal adoption consent papers are signed.

Many birthmothers prefer for the child to go from the hospital directly to the adoptive home and are very anxious about the concept of a foster home.

Other possible reasons the birthmothers may be strongly opposed to the concept of a foster home are possible guilt feelings related to their decision and negative articles in the media about foster children who were abused. They may fear their newborn child could be abused, too, despite reassurances from the caseworker and promises that they can visit the child in the foster home. (Most adoption agencies have their own private foster care systems that are operated separately from the state. Although the state may certify the agency's foster homes, the agency itself manages them.)

Risks of Independent Adoption Just as independent adoption has its advantages, so also it has risks, including major financial and emotional risks.

In many states, adoptive parents may pay for private prenatal care, legal fees, and support money for the pregnant women. If the woman changes her mind before or after the baby is born and before signing any formal consent papers, she has the right to parent the child, and no state will take that right away from her.

Any money the prospective adoptive family may have paid will probably be lost, because most pregnant women considering adoption for their children are indigent and cannot repay money expended for medical care, food and other necessities. In addition, most state laws preclude the money being legally recovered.

If the pregnant woman was on MEDICAID when she entered the hospital, Medicaid will cover the cost of the hospital bill and delivery. In addition, even if the birthmother follows through with the plan to place the baby for adoption, Medicaid will still pay for the delivery and the mother's medical bills.

Although the financial risk may be great, most adoptive parents agree the emotional trauma of a birthmother changing her mind is far worse than the money they've lost. And, of course, the euphoric adoptive parents who succeed consider the emotional roller coaster well worth the ride.

Independent adoption can be an extremely stressful process and experience for adopting parents. They are aware for months that they may receive their most heartfelt dream—a baby. Or they may not.

Often they are too afraid of jinxing the adoption to tell any of their friends and relatives about the impending adoption; consequently, they suffer the emotional highs and lows alone. If the birthmother changes her mind, it is a very painful experience for the couple, similar to a miscarriage.

Most birthmothers who do change their minds about a private adoption do so just before or immediately after the birth; however, in some states, the birthmothers may change their minds after placement, which is an even greater trauma to adoptive parents and also to the child who has bonded to them.

Even if the birthmother never considers changing her mind, the adoptive parents are greatly stressed by the knowledge that she may do so, and this fear can potentially affect and inhibit the bonding process and hence feelings of ENTITLEMENT.

Adoption agencies often will not inform a prospective couple about a child until all consent papers have been signed. Then they will call and give the couple a few days to arrange to pick up their child. As a result, the couple avoids the stress-filled months of anxiety; conversely, they are also deprived of the intense months of active and positive fantasizing before the child's arrival.

Intermediaries Pregnant women find lawyers through Yellow Pages advertisements, classified ads and networking with their friends (which is also the way prospective adoptive parents find their attorneys.)

Some physicians serve as intermediaries. A woman's obstetrician is likely to know infertile couples or can easily identify several through his or her own contacts.

Adoptive parents may also find a pregnant women on their own through networking or advertising and then contact the attorney and ask him or her to facilitate the adoption.

It is still extremely advisable to rely only on experienced and ethical attorneys, even if the adoption appears very straightforward and simple.

Neither a pregnant women nor prospective parents should accept any pressure from an attorney or other intermediary to accept a particular situation such as adoptive parents who don't sound like the type of family the birthmother was looking for or a birthmother who doesn't resemble what the parents want. If either party begins to feel pressured, they should leave and contact another intermediary or an adoption agency.

Some families adopting independently wish to adopt a girl or a boy, and ultrasound techniques often make it possible to identify the sex of the child before birth. However, most attorneys don't like the idea of a couple demanding one sex or another and think the couple should be happy with a healthy infant.

Costs The cost of an independent adoption varies greatly from state to state, and may be less than $5,000 or well over $10,000, depending on the individual case and the state laws. In addition, obstetrician fees and hospital expenses vary from area to area. If the birthmother must have a Caesarean section and the adoption parents are paying the medical bills, this will increase costs by several thousand dollars. About 20% of all births are by Caesarean section.

If the baby is not healthy and suffers from a range of disabling diseases, the couple may chose not to adopt the child. However, they will probably lose any money they have paid for prenatal care, attorney's fees and other expenses.

Birthmothers and pregnant women should never pay attorneys to arrange an adoption, and an attorney who asks a pregnant woman for a fee should be avoided. Adoptive parents pay all legal fees.

Before giving an attorney thousands of dollars, prospective adoptive parents should understand exactly what the lawyer is promising, the timeframe involved, what losses they could incur and so forth. State laws on adoption are available at most large public libraries, and a reference librarian can direct readers to their exact location.

In some instances, the adopting parents will be represented by one attorney, and they will hire a different attorney to represent the birthmother; however, probably in the majority of cases, one attorney is retained to represent both parties.

Interstate Independent Adoptions Many independent adoptions occur across state lines; for example, the birthmother may reside in one state, and the adoption parents may live in a neighboring (or faraway) state. It's important to understand that the provisions of the INTERSTATE COMPACT ON THE PLACEMENT OF CHILDREN must be followed. This is a sort of treaty between states that regulates interstate adoption, and each state has a compact administrator headquarters at the state public welfare office.

Generally, the laws of the "receiving" state, or the state where the child is placed, prevail; however, compact administrators strive to ensure that the laws of both states are complied with. Adoptive parents should not remove a child from another state without the permission of the compact administrator. (See INTERSTATE ADOPTION.)

Most independent adoptions are lawful and probably successful, and the prevailing number of attorneys and other intermediaries engaged in facilitating independent adoptions appear to be ethical. (See also AGENCIES; ATTORNEYS; PHYSICIANS.)

Adoption Factbook (Washington, D.C.: National Committee for Adoption, 1989).

Christine Adamec, *There ARE Babies to Adopt: A Resource Guide for Prospective Parents* (Lexington, Mass.: Mills and Sanderson, 1987).

Paul T. Fullerton, "Independent Adoption: The Inadequacies of State Law," *Washington University Law Quarterly,* 63(Winter 1985) 753–775.

Joan H. Hollinger, editor-in-chief, *Adoption Law and Practice* (New York: Matthew Bender, 1989).

Robert K. Landers, "Independent Adoptions," *Congressional Quarterly's Editorial Research Reports,* 2:22(1987).

William Meezan, S. Katz and R. Manoff-Russo, *Adoptions Without Agencies: A Study of Independent Adoptions* (New York: Child Welfare League of America, 1978).

Susan B. Price and Jody McElhinny, "Substantive Changes in Adoption and Relinquish Law in Colorado," *Family Law Quarterly Newsletter,* December 1987, 2183–2185.

Natalie Haag Wallisch, "Independent Adoption: Regulating the Middleman," *Washburn Law Journal,* 24(1985): 327–359.

Helen L. Witmer, Elizabeth Herzog, Eugene Weinstein and Mary E. Sullivan, *Independent Adoptions: A Follow-up Study* (New York: Russell Sage Foundation, 1963.)

India A Third World country and one of the countries from which children are adopted by Americans as well as by people from other countries. Single adoptive parents also adopt from India because they are not restricted from adopting, as is often the case elsewhere.

According to the Immigration and Naturalization Service, 698 Indian children were adopted by Americans in fiscal year 1988—264 boys and 434 girls. (See GENDER PREFERENCE for more information on why many adoptive parents choose to adopt girls rather than boys.) In fiscal year 1989, 677 Indian children were adopted by U.S. citizens, and it is likely the boy/girl ratio was the same, although a gender breakdown was not available as of this writing.

It should be noted that although India does not prohibit singles from adopting as of this writing, the international adoption scene is very changeable. Prospective adoptive parents are advised to gain current information from agencies and support groups. In addition, the INTERNATIONAL CONCERNS COMMITTEE FOR CHILDREN offers valuable and updated information. (See also INTERNATIONAL ADOPTION.)

Indian Child Welfare Act of 1978 A law enacted by Congress in 1978 that mandates special provisions for Native American children and their placement into foster or adoptive homes. Under the act, an Indian child's tribe or the Bureau of Indian Affairs must be informed before the child is placed for adoption and preference in placement must be given first to the child's tribe and last to another culture.

There are an estimated 1.4 million Native Americans in the United States and about 300 different tribes in 27 states. About one-half of them live on Indian reservations.

Supporters of the law say that, prior to its passage, as many as 25% of Native American children were placed into foster or adoptive homes because of such reasons as a lack of indoor plumbing in the biological parents' home, small houses or other conditions of poverty or social problems.

They believe TRANSRACIAL ADOPTION is not a good policy and believe placing an Indian child with a non-Indian family ultimately causes confusion in the child's sense of identity.

The law requires agencies or anyone involved with placing an Indian child to first inform the tribe or the Bureau of Indian Affairs. Even birthmothers who wish to transfer parental rights to an adoptive family fall under this law, and they must first receive permission from the tribe before an adoptive placement may occur.

It is not always clear whether a person is considered an Indian or not if the person is of mixed race, and definitions vary from tribe to tribe.

If a prospective adoptive parent believes he or she has American Indian ancestors, he or she should contact the tribe's headquarters, who (after verification) will issue a formal document or a letter on official stationery stating that a person is of Indian ancestry. In addition, the state historical society may maintain information enabling a person to track down ancestry, using Indian Census data.

The Pan American Indian Association (PAIA) also provide assistance in genealogy, and the local Bureau of Indian Affairs should be asked for assistance. (The PAIA is at P.O. Box 244, Nocatree, FL 33864.)

A family with no Indian ancestry may be able to qualify as "Culturally Indian" and hence be able to adopt an Indian child. Some possible criteria for being defined as "Culturally Indian," according to *OURS* Magazine, include the following: at least one parent has an Indian ancestor; the adopting parents live in a state with a large Indian population; the family has Indian friends; the parents read books about Indian culture. (Eligibility for "Cultural Indian" status is determined on a case-by-case basis.)

Charlotte Goodluck, a Navajo, has written about this issue. According to Goodluck, "The placement preference section of the ICWA [Indian Child Welfare Act] considers only immediate family members and then other tribal members as a source for the child; placement with another culture is only a last alternative . . . In many areas, there is an urgent need to develop a pool of Indian foster and adoptive parents in order to achieve more fully the goal of same-culture placement, and to develop reservation and urban-Indian resources such as guardianship programs that will minimize the mental health consequences."

In those cases where Indian children are placed in non-Indian homes, Goodluck writes that these children "need sensitive and caring adoptive parents who will advocate and address the child's need for a tribal-cultural identity as well as address the special issues of adoption itself."

There have been several cases of parents (non-Indian and Indian) fighting in court to keep a particular Indian child they have adopted. The tribe has prevailed and overturned adoptions in several cases, including one in which the adoptive parents were of the child's tribe.

However, in one case of a school-aged Indian child who had been adopted and was being raised in a Caucasian, Mormon home, the tribe allowed the child to remain in the former adoptive home despite the overturning of the adoption. Media attention and the child's expressed desire to remain in the home probably contributed to this decision.

Those who disagree with the implementation of the Indian Child Welfare Act generally also support transracial adoption. They usually believe that a home in the child's own culture is the first and best choice; however, when a suitable home is unavailable, then a home with a family of another race would be an alternative to consider before making a child wait.

Social workers and proponents of the act argue that there are Indians who are interested in adoption and complain that social workers don't spend enough time on active recruitment.

According to an article in *Children Today*, the Indian Child Welfare Act is not always followed, despite its federal status. The writers described a 9-year-old child who was placed in several different non-Indian foster homes and remained in care until he was 13, although his parents had apparently met the goals set for them.

The writers also noted that permanency is not always implemented as readily by Bureau of Indian Affairs officials as by public agencies. Instead, the writers contend that Indian children remain in foster care longer than non-Indian children. They urge a transfer of cases to trial programs from the under staffed Bureau of Indian Affairs social service office.

For a legal discussion of the Indian Child Welfare Act, see "Beyond the Best Interests of the Tribe: The Indian Child Welfare Act and the Adoption of Indian Children," by Joan Heifetz Hollinger, in the *University of Detroit Law Review*. The topic is also covered by Hollinger in her book *Adoption Law and Practice*.

In addition, an article by Michelle L. Lehmann in *Catholic University Law Review* entitled "The Indian Child Welfare Act of 1978: Does it Apply to the Adoption of an Illegitimate Indian Child?" provides a detailed discussion of this act. (The author's answer to the question posed in her title is "yes".)

Resources concerning Native American children, listed in the September/October 1988 issue of *OURS*, include the following organizations:

The Native American Adoption Resource
   Exchange (NAARE)
200 Charles St.
Pittsburgh, PA 15238

Indian Adoptive Family Circle
New Mexico, DHS—Adoptions
P.O. Box 2349
Santa Fe, NM 87503-2348

Indian Child Adoption Network
611 12th Ave. S, Suite 300
Seattle, WA 98144

Rocky Mountain Adoption Exchange
5350 Leetsdale Dr., Suite 10
Denver, CO 80222

The CAP Book
700 Exchange St.
Rochester, NY 14608

Films, slide shows and videotapes on American Indians, including such titles as "In the Best Interest of the Child: The Indian Child Welfare Act," "Ways of Our Fathers," and others are available for sale or rental through

Shenandoah Film Productions
538 G St.
Arcata, CA 95521
(707) 822-1030

Charlotte Goodluck, M.S.W., "Mental Health Issues of Native American Transracial Adoptions," in *Adoption Resources for Professionals* (Butler, Pa.: Mental Health Adoption Therapy Project, September 1986): 194–208.

Joan Hollinger, *Adoption Law and Practice* (New York: Matthew Bender, 1988).

Joan Heifetz Hollinger, "Beyond the Best Interests of the Tribe: The Indian Child Welfare Act and the Adoption of Indian Children," *University of Detroit Law Review*, 66(1989): 450–501.

"ICWA Works for Native American Children," *OURS*, September/October 1988, 22–23.

Michelle L. Lenmann, "The Indian Child Welfare Act of 1989: Does it Apply to the Adoption of an Illegitimate Indian Child?" *Catholic University Law Review*, 38(1989): 511–541.

Margaret C. Plantz, Ruth Hubbell, Barbara J. Barrett and Antonia Dobrec, "Indian Child Welfare: A Status Report," *Children Today*, January–February 1989, 24–29.

Anne Welsbacher, "Inside the Indian Child Welfare Act," *OURS*, September/October 1988, 20–21.

infant adoption The adoption of newborns or babies or toddlers under the age of two years.

Most people who wish to adopt an infant are seeking a healthy newborn or a child who is at most only several months in age. It is not clear how many people are actively taking steps to adopt, but for a variety of reasons, including ABORTION, birth control and the rise in single parenthood, it is clear there are insufficient numbers of adoptable infants to meet demand.

It has been hypothesized by some that if the U.S. Supreme Court decision on *Roe v. Wade* were overturned and abortion again made illegal, the number of infants available for adoption would increase to what it was before *Roe:* It remains to be seen what would happen should abortion be banned or limited.

Infant adoption is a relatively new phenomenon in the United States, and prior to the late 1920s, few newborn infants were adopted. Children who were adopted were primarily older children who were homeless or had lost one or both parents or whose parents were financially or emotionally unable to care for them.

When infant formula became widely available in the late 1920s, this development made it possible for pregnant women to place their babies with adoptive couples shortly after the baby's birth. Prior to the perfection of infant formula, newborn babies were breastfed and could not survive without mother's milk. (Wet nurses were sometimes used for infants who were boarded out, but many babies died.)

Infants who need adoptive families are placed through AGENCIES, ATTORNEYS or through other intermediaries, such as physicians or even friends of the birthmother, with the counsel of a state, county, or private social worker.

Ironically, it is often easier to adopt a newborn infant than it is to adopt a child of one, two or even three years of age. The reason for this is that an adoption decision regarding a newborn infant is usually made by the birthmother, and most birthmothers make this decision during their pregnancies or shortly thereafter. Few make a voluntary decision in favor of adoption when the child is two or three years old because they then have a relationship with the child.

As a result, small children and infants who are in state custody are usually there because of ABUSE, ABANDONMENT or NEGLECT. They are placed in FOSTER CARE, often for at least a year, with the state agency seeking to solve the problem in the biological family that required the removal of the child.

If the problem cannot be solved, for example, if an abandoned infant's biological relatives do not wish to adopt him or if an abused infant's parents cannot be rehabilitated, the state will ultimately go to court to terminate parental rights.

Often the child will be at least six or seven years old by the time the state terminates the rights of the parents. The reason for this is that abuse or neglect is frequently not discovered by the agency until the child is in kindergarten or some public setting.

As a result, few healthy toddlers are ready to be adopted. (Minority and mixed race toddlers are sometimes waiting for adoptive families.) (See TRANSRACIAL ADOPTION.)

There are, however, some number of older infants and toddlers available through international adoption agencies and orphanages in other countries. As a result, families who are insistent on adopting toddlers may opt to adopt internationally.

Primarily because of the long wait to adopt infants at many adoption agencies, thousands of U.S. and other citizens who wish to adopt babies have turned to INTERNATIONAL ADOPTION. These babies are generally at least four months old because of the time lag between the birth of the child and the matching with a particular couple, who must then travel to the infant's country to follow foreign and American immigration requirements.

But in some cases, infants may be only a few days old, especially if the adoption has been facilitated by an attorney in the child's homeland.

Health of Newborn Infants Most U.S.-born adopted babies are healthy, although a substantial number of those placed for adoption are of low birth weight (less than 5.5 pounds), and many are premature. The birthmother may have received little or no prenatal care and may or may not have had adequate nutrition during her pregnancy.

Many U.S. birthmothers also smoke, which can account in part for their low birth weight babies.

Increasing numbers of women, including pregnant women, abuse drugs such as cocaine, a drug that can directly affect the child's physiology. COCAINE BABIES may be premature, hyperactive, easily upset and unusually small. (See DRUG ABUSE.)

AIDS is an increasing societal problem in the United States, and an estimated 1,000 infants each year are born to women who test HIV-positive. It is not clear how many of these women place their babies for adoption, although it is certain that some of them do opt for adoptive placement.

Adoptive parents whose infants have AIDS or the potential to develop AIDS because of mothers with the syndrome may be unwilling to share this information with relatives, friends and neighbors, fearing social ostracism.

infertility Most people who adopt children, particularly people who adopt infants, are infertile or believe themselves to be infertile. The infertility may be correctable by modern and often expensive techniques, may be a more serious problem requiring surgery, may be incurable or, in about 20% of the cases, may be of undetermined causes, in which case the situation is called "unexplained infertility."

Despite dramatic newspaper stories about a skyrocketing infertility rate, experts at the National Center for Health Statistics say the infertility rate is about the same as it was 20 years ago. The reason infertility is highlighted today is primarily because of large numbers of "Baby Boomer" couples who delayed childbearing until their late twenties or their thirties and now have decided to start a family. (Fertility declines with age. For more information, see FERTILITY RATES.)

There are probably also a greater percentage of individuals seeking treatment, aware of a variety of fertility treatments available today that were unknown a decade ago.

Couples who have been unable to conceive after one year should see a fertility specialist because many causes of infertility can be treated today. They should also contact a support group, such as RESOLVE INC., which can provide practical information and emotional support.

Author Sharon Covington says dealing with infertility can be difficult because the medical community is sometimes unsympathetic, not realizing that patients feel their body is inadequate or has betrayed them. Covington says such feelings can be amplified by medical terminology that "describes reproductive functioning as hostile (cervical mucous), incompetent (cervix), defective (luteal phase), or poor (semen.)"

Patricia Conway and Deborah Valentine wrote about the lack of sympathy given to infertile couples by their friends and family. Infertile men are advised to eat oysters or relax. Some friends are nonsupportive because they are uncomfortable around the infertile couple—they may be afraid or embarrassed to discuss their own pregnancies. Thus, the couple may be deprived of the opportunity to talk about their infertility and feel they should suppress their feelings.

Because of this lack of support, many infertile couples find great comfort and empathy in support groups (also known as "mutual aid groups"), whose members not only understand the problem but also provide information about REPRODUCTIVE TECHNOLOGIES and adoption.

The infertile couple may have attempted to achieve a pregnancy for years, even as long as a decade or more, before finally deciding what they really want is to be parents and then being able to give up the idea of a pregnancy and a biological child.

If the desire for a genetic link is not a paramount concern, infertile couples turn to adoption agencies at this point. Unfortunately, they often find, to their dismay, the waiting period for an infant is likely to be a matter of at least two to three years and perhaps even longer.

They may feel an oppressive sense of time pressing in on them, particularly if they are in their mid- to late thirties or older. In addition, many adoption agencies will not accept applications to adopt infants from people over age 40.

They may be urged to adopt a child with SPECIAL NEEDS and may opt to do so. Some "older" couples turn to INTERNATIONAL ADOPTION, successfully adopting their child from another country. Others may turn to INDEPENDENT ADOPTION. And still others will locate an adoption agency willing to work with them.

Hopefully, the social worker who counsels the adoptive couple will have a basic understanding of the pain of infertility; unfortunately, some social workers believe this pain should be completely resolved before the couple seeks to adopt.

Author Patricia Johnston describes this problem in her book *An Adoptor's Advocate*. According to Johnston, the social worker may presume that the adopting couple should have put the pain of their infertility behind them forever, completely having resolved all issues. Yet the scars from the pain of awareness of infertility do not dissolve overnight with the decision to adopt a child, and infertile couples who choose to adopt need to realize feelings of anxiety over infertility may never disappear altogether. Still, anguish over an inability to reproduce may fade away as the happy adoptive couple sees their child for the first time and lives a normal family life.

Later on, perhaps in adolescence when a child's sexuality and probable fertility becomes apparent, the parent may again mourn over his or her own infertility.

Stephanie Siegel, a family therapist, provides a basic checklist for adoptive parents in her book *Parenting Your Adopted Child*. This list is meant to help adoptive parents determine whether they have truly accepted their infertility and includes several questions: "Do you find yourself wondering if the biological mother could do it better?" "Do you believe that you were not meant to be a parent because of your infertility?" "When family and friends question your parenting style, do your own doubts consume you?" "Do you become angry or sad when you see a pregnant woman?"

Therapists Judith Schaffer and Christina Lindstrom agree that infertility issues can be long-term, although they also concur with Siegel that counseling should be sought if the adoptive parent is obsessed or haunted by his or her infertility.

Say Schaffer and Lindstrom to adoptive parents in their book *How to Raise an Adopted Child*, "If infertility still bothers you, you're not alone. Many adoptive parents struggle to deal with it. It will probably always be in the back of your mind. To keep infertility from growing into a major problem that interferes with your becoming an effective parent, talk it out whenever you realize that it's troubling you." (See also FERTILE ADOPTIVE PARENTS.)

Patricia Conway and Deborah Valentine, "Reproductive Losses and Grieving" in *Infertility and Adoption: A Guide for Social Work Practice* (New York: Haworth Press, 1988).

Sharon N. Covington, "Psychosocial Evaluation of the Infertile Couple: Implications for Social Work Practice," in *Infertility and Adoption: A Guide for Social Work Practice* (New York: Haworth Press, 1988).

Robert R. Franklin, M.D., and Dorothy K. Brockman, *In Pursuit of Fertility: A Consultation with a Specialist* (New York: Henry Holt, 1990).

Patricia Irwin Johnston, *An Adoptor's Advocate* (Indianapolis: Perspective Press, 1984).

Judith Schaffer and Christina Lindstrom, *How to Raise an Adopted Child* (New York: Crown, 1989).

Stephanie E. Siegel, Ph.D, *Parenting Your Adopted Child: A Complete and Loving Guide* (New York: Prentice Hall Press, 1989).

informal adoption The rearing of a child as one's own, without benefit of legally adopting the child through the courts. Ever since and even before the pharaoh's daughter chose to raise Moses as her son, informal adoption has been a constant in our society. No longer popular among whites, it appears that many blacks still rely on informal adoptions. (This may be partly a function of necessity rather than desire. See BIRTHMOTHER.)

The problem with an informal adoption is that the child has no rights to the "adoptive" parents' social security benefits, inheritance, and so forth, and the "parents" have no legal status as parents unless or until they formally adopt the child. In addition, birthparents and relatives may come back months or even years later and reclaim the child, with no recourse to the informal adopters. (See also RELATIVE ADOPTIONS.)

inheritance Although it would seem logical that a child adopted by nonrelatives would inherit from the adoptive parents and not from birthparents (and indeed this is true in most cases), there are many ramifications of the laws regarding inheritances, and statutes vary from state to state.

Generally, an adopted child inherits from adoptive parents and may not inherit from biological parents unless specifically named in a will; however, in the states of Colorado, Louisiana, Rhode Island, Texas, Vermont and Wyoming, the adopted person's right to inherit from birthparents and birth relatives is retained. In some states (for example, Kansas, Mississippi and Oklahoma), whether or not an adopted person is excluded from inheriting from birthparents is not addressed while in many states the adopted person is specifically excluded from inheriting from birthparents.

Although an adopted person may inherit from adoptive parents, whether or not the adopted person will also inherit from adoptive grandparents is not always clear and depends on state laws.

It is best to review current state law and consult an attorney in the event of a question or a desire to provide an inheritance for an adopted-away child. (Two legalistic terms used when discussing inheritance are "adopted-away" and "adopted-in." An adopted-away child is a child who is born to a family and then leaves the birthparents because of adoption. An "adopted-in" child is a child that enters a family by adoption.)

If the child is adopted by nonrelatives, inheritance generally must come through adoptive parents; however, as recently as 1986, a challenge was made to this assumption in New York. Jessie Best wrote her will in 1973 and provided for her assets to be given to her "issue." Her daughter had given birth 21 years earlier to a son who had been adopted by nonrelatives.

The executor's of Best's will discovered the existence of the adopted child. With the permission of the birthmother, who also had a child born within wedlock, the trustees asked the adoption agency for identifying information since the adopted adult might stand to inherit a considerable sum.

The adoption agency told the adoptive parents, who disclosed the son's legal name. When the birthmother died in 1980, the trustees asked the court to determine whether the adopted child would share in the division of assets with the child born within wedlock and not adopted.

The court decided the adopted child was "issue" and could inherit; however, the court of appeals overturned this decision.

In a very unusual case, adopted adult Cathy Yvonne Stone alleged she was the birthdaughter of Hank Williams, the late singer. Stone sued to receive part of the royalties accruing to Williams' estate. Her suit was rejected at a lower court level, but, on appeal, a federal court decided she was entitled to have her case heard by a jury. In 1990, the U.S. Supreme Court affirmed this decision. In addition, the Supreme Court refused to overturn an Alabama Supreme Court decision that decreed Stone was a lawful heir to the estate of Williams.

In the case of a STEPPARENT ADOPTION, the adopted child may inherit from both birthparents and the stepparent in some states, but in other states, the adopted child may only inherit from the custodial parent and stepparent. (See STEPPARENTS.) Author Anne Wiseman French wrote, "In stepparent adoption situations, many states' statutes mirror New York's law before the 1987 amendments and preserve the child's inheritance rights only from and through the biological parent having custody of the child. Other states, however . . . preserve the child's inheritance rights from both biological parents.''

The intent of the donor is significant in determining whether an adopted child may inherit, and how intent is determined varies from state to state.

Anne Wiseman French, "When Blood Isn't Thicker Than Water: The Inheritance Rights of Adopted-Out Children in New York," *Brooklyn Law Review*, 53(Winter 1988): 1007–1049.

Joan Hollinger, ed.-in-chief, *Adoption Law and Practice* (New York: Matthew Bender, 1988).

Timothy Hughes, "Intestate Succession and Stepparent Adoptions: Should Inheritance Rights of an Adopted Child Be Determined by Blood or Law?'' *Wisconsin Law Review*, (1989):321–351.

insurance The primary insurance concern of most adoptive parents is health insurance. State laws vary greatly on when an adopted child is covered by health insurance, and many companies may disallow certain claims made for an adopted child because they evolve from pre-existing conditions.

Adoption agencies, attorneys and adoptive parents themselves should determine in advance what type of insurance coverage is mandated in their state for adopted children. If no law on insurance and adopted children is in the statutes, then individual insurance companies or employers must be contacted to determine the extent of coverage and the timing.

Some adopted children are covered by MEDICAID, which adoptive parents may be able to use indefinitely or at least until they are able to use their own private insurance.

Adoptive parents have become increasingly active in lobbying for changes in insurance laws. Dr. Larry Schreiber, a New Mexico physician, successfully changed the laws on insurance in his state to cover adopted children from the time of placement. He wrote a how-to article on lobbying for changes that was published in *OURS,* a magazine published by Adoptive Families of America.

Schreiber explained his actions:

At first glance, legislation seemed unnecessary, because all states but Illinois have statutes stating that an adopted child is to be treated the same as a birth child—and Illinois has a caselaw to this effect. However, health insurance companies freely violate the spirit of these state laws.

In 1988, Florida passed a law requiring insurance companies in Florida to provide insurance coverage to adoptive parents from the point of the birth of the newborn infant if there was a written agreement to adopt the child prior to birth, whether or not the agreement was enforcable. If the child was not placed with the family of the insured person, then coverage would not be required.

As a result, the child's hospital bill would be covered as well as any medical expenses the child incurred after birth. In at least one case to date, a child with serious medical problems was born and adopted, and the insurance company covered the expenses.

Some states mandate coverage for adopted children from the time of placement while others don't address the issue of adoption. As a result, insurance companies can deny coverage to children with a previously existing health problem.

Several states, including Arkansas, Florida, Georgia and Kansas cover adopted infants from birth. In 1990, the state of Kansas passed a law requiring insurance companies to cover the delivery of infants who are to be adopted. This law is perhaps the broadest in scope of any law mandating coverage of an adopted child. (Provisions of each state law should be checked by adopting parents to determine they comply with various requirements, such as, filing time deadlines.)

Many states cover adopted children from the time of placement; for example, Louisiana passed a law in 1988 mandating coverage at placement. Minnesota and New Mexico also passed similar laws in 1988.

Laws in some other states specifically allow for pre-existing conditions; for example, according to the *Adoption Factbook,* New Hampshire law recommends insurance companies charge adoptive parents on a sliding scale, depending on the severity of a child's disability. But some states do not address the issue of health insurance at all.

Because of the difficulty in obtaining health insurance coverage, many children with SPECIAL NEEDS are covered under MEDICAID, a federally-funded health insurance program; however, many physicians refuse to accept Medicaid. As a result, it is quite likely that in states allowing pre-existing conditions to exempt insurance companies from coverage, prospective adoptive parents are scared away from adopting infants and children with disabilities. Such children will remain in foster care, supported by state and federal taxpayers and never placed in a permanent home.

One argument in favor of requiring coverage upon placement is that adopted children enjoy virtually the same legal rights and privileges as children who come into the family by birth and should be treated the same by insurance companies. (See also EMPLOYMENT BENEFITS.)

Larry Schreiber, M.D., "How to Organize and Lobby for State Law Changes," *OURS,* July/August 1989, 18–19.

intelligence Although children's genes set forth their basic potential intelligence and the best adoptive family environment can never hope to transform a retarded child into a genius, there are some indications that a positive adoption experience can increase IQ (intelligence quotient) levels by as much as 15 points or more.

A study by Christiane Capron and Michel Duyme, French researchers at the University of Paris, looked at the socioeconomic status (SES) of birthparents and adoptive parents and found an apparent environmental impact of adoption on adopted children.

All the adopted children studied were adopted before the age of six months, and the average age of the adopted person at the time of the study was 14. (It would be fascinating to learn if the IQ differences remained constant when the adopted adults grew up and moved away from home. Some researchers speculate the effect of the adoptive parents' SES wanes as the adopted person ages.)

Considering only "high" and "low" SES of birthparents and adopters, with high SES individuals being physicians and executives and low SES being farmworkers and unskilled laborers, the researchers found clear-cut differences in the adopted children's scores.

"Children reared by high-SES parents have significantly higher IQs than those reared by low-SES parents," stated the researchers, referring to adoptive parents.

The highest IQs of adopted children were recorded when the SES of both the birthparents and the adoptive parents were high, and researchers found a mean IQ score of nearly 120. The lowest scores occurred when both the birthparents and adoptive parents were of low SES, and the average IQ was 92 points.

Probably the most likely actual scenario is the low SES birthparent and the high SES adoptive parent: In this case, the mean IQ score was about 104 points. (A person with an IQ score of about 100 is generally considered of "average" intelligence, and incremental increases of 10 points are significantly important.)

It appears the intelligence level of adopted children can be raised by nearly 16 points or more when the adoptive parents are of a high SES, despite the birthparents' SES. This difference can mean the difference between topping out educationally with a high

Intelligent Quotient of Adopted Children

		SES of Adoptive Parents	
		High	Low
SES of Birthparents	High	120	108
	Low	104	92

IQ levels are means and are rounded off.

school diploma or going on to obtain a college degree.

Capron and Duyme don't explain why or how higher adoptive SES homes apparently produce children with higher IQs. Said psychology professor Matt McGue in *Nature*, "It remains unclear whether the SES effect is related to access to quality education, the variety and complexity of intellectual stimulation in the home, the parents' press for scholastic achievement, or some other factor that differentiates between high- and low-SES homes."

According to McGue, other studies have correlated the adoptive mother's encouragement of the child to confidence and subsequent test performance.

Earlier studies found a stronger contribution from genetic factors, when some studies found the adoptive parents' contribution is greatest during the early years of childhood and decreases as the child grows older.

A longitudinal study reported in 1949 by Marie Skodak and Harold Skeel found a strong correlation between birthmothers and their adopted-away children. This study also indicated the genetic influence increased until the children became adolescents.

According to the findings of a study done by Joseph M. Horn on 300 adoptive families and the birthmothers of the adopted children, Horn concluded, "Adopted children resemble their biological mothers more than they resemble the adoptive parents who reared them from birth."

He found that children with higher-IQ birthmothers were more intelligent, saying, "Children from higher-IQ unwed mothers surpassed those from lower-IQ unwed mothers, even though the intellectual potential in their environments was comparable."

A study by Sandra Scarr and Richard A. Weinberg looked at the IQ levels of children adopted transracially and reported on their findings in *Child Development*.

According to the researchers, "Black and interracial children scored as well on IQ tests as adoptees in other studies. Individual differences among them, however, were more related to differences among their biological than adoptive parents."

The researchers also compared black children adopted transracially to black non-adopted children. The black adopted children scored above average in intelligence, with an average IQ of 110. The researchers also speculated that the transracially adopted children had an average IQ greater than their biological parents.

The researchers concluded that the high intelligence quotients of the adopted children indicated two key points: first, that race does not indicate for intelligence differences and, secondly, that "black and interracial children reared in the culture of the tests and the schools perform as well as other adopted children in similar families."

They also concluded that the children who were transracially adopted were responsive to the familial environment, and the adoptive parents provided "intellectual stimulation and exposure to the skills and knowledge sampled on IQ tests." (See also FETAL ALCOHOL SYNDROME; GENETIC PREDISPOSITIONS.)

Christiane Capron and Michel Duyme, "Assessment of Effects of Socioeconomic Status on IQ in a Full Cross-Fostering Study," *Nature*, 340(August 17, 1989): 552–553.

Joseph M. Horn, "The Texas Adoption Project: Adopted Children and Their Intellectual Resemblance to Biological and Adoptive Parents," *Child Development*, 54(1983): 268–275.

Matt McGue, "Nature-Nurture and Intelligence," *Nature,* 340(August 17, 1989): 507–508.

Robert Plomin and J. D. DeFries, "The Colorado Adoption Project," *Child Development,* 54(1983): 276–289.

Michael Rutter, Patrick Bolton, Richard Harrington, Ann Le Couteur, Hope Macdonald and Emily Simonoff, "Genetic Factors in Child Psychiatric Disorders—I. A Review of Research Strategies," *Journal of Child Psychology and Psychiatry,* 31(January 1990) 3–37.

Sandra Scarr and Richard A. Weinberg, "The Minnesota Adoption Studies: Genetic Differences and Malleability," *Child Development,* 54(1983): 260–267.

intercountry adoption   See INTERNATIONAL ADOPTION.

intermediary   Person who facilitates or who acts to put together an INDEPENDENT ADOPTION; a "broker" as middleman in an adoption; May be an ATTORNEY or PHYSICIAN or other person, as determined by state law.

international adoption   The adoption of a child who is a citizen of one country by adoptive parents who are citizens of a different country.

U.S. citizens adopt thousands of infants and children each year from Korea, Asia and Latin America. In fiscal year 1990, 7,088 children from other countries were adopted by U.S. adoptive parents. The children sometimes travel halfway around the globe until they meet their FOREVER FAMILY for the first time.

In almost all cases, the children involved have been living in orphanages or were considered abandoned by their parents. In some cases, they are biracial or physically handicapped, which is a great stigma in the view of some Asians just as mixed race or physical handicaps are a stigma in the view of some Americans.

Prior to World War II, few children and very few infants were adopted from other countries by U.S. citizens. It was World War II and subsequently the Korean War that brought home the plight of orphaned children to U.S. soldiers stationed overseas.

From 1935 to 1948, only about 14 immigrants per year in the category of "under 16 years of age, unaccompanied by parent" entered the United States. It is unknown how many of these children were actually adopted. Americans generally adopted American children during the pre-World War II years, and agencies strongly emphasized the concept of matching the child to the adoptive parents as closely as possible so the unknowing stranger would presume the child was a birth child of the adoptive parents. As a result, international adoption and the obvious distinctions between some children and their adoptive parents would have been viewed negatively during those years.

After World War II, when Americans first became very interested in international adoption, it was primarily U.S. immigration laws and quotas that held them back. Initially, the laws were changed to allow service members to adopt limited numbers of children.

In 1948, the Displaced Persons Act was created by Congress to enable over 200,000 European refugees to emigrate to the United States. The act also allowed 3,000 "displaced orphans" to enter the United States, regardless of their nationality. A sponsor did not have to promise to adopt the child but only to promise the child would be "cared for properly."

The orphan provisions of the Displaced Persons Act were temporary but were periodically renewed by Congress with expiration dates varying from one to three years.

During this time after World War II, American interest in and desire to adopt increased beyond the number of infants and children who needed families in the United States.

During and after the Korean War, many American servicemen became interested in adopting Korean orphans, and in 1953 Congress allowed up to 500 special visas for orphans who would be adopted by American servicemen or civil servants of the federal government. At this time, immigration was open to orphans from any nation: Prior to that time, immigration of orphans had been limited to European orphans.

The Refugee Relief Act of 1953 was subsequently passed, allowing for 4,000 orphan visas over the next three years. Yet this act, combined with the earlier provisons for special visas, was insufficient to accommodate all the orphans that service members and federal employees wished to adopt.

In 1957 Congress lifted all numerical quotas from orphan visas, but this action too was limited in time because Congress perceived the need and desire to adopt orphans from other countries as a short-term situation. Finally, in 1961, the Immigration and Nationality Act incorporated a permanent reference to the immigration of orphans from other countries to be adopted by Americans.

The Vietnamese "Baby Lift" occurred in 1975 after the fall of Saigon, South Vietnam, and thousands of Vietnamese children presumed to be orphans were flown to Western nations. It was later discovered that some of those children had living parents who did not wish their children to be adopted but only wanted their safe removal from the country. As a result, U.S. immigration laws were tightened.

International adoption has continued to date, and tens of thousands of children from other countries have been adopted by U.S. citizens. At least half of all children adopted from abroad over the past 10 years have emigrated from Korea, although Korea began cutting back the number of adoptions in 1988. (There were 4,942 adoptions of Korean children by U.S. citizens in fiscal year 1988 and 2,620 in 1990.) Both Korean officials and adoption experts predict this number will continue to decline. (See KOREAN ADOPTED CHILDREN.)

International adoption is extremely changeable and highly driven by the policies of the foreign countries as well as by U.S. immigration law. Most of the countries that allow the emigration of their orphans to the United States and other Western nations are considered Third World nations and have great difficulty with poverty and economic and social problems.

It's also very important to understand that many Third World nations do not share the philosophy or the understanding of adoption that most Americans take for granted. For example, in some countries, the birthmother of a child need not execute a written consent to relinquish her child. She may or may not receive any counseling, depending on the the laws of the nation.

Richard R. Carlson described a variety of international adoption issues in his comprehensive article, "Transnational Adoption of Children," published in the *Tulsa Law Journal*. One issue Carlson discussed was the "convergence" of federal and state laws in the case of international adoptions.

United States citizens cannot adopt children from other countries unless they follow the requirements of the U.S. Immigration and Naturalization Service (INS). Although they are not a child welfare agency, the INS strives to determine if the prospective adoptive parents are suitable and if the child to be adopted is "adoptable." The INS sets requirements that are not always imposed on parents who adopt children from within the U.S.

The INS does require a HOME STUDY, even if the state does not require a preliminary home study of the adopting parents before placement, and sets 25 as the minimum age for prospective adoptive parents.

The INS must also consider whether the child is "adoptable" based on the age of the child, the child's orphan status and other criteria.

The final adoption, however, is subject to state laws and regulations. Even when the child is formally adopted overseas in a foreign court, Carlson recommends the adoptive parents readopt the child in their home state.

Problems with state laws may occur when the state legislatures fail to understand that laws in other countries may be very different from adoption laws in the 50 states of the United States and when the state legislatures create laws that cannot be fulfilled by international adoption agencies.

If a state court demands a written relinquishment from the birthmother, such a document may be unavailable. Carlson says it is also highly unlikely that the consent was executed in a court. In addition, the relinquishment will almost certainly not include special language required by a state law.

A 1986 Ph.D. dissertation by Robert Charles Matthews recognized these and other problems and recommended that international adoption be given a special status. Matthews' dissertation suggested changes in the U.S. code "to eliminate the interjurisdictional confusion in which 50 systems of orphan immigration take the place of a unitary Federal system of immigration. It uses Supreme Court opinions with a more traditional policy analysis to show that the current system conflicts with fundamental constitutional values of individual rights and federalism."

Matthews stated that since adoption was strictly regulated by the U.S. Immigration and Naturalization Service, the State Department and foreign countries, the additional role of the individual state is "duplicative and based on less than compelling constitutional grounds." Said Matthews, "The State role adds to delays and costs incurred by citizens, with no additional public benefit."

Why Some Americans Adopt Minority Children from Other Countries Some have asked why U.S. citizens do not adopt more biracial minority members within the United States, where there are many infants and children needing families.

The answer is that TRANSRACIAL ADOPTION has been actively fought by such groups as the National Association of Black Social Workers, who state that transracial adoption is a form of "racial genocide." As a result, individuals wishing to adopt and to whom race is not a major factor have investigated international adoption, and many have successfully adopted children of all races from throughout the world.

It is also interesting to note that some international adoption agencies place black children from other countries, for example, Haiti, with white families, believing that the children are far better off in a happy adoptive family than they would be living in an orphanage.

Some individuals have investigated international adoption because they do not wish to wait three years to adopt a healthy white infant; however, they should be aware that children from other countries may be perceived as belonging to another race or ethnicity and consequently may experience racial or ethnic slurs in school or later at work.

Families to whom SKIN COLOR is a very important feature of the child to be adopted probably should not adopt a child from another country. Children from many of the countries that allow emigration are likely to be of Asian, African or a mixture of races. The race of the child's birthfamily may be unknown, especially if the child was abandoned as a foundling to the orphanage.

Some adoptive parents who adopt children from other countries are OPTIONAL ADOPTERS, that is, they are fertile but believe in providing a home for a child who is "already here." (See FERTILE ADOPTIVE PARENTS.) They may also be individuals who are over 40 years old or who do not fit the criteria of the average adoption agency placing infants.

Individuals may also seek to adopt children from abroad because they are seeking to adopt a child of their own cultural heritage; for example, a couple of Greek origin may wish to adopt a Greek orphan. It should be noted that some countries require at least one of the adoptive parents to be of the same national origin as the child.

Countries that allow intercountry adoption may set numerous restrictions on adoptive parents beyond what adoption agencies set; for example, they may accept only married couples and prohibit singles from applying. They may have age limits and religious requirements.

Many Latin American countries require adopting parents to travel to their countries and stay at least a few days until various paperwork and legal requirements are satisfied. Such a stay can be difficult for some Americans, particularly those who have never left their own state or city. (See CULTURE SHOCK.)

Other countries have their own way of accomplishing bureaucratic tasks, and sometimes Americans can become very impatient and frustrated with foreign officials. As a result, international adoption should never be considered the "easy" way to adopt.

Most of the children adopted from other countries are infants and small children; however, older children and siblings are also available for adoption. The INTERNATIONAL CONCERNS COMMITTEE FOR CHILDREN in Boulder, Colorado maintains a photolisting of school-age children with handicaps (some correctable) and healthy normal children in other countries who need families.

The International Adoption Process A family (or single person) in the United States can adopt a child from another country in two basic ways: by adopting through a licensed U.S. adoption agency or through a form of INDEPENDENT ADOPTION called PARENT-INITIATED ADOPTION (if the state in which they live allows INDEPENDENT ADOPTION).

Parents who choose this second form of adoption usually do so because they may adopt a child younger than usually available through an agency, or they may wish to adopt a child from a country with which U.S. agencies do not work. Some adopting parents find themselves forming their own adoption agencies to facilitate further adoptions in the country they have penetrated. Even when the family identifies an attorney or intermediary from another country, they must still undergo a home study, based on requirements of the U.S. Immigration and Naturalization Service.

Subsequent to approval of the family, the agency or the family's intermediary attempts to identify a child for the family. Most of the children in other countries who need adoptive families live in orphanages; however, in some cases, a birthmother may relinquish her child directly to an attorney shortly after the child's birth.

After the agency or intermediary notifies the family of an available child, they must decide then whether to adopt the child. If the child is living in an institution, the agency will attempt to obtain a photograph of the child along with social and medical information. Often families report that they feel they "bond" to these photographs, which is a problem if, for some reason, the adoption does not occur.

The child is usually adopted in the adoptive parents' home state. The child later becomes a naturalized U.S. citizen, based on the parents' citizenship and the child's dependent status. (Important note: U.S. citizenship is *not* automatic to children adopted by U.S. citizens: it must be applied for. Contact the U.S. Immigration and Naturalization Service for further information, or request their pamphlet *The Immigration of Adopted and Prospective Adoptive Children,* which was revised in 1990.)

Immigration laws include a special provision for children who have lived at least two years with U.S. citizens. It could be used, for example, by military members or individuals living abroad who have adopted children overseas. In such a case, no home study by a U.S. agency is required.

Adjustment Challenges for Children Born Overseas According to the 1990 *Report on Foreign Adoption,* a book published by the International Concerns Committee for Children, most of the children overseas needing U.S. families reside in orphanages, and adopting parents need to try to understand what such a life was like in order to help the child adapt.

Says an article within this book, "An institutionalized child's world is of necessity a very orderly and limited one. Many have never ridden in a car or even been outside the grounds of the orphanage. Wise parents will introduce new people, activities, and events slowly."

According to an Open Door Society of Massachusetts publication by Betty Laning and Mary Taylor entitled *A Parent's Guide to Intercountry Adoption,* parents should learn as much as possible about how their child was cared for abroad, for example, whether the child slept in a crib or on a floor mat, slept on his back or stomach, slept wrapped tightly in a blanket or loosely and so on. In addition, perhaps his formula was very sweet. The child may have been carried on the caretaker's back. Whenever possible or reasonable, the adoptive parent can try to create similar situations so the child will feel comfortable.

The authors also advise that parents learn some basic words in the child's native tongue before the child arrives home, such as "mother," "father," "toilet," "time to eat," and "I love you."

Laning and Taylor also describe "orphanage syndrome," which is survival behavior learned at the orphanage. Say the authors, "an orphanage child can become very competitive, always looking out for himself, pushing himself ahead of others to get the most food or attention . . . It takes a great deal of patience to teach sharing, being considerate of others, taking turns, and loyalty to the family."

Children may have dental decay, because bottles, propped up for hours at a time, are common in orphanages. Other medical problem are also possible.

The child adopted from another country will have plenty of new cultural experiences to absorb and assimilate; for example, most children who live in orphanages abroad receive sponge baths and may be frightened by their first sight of a tub full of water. They may also be initially fearful of flushing toilets, noisy vacuum cleaners and a host of experiences common to the everyday U.S. household but not common to the child from abroad.

The International Concerns Committee for Children article on children raised in orphanages concludes, "A child in an institution has had a succession of caretakers. Even the most loving caretakers vanish for hours of each day or night. A newly adopted child usually assumes that you are just like his old caretakers. Watching a child blossom under the slow-dawning realization that he or she is the center of someone's life is one of the most exquisite joys of adoption."

A pamphlet published by the Holt International Children's Services in Eugene, Oregon discussed newly-adopted children who previously lived in orphanages.

According to this pamphlet, "Many of the children who have lived in orphanages for years and have seen other children leave for adoption may have wondered why they could not go too. They may have developed a feeling of being unloved and unloveable. When they do go for adoption, they are apt to have mixed feelings toward their new parents. They are happy they finally have a home, but they may be unhappy they had to wait so long. If your child hangs back from giving you his whole love, this anger over the delay may be partly responsible. Sometimes it helps if the parents take the initiative and express their regret that they did not apply sooner to adopt him."

Some individuals have expressed concern that children displaced from their native land may experience adjustment problems as they grow into adulthood. Studies do not support this fear and indicate that most of the children integrate successfully. A study of severely deprived Vietnamese infants who were later adopted showed very dramatic improvements and revealed the children were not developmentally delayed despite the initial trauma they faced.

A 1988 Ph.D. dissertation by Lois Lydens studied Korean children at both adolescence and adulthood and found them to be well adjusted and successful. She also found the children adopted in infancy or early childhood experienced the least anxiety or questions about their racial or ethnic heritage. Said Lydens, "The findings suggest that most early and later crossculturally adopted children develop normally and adjust positively to a socially arranged interracial family situation."

A 1990 doctoral dissertation by Eulalio Gonzalez compared the effect of the age of placement on children adopted from within and without the United States. Gonzalez studied 275 children adopted from abroad and 47 children adopted within the United States. Using parental ratings, he found that, in general, the earlier the age at placement and the longer the time the child had been placed, the higher the parental satisfaction rating. (This finding tracks many other studies that reveal early placements of children have the highest rates of positive outcomes.) Gonzalez found that parents rated their children comparably, despite whether the child was adopted internationally or from within the United States.

He also found that children adopted internationally identified more strongly with their adoptive parents' ethnic backgrounds than with their own birth cultures. In addition, Gonzalez did not find a difference between the adopted children's ethnic identity and their "psychosocial" adjustment.

Disinformation Disinformation is propaganda that is purposely untrue and/or misleading and has a hidden negative agenda behind its perpetuation.

Sometimes competing governmental groups or foreign-based groups plant or leak disinformation about international adoption. For example, it has periodically been alleged that Americans and other affluent Westerners are adopting children from other countries in order to secretly use them as sources of "body parts" and "organ transplants" for domestic medical experiments or to use children as vehicles to smuggle drugs into the adoptive parents' countries.

When these stories are investigated by reputable journalists (or agency directors), no basis in truth whatsoever is found. Virtually all Americans adopt children from abroad because of their desire to love a child. They have no evil or secret motives behind the adoption.

Yet such disinformation is sometimes believed, particularly by sending countries, because they do not understand why Americans or persons in other receiving countries wish to adopt.

Their orphanages may be overcrowded, much of their population may be mired in poverty, and they do not have a frame of reference to understand why people from another country would desire children that their own country cannot provide for and who are sometimes devalued. It may be especially difficult to understand why older children or handicapped children are adopted by Americans and other Westerners. As a result, negative propaganda is more readily believed.

Partly because of such basic fears and suspicions generated or believed by various nations who use disinformation, adoption agencies who place children from abroad urge adoptive parents to mail the sending orphanage or agency photos of their children periodically, without their name or return address, so orphanage directors, agency staff, government officials, the media and others can see the children are healthy and thriving. See MEDICAL PROBLEMS OF ADOPTED CHILDREN for a detailed discussion of medical issues in international adoption. (See also INDIA; KOREAN ADOPTED CHILDREN; LATIN AMERICAN ADOPTIONS.)

Adoption—A Family Affair, (Eugene, Or.: Holt International Children's Services, April 1986).

Richard R. Carlson, "Transnational Adoption of Children," *Tulsa Law Journal,* 23(Spring 1988): 317–377.

John Gittelsohn, "Film's Adoption Horror Tale Angers Koreans," *Boston Sunday Globe,* February 25, 1990.

International Concerns Committee for Children, *Report on Foreign Adoption* (Boulder: International Concerns Committee for Children, 1990).

Intercountry Adoptions 1981–1990

Region and Country of Birth	1981	1982	1983	1984	1985	1986	1987	1988	1989	1990
All countries	4868	5749	7127	8327	9286	9945	10097	9120	7948	7093
Europe	96	71	96	79	91	103	122	99	120	262
Poland	21	12	31	26	29	32	54	51	68	66
Portugal	9	13	17	16	19	19	24	17	16	20
Other Europe	66	46	48	37	43	52	44	21	36	176*
Asia	3216	4189	5334	6251	6991	7679	7614	6484	5112	3815
China, Total	**	84	91	92	139	140	137	157	142	66
Hong Kong	**	18	29	30	51	40	56	49	47	29
China, Mainland	19	31	7	6	16	10	15	52	81	36
China, Taiwan	75	35	55	56	72	90	66	56	14	131
India	314	409	409	468	496	588	807	698	677	348
Japan	38	30	36	45	57	46	64	69	74	57
Korea	2444	3254	4412	5157	5694	6188	5910	4942	3552	2620
Lebanon	15	6	14	15	20	19	21	23	21	16
Pakistan	6	5	9	14	8	12	9	10	14	14
Philippines	278	345	302	408	515	634	593	476	481	421
Thailand	11	19	12	19	28	27	31	75	99	100
Other Asia	91	37	49	33	34	25	42	34	52	108
Africa	11	7	12	8	11	22	22	28	36	52
Oceania	9	7	9	9	9	21	3	15	13	10
North America	635	678	761	1026	1012	885	973	844	910	959
Canada	48	14	8	9	11	13	17	12	5	8

international adoption

Mexico	116	98	110	168	137	143	178	123	107	112
Caribbean	82	103	86	93	118	102	124	140	202	156
Dominican Rep.	21	45	42	44	47	31	52	54	69	58
Haiti	8	14	10	13	12	19	25	41	80	64
Jamaica	42	33	18	16	47	38	37	38	43	28
Other Caribbean	11	11	16	20	12	14	10	7	10	6
Central America	389	463	557	756	746	626	654	568	595	683
Belize	3	12	13	5	4	5	12	6	7	10
Costa Rica	48	108	90	99	59	72	72	73	78	105
El Salvador	224	199	240	364	310	147	135	88	92	103
Guatemala	82	98	105	110	175	228	291	209	208	257
Honduras	13	22	97	148	181	135	114	161	191	197
Nicaragua	6	4	2	10	0	14	5	8	9	7
Panama	13	20	10	20	17	25	25	23	10	4
Other N. America	0	0	0	0	0	1	0	1	1	0
South America	901	797	915	954	1172	1235	1363	1650	1757	1995
Bolivia	12	9	27	24	14	25	25	21	28	30
Brazil	62	72	55	117	242	193	148	164	180	228
Chile	106	113	172	153	206	317	238	252	254	302
Colombia	628	534	608	595	622	550	724	699	735	631
Ecuador	20	11	10	12	25	25	31	41	19	59
Paraguay	1	8	11	8	15	32	90	300	254	282
Peru	54	35	19	31	34	71	84	142	269	440
Other S. America	18	15	13	14	14	22	23	31	18	23

*Of these adoptions, 121 were children adopted from Romania
**Prior to FY 1982 data from mainland China and Taiwan were consolidated.
Source: U.S. Immigration and Naturalization Service

Eulalio Guadalupe Gonzalez, "Effects of Age at Placement and Length of Placement on Foreign and Domestic Adopted Children (Foreign Adoption)," Ph.D. diss., University of Akron, 1990.

Lois Adele Lydens, "A Longitudinal Study of Crosscultural Adoption: Identity Development Among Asian Adoptees at Adolescence and Early Adulthood," Ph.D. diss., Northwestern University, 1988.

Robert Charles Matthews, "The Littlest Immigrants: The Immigration and Adoption of Foreign Orphans," Ph.D. diss., Virginia Polytechnic Institute and State University, 1986.

Parent's Guide to Intercountry Adoption (Boston: Open Door Society of Massachusetts, n.d.)

"Preparing for a Child from Abroad," in *1990 Report on Foreign Adoption* (Boulder: International Concerns Committee for Children, 1990).

U.S. Department of Justice, Immigration and Naturalization Service, *The Immigration of Adopted and Prospective Adoptive Children*, revised 1990.

U.S. Department of State, *Soviet Influence Activities: A Report on Active Measures and Propaganda, 1987–1988*, August 1989.

International Concerns Committee for Children

An educational nonprofit organization that provides information and assistance—with a strong emphasis on international adoption—to families interested in adopting children. The organization is not an adoption agency and provides referrals to licensed agencies.

The organization was founded in 1979 by Betty Laning, AnnaMarie Merrill and Patricia Sexton, who currently serve on the board of directors.

The ICCC publishes a listing of international adoption agencies located throughout the United States, the annual *Report on Foreign Adoption*, which includes nine updates. The ICCC also publishes a photolisting of children from other countries who are legally available for adoption, the *ICCC Listing Service*.

The organization coordinates information with adoptive parent support groups and works to educate the general public on international adoption and related adoption issues.

For more information, contact

International Concerns Committee for Children
911 Cypress Dr.
Boulder, Co 80303

International Soundex Reunion Registry

(ISRR) Formed by the late Emma May Vilardi in 1975 and currently managed by registrar Tony Vilardi, this nonprofit organization provides a mutual consent registry and assists adopted adults, birthparents and adoptive parents who are seeking biological relatives as well as other individuals who are next of kin by birth and wish to locate each other.

Adopted individuals who wish to register themselves must be over age 18, although birthparents who register may be under age 18. Registration is free, but donations are accepted. The organization is not a SEARCH GROUP and will not actively seek out individuals beyond the registry; instead, it is a strictly voluntary registry.

If two related adults register, then ISRR will provide this matching information to the parties involved. It also assists adults who were separated from biological parents through divorce to find adult siblings and other birth kin. Free registration forms are available upon request.

Over 2,600 people have been matched since the organization's inception, according to ISRR. Professional counseling is also available through the organization.

It cooperates with adoption agencies and social services departments, and most search groups recommend that their members register with ISRR, regardless of other steps they may have taken or other registries they may have used.

The organization is based in Carson City, Nevada and has international affiliates.

For more information, contact

International Soundex Reunion Registry
P.O. Box 2312
Carson City, NV 89702-2312
(702) 882-7755

interracial See TRANSRACIAL ADOPTION.

interstate adoption The adoption of a child who lives in one state by adoptive parents who reside in another state. The INTERSTATE COMPACT ON THE PLACEMENT OF CHILDREN (ICPC) is an agreement between the states that delineates how interstate adoption should be handled. All states in the United States are members of the compact at the time of this writing.

State social services departments in each state administer the compact and ensure compliance with state laws.

A 1989 article by Bernadette W. Hartfield in the *Nebraska Law Review* delineated some of the problem areas of the interstate compact.

According to Hartfield, a key problem in such adoptions is a lack of awareness of the compact and a consequent lack of compliance. The compact is not described or even referred to in most state adoption laws. In many states, the compact is not cross-referenced under "adoption." As a result, there is a problem with "unintentional noncompliance."

Hartfield says the problem is especially significant in INDEPENDENT ADOPTION. She says noncompliance may be unintentional or purposeful.

If purposeful, an attorney may choose not to comply knowing one of the states places restrictions on independent adoption. In addition, noncompliance might occur because it is presumed compliance would take too long and the individuals wish to place an infant immediately. Finally, the penalties for noncompliance are either nonexistent or not very severe. (Hartfield does cite one case in which an adoption was overturned because of noncompliance with the ICPC: *In re Adoption of T.M.M.*, a 1980 case wherein the Montana Supreme Court overturned an adoption because of noncompliance and the child was returned to the birthmother.)

According to Hartfield, in some cases a pregnant woman may cross state lines to have her child in another state where the adoption laws are more favorable or where the adoptive parents live. Yet this would still be considered an "interstate adoption" by the provisions of the *Compact Administrators' Manual,* which states, "Where the expectant mother crosses a state line as part of the placement plan and arrangement, the transaction should be viewed as an interstate placement."

Another problem identified by Hartfield is that compliance with the "sending" state's adoption laws is not required, but she admits, "In usual practice, the compact administrator in a receiving state is unlikely to approve a placement that is violative of the sending state's laws."

Yet in some instances, a revocation of adoption that could have occurred in the sending state was denied by the receiving state. Hartfield cites the case *In re Male Child Born July 15, 1985.* A child was born in Montana and placed with an Idaho family. The mother wanted the child placed immediately, which occurred after ICPC approval was requested but before it was received. Three days after the placement however, the mother changed her mind. While the mother was attempting to revoke her consent in the Montana courts, ICPC approval was granted in Idaho, and the adoption was finalized there.

The mother lost her case because in Idaho, her original parental consent was sufficient to uphold the adoption. As a result, the Idaho law prevailed over the Montana law.

In another case, *In re Adoption of C.L.W.*, a child was placed with an adoptive couple. The birthmother in Pennsylvania then changed her mind, but the adoptive parents returned to their home in Florida and sought the adoption. The birthmother alleged the adoption should be overturned because the ICPC was not complied with. The Florida Court of Appeals agreed that the ICPC had not been complied with but said, "No harm was suffered by the failure to comply". The court also said the birthmother as a "sending agency" had a responsibility to comply with the ICPC, and the adoption was upheld.

Attorney Alice Bussiere has also discussed serious problems involved in facilitating interstate adoptions. According to Bussiere, there are an array of issues to resolve in interstate adoption: how adoptive parents should be identified, how home studies should be handled, how legal and financial responsibilities are overseen and how assurance of a proper placement is made.

Another problem is that many adoptive parents who relocate may have difficulty using a MEDICAID card from the state they left, and the state they enter may refuse to issue a Medicaid card. In addition, what is covered by Medicaid varies from state to state; for example, physical therapy may be offered in the original state but not in the state to which the adoptive parents relocate. The INTERSTATE COMPACT ON ADOPTION AND MEDICAL ASSISTANCE was formed to solve this problem, although a majority of states have not joined this compact as of this writing.

Other problems include difficulty finding adoptive parents in other states and aversion or confusion over using state exchanges (using a COMPUTER may seem too cold and impersonal for a social worker trained in one-on-one communication; however, a state or national exchange may often be the only way to locate suitable adoptive parents from other states).

Because each state has its own adoption laws, there are numerous problems when these conflict; for example, the time allowed a birthparent to revoke CONSENT (TO AN ADOPTION), in the case of an infant adoption and the type and timing of actions required to terminate parental rights and other problems. (The interstate compact on the placement of children can help resolve many of these problems.)

There is protection for children with SPECIAL NEEDS regarding adoption assistance agreements. The agreement should state that it applies without regard to the state residence of the adoptive parents. For example, if the parents move, the agreement should still apply; however, if a child has specific medical or social needs covered under Medicaid, parents should request those needs be written into the agreement in the event they relocate and those needs are not normally covered by the other state.

Alice Bussiere, J.D., "Issues in Interstate Adoptions," in *Adoption of Children with Special Needs: Issues in Law and Policy*, edited by Ellen C. Segal with Mark Hardin (Washington, D.C.: American Bar Association, 1985).

Bernadette W. Hartfield, "The Role of the Interstate Compact on the Placement of Children in Interstate Adoption," *Nebraska Law Review*, 68(1989): 292–329.

Joan H. Hollinger, editor-in-chief, *Adoption Law and Practice* (New York: Matthew Bender, 1988).

Interstate Compact on Adoption and Medical Assistance (ICAMA) An agreement between member states that governs the interstate delivery of medical services and adoption subsidies for adopted special needs children.

This compact is newer than the Interstate Compact on the Placement of Children. Adopted in 1986 by nine states, the following twenty-four states are members as of this writing, according to the American Public Welfare Association:

Arkansas, Colorado, Delaware, Georgia, Hawaii, Kansas, Kentucky, Louisiana, Maine, Massachusetts, Minnesota, Mississippi, Missouri, Nebraska, Nevada, New Hampshire, New Mexico, Oklahoma, Rhode Island, South Carolina, South Dakota, Utah, West Virginia and Wisconsin.

The reason for the creation of ICAMA was to protect special needs children who move across state lines and ensure they continue to receive appropriate medical assistance and subsidies. According to a booklet published by the American Public Welfare Association, "Adoption opportunities for children with handicaps or other special needs are limited at best. It is often necessary to expand the search for prospective adoptive parents to other states."

When a family moves or a child is relocated to another state, the child has a Medicaid card from the placing state; however, medical providers are often reluctant to accept Medicaid from another state. As a result, member states will provide a Medicaid card from the state to which the child has relocated.

States may either join ICAMA by an enaction of the state legislature, or an executive branch official may act for the state and sign the compact. (See also INTERSTATE ADOPTION.)

For further information on ICAMA or to request a copy of *A Guide to the Interstate Compact on Adoption and Medical Assistance,* contact

Secretariat to the AAICAMA
American Public Welfare Association
810 First St. NE, Suite 500
Washington, DC 20002-4205
(202) 682-0100

Interstate Compact on the Placement of Children An agreement between states that governs the placement of children for adoption or foster care across state lines. Drafted in the late 1950s, New York was the first state to join the compact. According to the American Public Welfare Association, as of this writing, all states are members of the compact.

The compact is a safeguard for children. It ensures that the laws of both states involved have been complied with and that the child will receive appropriate supervision and required home studies will be done and followed up.

Each state appoints a compact administrator, who is within the state social services arm of the public welfare department (commonly known as the welfare department.)

Compact administrators need about six weeks or more from the time the receiving compact office is notified of the proposed placement to process the various papers. (Some cases may take more or less time, depending on individual situations.)

The sending agency retains financial and legal responsibility for the child until the interstate placement ends due to adoption, the child reaching the age of majority or some other change. Violations of the compact are rare, but penalties do exist and children have been returned to the sending state when they were illegally placed.

The compact includes ten articles.

See also INTERSTATE ADOPTION for a discussion of problems with the Interstate Compact.

For further information or to obtain a copy of *Guide to the Interstate Compact on the Placement of Children,* contact

American Public Welfare Association
810 First St. NE, Suite 500
Washington, DC 20002-4205
(202) 682-0100

J

jargon used in adoption See TERMINOLOGY.

judge Elected or appointed individual, usually also an attorney, who grants the FINALIZATION of an adoption and gives the adopted child all the legal rights of a child born to the family. Usually this procedure is performed in the judge's chambers or a private waiting room, although some adoption proceedings are held in a courtroom.

When protective services social workers recommend that parental rights of an abusive or neglectful parent be terminated, it is the judge who will decide whether or not to terminate these rights. (See also CUSTODY; TERMINATION OF PARENTAL RIGHTS.)

K

kin See BIRTH KIN.

Korean adopted children Thousands of Korean children have been adopted by U.S. citizens since the Korean War period of the 1950s. (See INTERNATIONAL ADOPTION for chart with numbers of international adoptions from 1981 to 1989.) Nearly 100,000 Korean children have been adopted by U.S. citizens since 1953.

The numbers of adopted Korean children adopted has steadily declined since fiscal year 1987, from nearly 6,000 children in 1987 to about 5,000 in 1988 to 3,552 in 1989, and it is anticipated that this decline will continue. However, the numbers of adoptions have gone up and down since 1978; for example, there were only 2,444 adoptions in 1981 and 2,620 in 1990.

According to Holt Children's Services officials, one key reason for the current decline is that infertile Koreans are increasingly interested in adoption. (Holt is the primary U.S. agency that arranges international adoptions from Korea. The agency also arranges adoptions within Korea as well.)

Susan Cox, director of development for Holt, says many Koreans are adopting infants independently. Although agency adoption statistics are available in Korea and these numbers have not dramatically increased, independent adoption statistics are not compiled in Korea, even as they are not compiled in most states of the United States. This argument cannot therefore be supported or refuted, but it seems likely that Cox is correct because her agency has also increased agency placements within Korea (for example, in 1985, the agency placed about 400 children with Korean families, and by 1990, that number doubled to 800, clearly indicating more acceptance of adoption).

In addition, more abortions and a greater use of birth control has cut back the number of out-of-wedlock births in Korea, according to Cox and other experts. An *OURS* magazine article in January/February 1990 quoted David Pilgrim, adoption program director for the Children's Home Society in Minnesota, "Family planning is receiving much interest (in Korea). There are family planners in every neighborhood. They need to do that—Korea is one of the most populated nations in the world."

The Olympic games held in Seoul in 1988 negatively highlighted Korean adoptions, and this publicity may also have had an impact on Korean adoptions overseas. Korean Consul Baek-Sang Cho of the Korean Embassy stated that after the Olympic press coverage, the Korean government and people decided to rethink international adoption policies and the responsibilities of the government toward orphaned children.

One problem still remaining in Korea is that Confucian dictates have for many years concentrated on blood lines and genealogical heritage. As a result, an adopted child cannot be considered a true family member. Cox says this attitude still exists, which is why Koreans who adopt children often do so in secrecy.

Before 1952, according to a dissertation by Lois Lydens, adoption was illegal in Korea. Now legal, it is still a source of shame and embarrassment for many Koreans. In one incident, a businessman planned to adopt a child, and his wife feigned pregnancy for nine months, pretending that the adopted child was her birth child. Unfortunately, the truth was discovered, and this great loss of face forced the embarrassed couple to move away from their neighborhood.

The South Koreans have also been continually taunted by the North Koreans, who have accused them of baby selling. But, in truth, the fee for adopting an infant from Korea has generally been far lower than that charged by other countries.

In addition, the Korean orphanages have generally ensured the children are healthy and well cared for.

Officials who support adoption believe that international adoption is a much better solution than maintaining children in orphanages for years—or allowing the children to live in the streets, as some countries do. And the issue of abortion rather than adoption is a factor in international adoption, just as it is in domestic placements.

U.S. servicemen began adopting Korean orphans after the Korean War, and later Americans within the United States began adopting Korean infants and children. (See INTERNATIONAL ADOPTION.)

The primary U.S. adoption agency that has arranged international adoptions in Korea since 1956 is Oregon-based Holt International Children's Services.

Founded by Harry and Bertha Holt, the agency has placed thousands of orphaned children, both in the United States and also with Korean families in Korea. Holt has branch offices throughout the United States. Holt also places children from other Asian and Latin American countries with U.S. families, as well as a small number of U.S.-born children whose birthmothers choose adoption for their infants.

Parents of children adopted from Korea vary in their commitment to provide the child with information about his or her birth country. Some parents have joined support groups, enabling their child to meet other Asian children. Others have encouraged their child to attend CULTURE CAMPS, where the child can learn about his cultural heritage. And other parents believe that the best course of action is to raise the child as an American, believing that America is a nation of immigrants.

Some adoption experts are concerned when they hear adoptive parents constantly refer to their child as "my adopted Korean daughter," rather than "my daughter." These experts believe this reference could seem alienating and separates the child from feeling a part of the family. Although the Korean (or other nationality) heritage should never be a source of shame or embarrassment, it need not constantly be mentioned.

The adoption of a Korean child by a white family or other non-Asian family is a TRANSRACIAL ADOPTION. Some people believe adoptive parents should only adopt within their race, while others believe the prevailing concept should be that if a same-race family is not available to adopt a child, a loving family of another race should be considered.

Lois Adele Lydens, "A Longitudinal Study of Crosscultural Adoption: Identity Development Among Asian Adoptees at Adolescence and Early Adulthood," Ph.D. diss., Northwestern University, 1988.

Peter Maass, "Orphans: Korea's Disquieting Problem; National Embarrassment Over Letting Foreigners Take Children," *Washington Post,* December 14, 1989.

Leslie Maggi, "Korea Closes Its Doors," *OURS* magazine, January/February 1990, 20.

Hei Sook Park Wilkinson, Ph.D., *Birth is More than Once: The Inner World of Adopted Korean Children* (Bloomfield Hills, Mich.: Sunrise Ventures, 1985).

L

language See TERMINOLOGY.

large families The size of a "large" family is a judgment call; however, most people would consider families of four or more children to be large families.

Some adoptive parents have even more children, and there are differing views on whether large families should be allowed to adopt more children or how many children is "enough."

Those who believe large families are not healthy describe adoptive parents in such large families as "child collectors" and believe that the children do not receive adequate individual attention.

Supporters believe the children provide each other with a great deal of attention and a large family can be particularly nurturing for a child with SPECIAL NEEDS.

Sometimes a family is large because it adopts four or more siblings. Researchers and social workers Dorothy LePere, Lloyd Davis, Janus Couve and Mona McDonald studied adoptions of large sibling groups and reported their findings in the booklet *Large Sibling Groups: Adoption Experiences.*

The majority (87%) of the siblings studied were adopted together in groups of three or more children.

According to the researchers, parents with experience are good candidates for becoming well-functioning adoptive parents. "Those who are already parenting four or more children, or who have come from large families of origin, seem to have fewer adjustment problems."

Researchers noted that families who adopt large sibling groups sometimes cannot depend on their extended family or friends for support and should have the capacity to develop new support systems.

The authors concluded that large families can work effectively and stated, "The results of the questionnaire and the authors' research and experiences have demonstrated that the adoption of a large sibling group is rewarding and challenging both for the family and for the adoption worker."

Dorothy W. LePere, A.C.S.W., Lloyd E. Davis, A.C.S.W., Janus Couve, A.C.S.W., and Mona McDonald, A.C.S.W., *Large Sibling Groups: Adoption Experiences* (Washington, D.C.: Child Welfare League of America, 1986).

Latin American adoptions The adoption of children in Central and South America and the Caribbean. According to the U.S. Immigration and Naturalization Service, 1,757 orphans were adopted from South America by Americans in fiscal year 1989. Most of the children (735) immigrated from Colombia.

An additional 595 children were adopted from Central America with the largest number of adoptions (208) from Guatemala. An additional 202 children were adopted from the Caribbean.

Criteria for prospective parents, including the upper limit on age of adoptive parents and number of children already in the home, vary greatly. Some countries will allow adoptive parents as old as 55 years to adopt infants and have no limits on the number of children in the home already. Most Latin American countries require adopting parents to travel to the country and stay at least several days until legal paperwork is accomplished. In some cases, the stay may last weeks.

International adoption is very changeable, and prospective adoptive parents are urged to thoroughly investigate this form of adoption before applying to an agency or identifying a foreign attorney. An adoptive parents support group is a good start. The INTERNATIONAL CONCERNS COMMITTEE FOR CHILDREN also provides valuable and updated information. (See also IMMIGRATION AND NATURALIZATION; INTERNATIONAL ADOPTION.)

laws, federal See ADOPTION ASSISTANCE AND FAMILY WELFARE ACT OF 1980; FEDERAL GOVERNMENT; INDIAN CHILD WELFARE ACT OF 1978.

laws, state Each state has its own set of laws that govern who may adopt, who may be adopted and under what conditions adoptions may occur. Other issues, such as whether information on the adoption may be made available, whether or not adoption must be confidential and how adoptions are to be administered are also issues the state decides.

The states must follow federal rules and regulations regarding adoption or risk losing federal funds. Probably the most important federal law to impact adoptions has been the ADOPTION ASSISTANCE AND CHILD WELFARE ACT OF 1980, which requires review of foster children's cases every six months and a judicial review after 18 months. States have mixed results in adhering to these requirements.

Adoption laws are not static, and changes to state laws are common; for example, as of this writing, the social services department in Minnesota seeks for legislation to be passed that would regulate independent adoption and, among other factors, require a home study to be performed prior to a child's placement with the adoptive family. In 1990, independent adoptions were not addressed except as an exclusion to existing law, and home studies were performed subsequent to placement.

In some states, only agencies may arrange adoptions: as of this writing, in Connecticut, Delaware, Massachusetts, Michigan and North Dakota, an agency involvement is mandatory. It should be noted, however, that in virtually every state with the exception of Michigan, birthparents and prospective adoptive parents may decide they would like an adoption arranged and request an agency to perform a DESIGNATED ADOPTION. Because the adoption was originally planned by the birthparents and adoptive parents, it is also considered a DIRECT PLACEMENT and an INDEPENDENT ADOPTION, despite any agency involvement. (See MODEL STATE ADOPTION ACT.)

lawsuits See ATTORNEYS; BLOOD TIES; INHERITANCE; SURROGATE MOTHERHOOD; TERMINATION OF PARENTAL RIGHTS; WRONGFUL ADOPTION.

lawyer See ATTORNEYS; INDEPENDENT ADOPTION; WRONGFUL ADOPTION.

learning disabilities Also known as "specific learning disabilities". The federal definition of a learning disability, as set forth in U.S. P.L. 94–142 is as follows:

> Specific learning disability means a disorder in one or more of the basic psychological processes involved in understanding or using language, spoken or written, which may manifest itself in an imperfect ability to listen, think, speak, read, write, spell, or to do mathematical calculations.

Just as any other child, adopted children may suffer disabilities in learning. Some, but certainly not all, children with DEVELOPMENTAL DISABILITIES may also have learning disabilities and need assistance from parents and the educational system.

Children are generally screened prior to kindergarten; however, if a parent suspects a child may have a learning disability, this possibility should be brought to the attention of the school for possible testing.

There is evidence that some children born exposed to such drugs as cocaine may ultimately suffer learning disabilities, although this is by no means certain. The child may suffer memory deficits, inability to understand certain concepts, emotional conflicts and a wide array of problems that are attributed to the prenatal environment. The National Association for Perinatal Addiction Research in Education (NAPARE) believes that as many as 11% of U.S. newborns were exposed to drugs in the womb. Senator Christopher Dodd, chairman of the Senate Subcommittee on Children, Families, Drug and Alcoholism, estimates that in the year 2000, there may be 4 million children who have been born with cocaine or crack cocaine in their systems, at a societal cost in the billions of dollars. In addition, although the problem of drug addiction and drug-addicted babies appears more dominant in the working class areas, it is a problem that cuts across socioeconomic lines. A pilot project in Los Angeles is designed to help these children cope successfully and learn.

Some researchers challenge the assumption that all or most infants whose mothers were drug users will suffer severe developmental disabilities. Richard P. Barth, Ph.D., indicated there are many variations among children born to drug-using mothers. (See DRUG ABUSE.)

Parents who choose to adopt children whose birthmothers abused drugs or alcohol should be prepared to help the children with learning disabilities that may be present. It should be noted that some drug-addicted children are very bright and considered "gifted" and low intelligence is apparently not always a result of drug abuse. Prenatal alcohol abuse, however, can lead to FETAL ALCOHOL SYNDROME in the child and varying degrees of retardation in the child.

The field of learning disabilities is very complex, and there is a firestorm of controversy over how to evaluate children and how to treat them. For example, should a learning disabled child be removed from the classroom for sessions with a specialist in learning disabilities, or should the child remain in the classroom, where the teacher deals with the child and uses outside consultations for help? If a child has difficulty processing ideas with sound, should his visual abilities be allowed to substitute, or should the problem area be worked on instead?

It may be very difficult to determine the cause of a learning disability. Having a learning disability could frustrate a child enough to create an emotional problem, and because children with emotional problems often have trouble paying attention to information and therefore learning, an unfortunate cycle is created.

In some cases, a parent may believe a child does not have a learning disability and a teacher insists the child does. In such a case, the adoptive parent should consider whether or not the child's adopted status is affecting the evaluation.

A study on teachers indicated that teachers may perceive adopted children as pathetic individuals who merit special protective treatment, presumably because of the child's adoptive status. (See TEACHERS AND ADOPTED CHILDREN.) Of course, parents can be wrong about a learning disability and deny a disability that does exist and for which the child should receive help. (See also SPECIAL NEEDS.)

The Association for Children and Adults with Learning Disabilities Inc. (ACLD) is an organization of over 60,000 parents, professionals and others interested in learning disabilities. It serves as a resource for individuals interested in more information. Individuals needing assistance or information should contact

The Association for Children and Adults
  with Learning Disabilities Inc. (ACLD)
4156 Library Rd.
Pittsburgh, PA 15234
(412) 341-1515

(See also SPECIAL NEEDS.)

Richard P. Barth, "Educational Implications of Prenatally Drug Exposed Children," *Social Work in Education,* 13(1991): 130–136.
"Crack Babies Overwhelm Child Welfare System," *The Brown University Child Behavior and Development Letter,* April 1990.
Carl K. Deutsch, James M. Swanson, Jan H. Bruell, Dennis P. Cantwell, Fred Weinberg and Martin Baren, "Overrepresentation of Adoptees in Children with the Attention Deficit Disorder," *Behavior Genetics,* 12:2(1982): 231–238.
Susan Jenks, "Drug Babies: An Ethical Quagmire for Doctors," *Medical World News,* February 12, 1990.
Cathy Trost, "As Drug Babies Grow Older, Schools Strive to Meet Their Needs," *Wall Street Journal,* December 27, 1989, A1.

legal custody See CUSTODY.

legal father The man legally recognized as the father of a child, irrespective of whether he is the biological father or not. When a couple is married, and the wife bears a child, the law generally presumes her husband is the biological father of the child, even though he may not be. (See BIRTHFATHER for more information on the 1989 challenge to this status, which the U.S. Supreme Court denied.)

In a few states, this presumption cannot be challenged, and the U.S. Supreme Court has upheld such laws (*Michael H. v. Gerald D.*, 57 U.S.L.W. 4691, June 13, 1989). In many states, however, the presumption of paternity can be legally challenged with strong evidence, such as genetic testing. If there is no challenge to the legal father's status, then it stands.

Also, in about half the states, the husband is specifically described as the legal father in the case of artificial insemination.

As a result of statutes regarding legal fathers, if a married woman wishes to plan adoption for her child, her husband, as the presumed legal father, must also sign the consent for adoption forms. Some agencies and attorneys may seek consent from the alleged biological father as well as the husband if the mother states that the child's father is someone other than her husband.

If the name of a man not married to the child's mother is listed on the birth certificate of a child with his consent and if the mother is not married to someone else, then he is the presumed father. Some states, however, permit rebuttal of this presumption by proof (usually genetic tests) showing that the presumed father is not the biological father.

Adoptive fathers become legal fathers upon finalization of an adoption when a new birth certificate is issued with the adoptive father's name appearing as the father. (See also SEALED RECORDS.)

Joan H. Hollinger, editor-in-chief, *Adoption Law and Practice* (New York: Matthew Bender, 1989).

legal risk adoption See AT RISK PLACEMENT.

lifebook As used in an adoption of an OLDER CHILD especially, a scrapbook documenting a child's life to date and created for and with a child with the assistance of a social worker, psychologist, foster parent and/or other individuals. The lifebook may be one of the few possessions the child can call his own prior to his adoption.

The purpose of the lifebook is to provide meaning and continuity to a displaced child whose life may have been extremely disrupted. It is designed to capture memories and provide a chance to recall people and events in the child's past life, to allow for a sense of continuity. The lifebook can also serve as a focal point to explore painful issues with the child that need to be resolved.

Children who grow up as members of one family usually have ready access to birth certificates, baby and family pictures, and other evidences of growing up, as well as items that would be placed in a scrapbook.

Foster children often do not have tangible information about their growing up, and the lifebook can serve to help them feel important and "connected" in time. Lifebooks also may cover and explain major events and developmental milestones, such as when the child first walked, talked and so forth. (See also PREPARING A CHILD FOR ADOPTION.)

loss A feeling of emotional deprivation that is, at some point in time, experienced by each member of the ADOPTION TRIAD.

No matter how certain a birthparent is that adoption is the right decision for a child, there will be times when the loss of the child is keenly felt. The initial loss will usually be felt at or subsequent to placement of the child. Caring social workers realize that when a birthmother goes home from the hospital, she must contend with feelings of loss and separation in addition to any hormonal imbalance she may also suffer. Birthmothers also report that they think about the child on the child's birthday.

If the birthmother was not pressured into her decision to place the child for adoption and believes it was primarily her own decision, she is more able to cope with the feelings of loss she will experience. She will also realize that whatever the resolution of a pregnancy, particularly if it is unintended, some feeling of loss is inevitable.

Adoptive parents who are infertile feel a loss as well, and their loss is the ability to bear a genetic child. Individuals who are actively seeking to achieve a pregnancy have reported feeling anger or despair when they see pregnant women in public and a terrible sense of a lack of control over their own destinies. Hopefully, they will have resolved most of their own anxiety over infertility prior to adopting a child so they can fully accept a child who does not share their genes. (See INFERTILITY.)

An adopted child may feel a sense of loss at various points in time; for example, if a child is adopted at infancy, the first time the child realizes he is adopted, perhaps at age five or six, and this means his adoptive mother was not pregnant with him can be painful because the child loves the mother and wants to be as close as possible to her. Another possibly difficult time for an adoptive child is adolescence, when questions of identity and questions about life become important to the average teenager, adopted or nonadopted. Although most adopted children who were adopted as infants are as well-adjusted as the average nonadopted person, if there will be an identity crisis, it will probably be during adolescence. (See ADOLESCENT ADOPTED PERSONS; IDENTITY.)

Katherine Gordy Levine, M.S.W., director of group homes, SCAN, in New York and also adjunct professor at the Columbia University School of Social Work, points out that it should not be presumed that children adopted as adolescents who are ACTING OUT are unhappy with their parents or feel their parents are inadequate. Instead, she says, "The adjustment of children to a foster home before becoming adolescents is a good barometer of whether the problem originates in parental problems or the adolescents' shifting thoughts."

In some cases, Levine says, the adolescent may blame adoptive parents for problems stemming from treatment received by birthparents. "The tendency to blame the current parents and to focus on their limitations is often simultaneously used by placed adolescents to negate biological parents' failings. If all parents are bad, biological parents are not so bad."

Levine says adolescents "need to mourn and make sense of the experiences of their lives . . . when the wounds created by placement can be closed, peace can be made with the past, and life can move forward once again."

Adopted adults may again experience a sense of loss when they marry and have children themselves, wondering about their genetic links to their birthparents. If the adopted adult is infertile, the infertility may be even more painful than for the non-adopted infertile person; however, presuming the adopted person felt positively about his or her own adoption, he or she may perceive adoption as a very good way to create his or her own family.

Older adopted children may experience feelings of loss, not only from their birthparents, if they were old enough to remember when they separated, but also from foster parents, if they are adopted by another family. Adoptive parents are advised to recognize these feelings and help the child resolve them. If possible, adopting parents should initially meet the child at the foster parents' home.

Many experts recommend the use of a LIFEBOOK, which is a special scrapbook for adopted older children, chronicling the child's life. It is also helpful to allow the child to talk about the past and reflect upon it. Talking about previous experiences need not mean the child is unhappy with the adoptive parents but is more likely to mean the child feels comfortable and safe about talking about important events in his or her life. (See also BIRTHMOTHER.)

Vera Fahlberg, M.D., *Attachment and Separation: Putting the Pieces Together* (Chelsea, Mich.: National Resource Center for Special Needs Adoption, 1979.)

Claudia Jewett, *Helping Children Cope with Separation and Loss* (Boston: Harvard Common Press, 1982).

Katherine Gordy Levine, "The Placed Child Examines the Quality of Parental Care," *Child Welfare*, 67(July–August 1988): 301–310.

M

married birthparents An estimated 6% or more of all infants placed for adoption were placed by their married parents, according to studies by the National Center for Health Statistics.

Married birthparents place their infants for adoption primarily because they do not believe in abortion but feel unwilling or unable to parent the child. Often they may have other children and suffer severe financial problems.

They may also be on the verge of a divorce or a separation and not want the child as a constant reminder of their former relationship together.

When married birthparents decide on adoption for their infants, they are often viewed with contempt and suspicion by the rest of society, who cannot understand how or why a married birthparent would do such a thing; ironically, it is perfectly understandable and acceptable to many that married people might choose to abort a fetus.

Sometimes the child who is placed for adoption is a toddler, and the reasons for placement are similar to the reasons for making an adoption decision for a newborn infant: financial problems, marital problems, child abuse or neglect or career goals that conflict with parenting a child.

The married birthparent might also face debilitating health or personal problems that his mate also finds difficult to cope with; as a result, both feel that having the child adopted by a loving couple is a viable solution.

For married birthparents, confidentiality and anonymity may be particularly important, given the lack of understanding society often has for their dilemma.

matching The attempt to select adoptive parents similar to the child to be adopted. The selected parents and children may be similar in appearance, interests, intelligence, personality or other traits. This practice has also become known more recently as trying to achieve a "good fit" when choosing a family for a specific child. Other components may be included in the parent selection process, such as the ability to meet a child's unusual or specific needs (for example, if the child has a medical problem with which the parents have experience).

Religion Some agencies attempt to match a child based on religion, although religious matching is more often based on the preference of the birthmother. (Most sectarian agencies limit applications to couples with certain religion backgrounds.)

State adoption laws prior to the 1970s were very restrictive in some states and mandated matching despite the wishes of the birthmother. (Several cases are covered in *The Law of Adoption and Surrogate Parenting* by Irving J. Sloan.)

In 1954, in the Massachusetts case of *In re Goldman,* a Jewish couple attempted to adopt twins whose birthmother was Catholic. Although the children had lived with the couple for three years, the court decreed they could not adopt the children because Catholic couples waited to adopt children. The court refused to consider the birthmother's wishes.

In contrast, a birthmother today may often specify the religion of the family that will adopt her child.

In a 1957 case, the Ellis family, a Jewish couple, adopted a newborn child in Massachusetts. State officials later demanded the child be returned since the birthmother was Catholic. The adoptive parents fled to Florida. (The birthmother did not wish to revoke consent.)

Governor Collins of Florida, who received more than 9,000 calls, letters and telegrams both pro and con, refused to extradite the couple, stating that "the controlling question . . . must be the welfare of the child."

In 1971, a trial court held that a couple could not adopt because of a "lack of belief in a Supreme Being rendered them unfit to be adoptive parents." The adoption agency had insisted the prospective adoptive parents were people of high moral standards and argued they should be allowed to adopt. The New Jersey Supreme Court reversed the lower court.

Some states still have religious matching laws on the books; for example, in Delaware, the child must be placed in the home of the same religion as the birthparent unless the birthparent states that placing outside the religion is acceptable.

In Pennsylvania, the adopting parents should be of the same religion as the birthparent if at all possible. (This is a recommendation in the law, not a mandate.) A similar provision is incorporated into Rhode Island adoption law and Wisconsin law.

Ethnic Matching and Physical Appearance If the child to be adopted is an infant, the social worker will compare the birthparents to the adoptive parents in an attempt to make a suitable match; for example, if the birthmother is very musically inclined, the social worker will not place the infant in a home where both adoptive parents are tone-deaf. (Note: Some caseworkers do not believe in physical matching, and adopting parents should not depend on adopting a child who resembles them.)

When attempting to match for personality (if such matching is tried), a social worker will not place the child of a serious and bookish birthmother with a family who lives for weekend football.

Sometimes a factor to be considered in making a match is socioeconomic status: The child of a college student will probably not be placed with a blue collar worker, particularly in the case of an OPEN ADOPTION. (On the other hand, the child of a blue collar worker will be placed with an upper middle class family.)

Proponents of matching point to studies that indicate similarities between the adoptive parents and their adopted offspring lead to greater harmony and happiness. Adoption experts, such as Ruth McRoy, Ph.D., say the "goodness of fit" is important, and the more closely the child fits in with the family, the more he or she will thrive.

Dissenters insist it is often impossible to achieve realistic matches, and just because a birthmother is musical does not mean her child will also be musically talented nor will the child's personality necessarily be anything like the parents. They also point out that biological children often do not resemble their parents.

Opponents of matching add that painstakingly trying to match an adopted child to an adoptive family is a form of denial and a way to make it easier for the adoptive family to pretend the child is their biological child. (See also GENETIC PREDISPOSITIONS; RELIGION.)

Robert W. Delaney, "1957 Decision Puts Baby-Swapping Case in Perspective," *Florida Today,* November 17, 1988, 10B.

Ruth G. McRoy, Harold D. Grotevant, Louis A. Zurcher Jr., *Emotional Disturbances in Adopted Adolescents: Origins and Development* (New York: Praeger Press, 1988.)

Irvine J. Sloan, *The Law of Adoption and Surrogate Parenting* (New York: Oceana Publications, 1988).

maternity homes Residences for pregnant women. The number of homes has decreased over the past two decades, and existing homes often have a waiting list of women. In the mid-1960s, there were about 200 maternity homes nationwide, but by 1981, there were only about 100, according to the Interagency Task Force on Adoption's report, *America's Waiting Children*.

Concerning the problems faced by maternity homes, the task force said they "are challenged by rising costs due to the state and local codes for residential, educational and medical facilities. Many have had to close their doors due to high costs, and little, if any, reimbursement is available from the state level."

In California, the "Pregnancy Freedom of Choice Act" of 1978 enabled state reimbursements to licensed nonprofit maternity homes, and the task force recommended other states follow this lead.

Some newer maternity homes are small group homes, and some organizations have recruited families who volunteer to house women in crisis pregnancies.

The women who live in a maternity home may pay a small fee or no fee to live in the home and they often apply for public assistance and MEDICAID payments.

Women who use maternity homes may be adults or adolescents. They may also be teenage foster children who are wards of the court, if the maternity home has a license for group foster care.

The services provided by a maternity home usually include counseling, aid in applying for public assistance programs such as Aid to Families with Dependent Children, food stamps and Medicaid, nutritional advice and encouragement and assistance in continuing education or identifying career opportunities.

Most maternity homes utilize volunteers who will drive women to the physician, supermarket, welfare office and other sites where she must go.

The primary need of the homeless pregnant woman is for food and shelter, and the number of women with this need is not completely met by existing agencies or maternity homes. Organizations such as the NATIONAL COMMITTEE FOR ADOPTION support a voucher system, whereby women with crisis pregnancies can choose the appropriate shelter for themselves and pay for services with the vouchers. The NCFA believes more maternity homes would open if such a system were devised by the federal or state governments. (See also CRISIS PREGNANCY.)

Presidential Task Force, *America's Waiting Children: A Report to the President from the Interagency Task Force on Adoption,* (Washington, D.C.: May 12, 1988).

maternity leave An extended time of absence from employment granted by an employer to a woman who will soon give birth to a child and/or who has recently given birth to a child.

As of this writing, there is no federal parental leave policy in the United States for biological or adoptive parents, although Congress has seriously considered such proposals. Representative Patricia Schroeder (D., Colo.) has spearheaded these efforts. Policies on maternity leave vary from state to state. In the absence of a state law, the parental leave policy varies from employer to employer.

Contrary to popular belief, pregnant women are not automatically entitled to maternity leave nor are women (or men) who adopt children entitled to leave.

According to a 1990 Congressional Research Service Issue Brief on parental leave, the Pregnancy Discrimination Act of 1978 is part of the Title VII of the Civil Rights Act of 1964. Under this act, "Employers are not required to provide specific benefits of any kind, but if employers do provide benefits, they may not discriminate between protected classes of workers or on the basis of pregnancy."

In addition, the Pregnancy Discrimination Act requires women who are "affected by pregnancy, childbirth, or related medical conditions be treated the same for all employment purposes, including receipt of benefits under fringe benefit programs, as persons not so affected but similar in their ability or inability to work."

The problem with maternity leave for adoptive parents is that maternity leave is considered a form of disability leave and is not provided to assist the new mother with bonding but rather to allow time for "recuperation" from pregnancy and childbearing.

Since an adoptive mother is not "disabled" by pregnancy, she is therefore not eligible for maternity leave. Several states have passed laws mandating parental leave for adoptive parents, but these laws have been overturned because they were said by the courts to discriminate against biological fathers. (A broad parental leave policy for biological parents and adoptive parents would solve this problem.)

See PARENTAL LEAVE for a detailed discussion of the issues facing adoptive parents in this area. (See also EMPLOYMENT BENEFITS.)

Lelie W. Gladstone, "Parental Leave: Legislation in the 101st Congress," *CRS Research Brief*, updated January 8, 1990.

maternity services See MATERNITY HOMES.

mature women planning adoption
Although most women with crisis pregnancies who choose adoption are in their late teens or early twenties, there are also women in their late twenties and thirties and even forties who choose adoption for their children.

They may be married and already have three, four or more children. Faced with an unplanned pregnancy but morally opposed to abortion, they view adoption as a loving solution. Other mature women may be divorced or divorcing, or they may be single women.

Few adoption agencies are structured to deal with mature women; instead, their informational packets and counseling are more oriented to teenagers with crisis pregnancies. There are, however, agencies that offer separate living quarters and specially designed programs for this age group.

Social workers should realize that mature women with unplanned pregnancies also need positive support and do not desire patronizing attitudes.

Some mature women have asked agencies for help only to be turned away and told to come back in their last trimester if they still want help. Such action does not allow the woman a chance to receive counseling and other services. If she is turned away, she is deprived of needed assistance to plan for her child's future and her own future as well, and this action can severely inhibit the success of an adoption plan should the birthmother desire adoption.

Whether they are considering adoption or not, such women need information and assistance to help them gain necessary prenatal care. They may also need income and shelter to avoid the plight of homelessness or physical abuse by the father of the baby.

The Nurturing Network was formed by Mary Cunningham Agee to assist college-age and career women facing a CRISIS PREGNANCY. Founded on Mother's Day in 1987, Agee and her network of families and individuals nationwide provide housing, financial assistance, medical assistance, prenatal classes and other needs.

Agee founded her organization when she realized women over age 20 faced the greatest difficulty in obtaining assistance during a crisis pregnancy. Some of the women Agee has assisted have made adoption plans while others have chosen to parent their children. Agee and her fellow networkers have helped over 700 women since the inception of the program.

For further information about the Nurturing Network, contact

The Nurturing Network
910 Main St. #360

P.O. Box 2050
Boise, ID 83701
(208) 344-7200

media Society's overall views on adoption are affected by a variety of factors, including individuals' personal experiences with adoption, either first-hand or through knowing someone who adopted or was adopted, discussions about adoption with other people, and the media and its depiction of adoption as a positive or negative experience.

Although it is not possible to quantify the overall effect of the media on people's views about adoption, some effect is very likely, particularly when considering the television media and its extensive reach to all segments of society. The effect of movies is also important on a lesser segment of society. Print media, albeit more selective, also impacts numerous individuals, as does radio broadcast media.

A 1988 study of the media and its depiction of adoption revealed a heavily negative bias. This study, performed by Dr. George Gerbner of the Annenberg School of Communications at the University of Pennsylvania, concentrated on television, film and print coverage of adoption. The study was funded by the Catholic Adoptive Parents Association Inc. in New York City.

Television According to Gerbner's report,

> Americans encounter vivid images of adoption, adopted children, and adoptive parents most often in television drama. Significant dramatic portrayals occur, on the average, at least six times a year.

According to Gerbner's analysis, "The treatment of adoption ranged from the highly sensitive and thoughtful to the hackneyed and stereotypic." He found the legal process of adoption as the predominant theme, appearing in nearly half of the television programs offering adoption themes.

Next most prominent, with almost one-third of the programs depicting some variation on this theme, was the "shady deal": baby buying, cheating birthmothers, stealing babies. Although illegal activities do occur in the real world of adoptions, they represent a tiny minority of all adoptions, and most infant adoptions are lawful; however, a primary purpose of electronic media such as television and movies is to entertain and dramatize. The average successful adoption would probably seem very boring to a television producer.

As a result, when the public continually views adoption scams, it is highly probable viewers will conclude that shady adoptions are an everyday occurrence. In addition, adoption itself is viewed more suspiciously, as are birthmothers considering adoption and prospective adoptive parents.

Films Portrayals of adoptions in 87 films from 1927 to 1987 were analyzed. Of these movies, 60% concentrated on the process of adoption, a pattern also seen in television. The researchers selected movies that seemed to typify plots over the long-term. "Bad Seed" themes were considered: In fact, a film entitled "Bad Seed" was released in 1956 and depicted an adopted child with evil inherited traits.

These and similar films may have profoundly affected viewers' attitudes toward adoption, particularly the attitudes of Baby Boomers who were then children. Such film treatments cause concern over possible genetic predispositions toward "evil" and inherited bad genes.

Researchers stated that film coverage appeared to be less bound to "formulas" than is television coverage in depiction of adoption.

Adoptive parents have had some impact on media; for example, in 1989 when adoptive parents complained to the producers of a Disney movie about negative adoption remarks made by a character, the remarks were deleted from the movie.

Print Media An analysis of adoption articles in the *Reader's Guide to Periodical Literature* revealed a similar pattern to television storylines on adoption.

Nearly one-third of the articles covered problem areas: obstacles to adoption because of the prospective parents' race, religion, marital status and so forth; negative behavior by adopted persons; baby or child selling; adopted children confronted with two mothers; birthparents "giving away" a child; adoptive parents committing crimes against adopted children; and lawsuits brought by adoptive parents.

An analysis of the *New York Times Index* revealed that criminal activities or court stories represented as much as one-third of all adoption-related stories in the *New York Times*.

"Litigation, rackets, abuses, and other illegalities linked to adoption, including suits over parenthood, claims of baby-switching and selling, race-related disputes, and various scandals are the most likely to make the subject of adoption—as indeed many other subjects—newsworthy," said Gerbner.

Concluded Gerbner, "Adoption is depicted as a troubling and troublesome issue . . . Useful and helpful information is available to those who seek it. But images and messages most viewers and readers encounter most of the time are more likely to project than to deflect the common problems adopted persons and their families face in our culture."

One common complaint of adopted individuals and adoptive parents about articles in print is the frequent singling out of a celebrity's adopted children and children born to the family when adoption plays no role whatsoever in the story. (See also ATTITUDES ABOUT ADOPTION.)

In 1991, a new group was formed to promote "decency and equality of treatment" of adoption by the media. The organization is Positive Adoption Attitudes in the Media (PAAM). Contact PAAM at
Box 15293
Chevy Chase, MD 20825
(202) 244-9092.

George B. Gerbner with the assistance of Sr. Elvira Arcenas and Marc Rubner, *Adoption in the Mass Media: A Preliminary Survey of Sources of Information and a Pilot Study,* unpublished, The Annenberg School of Communications, University of Pennsylvania, Philadelphia, November 21, 1988.

Medicaid Medical assistance program for individuals categorically eligible for public assistance, including low-income pregnant women, low-income parents with dependents (both are eligible under Aid to Families with Dependent children [AFDC]) and other categories. The program is funded with both federal and state money and originated with the 1965 amendments to the Social Security Act (Title XIX).

Adoptive parents of children with special needs are eligible to receive Medicaid for their adopted children. Problems have arisen when a Medicaid card was issued to a child in one state and the parents then moved to another state or when the child was adopted by parents from another state. Many of these problems have been resolved by issuing the parent a card from the state in which he or she lives; however, problems still occur. (See INTERSTATE ADOPTION.)

medical history Information on childhood diseases, allergies and major ailments suffered by the birthparents and their parents, siblings, uncles, aunts, and grandparents or by the child himself; also includes information on immunizations in the case of an older child.

Adoptive parents should obtain as much medical information as possible on the child(ren) they adopt. Not only will this information assist their pediatrician, but it will ultimately serve to reassure the adopted adult later in life. Adult adopted persons often report anxiety about a lack of medical history information, particularly women when they are pregnant. This information could alleviate much anxiety about their heredity and the genes they may be passing on to their child.

When adoptive parents are applying to adopt, social workers usually supply a checklist of which ailments, disabilities and other conditions they would be willing to consider or would not accept; for example, mental illness in the birth family, incest, rape of the birthmother, heart disease, allergic reactions to antibiotics and a broad spectrum of possible diseases or conditions. Prospective parents may be asked to state yes, no or maybe to each condition.

In addition, when parents will be adopting an infant, the caseworker will want to know if they are willing to accept an infant whose birthmother abused drugs or alcohol during her pregnancy because such conditions can lead to either permanent birth defects or temporary conditions that ultimately improve.

The adoptive parents should be thoroughly briefed on the condition of the child they adopt, despite their prior written acceptance of conditions: Parents sometimes may be too open-ended for their individual situation, in their eagerness to adopt a child, or they may believe they should tell the agency what they think the agency wants to hear.

After approval of the adoptive parents and before the child is placed with them, the parents will be told of a child in need of adoptive parents and given medical information on the child's genetic ancestry as well as on the child himself. The child's birth weight, height, condition at birth and other factors will also be shared.

If it is an older child who is being adopted, the adoptive family should be provided with as much social, developmental and medical information as available. Any broken bones or major ailments as well as learning disabilities should be explained. In addition, any history of physical or sexual abuse should be discussed as completely as the social worker's information allows. Agencies can and should go back to obtain all possible additional information from foster families, schools and others who have had contact with the child through the years.

In the case of an INTERNATIONAL ADOPTION, medical history information may be sorely lacking or unavailable, and frequently only the current physical condition of the child can be provided. As a result, adoptive parents should seek out a pediatrician or physician knowledgeable about medical problems that may sometimes occur in foreign lands, for example, intestinal parasites and malnutrition.

The adopted child is not the only person on whom medical information is gathered: The adopting parents are medically evaluated as well, and an adoptive parent must usually undergo a complete physical and a discussion of his or her own medical history with the doctor. This medical history information will be provided to the social worker, who will evaluate whether there are any medical conditions that would make it difficult or impossible for the prospective adoptive parent to properly care for the child.

Recent disabling accidents, major surgery and other serious medical problems will be thoroughly analyzed before placement to ensure the child's best interests are met.

Handicapped parents have often found agencies prefer to match handicapped children to them, believing they would have a certain affinity to each other; however, if a disabled prospective parent feels he or she is capable of parenting a healthy infant or child, that person should seek an agency interested in working with them. (See also BACKGROUND INFORMATION; GENETIC DATA; MEDICAL PROBLEMS OF ADOPTED CHILDREN.)

medically fragile Term used by child welfare experts, usually to denote a child with a very severe medical problem; for example, pediatric AIDS or an addiction at birth to crack cocaine. (See also BOARDER BABIES; DRUG ABUSE; AIDS; SPECIAL NEEDS.)

medical problems of adopted children

Before adopting a child of any age, adoptive parents should gain as much information as possible about a child's MEDICAL HISTORY and that of his or her birthparents.

A medical problem in a birthparent or relative may or may not be an indicator of a potential problem in an adopted child, depending on the type of condition. Armed with knowledge, adoptive parents can consult with physicians to determine if this medical problem could occur in the adopted child and what to do if it does occur. In addition, it may be possible for tests to determine whether or not a child is a carrier or afflicted by a genetically-transmitted condition.

If at all possible, parents should locate a physician with a positive attitude about adoption before they adopt a child. If the parents are adopting a child from overseas, they should contact adoptive parent groups for recommendations of physicians experienced in treating children from abroad. (Or, if no physicians experienced in the medical problems of children overseas are available, recommendations should be sought on physicians willing to research and learn about ailments beyond what they usually see.)

Medical Problems of Children in the United States Adopted infants could have a variety of medical problems, severe or minor, ranging from DOWN SYNDROME to cocaine addiction to congenital defects to the less-serious jaundice many newborn babies have, which can usually be treated and resolved in a hospital. Pediatricians screen newborn infants for severe birth defects and may also test for the presence of drugs or AIDS.

Even children who seem perfectly healthy may later develop a heart murmur or other medical problem, just as children born into the family sometimes develop health problems. Physicians attempt to screen major health problems and risks, but there are no guarantees, whether one has adopted or a child is born to the family.

Older children who are adopted may have handicapping conditions resulting from physical or sexual abuse. They may have temporary problems, such as parasites, because of previous neglectful care. Most U.S. physicians should be able to evaluate the physical condition of a U.S.-born child.

Children with severe handicaps, such as blindness or cerebral palsy, are often difficult to place, yet there are adoptive parents who are willing and eager to adopt handicapped children.

Probably the hardest categories for whom to find suitable families are children who suffer from pediatric AIDS, FETAL ALCOHOL SYNDROME and cocaine withdrawal.

Even when the adoptive parents do not fear they will contract AIDS, many feel they cannot bear to grow to love a child and watch that child deteriorate and die. It's also true that babies born addicted to cocaine require special and intensive care, and such care is not a normal parenting experience. Many may also need later assistance with LEARNING DISABILITIES.

Medical Problems of Children Born Outside the United States Nearly 8,000 children were adopted by U.S. citizens in intercountry adoptions in fiscal year 1989. Children arriving from abroad may carry diseases and parasites that are virtually unknown in the United States, making diagnosis challenging for the average pediatrician. In addition, medical information provided to adoptive parents on the child and his genetic ancestry can be extremely sketchy or nonexistent.

According to the *Report on Foreign Adoption, 1989,* it is important to obtain medical information before the child leaves his or her country, and adopting parents are urged to "get at least two or three medical and psychological evaluations by professionals who are recommended by the U.S. Embassy or Consulate, and not to depend only on those evaluations done by persons the lawyer recommends."

Hepatitis B is another concern because of high rates of infection in many Asian countries. Dr. Margaret Hostetter, a physician at the International Adoption Clinic in Minnesota, points out that 15% to 20% of all Koreans have hepatitis B. Thus it is very important that families who adopt Korean-born children have the child tested. (The International Adoption Clinic is based at the University of Minnesota Hospital and Clinics, Box 211, Harvard St. at E. River Rd., Minneapolis, MN 55455; telephone 612-626-6777 or 612-626-2928.)

In a study of 52 internationally adopted children and disease published in the April 1989 issue of *Pediatrics,* the authors reported that even when children who had already been examined were evaluated, physicians found a high rate of medical problems undetected by the initial physical examination.

The lack of administering screening tests was the greatest reason for undetected diseases, primarily diseases that were infectious.

The following diagnoses were missed in 67% of the cases by other physicians: two cases of acute hepatitis B, five cases of chronic hepatitis B, three cases of intestinal parasites and seven cases of asymptomatic cytomegalovirus. Noninfectious ailments that had been undetected included developmental delays in three children and a number of other disorders.

According to the article, had the testing been confined to only three tests recommended by the American Academy of Pediatrics for refugees, 16 children with medical problems would not have been diagnosed and treated.

Based on this study, the researchers recommended the following tests: "A hepatitis B profile that includes serologic testing for the heptatitis B surface antigen and for antibodies to hepatitis B surface antigen . . . urine culture for cytomegalovirus, which is a contagious disease; an intradermal skin test for tuberculosis rather than the Tine test; testing for intestinal parasites; and testing of the child's vision and hearing."

Many adopted infants born abroad are malnourished, and the physician will need to evaluate the extent of the problem. According to the *Report on Foreign Adoption,* about 20% of infants born in other countries have some type of nutritional deficiency.

As a result (and also because the children may come from families of physically smaller stature than many Americans), children adopted internationally are often smaller than U.S. babies, and their growth rates will not track expected growth rates for a U.S. infant. In some cases, the child's age may be underestimated because of size. Bone tests and dental x-rays can better determine a child's actual age.

Newly adopted children from lands abroad may be healthy but have difficulty digesting cow's milk or other foods that are American staples. The *Report on Foreign Adoption* recommends, "A healthy, vitamin-fortified diet high in protein will surely help, but keep it plain for a while, gradually adding the richer American foods."

The report also notes that as of December 1, 1987, the U.S. Immigration and Naturalization Service requires all immigrants to the United States to have a physical exam and an exam to detect symptoms of AIDS. (Immigrants over age 15 must also be tested for syphilis and must have a chest x-ray.)

International Adoptions of Children with Special Needs Although many children from other lands may have curable problems, some children have more serious ailments that are considered SPECIAL NEEDS, for example, a child with a cleft palate or club foot. American surgeons may be able to correct or cure many defects and diseases that would go uncured had the child remained in the overseas orphanage.

The child could have a medically controllable form of epilepsy or a delayed development as a result of a variety of conditions. Some ailments cannot be corrected; for example, deafness or blindness may be uncorrectable or correctable, depending on the nature of the problem causing the deafness or blindness.

Other children overseas with special needs are over age five or six or part of a sibling group, which are harder categories of children to place than healthy infants. They may be very healthy children—their special need is their age or membership in a sibling group. (See also INSURANCE.)

Margaret K. Hostetter, M.D., "Adoptive Parents: A Physician's Perspective," *OURS,* March/April 1989, 20–21.

Margaret K. Hostetter, M.D., Sandra Iver, R.N., Kathryn Dole, O.T.R., and Dana Johnson, M.D., Ph.D., "Unsuspected Infectious Diseases and Other Medical Diagnoses in the Evaluation of Internationally Adopted Children," *Pediatrics,* 83:4(April 1989): 559–564.

International Concerns Committee for Children, *Report on Foreign Adoption, 1989,* (Boulder: International Concerns Committee for Children, 1989).

mental health of adopted children and adults   See PSYCHIATRIC PROBLEMS OF ADOPTED PERSONS.

military members and adoption
Adoption may be difficult for members of the military and their spouses who are subject to frequent transfers to other states or even other countries, particularly if they wish to adopt a healthy newborn. Numerous agencies have waiting lists for years; consequently, military families are never in one place long enough to make it to the top of many agencies' waiting lists.

In addition, few home studies are "transferable," thus often a person in the armed forces must start over again at square one in the new location.

The picture is not entirely bleak: Military families who are willing to actively network and seek out agencies willing to work with them have a good chance of successfully adopting a child. In addition, some agencies will accept home studies from other agencies. Military members may also adopt through public agencies or may opt to adopt independently.

Because of the diverse ethnic and racial mix of the military, many military members are good candidates as adoptive parents, particularly since it is more difficult to place black and biracial children. Many military families have traveled abroad and have far more cosmopolitan and accepting attitudes than families who have never left their home areas.

Some adoption agencies are biased against military members; for example, because of the "macho" image of the military, some agencies may believe that such parents may be harsh disciplinarians, authoritarian or even physically abusive. This is an unfair stereotype and hard to counter if individuals are turned away, ostensibly for other reasons.

Another problem faced by military parents who adopt is that health insurance benefits for their children are not available until finalization of the adoption, however, finalization could take up to a year, depending on the state in which the family resides. Most private corporations provide medical insurance to their employees for adopted children as soon as the child joins the family, and several states have passed laws mandating coverage upon placement. (See INSURANCE).

According to a release from the American Forces Information Services, published in the *Missileer* at Patrick Air Force Base on April 14, 1989, military members may be able to obtain limited medical benefits for their adopted child before finalization if they obtain a secretarial designee letter.

Base personnel officers can assist military families who are adopting with information and enrollment forms and can also provide other information on short-term health insurance.

According to an article by author Linda Taylor for *Military Lifestyle,* a Coast Guard attorney she interviewed applauded "any measure to eliminate the 'ward' status all military services use to classify a child placed in the home prior to finalization.

" 'It's a distinction that allows pre-adoptees dependent benefits, but prevents them from receiving full medical care,' he says. 'This puts a family's savings and future at risk until after the adoption is finalized. When a child is placed in the home by a qualified agency or state, then that child should be treated as a dependent.' "

For several years (1987–1990), military members were eligible for a $2,000 reimbursement upon finalizing an adoption of a child, whether the child was adopted through a private adoption agency, attorney, international adoption agency or any other legal means of adoption. If the family adopted more than one child in one year, they could be eligible for up to $5,000 in reimbursement expenses.

The reimbursement program was authorized as a test by Congress. It began October 1, 1987, and ended September 30, 1989. In 1989, Congress extended the reimbursement test to September 30, 1990, but the program was subsequently terminated.

Prospective adoptive parents in the military are advised to join local and national adoptive parent support groups, who can help them steer through the sometimes confusing morass of adoption rules and regulations and help them find the agency or attorney who can help them adopt.

Armed Forces Information Service, Patrick Air Force Base, "Adoptive Parents Need Interim Health Coverage for Children," *Missileer*, April 14, 1989.

Linda Taylor, "Strategies for Adoption," *Military Lifestyle*, June 1989, 19–20, 39–40.

minority adoption See BLACK ADOPTIVE PARENT RECRUITMENT PROGRAMS; BLACK FAMILIES; HISPANICS/LATINOS; INDIAN CHILD WELFARE ACT OF 1978; NATIONAL COALITION TO END RACISM IN AMERICA'S CHILD CARE SYSTEM INC.; SPECIAL NEEDS; TRANSRACIAL ADOPTION.

mixed families Families that include both adopted children and children born to the families, i.e. "biological children," are referred to as "mixed." (Biological children may also be known as "natural" children in some contexts, especially legal writings.)

Studies by the U.S. Census in 1985 of married couples with biological and adopted children revealed 1.3% of all married couples with children had adopted children only and another .9% had adopted children and biological children. (There were other combinations including adopted children, for example, "joint step-adoptive," "joint bio-step-adoptive.")

Therefore, more than 2.2% of American married couples included at least one adopted child in their family. (See also ADOPTIVE PARENTS for more information.)

It's important to note there are also adopted children in single families, divorced families, widowed families, and so forth, although the numbers are undoubtedly less than the numbers in married families.

The impact of an adopted child on a biological child depends on a variety of factors, including which child is older, which child arrived first in the family and problems of both the adopted child and the biological child.

Experts disagree on whether adopted children in mixed families fare better or worse than do families with only biological children.

Marilyn Ternay, Bobbie Wilborn and H. D. Day reported on child adjustment in families with both adopted and biological children. The researchers compared families with only adopted children with families with adopted and birth children and also with families with only biological children.

Studying 133 families, the research did reveal a difference. Said the authors,

Although the effect was small, children in all-adoptive families reported lower adjustment scores than children in natural families; however, the adopted children in mixed families were similar to the natural children in both the mixed and natural families on all measurements. These results suggest that the placement of an adoptive child in a mixed family does not affect the overall adjustment of the natural child.

Although adopted children in mixed families scored higher on adjustment scales, the researchers add that families with only adopted children should not worry unduly because "the actual differences between these two groups were small.

"These small differences, coupled with the logical limitations inherent in a correlational study of this type, do not justify the conclusion that the adoptive setting provides a serious hindrance to the overall adjustment of the adopted child."

(See SIBLINGS for further information on mixed families.)

Margaret Ward and John Lewko studied the impact of adopted school-age children on biological adolescents and reported, "Difficulties with all siblings were seen primarily as hassles. The adoptee was, however, reported as creating more problems than the 'old' siblings."

Adolescence is an extremely difficult period for many children, and the introduction of a new sibling can cause major stresses. One problem identified by Ward and Lewko was that the adopted child was unfamiliar with acceptable behavior in this particular family and the adolescent biological child, very familiar with the "rules," may be unwilling to teach them.

In addition, the adoptive parents may have stressed the very hard life the newly-adopted child has led up to this time. The adolescent biological child may initially put a great deal of effort into making the new family member feel welcome, but the adopted child may act out, test the parents and the entire family and generally act very ungrateful for being "saved" from his previous unhappy life. This behavior can lead to resentment in the adolescent biological child.

Seeing the new family member fussed over can cause resentment in a child of any age; for example, one biological child, upon learning that some parents celebrate both an adopted child's birthday and the day the adopted child arrived in the family, felt very annoyed that adopted children received the equivalent of two birthdays, whereas biological children only receive one.

As a result, it's important for adoptive parents to sensitize themselves to the feelings of everyone in the family.

Marilyn R. Ternay, Bobbie Wilborn and H. D. Day, "Perceived Child-Parent Relationships and Child Adjustment in Families with Both Adopted and Natural Children," *The Journal of Genetic Psychology,* 146: 2(1985): 261–272.

Margaret Ward and John H. Lewko, "Problems Experienced by Adolescents Already in Families that Adopt Older Children," *Adolescence,* 23(Spring 1988): 221–228.

Model State Adoption Act A 1981 act offering recommendations to state legislatures for facilitating the adoption of children with SPECIAL NEEDS. This act, which does not have the force of law, was issued by Richard S. Schweiker, secretary of the Department of Health and Human Services at that time.

Key recommendations included such provisions as offering financial assistance to families who adopt children with special needs and who need such assistance; expanding grounds for TERMINATION OF PARENTAL RIGHTS, thus freeing children for adoption so they will not remain in foster care or institutions for years or indefinitely; creating state adoption administrations that will cut red tape and enhance cooperation between public and private adoption agencies; and considering the wishes of the PSYCHOLOGICAL PARENT regarding adoption. Some of these recommendations have been enacted into law by some states.

The American Bar Association had previously attempted to formulate similar suggestions, but the multi-year effort resulted in such a level of controversy that no draft was approved. As of this writing, the National Conference of Commissioners on Uniform State Laws (NCCUSL) is drafting an adoption act. The drafting committee, chaired by Orlan L. Prestegard, is hopeful to have an act ready for consideration by the end of 1991. Joan H. Hollinger, Esq., serves as reporter for the drafting committee.

For further information, contact

National Conference of Commissioners on
  Uniform State Laws
676 N. St. Clair St.,
Suite 1700
Chicago, IL 60611
312-915-0195.

National Committee For Adoption, *Model Act for the Adoption of Children with Special Needs* (Washington, D.C.: National Committee For Adoption, 1982).

multiethnic   A child of mixed cultures or nationality backgrounds; for example, the child may have one Hispanic parent and one Anglo parent. The term is frequently misapplied to the child who is biracial and has instead a racial heritage of two different races. (Most often the term "biracial" is used to describe a child who has one black and one white parent.)

In the strictest sense, most Americans are "multiethnic" because few can trace their heritage solely to one country or culture.

mutual aid groups   See SUPPORT GROUPS.

mutual consent registries   Because some adopted persons and birthparents do SEARCH for each other after the child has grown into adulthood, many states have established registries that will provide identifying information if both the birthparent and the adopted adult are registered. (Some registries also require the registration of the adoptive parents.)

Groups that support OPEN RECORDS, or the ready availability of identifying data to adopted adults and birthparents, such as the CHILD WELFARE LEAGUE OF AMERICA INC., do not believe mutual consent registries go far enough, but supporters of the registries, such as the NATIONAL COMMITTEE FOR ADOPTION, believe it is important to protect the confidentiality of both the adopted person and the birthparents, and unless both wish to meet, then information should not be shared. On the other side of the spectrum are some groups, mostly state-based, that believe registries go too far and merely set the stage for further intrusions into family and personal privacy.

The following 24 states have established mutual consent registries as of this writing: Arkansas, California, Colorado, Florida, Idaho, Illinois, Indiana, Louisiana, Maine, Maryland, Massachusetts, Michigan, Nevada, New Hampshire, New Jersey, New York, Ohio, Oregon, South Carolina, South Dakota, Texas, Utah, Vermont and West Virginia.

Twelve states have enacted "search and consent" laws, allowing adopted adults to contact the state social services department or an adoption agency and request the birthparent(s) be located. If the birthparent(s) are located, consent is sought to provide identifying information to the adopted person. The following states have search and consent laws: Alabama, Connecticut, Georgia, Kentucky, Minnesota, Missouri, Montana, Nebraska, North Dakota, Pennsylvania, Tennessee and Wisconsin.

Three states have open records as of this writing: Alaska, Hawaii and Kansas.

The INTERNATIONAL SOUNDEX REUNION REGISTRY provides an international listing. (See also REUNION.)

N

naming When a child is adopted and the adoption is "finalized" in court, the adoptive parents have the legal right to change the child's entire name, including first, middle and last names. After the finalization, the original birth certificate becomes a SEALED RECORD in most states, and the name given by the adoptive parents is placed on a new birth certificate.

The name given to every child, adopted or not adopted, is very important to that child, because the name is an integral part of the identity. Even perfect strangers respond to a person's name with preconceived ideas of what a "Larry" or a "Francis" is like; consequently, the choice of a name should be made very carefully.

Naming an Infant If the child is a newborn infant, he or she probably has not been given a name by the birthparents. Even if the birthparents do choose to name the child, it is unlikely a name change would be detrimental to the adopted infant.

In some cases of OPEN ADOPTION, the adoptive parents and birthparents both choose the child's name or share the naming of the child. Opponents of this practice believe it could create a problem of ENTITLEMENT for the adopting family and a false sense of control for the birthparents. Supporters believe it is a positive act of sharing and acceptance. In the majority of cases, adoptive parents choose the child's name.

Adoptive parents may choose a name for the pleasant sound of it or may choose a name with Biblical or religious meaning; for example, "Matthew" means "gift of God" in Hebrew.

Other parents may choose the names of a favorite relative, such as a grandparent or cousin, thus adding a sense of family belonging, not only to the adoptive parents and later to the child but also to the extended family.

Says author Cheri Register,

Giving a family name to an adopted child also makes a statement to the extended family: The parent claims the right to share the family heritage with a child who is not a blood relative.

Occasionally, relatives will disagree with the choice of name, believing "family names" should only be reserved for blood relatives. Register describes an incident in which an adopted child was a named after the adoptive parents' fathers. Later, when a child was born to the family, an uncle was angry that the names had not been "saved" for the child with the genetic link.

If the child has been adopted internationally, the family may opt to choose a name that is common or acceptable in the birth country of the child. Some families who have adopted Korean-born children have chosen to use a Korean middle name; for example, Register named her daughter "Grace" and "Keun Young" for her first and middle names. According to Register, some countries require adoptive parents to name their child with at least one name common to the country of origin. (This requirement is, however, probably unenforceable once the child has relocated to the United States.)

Naming an Older Child When the child who is adopted is not an infant, the child almost invariably has been given a name by others. As a rule, if the adopting parents can retain the child's original first and middle names, it would probably be best for the child. Almost inevitably, the child's last name will be changed. To change a child's first and middle names, along with changing the child's environment, could theoretically affect the child's identity as well.

Although she was not adopted, actress Patty Duke has discussed and written about the dissonance and the dismay she felt when her original name "Anna" was replaced by "Patty" and how this name change affected her identity and feeling of selfhood. It seems likely that an adopted child whose name is changed against her wishes or desires would also feel negative or confused about her identity.

There are exceptions; for example, if the child detests his first name or normally goes by his middle name, then he may desire a legal name change. Sometimes the adoptive family will retain the child's first birth name and opt to give the child a family middle name, in an effort to retain the child's original identity and also bond the child with the new family.

One adoptive family finalized the adoption of their 10-year-old child over the summer vacation. She was very eager to have her last name changed to match the name of her parents because she wanted to go to school with the same last name as theirs.

Cheri Register, *"Are Those Kids Yours?": American Families with Children Adopted From Other Countries* (New York: Free Press, 1990).

National Adoption Exchange See NATIONAL ADOPTION NETWORK.

National Adoption Center Founded in 1972, this organization promotes adoption opportunities for children throughout the United States, particularly for children with SPECIAL NEEDS. Two of its main programs are

1. The NATIONAL ADOPTION NETWORK, a telecommunications system that links social workers, social agencies and prospective parents around the country. For example, through the network, a social worker in Ohio can place a child with a family in Pennsylvania.

2. National public awareness. The center works closely with national and regional media, community and professional organizations, libraries and corporations to spread the word about WAITING CHILDREN and the adoption process. The organization also offers a special program to heighten consciousness about children in minority cultures who need families.

A study called *Who Adopts Children with Special Needs*, funded by the Department of Health and Human Services and conducted by the center, analyzed the characteristics of people who adopt children with SPECIAL NEEDS.

According to the November 1986 issue of *National Adoption Center News*, the "average" family seeking to adopt a child with special needs is "a white, married couple in their mid-thirties who have one child and prefer to adopt a younger child. While this is the 'average,' included among those waiting to adopt are black single women, unmarried men, and families with more than two children."

For more information, contact

The National Adoption Center
1218 Chestnut St.
Philadelphia, PA 19107
(215) 925-0200

The National Adoption Information Clearinghouse A government-funded organization that provides information and referrals on adoption but is not a child-placing agency. The clearinghouse was established by Congress in 1986 under the Omnibus Budget Reconciliation Act of 1986 (P.L. 99-509).

At this writing, CSR Inc. in Washington, D.C. manages the clearinghouse, together with the National Adoption Center in Philadelphia, Pennsylvania.

Available services include: adoption publications; a computerized database of information on adoption articles that clearinghouse staff will search upon request; full-text listings of federal and state adoption laws; a listing of adoption experts in many areas; a listing of films and videotapes of interest to adoptive parent support groups, adopted persons and others, available for rent through the National Adoption Center.

The clearinghouse also maintains directories of crisis pregnancy centers, shelters for pregnant women and licensed adoption agencies.

Some services are free while there is a charge for other services.

The clearinghouse is funded by the Administration for Children, Youth and Families, Office of Human Development Services, U.S. Department of Health and Human Services.

For more information, contact

National Adoption Information Clearinghouse
1400 Eye St. NW, Suite 1275
Washington, DC 20005
(202) 842-1919

National Adoption Network A computerized telecommunications system operated by the National Adoption Center that links adoption professionals and prospective adoptive parents and parent groups throughout the United States.

Children with SPECIAL NEEDS are listed and detailed information is available to adoption professionals. Families who have completed home studies may also request that their names be placed in the database for possible matches with children. Requests by families need not be processed through an adoption agency but may be sent directly to the center after the home study has been completed and individuals have been approved.

"Bulletin board" information is available to subscribers, as well as users, in the form of electronic mail that allows them to communicate with each other in confidence.

Members need a personal computer or communicating word processor and a 300 or 1200 baud modem. (A modem is a device that enables the computer to use the telephone lines to "call" another computer. Subsequently, users can communicate by typing in messages or receiving typed messages that were saved for them.)

As of this writing, a one-time hook-up is $200, and monthly maintenance fees are $30 per month. An hourly usage fee of $21 is also charged. Federal grants are available to parent groups. Members receive their own access codes and a detailed instruction manual.

For further information about this service, contact Yvonne Kay at the National Adoption Center:

National Adoption Center
1218 Chestnut St.
Philadelphia, PA 19107
(215) 925-0200

National Adoption Week Celebrated on the Sunday preceding Thanksgiving to the Saturday following the holiday. According to the NORTH AMERICAN COUNCIL ON ADOPTABLE CHILDREN (NACAC), National Adoption Week was first proclaimed in Massachusetts in May of 1976. President Ford proclaimed the first federal National Adoption Week later that year.

Each year, increasing numbers of adoptive parent support groups, adoption experts and other proponents have worked to promote adoption during National Adoption Week. The adoption of children with SPECIAL NEEDS who wait for parents to adopt them is especially promoted at this time.

Adoptive parent support groups and state social services departments celebrate National Adoption Week in different ways: organizing a "CALLING OUT" of the first names of WAITING CHILDREN in their states; holding adoption seminars, picnics or fairs with information about special needs adoption available to the general public; coordinating letter campaigns to encourage adopted children to write about how they feel about adoption.

The NATIONAL COMMITTEE FOR ADOPTION distributes a press kit that stresses the full range of adoption options: healthy infants, children from other countries, children with special needs, as well as information on pregnant women's needs.

Celebrants of National Adoption Week do their best to obtain media coverage, although coverage is spotty, perhaps because of the time of year during which it occurs.

Chase's Annual Events (Chicago: Contemporary Books, 1989).

National Association of Black Social Workers See TRANSRACIAL ADOPTION.

National Association of Social Workers Inc. (NASW)
Organization of over 127,000 professional social workers, dedicated to uniting the profession and providing optimal services to clients. According to its publications catalog, the NASW "works to enhance the professional growth and development of its members, to create and maintain professional standards, and to advance sound social policies."

Regular membership is limited to individuals with a graduate or undergraduate degree from a Council on Social Work Education accredited program. Associate membership is available to those who are employed as social workers but hold a degree from a discipline other than social work. Retired memberships and student memberships are also available.

The organization produces *NASW News* ten times a year and *Social Work* six times per year. Other quarterly publications include *Social Work Research & Abstracts*, *Social Work in Education* and *Health and Social Work*. The NASW Press also offers over 100 titles of books, available to members and nonmembers.

The organization holds annual conferences each fall.

For more information, contact

National Association of Social Workers
7981 Eastern Ave.
Silver Spring, MD 20910
(301) 565-0333; 800-565-0333
Publications catalog or ordering number: 1-800-752-3590

National Coalition to End Racism in America's Child Care System Inc.
Founded by president Carol Coccia and seven other foster parents in 1984, this nonprofit organization strives to change policies at the national and state levels and supports TRANSRACIAL ADOPTION and foster parenting of children.

Coccia is a foster parent who fosters children of all races. She and her members believe the concept of "the best interests of the child" is ignored when racial matching is mandated. Although she supports placing children with a family of the same race whenever possible, Coccia insists it is not always possible to find a match, and in such cases, the child should be placed with a suitable family regardless of his or her race.

She and her members believe racial matching violates the U.S. Constitution as well as the Civil Rights Act of 1964. Coccia's organization provides material to adoptive parents, prospective adoptive parents, foster parents and anyone else interested in overturning policies that she and some others consider are racist and unreasonable.

The organization is also supported by Sandi Ililonga, a woman of mixed ancestry who needed adoptive parents at age two and a half but who was not adopted until she was 12 years old. Ililonga is an adult of above-normal intelligence and attractiveness and suffers no handicaps.

Ililonga has publicly stated that she is convinced her adoption was delayed so long solely because of her mixed race and policies preventing Caucasian couples from adopting her.

The National Coalition produces a quarterly newsletter.

For more information, contact

National Coalition to End Racism in America's Child Care System Inc.
22075 Koths
Taylor, MI 48180
(313) 295-0257

National Committee For Adoption

Founded in 1980, the National Committee For Adoption (NCFA) is a national, nonprofit advocacy and information group with a membership of 152 adoption agencies in 45 states and the District of Columbia and over 2,000 individual members. It has more voluntary sector adoption agencies as members than any other national nonsectarian umbrella organization in the United States.

Barbara Bush, the first lady of the United States, serves as the honorary chair of the NCFA.

The association provides information and assistance on all areas related to adoption—from the adoption of healthy infants to children with SPECIAL NEEDS to INTERNATIONAL ADOPTION to MATERNITY HOMES to INFERTILITY.

The media uses the NCFA's information clearinghouse as a resource for information on a variety of topics, and NCFA draws on its staff and on members of the organization as well as federal and state agencies and members of Congress for data. Its members frequently are asked to speak on adoption issues on television and radio programs and are often interviewed by the print media.

The NCFA is frequently invited to provide information and testify before Congress on adoption-related issues. Lobbying on adoption issues is another facet of the NCFA's purpose.

The Adoption Factbook, the NCFA's 1989 compilation of statistics on all facets of adoption, is a comprehensive update and expansion of its 1985 *Factbook.* In addition, the NCFA produces a bimonthly report for members entitled *National Adoption Reports,* which informs readers about the latest research on adoption as well as pending legislation related to adoption issues and discusses media reports on adoption and current issues and problems.

The NCFA performs the following services and activities:

- promotes adoption to the public as a positive option for individuals with crisis pregnancies
- protects children by encouraging that adoptions be facilitated by public or licensed nonprofit agencies
- promotes ethical practices in adoption through contacts with the MEDIA, legislators, policymakers, people in the human services field and the public
- supports confidentiality for members of the adoption triad and also supports the creation of state-level mutual-consent voluntary adoption registries
- monitors state adoption legislation
- operates a variety of informational services for individuals or organizations interested in INFANT ADOPTION, America's WAITING CHILDREN and INTERNATIONAL ADOPTION; provides information and recommends counseling resources for young, single or troubled parents
- publishes the bimonthly *National Adoption Reports,* a newsletter specifically tailored to the needs of adoptive parents; *Unmarried Parents Today,* a newsletter on adoption and maternity services; *Legal Notes,* a newsletter on legal issues; the biweekly *MEMO,* an advisory bulletin especially for member agencies; and various analyses, manuals, directories and posters; provides discounts on materials, books and other resources published by others
- tracks and offers information on current developments in court cases and legisla-

tive developments that affect adoption and adolescent pregnancy
- plans and offers public service television and radio advertisements, such as the NCFA's well-received "Adopted Kids Have Great Expectations" campaign
- promotes excellence in practice through appropriate standards and accreditation
- provides information and training needed to empower agencies and individuals to cope with changes in practice
- supports continuation of the Adolescent Family Life Demonstration Projects Law or its equivalent
- reviews existing research and performs and publishes new research
- responds, when necessary and appropriate, to events affecting adoption of infants; young, single or troubled parents; America's waiting children; and children from other countries

Membership availability, services, dues and benefits vary, depending on the member's status. For further information, contact

National Committee For Adoption
1930 17th St. NW
Washington, D.C. 20009-6207
202-328-1200

National Photo History of Children Waiting for Adoptive Parents See CAP BOOK.

Native Americans See INDIAN CHILD WELFARE ACT.

Naturalization See IMMIGRATION AND NATURALIZATION.

natural parents The man and woman who conceived a child together; also known as "birthparents" or "biological parents," usually used when the child is placed for adoption and parental rights and obligations are transferred to the adoptive parents.

The terminology "natural parents" is out of favor with many adoptive parents and adoption professionals, who point out that the opposite of "natural" is "unnatural." As a result, many adoptive parents prefer the words "birthparents" or "biological" or "genetic" parents. (See also BIRTHPARENT.)

neglect Failure to provide adequate care and supervision for a minor child by a parent or adult caretaker. Neglect may be more traumatic to a child than physical abuse and is a serious problem in the United States and the world.

The National Center on Child Abuse and Neglect classifies neglect as physical neglect, educational neglect and emotional neglect.

Physical Neglect Physical neglect primarily includes such subcategories of mistreatment as abandonment, refusal to provide health care, delay in health care, expulsion and inadequate supervision. These forms of neglect are most prevalent in families with incomes below $15,000. Children from these families are nearly 12 times more likely to be neglected than are children from families with greater incomes.

Family size is also a factor in physical neglect, and the rate for families with more than three children is nearly double the rate for smaller families.

Emotional Neglect Emotional neglect, as defined by the National Center on Child Abuse and Neglect, includes seven specific categories:

1. inadequate nurturance/affection—a marked inattention to the child's needs for affection, emotional support, attention, or competence
2. chronic/extreme spouse abuse—spouse abuse or domestic violence in the presence of the child
3. permitted drug/alcohol abuse—allowing the child to use drugs or alcohol
4. permitted other maladaptive behavior—encouragement or permitting of other maladaptive behavior (e.g., severe as-

saultiveness, chronic delinquency) under circumstances where the parent/guardian had reason to be aware of the existence and seriousness of the problem but did not attempt to intervene
5. refusal of psychological care—the "refusal to allow needed and available treatment for a child's emotional or behavioral impairment or problem which any reasonable layman would have recognized as needing professional psychological attention (e.g., severe depression, suicide attempt)
6. delay in psychological care
7. other emotional neglect

Educational Neglect The center lists three categories of educational neglect, including "permitted chronic truancy," which means the child had missed school at least 5 days in one month and the parent did not intervene after being notified of the problem; "failure to enroll the child" in school or other problems causing the child to miss school fall under the second category (for example, if the parent continually makes the child stay home to take care of a sibling); and "inattention to Special Educational Need," which refers to the parent's failure to follow through with a course of action that will help the child, for example, treatment of a learning disability. (See also ABUSE.)

U.S. Department of Health and Human Services, *Study Findings: Study of National Incidence and Prevalence of Child Abuse and Neglect: 1988,* prepared by National Center of Child Abuse and Neglect, Office of Human Development Services, Administration for Children, Youth and Families Children's Bureau (Washington, D.C.: 1988).

nonidentifying information Information provided to adopting parents, birthparents, adopted persons or others, excluding identifying data; for example, a birthparent may be told the adopting parents are athletic and given general information about their occupation, ethnic and racial background and religion. Similar information about the birthparents is shared with the adopting parents.

Identifying data, such as names, city where the person lives, and other information that could help identify a person, is not revealed in a traditional adoption.

Identifying information IS revealed in an open adoption. (See also CONFIDENTIALITY; GENETIC DATA; MEDICAL HISTORY; OPEN ADOPTION; TRADITIONAL ADOPTION.)

nonsectarian agencies See AGENCIES.

North American Council on Adoptable Children (NACAC) Formed in 1974 as a result of adoptive parents' desire for a national coalition and voice. The original and continuing purpose is to advocate for the rights of WAITING CHILDREN to permanent placements in loving adoptive homes; concentrates on children with SPECIAL NEEDS.

According to brochure information, NACAC is "a non-profit, broad-based coalition of volunteer adoptive parent support and citizen advocacy groups, caring individuals, and agencies committed to meeting the needs of waiting children in the United States and Canada."

There are about 1,500 members in the organization: about half are adoptive parents and half are social workers.

The number one priority for NACAC through the early 1990s is advocating for the placement of waiting children, particularly children who are black, Hispanic and Native American. The organization also plans to strive for implementation of existing federal adoption laws limiting the length of time a child may remain in foster care and press for full implementation of subsidy programs for special needs adoptive families.

The NACAC board meets three times per year, and the organization holds an annual conference each August. The conference offers over 100 workshops led by many nationally known adoption experts.

The organization publishes *Adoptalk,* a quarterly newsletter.

For more information, contact

North American Council on Adoptable Children (NACAC)
1821 University Ave., Suite N-498
St. Paul, MN 55104
(612) 644-3036

notice Information on a pending court action, for example, a hearing to place a child for adoption or to finalize an adoption, that is given to specific interested parties.

Generally, it is those parties from whom CONSENT is required who must be notified of an impending adoption. Other parties may also be designated by the state to receive notice. States differ on who must be given notice. (Also, laws change, and readers should review current state laws to ensure notice requirements have not changed.)

In Arizona, the person or agency conducting an adoption investigation must be notified before the adoption occurs. In Delaware, "all interested parties shall be duly summoned" if an adoption hearing is held. In Florida, the state social services office or child placement agency must be notified as well as those who provided consent and anyone seeking to revoke consent.

In Georgia, parents whose parental rights have been terminated are notified of an adoption petition and grandparents who have been granted visitation rights are also entitled to notice.

Some states require that notice be given within a certain timeframe prior to the adoption hearing; for example, Connecticut requires notice be given 10 days before the hearing, and Colorado requires notice be given 30 days beforehand. Alabama requires proof that notice has been given to parties entitled to notice.

Failure to give proper notice can be grounds for overturning an adoption in the states of Alaska, Arkansas, Illinois, Massachusetts, Mississippi, North Dakota, Ohio and West Virginia. (See also REVOCATION; RELATIVE ADOPTIONS.)

Nurturing Network See MATURE WOMEN PLANNING ADOPTION.

O

obesity Overweight individuals report greater difficulty in adopting a child. Some agencies will reject applicants who are obese, fearing that they are unhealthy or may have a reduced life expectancy. They may also fear obese parents will raise overweight children and may not wish children to be subjected to taunts of others, particularly schoolmates.

According to an article in the *NAAFA Newsletter,* one woman "found that, with a few exceptions, most agencies didn't want to deal with her because of her size." (The *NAAFA Newsletter* is published by the National Association to Advance Fat Acceptance Inc. and is based in Sacramento, California.)

The article further states, "The weight of a parent can be a very serious consideration in the eyes of some adoption agencies. Eleven years ago, a lawsuit in Wisconsin received national attention when a couple, each weighing 200 pounds, were denied adoption by a state agency. The matter was resolved by the governor, who declared that his grandmother had been fat, and with no ill effects."

Obese individuals can either lose the weight or seek an adoption agency or attorney who is willing to work with overweight adoptive parents.

Frances M. White, "Adoption," *NAAFA Newsletter,* November 1989, 6.

older child Generally, school-age children are considered SPECIAL NEEDS children by virtue of their age alone. The age threshold at which a child is considered hard to place varies according to the state and may be six or eight years—or older or younger.

Older children are usually known to and listed by the state social services department, and sometimes their adoptions are arranged through adoption agencies. Attorneys and other intermediaries are rarely involved with adoptions of children who are not infants.

Most older children have entered the child welfare system as foster children and were removed from their parents' homes due to ABUSE, NEGLECT or ABANDONMENT. When attempts by a social worker to reunify the family fail, the worker ultimately will request the court to terminate parental rights and place the child in an adoptive home or will find a group home for the child if adoption doesn't seem likely or feasible.

In the recent past, the prevailing feeling among many in society was that adoptive families for older children could not be found; however, many adoption professionals and adoptive parent groups believe today that older children can and should be adopted. But the older the child is, the more difficult it is to identify a suitable family.

The adoption of older children, including teenagers, is supported today because every child deserves a family to love and one to whom the young adult can return for holidays, in crises and at other times.

Many older children are a part of a sibling group, and if the sibling group is large (three or more children), placement is further complicated. Most adoptions of older children are successful, according to adoption experts and researchers although they do have a higher rate of problems than infant adoptions. (See DISRUPTION.)

The older adopted child may show some initial negative reactions, and possible behavior should be discussed with adopting parents. Psychologist Earl Braxton says a newly adopted older child who immediately expresses anger and rejection may be exhibiting such behavior because of a fear of rejection or because of a misguided attempt to "connect" with the adoptive parent. (See ADJUSTMENT; BONDING AND ATTACHMENT.)

Braxton advises adoptive parents to reassure the child and "try to discover what the fear is underneath."

It is also very common for children to test parents, whether they are biological parents or adoptive parents. A newly adopted child is often in a honeymoon phase and strives mightily to please the adoptive parents and be a perfect child, but after the honeymoon period may come a very trying time for the adoptive parents—extensive testing by the child of the limits of what is accepted behavior.

Ann Hartman also describes the period after the honeymoon stage and says a minor altercation can be exaggerated in the child's mind as a fear of being sent away, driving the child to even further negative actions. She says the adoptive parent needs to know that such behavior is not a negative sign but actually symbolic of the beginnings of the attachment of the child to the family.

A 1989 doctoral dissertation at Yeshiva University studied factors related to succcss in the adoption of older children. Researcher Eve Pearlman Smith defined "success" in terms of parental satisfaction and kinship behavior of the child.

Studying 69 families who had adopted 98 children, Smith found the following predictors of success: "discussion of parents' expectations with the child"; "contact during the homestudy process with parents who had already adopted older children"; and a provision for agency services after finalization (also known as post-legal services).

Demographic predictors for success were "parent over age 40"; "non-professional father"; "child had no or mild emotional disability at placement"; and "child is a girl." (See also GENDER PREFERENCES; PREPARING A CHILD FOR ADOPTION; SIBLINGS; SPECIAL NEEDS.)

Earl T. Braxton, Ph.D, "Parental Management of Anger and Emotional Anxiety in the Adopted Child," in *Adoption Resources for Mental Health Professionals* (Butler, PA: Mental Health Association, 1985)

Ann Hartman, "Practice in Adoption," in *A Handbook of Child Welfare: Context, Knowledge, and Practice* (New York: Free Press, 1985).

Eve Pearlman Smith, "The Relationship of Services to Success in Older Child Adoption," D.S.W. diss., Yeshiva University, 1989.

One Church, One Child Program initiated on a local basis in 1981 by Rev. George H. Clements in Chicago at the Holy Angels Church, a predominantly black Catholic church. Clements' goal was to recruit black adoptive parents through local churches. Rev. Clements was named to the National Committee For Adoption's Hall of Fame in 1989 for his outstanding leadership and the great interest he generated in black adoptions.

Some social workers believe the social work system is dominated by whites who do not provide sufficient assistance to blacks interested in adoption. According to an article in *Ebony* magazine, blacks face numerous obstacles in their attempts to adopt, and as a result, "many begin the adoption process, become exasperated and then just forget about the whole idea." Recruitment efforts specifically targeted at blacks are designed to overcome such institutional rigidity when and where it exists.

The One Church, One Child program became a national recruiting effort in 1988, and 32 states are using all or portions of the program. Its originally envisioned mission was to combine the resources of the church and the state to the end of recruiting black adoptive parents to provide permanent homes for black children awaiting adoption.

In most states, the state social services agency (Children, Youth and Families) manage the program, while in some states the responsibility for administration of the program is contracted out to private nonprofit agencies.

According to national staff director Patricia O'Neal-Williams, the Florida office leads the most successful program, having placed 805 children from March 1, 1988, to September 30, 1990.

The president for the period September 30, 1990, to September 30, 1992, is Rev. R. B. Holmes Jr., pastor of the Bethel Baptist Missionary Church in Tallahassee, Florida. (See also BLACK ADOPTIVE PARENT RECRUITMENT PROGRAMS.)

For more information, contact

Patricia O'Neal-Williams
National Executive Director
1317 Winewood Blvd., Bldg. 8
Tallahassee, FL 32301
(904) 488-8251

Walter Leavy, "Should Whites Adopt Black Children?," *Ebony*, September 1987, 76–82.

only child adoptive families There are indications that as many as 50% or more of all adoptive parent couples (or singles) adopt one child only. Many parents adopt only one child because the agency they dealt with will only place with childless couples. (Many agencies are moving away from this stance and will place two children in a home.) Other parents want one child only and are satisfied after the adoption. Other parents cannot afford to adopt more than one child.

When only one child is adopted and there are no biological children, the adopted child's situation is similar to the situation of an only biological child, and there may be a risk of overindulging the child or expecting too much of the child.

Researchers disagree on the negative effects of being an only child; for example, a 1984 study of only children by Norval D. Glenn and Sue Keir Hoppe at the University of Texas found adults who were only children enjoyed lives as satisfying or even more satisfying than adults who grew up with siblings.

They did find a sex difference: Adult males who grew up as "onlies" were more likely to report being "very happy" than men who grew up with siblings while adult women who had been only children reported they were "very happy" at about the same levels as adult women who grew up with brothers and sisters.

Said the researchers, "If reluctance to have an only child is based primarily on fear that he or she will be unusually likely to become a maladjusted and unhappy adult, we believe that the best available evidence indicates that the reluctance is ill-founded."

This advice could also be extended to adoptive parents who prefer to adopt one child.

Adoptive parents would probably also be interested in the results of a study of BIRTH ORDER and academic achievement, although adopted children were not studied. Researcher Varghese I. Cherian studied over 1,000 children and found a direct relationship between birth order and academic achievement, with the oldest child or the only child usually achieving the best grades. (See ACADEMIC PROGRESS.)

Varghese I. Cherian, "Birth Order and Academic Achievement of Children in Transkei," *Psychological Reports,* 66(1990) 19–24.

Norval D. Glenn and Sue Keir Hoppe, "Only Children as Adults," *Journal of Family Issues,* September 1984.

open adoption An adoptive placement, less commonly known as a "full disclosure" adoption, in which the BIRTHMOTHER and sometimes the BIRTHFATHER exchange specific identifying information with the adopting parents, such as names, addresses and other data, so ongoing contact between the adopting and birth families is possible. Whether that ongoing contact is monthly, annually or sporadic depends on the parties and is decided by them rather than an agency or attorney.

Open adoption differs from COOPERATIVE ADOPTION, in which an active and continued involvement on the part of the birthparent(s) with the child is presumed, with parental decisions shared or the birthparents consulted about major issues. Visits are common in cooperative adoption and may or may not occur in an open adoption.

In some cases, contact between the adoptive parents and birthparent(s) may continue after finalization of the adoption in an open adoption, and in some cases, it may subside (through letters, phone calls, or other means) or end.

Determining the Number of Open Adoptions Because the federal government does not collect adoption statistics as of this writing, it is difficult to determine how many adoptions have occurred, let alone how many open adoptions. It is possible, however, to use other research and statistics to estimate the percentage of open adoptions.

The National Committee For Adoption reports there were 24,589 infant adoptions in 1986. In California, where all independent adoptions are open by law, there were 1,802 independent adoptions in 1986. As a result, at least 7.3% of all adoptions were open in 1986. The National Committee For Adoption estimates the number of open adoptions nationwide at about 10%. (Most states mandate confidentiality rather than open adoptions.)

The definition of open adoption is critically important because tremendous confusion about the definition of this phrase abounds nationwide. Some agencies consider degrees of "openness" as open adoptions, for example, when the pregnant woman is given nonidentifying resumes to review, while other agencies consider a brief meeting with no exchange of identities to be an open adoption, and still others insist that only a disclosure of identities is an open adoption.

Consequently, until more universal agreement on a definition is achieved, it's very important to obtain an exact definition from the agency or attorney of what they mean by "open adoption."

History Open adoptions or direct placements were once the norm, and in the 1920s, women actually advertised their own children for adoption. Primarily indigent women, they performed their own screening and decided for themselves if the placement would occur.

Social workers were understandably distressed by this practice, both because they felt the parents might have considerable difficulty in adequately screening the people who would adopt their children and also because they were concerned about people who might actually sell their children.

As a result, social workers in Massachusetts and other states actively sought to ban parents from ADVERTISING their own children for adoption, and today most states that allow adoption advertising only allow adoption agencies, attorneys or prospective adoptive parents to advertise. (See ADVERTISING AND PROMOTION.) Some states prohibit advertising altogether, whereas other states require specific wording or limit advertising to agencies or attorneys only.

With the advent of new adoption laws and a strong support of confidentiality among social workers, confidential adoptions became the norm by the 1930s. There has been an upturn in the number of open adoptions since 1970, primarily because of the growing presence of lawyers as adoption intermediaries.

Today, choices within a framework of confidentiality are commonplace. In addition, more adopting parents are willing to provide nonidentifying information about themselves or to meet with a pregnant woman considering adoption.

One reason for this willingness is a belief it will be easier to adopt and the waiting period will be shorter if the prospective parents comply with such demands. Another reason is the belief that it is reasonable to give a birthmother considering adoption information about the couple who would like to adopt the child. Individuals who support this rationale believe the birthmother merits more control (in the form of information) than a confidential adoption will allow and should not have to rely on the word and reputation of agencies and their employees that the adopting parents are "good people."

A key reason for some agencies (and attorneys) offering open adoption is that there are fewer babies available for adoption than 20 or more years ago, thus birthparents have greater bargaining power and more control than in the past.

Another trend impacting open adoption is the desire of some birthparents and adopted adults to SEARCH for each other. Proponents of open adoption point out that searches are unnecessary in the case of open adoptions: The people already know each other's identities.

The risks and benefits of open adoption continue as a source of hot debate between proponents and dissenters. No longitudinal studies have been performed on the well-being of individuals adopted through open adoptions, and it will be at least 10 years before sufficient evidence is available to support a change from standard practices involving confidentiality.

Critics insist that it would be very unwise to actively promote open adoptions until we can see the effects of existing open adoptions; proponents of open adoption are eager to change practice immediately.

Arguments in Favor of Open Adoptions Advocates of open adoptions insist that openness is best for the child, who will not spend his or her life wondering what a birthparent looked like or why he or she was "given up." (Even in traditional "closed" adoptions offering choices, the adopting parents are rarely given a photograph of the birthparent.)

Proponents cite studies of adopted adults who were institutionalized or who required psychotherapy and conclude that the secrecy inherent in traditional adoption contributed to or caused the mental illness. On the other hand, studies of adopted adults indicate most who were adopted under age five, and especially those children adopted as infants, are well adjusted.

In addition, if the adopted person suffers any health problems as a child or as an adult, the birthparent can readily be contacted. In a traditional adoption with confidentiality, the adopted person would need to contact the agency or attorney to search for the birthparent or would need to request an unsealing of the birth records by a court.

Open adoption proponents insist the commonly felt experience among many new adoptive parents of wondering whether every young woman in the supermarket is the birthmother is not a problem in an open adoption when the adopting parents know exactly who the birthmother is.

They also add the fear of the unknown birthmother coming back to "reclaim" the child by kidnapping him or her disappears when an adoption is open. Despite the fact that a birthmother could theoretically take such action when she knows the identities of the adoptive parents, few have actually done so.

Advocates of open adoption argue knowing where the child is and with whom alleviates fears the birthmother has about the adoptive placement, and her confidence is transmitted to the adoptive parents.

Kenneth Watson, a well-known advocate of open adoption and the chair of the adoption task force of the CHILD WELFARE LEAGUE OF AMERICA, does not believe open adoption should be mandated, nor does he believe confidentiality should be required. However, believing that open adoption enables an adopted person to have a better sense of his or her identity, Watson holds that open adoption helps a child better cope with the loss of a birthparent as well as helps birthparents and adoptive parents cope with their sense of loss.

Says Watson, "Any attempt to make the adoption relinquishment a clean and total break denies the possibility of further contact and restricts the grief process from following its natural sequence. Openness, on the other hand, accepts the possibility of ongoing or subsequent contact and allows the relinquishing parent to face the real loss, the loss of the role of the nurturing parent."

He also believes an open adoption forces the adoptive parents to work through the loss they may feel about being unable to have a biological child and says, "The clearer adoptive parents are that their adopted child also has other parents and the more real those parents are, the greater the pressure on them to confront and work through their feelings about their own loss."

Although formerly a proponent and practitioner of confidential adoptions, Watson now compares himself to the salesman of asbestos 25 years ago who now knows asbestos is dangerous and who warns former customers about the danger.

Open adoption advocates also believe adoptive parents gain a strong respect for the birthmother when they actually know who she is. They say the sense of ENTITLEMENT adoptive parents feel towards the child is stronger when the adoptive parents are personally chosen.

Some attorneys believe their open adoptions are better than agency adoptions because agencies generally prescreen individuals before they share data about them (or arrange meetings) with birthparents. As a result, they believe birthmothers in open adoptions have a much broader pool of potential parents to choose from. Agencies, however, believe it is safer for both the adoptive parents and the birthparents if the prospective parents have been screened and have already received counseling.

Kathleen Silber and Phylis Speedlin, authors of *Dear Birthmother: Thank You for Our Baby,* argue against confidential adoptions, saying that birthmothers, adoptive parents and adopted children are forced to accept whatever information an intermediary was willing to provide in a confidential adoption. Hence, adoptive parents see birthparents as "shadowy figures," and birthparents wonder intensely whether or not their children are all right.

Arguments in Favor of Confidential Adoption Supporters of traditional adoption have numerous reasons for their objections to open adoption, and many are the reverse side of the arguments offered in support of open adoptions.

Opponents fear that women might choose unwanted abortions if they do not have the option of maintaining confidentiality. They (or the biological fathers) may be fearful of the child searching for them in later years and choose ABORTIONS over an open, nonconfidential adoption. Those who do not support open adoption also argue that the birthmother should not have a say in choosing adoptive parents because she is often in a highly emotional state and not always the best judge of what kind of people would make good parents. An adopting couple might also feel less entitlement to a child, rather than more, when the birthmother is known and she also knows who the parents are. Many argue that this could raise difficulties with adoptive parents bonding to the child. The adoptive parents may not feel like "real" parents and instead feel more like foster parents, despite the emotional, legal and financial commitment they incur with adoption.

It is also argued that the birthmother will not psychologically relinquish her own feelings of entitlement toward the baby in an open adoption, and it may become difficult or impossible for her to disengage from the child. What she originally considered acceptable, for example, photographs sent to her every few months, may become unacceptable, and she may seek or demand more involvement with the child. One study appears to refute the hypothesis that the birthmother will experience less grief when she knows the identity of the adoptive parents.

A study of 59 birthmothers by Terril Blanton, M.S.S.W., C.S.W., crisis pregnancy counselor at Buckner Baptist Benevolences in Dallas, Texas, and Jeanne Deschner, Ph.D., associate professor at the Graduate School of Social Work at Arlington, Texas, was reported by the two researchers in 1990.

The researchers compared birthmothers who had chosen an open adoption (defined as at least having personally met the adoptive parents) to birthmothers who had chosen traditional confidential adoptions. These two groups were also compared to bereaved women whose children had died.

The birthmothers were an average age of 21.3 for the 18 open adoption birthmothers and 25.6 years for the 41 traditional adoption birthmothers. The researchers modified the Grief Experience Inventory; for example, modifying the question "The yearning I have for the deceased is so intense that I feel physical pain in my chest" to "The yearning I have for the relinquished child is so intense that I feel physical pain in my chest."

The researchers found that the birthmothers who placed their children in an open adoption suffered more than mothers whose children had died. Said the authors, "Indications were strong that biological mothers who know more about the later life of the child they relinquished have a harder time making an adjustment than do mothers whose tie to the child is broken off completely by means of death. Relinquishing mothers who know only that their children still live but have no details about their lives appear to experience an intermediate degree of grief."

The authors hypothesized that the birthmothers in an open adoption could be compared to divorced women who may have more difficulty adjusting to their loss than bereaved widows.

In addition, the birthmother may not fully accept the loss of her nurturing role. Said A. Dean Byrd, Ph.D., executive director of LDS Social Services in Frederick, Maryland, "Open adoption may encourage birth parents to avoid experiencing the loss, to postpone or prolong the separation and grieving process. Ongoing contact may serve as a continuous reminder of the loss, or as a stimulus for the fantasy that relinquishing a child is not really a loss at all."

In addition, her own personal situation may change, and the birthmother may marry and feel she can provide a stable home life. She then could theoretically argue for visits with the child.

Pregnant women may sometimes make demands adopting parents agree to out of desperation or fear because they want to adopt the child so greatly; for example, they may agree to a letter once a week or a phone call every other week.

After placement and especially after finalization, the adopting parents may lose their eagerness to communicate with the birthmother. Perhaps they were dishonest with the birthmother or perhaps they lost their enthusiasm for the previously agreed upon open adoption, especially as the child grew older and became aware of "two Mommies."

This has actually happened, with differing results depending on the state. In a 1986 California case, the adoptive parents failed to follow through with promises made to a birthmother, and she sued for the return of the child. The child was returned to her, and she placed the child with another couple willing to meet her demands. In a similar case in Georgia, the adoptive parents prevailed because the court reasoned that "riders" may not be attached to an adoption agreement, and the birthmother had no legal standing.

Yet if the baby has been placed in an open adoption and the adoptive parents later "slam the door shut," this action could be very traumatic for the birthmother. In some cases, she may not have placed the child for adoption at all and would have opted to raise the child as a single parent had open adoption not been presented to her as a very positive option. Without the inducements offered through open adoption, she would have chosen to parent the child.

Another problem with open adoption is that human nature being as it is, there will be stress and disagreement (even between a married couple) on how to rear a child. Even if the child has no contact with the birthmother but perhaps sees the parent receiving cards, letters and photographs from the birthparent, this raises questions about who is or should be making parenting decisions, and the responses could generate discord and uncertainty in the child's mind. (Supporters of open adoption would greatly disagree with this point.)

In addition, if the child should have some contact with the birthparent, the child might then feel torn between his or her parents and birthparents.

Critics also fear some birthmothers may make unreasonable financial demands on a couple, either before the adoptive placement or in the future, playing on their guilt feelings over "taking her baby." (If the couple offers or gives the birthmother any money directly before placement or even finalization, this could be construed as BABY SELLING and is very dangerous and should be avoided.)

A past strong advocate of open adoption was Reuben Pannor, a retired agency-director who formerly oversaw adoptions at Vista Del Mar, an agency in California.

In the article "Open Adoption as Standard Practice," which Pannor co-authored in 1984 with therapist Annette Baran, the authors described their views that open adoptions are highly preferable to confidential adoptions.

But in a striking change, both Baran and Pannor renounced open adoption in an article written in 1990 for *Orphan Voyage*. Said the authors, "Open adoption, which we helped pioneer, is not a solution to the problems inherent in adoption. Without legal sanction, open adoption is an unenforceable agreement at the whim of the adoptive parents."

Renouncing adoption altogether, both traditional and open, Baran and Pannor instead opt for a "simple adoption," or a form of guardianship, for those parents who are unable to care for their children.

Sometimes the age of the birthmother can be an important factor; for example, some experts, such as Adrienne Kraft and others, argue that adolescent birthmothers would have considerable difficulty with open adoptions and are unprepared to determine whether or not they should continue contact with a child through an open adoption. In addition, the adolescent birthmother may not understand that she is irrevocably transferring her parental rights.

(Some proponents of open adoption insist that a birthmother's continued contact with a child is only seen in COOPERATIVE ADOPTIONS and is not a feature of open adoption. It seems possible that the lines may blur from an open adoption into a cooperative adoption.)

Finally, open or fully-disclosed adoption is perceived by some critics as simply another social fad that has the potential to greatly damage children.

Adult Adopted Persons and Open Adoption Adopted adults are mixed in their feelings about open adoption. Studies have revealed that adopted persons who are actively seeking contact with their birthparents generally favor openness, primarily because it would ease their search.

Adopted adults who feel no need or interest in searching are less likely to favor open adoptions, although they may support the provision of nonidentifying information, especially if the information was updated.

The Open Adoption Process The first step to an open adoption may be a contact with a social worker, attorney or a friend of the pregnant woman or adopting couple. The pregnant woman may view photographs and resumes of prospective adoptive couples and select one or more couples she'd like to meet. She may choose a family she thinks physically resembles herself, or she may simply like the way the husband and wife look in their photograph.

If she meets the couple, she may decide they appear to have good parenting skills and generally appear to offer security for the child to develop to his or her full potential.

The birthmother may also think the couple's hobbies and interests are similar to her own; for example, they may have expressed a love of travel, which she shares and values.

The adoption may not start out as open during the period when the birthmother reviews resumes and/or photographs. When states mandate confidentiality, the social worker or attorney may not lawfully disclose identities.

If the pregnant woman opts to meet the couple, and especially if she meets them more than once, it becomes extremely difficult to maintain confidentiality.

Some adoption agencies have devised a unique and controversial way to both house the pregnant woman and maintain the option of confidentiality: They place a pregnant woman in the home of a prospective adoptive couple, but NOT the woman whose child the couple would adopt. This practice is meant to foster a greater understanding into the decision-making process of birthparents and the emotions a birthmother experiences when she considers adoption.

As a result, the couple and the pregnant woman would theoretically develop empathetic feelings for each other without the pressure involved in an open adoption.

It is also important to understand a FOSTER PARENT ADOPTION is sometimes open, and many foster parents know identifying information about the birthparents, especially if the child is over six. Even if the social worker doesn't share this information with the foster parents, the child may.

Some foster parents have allowed visitations in their own home during foster care and may have telephone or written communication with the birthparents after the adoption occurs.

There are also a very limited number of open adoptions occurring in INTERNATIONAL ADOPTION; however, this does not appear to be a trend at all. In fact, some adoptive parents have stated they wish to adopt a child from another country because they won't have to worry about the birthmother showing up at some time in the future.

In one unique case, adoptive parents in Oregon adopted a teenage girl and her child, making them both parents and grandparents, at the same time.

RELATIVE ADOPTIONS are generally open and are a special category of adoption with unique pros and cons; for example, the child may resemble the adoptive parents. Sometimes relative adoptions are adversarial, resulting from a court battle. In some cases, there will be no counseling or social work assistance to help with the reorganization of kinship role and status and the concomitant feelings that occur. Emergent negative feelings among battling relatives can be extremely painful for the adopted child and affect him or her even to adulthood. (Gloria Vanderbilt wrote an intense account of her mother's battle to gain custody of Gloria, which she lost.)

STEPPARENT ADOPTIONS are, by their nature, open adoptions, and may sometimes involve additional acrimony as may occur in other forms of relative adoptions. (See also CONFIDENTIALITY; TRADITIONAL ADOPTIONS.)

Annette Baran and Reuben Pannor, "A Time for Sweeping Change," fax copy of article sent to *Orphan Voyage*, June 1990.

Terril L. Blanton and Jeanne Deschner, "Biological Mothers' Grief: The Postadoptive Experience in Open vs. Confidential Adoption," *Child Welfare*, 69 (November–December 1990): 525–535.

A. Dean Byrd, "The Case for Confidential Adoption," *Public Welfare*, Fall 1988, 20–23.

Carmello Cocozzelli, "Predicting the Decision of Biological Mothers to Retain or Relinquish Their Babies for Adoption: Implications for Open Placement," *Child Welfare*, 68 (January–February 1989): 33–44.

Adrienne D. Kraft, M.A., Joseph Palombo, M.A., Dorena L. Mitchell, M.A., Patricia K. Woods, M.A., Anne W. Schmidt, M.A., and Nancy G. Tucker, M.S.W., "Some Theoretical Considerations on Confidential Adoption," (A four-part series), *Child and Adolescent Social Work*, 2:1,2,3 and 4:1(1985, 1986).

Jeanne Warren Lindsay, *Open Adoption: A Caring Option* (Buena Park, Calif.: Morning Glory Press, 1987).

Ruth G. McRoy, Harold D. Grotevant and Kerry L. White, *Openness in Adoption: New Practices, New Issues* (New York: Praeger, 1988).

Reuben Pannor and Annette Baran, "Open Adoption as Standard Practice," *Child Welfare*, May–June 1984, 245–250.

Kathleen Silber and Phylis Speedlin, *Dear Birthmother: Thank You for Our Baby* (San Antonio, TX: Corona, 1982).

Jerome Smith, Ph.D., and Franklin I. Miroff, *You're Our Child: The Adoption Experience* (Lanham, Md.: Madison Books, 1987).

Kenneth W. Watson, "The Case for Open Adoption," *Public Welfare*, (Fall 1988): 24–28.

Open Door Societies Adoptive parent support groups who have chosen to incorporate the phrase "open door" in the title of their organizations. The various Open Door organizations are not tied together by any central core.

The Open Door Society of Massachusetts claims to be the oldest adoptive parent support group in the United States. (The Open Door Society of Montreal is believed to be the oldest adoptive parent support group in North America.)

The ODS of Massachusetts was formed in 1967 by a group of adoptive parents who adopted children with SPECIAL NEEDS from the New England Home for Little Wanderers. Later the organization expanded to include adoptive families of children born overseas and healthy children born in the United States. Over 1,500 adoptive families are members of the ODS of Massachusetts, which has chapters throughout the state, publishes a bimonthly newsletter and holds an annual conference each spring.

For more information, contact

Open Door Society of Massachusetts Inc.
867 Boylston St.
Boston, MA 02111
(617) 527-5660

"openness" A commonly used and confusing term that refers to a wide spectrum of information-sharing practices. Such information may, at one extreme, simply refer to offering a birthmother (and birthfather) nonidentifying information to help choose adoptive parents while at the other extreme providing birthparents and adopting parents with identifying information about each other. Some adoption professionals see a sort of openness continuum.

Until the mid-1970s, birthparents were given almost no information about adopting parents. Today most agencies offer birthparents choices; for example, the birthmother may often be able to specify the religion of the adopting couple as well as their interests, age (within certain guidelines) and other factors. Many agencies offer birthparents nonidentifying resumes of prospective adoptive parents, and the birthparents then select the adoptive parents for their child.

Other agencies encourage actual meetings between prospective adoptive parents and birthparents, and still other agencies would like to eliminate CONFIDENTIALITY altogether.

OPEN ADOPTION refers to a full disclosure of identities between the parties involved. Some agencies are using the word "openness" as a kind of "soft" definition of open adoption. It's very important for prospective adoptive parents and birthparents to request a clear definition of "openness" or "open adoption" when contacting an adoption agency to ensure the agency's policies are compatible with their own beliefs and desires. (See also GENETIC DATA; MEDICAL HISTORY; NONIDENTIFYING INFORMATION; OPEN RECORDS.)

open records Refers to a variety of confidential and sealed adoption information that has been made available to a member of the adoption triad, usually the adopted adult or adoptive parents. Such records can include an original unamended birth certificate, court records, adoption agency case records and other confidential information, including professional working notes or files, that were "sealed" or closed subsequent to an adoptive placement. A new birth certificate is issued after finalization with the adoptive parents listed as the parents.

It's important to note that there is considerable confusion in the minds of open records advocates and some adopted adults about the difference between obtaining identifying information, which enables a triad member to seek out another triad member, and a court request to provide confidential sealed records.

Access to the original court records is a vastly different process from opening sealed records. Many searchers who have located a triad member never sought or needed the court's permission to open sealed records in order to locate a birthparent or adopted adult.

The original birth certificate and adoption records are not available or accessible to anyone in most states, including the adopted person, adoptive parents or birthparents, without a court order or special action. Only three states as of this writing offer open inspection of original birth records: Alaska, Hawaii and Kansas. (Alabama rescinded their open records statute in 1990 and became a "search and consent" state, while Hawaii passed an open records law in 1990.) These three states will provide an original birth certificate on demand to adult adopted persons. (In no state may the birthparent obtain sealed records without a special court order.)

Some states require an agency to do a "search and consent" procedure whereby the agency contacts the birthparent or adopted adult and determines if that person is willing to have his or her identity revealed. (Critics of this approach call it "search and confront" and point out several weaknesses in the way it is usually carried out, especially when there are insufficient funds or trained sensitive staff to provide postadoption services.)

If she (or he) is willing to share identifying data, then it is provided. If the individual sought is unwilling to provide identifying data, he or she might be willing to update medical information to alleviate any fears or concerns the adopted adult may have. Yet search and consent laws do not satisfy proponents of open records because the control is in the hands of the agency doing the search and confidentiality will be maintained if the sought person requests it.

Twelve states have passed laws on searching for a birthparent to seek consent for a meeting: Alabama, Connecticut, Georgia, Kentucky, Minnesota, Missouri, Montana, Nebraska, North Dakota, Pennsylvania, Tennessee and Wisconsin. The birthparent is contacted to determine if she or he is willing to have identifying information provided to the adopted adult.

Mutual Consent Registries The most popular approach to the search issue has been the establishment of mutual consent registries. Twenty-four states as of this writing have formed MUTUAL CONSENT REGISTRIES, which match information on adopted persons with birthparent information. In most states, when both the birthparent and the adopted adult register, identifying information is then shared with each.

States with registries include Arkansas, California, Colorado, Florida, Idaho, Illinois, Indiana, Louisiana, Maine, Maryland, Massachusetts, Michigan, Nevada, New Hampshire, New Jersey, New York, Ohio, Oregon, South Carolina, South Dakota, Texas, Utah, Vermont and West Virginia.

For more than a decade, Sen. Carl Levin (D, MI.) has been seeking to enact some form of federally-funded national adoption registry to facilitate matches. (Several national registries, most notably the INTERNATIONAL SOUNDEX REUNION REGISTRY (ISRR) already exist without the support of tax funds.) Many people move at least several times during an 18 to 21 year span, and thus a birthparent or the adoptive parents may no longer reside in the state where the child was adopted.

Concerns about Sen. Levin's bill range from whether and how confidentiality would be sufficiently preserved and whether a federal registry would merely duplicate the efforts of existing state or voluntary national registries.

Most open record advocates are dissatisfied with mutual consent registries because they think they do not go far enough and it is too difficult to make matches because of restrictions. In addition, some state registries, for example, in New York, require the permission of the adoptive parents, the adopted person and both birthparents. It is less likely that so many people will register, some critics observe.

Some states have taken the path of moving away from a mutual consent registry to providing information to the adopted adult unless there is a nonconsent document by the birthparent on file. If a birthparent has not filed such an affidavit, it is presumed that he or she is willing to have confidential information released.

Minnesota took such an approach for adoptions arranged after August 1, 1982. Nebraska changed its adoption laws in 1988 to require that an original birth certificate be provided to an adopted adult unless a nonconsent document was on file. The obvious problem is that birthparents may be unaware of these legal changes because they have relocated or have not read about changes even when they continue to reside in the state.

In ALMA Society v. Mellon, 601 F2d. 1225, cert. den. 444 U.S. 995, (1979), adopted adults sued for identifying information, stating they were being unfairly denied information and treated as a special class when it did not serve the state's interests or the adopted person's interests. The Court found that the New York laws did not "unconstitutionally infringe upon or arbitrarily remove appellants' rights of identity, privacy, or personhood."

In a state court case, a physician's estate was successfully sued by a birthmother for revealing identifying data that enabled an adopted woman to seek out her birthmother. In the Oregon case of *Humphers v. First Interstate Bank* in 1985, the court ruled the physician had breached his professional responsibility to maintain confidentiality.

Arguments in Favor of Open Records
Many and probably most adoption search groups, composed primarily of adopted adults and birthparents who have searched or are engaged in searching, are proponents of open records and believe birthparents and adopted persons should have access to identifying information. They believe such information will make it easier to locate a triad member; however, even with identifying information, it could still take years to locate a person.

An adoption search group is a group that seeks to help an adopted person or birthparent locate birthparents or birthchildren, respectively, or provides them with the techniques or information to enable them to perform their own search. They may also support the searcher emotionally.

The best-known adopted persons' search group is ALMA (see ADOPTEES' LIBERTY MOVEMENT ASSOCIATION), and CUB is the best-known birthparents' search group (see CONCERNED UNITED BIRTHPARENTS). The AMERICAN ADOPTION CONGRESS (AAC) is an umbrella group with which most of the major groups (with ALMA as the most notable exception) are loosely affiliated. Occasionally search groups also help an adoptive parent locate a birthparent, although many adoptive parents are unaware of search groups.

Search groups believe adopted persons have an inviolable right to information concerning their genetic origins and have difficulty understanding why this information can or should be denied. Some adopted adults cannot understand or do not believe that 20 or more years ago, unwed motherhood was considered reprehensible or shameful by many segments of society who shunned unwed pregnant women. All they would need do is talk with unmarried women who became pregnant at that time to verify the emotional climate.

Whether meeting an adult birthchild would lessen these powerfully negative feelings is a matter of much heated debate between open birth record advocates and proponents of confidentiality.

Some advocates of open records believe adoption information should not be available to an adopted person until adulthood (or the age of 18 or 21 years old). Others believe minor children and all the members of the ADOPTION TRIAD (adopted child, birthparents and adoptive parents) should have access to identifying information from the point of adoptive placement.

In the case of an OPEN ADOPTION, identifying information is shared, and there is less reason for adopted persons or birthparents to prepare an elaborate search strategy because this information is already known. However, it is estimated that only about 10% of all infant adoptions are open adoptions. (An open adoption allows for complete disclosure of identities. See entry on open adoption.)

Open record proponents argue that adopted adults are treated as if they were children and forced to adhere to a contract they never agreed upon when confidentiality is mandated.

Adopted adult and attorney Heidi A. Schneider has stated the state's efforts to protect confidential information from curious or prying eyes has also prevented adopted adults from obtaining background information, which Schneider believes should rightfully belong to the adopted person. Schneider believes most of the courts are unreasonably hard on adopted adults who seek information. She adds that even in the case when both adoptive parents and birthparents agree with the opening of confidential adoption records, some courts will mandate an investigation as to whether the information should be turned over.

Those who favor open records include adopted persons who have begun search groups, birthparent support groups and activist social workers, such as Reuben Pannor, retired director of adoption services for Vista Del Mar, a California child welfare agency. In addition, some adoptive parents favor open records, although many adoptive parents remain skeptical.

Arguments Against Opening Identifying Information Advocates of continued confidentiality are concerned that opening birth records would violate the confidentiality that was promised to most birthparents and adoptive parents as well.

Many birthparents have married or remarried and have other children and may or may not have told their families about the child or children they placed for adoption.

Proponents of sealed records also argue that most adopted persons do not opt to search and are satisfied with the nonidentifying medical, social and other information provided to them by their adoptive parents or the agency. In the event of some compelling need to locate the birthparent, for example, a life-threatening problem requiring the birthparent be contacted, an adopted person or the adoptive parents can seek a court order to unseal the records.

Jerome Smith and Franklin Miroff, authors of *You're Our Child: The Adoption Experience,* argue that adopted persons have no constitutional right to know about their biological roots—and that open records may violate the birthmother's constitutional right of privacy. Among the courts to reject open records arguments is the U.S. Supreme Court in *ALMA v. Mellon Society.*

Proponents of sealed birth records also argue that despite the joyous "reunion" stories published in magazine and newspaper articles, some adopted persons who are trying to locate birthparents are devastated by the results of the search, particularly if they are rejected by a birthparent. (Open birth record advocates insist it is better to know the truth, even when the truth is very painful and doesnt live up to the fantasy the adopted adult may have created about birthparents and his or her genetic origins.) (See REUNION.)

Court Order to Unseal Adoption Records When courts are asked to provide sealed records, the requester must usually provide a "good cause." Good cause includes a need for critical medical information.

If the adopted person is mentally stable and the driving force appears to be curiosity, many courts would not consider that to be sufficient "good cause" to open up adoption records and court proceedings.

Adoptive Parents and Open Records Although adoptive parents would seem to be and are usually depicted as the most resistant to open records, some are in favor of opening adoption records in certain cases.

Two Canadian studies of attitudes toward open records were published in 1989. Both studies were somewhat limited in terms of numbers of subjects. The adoptive parents were selected from three different periods: 1958, 1968 and 1978. The birthmothers were selected from 1968 and 1978 because of a lack of information on birthmothers from the 1958 period.

Although a significant percentage of adoptive parents (nearly 70%) expressed support for the releasing of confidential information, researcher Paul Sachdev found the "adoptive parents' support was more apparent than real." In general, the parents supported open records, but when they were asked about their own adopted children, they were more conservative.

The adoptive parents who supported release of identifying data also wanted to set conditions; for example, they wanted to ensure the adopted adults were motivated by a true need for information rather than overall curiosity. They also wanted to ensure that the adopted adults were positively motivated and were not "driven by the need to express negative feelings or to cause harm to the biological parent."

The majority of the birthmothers were in favor of opening records. Yet they also wanted to set conditions. Sachdev said the birthmothers wished to ensure the adopted adult's motives were not negative ones, such as resentment or vengeance. In addition, a large percentage of the birthmothers (75.4%) wanted to be sure the birthmother's consent was obtained before any identifying information was provided.

The adopted adults were the most conservative group among the triad. Over half (56.7%) were in favor of releasing identifying data to their birthmothers. The majority (80%) expressed their desire that the adopted adult's consent be obtained before the release of any identifying information.

Nearly 91% of the adopted adults favored limiting identifying information to adults only. In fact, adopted adults were more in favor of a legal age requirement for information than were adoptive parents or birthmothers. (See also SEARCH.)

Betty Jean Lifton, *Lost & Found: The Adoption Experience* (New York: Harper & Row, 1988).

Jeffrey Rosenberg, "1988 Survey of State Laws on Access to Adoption Rcords," *The Family Law Reporter*, 13:42(August 16, 1988): monograph no. 3.

Paul Sachdev, "The Triangle of Fears: Fallacies and Facts," *Child Welfare*, 67(September/October 1989): 491–503.

Heidi A. Schneider, "Adoption Contracts and the Adult Adoptee's Right to Identity," *Law and Inequality,* 6(1988): 185–229.

Jerome Smith, Ph.D., and Franklin I. Miroff, *You're Our Child: The Adoption Experience* (Lanham, Md. Madison Books, 1987).

optional adopter See FERTILE ADOPTIVE PARENTS.

orphan A person whose parents have died or who are presumed dead; usually refers to a dependent child. Few of the infants and older children who are adopted in the United States are orphans. Instead, most are voluntarily placed for adoption by living birthparents, or parental rights are involuntarily terminated by the state (because of abuse, neglect, abandonment or another reason), and the child is subsequently adopted.

The term "orphan" has a different meaning to the U.S. Immigration and Naturalization Service (INS), the federal agency that oversees international adoption.

To the INS, an orphan is a child from another country with no parents or with only one parent who has signed an irrevocable consent to an adoption. There is also an upper age limit on orphans from other countries who may be adopted by U.S. citizens: The orphan petition must be filed before the child's 16th birthday.

Once the petition is approved, the child is considered as a relative of a U.S. citizen (at least one of the parents must be a U.S. citizen; in the case of a single parent, the single parent must be a U.S. citizen).

U.S. Department of Justice, Immigration and Naturalization Service, *The Immigration of Adopted and Prospective Adoptive Children,* 1990, Government Printing Office, Washington, D.C.

orphanage Institution that houses children whose parents are deceased or whose whereabouts are unknown. The term is generally considered outmoded in the United States, although it is frequently used to describe institutions abroad, where it is a more accurate term, since the word ORPHAN has a different definition in international adoption.

GROUP HOMES is the phrase used to describe the types of institutionalized residences that usually fulfill this function; however, the group homes of today have smaller numbers of children than did the orphanages, and the children have live-in house parents. Children enter this alternative living arrangement because of a parental inability to control their behavior or because of parental abuse, abandonment or neglect. Many group homes have a therapeutic or treatment component, although they differ from RESIDENTIAL TREATMENT CENTERS.

Some experts believe that group homes would be more efficient and preferable to foster homes. According to an article in the *Washington Post,* child welfare officials are experiencing great difficulty in recruiting sufficient numbers of foster parents and must send increasing numbers of children to long-term residences.

Some cities are using group nurseries for drug-exposed babies, while others place children with severe emotional or behavioral problems in group homes.

Marcia Slacum Greene, "Rebirth of Orphanages is Reviving Old Fears; In D.C., the Ghost of Junior Village Haunts Talk of New Orphanages," *Washington Post,* January 9, 1990.

"orphans of the living" A phrase to describe the many children in foster care in the late 1950s and early 1960s and before the movement for PERMANENCY PLANNING began in the mid-1970s. The phrase was also used to describe children who were stigmatized by illegitimacy in past years.

Social workers in the early 1960s became increasingly concerned that many children were remaining in foster homes throughout their childhood and never returning to their biological families or being placed in adoptive homes. Nor would they necessarily remain in one foster home. Children could be moved numerous times and never form strong attachments to parent figures.

This temporary home status of the children was perceived as a serious problem; however, little action was taken until testimony before Congress in the 1970s, and the first steps were taken to place children with SPECIAL NEEDS back with their parents, in adoptive homes or in long-term foster care with the same caretakers or institutional care.

Orphan Train Refers to the era of 1854–1929 when an estimated 150,000 homeless children were placed on trains and taken to rural sites concentrated in the Midwest and West in search of homes where the children could live and work. The children ranged in age from as young as about one year old to age sixteen or seventeen.

Limited follow-ups of the children revealed that then, as now, the children who adapted the most readily were usually the younger children and the older teenagers faced the greatest difficulty in adjusting to a radically different environment.

These homeless children came primarily from large cities on the Eastern Seaboard, such as New York City. Most were poor, and many had been involved with minor or serious infractions of the law. Many also had siblings and were separated from them for life as a result of the move. Yet most of the children made successful new lives for themselves, leaving behind them severe poverty and desolation.

The Orphan Train era was initiated by social welfare reformer, Charles Loring Brace of the Children's Aid Society in New York.

Brace urged that children of paupers not be left to languish in large crowded institutions but instead be given an opportunity to live and work in a family home.

Homelessness was a severe problem in Brace's society, and thousands of children often engaged in petty crimes, such as picking pockets, in order to survive. Police reports in New York City in 1852 revealed that in 11 wards, 2,000 homeless girls ages 8 to 16 were arrested for theft.

Children arrested for "vagrancy" and other infractions were housed together with pauper children in large institutions, influencing each other. These children were referred to as the "dangerous classes."

Part of the problem was that there was almost no need for "honest labor" in the large cities, which was why the children had turned to dishonest labor. Large numbers of immigrants had teemed into the major Northeast cities, especially New York City, between 1847 and 1860.

There was insufficient demand for the labor of this huge influx of adults, let alone children. (This was prior to the child labor movement, and at this time, everyone worked.)

But at the same time, the midwestern and western farmers suffered a severe labor shortage. Brace saw the answer in Christian terms as well as in economic terms: provide children to the farmers—children who would work in exchange for a home—get the children out of their evil urban environments and into rural America.

Brace contrasted the chance to live with a family to what he saw as the demoralizing effects of growing up in an institution, and to him, the choice was clear.

He was supported in this movement by organizations within the Catholic Church and other groups; for example, the Sisters of Charity of St. Vincent de Paul and the New York Foundling Hospital were both actively involved in the Orphan Train movement.

The children were accompanied on the train by adults, often Catholic nuns, who rode with the children to their destinations and destinies.

The movement was also known as the "Placing Out" program and preceded adoption as we know it today.

The children left the train at each stop and were chosen or not chosen by people who came to the station to see them. In some cases, the match was made ahead of time, and the couple would present a number to the children's chaperon who would match the number to the child wearing the same number.

In other cases, the matches were far more informal. One train rider reported that her adoptive mother wanted a brunette girl, but the child with the right number refused to leave the nun. The red-haired and fair-skinned 18-month-old train rider happened to look at the woman and say, "Mama." She was chosen.

Some of the Orphan Train riders were ultimately adopted, while others were not. Some were "indentured," which means their labor was sold to waiting farmers, but many were taken in as one of the family and raised as if they had been adopted, whether or not an adoption was ever legitimized.

Brace was opposed to indenturing children because it didn't work and too often the children ran away. Instead, he believed the children should be treated with dignity and respect, and they would respond admirably.

Wrote Brace in 1859 in his book *The Best Method of Disposing of Our Pauper and Vagrant Children,*

> The children of the poor are not essentially different from the children of the rich; the same principles which influence the good or evil development of every child in comfortable circumstances, will affect, in greater or less degree, the child of poverty. Sympathy and hope are as inspiring to the ignorant girl, as to the educated; steady occupation is as necessary for the street-boy, as the boy of a wealthy house; indifference is as chilling to the one class, as to the other; the prospect of success is as stimulating to the young vagrant, as to the student in college.

The Orphan Train riders continued their treks west until about 1929. Although today the idea of sending out homeless children to strangers in other states may sound cruel and inhuman, it must be remembered that diseases abounded in the almshouses and orphanages and that yesterday's orphan trains were not all that different from today's "Adoption Fairs," wherein caseworkers bring adoptable children to a picnic or party that is attended by previously-approved prospective adoptive parents.

Poor children were often not taught to read and write and had little hope for a successful future. Brace envisioned the children sent out on the trains as having a better life, growing up to be farmers and farmer's wives.

Yet there were critics of Brace and the New York Aid Society. Brace's organization did not attempt religious-matching, and often children of Catholic immigrants were placed in Protestant homes. Concern over this practice grew and ultimately resulted in attempts to place children in homes with the same religious background as their parents.

Critics also said Brace did insufficient investigations of the foster or adoptive homes and little follow-up or documentation. In Brace's defense, communications and transportation of his era had little resemblance to our society today.

Today the history of the Orphan Train era is kept alive by the ORPHAN TRAIN HERITAGE SOCIETY OF AMERICA INC., based in Springdale, Arkansas. Members assist each other in finding birth families and in reminiscing about their shared history.

Orphan Train Heritage Society of America Inc. (OTHSA) An organization formed in 1987 to provide a clearinghouse of information on the estimated 150,000 children who were "placed out" from 1854 to 1929.

The OTHSA collects historical information on the period in an effort to preserve the family histories of children "placed out" on the Orphan Train and the families who raised them. The group also attempts to reunite Orphan Train riders and their descendants with biological relatives. The OTHSA holds an annual reunion of members and guests.

The organization publishes *Crossroads*, a quarterly newsletter describing current activities as well as true life stories of train riders. In addition, the group sells books about this era and informs readers of recent articles or upcoming television programs on the Orphan Train era.

For more information, contact

Orphan Train Heritage Society of America
Route 4, Box 565
Springdale, AR 72764

OURS Former name of the ADOPTIVE FAMILIES OF AMERICA INC.; name change occured in 1989.

outreach An effort, usually by a human service agency, to reach out to enlist clients in the community who need services but have not yet sought such services. Individuals who need assistance may be unaware the agency exists or not know the range of the services offered by the agency.

Some agencies promote their services to the general public as well, not only educating the entire community about what the agency achieves but also reaching potential clients needing service who are unknown to the agency.

In the case of an adoption agency, outreach could include programs open to the public, articles in the newspaper, visits to clubs and high schools and other attempts to reach particular people.

Agencies who are interested in reaching out seek to extend their services beyond the usual 9 to 5 working day, will often answer questions and provide counseling during evening hours or on weekends and frequently utilize volunteers to supplement staff. (See also AGENCIES.)

P

parens patriae The concept that the state has responsibility for a child when the parent or guardian cannot effectively continue in a parental role. As a result, if a parent abuses or neglects a child, the state has the right to remove the child from the home. If the state determines the parent cannot or will not become an adequate parent, then the courts may terminate parental rights without the consent of the parents and place the child in an adoptive home. (See TERMINATION OF PARENTAL RIGHTS.)

Parens patriae was based on the English common law whereby the king protected children within his kingdom. According to Lela B. Costin, one of the contributors to *A Handbook of Child Welfare,* the concept of *parens patriae* was given a more liberal interpretation in America during the frontier period, when children were at great risk for being orphaned, abandoned or neglected. As a result, *parens patriae* came to be interpreted as a rationale for the state stepping into the parent-child relationship when needed.

Parens patriae is a principle also used beyond the field of adoption; for example, the state requires children to go to school up to a certain age, and parents and children must comply with this requirement. (Some states recognize home schooling as acceptable.)

Up to about a century ago, the parents were usually seen as the supreme arbiters of the children's fate, and it was not up to neighbors or society in general to set rules or standards for parents. Child labor laws did not exist, and many children worked long hours at low wages. Social reforms were passed, and today children occupy a special role in society.

Lela B. Costin, "The Historical Context of Child Welfare," in *A Handbook of Child Welfare: Context, Knowledge, and Practice* (New York: Free Press, 1985).

parental leave Time taken off from work by a mother or father to care for a child.

Although many companies allow for MATERNITY LEAVE for pregnant women or women who have just borne children, far fewer offer maternity leave or parental leave to adoptive parents.

A late 1989 General Accounting Office study of parental leave policies for adoptive parents at 77 employers who provide some form of adoption benefit revealed that 75 of the companies allowed employees to use paid leave and 74 allowed them to use vacation time. (Employers included 67 private companies, 7 government organizations and 3 nonprofit agencies; 60% of the companies surveyed were large U.S. corporations.)

Seven of the companies had specific leave for parental leave or adoption leave, and four companies allowed adoptive parents to use maternity or paternity leave in the case of adoptions.

Fifty-three of the companies allowed for unpaid leave in the form of "personal leave" or an unpaid leave of absence.

Most paid leaves ranged between one to three months. More time off was allowed with unpaid leave, and 37 companies allowed six months or more of unpaid leave.

According to information published in *Family Affairs,* published by the New York-based Institute for American Values, 13 states allow for maternity or parental leave. Some states, such as North Dakota and Oklahoma, limit parental leave to state employees. West Virginia law allows leave for an adoption by a state or county school board employee.

States that mandate a provision for parental leave require employers with a certain number of employees to provide unpaid leave; for example, Minnesota law allows up to six weeks parental leave for a birth or an adoption if the company employs 21 or more workers. Oregon law stipulates 12 weeks leave for a birth or adoption if the company has 25 or more employees. Connecticut's employee base is 75, Pennsylvania's is 10, Washington's is 100, Wisconsin's is 50, and Maine's is 25.

Whether or not health care benefits are continuous during parental leave depends on the state. Health coverage must continue in Connecticut, Minnesota, North Dakota, Oregon, Pennsylvania, Rhode Island, Vermont and Wisconsin. Continuous health care benefits during parental leave are not required in Tennessee and Washington. Health care benefits may be continued during parental leave if the employee pays the expense in Maryland and Maine.

In 1990, New Jersey passed a parental leave act for individuals with newborn or newly-adopted children who had been employed for at least a year with a company employing at least 50 workers. Leave of up to one year was allowed and could be paid, unpaid or a combination of paid and unpaid.

Because these family leave laws have been passed since 1987, it is likely even more states will begin to offer parental leave benefits.

Adoptive parents need parental leave to bond with their children, whether the children are infants or older children and whether the children are from another country or the United States. In fact, extra time with older children may be even more critical than for infants.

Children who have spent years in foster care or foreign orphanages cannot or should not be sent directly to a daycare center. Instead, they need time to adjust to a new home and new parents, just as parents need time to adjust to the child.

Parental leave for adoptive parents is equitable because many corporations provide health coverage and time off for pregnancy and childbirth. In some cases, corporations who cannot or choose not to provide parental leave to adoptive parents will instead provide a cash payment to cover adoption expenses.

The General Accounting Office estimated that the total overall cost to employers to cover health insurance for workers on unpaid leave to care for new children would be about $90 million annually. To the extent that firms already offer unpaid leave similar to proposed federal legislation and to the extent that some states already have comparable leave laws, the actual cost of proposed federal legislation to employers of providing continued health insurance coverage would be less than the $90 million estimate.

The General Accounting Office believes that leave to care for new children will be used predominantly by women. In 1986, 840,000 working women would have qualified for unpaid leave for the birth or adoption of a child. Based on current adoption statistics, less than 5% of these parents would be new adoptive parents.

Because adopting parents often receive very little notice that a child is available—perhaps only a few days—it's impossible for employees to give their employers even two weeks notice about an impending leave. Consequently, adoption leave is perceived negatively by many employers.

The reason most adopting parents are given very little notice by agencies is that the agencies don't want to tell prospective adoptive parents about a child until all the appropriate papers are signed in case the birthmother changes her mind.

One tactic a prospective adoptive parent can employ if she or he wishes to take parental leave is to simply ask for an exception or to prepare information on his or her value to the company and attempt to convince the employer that because the adopting parent is so valuable, an exception should be made in her or his case. Exceptions to the rule are generally far easier to obtain than changing the rule itself—no matter how desirable it would be to change that rule. (See also EMPLOYMENT BENEFITS; INSURANCE.)

"Family Leave Act," P. L. 1989, Chapter 261, approved January 4, 1990, state of New Jersey.
"Family Leave Legislation Since 1987," *Family Affairs*, 2(Summer/Fall 1989).
Beverly Lempicki, "Parental Leave a Reality with Your Help," *F.A.C.E. Facts,* May/June 1989, 37–38.
U.S. General Accounting Office, "Adoption Assistance Provided by Selected Employers to Adopting Parents," GAO/HRD-90-47FS, December 1989.
U.S. General Accounting Office, "Parental Leave: Revised Cost Estimate Reflecting the Impact of Spousal Leave," report to congressional requesters, GAO/HRD 89-68, April 1989.

parental rights Parents have the right to choose the religion of their child, place the child in public or private schools (or home school), select health care providers and make a myriad of decisions affecting a child's life. Parents do not have the right to abuse a child, and if state social service officials believe parents are abusing their children physically or sexually or are neglecting the children or have abandoned them, state workers have the right to remove the children from the home and place them in foster care or institutional care.

Parents may voluntarily choose to place their children for adoption. This involves a formal termination of rights. Adoption author and expert Marietta Spencer sees this process as a "transfer" of parental rights, rather than a "surrendering" or "giving away" of a child. What the parent is relinquishing or giving up is parental rights to the child, not the child her- or himself.

States also have the right to terminate parental rights, although rights are usually only involuntarily terminated in the most extreme cases. Until the late 1970s, most children placed in foster care either remained in foster care or were returned to their parents. (For a detailed discussion of voluntary and involuntary ending of rights see TERMINATION OF PARENTAL RIGHTS.)

The passage of the ADOPTION ASSISTANCE AND CHILD WELFARE ACT OF 1980 by the federal government mandated that the cases of foster children be reviewed every six months and a PERMANENCY PLAN be made for children by the time 18 months had passed.

At that time, either the child would be returned home or steps would be initiated to terminate parental rights and place the child in an adoptive home.

In mose cases, if a biological parent expresses a desire to retain parental rights and appears willing to work toward correcting the condition which led to the child's removal, then parental rights will not be terminated. (See COURT-MANDATED CONTRACTS.)

Parents have the right to appeal when a child is removed from the home if they feel the charges of abuse or neglect were unfair; however, there are often periods of weeks or even months before a court will decide whether or not to return the child home.

If the state social services department decides to initiate action to terminate parental rights, then the parent may appeal these actions as well. If the court does terminate parental rights, the parent has no further recourse (presuming all appeals are exhausted.)

Most children needing adoptive families under the control and authority of the state social services system are over age eight, even if they entered foster care three or four years earlier, because few states comply with federal laws requiring action be taken on a child's case 18 months after entry into foster care.

Part of the problem is the difficulty in preparing a case for court to terminate parental rights, and another part of the problem is many casewokers and/or judges who are extremely hesitant to terminate parental rights, even in the face of extreme cruelty or obvious parental abuse or neglect.

Even if the parents have been imprisoned for major crimes or if the parents are mentally ill, such grounds may not be sufficient to terminate parental rights. (See also ABUSE; FOSTER CHILDREN; NEGELCT; PERMANENCY PLANNING; SPECIAL NEEDS.)

Associate Press, "Schizophrenic Mother Wants Son Adopted," *Florida Today*, October 6, 1989.

Adela Beckerman, "Incarcerated Mothers and Their Children in Foster Care: The Dilemma of Visitation," *Child and Youth Services Review*, 11(1989): 175–183.

parent-initiated adoption See INTERNATIONAL ADOPTION.

pathology and adoptive status The theory that there are problems in a person that are related to adoptive status, either directly or indirectly. These could include problems with identity, psychiatric problems, alcohol abuse or criminal behavior.

Some adoption experts believe adopted persons are at risk for developing certain problems. Psychologist David Kirschner has stated that 5% to 10% of adopted children develop "adopted child syndrome," which includes such behaviors as lying, stealing, learning difficulties and occasional violent acts.

Other adoption experts believe adopted persons are not necessarily at risk for developing behavioral problems.

Some adopted persons believe traditional adoption is the problem, not the answer, and are pressing for OPEN RECORDS. Other experts feel open records would cause more problems than they would solve. The debate on these issues is likely to continue for some time. (See also ADOLESCENT ADOPTED PERSONS; ADULT ADOPTED PERSONS; ALCOHOL ABUSE AND ADOPTED PERSONS; CRIMINAL BEHAVIOR IN ADOPTED PERSONS; IDENTITY; OPEN RECORDS; PSYCHIATRIC PROBLEMS OF ADOPTED PERSONS.)

National Committee For Adoption, "Experts Debate 'Adopted Child Syndrome' at A.C.C.," *National Adoption Reports*, May-June 1987.

pediatric AIDS See AIDS.

permanency planning Refers to a movement, which developed in the late 1970s, to either return foster children to their biological homes or terminate parental rights and place the child for adoption. This movement led to the ADOPTION ASSISTANCE AND CHILD WELFARE ACT OF 1980, which mandated permanency planning for all states.

Prior to this time, most older children who were placed in foster care remained in the system until they "aged-out" at 18 years old. Caseworkers began to realize that children over age eight were adoptable and there were also families for children in sibling groups, handicapped children, minority children and other categories of children previously considered UNADOPTABLE.

Although many children still remain in foster care for years, the numbers appear to have dropped, and states are making increasing efforts to find permanent homes for foster children. (See also FOSTER CARE; FOSTER PARENT; FOSTER PARENT ADOPTIONS; SPECIAL NEEDS.)

photolistings Refers to photographs and descriptions of children available for adoption, who are also known as WAITING CHILDREN.

Starting in 1971 the Adoption Listing Service in Illinois was the first organization to use a photolisting service to find families for older children. Subsequently, the Massachusetts Adoption Resource Exchange (MARE) and the Council of Adoptive Parents (CAP) also began using photolistings in 1972. (See CAP BOOK.) In 1975, New York law ordered that all children needing adoptive families be photolisted.

Each state social service agency has a photolisting book, usually available to individuals who have completed their home study or who are considering adopting a child with SPECIAL NEEDS. How updated these listings are varies from state to state. Photolistings are used in conjunction with VIDEOTAPES of children needing families, media campaigns, adoption fairs and picnics and a variety of tactics to recruit adoptive parents.

Adoptive parent support groups often include photographs of waiting children in their newsletters. Prospective adoptive parents may also purchase photolisting books through such organizations as Children Awaiting for Adoptive Parents (CAAP) in Rochester, New York, which offers photolistings of domestic children, or through the International Concerns Committee for Children in Boulder, Colorado, which includes photolistings of children from other countries.

Most photolistings are of children with special needs who are black or mixed race, are over age 8 or have siblings and need to be placed together. Some photolisted children may suffer mild to major handicaps.

Jack Brennan of Family Focus Adoption Services in Little Neck, New York analyzed the status of over 7,000 children listed in the "Blue Books" of New York (New York's photolisting books of adoptable children).

According to Brennan, 75% to 80% of the children whose photos leave the books are placed for adoption. Brennan also noted the necessity of keeping children in the books until placement and stated, "In examining the specific years of 1978, 1983, and 1988, to look at trends, we found further proof of the necessity of keeping children listed: In each year we examined there were children that moved into adoption from the age of under one year old all the way up to over seventeen years old."

The analysis also revealed that the sex ratio throughout the years was 60% male and 40% female. (Because many adopting families specify they want to adopt girls, it is not surprising that there are fewer girls listed in the photolisting book than boys. The girls who do become available for adoption are quickly adopted and often never make it to a photolisting book.)

Racially, Brennan found that black placements increased from 13% in 1978 to 22% of all the placements by 1988. Caucasian placements declined, especially placements of Caucasian girls, from 20% in 1978 to 11% of all the placements that occurred in 1988.

According to Brennan's report, the photolisted child with the greatest probability of being placed was in the racial category of "other" and was not black, white or Hispanic. "Other" included all biracial children as well as Indian and Asian children. Of the children racially defined as "other," 90% of the boys and 84% of the girls were placed for adoption.

The largest category of children found by Brennan was black males, who represented 34% of the population listed in 1988. Next was black females, at 21%, followed by white males, at 18% in 1988.

It is clear from the efforts of the cap book as well as the many state photolisting services that photolisting children is an effective way to recruit adoptive parents. Giving a "face" and a description to a child inspires many adopting parents to select a particular child or at least ask for further information.

Public policy should mandate photolisting of all waiting children with the provision that public funds be used to underwrite this essential OUTREACH service. (See also RECRUITMENT.)

Jack Brennan, "1989 Fact Sheet: Another Look at the Blue Books" (Little Neck, N.Y.: Family Focus Adoption Services, August 11, 1989).

Jeff Seideman, *How to Publish a Photo Listing Book* (Boston: Adoption Exchange Association, 1984).

physicians Doctors play an important and broad role in the field of adoption. They are often the first to confirm a pregnancy in a teenager. They also diagnose and treat adopted children as they grow, and attitudes of the physician toward the adopted children are important. Physicians are also critically important in INTERNATIONAL ADOPTION because children who are being adopted from other countries may suffer ailments that are unknown or highly unusual in the United States.

Crisis Pregnancies Doctors vary widely in their opinions about adoption. As in the society at large, some physicians believe abortion is the best answer to most crisis pregnancies while others believe parenting should be chosen while others are supportive of adoption. Ideally, a physician will present the pros and cons of all the various options and enable a pregnant girl or woman to make her own informed decision.

Physicians are also affected by the attitudes of society at large; for example, if the average person believes an unmarried person should abort before she should consider having a baby and placing it for adoption, physicians too may be influenced by such an attitude. In turn, the opinions of doctors about adoption (and many other subjects) influence and affect the community at large. (See CRISIS PREGNANCY.)

Teen Pregnancies Because the physician may be the first adult an adolescent talks to about the pregnancy, the physician's response is very critical, and adoption is one option which should be discussed. To properly discuss adoption with the patient, the physcian should be aware of adoption agencies and counseling resources available in the community. Physicians should also be sure to talk to the pregnant adolescent in person rather than over the telephone to ensure privacy. (In some states, privacy rights cover adolescents, and diagnoses of pregnancy or other medical conditions may not be given to individuals other than the minor unless she has given her permission.)

Physicians as Intermediaries Some physicians actually arrange independent adoptions, particularly physicians who are also obstetricians. They may have patients who are infertile couples and arrange for the woman with the crisis pregnancy to place her child with one of these infertile couples.

Social workers argue that adoption agencies are much better suited to provide objective counseling to a pregnant woman considering adoption for her child than is her physician, whose expertise lies in the medical arena rather than the social work field. (This argument is also advanced against attorneys who are involved with placing children in independent adoptions: Social workers assert that lawyers are more qualified at handling legal matters than at counseling adopting parents or birthparents.)

An article in *The Journal of Family Practice* discussed the role of the physician as an intermediary or active party in facilitating an adoption.

Said Dr. Richard Anstett, "Physicians involved in these adoption-relinquishment situations have to assume a triple advocacy role. They are advocating for the birth parents, for the potential adoptive parents, and of course for the baby."

An adoption agency representative, Ms. Martin, urged the involvement of an adoption agency, which enables one social worker to be assigned to the birthmother and another to the prospective parents. She also urged physicians to repeat information at least several times because birthmothers are often so anxious that they may have difficulty listening to information.

Adoptive Parents and Physicians Adoptive parents who are adopting either an infant or older child should talk to the pediatrician they are considering to determine if he or she is generally favorable or neutral about adoption.

Studies of internationally adopted children have revealed that physicians may be unaware of medical problems foreign children may suffer. (See MEDICAL PROBLEMS OF ADOPTED CHILDREN.)

As a result, adopting parents should educate themselves as much as possible about necessary tests and should also seek out a physician at or near a major medical center whenever possible. (See also HOSPITALS' TREATMENT OF BIRTHMOTHERS; INDEPENDENT ADOPTION.)

Committee on Adolescence, "Counseling the Adolescent About Pregnancy Options," *Pediatrics,* January 1989, 135–137.

Sandy Wherley, M.A., Peggy Hauser, M.S.W., and Richard E. Anstett, M.D., Ph.D., "The Relinquishing-Adopting Patient and the Family Physician," *The Journal of Family Practice,* 83(March 1989): 257–261.

placement The point at which a child begins to live with prospective adoptive parents. After a certain period, depending on the state in which the adoptive parents reside, the adoption may be finalized, and the adopted child will have virtually all the rights and privileges of a biological child born to the family.

placement outcome Refers to the success or failure of an adoption, whether the adoption is disrupted or dissolved or successful. The overwhelming majority of adoptions are successful. (See also DISRUPTION; DISSOLUTION.)

post-legal adoptive services Also known as postadoption services, these are services provided by an adoption agency subsequent to legal finalization of the adoption. The adopted person, birthparents or adoptive parents may have questions soon after finalization or many years later.

Adopted adults may have questions about adoption in general or their own birthparents. Adopted persons, birthparents and/or adoptive parents may wish further information about genetic backgrounds or may wish an actual meeting to be arranged between the parties.

Families who adopt children with SPECIAL NEEDS may need further counseling. Even parents who adopt children as infants often find adoption issues arise later and may seek expert assistance and counseling.

Social worker Marietta Spencer has described how agencies can assist all members of the adoption triad well after finalization of an adoption. Spencer says the agency may share genetic information, assist in the exchange of nonidentifying information between triad members and provide an array of other services.

Mary Jane Fales reported on a survey of post-legal services in her booklet *Post-Legal Adoption Services Today*. According to Fales, there are primarily four types of post-legal services: social service agencies, private therapists, mental health clinics and self-help (support, mutual aid) groups.

Fales said most of the adoptive parents using post-legal services are white, and they generally seek aid when their children are adolescents. Says Fales, "The families either had no problems with the children prior to adolescence, or were able to solve them."

Mary Jane Fales, *Post-Legal Adoption Services Today* (Washington, D.C.: Child Welfare League of America, 1986).

Marietta E. Spencer, "Post-Legal Adoption Services: A Lifelong Commitment," in *Infertility and Adoption: A Guide for Social Work Practice* (New York: Haworth Press, 1988).

postplacement services The range of counseling and services provided to the adoptive parents, adopted child and birthparents subsequent to the child's adoptive placement and before the adoption is legally finalized in court.

Birthparents may need counseling to resolve feelings of loss after they've placed a newborn infant for adoption. Older children usually need counseling after an adoptive placement, no matter how positive the child feels about the adoptive parents. Postplacement services are provided to make the adoption experience as positive and satisfying as possible to all parties.

poverty Birthmothers who choose adoption are less likely to live in poverty than are single women who choose to rear their children, according to data available from the National Center for Health Statistics and numerous studies.

Birthmothers in the United States who choose adoption are also more likely to be middle-class women from stable homes. According to another study (McLaughlin, see BIRTHMOTHER), women who choose adoption generally have higher educational and/or career goals than those single women who parent their children. (See also TEENAGE PARENTS.)

Christine Bachrach, "Adoption Plans, Adopted Children, and Adoptive Mothers," *Journal of Marriage and the Family,* 48(May 1986): 243–253.

preadoptive counseling Counseling provided to prospective adoptive parents while they are being assessed and before they are approved to adopt a child. Another phrase in common usage for this process is the HOME STUDY.

pregnancy after adoption Although the majority of adoptive parents do not have a biological child subsequent to an adoption, virtually every new adoptive parent has heard about a person with this experience. It is unknown how many adoptive mothers become pregnant after adopting but probably well less than 10% have biological children after they adopt a child. In many cases, the pregnancy is unplanned because the mother presumed she was infertile.

In an extensive study performed by Michael Bohman, he found 8% of the adoptive parents ultimately had a biological child. According to Bohman, 8% of the infertile couples who had applied to the agency and then withdrew before adopting also later had biological children. Bohman discussed other studies, which indicate postadoptive pregnancies at a rate of about 3% to 10%.

The act of adopting a child cannot erase a woman's or man's infertility problem, and individuals who suggest adoption as a psychological "cure" to infertility are sadly misled. What is likely to happen in those instances is that infertility caused by unknown factors was somehow diminished. Since about 20% of infertile couples have "unexplained infertility" for their diagnosis, this is likely to account for such a phenomenon.

Adoption experts strive to ensure that prospective adoptive parents have resolved as much of their conflicts about infertility as possible prior to adoption so the adopted child will be fully accepted.

With increasing breakthroughs in REPRODUCTIVE TECHNOLOGIES, it may be possible for a greater number of adoptive mothers to successfully bear biological children, should they wish to do so. (See also MIXED FAMILIES; SIBLINGS.)

Michael Bohman, *Adopted Children and Their Families* (Stockholm, Sweden: Proprius, 1970).

pregnancy counseling A service provided to women with crisis pregnancies. Counseling may be offered by social workers at adoption agencies, counselors at family planning clinics, pregnancy centers or schools or other individuals.

The woman with a CRISIS PREGNANCY may need assistance in resolving her immediate needs, for example, verification that she actually is pregnant, location of a place to stay (if needed) and initiation of medical care. She may be eligible for public assistance, such as Aid to Families with Dependent Children (AFDC), food stamps and Medicaid.

She may also be uncertain as to whether or not she should continue her pregnancy and may feel compelled to abort because she is fearful of what her parents, friends and others will think when she becomes visibly pregnant.

Often she may have vague and erroneous ideas about adoption that need to be clarified after her immediate needs are met. Should she consider adoption or parenting (presuming she continues the pregnancy), she needs someone who can fully explore both options with her. The agency social worker is usually the best qualified person to provide this service. Whoever provides her counseling should be sure to include the adoption option as one possible choice, whether the woman appears interested or not.

In his study of counselors, Edmund Mech found that many counselors never discussed adoption with pregnant teenagers because they were convinced teens were completely uninterested. On the contrary, when Mech surveyed pregnant teens, he found the majority were interested in learning more about adoption. Yet this omission causes a problem for the teenager (or woman) who is interested: If she brings the subject up herself, will the counselor think she is a "bad" person? By not approaching the topic of adoption, the counselor implicitly conveys the idea that adoption is not acceptable—or at least not acceptable in this person's case.

In addition, a failure to discuss adoption shortchanges the woman who might consider it if she understood what it entailed.

Jerome Smith and Franklin Miroff describe feelings the birthmother faces as she makes her decision about whether to parent or make an adoption plan in their book *You're Our Child: The Adoption Experience*.

According to the authors, the birthmother may tell herself that an infertile couple will adopt her baby, and without her, they would be unable to adopt. If she is religious, she may see herself as "God's instrument." She may also try to think of the fetus or baby as the adoptive couple's child rather than her child. By such thinking, she defends herself against maternal attachment, thereby reducing the sense of anticipatory loss.

She will also swing back and forth between deciding to parent or to delegate parenting to others more prepared for it. Smith and Miroff explain the ambivalence of the woman (or girl) as a "head-heart" response.

The authors believe counseling is critically important and state, "A warm, supportive, nonjudgmental atmosphere will allow the woman to think through her situation and discuss the practical aspects of her planning free from coercion."

They add, "In assisting the woman in decision-making, the counselor must help her to separate fact from fantasy, help her to see the realities involved with raising a child alone and with relinquishing a child she may never see again."

Most birthmothers say they have some future plan for themselves after placement; for example, they plan to return to high school or college or they expect to resume their job or career. A study by Jane Bose and Michael Resnick revealed the teenagers who made an adoption plan had much higher educational aspirations than did the teenagers who chose parenting. (See TEENAGE PARENTS.)

Women who refuse to make future plans and who have no idea what will happen to them after the baby is born are far more likely to change their mind about placing the child for adoption, either just before or after the baby is born and before consent is signed, than is a woman with a plan for her future.

Stages of Counseling In a paper on pregnancy counseling, social worker and vice president of the NATIONAL COMMITTEE FOR ADOPTION Mary Beth Seader discussed stages of the counseling process, including assessment, decision-making, making an "action plan," mourning and acceptance and integration of the adoption experience.

According to Seader, it is the initial assessment that requires the most skill on the part of the pregnancy counselor. It is at this point when the counselor must learn about the woman or teenager, her family and her relationships and also evaluate at what intellectual and emotional levels she is. In addition, if possible, the counselor will actually involve the birthfather and the family of the birthmother (and sometimes the family of the birthfather as well), not only to help the social worker with assessment but to involve people who are intimately connected to the crisis at hand and who can help the pregnant woman with resolution, whatever her ultimate decision is.

Seader says it is dangerous to concentrate on the outcome (parenting or adoption) at this point because there are many other issues that more urgently need to be discussed (although the woman should be assured that the agency can assist with adoption, should that option be chosen).

During the decision-making phase of counseling, the pregnant woman begins evaluating the pros and cons of parenting and adoption as she explores each option and considers her own unique case.

When she is in the "action plan" stage, she is ready to formulate a plan; however, she cannot make a plan unless the counselor has fully explained both adoption and parenting to her. Says Seader, "If the client knew everything she needed and wanted, chances are she would not be in the counselor's office . . . She may not know the possible repercussions of any of her choices on herself, her baby or the adoptive family unless the social worker leads her through a thoughtful decision-making process after outlining all possible options and supports available to her."

The last stage of counseling is grief counseling. Some counselors may try to shorten this phase because it is painful; however, this well-meaning action could result in even more pain because it inhibits the resolution of the loss. (See LOSS.)

As she resolves the pain associated with the loss, the birthmother can accept that adoption was the best choice for herself and her child, particularly if she feels she was not pressured to make an adoption plan but personally believed it was the best decision. Counselors should be careful not to make adoption a scapegoat if the birthmother complains of problems and should instead seek out what the problem is, whether it be family problems, "unresolved problems of pregnancy" or other problems.

Edmund V. Mech, *Orientations of Pregnancy Counselors Toward Adoption*, U.S. Department of Health and Human Services, Office of Population Affairs, 1984.

Mary Beth Seader, M.S.W., "Pregnancy Counseling: Traditional and Experimental Practices," paper published by the National Committee For Adoption, 1988.

prenatal care Medical care provided by a physician to a pregnant woman during the course of her pregnancy.

Many women in crisis pregnancies, particularly teenagers, do not seek prenatal care early in the pregnancy. Consequently, problems with the fetus may not be identified, or the women herself may suffer untreated health problems.

There are several reasons women avoid prenatal care in the first trimester, including denial of the pregnancy and a conscious or unconscious desire to carry the fetus to term—a desire that is easier to realize if no one except the woman is aware of the pregnancy in the early months. Clinics have seen women in their last trimester of pregnancy who deny they are pregnant yet who are very clearly pregnant to even the most casual observer.

Poor women may not have health insurance and think they are ineligible for public assistance or Medicaid.

The lack of prenatal care contributes to the high rate of infant mortality in the United States. It is very important for every woman to see a physician for appropriate testing and care as soon as she suspects she may be pregnant.

preparing a child for adoption Although no preparation of the child is needed in an infant adoption, when older children are to be adopted caseworkers usually work together with foster parents and adopting parents to help the child get ready for the impending move.

Various means are employed to prepare a child for adoption. Many caseworkers use a LIFEBOOK, which is a special scrapbook describing the child's life, hobbies and relationships. The social worker also counsels the child abut what adoption will mean to him or her and makes it clear that an adoptive family is a permanent family. This explanation also necessitates the often-painful realization that the biological family ties will be severed prior to the adoption.

Social workers usually arrange a meeting between the propsective adoptive parents and the child before any home visits are arranged. The child may go to a park or a fast food restaurant with them, or they may meet in the social worker's office, or the meeting may occur at an adoption picnic. In some cases, the social worker will show the child a videotape the family has made of their home, family and lifestyle. Social workers who use such techniques say children ask to see the videos over and over.

If the prospective parents and the child appear to be a possible "match," the caseworker will arrange a visit within their home for a day or a weekend. Many times the child and the adopting parents are anxious for visits to end and for the child to move in permanently but caseworkers want to ensure as much as possible that the placement will work and that a DISRUPTION will not occur, causing the child further pain.

Whenever possible, foster parents are also employed to prepare the child for adoption and to speak positively about the adoptive placement. Sometimes foster parents have become very attached to the child and may resist the placement, thus making the child's transition even more difficult. Today many foster parents adopt their foster children, and it's likely to be an increasing trend. (See also FOSTER PARENT ADOPTIONS; SPECIAL NEEDS.)

preplacement visits Social worker visits to prospective adoptive parents before a child is placed within their home. The visits are made as a part of the HOME STUDY process, which is a preparation and evaluation of adopting parents.

private adoption See INDEPENDENT ADOPTION.

private agencies See AGENCIES.

prostitution Providing sexual services to a variety of individuals for pay; illegal in every state except Nevada.

Few prostitutes place their children for adoption, probably because most prostitutes are aware of methods of birth control; however, with the increasing rate of drug addiction, even well-informed prostitutes may fail to use birth control and become pregnant. If an abortion is not obtained within the first two trimesters, it becomes more difficult to obtain an abortion in some states, and a prostitute may opt to place the child for adoption.

Because of the high risk of AIDS and the high probability of drug use among prostitutes, few adopting parents are willing to adopt the child of a prostitute, and agencies may consider such a child to fit into the category of a child with SPECIAL NEEDS.

If a child born to a prostitute is ultimately adopted, it is likely the termination of parental rights by the state occurred after some timeframe during which the child had been removed from the home and placed in foster care. In a study of children born to teenage prostitutes, 38 of 55 infants had been placed in the protective custody of the state with most of the babies being referred to protective services either prior to the child's birth or at the time of delivery. Unfortunately, according to the researchers, in many of the cases the infant was placed in the home of the prostitute's mother, "in whose home the girl may still be living while prostituting."

Motherhood did not change the girls' lifestyles. According to the researchers, "These young women usually continue with prostitution, drug involvement and a destructive life-style. Many return to the streets within days of delivery."

Many adopted persons who fantasize about their birthmothers imagine the birthmother at two ends of the spectrum: either a prostitute or a wealthy socialite. The reality is usually neither: Most are ordinary girls or women who became pregnant as the result of a long-term relationship. (See also DRUG ABUSE; FANTASIES OF ADOPTED CHILDREN; AIDS.)

Robert W. Deisher, M.D., James A. Farrow, M.D., Kerry Hope, M.S.W., and Christina Litchfield, R.N., B.S.N., "The Pregnant Adolescent Prostitute," *American Journal of Diseases of Children,* 143(October 1989): 1162–1165.

protective services Child welfare services, usually provided by state, county or other public child welfare agencies, assigned to investigate allegations of child abuse, neglect or abandonment. Protective service workers who believe a complaint is founded may remove a child from the home immediately and place the child in an emergency shelter home or foster home. A judge will shortly thereafter determine if continuous foster care is in the best interests of the child. Reports of suspected abuse may come from teachers, physicians, emergency room doctors and other sources.

If the complaint was unfounded, the child will remain in the home. Unfounded complaints may come from ex-spouses, jealous neighbors and similar other sources. Protective services workers should be trained in techniques to detect abuse and injuries most likely to have occurred from abuse.

Protective services is a high-pressure, stressful job, and many social workers working in this unit transfer to other jobs that are less stressful.

Workers report that even when they remove a child from his or her home because of severe abuse, the child is angry at the caseworker rather than the abusive parent. In addition, the abusive parent often denies the abuse and believes the caseworker is persecuting the parent.

Often protective workers are given little time to investigate and must visit the accused person with 24 hours or 48 hours, so the pressure of time is another constraint on the worker.

Ultimately, many of the children seen by protective services workers and judged by the workers to have been abused, neglected or abandoned will enter the child welfare system. Adoption will be the plan for some of these children. (See also ABANDONMENT; ABUSE; NEGLECT.)

psychiatric problems of adopted persons Mental health experts disagree among themselves on whether adopted persons evince a greater level of mental illness than nonadopted persons. Vastly differing percentages of adopted persons in the institutionalized population have been reported, ranging from 5% to as high as 25% or more, depending on which study is used.

The disproportionate number of adopted persons seems particularly evident when the population studied is composed primarily of adopted adolescents. Yet some experts argue that adoptive parents are more likely to seek professional help when faced with a difficult problem than the average person, and adolescence is difficult for many children. (Indeed, it has been said that adolescence is the closest most of us come to psychosis.)

Many adoptive parents also enjoy a higher socioeconomic level than the average person and can thus afford psychiatric treatment, both inpatient and outpatient.

The Schecter Study One of the earlier studies on adopted persons and mental disturbances was reported in 1960 by psychiatrist Marshall Schecter who concluded about 13% of his psychiatric patients over five years had been adopted. His findings were used as a basis for concluding that adoption causes or contributes to psychiatric problems, and this study is still cited 30 years later.

Schecter studied a small population of adopted persons, 16 of 120 mental patients. Of these, at least three were over age nine at the time of adoption. Studies by Dr. Richard Barth and others have revealed the older the child is at the time of adoption, the more likely there will be problems with the adoptive placement. As a result, it is almost certainly unfair to include children adopted as infants with children adopted as older, SPECIAL NEEDS adopted persons.

In addition, it is fairly evident that practices prevalent at the time of the Schecter study in the 1950s, and which were hardly intrinsic to the institution of adoption, contributed greatly to the adopted child's problems.

For example, a child studied by Schecter who was adopted at only 14 months from a foster home was not toilet trained. Today, it is rare that parents expect an infant to be toilet trained at this early age; however, at that time, it was commonly accepted by some physicians as possible and desirable. Schecter reported that a pediatrician told the parents they must "insist on complete control of the excretory functions immediately and forcibly. This, then, seemed to become the conditon for acceptance into the family."

The child had difficulty with this demand. In addition, the adoptive parents changed her name. Even to a toddler, one's name is part of one's identity. Today social workers advise adoptive parents that children need time to adjust to their new surroundings, and may actually regress in their behavior for awhile. It seems likely the trauma of relocating to a new family, hell-bent on potty training her, and also losing her name would ultimately cause behavioral and identity problems, and it did.

In another case, Schecter described a five-year-old girl who was phobic about going to school and had "severe temper tantrums."

Schecter concluded that the child was threatened because she had been "sent away" from her "original mother" at age 17 months. It would be interesting to speculate on how many nonadopted children of age five also experience severe difficulties surrounding entering school for the first time.

Another case cited by Schecter seems to be an obvious problem of attachment, wherein the child responded as well to strangers as to the adoptive parents. In yet another case, a child who was not hypothyroid had been placed on thyroid medication.

What is not revealed about these children and their families is fascinating to speculate, considering what disturbing information is offered. It is hoped that social workers and others associated with adoption and children have gained from the mistakes of the past and that how adopted children of today are raised will not be viewed with amazement by future generations.

The "Adopted Child Syndrome" Some adoption experts argue there is an "adopted child syndrome" with specific behavioral disorders found in some adopted children.

Psychologist David Kirschner estimates that 5% to 10% of adopted children will develop mental problems related to being adopted and he coined the phrase "adopted child syndrome."

Kirschner says the syndrome includes such behavioral problems as "lying, stealing, learning problems, threats of running away and occasionally, violent actions." Mental health practitioners have discussed at length the existence (or nonexistence) of the syndrome.

According to Kirschner, who spoke at the May 30, 1987, conference of the AMERICAN ADOPTION CONGRESS, he has treated over 250 adopted individuals over 25 years and never meant to imply the syndrome was typical. (His and other comments were included in the May–June 1987 issue of *National Adoption Reports*).

Said Kirschner, "While the term adopted child syndrome may seem to imply that most adoptees have it, that is certainly not my position. Adoption is clearly a very positive alternative for many children."

According to Kirschner, the "adopted child syndrome" includes such antisocial behavior as shallow attachment, stealing, manipulativeness, running away, promiscuity, academic underachievement or learning problems and fire-setting.

Dr. Kirschner was challenged by William Feigelman, Ph.D., who said, "Why not the Jewish boy syndrome or the Italian father syndrome? It's disturbing if we do not see any hard evidence to substantiate the claim."

Feigelman contended that, when adoptive families encounter problems, they are likely to seek psychiatric or psychological help because they are used to dealing with agencies and they have the economic resources to afford counseling.

Other Studies Since Schecter's work in the 1950s and 1960s, the psychiatric problems of adopted persons have been the focus of a considerable amount of research, some of which is reported below. A Canadian study of 57 adopted children referred to a psychiatric service found a greater incidence of referrals than would be expected for the general population.

According to the researchers, adopted children "presented more with conduct disorders and less with anxiety disorders and were significantly more impaired than the controls."

The researchers also discussed apparently conflicting findings of researchers on the incidence of mental problems among adopted persons.

Their explanation was that "while adopted children and adolescents may experience psychosocial problems at a relatively increased rate, these are early problems that are probably not associated with increased risk for mental illness in adulthood."

It is also interesting to note that the researchers found a significant number of the adopted children came from families of a higher socioeconomic level than the control patients' families. The researchers stated, "This probably reflects the selection policy for would-be adoptive families by the adoption agencies." Other researchers have speculated that perhaps adoptive families are more likely to seek assistance when their child has a problem than nonadoptive families, in part, because they can afford it.

A 1977 study by Melissa Norvell and Rebecca Guy compared and contrasted the self-concept of adopted persons to the self-concept of nonadopted persons. The hypothesis was that the adopted individuals would have a more negative self-concept than the nonadopted persons. Seven-hundred-twenty-one males and females were sampled from psychology and sociology students at two universities. Of these, 38 identified their adoptive status. The researchers drew 38 nonadopted subjects from the population, matching for age, marital status, race and sex. No significant differences were found between the self-concepts of the adopted subjects and the nonadopted subjects.

A 1985 study by Andrea Weiss compared the symptoms of adopted and nonadopted children who were admitted to a psychiatric hospital and found significant differences: Most of the adopted children who were admitted were far less disturbed than were the nonadopted children. (There were no significant differences in age, gender or social class.)

According to Weiss, the adopted children did not receive diagnoses of personality disorders at greater frequency than the nonadopted children. In addition, they were not more likely to have been hospitalized because of exhibiting antisocial behavior. One difference Weiss did note, however, was that the adopted children were admitted to the hospital at younger ages than the nonadopted children. (15 to 16 years) In addition, the adopted children were diagnosed as psychotic in significantly *less* cases than the nonadopted children. Finally, the adopted children were more frequently (and statistically significantly) identified as suffering from adjustment reaction. Weiss reported that upon discharge only 25.5% of the 47 adopted persons had been diagnosed with psychoses compared to 46.2% of the 93 nonadopted persons who had been admitted.

One wonders to what extent psychiatrists themselves are biased about adoption and adopted persons. Would knowledge of an individual's adoptive status increase the probability that a child might be admitted to an institution?

In an earlier report Weiss found that psychiatrists limited visitations by adoptive parents more than they limited visitations by biological parents. They also labeled adoptive parents as "precipitants" to the hospitalization more frequently.

Said Weiss, "It was concluded that parent-child relations may be more problematic among hospitalized adopted, as compared with nonadopted, adolescents. It was also suggested that psychiatric bias concerning 'typical' adoptive family dynamics might have contributed to the observed differences."

In one of the largest studies to date Paul Brinich and Evelin Brinich studied 113 adopted persons who had received psychiatric services during 1969 to 1978 at the

Langley Porter Psychiatric Institute (LPPI) in San Francisco, California and compared them to nonadopted individuals who were also registered as patients.

The authors concluded, "Adoptees are not generally overrepresented in psychiatric samples, though it is true that they may be seen somewhat more frequently in child psychiatry clinics . . . while adoption may serve as a focus for psychopathology in individual cases, adoption itself cannot be seen as specifically pathogenic."

Unfortunately, most of the psychiatric studies comparing and contrasting adopted and nonadopted persons concentrate on institutionalized or clinical populations rather than individuals in the general population. In addition, most studies fail to include any data on the age of the children at the time of adoption, a very significant factor, particularly in today's world when many individuals are adopting older children rather than infants.

If a child were sexually abused and lived in five foster homes prior to his adoption at age 12, it seems likely that he would face a higher probability of adjustment problems and the need for therapy than would an infant placed for adoption at the age of three weeks.

This seems a logical conclusion, based on the facts that the older a child is at placement and the greater number of foster homes the child resided in prior to adoption, the higher the probability the adoption will disrupt. (See DISRUPTION.)

Problems with Finding Competent Therapists Some authors insist that mental health professionals tend to blame the family too frequently or blame adoption itself for a problem when the underlying problem may have resulted from experiences the child had before he came to this family. In addition, the adoptive family may be struggling mightily to succeed and stay together. (See THERAPY AND THERAPISTS.)

Genetic Factors and Psychiatric Problems A genetic predisposition is a critically important factor to consider in psychiatric ailments, and increasing evidence is revealing there are genetic markers for schizophrenia, Alzheimer's disease and other psychiatric ailments. (See also GENETIC PREDISPOSITIONS.)

As a result, even a child adopted as a healthy infant may ultimately develop psychiatric problems. These problems may have nothing to do with adoption per se but instead have to do with the child's genetic inheritance, or the problems could be a combination of adjustment and hereditary factors.

A 1989 issue of the *American Journal of Psychiatry* included a discussion of genetic issues and disorders in birthparents in relation to disorders in adopted children. The findings do not mean there is support for the "bad seed" among adopted children.

It seems apparent that much more scientific research is needed on psychiatric problems and adopted persons, and it would also be interesting to study psychiatrists and their attitudes toward adopted persons in a blind study.

If and when adoptive parents see that their adopted children need therapy, it is essential that they identify therapists in the community who understand general issues in growing up, particularly adolescence, as well as issues of separation and loss or identity that may result from an adoption issue. As adoptive parent self-help groups expand, it is likely such groups can recommend knowledgeable therapists who can assist the child and his family. (See also ADOLESCENT ADOPTED PERSONS; ADULT ADOPTED PERSONS; EXPLAINING ADOPTION; MEDIA.)

Paul M. Brinich, Ph.D, and Evelin B. Brinich, M.A., "Adoption and Adaptation," *The Journal of Nervous and Mental Disease*, 170:8(1982): 489–493.

"Experts Debate 'Adopted Child Syndrome' at A.A.C.," *National Adoption Reports*, May–June 1987.

Pamela V. Grabe, editor, *Adoption Resources for Mental Health Professionals* (Butler, Pa.: Mental Health Adoption Therapy Project, 1986).

Kenneth Kaye, "Turning Two Identities into One," *Psychology Today,* 22(November 1988): 46–50.

Sotiris Kotsopoulos, M.D., Ph.D, Andre Cote, M.D., Llewelyn Joseph, M.D., Neomi Pentland, M.D., Chryssoula Stavrakaki, M.D., Patrick Sheahan, M.S.W., Louise Oke, B.A., "Psychiatric Disorders in Adopted Children: A Controlled Study," *American Journal of Orthopsychiatry,* 58(October 1988): 608–612.

National Committee For Adoption, *1989 Adoption Factbook* (Washington, D.C.: National Committee For Adoption, 1989).

Melissa Norvell and Rebecca F. Guy, "A Comparison of Self-Concept in Adopted and Non-Adopted Adolescents," *Adolescence* 12(Fall 1977): 443–448.

Herbert Pardes, M.D., Charles A. Kaufmann, M.D., Harold Alan Pincus, M.D., and Anne West, "Genetics and Psychiatry: Past Discoveries, Current Dilemmas, and Future Directions," *American Journal of Psychiatry,* 146(April 1989): 435–443.

Marshall D. Schecter, "Observations on Adopted Children," *Archives of General Psychiatry,* 3(July 1960): 21–32.

Naomi Thiers, "Controversy Surrounds Adoption's Effects," *Guidepost,* May 29, 1989.

Andrea Weiss, "Parent-Child Relationships of Adopted Adolescents in a Psychiatric Hospital," *Adolescence,* 19(Spring 1984): 77–88.

Andrea Weiss, "Symptomology of Adopted and Nonadopted Adolescents in a Psychiatric Hospital," *Adolescence,* 20(Winter 1985): 763–774.

psychological parent Also known as de facto parent; person to whom the child has bonded in a parental relationship but with whom the child does not necessarily have a biological, adoptive or legal relationship.

This may be a person who has "informally" adopted a child; for example, a foster parent or a relative who is caring for a child but who does not have legal custody. A psychological parent could also be the live-in friend of an actual parent.

public assistance Programs such as Aid to Families with Dependent Children, food stamps, MEDICAID and other payment or in-kind programs for categorically eligible families. Indications are that unwed mothers who choose to parent their infants and children have a higher probability of applying for and receiving public assistance than do birthmothers who choose adoption for their children. (See also BIRTHMOTHER.)

putative father A man who claims to be or who is alleged to be the father of a "nonmarital" child.

After a man is proven, usually by genetic tests, to be the father of a child, he is more often known as the biological father or BIRTHFATHER.

A number of states have established putative father registries, wherein a man who believes himself to be the father of a child may register his alleged paternity with the state. Men on this registry must be notified before a child may be placed for adoption. Putative fathers are usually not married to the mother of the child nor are they named as the father on the child's birth certificate.

The registry approach in New York State's law was upheld by the U.S. Supreme Court in *Lehr v. Robertson.* (See also BIRTHMOTHER; CONSENT (TO AN ADOPTION); UNWED PARENTS.)

R

race Refers to the racial heritage of a child and his or her parents. Primary races that are considered are black, Caucasian and Asian. Hispanics/Latinos are sometimes inaccurately considered as a separate race, although they are actually an ethnic group. There is broad difference among Hispanics, who may be of Caucasian, American Indian or black descent or various mixtures.

Some children needing adoptive families are also of mixed race or BIRACIAL. Although the term "biracial" connotes two races and includes Caucasian/Asian and Asian/black, most social workers use the term to refer to black/white children.

Whether or not race is an important aspect in the child to be adopted must be considered by adopting parents.

Studies have indicated that TRANSRACIAL ADOPTION can work very effectively for both the child and the family; however, the family must be able to tolerate criticism from family and strangers. In addition, many social workers and adoption agencies are adamantly opposed to placing a black or biracial child in a white family. (See also BLACK ADOPTIVE PARENT RECRUITMENT PROGRAMS; BLACK FAMILIES; HISPANICS/LATINOS; INDIAN CHILD WELFARE ACT OF 1978; NATIONAL COALITION TO END RACISM IN AMERICA'S CHILD CARE SYSTEM INC., SPECIAL NEEDS; TRANSRACIAL ADOPTION.)

rainbow families An upbeat phrase adoptive parents sometimes use to describe their families when their children are of mixed or different races or ethnicity.

rape Forcible sexual intercourse; also includes statutory rape and "acquaintance rape" or "date rape."

Some children are conceived as the result of rape, which is one of the key arguments in favor of legal abortion. Should the woman wish to continue her pregnancy, she may opt to arrange an adoption for her child.

If the mother does not know her attacker and never identifies him, she cannot provide important medical and social information for social workers to pass on to adoptive parents.

Whether or not the circumstances of the adopted person's birth should be revealed or how it should be phrased are open to argument; however, this information certainly should not be shared until the child is an adolescent or an adult. If at all possible, the information should also not be provided to friends or relatives who may inadvertently leak it to the adopted person.

"real parents" A phrase in wide popular use to indicate the birthparents of an adopted child. It alludes to shared genetic descent. This label is particularly disliked by most adoptive parents who feel it denigrates and verbally invalidates their relationship to the child.

The term is also technically incorrect, because parental rights, obligations and activities have been transferred in the case of adoption.

As a result, most adoptive parents and adoption experts advise the words "birthparents" or "biological parents" (or, less frequently, "genetic parents") be used when referring to the man and woman who conceived the adopted child.

recruitment Adoption agencies, adoptive parent support groups and others use a variety of means to encourage the adoption of children, particularly children with SPECIAL NEEDS. ADVERTISING AND PROMOTION, NATIONAL ADOPTION WEEK, seminars, WEDNESDAY'S CHILD, PHOTOLISTINGS and VIDEOTAPES are primary techniques.

Adoption advocates may also use bumper stickers, T-shirts and many other creative tactics to promote adoption.

Various BLACK ADOPTIVE PARENT RECRUITMENT PROGRAMS have been established to help cope with the large numbers of black children waiting for adoptive parents.

Meetings When parents are adopting an older child, agencies arrange for the parents to meet the child before committing to an adoption.

The meeting may be at a social event, such as an adoption picnic, or it may be in the agency office or at another location. Some agencies try to make the meeting appear accidental or casual, so the child will not feel threatened or feel like he or she is being examined.

Adoption "fairs," parties or picnics are used by some agencies to introduce children to prospective parents. Children are dressed casually and given balloons, and games and activities are planned for the children. The disadvantage of these events is that many of the children know they are on display and may feel anxious. The advantage of such events is that parents do have a chance to meet kids one-on-one, and children have been adopted through this process.

If and when adopting parents are interested in an older child, the agency will often arrange for them to spend a day or weekend with the child in their home. The adoptive parents' interest in the child must be very strong before the agency will commit to such a meeting because they want to minimize the pain of rejection should the weekend not work out.

When an agency is attempting to match a particular child with a particular family, they talk to the family first to make sure the family has an interest in the child.

Usually prior to the showing of the child, if it's a personal meeting, the social worker will "talk up" the family to the child and provide general and specific information about the family to whet the child's curiosity and interest in them.

If the weekend visits seem to work out well, more visits will be planned until the child is transitioned to the new home and family.

registries See MUTUAL CONSENT REGISTRIES; PUTATIVE FATHER.

reimbursement See EMPLOYMENT BENEFITS; MILITARY MEMBERS AND ADOPTION.

relative adoptions Most relative adoptions are GRANDPARENT ADOPTIONS or adoptions by STEPPARENTS, although aunts, uncles, cousins or other relatives may also adopt a child.

Many states do not require a complete home study if the child is adopted by a close relative, such as a stepparent, grandparent, sister, brother, aunt or uncle.

Relative adoptions are of necessity OPEN ADOPTIONS. In some cases, however, the adoptive parents have concealed the relationship and even the adoption itself from the child.

The primary advantage of a relative adoption is the birthmother feels confident the child will be safe and loved by a family member. Such an adoption does not preclude the relative from death or divorce, and the child may ultimately end up with individuals over whom the birthmother can exert no control.

The main disadvantage of a relative adoption is that if other family members are also aware this is a relative adoption, constant comparisons may be made between the child and the birthparent, and it may be difficult for the adoptive parents to forge a strong sense of ENTITLEMENT to the child.

The NATIONAL COMMITTEE FOR ADOPTION found a substantial decline in relative adoptions over a short period: from 91,141 in 1982 to 52,931 in 1986. One probable cause is that remarriage rates also declined over this period.

It is also possible that stepparents have not adopted children because of financial reasons—Child support payments from the ex-spouse, which have become more collectible in recent years because of changes in federal and state laws and benefits. Adoption of the child by the stepfather could end child support payments.

There is also a strong trend for single women as heads of households to remain single longer; for example, according to the Census Bureau, in 1980, 15% of white children and 46% of black children lived in female-headed households. By 1988, this number had increased to 19% of white children and 54% of black children living in female-headed households. (See also INFORMAL ADOPTION.)

Adoption Factbook (Washington, D.C.: National Committee For Adoption, 1989).

religion Religion has played a strong role in the history of United States adoption from the early days of the ORPHAN TRAIN era of the late 19th century, when well-meaning Protestant reformers sent thousands of children from the Eastern Seaboard to Protestant families in the Midwest and West. Some of the children were formally adopted, but many were indentured to the families who chose them from the train platform, where they were "put up" for people to see (hence the expression, "put up for adoption").

Most of the children were orphans of immigrants of Jewish or Catholic descent, and eventually Jewish and Catholic organizations objected to these placements in Protestant homes. The ultimate result of such protests was the formation of sectarian agencies that concentrated on serving their own particular faith groups; as a result, Catholic, Jewish, and Protestant agencies evolved that accepted applications for adoption from people of these respective faiths or particular denominations.

If a child were left as a foundling on a Jewish agency's doorstep, it was presumed the birthmother wished the child to be placed with a Jewish family, and this wish was respected.

Subsequent to the legalization of ABORTION and with increased acceptance of single parenthood, fewer babies were placed for adoption by their birthmothers in the 1970s and to date than in past years.

With the increase of INDEPENDENT ADOPTION, DESIGNATED ADOPTION and TARGETED ADOPTION, agency adoptions of healthy newborns began to decline, and the sectarian agencies became dominant among the agencies that continued to play significant roles.

The sectarian agencies and other interested individuals were also successful in passing religious matching laws in some states, requiring a child to be placed with a family of the same religion as his birthparents.

Because sectarian agencies usually have a religious requirement, prospective adoptive parents who are not of the religion of the agencies in their state may find themselves "shut out" of adoption; for example, if there are only Christian adoption agencies within a state, a Jewish family would generally only be able to adopt a child through the state social services department. (They could apply to an adoption agency in another state, which can be a complex process.)

In addition, individuals who profess no particular religious faith or who state they believe in a deity but do not attend religious services, also could find themselves unable to adopt through a sectarian agency. Another type of family that may have difficulty is the couple wherein the wife is one religion and the husband is another; for example, the wife may be Catholic and the husband Jewish. In such an instance, they would generally be denied the opportunity to adopt a child through either a Catholic agency or a Jewish agency.

As a result of this difficulty, individuals who cannot or choose not to apply to a sectarian agency have increasingly and actively lobbied state legislatures to approve IDENTIFIED ADOPTIONS or DESIGNATED ADOPTIONS, which are adoptions arranged by the adoptive parents themselves and subsequently approved by an adoption agency or adoption facilitator.

In some cases, individuals have sued the sectarian agency, stating that they have been discriminated against because of their religious faith. As a result, some agencies will now accept applications from individuals who are not members of the faith group the agency primarily represents. For instance, a Jewish family should not presume that Catholic Social Services will not accept their application. Policies vary from state to state and agency to agency, based on many factors, including the source of financial support of the agencies. As a result, in some cases the Jewish family would be turned down by Catholic Social Services while, in other cases, they would be served.

Although the obvious solution to religious or denominational "matching" appears to be laws requiring any otherwise suitable family to be served, there are problems.

One potential problem with requiring sectarian agencies to accept members of another faith group is that most agencies wish to give birthmothers a choice in designating the adoptive parents and how their children will be religiously reared. As a result, it is likely that a Catholic birthmother (or Jewish or Protestant birthmother) would wish her child to be raised in the same religion, and if she specifically makes this request, most agencies would do their best to honor it.

The other major problem is that birthmothers who consider religious matching important would simply do what many are already doing: They would go to an attorney or other intermediary (or to an agency in a state with different laws) who would arrange a direct placement with adoptive parents of the specified religion.

They might also decide they will need to parent the child themselves in order to carry out what they believe is in the best religious interests of the child, according to the dictates of their conscience. (See the entry on BIRTHFATHER for other reasons why birthmothers who would otherwise choose adoption decide to parent a child.) (See also AGENCIES.)

Three of the largest networks of sectarian agencies are

Association of Jewish Children & Family
  Agencies
3084 State Hwy. 27, Suite 1
P.O. Box 248
Kendall Park, NJ 08824-0248
(201) 821-0909

Catholic Charities USA
1319 F St. NW, 4th Floor
Washington, DC 20004
(202) 639-8400

LDS Social Services
50 E. N. Temple, 7th Floor
Salt Lake City, UT 84150
(801) 240-3339

relinquishment Voluntarily forfeiting or terminating one's parental rights to a child for the purpose of adoption. This term is considered negative by some adoption professionals who believe it implies the birthparent has not considered the child's future when, in fact, the birthparent usually has given very serious and lengthy consideration to the child's future life. Those who are critical of the word "relinquishment" may prefer "giving consent" for an adoption or "transferring parental rights and obligations."

An involuntary forfeiture of rights is called TERMINATION OF PARENTAL RIGHTS and usually results from the caretaker's abuse or neglect of a child and the inability of the parent or caretaker to overcome the problems that led to the child's removal from the home.

reproductive technologies The scientific breakthroughs that have been achieved and continue to be achieved to enable infertile couples to bear children.

Techniques include in vitro fertilization, surgery and microsurgery. In limited cases, it is possible for a woman to serve as her own "surrogate mother" by the physician implanting an embryo or fertilized egg in the woman. Such women have uteruses but do not ovulate or have damaged tubes or some other problem preventing them from creating a pregnancy themselves. (See SURROGATE MOTHERHOOD.)

The embryo may be the result of donor sperm and donor ovum or the woman's husband may have contributed his sperm.

With developing reproductive technologies have come confusing ethical and moral problems, and most state laws have not yet caught up. For example, if a woman carries the fetus of another woman, should the woman carrying the fetus have to formally adopt the child after birth? (See BIOETHICS.) And if a woman is able to create ova but her uterus has been surgically removed, if her own fertilized egg and her husband's sperm is implanted in another woman, should she then have to adopt her own genetic child?

Doctors have also been able to freeze embryos, and the morality of what should be done with the unused embryos is hotly debated. In addition, some doctors implant numerous embryos into a woman, presuming one or two will "take." If the woman has a multiple pregnancy of four or more children and it is presumed they cannot all survive (or she does not wish this many children), is it moral to abort some of the fetuses?

As technology advances even further, it is likely the ethical issues will become even more difficult to resolve.

research While rigorously designed and mounted studies of adoption are rare, interest in studying members of the adoption triad (adoptive parents, birthparents and adopted persons) and adoption itself appears to be increasing. This is a good sign because the more valid research conducted on adoption, the more reliable information adoption professionals have upon which to make sound policy decisions. In addition, such information would be very helpful to triad members.

The difficulty in studying individuals who were adopted, adoptive parents or birthparents lies primarily in that CONFIDENTIALITY protects their identities. As a result, individuals who come forward in response to requests from adoption agencies or advertisements may well be significantly different from individuals who prefer to retain their privacy and anonymity.

Another difficulty lies in finding a way to interview young adopted persons without risking affecting their views and psychological well-being; any research involving human subjects is sensitive.

The interpretation of data may also be difficult; for example, some researchers have generalized from small groups of people to large groups of adopted individuals. Some researchers have studied institutionalized adopted persons or persons receiving therapy and generalized their results from this population to all or most adopted individuals. Others argue that adopted adults (or children) should be compared to nonadopted adults or children in the general population.

Adoption research is expensive, which is why so many studies use small samples. Presuming that hundreds of adopted individuals, birthparents or adoptive parents could be identified, it would be expensive and time-consuming to interview and test them all. Funding must be available in order to cover this cost.

Another problem with research is that researchers cannot always determine causal factors; for example, if children are emotionally disturbed, are they disturbed because of an adoption issue or because of a problem that occurred before they were adopted? Some researchers fail to determine the age at which the child was adopted, which is an important factor.

Terminologies often vary, and it is important for researchers to share a common frame of reference; for example, many researchers have differing definitions of OPEN ADOPTION, varying from those who believe providing the birthmother nonidentifying information about prospective parents is open to those who believe only a total disclosure of identities is open.

Timeliness is a problem as well. Because a large study may take extensive time, the information garnered may not be available for years. Some researchers undertake longitudinal studies, which study the same population at different points in time; for example, children at age 3, 7, 11 and 15. Researchers try to determine what factors have changed in the child's life, if the child is still adjusted (or maladjusted) and so on. Longitudinal studies have been performed to determine changes in adjustment, intelligence and numerous other areas.

residential treatment centers Out-of-home placements where the child receives help with many areas of his or her life that have gone awry, particularly psychological and/or behavioral problems. Centers are funded either through public or private funds or a combination of both.

According to the book *Residential Treatment: A Tapestry of Many Therapies,* edited by Dr. Vera Fahlberg, "Residential care is usually reserved for the child who is having problems in all three major areas of his life—family, school and peers—and even then only when the problems have not been amenable to out-patient treatment."

Residential treatment is 24-hour care and is different from a GROUP HOME, which is usually staffed by one couple and where the children are able to attend local schools. (Some children in group homes may need residential treatment or will need it in the future.)

A residential treatment center is also different from psychiatric hospitals, which are generally used for severely disturbed children who are suicidal or who are undergoing detoxification, receiving treatment for psychoses and so forth.

Residential treatment is not a short-term solution to a problem, and the average child who needs residential treatment remains at the facility for eighteen months to two years.

Says Sandra Mooney, chief clinical social worker at Episcopal Child Care of North Carolina, "Usually the child comes to the program with numerous problems which have been identified by various community agencies, police, foster families, schools and sometimes biological parents."

Common problems of children placed in residential institutions include low self-esteem, inability or inadequacy at forming relationships with others, poor control of emotions, learning disabilities and other problems.

Fahlberg's book also discusses a variety of children who have done well in a residential treatment center where she has had extensive experience: Forest Heights Lodge in Evergreen, Colorado. These include children with attachment problems, children who have suffered a parental loss or separation, children who are "stuck" at a childhood stage earlier than their chronological age and children with perceptual problems. Children who are not suitable for the facility are handicapped children or teenagers who are sociopathic or have other personality disorders.

It is partially the milieu as well as separation from the primary caretakers as well as other factors that will, hopefully, lead the child to recovery and an ability to function in the world. The "milieu" refers to the daily environment and its structure, and in a residential treatment center, the milieu describes a setting in which the child can grow to trust the caretakers of the center, empowering the child to change.

Children placed in residential treatment may be placed by a social worker, their biological parents or their adoptive parents or other guardians.

According to social workers Judith McKenzie and Drenda Lakin, such children "are often youngsters for whom no other resource has been available or whose medical, cognitive, behavioral and emotional difficulties have led to residential placement usually after they have experienced many moves in the foster care system."

The children may be able, with time, to return to their adoptive or biological homes; however, therapists often have biases against adoptive parents who wish to temporarily place their children in a residential treatment facility. There may be biases against adoption on the part of the staff and an overeagerness to "rescue" the child and the adoptive parents from each other.

Children from adoptions that have disrupted or dissolved may be placed in residential treatment and will hopefully learn to cope with the pain and rejection they may feel. They may have problems with attachment to adults and sometimes may find it difficult to attach to more than one adult.

Adopting parents need to be aware of the problems of the child who has previously resided in a residential treatment center. The adoption agency and the residential treatment center should both fully educate the adopting parents on the child's problems.

Adoptive parents who expect the child to be grateful he or she was "saved" from the institution will be disappointed, because the child will probably not bond readily: He or she has been disappointed too many times before.

Other issues include the capacity of the child to attach to new parents. Because of past problems forming strong relationships, the child is wary of familial-type relationships. The child may also have difficulty in attaching to both parents.

In addition, the child may have formed relationships with residential treatment center staff and suffer separation anxiety when it's time to leave the residential treatment center. (See also ADOLESCENT ADOPTED PERSONS; BONDING AND ATTACHMENT; PSYCHIATRIC PROBLEMS OF ADOPTED PERSONS.)

For assistance in locating a residential treatment center, the following organizations may be consulted:

American Association of Children's Residential Centers
440 First St. NW, Suite 310
Washington, DC 20001
(202) 638-1604

National Association of Psychiatric Treatment Centers for Children
2000 L St. NW, Suite 200
Washington, DC 20036
(202) 955-3828

Vera Fahlberg, M.D., editor, *Residential Treatment: A Tapestry of Many Therapies* (Indianapolis, IN: Perspectives Press, 1990).
Joan Laird and Ann Hartman, editors, *A Handbook of Child Welfare: Context, Knowledge, and Practice* (New York: Free Press, 1985).
Judith K. McKenzie, M.S.W., and Drenda Lakin, M.S.W., "Residential Services on the Continuum of Adoption Services," *The Roundtable: Journal of the National Resource Center for Special Needs Adoption*, 4:1(1989): 1–2.
Ruth G. McRoy, Harold D. Grotevant and Louis A. Zurcher Jr., *Emotional Disturbance in Adopted Adolescents: Origins and Development* (New York: Praeger, 1988).
Sandra Mooney, "Coordination Among the Residential Treatment Center, Guardian Ad Litem, and the Department of Social Services," in *Adoption for Troubled Children: Prevention and Repair of Adoptive Failures Through Residential Treatment* (New York: Haworth Press, 1983).

RESOLVE Inc. A national support organization founded in 1973 by Barbara Eck Menning for people experiencing the crisis of infertility. Based in Arlington, Massachusetts, the organization has over 15,000 members in chapters throughout the United States.

RESOLVE offers medical information and referrals, counseling, journal articles on infertility and backing for reforms in such areas as medical insurance coverage for the expenses of infertility treatment and adoption. The organization also provides mental health experts with infertility information to help with treatment of anxiety that may result from infertility.

Local chapters provide local telephone contacts, support and information and referrals to physicians, adoption agencies and other resources.

The majority of RESOLVE members are infertile couples, but membership also includes social workers, physicians and other professionals who help couples with problems of infertility.

According to RESOLVE brochures, infertility is linked to a medical problem in 90% of the cases, and feelings of stress are caused by infertility and are not the cause of infertility. (Many couples have been urged to "just relax" by well-meaning friends, placing the blame on their anxiety—which could lead to more anxiety.)

The organization publishes a newsletter five times a year.

The national organization holds one annual meeting, and local chapters hold periodic meetings. RESOLVE leaders hope to expand membership and create a strong public awareness.

For more information contact

RESOLVE Inc.
5 Water St.
Arlington, MA 02174
(617) 643-2442

resume A written description of a prospective adoptive family, usually written by the couple or single person wishing to adopt; also known as a "profile". Agencies that offer birthmothers choices in adoption often use resumes of prospective adoptive parents to assist the birthmothers in their selection of adoptive parents. A caseworker will generally review the resume to offer suggestions for changes and improvements before showing it to a birthmother.

Some couples who wish to locate their own birthmothers will independently circulate hundreds or even thousands of resumes nationwide to obstetricians, lawyers and other professionals who come in contact with pregnant women considering adoption for their babies. Couples who succeed with this method swear by it.

It is difficult to impossible to maintain confidentiality when sending out resumes to people throughout the United States; therefore, couples who do not want to take part in an OPEN ADOPTION should use more traditional means to succeed at adopting their child.

Proponents of using resumes in INDEPENDENT ADOPTION see them as very effective and speedy while detractors believe they are costly and inefficient and contend that physicians are most interested in assisting people they already know.

After the prospective parents have completed the HOME STUDY process, they may prepare their resume. This document, sometimes accompanied by photographs of the prospective parents, will be shown with other resumes to pregnant women considering adoption. The social worker will usually show the pregnant woman three or four resumes of couples who seem most appropriate to parent the child, although some agencies open their entire file of resumes to pregnant women.

The pregnant woman will then select the family she feels most closely resembles the type of family she is seeking for her child. Some pregnant women seek childless couples while a lesser number hope to place their child with a family who already has siblings or who intend to adopt other children after this child.

In some cases, the religion of the adoptive family is important, and in other cases, it is their lifestyle that matters most, for example, if they are active outdoors people, literary people or some other pattern the pregnant woman sees as desirable.

If the prospective adoptive family has no children but has a dog or cat or other pets, this information should be included because the couple may be perceived as nurturing by the pregnant woman.

Sometimes the agency may use resumes to help the birthmother choose the adoptive parents but wait until after the birthmother has delivered to show her any of the resumes. These agencies believe it would be a form of pressure to show the woman resumes before she has her baby. The agencies that show the pregnant woman resumes, usually in her last trimester, believe it will ease her mind to know something about the adoptive family and will give her a feeling of control over a crisis situation.

Adoptive parent resumes differ from job resumes in that it is important for the prospective parents to convey both information and emotion; they need to describe themselves factually as well as explain why they want to adopt a child.

Resumes may include such information as a physical description of the couple, their hobbies and interests, whether they live in the city, country or suburbia, whether or not they have children already and other general information.

If the prospective adoptive mother plans to stop working outside the home in order to stay at home with the child, this information should be included. If the prospective grandparents greatly anticipate the adoption, this information is valuable as well.

Many women who are considering an adoption are very concerned about how the child will be accepted by the adoptive parents' own parents and relatives; therefore, if the future extended family is very eager and anxious for the child, this information should be included in the resume.

A critical portion of the resume is why the couple or single person wishes to adopt—beyond any information about infertility. In fact, detailed information on infertility is unnecessary. Most pregnant women presume a couple who wishes to adopt is infertile and are not interested in details of the infertility or expenses related to infertility testing. Instead, they are most interested in why the adopting couple wants a child and what kind of home they will provide for that child.

Resumes should be no more than a page or two in length. They can be difficult to write; however, most social workers will provide assistance.

reunification A currently prevailing concept in child social welfare that dictates caseworkers should do whatever is necessary to return a child to the biological home when the child or children were removed by the state due to abuse, neglect or abandonment.

It is presumed that the biological home is the best home for a child and that the biological parents can and should be rehabilitated from whatever caused them to abuse, neglect or abandon the child, whether causal factors were drug or alcohol abuse, psychiatric problems, homelessness or a combination of these and other factors.

It should be noted that most children actually wish to be reunited with their biological families, even when they have been abused or neglected. This does not mean such a reunification is in the child's best interest, and caseworkers must make a determination and recommendation to the court, which will make the final decision.

While a child is in foster care, social workers attempt to arrange visits with the biological parent. If the parent appears to show improvement, caseworkers may arrange weekend visitations with the parents, and if these visits appear to go well, the child may be returned to the home. It is likely, however, that a child who enters the foster care system will remain in care for at least several months.

Although social workers are supposed to monitor parental progress to ensure children are not returned to abusive homes, severe errors occur. For instance, a two-year-old Lakeland, Florida child died in July of 1989 when social workers returned him to his biological mother and stepfather. Repeated allegations of abuse had been made, and other evidence had indicated that the placement was inadvisable.

The child suffered a brain hemorrhage after repeated dunkings in the toilet in an alleged attempt to "toilet train" him. The parents were charged with first degree murder, and a child already in the home was removed.

The judge, apparently horrified by the incident, opened the case to public scrutiny. An estimated 1,100 children are fatally abused each year in the U.S., although it is unknown how many of these were returned to their biological parents from foster care.

Sometimes it is not clear why a child is not returned to his birthparents, and sometimes it is unclear why he is returned. Experts recommend children be returned to their parents if the parents can properly care for the children; however, there should be clearcut evidence that the parents do have the capability to care for the children and are no longer drug or alcohol dependent or abusive or no longer have the problem that led to the child's removal from the family.

According to experts, the problem with the reunification concept is not the concept itself but the amount of time allowed to elaspe before termination of parental rights is effected when it is determined reunification cannot occur or is not in the best interests of the child.

Many children who enter the foster care system may not be legally adopted for years. Although two or three years may not seem like much time to an adult, to a six-year-old child this time span represents a significant portion of a child's life.

A child who enters the foster care system as an infant or toddler will usually become attached to the foster parents. It is very painful for the child to leave the people who are his psychological parents and return to his birthparents.

In addition, the older the child becomes, the more difficult it is to place the child in an adoptive home. Also, if the child has been in numerous foster homes, she may also have acquired a host of emotional problems as well, thus making her more difficult to adopt.

Because reunification is seen as the best solution for a foster child, adoption is perceived as the next best solution. "Permanency" is the stated goal for all children, whether through returning to their families or relatives or being placed in an adoptive family. The reality, however, is that thousands of children languish in foster homes and group homes.

Experts argue that these children who are victimized today by repeated moves will become the juvenile delinquents and criminals of tomorrow. (See also ADOPTION ASSISTANCE AND CHILD WELFARE ACT OF 1980; FOSTER CARE; FOSTER PARENTS; PERMANENCY PLANNING; TERMINATION OF PARENTAL RIGHTS.)

Andrew Stein, "Paradise Lost: How Foster-Care Children Are Being Removed From Loving Homes," *New York Magazine,* October 1989.

reunion Term used, perhaps inaccurately, to describe the meeting between a birthparent and an adult adopted person. (True reunions generally occur between people who have known each other, as in a class reunion where former schoolmates return to the institution to renew their friendship.) Often the adopted person was placed as an infant and has no memory of the birthparent.

Many newspaper articles describe the fond meeting between a birthmother and adopted adult. Hopefully, most meetings are a very positive experience; however, sometimes the birthparent or the adult adopted person is opposed to the meeting and will refuse or block it. The person may need time to adjust to the idea. In a birthparent's case, the birthparent may never have told his or her spouse or other children about the adoption.

Some adopted adults wait until their adoptive parents are very elderly or even deceased before they seek to locate birthparents, fearful that the adoptive parents would feel offended.

A study by Janet Rosenzweig-Smith, a project specialist for the New Jersey Department of Human Services and a doctoral candidate in social work at Rutgers, examined the factors related to successful meetings between birthparents and adopted adults. She found individuals over age 22 were more likely to have successful reunions than younger adopted persons.

According to Rosenzweig-Smith, the most difficult and tumultuous time a reunion could occur is during adolescence, which may well be an inappropriate time for an adopted person to seek out birthparents. Instead, she recommends individuals wait until adulthood and achieving a certain competency and self-confidence before attempting to locate birthparents.

The author also found a correlation between blaming a birthparent and an unhappy reunion. "The supported hypotheses regarding attribution can provide some direction in preparatory counseling with adult adoptees. Clinical techniques might be used to mitigate attribution of blame to the biological mother."

The author also found a correlation between blaming the biological father and successfully meeting with the birthmother. Adopted children may perceive the birthfather as a villain and a victimizer of the birthmother, or they may have no image of the birthfather at all.

In his report on Canadian studies of adopted adults, published in the September–October 1989 issue of *Child Welfare,* Paul Sachdev reported on adopted adults who did meet their birthparents. According to Sachdev, the studies reveal that the adopted adults recognize the importance of their adoptive parents and perceive them as "real" parents with whom they have an unbreakable bond, a bond stronger than the tie to the biological parents.

Sachdev found that almost two-thirds of the adopted adults confided in their parents prior to searching for the birthparents. The remainder who did not discuss the search with their parents expressed a fear of hurting their feelings.

The researchers also asked the 107 adopted adults to evaluate the relationship that had developed between them and their birthparents. According to Sachdev, nearly half became friends with their birthparents, about one-third perceived the relationship as similar to that between acquaintances, and about one-fifth described the relationship as a mother-child relationship.

In research for a doctoral dissertation in 1988, Janet Susan Waner studied the adjustment of a small sample of adopted adults (14) who searched for and found their birthmothers. According to Waner, the subjects experienced an initial euphoria or despair, depending on the rejection or acceptance of them by their birthmothers. In addition, all subjects felt a "let down" that Waner said was related to "the process as well as guilt for searching and anger towards the birthmother."

About half her subjects developed a "close relationship" with their birthmothers. According to Waner, some factors in forming this close relationship were that the birthmother was accepting, able to relate to the adopted adults and willing to "work through the past." (See also SEARCH; ADULT ADOPTED PERSONS; BIRTHMOTHER.)

Paul Sachdev, "The Triangle of Fears: Fallacies and Facts," *Child Welfare,* 68(September–October 1989): 491–503.
Janet Rosenzweig-Smith, "Factors Associated with Successful Reunions of Adult Adoptees and Biological Parents," *Child Welfare,* 67(September–October 1988): 411–422.
Janet Susan Waner, "A Study of Post-Reunion Adjustment in Adoptees Who Have Found Their Birthmothers," Ph.D. diss., California School of Professional Psychology, Berkeley/Alameda, 1988.

revocation When the birthparent or custodial relative formally changes his or her mind after signing a voluntary CONSENT. How long a person has to change his or her mind after signing consent and under what conditions varies from state to state.

States may allow revocation of consent if proper NOTICE has not been given to involved parties, such as the birthfather. Most states allow for revocation of consent because of fraud or duress on the part of the attorney, agency or adoptive parents.

If proper legal procedures were not followed, revocation of consent may be allowed in many states.

It is important for pregnant women and birthparents considering adoption to understand revocation of consent is not an easy and automatic matter and will usually require the hiring of an attorney. It may also involve a long and expensive court battle.

Roe v. Wade See ABORTION.

S

screening See HOME STUDY.

sealed records The original birth certificate of an adopted person as well as records of court proceedings, adoption agency reports and other matters surrounding a confidential adoption.

The original birth certificate and these records are sealed to protect the CONFIDENTIALITY of the birthparents, adoptive parents and adopted child.

In those states that have SEALED RECORDS (the majority of states), after an adoption is finalized, the adopted child's original birth certificate is made inaccessible to all persons, and a new birth certificate reflecting the transfer of parental rights, with the adoptive parents listed as the now responsible "parents," is issued.

The circumstances under which the original birth certificate may be obtained vary according to the state; however, most states require the adopted person to be at least 18 years old and may also require a court order before the original birth certificate may be released.

Some groups have sought to OPEN RECORDS. As of this writing, only adopted adults in three states may obtain records on request and without a cout order: Alaska, Hawaii and Kansas. In Alaska and Kansas, only the original birth certificate may be obtained upon the request of the adopted adult. In Hawaii, the entire court record may be obtained upon request of the adopted adult. As of this writing the National Committee for Adoption plans to seek an injunction against the open records provision in Hawaii.

search Term used to describe an attempt, usually by a birthparent, adopted person or adoptive parent but sometimes by volunteers or paid consultants, to make a connection between the birthparent and the biological child. Searches are usually accomplished by adopted adults or birthparents of adopted adults but may also be made by adoptive parents to assist the adopted person. Sometimes searches occur when the adopted person is a minor, although most searches are not made until the adopted person is considered an adult and is at least 18 years old.

Although it is not known how many adopted individuals ultimately search for their birthparents or how many birthparents actively seek their birthchildren, searching appears to be on the increase, at least based on the number of SEARCH GROUPS that exist nationwide, although reliable statistics are not available.

In addition, a great deal of media attention has focused on this issue, and numerous newspaper features about "reunions" of individuals adopted at birth and their birthmothers have been published.

Speculation has centered around such key issues as whether the person should be contacted for consent to disclose his or her identity prior to an actual meeting; whether OPEN RECORDS would be more humane than traditional adoption, thus negating the need for a search; whether adopted persons who search for birthparents are better or less adjusted than adopted adults who do not search; and many other issues.

In addition, most states seal adoption records permanently or at least until the adopted person reaches the age of majority, and it is extremely difficult to obtain a court order to unseal adoption records in most states. As a result, many searchers use a variety of methods—sometimes legal, sometimes not—to locate and identify the person sought, including both open and covert searching techniques.

To date, 24 states in the United States have established MUTUAL CONSENT REGISTRIES, wherein if both the birthparent and the adopted person agree that information should be shared, then identifying information shall be provided. There has also been an effort, led by Sen. Carl Levin (D, Mich.) to establish a national Reunion Registry, although no federal registry has been established as of this writing.

Several studies have compared and contrasted adopted adults who search for their birthparents with adopted persons who have no desire to search. Canadian researchers Michael P. Sobol and Jeanette Cardiff located adopted adults through newspaper advertisements and through ParentFinders, a Canadian search group.

Respondents were administered a questionnaire devised by the researchers as well as previously-designed tests on self-esteem and adjustment.

In contrast to other research findings, the researchers did not find women searching more than men nor did they find a significant correlation between age and the decision to search; however, they did discover several significant correlations. For example, the older the person was at the time of the adoption, the greater probability the person would conduct a search as an adult.

The more the adopted person remembered being told about the adoption and the more negative early feelings about adoption were, the higher the probability the adult adoptee would search for a birthparent. A doctoral dissertation by Robert Allen Adelberg at Boston University in 1986 supports these findings.

Adelberg compared searching and nonsearching adopted adults and found searchers perceived their families as less open in discussing adoption than did nonsearchers. According to Adelberg, "The findings indicated that more closed adoptive family communication was associated with the decision to search and with lower self-esteem." He did not find searchers to be less adjusted than nonsearchers.

A master's thesis by Rosie Ann Kauffman in 1987 at the University of Texas at Arlington found high self-concept scores in both searchers and nonsearchers and no significant differences. Adoptees with the highest self-concept scores were those placed in an adoptive home at an early age.

Research on adjustment levels of searchers versus nonsearchers has yielded conflicting results. A 1981 M.S.S.W. thesis by S. A. A. Aumend did find significant differences between searchers and nonsearchers. Comparing 49 nonsearchers to 71 searchers, Aumend found nonsearchers to have higher self-esteem, more positive attitudes toward their adoptive mothers and more positive feelings about adoption.

A study by J. Triseliotis reported in 1973 discussed 70 adopted adults who used the open records available in Scotland and compared these individuals with nonsearchers. His findings were

"Adoptees who have experienced a happy home life and to whom the circumstances of their adoption has been made available by the adoptive parents, and who have not experienced a recent intense crisis, are less likely to feel the need to seek reunions."

A surprising finding by Michael Sobol and Jeanette Cardiff was that the greater the information provided on the birthparent, the higher the probability the adult adopted person would initiate a search. This finding conflicts with other studies, which have found that a lack of information is correlated with a desire to search.

How the adopted person felt about the information provided was significant; for example, if the adopted adult was satisfied with the information on the birthparent, he was unlikely to search. In addition, the ability to freely discuss adoption in the adoptive home was negatively correlated with searching: The less the adopted person felt he or she could ask questions, the greater the compulsion to look outward for answers and initiate a search.

Nonsearchers were asked why they chose not to search. Of these, 29.1% were concerned about hurting the feelings of their adoptive parents, and 20% saw no reason to search beyond their adoptive family. Other reasons included fear of unknown consequences, insufficient money or time to accomplish a search, lack of knowledge and fear of rejection.

Of those who did opt to search, nearly 51% wanted factual information, and 21% were curious about their birthparents. Other answers revealed a more emotional basis for searching; for example, about 29% stated they were searching for reasons of identity and fulfillment.

About 25% of the respondents who searched had wished to create a relationship with their birthparents, and about 9% wanted to create a relationship with birth siblings. Another 9% wanted to contact birthparents to reassure them about the outcome of the adoption and that they had in fact done the right thing.

Events triggering a search ranged from identifying a search group to having children born to them to discovering a health problem that may have been inherited to the death of the adoptive parents.

Katherine A. Kowal and Karen Maitland Schilling described their study of adult adopted persons who had contacted adoption agencies or a search group, asking searchers why they had searched or were currently searching.

"The most commonly mentioned precipitants were pregnancy, birth, or adoption of a child (24%). In addition, six subjects listed a pregnancy, abortion, birth or adoption of a child as having occurred within the last year even though they did not identify these events as precipitants for searching."

Other "precipitants" for searching found by Kowal and Schilling included "the encouragement of a significant other," "medical conditions in oneself or one's child" and "some disruptive change in the relationship with or between the adoptive parents—their death, divorce, or estrangement from the adoptee". Others reported the time seemed right.

The type of information most sought after by Kowal and Schilling's study group was medical information—75% sought this information. Other key pieces of information desired by adopted persons (in descending order), were personality traits of birthparents, a physical description of the birthparents, the names of birthparents, birthparents' ethnic background, information on the adopted person's early medical history, interests and hobbies of birthparents, the reason the child was placed for adoption, current marital status of birthparents, education and occupation of birthparents, marital status of birthparents when the adopted person was born and where the adopted person lived before the adoption.

Since much of this information, with the exception of the name of the birthparents, is available to adoptive parents today, it is clear such information should be shared with adopted children. In addition, it is also clear such information should be offered before the adopted person asks, in the event the adopted person is fearful of hurting the feelings of adoptive parents.

A study of birthparents initiating a search for their biological children who were adopted was reported in the November/December 1988 issue of *Social Work*.

Researchers found that birthparents who searched were less likely to be married and more likely to have a higher income than birthparents who had been sought out by their birthchildren. Birthparents from each group were about the same age when the child was adopted.

According to *Clinical Practice in Adoption,* by Robin C. Winkler, Dirck W. Brown, Margaret van Keppel and Amy Blanchard, there are distinct phases to the search process. (The authors have also drawn upon books written by adopted person Betty Jean Lifton.)

"The initial stage, *crossing the threshold,* often takes place only after a lengthy period of hesitation and ambivalence about whether or not to search." The authors believe this stage can be caused by a life change, such as the birth of a child or death of an adoptive parent.

Obsession is the second stage. "Hours are spent examining records, researching leads; it is like working on a major mystery." This stage is complete once the birthparent has been identified but before contact occurs.

Limbo is the third stage, when the adopted person steps back and assesses feelings. "Feelings of ambivalence are strongly felt: 'How can I take the final step and call my birth mother?' 'I'm afraid she will reject me again.' 'What if she is married and hasn't told her husband about me?' 'What if I call and find she is dead?' "

Adopted persons have built up many fantasies over the years about the birthmother. What if reality clashes painfully with the fantasy? Would it be better to hold onto the fantasy or learn the truth? The adopted person must (or should) resolve conflicts in this stage before contacting a birthparent.

The final stage is dramatically labeled *penetration of the veil*, and this is the stage at which the adopted adult makes contact by a visit, phone call or a letter to the birthparent. (See also REUNION.)

Robert Allen Adelberg, "A Comparison Study of Searching and Non-Searching Adult Adoptees," Ed.D diss., Boston University, 1986.

S. A. A. Aumend, "Self-Concept, Attitudes Toward Adoptive Parents," M.S.S.W. thesis, University of Texas at Austin, 1981.

Rosie Ann Kauffman, "Reunion and Non-Reunion Searching Adult Adoptees: A Comparison of Identity, Physical Self and Family Self," Master's thesis, University of Texas at Arlington, 1987.

Katherine A. Kowal, Ph.D., and Karen Maitland Schilling, Ph.D., "Adoption Through the Eyes of Adult Adoptees," *American Journal of Orthopsychiatry,* 55(July 1985): 354–362.

P. R. Silverman, L. Campbell, and P. Patti, "Reunions between Adoptees and Birthparents: Birthparents' Experience," *Social Work,* 33(November/December 1988): 523–528.

Michael P. Sobol and Jeanette Cardiff, "A Sociopsychological Investigation of Adult Adoptees' Search for Birth Parents," *Family Relations,* 32(October 1983): 477–483.

J. Triseliotis, *In Search of Origins: The Experience of Adopted People* (London: Routledge and Kegan Paul, 1973).

Robin C. Winkler, Dirck W. Brown, Margaret van Keppel and Amy Blanchard, *Clinical Practice in Adoption* (Elmsford, N.Y.: Pergamon Press, 1988).

search and consent laws As of this writing (1991), 12 states (Alabama, Connecticut, Georgia, Kentucky, Minnesota, Missouri, Montana, Nebraska, North Dakota, Pennsylvania, Tennessee and Wisconsin) have passed search and consent laws, which enable an adopted adult to contact the state social services department and request a search of the birthparent. Alabama had previously been an OPEN RECORDS state; however, in 1990, the state changed the adoption laws, and Alabama became a search and consent state.

If the birthparent is found, the agency is to ask the birthparent if s(he) wishes to release identifying information. If the birthparent consents, then the information will be given to the adopted person.

Search and consent laws differ from the registry concept. With an adoption registry, the adopted adult independently registers the desire for information about a birthparent. If the birthparent also registers, the information is shared with both parties. (See MUTUAL CONSENT REGISTRIES.)

Some advocacy groups opposed to search and consent laws consider them intrusive and contend they should be more properly be called "search and confront" laws.

Twenty-four states utilize the concept of mutual consent registries, including Arkansas, California, Colorado, Florida, Idaho, Illinois, Indiana, Louisiana, Maine, Maryland, Massachusetts, Michigan, Nevada, New Hampshire, New Jersey, New York, Ohio, Oregon, South Carolina, South Dakota, Texas, Utah, Vermont and West Virginia.

Adoption Factbook (Washington, D.C.: National Committee For Adoption, 1989).

search groups Organizations that assist adopted people, birthparents, adoptive parents and others in identifying and locating birth relatives. National organizations include the ADOPTEES' LIBERTY MOVEMENT ASSOCIATION, CONCERNED UNITED BIRTHPARENTS INC. and Triadoption Library Inc. in Westminster, California. The INTERNATIONAL SOUNDEX REUNION REGISTRY, while not a search group per se, has a philosophy that makes it more than simply a passive registry. It is clearly linked to most of the search groups.

There are also many other small organizations within states. The AMERICAN ADOPTION CONGRESS serves as an umbrella for many of the search groups.

The first search group was Orphan Voyage and was founded by adopted adult Jean Paton in 1953.

Search groups may also seek to change state laws; for example, many search groups are in favor of OPEN RECORDS. Groups vary in their policies.

Most groups will only help adult adopted persons seek birthparents or help birthparents seek adopted adults. Other groups assist adoptive parents who wish to seek birthparents when their adopted children are still minors.

Each group's policies and procedures should be considered before joining a particular organization. Most groups provide helpful hints on searching and recommended readings as well as emotional support from successful searchers. Others charge extensive fees and perform the actual searches.

It is also true that some adoption agencies charge searchers. Adopted people, birthparents or adoptive parents considering the use of such a search should find out what the fee (or estimated fee) will be. If agencies provide an hourly rate, then the customer should request an estimated number of hours the search will take as well as estimated length of time.

Books on the advisability of searching or actual search techniques written from the perspective of search groups include *The Adoption Triangle* by Arthur D. Sorosky, Annette Baran and Reuben Pannor (Anchor Press/Doubleday, 1984) and *The Adoption Searchbook* by Mary Jo Rillera (Triadoption Publications, 1985). (See also SEARCH.)

Anne Welsbacher, "When Your Child Decides to Search," *OURS,* July/August 1988, 6–10.

sectarian agencies See AGENCIES.

self-esteem An individual's regard and respect for himself or herself and his or her sense of identity and self-worth. Individuals with high self-esteem perceive themselves as valuable, and those with low self-esteem denigrate themselves, their self-worth and their achievements.

A person with high self-esteem has a realistic view of his strengths and weaknesses and accepts himself as he is. It is often difficult for the average person to develop a healthy self-esteem and is especially difficult for the child who was adopted at an older age—difficult, but by no means impossible.

Self-esteem is not only important to the individual but also affects his family, his friends (and whether or not he has friends) and his entire life. Most criminals have very low self-esteem. People who never fulfill their potential often hold themselves back from fear of failure traceable to a lack of self-esteem.

Adopted children who were adopted at an older age are particularly prone to low self-esteem in the early stages of their adoption. According to family counselor and author Claudia Jewett, "Low self-esteem is one of the most common characteristics in newly adopted older children."

Often these children have been abused or neglected by their biological parents who may also have verbally abused them, and the children have internalized the negative feedback.

Opponents of TRANSRACIAL ADOPTION have stated that low self-esteem is a key reason they disapprove of such adoptions, particularly involving whites adopting black or biracial children. Studies have not borne out this prediction, and children who are transracially adopted appear to have a positive self-esteem for the most part.

When a child (or an adult) has a very low opinion of herself, then she may have exhibited a variety of behavior, including ACTING OUT in frustration, or underachieving in school. The child may find it difficult to understand or even be suspicious that someone would want to adopt and love her. To paraphrase an old Groucho Marx saying, she's not sure she'd want to live with any people who would find her acceptable.

Self-esteem can be encouraged and built up, but it also comes from within. If a child has very low self-esteem, the parent (adoptive or biological) must strive to bring the child's self-esteem level up to a realistic point.

Jewett says praise may not work well with the child adopted at an older age, particularly generalized praise, "You're a good girl" or "You're a wonderful boy." Instead, Jewett recommends praising actions and tasks that are performed well.

She also recommends the parent teach the child self-praise. "Teaching the child to engage in self-praise not only reinforces his positive behavior, it also teaches him a new set of self-referent ideas . . . This skill of praising oneself can be nurtured by asking the question, 'Don't you think you did well on that?' The child's response can then be linked with a statement of praise, such as, 'I think you did a tremendous job, too' or 'You must feel good about that.' When the child becomes more accustomed to giving self-referent verbal reinforcement, the adult can ask, 'What do you think you should say to yourself?' If the child replies that he doesn't know, the adult can ask, 'What do I say to you?' or a similar question to help involve the child in the evaluative, praising process and to give him permission and encouragement to feel pride in himself."

Therapists should also be able to provide many helpful hints. It's important to note, however, that some therapists presume a person is disturbed for the sole reason that she is adopted when in fact other issues may be causing the problems. The child may not have low self-esteem because he wonders why his mother "gave him up" or physically abused him—his difficulty with math or reading may make him feel stupid, and tutoring can help.

Sometimes it *is* an adoption issue that disturbs a child and lowers his self-esteem. Author Stephanie Siegel described a 12-year-old boy who ran away from home because he could not resolve a conflict in his mind. He could not understand why his birthmother had chosen adoption for him and concluded that he must have been a defective child. He reasoned that his adoptive parents, then, must also have something wrong with them, or they wouldn't have adopted a defective child.

With therapy, the child was able to resolve his anxiety, accept his adoption and improve his self-esteem and self-worth.

One possible way to handle such a situation is for the adoptive parents to bring up the subject of adoption and ask the child if he has any questions about his birthparents. The child may have questions but be afraid to ask the adoptive parents for fear they will feel offended or unloved. (See also EXPLAINING ADOPTION.)

Claudia L. Jewett, *Adopting the Older Child* (Boston: Harvard Common Press, 1978).
Stephanie E. Siegel, Ph.D., *Parenting Your Adopted Child* (New York: Prentice Hall, 1989).

self-help   See SUPPORT GROUPS.

separation and loss See LOSS.

sex of child, preference of adoptive parents See GENDER PREFERENCE.

sexual abuse According to the National Center on Child Abuse and Neglect, sexual abuse is the least frequent form of ABUSE among the three major categories of abuse—physical, emotional and sexual. The National Center estimates 155,900 children were sexually abused by adults or teenagers in 1986.

There are various forms of sexual abuse, according to the National Center on Child Abuse and Neglect: intrusion, which refers to actual penile penetration, genitally, orally or anally; molestation with genital contact but no penetration; and other sexual abuse, such as fondling of the breasts or buttocks or other inappropriate sexual behavior.

It was estimated there were 48,400 children suffering intrusion, 70,300 cases of genital molestation, and 37,600 children suffering other sexual abuse in 1986. Girls were (and are) much more likely to be the victims of sexual abusers: 121,000 girls suffered some form of sexual abuse versus 34,300 boys.

Children are more likely to be sexually abused if their family income is low. Families earning less than $15,000 per year were four times more likely to commit acts of sexual abuse than families earning incomes greater than $15,000.

When foster children have been sexually abused, they may have been abused by their birthparents, a stepparent or even another child in a foster home or group home. They may have kept the abuse secret from everyone and been removed from their parental home for other reasons, such as neglect or physical abuse.

They may have lived in many different foster homes, trying to assimilate changes in families and lifestyles along with coping with the sexual abuse that happened to them. Sometimes they may relive the abuse in their minds like a videotape inside their heads.

They often suffer low SELF-ESTEEM, believing that at least part of the sexual abuse was their fault. The abuser may have told them that the abuse was, in fact, their fault. They may also have enjoyed some of the sexual activities that occurred and then felt guilty and bad for liking it.

Social workers have an ethical and moral responsibility to report incidences of sexual abuse that have happened to a child a family is considering adopting so the family can be fully aware of whether they wish to adopt the child as well as how they can formulate plans to help the child. The social worker need not tell who was the perpetrator but should tell what happened in as much detail as confidentiality will allow.

Unfortunately, in many instances the social worker may not know of incidents of sexual abuse that have happened to the child, and it may not come out until much later, when the child feels comfortable enough with the parent to tell the parent what happened.

One reason the child may not tell anyone about the abuse is because the child presumes he or she deserved it. Says author Marian Sandmaier in her book, *When Love is Not Enough: How Mental Health Professionals Can Help Special-Needs Adoptive Families*.

"This is particularly true of sexually abused children, some of whom also have learned to equate love with sex and may not consciously feel they were maltreated."

Sandmaier says a child who has been sexually abused in the past may exhibit seductive behavior that can cause "outright panic among family members. Although the child may be looking for the only form of nurturance he or she knows, the parents are likely to view the child's behavior as a profound threat to family stability."

Not all sexually abused children exhibit provocative behavior and other symptoms of previous abuse. Joan McNamara of the Family Resources Adoption Program in Ossining, New York has written an informative pamphlet for prospective adoptive parents and adoptive parents entitled *Tangled Feelings: Sexual Abuse & Adoption.*

McNamara describes symptoms common to sexually abused children, including "sexual knowledge or behavior beyond the child's age level, aversion to touch, or, conversely, seductive or clinging behavior, marked sensitivity to body exposure (aversion or excessive interest), self-exposure and excessive masturbation."

According to McNamara, sexually abused boys are confused about their identity and act out, but girls internalize the guilt of the abuse. In addition, the child may be emotionally "stuck" at the developmental stage he or she was in at the time of the abuse

McNamara says that in working with adopted children who had been sexually abused, the therapist must realize that older children sometimes believe the abuse somehow validated their own feeling of extremely low self-esteem.

Counseling may be necessary for the family as well as for the abused child. Says Sandmaier, "Without counseling to help them [the family] understand the emotional and behavioral consequences of sexual abuse, a family may declare the child incorrigible and prematurely disrupt the placement."

Another problem is that no matter how well-prepared an adoptive parent feels he is, if a beloved child suddenly describes sexual abuse from the past, many parents would understandably feel enraged and may well have to struggle not to voice their condemnation of the perpetrator.

The danger is that the child could internalize the guilt for what happened to him or her as well, further damaging an already battered ego. It's very important the child realize that what happened was not his fault. Even if he or she enjoyed some of the sexual activities that occurred, it was the perpetrator's fault for introducing the child to sex before she or he was ready, and it was the perpetrator's fault for inducing his will over the child's will.

Another problem is that the child may accuse someone who did not abuse him, perhaps a former foster parent. He may not be lying on purpose but may be confused and insecure. Perhaps admitting he was abused by a person who was supposed to protect him, such as a parent, is too painful.

Children need a safe environment where the rules are known. They need a great deal of positive reinforcement, and they may have a very difficult time accepting that they are intrinsically worthy to the parent.

Concludes McNamara, "When hurt children enter a new family through adoption, past events and feelings are fused with current realities for these children and families. To help heal the hurt takes time, loving commitment, and willingness to be open to another person's pain." (See also NEGLECT.)

Jane Marks, "We Have a Problem," *Parents,* March 1990, 63–69.

Joan McNamara, *Tangled Feelings: Sexual Abuse & Adoption* (Ossining, NY: Family Resources Adoption Program, 1988).

Marian Sandmaier, *When Love is Not Enough: How Mental Health Professionals Can Help Special-Needs Adoptive Families* (Washington, D.C.: Child Welfare League of America, 1988).

U.S. Department of Health and Human Services, National Center on Child Abuse and Neglect, Office of Human Development Services, Administration for Children, Youth and Families, Children's Bureau, *Study Findings: Study of National Incidence and Prevalence of Child Abuse and Neglect: 1988.*

showing of the child   See RECRUITMENT.

siblings   People who are brother or sister to one another, either through a birth or an adoptive relationship (by sharing the same birthmother or through adoption). An adopted child who is unrelated to children already in a family or who follow him through birth or adoption does *not* refer to these children as his "half" brothers or sisters: They are his brothers or sisters.

A child who is adopted may be placed with his or her other full or half siblings or may be placed in a family that already has adopted children or children by birth. In addition, the parents may adopt more children in later years or may have additional children by birth. (It is a myth that a good way to cure infertility is to adopt children. See PREGNANCY AFTER ADOPTION.)

Many children who are adopted are only children because the adoptive parents do not already have children and do not adopt again. Consequently, these children will not have siblings in the adoptive family. They may, however, have full- or half-genetic siblings within their birth family. (See ONLY CHILD ADOPTIVE FAMILIES.)

In other cases, sibling groups are placed in an adoptive family, and the consensus among adoption professionals is that siblings should be adopted together whenever possible. In a paper on siblings, social worker Kathryn Donley has said, "Only under the most extraordinary circumstances should prospective parents consider the placement of just one of the children from a family group."

She also urges that existing sibling relationships should be considered and their meanings fully explored. Children's wishes should also be considered. Donley says it's important to remember that sibling relationships can be lifelong and often when adopted adults search, they search for a sibling.

Margaret Ward, an instructor at Cambrian College in Ontario, Canada, describes several key characteristics adoption workers should look for when fitting sibling groups into their new families. One is administrative ability and the capability of juggling Boy Scout meetings with dance classes, doctor appointments and so forth, along with the basics of running a home.

The ability to cope with emergencies was also seen as important, and the more children in the family, the greater the probability there will be emergencies. According to Ward, "Parents need to possess, or to develop, a relative unflappability. If they become too excited or panicky, the crisis will be escalated by an additional behavioral or emotional chain reaction in the rest of the family."

The ability to promote healthy family interaction and cope with sibling rivalry and group dynamics is also important when siblings are newly added to a family. Parents must be sensitized to existing relationships between children.

Other characteristics Ward identified as important included the "ability to survive in the community" and deal with the school system and other institutions; the availability of support systems, such as adoptive parent support groups, relatives, friends; the ability for the wife and husband to provide each other mutual support and not heap all parental tasks on one person; and the ability to adapt.

When children are adopted into an already-existing family, the BIRTH ORDER is altered, and the former child who was the "baby" of the family may well find himself the "middle child," while the oldest child could lose his authority and become a middle child.

Adopting parents should prepare children already in the home as much as possible for the inevitable changes, whether the child to be adopted is an infant or an older child. The whole family needs to understand that there will be frustrations and stresses, particularly when adopting an older child.

Many people who adopt older children already do have children in the home, or they may have raised a family at a relatively young age and opted to parent another family through adoption.

When parents adopt a school-age child, siblings in the home may have unreasonable expectations placed on them; for example, they may be told of the deprived conditions the child lived under and are urged to be understanding.

This may be difficult when the new child moves out of the honeymoon stage of the initial phase of adoption, when she is on her best behavior, to the testing stage when misbehavior is very common.

In addition, the newly adopted child may not feel very grateful about her adoption, which can annoy the "old" siblings who are trying to feel sorry for her and expect her to appreciate it. When siblings or when one newly-adopted child is placed in a home with children, there is a great deal of adjustment to be made by everyone.

Social worker Carole Depp says sometimes one or more of the siblings in an adoption of siblings may have severe problems. In such a case, she advises, "the best plan may be to stagger the placement of the children with the family . . . visits of a sibling with the child or children not yet placed should be arranged. If the most needful child is placed first, then some of the healing process can begin before the family assumes responsibility for additional siblings."

Adolescence As with most other facets of adoption and indeed with life in general, adolescence appears to be the most difficult stage for both adopted persons and siblings of adopted persons. (See ADOLESCENT ADOPTED PERSONS for a further discussion of adopted teenagers.)

Margaret Ward and John H. Lewko studied families adopting school-age children after they already had existing adopted or biological children, concentrating on adolescents.

Using a questionnaire for adolescents who already lived in the home, the researchers identified several problem areas. According to Ward and Lewko, "Difficulties with all siblings were seen primarily as hassles. The adoptee was, however, reported as creating more problems than 'old' siblings."

The respondents complained the most about the newly adopted child's lying, interfering with privacy and failing to obey rules. "Old" siblings were also rated by other old siblings, and sisters were accused of using bad language while brothers were "more likely to practice inadequate hygiene" and not "pay attention to the rules" more than the new adopted child.

According to the researchers, "The appropriate behavior for a resident adolescent is to teach the new child the rules of the family game. Yet the behavior of the new child can upset the adolescent. The daily hassles can add up to severe stress, as indicated by the respondent who stated that she wanted no children at all as a result of the adoption . . . instead of establishing a helpful attitude toward the new child, the adolescent may become alienated."

Adopting Sibling Groups Although once it was considered acceptable or necessary to separate siblings and to place them into different adoptive families, agencies make strenuous attempts to place sibling groups together into the same family so they will not undergo a further trauma of separation.

When sibling groups are small, with two siblings of a relatively young age, placement is far easier than when sibling groups of three or more need to be placed. (Groups may be as large as seven or more!)

Sometimes siblings are separated when one wishes to be adopted and the other does not wish to be adopted or is unready to make a commitment. If it is felt by the social worker to be in the child's best interests, then the children may be physically separated. Of course if siblings are abusive to one another, they will be separated.

Twins In the past, particularly during the Depression era (the early 1930s), it was deemed acceptable to separate twins into different adopting families. Usually this was done because the couple could not handle the stress and financial cost of raising twins.

Social workers today believe it is cruel and unreasonable to separate twins and actively seek to identify adoptive families willing and able to rear both children.

Birth and Adopted Children (Also known as BLENDED FAMILIES.)

Some people have hypothesized that when adopted children join birth children already in the family, the adopted child is the "odd man out," while the birth children are the favored ones.

Studies of such families have not borne out this fear, and instead, adopted children in families with birth children seem to have a higher self-esteem than adopted children whose siblings in the family are also adopted.

According to a study by Janet Hoopes and Leslie Stein, adopted children may feel more positive. They said, "The presence of biological siblings was viewed advantageously, i.e., as confirmation of own self-worth enhanced by the realization of their egalitarian treatment within the family."

In other words, if the adopted child felt as well-treated as the biological child(ren), self-esteem was high. Conversely, the adopted child in a family with only other adopted children doesn't know how his adoptive parents would treat biological children and may imagine that they would treat them better.

When the adopted child precedes the birth child, people may make disturbing remarks, such as "At last! Now you have a child of your own!" If the child is old enough to understand, this is a painful message, indicating the other child is more important, when in most cases the adoptive parent loves both children very much.

Disabled New Siblings If the newly adopted child is disabled, the stress on the "old" children may be even greater than otherwise because there's more than just a new child to get used to.

Susan Maczka, director of Project S.T.A.R., a licensed adoption agency for children with developmental disabilities in Pittsburgh, Pennsylvania wrote "A Head Start" for *OURS* magazine on how to prepare a sibling already in the home for the new child who is disabled.

According to Maczka, it is important to provide "old" siblings with information about the disability. As a result, the child will be more prepared for new needs that must be met or for disturbing behavior that may occur. Maczka also recommends adopting parents take the child to a Special Olympics or visit with a family whose child is disabled.

In addition, she advises discussing with the child ahead of time any changes that may need to be made. "Figure out ways that your children can signal you about frustrations they may feel over those changes. Ask for your children's help in making adjustments," she advises.

Maczka says parents must not place too heavy a burden on their children when the newly adopted child arrives.

"Girls notoriously 'overdo it' in the helping area, and sometimes feel angry about it later," she says.

Sibling Rivalry Whether siblings are genetically related or are related by adoption, it is virtually inevitable that they will disagree and argue.

Sometimes the sibling rivalry can be very intense, and although caseworkers generally strive to place biological siblings together, if the rivalry is very strong, the children may be separated.

The authors of *Large Sibling Groups* argue with this policy and believe such separation teaches a child that the way to resolve conflict is to leave or to separate the individuals involved rather than actually dealing with the problems surrounding the conflict. (See also SPECIAL NEEDS.)

Carole H. Depp, M.S.W., "Placing Siblings Together," *Children Today,* 12(March–April 1983): 14–19.

Kathryn Donley, M.S.W., "Sibling Attachments and Adoption," paper available from the National Resource Center for Special Needs Adoption, Chelsea, Michigan.

Gwen Fodge, "Bringing Home Joy," *OURS,* January/February 1989, 14–15.

Pam Havel, "The Geometric Component of Two," *OURS,* January/February 1989, 12–13.

Dorothy W. LePere, A.C.S.W., Lloyd E. Davis, A.C.S.W., Janus Couve, A.C.S.W. and Mona McDonald, A.C.S.W., *Large Sibling Groups: Adoption Experiences* (Washington, D.C.: Child Welfare League of America, 1986).

Susan Maczka, "A Head Start," *OURS,* January/February 1989, 10–11.

National Committee For Adoption, "Adolescent Adoptees' 'Identity Formation' is Normal, Study Says," *National Adoption Reports,* 6(March–April 1985): 6.

Michael Rutter, Patrick Bolton, Richard Harrington, Ann Le Couteur, Hope Macdonald and Emily Smirnoff, "Genetic Factors in Child Psychiatric Disorders-I. A Review of Research Strategies," *The Journal of Child Psychology and Psychiatry and Allied Disciplines,* January 1990, 3–37.

Margaret Ward, "Choosing Adoptive Families for Large Sibling Groups," *Child Welfare,* 66(May–June 1987): 259–268.

Margaret Ward and John H. Lewko, "Problems Experienced by Adolescents Already in Families that Adopt Older Children," *Adolescence,* 23(Spring 1988): 221–228.

simple adoption A form of adoption, also known as "adoption simple," based on the Napoleonic code; present in some countries in Latin America and former French colonies.

A simple adoption does not lead to a complete dissolution of the ties with the biological family and corresponds most closely to INFORMAL ADOPTION or legal guardianship in the United States. Simple adoption is differentiated from informal adoption in that legal action must be taken to achieve the simple adoption. This and other old approaches are receiving new attention in the United States by some influential people in the field of adoption, notably Reuben Pannor and Annette Baran, who have called for their equivalents to be established in the United States.

Annette Baran and Reuben Pannor, "A Time for Sweeping Change," fax copy of article sent to *Orphan Voyage,* June 1990.

J. H. A. van Loon, *Report on Intercountry Adoption,* paper presented at Hague Conference on Private International Law Intercountry, The Hague, Netherlands, April 1990, 23–24.

single adoptive parents Because of much media attention to single biological parents, many of whom are low-income and struggling, single adoptive parents have found they have often been mistakenly categorized with this group. Yet this stereotype is unfairly applied to the average single adoptive parent, according to the COMMITTEE FOR SINGLE ADOPTIVE PARENTS, a support group that says most single adoptive parents familiar to the organization are middle-class females and nearly half are members of the "helping professions": teachers, social workers, nurses and other career fields.

Many are very well-educated, according to the group, which says that the overwhelming majority of the people it surveyed are college graduates with many having earned postgraduate degrees. Most of the single adoptive parents adopt their children while they are in their thirties or early forties. (Single adoptive parents are still in the minority, and most adoptive parents are couples.)

Until the 1980s, it was difficult to impossible for the average single woman or man to adopt a child of any age. If the single person was considered as a prospective adoptive parent, she or he was usually only considered for the most difficult to place children, often children needing extensive care and attention. Yet single individuals usually were (and are) employed full-time and may find it very difficult to care for children with severe physical handicaps.

Lori Kellogg, founder of a North Miami-based adoption agency, Universal Aid for Children, wished to adopt and was amazed to learn that her divorced marital status made it impossible in 1973. She and other prospective single parents lobbied actively to change laws. One single woman filed suit claiming discrimination based on marital status. The end result of these combined actions was that Kellogg and others were subsequently able to adopt their children.

Some experts believe couples should still be given priority in adopting children. They argue that just because a single woman or man wants a child doesn't mean they are automatically entitled to a child or would make a good parent.

Yet it is important to note that many single adoptive parents adopt older children, handicapped children and children who are considered to have SPECIAL NEEDS. Even when single parents choose to adopt an infant, it is usually an infant from another country and often an infant urgently needing a family and yet considered hard to place because of race, medical problems or other factors. As a result, the child gains a much-needed parent.

Single Men It may still be difficult for a single man to adopt an unrelated child, either in the United States or internationally. Experts hypothesize that women are perceived as nurturing and adoption is a nurturing act. But the motivations of a man who wishes to adopt may be suspect. In addition, some overseas nations will accept applications from single adoptive women but not single adoptive men.

Mary Ann Curran of Adoption Services of WACAP in Seattle, Washington explained the problem:

"Not many countries accept men. We have had some very successful placements with single men, but unfortunately our options are very limited" (by the necessity of complying with the criteria of the overseas nation.)

Agencies and Support Groups Although some agencies refuse to accept applications from single adoptive parents, other agencies concentrate on working with singles, because of very positive experiences with single adoptive parents. The Committee for Single Adoptive Parents offers periodic newsletters with listings of agencies that work with singles, and other support groups are also highly aware of which agencies are responsive to single adoptive parent applicants and which are less responsive.

There are also support groups specifically geared to singles, such as the Committee for Single Adoptive Parents, SINGLE PARENTS ADOPTING CHILDREN EVERYWHERE (SPACE) and other groups nationwide. (The Report on Foreign Adoption, published by the INTERNATIONAL CONCERNS COMMITTEE FOR CHILDREN, includes information on support groups for singles.) In addition, many adoptive parent groups have subgroups of singles who are seeking to adopt or already have adopted a child.

Motivations The primary motivation of a single person wishing to adopt is congruent with the primary motivation of a married couple who wishes to adopt: the desire for a child to love and cherish. The difference is that most couples who adopt are infertile, whereas the single person may or may not be infertile.

Singles may be given support from their families and friends, or they may be treated with incredulity.

Agencies cannot presume couples will stay married, nor should they presume singles will forever remain single. Instead, say singles, what should be looked at is the individual person and his or her potential parenting capacity.

Christine Adamec, *There ARE Babies to Adopt* (Lexington, MA: Mills & Sanderson, 1987).

Committee for Single Adoptive Parents, "Who Wants to Be a Single Adoptive Parent?" (Chevy Chase, Md.: CSAP, 1990).

Hope Marindin, editor, *The Handbook for Single Adoptive Parents* (Chevy Chase, Md.: Committee for Single Adoptive Parents, 1987).

Marylou Sullivan, "Perceptions of Single Adoptive Parents: How We View Ourselves, How Others View Us," *OURS,* November/December 1989, 34–35.

Kathryn Watterson, "You Can't Keep Me From This Child!" *Working Mother,* November 1989, 26, 28, 31.

Single Parents Adopting Children Everywhere (SPACE) Organization formed in 1974 to provide support and information to singles considering or planning to adopt, those who have already adopted and also to the adopted children.

About 250 people are members of SPACE. Dues are $20 the first year with a renewal fee of $10. The organization holds meetings about six to eight times per year, regional meetings are held once a year, and a national meeting is held every other year.

Members receive a newsletter three times per year.

For more information, contact

SPACE
6 Sunshine Ave.
Natick, MA 01760
(508) 655-5426

skin color Children who need permanent, loving families through adoption come in all colors. Many adopting parents prefer to adopt children with a skin color similar to their own, although skin color and/or race is immaterial to other parents.

When people plan to adopt children internationally, they may expect the children to be Caucasian in appearance, particularly if they plan to adopt South American children; however, South American children range from light-skinned to dark-skinned and many are racially mixed.

As a result, prospective adoptive parents who are sensitive to the issue of skin color should carefully evaluate their position before adopting a foreign child. (The *Report on Foreign Adoption* prepared each year by the Boulder, Colorado-based INTERNATIONAL CONCERNS COMMITTEE FOR CHILDREN, includes general information on skin color, appearance and other features of adoptable children in countries worldwide.)

sliding scale fees Some adoption AGENCIES peg their fees to the prospective adoptive parent's income, for example, 10% of their gross income with a minimum fee and a maximum "ceiling" fee.

The purpose of this policy is to enable individuals who are not wealthy to adopt, while people who are more affluent offset the difference with their greater fee. Whether to charge a flat rate fee or a sliding scale fee is left up to the policy of each agency.

Sliding scale fees are lawful in every state but Pennsylvania, whose Supreme Court decided such fees were unlawful in a 1986 court case that equated sliding scale fees with a form of baby selling. The Pennsylvania state legislature subsequently banned sliding scale fees.

social workers Men and women trained in the field of social sciences, usually social work specifically, although college graduates in sociology, psychology and other fields may be employed as social workers. (Some social work graduates take umbrage when a person without a social work degree is referred to as a "social worker"; this definition is given in its broadly understood sense.)

Adoption social workers may counsel birthparents, prospective adoptive parents, older children who will be adopted, birth-grandparents and other individuals involved and actively interested in adoption.

Social workers perform home studies of individuals who have applied to adopt a child or children. A HOME STUDY may include group classes, depending on the agency and the situation. The social worker will also visit the home of the prospective parents to interview the adopting parents and verify they would make suitable parents for the child and to ensure the home is safe and relatively clean.

After the child is in the family, follow-up visits to the home are made.

The primary goal of the social worker involved in adoption is to find good families for children and to protect the rights of the children. If a SPECIAL NEEDS adoption is planned, the social worker wants to fully educate the adopting parents so they will understand the needs and problems of the child. The social worker will also often arrange for the adoptive parents to meet the child and will prepare the child prior to the meeting.

Social workers work for both public and private agencies, as well as for lawyers and others doing independent adoptions. Some social workers are self-employed individuals who perform home studies on demand in states that allow it. (Many states require adoption agencies to administer home studies.)

Social workers are also involved in other aspects of child welfare. Protective services social workers remove children from families that are abusive or neglectful; foster care social workers oversee children in foster care; other social workers oversee the cases of individuals receiving Aid to Families with Dependent Children (AFDC) and Medicaid. And there are other types of social workers.

Pay in the professional field of social work is generally modest, and most people who remain in this field are self-motivated and dedicated people who want to make a positive difference in society and people's lives by their help. (See also NATIONAL ASSOCIATION OF SOCIAL WORKERS, INC.)

socioeconomic status Many adopted people are adopted from families with a lower socioeconomic status than the families who adopt them; for example, the birthparents may be both blue collar and lower middle-class people whereas the adoptive family is middle class or even upper class.

Not all birthparents are lower middle class, however, and not all adoptive parents wear "white collars." Many foster parents opt to adopt their foster children, and the average foster parent is a working-class person.

Some birthparents are middle-class or upper-class girls in high school or college who don't wish to parent a child and instead opt to place it for adoption. It is likely they will seek out an agency they feel would place their child with a socioeconomic background similar to their own, and many agencies do such socioeconomic matching.

When agencies allow birthparents to choose adoptive parents from nonidentifying resumes or to meet them, birthparents generally choose a family that is more affluent than their own, wanting "something better" for their child. They are not necessarily seeking a rich family, but they don't want their children to suffer any economic privation.

Studies indicate that socioeconomic status and criminality of adopted individuals are linked inversely: The higher the socioeconomic status of the birthparent and/or the adoptive parent, the lower the probability the child will commit any criminal violations. (See CRIMINAL BEHAVIOR IN ADOPTED PERSONS.)

Many agencies inadvertently screen out poor or working-class applicants for adoption by virtue of the fees they must charge. If a family cannot afford a total fee of $6,000 and up, the agency frequently will not accept their application. As a result, many working-class families give up altogether, while others work two jobs and save their money for years in order to pay for the adoption.

Some agencies, however, will allow these families to make payments on a regular schedule. Still other agencies offer SLIDING SCALE FEES, which are dependent on a percentage of the adopting parents' income.

SPECIAL NEEDS adoptions are usually lower cost than adoptions for healthy white infants, and many agencies are especially willing to work with families in these situations. In addition, state agencies charge minimal or no fees, and often offer SUBSIDIES for adopting special needs children.

Consequently, it is more likely that blue collar workers will adopt older children or children with special needs and white collar and middle-class workers will adopt healthy infants by virtue of the economics of adoption. (See also ADOPTION ASSISTANCE PROGRAM; COSTS TO ADOPT.)

Soundex, International Reunion Registry See INTERNATIONAL SOUNDEX REUNION REGISTRY.

special needs Conditions or characteristics that make a child difficult to place by the state adoption unit or an adoption agency, some of which have nothing to do with the health or temperament of the child. Most agencies consider children and infants who are black or biracial to be children with special needs.

Other categories of special needs include sibling groups, children over age six or eight and children who have been physically or sexually abused, Many children with special needs have lived with foster parents for at least a year, and some social workers consider a child to have a special need simply because he or she has lived in a foster home.

Handicaps Children with special needs may suffer permanent or temporary disabilities, for example, cerebral palsy or a club foot. If the birthmother was a drug or alcohol abuser, her child may have been affected in utero and be a COCAINE BABY or suffer FETAL ALCOHOL SYNDROME. A baby or child born to a mother with AIDS is definitely considered a special needs child. (See DEVELOPMENTAL DISABILITIES.)

Some social workers consider the background of the birthmother in evaluating a child as a potential special needs child, but if the pregnant woman abused alcohol or drugs during her pregnancy, the caseworker may wait until the child is born before making a determination on whether the baby will be categorized as having special needs or not.

In other cases, if the birthmother or birthfather or their parents were schizophrenic, alcoholics, criminals, drug abusers or exhibited other diseases or maladaptive syndromes, the social worker may automatically categorize the child as special needs, based on suspected GENETIC PREDISPOSITION.

Siblings Children with special needs may be healthy physically and mentally but belong to a sibling group. A sibling group of just two siblings will cause the children to be categorized as "special needs," and the more siblings in the family, the more difficult the placement. (See SIBLINGS.)

The reason behind the difficulty in placing the children is that most social workers strive to keep siblings together, believing the trauma they experienced in separating from their birthparents could be unbearably complicated if they are forced to separate from each other. If siblings are sexually or physically abusive with each other, this guideline is relaxed, and siblings are separated.

Many children with special needs are siblings, and consequently, a 10-year-old female and her 12-year-old brother would usually be categorized as special needs because they are siblings as well as because they are over age eight. (Children over age six or eight are considered to have special needs by many states; others raise the age level to age 10 or older, depending on the difficulty in placing the children.)

Teenagers Teenagers are one of the most difficult categories of children to place, yet a suitable family can be found, and many social workers are very successful at finding good homes for adolescents.

In his article, "Born Again Through Adoption," Father Paul Engel, mission director of Downey Side in Springfield, Massachusetts, describes his agency, which was formed in 1967, as "one of the first adolescent adoption agencies in the country."

Says Engel, "We've been involved with well over 1,500 children. The Downey Side credo is that all children need and deserve a permanent home of their own, and that no matter what age a child happens to be, he or she can be adopted into a 'forever family.'"

Parents who adopt older children must understand that the experience of adopting and raising these children will not be the same as adopting an infant, nor will it be the same as adopting the 10-year-old child next door who was always raised in a happy loving home. (See ADJUSTMENT.)

Older children often remember their biological parents and may initially resent being adopted. They may exhibit reclusive behavior or may be unusually clingy with the adoptive parents. They may shun affection or demand it. They will often exhibit behavior considered inappropriate for their age, either too childlike or too adult.

The adoptions of older children are considered a greater risk than adoption of infants, and an estimated 25% to 40% of such placements fail. Studies have revealed, however, that older children who are adopted can adapt very successfully to their new homes. Studies have also found a strong correlation between large families and successful placements. (See MIXED FAMILIES.)

Behavioral Problems The child's own behavior, for example, precocious sexual behavior, aggressive or abusive behavior, chronic bedwetting or other actions that would require a great deal of understanding and adjustment on the part of adoptive parents, could categorize the child as one with special needs.

Foster Children and Developmental Delays Children who are developmentally delayed may or may not "catch up," depending on the situation. Social workers should provide as much information as possible to adopting parents; however, social workers cannot always predict how a child will respond and whether or nor a child's behavior will significantly change. In addition, very often social workers do not have access to information about the child. (See DEVELOPMENTAL DISABILITIES.)

Black and Biracial Children Black and biracial infants and children are considered to have special needs even when they are physically normal and of a normal intelligence. Unfortunately, race alone is often sufficient criteria to categorize these children as having a "special need."

There are apparently not enough black families interested in or aware of the need for families of many black and biracial children, and, as a result, many remain in foster homes until adulthood. Some social workers have strongly suggested that adoptive recruitment efforts in black communities have been woefully inadequate and hypothesize that greater numbers of black families would be interested in adoption if they had information on the need and the children. (See BLACK ADOPTIVE PARENT RECRUITMENT PROGRAMS.)

Many social workers do not wish to place black or biracial children in white homes; however, increasing numbers of adoption agencies and even state agencies are beginning to make these types of placements.

TRANSRACIAL ADOPTION is a hotly disputed topic in the field of social work today, and some families have sued agencies for violating their civil rights by refusing to allow them to adopt black or biracial children. Organizations such as the NATIONAL COALITION TO END RACISM IN AMERICA'S CHILDCARE SYSTEM have formed to fight what they perceive to be racism in adoption and foster care.

Social workers may be more willing to arrange an adoption for a child who is part Asian and part Caucasian or part Hispanic, part Caucasian in a Caucasian home. Policies vary from agency to agency and from state to state.

Children from Other Countries Children adopted through international adoption agencies or private sources may also suffer medical or mental problems and may be classified as special needs, although their disabilities are generally far more severe than an American-born child with special needs.

A child with hepatitis B, tuberculosis or other ailments not commonly found in the United States would be considered a special needs child. A child needing corrective surgery would also be considered to have special needs, for example, a child with a club foot or a cleft palate. If the child remained in the foreign land, this condition might never be corrected, yet the birth defect might be relatively simple for U.S. doctors to correct.

A child from overseas might have parasites, such as lice or scabies, or suffer from chronic diarrhea or other medical problems, but these problems would usually not be considered special needs because they are regarded as temporary and correctable.

Children adopted from other countries may also be categorized as special needs children for the same reasons as U.S. children are so labeled: over age eight, member of a sibling group, mixed-race child, and so on.

Definitions of "Special Needs" Vary
Prospective adoptive parents need to understand that the designation of "special needs" varies from agency to agency and state to state, and a child who is viewed as having a special need in one adoption agency may be perceived as a healthy child by another agency.

Agencies often list categories they consider to be special needs on an adoption application, asking prospective parents to indicate their willingness or unwillingness to accept specific special needs by checking yes, no or maybe for each condition.

In addition, when a pregnant woman states her desire to place her child for adoption, she is questioned closely on medical and possible mental problems in her family background.

A very common misperception about children with special needs dominates the views of many lay people: The average American frequently thinks a child with special needs is one who is profoundly retarded or severely disabled, such as a quadriplegic or a blind child.

Although seriously handicapped children are considered to have a special need, many children who are also considered to have special needs may be intellectually and physically normal. A significant number are "developmentally delayed," which means they are a year or more behind in school and their behavior is not equivalent to what would be expected of a child their chronological age. See ADOPTION ASSISTANCE PROGRAM for the definition of special needs under which such adoptions may be subsidized.

Families Who Adopt Children with Special Needs Barbara Moulden Reid compared and contrasted families who adopt infants with families who adopt children with special needs for her doctoral dissertation.

She found adopters of children with special needs place a greater emphasis on flexibility, patience and motivation to adopt, while those families who adopted healthy white infants greatly stressed the importance of their spousal relationship, a love of children and the desire for parenthood as their main reasons for wanting to adopt.

Families who adopt children with special needs are frequently older, more educated and married longer than the infant adopters. Many agencies have an upper age limit of about age 40 for infant adopters, but the age limit is relaxed considerably for special needs adopters.

Many families who adopt children with special needs already have children, and this experience is seen as a plus by numerous agencies. In contrast, a large number of adoption agencies who work with infant adoptions restrict their applications to childless couples or couples with only one child. Agency practices probably contributed greatly to this difference.

Single people are usually allowed to apply to adopt children with special needs, whereas they are often banned from adopting infants. Many singles have successfully adopted and raised children with special needs; others resent being offered only a child whose needs are complex, believing that a single person would have a harder time caring for a child with serious problems than caring for a healthy infant.

The federal government does partially subsidize the adoption of some special needs children. See ADOPTION ASSISTANCE PROGRAM. (See also ADOPTION ASSISTANCE AND CHILD WELFARE ACT OF 1980; ADOPTIVE PARENTS; DOWN SYNDROME; SIBLINGS; SUPPORT GROUPS; TRANSRACIAL ADOPTION.)

Fr. Paul Engel, "Born Again Through Adoption," *Restoration*, September–October 1988.

Joan Laird and Ann Hartman, editors, *A Handbook of Child Welfare: Context, Knowledge, and Practice* (New York: The Free Press, 1985).

Barbara Moulden Reid, "Characteristics of Families Who Adopt Children with Special Needs (Parenting, Traits)," Ph.D. diss., University of Texas at Austin, 1983.

Katherine A. Nelson, *On the Frontier of Adoption: A Study of Special-Needs Adoptive Families* (Washington, D.C.: Child Welfare League of America, 1985).

Marian Sandmaier, *When Love is Not Enough: How Mental Health Professionals Can Help Special-Needs Adoptive Families* (Washington, D.C.: Child Welfare League of America, 1988).

Stanley v. Illinois. See BIRTHFATHER.

Stars of David Massachusetts-based adoptive support group with over 1,000 members nationwide. Formed by Phyllis Nissen and Rabbi Susan Abramson in 1984, the organization provides a social and educational support group for Jewish and part-Jewish adoptive families and prospective adoptive families. (It is NOT an adoption agency.)

Most members are adoptive parents. Other members include grandparents of adopted children, adult adopted persons and nonwhite biological children.

The organization deals with specific identity issues faced by Jewish families and their adopted children, including such issues as conversion to Judaism, acceptance of the child and adoptive parents by the Jewish community, if, when and how to incorporate the child's biological heritage into the Jewish identity and related issues.

The organizational leaders hope to expand the group by creating more chapters and also by making the Jewish community and especially the synagogue community aware of the group and adoption issues.

For more information, contact

Stars of David
c/o Rabbi Susan Abramson
Temple Shalom Emeth
14–16 Lexington St.
Burlington, MA 01803

state laws See LAWS, STATE.

state social services department The public welfare agency responsible for children in foster care and also responsible for finding adoptive parents for waiting children. Each state has a central social service department that oversees various local or county divisions. Generally, the headquarters of the state social services department is in the state capitol.

It should also be noted that the state social service department's recommendations for changes to adoption law are considered very important by legislators. (See also PROTECTIVE SERVICES.)

statistics A key problem in determining adoption policy is a severe scarcity of numbers to work from. If the scope of adoptions is unknown or unclear, then problems related to adoption cannot be resolved effectively.

The federal government stopped gathering adoption data in 1975, but plans are underway, in response to a mandate of Congress, to create new federal statistical databases on adoption. However, statistics on the numbers of children placed, numbers of waiting children and other critically important numbers are still not collected by the federal government, as of this writing.

When the federal government removed the requirement on states to collect adoption statistics, many states no longer saw such data collection as a high priority and discontinued collecting the statistics. As a result, some states can only provide "best estimates" and piecemeal data on adoption statistics.

The NATIONAL COMMITTEE FOR ADOPTION mounted a serious effort to survey all states and assemble national adoption statistics on a state-by-state basis in 1982 (published in the 1985 *Adoption Factbook*) and again in 1988 (published in the 1989 *Adoption Fact-*

book). The limitations of this survey in each case were that some states provide very accurate data while others can offer only estimates.

In response to intense lobbying, Congress decided adoption data collection should resume and mandated a new system that is planned to begin operation by October 1991.

According to a report issued by the secretary for Health and Human Services in May of 1989, "The principal value of the adoption and foster care data collection system will be to provide comprehensive national information for federal policy purposes.

"Valid, reliable and timely information will be routinely available to assess on a continuing basis the incidence, characteristics, and status of children in adoption and foster care."

Data will be submitted electronically on a quarterly or annual basis to the Administration for Children, Youth, and Families.

One problem for the states to overcome is a lack of uniformity of definitions. Because each state has its own adoption laws as well as unique problems, each has also evolved its own definitions. For example, how states define a "waiting child" varies from state to state. A waiting child may be a child who has been freed for adoption or a child for whom the goal is adoption but who is not free for adoption or other definitions. In some states, parental rights may not be terminated unless a judge is convinced there is a family who will adopt a particular child. Whether or not this child would be considered "waiting" would depend on the definition.

Although public adoptions through the state social services department is readily available data, the problem that must be overcome is data collection on private agency adoptions and independent adoptions. A good amount of data on intercountry adoptions is already available through the efforts of the U.S. IMMIGRATION AND NATURALIZATION SERVICE. Such information will be very valuable to legislators, adoption professionals and child welfare experts.

In addition, by determining how many foster children there are in the system, how many wait to be adopted and other crucial pieces of the statistical puzzle, adoption professionals may more expertly help the children they aspire to serve.

Another aspect of statistics that should be considered is a combination of statistical and methodological failings in many studies related to adoption. Too many social scientists rely on sample sizes of less than 30 on which to base conclusions that are generalized to extremely large populations.

Studies of small and highly specialized samples and their data should always be interpreted with caution, especially if percentages are prominently cited. In addition, the interpretation of data may be skewed, depending on the researchers and their possible biases.

One need not be a statistician to be a critical reviewer of studies related to adoption. Although no study can be perfect and it cannot be expected that they will be, it is important for readers to understand that just because a study was performed by a prominent person does not mean it is a valid or reliable study.

The good news is that most social scientists who study adoption are careful researchers who do outstanding studies that can be replicated and that are very useful to the adoption community.

The bad news in statistics is that it is unlikely the federal government will comply with the intent of Congress. The 1991 target date for initiating adoption data collection in an operational system will probably not be met, and further congressional action may be required to prod federal and state agencies into responding adequately.

National Committee For Adoption, *Adoption Factbook* (Washington, D.C.: National Committee For Adoption, 1985).

———, *Adoption Factbook* (Washington, D.C.: National Committee For Adoption, 1989).

stepparents According to Census Bureau figures released in 1989, the number of stepparent households increased by 11.6% from 1980 to 1985, and the number of children living with both biological parents fell.

Nearly 6.8 million children lived with a stepparent in 1985. About 39.5 million children lived with both parents, down from 37.2 million in 1980.

Most stepchildren lived with a biological mother and a stepfather, and the Census Bureau found only about 11% of stepchildren lived with a biological father and stepmother in 1985.

Some stepparents adopt their spouse's children. In such adoptions, a home study may not be required, depending on state laws.

There has been a surprising lack of research performed on stepparent adoptions despite the increasing numbers of stepparent relationships. A 1988 doctoral dissertation in psychology was researched and written by Elizabeth Heiss on this subject, concentrating on stepfather attitudes toward adoption in their first year of marriage to the child's mother.

Heiss reported on 58 white middle-class stepfathers. Of these, 43 expressed an attitude for or against adopting their stepchildren: 10 stated they had a favorable attitude toward adoption, 18 did not wish to adopt, and the remaining 15 stated they would like to adopt their stepchildren but believed it would be impossible.

Differences were found between the groups; for example, the stepfathers in the "positive" group (wishing to adopt) had a closer and more parental relationship than did the other stepfathers. In addition, the biological father apparently had a weaker relationship with the children than in the groups that did not wish to adopt or felt they could not adopt. Each group stated the importance of the biological father's role in affecting their attitudes towards adoption.

No differences were found between the groups in the quality of the marriage or the age or sex of the children.

A 1987 study of 55 stepparents who had adopted their stepchildren indicated three primary reasons for the adoption. These were to change the name of the child, as a result of the adopted child's positive relationship with the stepparent and a desire for stability.

An earlier (1984) Ph.D. dissertation in psychology by Carrie Fancett studied predictors of satisfaction with the stepparent relationship among adolescents. Key factors determining the adolescents' attitudes toward stepparents were whether or not the adolescent believed the stepparent was interested in listening to him or her, whether the religion was the same or not, the frequency of communication between stepparent and stepchild, the stepchild's view of the marital relationship between the parent and the stepparent and other factors.

Factors found not significant were differing views toward discipline by parent and stepparent, contact with the biological parent, the adoption "orientation" (whether adoption was a possible consideration) and the relationship with half-siblings who lived in the household. Fancett recommended an emphasis on "the role that empathy and perception of shared stress play in the adjustment of teenage stepchildren to their stepparents."

Carrie Susan Fancett, "Predictors of Adolescent Stepchildren's Satisfaction with Their Stepparents," Ph.D. diss. University of South Carolina, 1984.

Elizabeth Gwen Heiss, "Stepfather Attitudes Toward Stepparent Adoption During the First Year of Remarriage," Ph.D. diss., Temple University, 1988.

P. A. Wolf and E. Mast, "Counseling Issues in Adoptions by Stepparents," *Social Work*, 32:1(1987): 69–74.

subsidies See ADOPTION ASSISTANCE PROGRAM.

success rates The other side of the coin to rates of DISRUPTION, or adoption failures. The overwhelming number of adoptions are successful, particularly placements of infants.

The adoption of children with SPECIAL NEEDS is successful in the majority of cases as well. (See DISRUPTION for more data).

According to a 1988 article in *Child Welfare* by Joan Ferry DiGiulio, one important criteria agencies should consider in selecting adoptive parents because it does affect the success of an adoption is the ability of the adopting parents to accept the child as a separate person. In addition, DiGiulio hypothesizes that a prospective adoptive parent's own self-acceptance is an important criteria in determining whether or not the parent can recognize the child's separateness.

In her study, she further hypothesized that the higher the score of an adoptive parent on a self-acceptance scale, the correspondingly higher the score on a parental acceptance of child scale.

Studying 80 couples who had adopted children under age three and whose children averaged nine years at the time of the study, the scales were administered.

The conclusion: "The study discovered that high self-acceptance of adoptive parents influenced high parental acceptance of the child."

The author concluded, "The importance of self-acceptance of adoptive parents can be stressed in the training of adoption professionals, who might then be more aware of the existence or absence of this trait in potential adoptive families." (See also DISSOLUTION.)

Joan Ferry DiGiulio, "Self-Acceptance: A Factor in the Adoption Process," *Child Welfare,* 67(September–October 1988): 423–429.

support groups Groups formed to help others with a similar interest or problem; also called mutual aid groups. There are adoptive parent support groups, adopted adult support groups and birthparent support groups.

The largest adoptive parent support group in the United States is the Minneapolis, Minnesota-based ADOPTIVE FAMILIES OF AMERICA (AFA), which has almost 15,000 members nationwide. (The former name of AFA was OURS.) It is impossible to determine the exact number of support groups existing nationwide, but virtually every state in the United States has at least one ongoing and active group.

Support groups are usually nonprofit organizations that may number their membership in the thousands or hundreds or may be just a handful of individuals who come together to form their group.

Some adoptive parent groups concentrate on the adoption of children with special needs, others are oriented more toward foreign adoption or infant adoption, and still others attempt to cover all ages and types of adoption.

Adoptive parent groups can be extremely helpful as information providers to prospective adoptive parents. People who have already adopted can advise them on agencies, attorneys and such issues as what a home study is really like and also can allay many of their fears about adoption.

The average person considering adoption has no idea where to turn for information, and usually friends and relatives are equally uninformed or baffled by the subject. As a result, support groups fill critical information voids.

After the adoption has taken place, other adoptive parents can provide advice and information to assist new adoptive parents through adjustment problems they may face.

Most groups are very aware of adoption issues and current federal and state legislation on adoption and keep their members informed on the latest adoption current events.

Actual lobbying of their state and federal legislators on adoption issues is another goal of many support groups, and groups have succeeded in convincing legislators at every level to pass a broad array of bills supporting adoption.

Support groups composed primarily of adopted adults or birthparents are also interested in legislation, and some actively lobby for OPEN RECORDS.

Most adoptive parent groups maintain a regular contact with their local adoption agencies and attorneys and build up a camaraderie between social workers and adopting parents. Groups invite social workers and attorneys to speak at meetings, and many plan an annual informational meeting when a variety of child-placing experts attend and explain their policies and the guidelines to follow in applying for a child.

Another goal of many adoptive parent support groups is to assist adoption agencies in recruiting adoptive parents for children with SPECIAL NEEDS. Some also raise money to buy food and clothing for foreign children and Christmas presents for foster children, and they perform other charitable activities.

Groups that concentrate on the adoption of children with special needs or larger groups that attempt to encompass all forms of adoption may assist local social services departments; for example, some groups will drive foster children who are legally ready to be adopted to a photographer to have their pictures taken for the state's WAITING CHILD PHOTOLISTING. Others actually VIDEOTAPE waiting children, and tapes are shown to prospective parents.

Reasons for Joining Support Groups
People who are in the process of adopting primarily join an adoptive parent group to learn and to obtain information and moral support. They often feel very anxious about identifying a good agency or attorney.

If they are in the midst of their home study, they may be concerned about whether or not they will ever "pass" the home study and be able to successfully adopt a child. Other members who have successfully adopted build their confidence and hope.

Often the relatives of an adopting family may be very nonsupportive and urge them to drop the idea of adoption altogether; consequently, the support group serves as a kind of family.

Members who already have adopted may join a support group because they want to adopt more children via a different method than they previously used; for example, they may wish to adopt through an agency although their first child came to them through an INDEPENDENT ADOPTION. Or they may wish to adopt internationally after already adopting an American-born child.

Some members join because they believe in adoption as a positive concept, and they wish to help others. They may also wish for their children to have the chance to meet and socialize with others who were adopted.

Support groups can be a good resource for adopted children, giving them an opportunity to meet other adopted children. This is especially important for families who have adopted children from other cultures, although all children can gain reassurance from learning that adoption is a good way to form a family. In addition, support groups can provide information on adoption issues, thus helping both adoptive families and their children.

Adopted adults or birthparents most often join a support group because they wish to meet other adopted adults or birthparents, especially those who have completed a successful SEARCH. They may wish to learn how to locate a birthparent or adopted person as well as hear about the experiences of others who have located birthparents or adopted persons, and they may also be searching for a biological sibling or other birth relatives in addition or instead of the birthparents. They may desire the moral support and camaraderie of people who share a common bond of adoption.

Adopted adults may wish to have a voice in lobbying state and federal legislators on a variety of adoption issues. (See ADOPTEES' LIBERTY MOVEMENT ASSOCIATION; AMERICAN ADOPTION CONGRESS.)

Most parent groups produce a monthly, bimonthly or quarterly newsletter offering information on children newly adopted by members, articles written by adoptive parents or adoption experts and information about upcoming events. The newsletter serves to inform and also to reinforce the importance of adoption to its members.

To locate the nearest adoptive parent support group, individuals should contact their state adoption office or national organizations, such as AFA or RESOLVE. Adopted adults should also contact their state social services office or adoption agency as well as national organizations, such as the American Adoption Congress or Adoptees' Liberty Movement Association. Birthparents may wish to contact the state social services office and local agencies as well as national organizations, such as CONCERNED UNITED BIRTHPARENTS.

surrender Refers to the voluntary act of TERMINATION OF PARENTAL RIGHTS to an agency or a court. Once the parental rights of a person are officially transferred to either an agency, attorney or other intermediary as allowed by state law, the child may be placed into an adoptive family within the limits of state laws.

This term has fallen out of favor with adoption advocates, who believe it has a negative connotation. Some adoption critics, however, purposely use the word to stress a negative message, for example, "I surrendered a child to adoption" rather than "I planned adoption" or the more neutral, "I placed a child for adoption."

surrogate motherhood Generally refers to the practice of hiring a fertile woman who agrees to become impregnated, usually through artificial insemination, and agrees ahead of time to give the child to the infant's biological father and his wife, according to terms of a contract signed before the woman becomes pregnant. The impregnated woman is called the "surrogate mother," although technically, it is the intended mother who is more accurately described as a "surrogate."

It is estimated that as many as 1,200 children may have been born to surrogate mothers with such a contractual arrangement since 1980.

In some very limited cases, a woman who is capable of producing ova but who cannot carry a child may opt to use a surrogate to carry a child with her genes as well as those of her husband. This is possible through modern reproductive techniques, such as embryo transfer. (See also REPRODUCTIVE TECHNOLOGIES.)

In such a case the surrogate would have no genetic link to the child; however, in the overwhelming number of cases, the surrogate does contribute her genes to the child.

Surrogacy has been practiced since Biblical times, but only recently has surrogate motherhood become a means for wealthy infertile couples to gain a "genetic link" to a child.

Most surrogate mothers receive income for their "services": at least $10,000 upon relinquishment of the child. If the surrogate does not become pregnant, she usually receives nothing. If she becomes pregnant but miscarries, she may receive a partial payment.

It is this aspect of surrogacy that most concerns those who disapprove of surrogacy: the money. Critics feel that planning to bear a child for a couple (or single person) in exchange for large sums of money is baby selling and should be banned.

As a result, at least nine states have banned commercial surrogacy, although one state, Nevada, has declared commercial surrogacy legal.

Surrogacy opponents are also concerned about the mother's right to change her mind about releasing the baby after the child's birth. They argue that she should have the same right to choose to parent the child as she would if she were a mother considering placing her child for adoption.

The "Father" of Surrogate Motherhood Michigan attorney Noel Keane developed the first contracts for surrogacy in 1976, and by 1988 Keane had arranged 302 births. According to *The Detroit News,* "One-third of all babies born through Keane contracts leave the United States. Many go to Germany.''

Keane also handled the first embryo transfer surrogacy, wherein a woman carried the genetic child of another woman and man. That child, implanted by Dr. Wolf Utian of the Mt. Sinai Medical Center in Cleveland, was delivered in 1986. According to *The Detroit News,* Dr. Utian did not realize the mother was a paid surrogate.

Numerous lawsuits have been filed in surrogacy cases. The most famous suit was the "Baby M" case between surrogate mother Mary Beth Whitehead and the people with whom she originally arranged to give her baby, William and Elizabeth Stern.

In this case, heard by the courts in 1987, the Sterns hired Mary Beth Whitehead to be a surrogate mother.

After Ms. Whitehead bore the child, she changed her mind about giving the baby to the Sterns, asked for the child back and ran away with the baby to Florida. Private detectives for the Sterns found Ms. Whitehead, and she was returned to New Jersey.

A lower court awarded custody of the child to the Sterns and made Mrs. Stern an adoptive mother. The New Jersey Supreme Court overturned the adoption in May of 1988 but left custody of the child with the Sterns. Whitehead was allowed visitation rights.

In a case reported by *The Detroit News,* a surrogate mother delivered twins, a boy and a girl, but the biological father wished to only parent the girl. The boy remained in foster care for a week, when the surrogate mother decided she wanted the child back and also sought custody of his sister. She won her case. This issue of the negative impact on siblings is another reason many critics oppose surrogacy arrangements. In addition, because most surrogates already have children, surrogacy usually separates siblings.

In a California case in 1990, a woman agreed to bear the genetic child of a couple. (The wife could create ova but could not carry a child.) The surrogate mother, who some groups have referred to as the "gestational mother" because she gave no genetic material to the child, sued for custody, arguing that she was a birthmother. The genetic parents prevailed.

Author Natalie Loder Clark has argued that surrogacy cases should be considered in the same light as paternity cases. She believes the paternity settlement contract can serve as a temporary solution to disputes in surrogacy cases until state legislatures can determine for themselves what legal changes to make.

According to Clark, the biological father and the surrogate mother have similar problems and risks of unwed parents or parents who are no longer married.

Problems with Surrogacy Most people who are worried about surrogate parent agreements are concerned that no one will want the child if it is handicapped and the child will become a ward of the state. This problem has occurred.

In addition, the potential emotional problems resulting from surrogacy are a concern to those opposed to the practice. One area of concern is the reaction of siblings to the child of the surrogate who then leaves the home. Psychologist Reuben Pannor says surrogates have contacted him about this problem.

According to an article in *The Detroit News,* "Pannor says more than two dozen surrogates have contacted him through his national counseling network.

" 'The thing that brought most of them in is their other children,' Pannor said. 'They began to develop serious problems: school phobias, unwillingness to leave their mother, nightmares, fear of leaving the house. They're deathly afraid that someone is going to take them away.' "

Another concern of surrogacy opponents is that there is no screening for people who wish to hire surrogate mothers nor is there any required screening of the surrogates. In addition, those who arrange surrogate contracts are unregulated and may be housewives, attorneys, social workers or anyone else. Beauticians need state licenses, they argue, but people who arrange births and transfers of infants need no licenses or required training.

In May of 1988, the Child Welfare League of America board found that surrogacy was not in the best interests of a child. According to an article in *Children's Voice,* "In order to minimize the opportunity for confusion in the child's lifelong relationships with his/her parents, the use of surrogacy which involves a third party in conception and birth, cannot be viewed in the best interests of children, and, therefore, cannot be supported."

In 1984 the National Committee For Adoption became the first organization to take a stand against surrogate motherhood. The group has been a vocal opponent of the practice itself and of the implications of surrogacy for adoption policy.

Surrogacy Versus Adoption The primary difference between surrogacy and adoption is that in nonrelative adoptions, the adoptive father is not the biological father nor has he contracted to create a child. In fact, if a man hired a woman to bear a child by another man for him, such an act would be illegal baby buying. Surrogacy is a planned pregnancy, usually for money; adoption is a humanitarian solution to an unplanned pregnancy.

Another difference is that every state has an adoption law, but laws on surrogacy are still evolving. In addition, in every state, if a woman in a crisis pregnancy who is considering adoption for her baby changes her mind about adoption before she signs consent (or within a certain timeframe of signing consent, depending on state law), she may legally choose to parent her baby.

Arguments in Favor of Surrogacy Advocates of surrogacy believe it is unfair for the government to interfere with individuals and their private behavior and argue that surrogacy and procreation should not be restricted. Some civil libertarians agree with this argument.

They also argue that even if surrogacy were completely banned, individuals would still arrange such contracts, albeit illegally.

In addition, supporters of surrogacy believe that if a person strongly desires a genetic link to his child and a fertile woman agrees to bear the child, then the surrogacy should proceed. They believe the surrogate mother is well-compensated for her services and see the situation as a "win-win" experience for both sides.

Arguments Against Surrogacy Critics argue that rich people are buying babies from poor women, and if the hourly rate is computed as a wage, the woman earns far less than the minimum wage. She also experiences the discomforts and the risks of pregnancy.

Critics dislike the idea of splitting half-siblings (in many cases, the surrogate already has a healthy child, which theoretically proves she is fertile). But the child she bears for surrogacy will in virtually all cases never know the children she parents.

In a 1987 doctoral dissertation, Daniela Rodda Roher studied the nature of surrogate motherhood and found a "lack of clarity in defining the social and reproductive roles of the people involved in surrogacy practices."

According to Roher, this ambiguity about their roles was especially apparent in the surrogates' presumptions about their roles and the roles of the others involved in the agreement.

Says Roher, "The figure of the surrogate mother appears to be anomalous, partaking of characteristics typical of other female reproductive and sexual roles, e.g., 'mother,' 'wife,' 'virgin,' and 'prostitute,' yet not fully belonging in any of them."

Roher says this ambiguous position "contributes to the maintenance of a socially and psychologically disturbing role."

Feminists are not united on the surrogacy issue. Some are very opposed, believing surrogacy is exploitation, but others are supportive, believing a woman has the right to choose what to do with her own body, including bearing a child for another person.

Lori B. Andrews, "Alternative Reproduction and the Law of Adoption," in *Adoption Law and Practice* (New York: Matthew Bender, 1988).

Natalie Loder Clark, "New Wine in Old Skins: Using Paternity-Suit Settlements to Facilitate Surrogate Motherhood," *Journal of Family Law*, 25:3(1986–87): 483–527.

"CWLA Board Finds Surrogacy Is Not in Best Interest of Children," *Children's Voice,* May 1988, 1.

Noel Keane and Dennis L. Breo, *The Surrogate Mother* (New York: Everest House, 1981).

Karen Lynn Migdal, "An Exploratory Study of Women's Attitudes After Completion of a Surrogate Mother Program," Ph.D. diss., University of Southern California, 1988.

William Pierce, "Survey of State Activity Regarding Surrogate Motherhood," *Family Law Reporter,* January 29, 1985.

Rebecca Powers and Sheila Gruber Belloli, "The Baby Business: Mothers and Other Strangers," special report to *The Detroit News,* September 20, 1989.

Rebecca Powers and Sheila Gruber Belloli, "The Baby Business: Shattered Dreams," special report to *The Detroit News,* September 17, 1989, 1C–4C.

Rebecca Powers and Sheila Gruber Belloli, "The Baby Business: Surrogacy's Big Daddy," special report to *The Detroit News,* September 19, 1989, 1G–3G.

Daniela Rodda Roher, "Surrogate Motherhood: The Nature of a Controversial Practice," Ph.D. diss., Wayne State University, 1987.

T

targeted adoption See DESIGNATED ADOPTION; OPEN ADOPTION; TRADITIONAL ADOPTION.

teachers and adopted children Some adoptive parents feel teachers, as part of society, may be biased against adopted children and recommend teachers not be told children are adopted unless absolutely necessary. Others disagree, particularly when older children are adopted. They believe a teacher needs to understand if a child has had problems in the past.

Researchers and authors Ruth G. McRoy and Louis A. Zurcher Jr. reported that sometimes teachers bend over backwards to be overly-nice to transracially adopted children. Said the authors,

"Overenthusiastic acceptance of the black child into the classroom has been characterized as discriminatory by some transracial adoptive parents. In such instances, the teacher has reduced performance demands for the black child while keeping those standards high for the white child. This behavior is likely to occur in situations in which the teacher has had very little, if any, experience teaching black students."

An excessive concern for the adopted students is not unique to black adopted children.

A 1987 doctoral dissertation by Lynn Friedman Kessler at the Fielding Institute was a study of school teachers and their attitudes towards 121 Caucasian preschool adopted children.

The study was intended not only to study the attitudes and possible biases of teachers but also to determine if attitudes affected evaluations of attractiveness, whether the child should be punished for misbehavior and how severely and other factors.

Kessler presented vignettes and photographs, and teachers were told children were adopted or nonadopted. Children were described as misbehaving in a major or minor way.

Findings indicated the teachers' attitudes about children were primarily affected by their described behavior and the perception of the child's aggressiveness and "callousness."

But the findings also revealed teachers frequently reacted to a child's adoptive status in relation to gender, physical attractiveness and the degree of the described misbehavior.

In addition, the perceived attractiveness, aggressiveness and intensity of punishment recommended by the teachers were all related to a child's adoptive status.

Kessler had hypothesized that teachers, as part of society, would react more negatively to adopted children than to nonadopted children. To her surprise, she found teachers reacted more positively to adopted children.

Said Kessler, "Teachers perceive an adopted child performing severe harmdoing as *less aggressive* than a non-adopted child performing severe harmdoing. Even more surprisingly, teachers do not identify the adopted child performing severe harmdoing as significantly more aggressive than the adopted child performing mild harmdoing."

Kessler interpreted her results to mean that teachers are still reacting to negative stereotypes about adoption but are bending over backwards to be nice to the child.

Said Kessler, "A possible interpretation for this finding is that teachers are reacting to certain aspects of the adoptedness stigma and stereotype which cause them to perceive the adopted child as pathetic rather than 'bad' (as originally predicted)."

Another finding was in relation to perception of attractiveness: The adopted child in the vignette who was described as performing some severe harmdoing was seen as more attractive than the nonadopted child doing the same thing.

Kessler also found the nonadopted girl was judged more harshly by the teachers, who saw her as more "callous" than the adopted girl, despite the degree of severity of harm.

In addition, the adopted male child was viewed as more callous than the adopted female child. Unsure how to interpret this data, Kessler said it may have occurred because of a preference for female adopted children versus male adopted children.

Psychologist Janet Hoopes believes adopted children may exhibit behavioral problems in school. She based her opinion on teacher ratings.

"In the course of my longitudinal research on adopted children, it became apparent to me that although adopted children, compared to a matched sample of biological children, did not manifest significantly more emotional problems or identity problems, they did manifest some subtle problems in school according to teacher ratings." (Hoopes did not think teachers were biased in their ratings.)

Studying 100 adopted children ages 10 to 15 and comparing them to biological children, she found no significant differences in IQ, personality or achievement. The one significant area of difference was in the ratings by teachers. Her findings: "The adopted child did not quite measure up to the comparison child, or, in other words, was not doing as well in school as might be expected on the basis of ability."

Early parental expectations were also negatively related to the child's later performance in school. "These findings clearly suggest that unduly high expectations of adoptive couples for the intellectual endowment of the adopted child are associated with later negative attitudes toward school (as rated by teachers) on the part of the adoptive child."

On the plus side, Hoopes found adopted children were accepted by peers. In addition, the rates of children referred for special class (learning-disabled) placement was about 10% versus 10% to 14% in the nonadopted school population.

Hoopes also discussed the societal bias against adoption. "Reflecting upon the attitude of the general public toward adoption, one 15 ½ year old boy in my recent study with Stein . . . on identity in the adopted adolescent poignantly stated, "It's not adoption that is the problem, but what other people think of adopted kids. They're always shown in movies as 'the druggie.' "

The implications for adoptive parents and social workers based on the studies are that it appears inadvisable to inform a teacher about a child's adoptive status unless necessary in order to ensure any unconscious biases about adoption will not interfere with the child's school experience.

If the child is of another race, such information is unavoidable; however, if the child is of the same race as the adoptive parents, and especially if the child was adopted as an infant or before beginning school, then his or her adoptive status need not be shared with teachers.

Although adopted children may be treated more leniently, such leniency is still unequal, an aspect children quickly pick up on. Dr. Hoopes said adoptive parents' expectations might be too high, and perhaps in some cases, teachers' expectations of adopted children are too low.

There is also the issue of positive bias among teachers; for example, many expect every Asian-born child to excel at math and science, based on stereotypical attitudes in the U.S. media.

It is clear more research needs to be conducted on this issue to determine if there are other factors that may affect teachers' perceptions of adopted children.

It is also important to note that many segments of society have evinced baises toward adopted children, and teachers are by no means unique if they are indeed biased. In addition, it's highly likely that as society becomes more understanding and accepting of adoption, so will teachers and other categories of professionals.

Janet L. Hoopes, Ph.D., "Psychologist Sees Adopted Children at Risk for Learning Disabilities," *Hilltop Spectrum,* Hill Top Preparatory School, Rosemont, Pennsylvania, June 1986, 1–4.

Lynn Friedman Kessler, "The Measurement of Teachers' Attitudes Toward Adopted Children," Ph.D. diss., Fielding Institute, 1987.

Ruth G. McRoy and Louis A. Zurcher Jr., *Transracial and Inracial Adoptees: The Adolescent Years* (Springfield, Ill.: Thomas, 1983).

teenage adopted persons See ADOLESCENT ADOPTED PERSONS.

teenage parents About 300,000 unmarried teenagers gave birth in 1987, according to figures provided by the National Center for Health Statistics. An estimated 5% of teenage mothers place their infants for adoption.

About one-third of all births to teenagers are to married teenagers, and consequently, the children from these births are often planned and can be considered socially beneficial. According to a report on "Wanted and Unwanted Childbearing" by the National Center for Health Statistics, married teenage women in 1982 had the highest rate of wanted births of all ages of mothers: 95%.

In considering wanted versus unwanted births among unwed teenagers, the National Center for Health Statistics found 24.4% stated they had not wanted a child at the time of conception. (The highest rate reported was the rate for black teenage girls—31.8%.)

The National Center for Health Statistics also reports on birth or "natality" rates. According to the National Center for Health Statistics' natality information on 1988 (the latest information as of this writing), the birth rate for women ages 15–17 years was 33.8 births per 1,000 in 1988, higher than in any year since 1977 (33.9).

Studies of Teenage Mothers One study revealed that some teenagers purposely became pregnant, which seems likely given the fact that so many teenagers have reported that the child was wanted at conception. Allan F. Abramse, Peter A. Morrison and Linda J. Waite reported their findings.

The researchers asked high school sophomores if they would consider having a child out of wedlock. The researchers found 41% of the black girls, 29% of the Hispanic respondents and 23% of the non-Hispanic whites said they would consider bearing a child while single. They followed up the students two years later and found that many of the girls who had said they would consider having a child did in fact have a child.

The researchers also considered the girls' "parenthood risk," taking into account factors such as socioeconomic background, race and living in a family headed by a female.

Over the next two years following the survey, the women who said they were interested or willing to become single mothers were much more likely to have already become single mothers.

Said the researchers, "In the group at highest risk, levels of childbearing were at least twice as high among those who had said they were willing than among the unwilling—29 percent compared with 14 percent among blacks, 20 percent compared with five percent among Hispanics and six percent vs. two percent among whites."

The researchers also found girls exhibiting problem behavior, such as cutting classes and causing disciplinary problems, were more likely to consider single parenting.

"Forty-one percent of whites with a high problem-behavior score expressed such willingness, compared with only 18 percent of those who scored low; among black respondents, the comparable proportions are 4 percent and 40 percent."

Depression was another factor in choosing to become a parent, and the authors stated, "Young white respondents who had felt depressed more than once in the preceding month were almost twice as likely to have been willing to consider single parenthood as were young women who reported no such instances of depression (30 percent compared with 17 percent)."

Many teenagers who become parents have difficulty completing high school, although the numbers who are graduating have increased in recent years. According to information provided by Child Trends Inc., "Among women in their twenties who had their first child at age 17 or younger, the proportion who graduated from high school was 19% in 1958, 29% in 1975, and 56% in 1986. Among women in their twenties who were aged 20–24 when their first child was born, 81% had graduated in 1958, 89% in 1975, and 91% in 1986." (This data included *both* married and unmarried teenagers. Presumably, it would be more difficult to parent a child as a single teen—whether that child was planned or not planned—than as a married teen parenting a child she strongly desired.)

Single teenage parents are also likely to bear more than one child out of wedlock. According to the authors of *Crisis of Adolescence: Teenage Pregnancy*, one study of 100 girls who were pregnant out of wedlock by the age of 15 revealed the group averaged 3.4 births before they were 20 years old. (Most of these were out of wedlock.) Only five of the girls had no repeat pregnancies by age 20.

Say the authors, "The high incidence of repeat pregnancies may suggest that there are psychological determinants along with social and economic factors. These girls were unable to develop beyond the level of immaturity that had made them vulnerable to an untimely pregnancy."

This data is apparently somewhat supported by an earlier study by Kathleen Ford of the Family Growth Survey unit. According to Ford's 1981 study, women who are under age 21 at the time of the birth of their first child have a 9% probability of having more children, women who are ages 21 to 23 have a 7% chance and women 24 years and over have a 5% chance of bearing more children.

Problems of Pregnant and Parenting Teenagers Single teens may also face an array of problems beyond parenting their children. A study of pregnant teens and teenage mothers in California revealed the several problems. According to *Youth Law News*, housing was the most serious problem, and "estimates of the proportion of minors with housing problems ranged from nearly zero in some counties to as high as 88%."

It was discovered that public housing was rarely an option for pregnant and parenting teenagers.

"Most who knew the policy in their areas stated that applications from minors were not accepted by housing authorities, although approximately half of those noted that an exception was made for emancipated minors. Many respondents noted that public housing waiting lists were so long as to make the option virtually non-existent for adults as well as minors."

Other problems included health care and the difficulty involved in applying for state assistance (Medi-Cal) as well as difficulties and confusion surrounding federal public assistance programs, such as Aid to Families with Dependent Children.

Teenagers in the U.S. today are seldom psychologically ready and very young teens are not physically suited for childbirth. Many teenagers do not obtain sufficient, or in some cases any, prenatal care, and as a result the pregnancy depletes their still-growing bodies and often deprives the fetus of valuable nutrients.

According to the National Center for Health Statistics, 13.7% of the teenage mothers under age 15 gave birth to infants of low birthweight (less than 5 pounds, 8 ounces, or less than 2,500 grams). This is the greatest percentage of low birthweights of any age group. Girls ages 15 to 19 had an overall risk rate of 9.3%, with the highest risk at age 15 years (11.5%) and declining thereafter to 8.5% having low birthweight babies at age 19. (The next highest risk rate, after teenage mothers, was mothers over age 45, who experienced 8% of all their births as low birthweight births.)

Studies performed by the National Center for Health Statistics reveal that an estimated two-thirds of pregnant teens receive no prenatal care in the first trimester of pregnancy, a critical time in fetal development.

Some teenage mothers are actually foster children themselves. The state social worker may try to place the teenage mother and her baby in the same home or may feel it would be better to place the infant in a separate foster home.

In some cases, parental rights of the teenage mother will be terminated, and the child will be placed for adoption. However, in most cases, the infant will remain in foster care until the teenager is 18 years old. At that time, the case may be re-evaluated, and her child may be placed with her, continue in foster care or be placed for adoption.

Some schools provide daycare for teenage mothers at the school. This issue is controversial because of the cost, the feasibility and many other factors.

Adoption and Teenage Parents Adoption is not a popular choice among most pregnant teenagers who continue their pregnancies. Reasons behind an apparent aversion to considering adoption include lack of pregnancy counseling by a person who is knowledgeable and positive about adoption, social pressure from parents and peers who are opposed to adoption, a desire to be loved by the infant and fill a void in the birthmother's emotional life, an attempt by the birthmother to induce a commitment from the birthfather and a variety of other reasons.

As a result, the majority of teenage mothers choose single parenthood over adoption. In some cases, the teenager's own parents may raise the teenager and her child, and the grandparents' relationship with the child is more parental than grandparental.

Although many teenagers reject adoption as a viable choice for their infants, some teenagers do actually make an adoption plan for their infants. More teenagers might choose this option if it were explored with them by counselors.

Edmund Mech, Ph.D., in a study for the ADOLESCENT FAMILY LIFE PROGRAM, researched pregnancy counselors and their presentations of adoption and found that often pregnancy counselors do not stress adoption as a valid option even when the counselor believes adoption is a choice that should be considered. The reason adoption is not mentioned or is skimmed over is the counselor's belief that teenagers do not wish to hear about adoption.

In fact, the teenager may be very interested in adoption but fear bringing up the subject with a counselor, feeling that people who "give up" their babies must not love them or that the counselor would think less of her if she should broach the subject.

Steven D. McLaughlin of the Battelle Human Affairs Research Center in Seattle, Washington did a comprehensive comparison of adolescent mothers who chose parenthood versus adolescents who placed their infants for adoption.

He found the "economic well-being" of "parenters" to be less than those women who chose adoption.

Says the author, "even after controlling for background characteristics, current employment status, and living arrangements (in particular, the presence of pre-school children in the household), relinquishment decision remains an important factor underlying the large difference in the per capita incomes of the two groups."

Characteristics of Teenage Mothers The following is an encapsulated profile of teenage girls who become pregnant and make adoption choices:

- Race. Black teenage girls are five times more likely to have babies out of wedlock than are white teenagers. According to a *Wall Street Journal* article, in one community in Los Angeles, 25% of the high school girls bear children. An estimated 80% of the black children of Watts in Los Angeles are born to single parents.

  Few black girls choose adoption for their babies, and if they do, they find their newborn infants will be categorized as children with "special needs." Black and biracial children are considered "hard-to-place" by some adoption agencies, who state they do not receive sufficient adoption applications from black parents.

  An informal system of adoption may prevail among black families; instead of planning adoption for her child via an adoption agency or an attorney, a black mother may opt to let her mother, sister or another female relative or friend raise the child.

- Socioeconomic status. Teenagers who become pregnant span the socioeconomic class structure; however, researchers have found a distinct difference in socioeconomic status between teens who choose to parent their babies and teens who opt for adoption.

  A study by Michael D. Resnick at the University of Minnesota revealed that "placers" tend to come from more affluent homes than those girls who opt for single parenthood. Teenage parents were more likely to have dropped out of school than girls who made an adoption plan for their children.

- Sexual abuse. Some teenagers who become pregnant have suffered a history of sexual abuse. The Resnick study revealed that 23% of the teenage girls had been sexually abused and 38% had been physically abused. As for the placers, 30% had been sexually abused and 28% had been physically abused.

- Peers who became pregnant. Many teenagers who become pregnant already have friends who were or are pregnant. In the Resnick study, 72% of the placers and 92% of the parents stated they had friends who were under 18 years of age when they became pregnant.

- Desire to be pregnant. The Resnick study also revealed that significant numbers of the pregnant teens became pregnant by design. Half the teen parents and 20% of the placers planned the pregnancy. Of those who planned the pregnancy, the prevailing reason was that the girl wanted to have a baby or both the girl and her boyfriend desired an infant, 7% wanted to be loved by the baby, and another 7% wanted to become pregnant to spite their parents. Also, 21% thought a pregnancy would help them hold on to their boyfriends.

Some teenagers forego birth control in the hope that they will become pregnant. Others are too fatalistic and with such low self-esteem that they feel they should not use birth control and will instead trust in fate.

The teenage mother may feel starved for love and affection and presume the infant will fulfill her emotional needs. The pregnancy may not have been an accident and in some circles is a badge of honor and symbol of adulthood, particularly in lower socioeconomic strata.

The pregnant teenager may presume that a baby of her own will make her an adult and provide her with the privileges of adulthood. In her attempt to separate from her own parents, she often does not realize the infant will burden her even more than her parents' restrictions.

The media's depiction of beautiful and independent women may also have an impact on the teenagers view of single parenthood. Most single parents on TV soap operas live in opulent circumstances and are well-dressed and healthy. They are seldom renounced by their parents and thrown out into the street, although some pregnant teenagers today do face such an appalling scenario.

Many teenage girls fantasize that the baby will bring them closer to the baby's father, and they envision marriage and a happy home in a vague but rose-colored setting. The reality rarely matches the fantasy.

Teenage Birthfathers Although very few well-designed studies have been made of teenage fathers of infants placed for adoption, interest appears to be on the rise, and more adoption agencies are attempting to include the birthfather with the birthmother in the counseling process.

In the case of teenage fathers where the birthmother chooses to parent the child, some studies have indicated problems resulting from the parenthood; for example, according to the book *Adolescent Fatherhood,* "Males who father children as teenagers are less likely to receive a regular diploma, more likely to receive a GED, and more likely not to receive high school accreditation by age 20."

According to the authors of *Crises of Adolescence. Teenage Pregnancy,* studies reveal teenage fathers suffer economic consequences of paternity. (Presumably these are fathers who did not choose adoption for the child.)

Ten percent or less of the teenage birthfathers completed college by age 29 versus 30% of men who delayed childbearing until after the age of 24 years. In addition, adolescent birthfathers have a lower probability of completing high school than nonfathers.

Feelings of Teenage Fathers In the past it was presumed that few or no birthfathers were interested in their offspring placed for adoption; however, recent studies indicate birthfathers may experience considerable feelings of guilt and stress. In some cases, however, the adolescent male is actually pleased by the pregnancy because he thinks it validates his masculinity and virility; however, once the girl is pregnant, she is no longer of interest.

One study has revealed an increased propensity to commit crimes among teenage men who father children. A study performed by Maureen Pirog-Good at Indiana University in Bloomington analyzed crime rates among 333 males under 18 who were named in paternity suits.

Although the teenage fathers who were studied were more likely to have committed criminal acts before fathering the child than their peers who were not fathers, the crime rate of the teenage fathers escalated greatly during the pregnancy.

The study found unwed teenage fathers committed more offenses in the first trimester of the pregnancy, then offense rates fell back in the second trimester, increasing again in the final trimester.

One year after the baby was born, the rate was 353 arrests per 1,000 people. The annual arrest rate of this group before the conception of their infants was 187 per 1,000, compared to 71 per 1,000 for all 17-year-old males.

The hypothesis for this radical increase in the number of crimes committed by birthfathers was that unwed fathers face extremely negative reactions from peers, teachers and parents.

Despite popular prejudices that black teenage fathers are more likely to commit crimes, the study found a stronger correlation between white teenage fatherhood and crime.

It should be noted that these teenage fathers were parents to children who were NOT placed for adoption. A study of teenage fathers whose children were adopted and a subsequent review of their criminal records before and after the child's birth and adoption would be greatly enlightening.

Some studies have indicated that teenage birthfathers do attempt to maintain a relationship with the birthmother and the child. According to the authors of *Crises of Adolescence,* about half of the adolescent fathers maintained contact during the first two years of the child's life. In addition, about 20% of the adolescent fathers married the teenage birthmothers. Unfortunately, other studies indicate that visitation and involvement with the mother and child plummeted after the child's second birthday.

In a study of the children of adolescent mothers, *Adolescent Mothers in Later Life,* the authors stated, "Adolescents whose mothers were teenage childbearers are at very high risk for school problems. They have a fifty-fifty chance of being held back a grade sometime during their school career, of having been expelled or suspended in the last 5 years, and of having their parents contacted about a problem. It is little wonder that so few have an above-average standing in class."

The children of teenage mothers were also more likely to exhibit behavioral problems such as skipping school and fighting, particularly male teenagers. (See also ABUSE; BIRTHMOTHER.)

Allan F. Abramse, Peter A. Morrison and Linda J. Waite, "Teenagers Willing to Consider Single Parenthood: Who is at Greatest Risk?" *Family Planning Perspectives,* 20(January/February 1988): 13–18.

Christine A. Bachrach, Ph.D., "Adoption Plans, Adopted Children, and Adoptive Mothers: United States, 1982," working paper for National Center for Health Statistics, series 22, 1985.

Frank G. Bolton Jr., *The Pregnant Adolescent: Problems of Premature Parenthood* (Beverly Hills, Calif.: Sage, 1980).

Kathleen Ford, Ph.D., "Societal Differentials and Trends in the Timing of Births," National Center for Health Statistics, February 1981.

Frank F. Furstenberg Jr., J. Brooks-Gunn and S. Philip Morgan, *Adolescent Mothers in Later Life* (New York: Cambridge University Press, 1987).

Group for the Advancement of Psychiatry, *Crises of Adolescence. Teenage Pregnancy: Impact on Adolescent Development* (New York: Brunner/Mazel, 1986).

Cheryl D. Hayes, editor, *Risking the Future: Adolescent Sexuality, Pregnancy and Childbearing* (Washington, D.C.: National Academy Press, 1987).

William Marsiglio, "Teenage Fatherhood: High School Completion and Educational Attainment," in *Adolescent Fatherhood* (Hillsdale, N.J.: Lawrence Erlbaum, 1986).

Steven D. McLaughlin, principal investigator, *Final Report: The Consequences of The Adoption Decision* (Seattle: Battelle Human Affairs Research Centers, 1987).

Edmund V. Mech, *Orientations of Pregnancy Counselors Toward Adoption,* Department of Health and Human Services, Office of Population Affairs, 1984, Washington, D.C.

Shelby H. Miller, "Childbearing and Childrearing Among the Very Young," *Children Today,* May–June 1984, 26–29.

National Center for Health Statistics, *Wanted and Unwanted Childbearing: United States, 1973–1982,* May 9, 1985.

National Center for Health Statistics, "Advance Report of Final Natality Statistics, 1987," *Monthly Vital Statistics Report,* 38:3(supplement), June 29, 1989.

National Center for Health Statistics, *Socioeconomic Differentials and Trends in the Timing of Births,"* National Survey of Family Growth, Series 23, No. 6, February 1981.

Maureen A. Pirog-Good, "Teenage Paternity, Child Support, and Crime," *Social Science Quarterly,* 69(1988), 527–546.

Eileen White Read, "Birth Cycle: For Poor Teen-Agers, Pregnancies Become New Rite of Passage," *The Wall Street Journal,* March 17, 1988.

Lillian Tereskiewicz, "Survey Documents Problems of Pregnant, Parenting Teens," *Youth Law News,* May–June 1987, 17–19.

teenage pregnancy See TEENAGE PARENTS.

teenagers, adopted See ADOLESCENT ADOPTED PERSONS.

termination of parental rights The overwhelming majority of adoptions require the voluntary or involuntary termination of the biological parental rights before the adoptive parents may formally and legally adopt a child. (If the birthparents are deceased and relatives have custody of the child, then the relatives may provide voluntary consent to an adoption, or, in some cases, a court may terminate their legal rights.)

In many cases, termination of parental rights is voluntary, and the birthparents willingly relinquish their parental rights by signing the appropriate consent forms. (The timeframe during which birthparents can "change their mind" about adoption after signing consent forms varies greatly from state to state; however, after the adoption is finalized, it is extremely difficult to overturn an adoption.)

Most birthparents who voluntarily make an adoption plan for their children do so when their children are infants or not older than toddlers; however, some parents feel compelled to take this action when the child is older. If the child has been in foster care for many years, the social worker may ask the parents if they wish to transfer parental rights so the child may be adopted.

In other instances, the state may request that parental rights be terminated by petitioning the court for permission to end these rights so the child could be ready for an adoption. Often the children have been in foster care for several years, and social workers have determined that the birthparents cannot adequately assume their parental responsibilities.

Courts understandably take the genetic ties of the children to the biological parents very seriously, and judges insist on strong supporting evidence before terminating any parental rights.

At least one and often many court hearings will precede any involuntary termination of parental rights. In addition, even if the biological parent is imprisoned for many years, it may still be difficult to terminate his or her rights.

When Termination Is Not Required In some unusual cases discussed by attorney Emily Patt, a child may be adopted without any voluntary or involuntary termination of the parental rights of the biological parents.

In a 1985 case in Alaska, the parents of the child wished to retain their parental rights and also allow a third person to adopt the child. The three individuals had shared parental duties. The court decided to allow the adoption, and the child then had three lawful parents, rather than two.

In a 1987 California case, two women applied to adopt a child through the department of social services. Their petition was granted. One of the women had previously adopted a child, and she and her partner wished to share legal and parental responsibilities. The court initially decreed that the adoptive mother must terminate her parental rights before her partner could adopt; however, the Superior Court overturned that decision and granted the adoption.

Delays in Terminating Parental Rights The ADOPTION ASSISTANCE AND CHILD WELFARE ACT OF 1980 mandates a court hearing be held once the child has been in foster care for 18 months. The child may be returned to the family of origin, may continue on in foster care or may be placed in institutional care or recommendations may be made to begin proceedings to terminate parental rights. In addition, in many cases, the court will delay making a decision at all.

Very few children are adopted after a mere 18 months of foster care, and it is far more likely the child will have been with foster parents for at least two or three years before court action has been taken to terminate parental rights.

There are many reasons for this, including a shortage of social workers, job turnover of social workers, judges' possible dislike of terminating parental rights, birthparents' statements that they will change and become "good parents" and a myriad of other factors. Attorneys handling termination cases may be inexperienced. In addition, if a lower court refuses to terminate parental rights, the action may not be pursued to a higher court, but in some cases, the highest court in the state may decide for termination of parental rights when lower courts were reluctant to take such action.

Grounds for Termination of Parental Rights When the state seeks to terminate parental rights, the child was usually neglected, abused or abandoned by the birth parents or the birthparents suffer some mental or physical incapacity, making it impossible for them to provide normal parental care. In addition, no relatives have been identified who are willing to assume permanent custody of the child.

According to the reference law book, *Adoption Law and Practice,* some states recognize other grounds for terminating parental rights; for example, nonsupport is grounds for termination in Colorado, Indiana, Montana, Ohio and Oklahoma. Stepparent adoptions may be granted on the grounds of nonsupport of the birthparent.

Some states recognize physical or mental illness (particularly mental illness) in the birthparent as sufficient grounds for terminating parental rights, but judges in other states may not recognize mental illness as sufficient grounds to terminate.

A mentally ill Miami woman who literally raised her small son as a cat until he was removed from the home refused to voluntarily consent to the adoption of her child years after he had lived in a foster home. Her lawyer said she should not be deprived of her parental rights just because she was schizophrenic. Fortunately, this story did have a happy ending. After the story appeared in the *Miami Herald,* the woman agreed to allow the child to be adopted by his foster parents.

Apparently the problem in the case of the Florida child was that the law stated parental rights could not be terminated if the failure to comply with a performance agreement was "the result of conditions beyond the control of the parent or parents." Since mental illness is beyond the control of a parent, it was reasoned that parental rights could not be terminated.

In 1990, the Florida Legislature rectified the apparent former error in wording of the statue, and the law was changed so that parental rights could not be terminated if the failure to comply with a performance agreement was "due to the lack of financial resources of the parent or parents or due to the failure of the department to make reasonable efforts to reunify the family." This change thus enabled state social workers to terminate parental rights in the case of mental illness and other situations formerly considered by some judges or attorneys as "beyond the control of the parent."

In addition, the legislators added a new category of "egregrious abuse," which refers to "conduct of the parent or parents that is deplorable, flagrant, or outrageous by a normal standard of conduct." If the parent(s) commit egregious abuse, no performance agreement is required, and parental rights may be terminated.

Some states recognize the imprisonment of a parent as sufficient grounds for termination of parental rights, but others refuse to recognize such grounds.

In a 1985 New Jersey case, cited in *Adoption Law and Practice,* a father was sentenced to 30 years in jail for the murder of his wife. His parental rights were terminated involuntarily because of the length of his sentence, which would not enable him to assume parental duties.

In a 1985 Michigan case, a father was sentenced to seven to twenty years for a sex crime. Because he would not be able to assume his parental rights for at least two years, his parental rights were terminated.

Incarceration in and of itself is not automatically grounds for termination. A 1989 article by Adela Beckerman of Sociology and Community Services at Clinton Community College in Plattsburgh, New York described the difficulties of arranging visits between foster children and their birthparents who were in jail. According to Beckerman, 7% to 12% of the children in foster care have mothers who are prisoners.

Beckerman says prisons are usually remote from the community, and visitations are hard to arrange. In addition, prisons are not sympathetic to the needs of children and parents, do not have special facilities or separate visiting areas for children and present many other obstacles.

She says a "common fear" is that the child's foster parent or caretaker will wish to adopt the children. But Beckerman cites states that do not presume imprisonment is tantamount to "abandonment" or "neglect"; for example, according to Beckerman, New York law does not allow imprisonment alone to be sufficient grounds to constitute "abandonment" or unfitness, nor is it alone adequate grounds to terminate parental rights to a child. Instead, it must be shown that the parents have not continued contact with their children and have been neglectful and also that the child welfare agency has attempted to maintain the parent-child relationship. It may be difficult to maintain that relationship; for example, the prison may be far from the city in which the child lives. Often there may be no special visiting facilities for children, who are accorded the same visitor treatment as adults.

Beckerman also discussed the dilemma of deciding when parental rights should be terminated, and says there are no guidelines on how long a child should remain in foster care if his father or mother is imprisoned. In some cases, a parent may have a very long prison sentence.

Parental unfitness is sufficient grounds in some states to terminate parental rights, especially when the parent has abused the child, another parent or other victims. Emotional instability could be a subcategory under "unfitness." In a 1985 case in Boston, Massachusetts, the mother was seriously disturbed, the family repeatedly relocated, and other problems existed. The court decided to terminate parental rights.

In a 1985 Wyoming case, the father's parental rights were terminated because he had been maintaining an incestuous relationship with his 12-year-old daughter.

Violence is often related to alcohol or drug abuse by the parents and increasingly is seen in cocaine and crack addiction.

Reporters Anita Manning and Karen S. Peterson quote Judge Leah Ruth Marks in Manhattan as saying, "I never thought I'd look back on the good old days of heroin. As bad as it was when parents were on heroin, they still remembered they were parents. Now, with the crack, they don't even know they have kids."

Leslie Mitchel of the Committee for Prevention of Child Abuse was also quoted as saying, "Crack and cocaine increase the level of violence. There are cases where a parent puts a child in an abandoned house and just forgets, or where one parent is brutally abusing a child and the other is just passively watching. Families seem just much more disturbed."

Social workers and the child welfare system have a difficult time reaching the goal of REUNIFICATION of the child with the birth family when also faced with the extreme difficulty of rehabilitating a crack addict. Another critical factor to consider is that many cocaine babies suffer a broad range of physical, neurological and psychological damage as a direct result of cocaine abuse by their mothers during critical stages of fetal development.

As a result, cocaine babies and older children from cocaine-abusing families are usually considered to be children with SPECIAL NEEDS. Even though it is probably likely parental rights will ultimately be terminated, it is not at all certain adoptive homes can be readily located.

In some states, the termination of parental rights and the adoption of a child are combined together in a joint proceeding. According to *Adoption Law and Practice,* such joint proceedings are risky for adopting parents because they may be challenged by birthparents.

Grounds for terminating rights vary from state to state. (See chart at end of entry.) Some states take into account the age of the child and his wishes, while others do not. In addition, some states consider the relationship the child has with foster parents, while others do not use that factor in determining termination.

Rehabilitation of Abusive Parents Louisiana attorney and author Richard Ducote believes a key problem is the common view of child abuse as a temporary stepping over the line. Instead, he says there are parents who will repeatedly, knowingly and dispassionately abuse their children.

The model of the parent who loses his temper doesn't explain such cases as parents ritualistically abusing their children—binding, gagging and beating them and performing other actions with premeditation. In addition, not all parents who neglect their children do so for reasons of poverty.

Ducote's contention that some parents cannot be "rehabilitated" is supported by a 1987 article in *Child Abuse and Neglect.*

Author David P. H. Jones contends that some families are "untreatable", and says, "In the field of physical abuse, 16–60% of parents reabuse their children following the initial incident. Sexual reabuse is estimated to occur in 16% of cases. Treatment of abusive families also aims to alter family functioning. From studies in physical abuse we find 20–87% of families are unchanged or worse at the end of treatment. In sexual abuse the equivalent figures are 16–38%."

Jones says factors particularly indicative of poor outcome to treatment are "parental history of severe childhood abuse, persistent denial of abusive behavior, refusal to accept help, severe personality disorder, mental handicap complicated by personality disorder, parental psychosis with delusions involving the child and alcohol/drug abuse."

In addition, says Jones, "Severe forms of abuse (fractures, burns, scalds, premeditated infliction of pain, vaginal intercourse or sexual sadism) are more likely to prove untreatable."

Jones adds, "The idea that some families do not respond appears to be anathema to some practitioners and researchers alike. Yet the reality for those who work in the field of child abuse is that some families cannot be treated or rehabilitated sufficiently to offer a safe enough environment in which children can live."

Ducote contends termination efforts should begin immediately in certain cases, for example, when abusive parents refuse to undergo psychotherapy or take other actions as required, when the child is abused again after return to the parents, when the parent is jailed for a major crime and will be unable to parent the child for many years, when it is unlikely the parents can become successful parents because of severe psychosis and when another child shows a serious aversion to the parent.

Many experts contend that the lengthy periods required to terminate parental rights severely damage the children the system is theoretically designed to protect.

Says attorney Richard Ducote, "We adopt a higher standard for proof in parental-termination cases than in criminal cases. With the same evidence that would enable a D.A. to send a parent away for 15 to 20 years for what he did to his kids, some juvenile- and family-court judges are still reluctant to terminate rights." (See also ABANDONMENT; ABUSE; BOARDER BABIES; CHILDREN'S RIGHTS; GAY AND LESBIAN ADOPTION; PARENTAL RIGHTS; REUNIFICATION.)

Adela Beckerman, "Incarcerated Mothers and Their Children in Foster Care: The Dilemma of Visitation," *Children and Youth Services Review,* 11(1989): 175–183.

Richard Ducote, "Why States Don't Terminate Parental Rights," *Justice for Children,* Winter 1986.

Celia W. Dugger, "When the Child Must Pay for the Crimes of the Father: Little Girl is Caught in a Legal and Moral Tug of War," *The Miami Herald,* October 1, 1989, 1A, 16A.

Joan H. Hollinger, editor-in-chief, *Adoption Law and Practice* (New York: Matthew Bender, 1989).

David P. H. Jones, MB.CHB., M.R.C. Psych, D.C. H.D. (OGST), R.C.O.G., "The Untreatable Family," *Child Abuse and Neglect,* 11(1987): 409–420.

Anita Manning and Karen S. Peterson, "Drugs Fuel Disintegration of Families," *USA Today,* March 6, 1989, 1A–2A.

Emily C. Patt, "Second Parent Adoption: When Crossing the Marital Barrier Is in a Child's Best Interests," *Berkeley Women's Law Journal,* 3(1987–88): 96–133.

Tom Seligson, "Who Speaks for the Lost Children? A Report on Foster Care in America," *Parade Magazine,* July 31, 1988, 4–5.

(This following essay is written by adoption expert and author Marietta Spencer, adoption triad consultant and founder of postlegal services for the Children's Home Society of Minnesota in St. Paul, Minnesota, and is reproduced here with permission.)

terminology Positive or negative messages can be conveyed through language. Sometimes language is purely descriptive and explanatory without seeming to carry any emotional baggage; however, words are symbols that often carry a deeper meaning and are instrumental in creating feelings and attitudes.

The constructive use of language requires discernment, thoughtfulness and skill. This essay offers insights and perspectives for individuals interested in mastering accurate, current and positive word choices supportive of birthparents, adopted children and adults as well as of families who have added sons and daughters via adoption.

There are different users of adoption language, and in some cases, language has become outdated and obsolete. The general public has inherited concepts, words and phrases from the past; for example, the phrase "put up for adoption" refers back to the old Orphan Train era, when children were actually put up on display so people could see them.

As changes occur, new speech patterns evolve and new words are coined. When considering adoption language, including sentences, phrases and single words, readers may find it surprising to note how uncritically words in common usage are accepted.

Subgroups within the general public are deeply involved in matters related to adop-

Summary of Major Components of State Statutes Concerning Involuntary Termination of Parental Rights

ISSUES CONCERNING RETURN TO HOME[3]
Significant relationships
Parent/parents
Foster parents
Child's preference
Age of child a consideration
Nature and depth of child's wishes are considered
Alternative placements
Custody/guardianship—caretakers not adopting
Other forms of long-term care (group home, etc.)
Court ordered permanent foster placement
Open adoption
LEGAL PROCEDURES/ISSUES
Notice and hearing requirements
Right of appeal
Right to counsel
For parents
For the child
Rights of putative fathers
Proof by clear and convincing evidence
Time frames for completing termination litigation
STATUTE RELATED TO INDIAN CHILD WELFARE ACT

3. Note that a number of states specify that the best interests of the child must be considered. Although specific issues are not designated in the statutory language, the factors listed on the chart are considered.
4. New Hampshire's burden of proof is beyond a reasonable doubt.

State Legislature Report 14, no. 7 (April 1989)
Credit: National Conference of State Legislatures

tion. There are those directly touched by adoption (adopted individuals, birthparents and adoptive parents) and their many extended family members. In addition, there are many other people who are part of the support system of the triad: neighbors, teachers, doctors, clergy and others with helping functions in the community.

Professional individuals are actively involved in adoption. The social worker is occupied with assisting in decision-making, information and community resource sharing and is trained and licensed by society to represent societal standards. Physicians and attorneys sometimes function as catalysts between the adult parties involved in the adoption contract, in such cases focusing more on their own expertise rather than that of the counseling process. Unfortunately, many of these professionals rely on adoption language currently in general use, disregarding the nuances and implications of these words. (Specific examples are provided at the end of this section.)

Another subgroup that uses adoption language is a growing component of advocacy or special interest groups who rally around emotional causes and purposefully express their messages in strong and emotionally-loaded and often negative words. These special interest groups, focusing on their pain and frustrations, point up the need for more constructive language.

Still another part of the public is an ever-growing body of adoptive parent support groups or mutual aid groups, organized around enhancing the successful family relationships of members, among many other goals. (See SUPPORT GROUPS.) While these groups and their members often have no special language tools at their command, they frequently grope for more constructive language to describe adoption and adoption-related subjects. They usually publicize positive terminology for adoption.

Adoptive parents who have been carefully prepared for adoption through the HOME STUDY process and who often have taken special adoption classes have carefully considered adoption-related words and phrases, and consequently, they help to disseminate constructive terminology as they use this language in their conversations with family, friends and others.

In addition, social workers add to and sharpen their skills by melding their expertise with what they learn from the clients they serve. That is why competent post-adoption services are so useful to adoptive families, allowing creative service providers the insight and ability to feed back what is needed in birthparent and adoptive parent preparation. Language is a critical part of this preparation and of the ongoing service process.

Words are used to convey feelings, options and activities. Writers use language to illustrate and describe thoughts, situations and factual content. Most writers and researchers, even if they are familiar with adoption language accepted by thoughtful adoption professionals, choose to instead use words whose purpose is to hold the attention of the readers to entertain or to fit commonly accepted (albeit inaccurate or negative) usage. They also often tend to fall back on colloquial expressions.

Constructively selected language benefits those who are directly involved in adoption: the man and woman who shared in a child's conception, for whom adoption was planned immediately after birth or later; the adopted individual; and the parent(s) who adopted and gave family membership to their child. These three parties are best referred to as the "ADOPTION TRIAD."

Following are some examples of appropriate (and inappropriate) terms.

The term *"adoptee,"* created as a convenience by writers, researchers and the media, has recently invaded the social service arena. It is interesting to note, however, that adoptive families instinctively avoid its use.

The word "adoptee" labels the whole person. Rather than helping the child and the community underline that he belongs to his family, it sets him apart, which countermands and contradicts the purpose and function of the institution of adoption. Adoption is not the sole meaning and purpose of any individual's life; instead, it is one aspect of life. Preferable terms are *"adopted adult," "adopted person," "adopted child"* or *"adopted individual."* In many cases, the person's adoptive status is irrelevant; for example, in reporting a celebrity's divorce, it is irrelevant whether the children were adopted or not adopted. Yet most of the time, if the adoptive status of the child is known, it is reported.

In addition, the phrase *"adoptive parents,"* although a descriptive and useful term, need only be used if adoption is an issue or of specific interest; for example, when an adopted person introduces a friend to her parents, she does not say, "I would like you to meet my adoptive parents" but merely refers to them as "my parents".

In everyday usage, children (or adults) should be referred to as "my son," "my daughter" or "my children," rather than "my adopted son," "my adopted daughter" or "my adopted children."

"My own" or *"their own"* are terms often used by the public to denote children born to the family as opposed to children who were adopted. Yet the child who was adopted becomes the parents' "own" because of the adoption and their assumption of parental rights and obligations in relation to the child. Parents also occupy the very same parental rights and obligations vis a vis their birth children—no more and no less than the rights and obligations they have assumed with children they adopt.

A reference to the shared genetic descent is the usual reason for the phrase "their own"; however, its use results in unconstructive implications for the adopted child, parents and siblings, making it sound as if he really does not belong.

Birthmother/birthfather. A recent term, now widely accepted by all adoption triad members as well as by the general public and popularized by women and men who "gave the child life," but whose offspring was adopted by other parents. The term "birthfather," while popular, lacks the air of authenticity, since males do not give birth.

Foreign child, foreign adoption. The word "foreign" connotes a person who is alien and outside the family. But whether a family adopts a child, from the United States or from another country, he becomes a part of that family. He will become enculturated through parenting and by community participation.

In addition, a child adopted from another land is "naturalized" on the basis of adoptive parental citizenship in the United States. Preferred terms are *"international adoption," "intercountry adoption"* or *"child adopted from another country."*

Genetic mother/father. A term that is appropriate when discussing heredity, genetic descent and lineage issues. It correctly discerns and yet accepts "difference" when aspects of nonshared genetic descent are considered and the locus of the child's genetic traits are discussed in relation to his genetic ancestry.

Home study. This old term has been rejuvenated and recast into the phrase *"family assessment"* or *"family study"* or *"preadoptive counseling"* used by contemporary adoption agencies. The problem with the phrase "home study" is that it conjures up the image of the social worker with white gloves and a judgmental attitude. It is not primarily the home that is being studied but the family. The family may change their domicile and move into a different "home."

Natural mother/father/parents. Originally coined and applied to the legal scene, this term predated the concept and term "genetic." Being highly structured and precedent-setting, legal language is often slower to change than are terms in every day use.

The term "natural parent" is often acceptable to the birthparent, but on deeper consideration, those birthparents who wish their birthchild really well might see otherwise. If the child who was adopted comes to assume that his parents are "unnatural," it will not help his comfort level. Adoptive parents also believe that they are made of natural substances and not of artificial material.

To "parent." Refers to the child-rearing process. This descriptive and constructive term finds frequent usefulness in adoption for everyone and should be a must for all those counseling pregnant women and those who have recently borne a child. "To parent" is a collective verb for all that is necessary in helping a child grow up and fulfill his potential.

In contrast, *to "keep"* a child does not connote the entire realm of child-rearing aspects that are involved in raising a child. In addition, the opposite of "to keep" is to *"give away,"* and this phrase implies that a person can own another person and thus is able to give that person away. There is an extremely strong negative aspect to the phrase "give away" in addition to its inaccuracy. Also, the adopted person who hears he was "given away" is left with a very negative image.

To terminate parental rights may be in the best interest of a child, especially when the parent is unable to fulfill parenting responsibilities and obligations.

"Real" parents. Those who have adopted the child are really his parents from that point on. Birthmothers and fathers are genetically related to the child forever, but they are not the child's "parents" subsequent to severing functional family ties and transferring family status and roles to other parents.

"Reunion". At first glance, REUNION sounds like a positive phrase for referring to a first meeting between a birthparent and an adopted adult, but it is misleading if the adopted person was adopted as an infant.

In an infant adoption, the birthmother/father remembers parting with a baby. Coming face to face with a now adult birthchild, they must learn to know him or her. In addition, the adopted adult has no recollection or memories of the birthparent(s). More positive terms are *"to meet with," "to learn to know," "to locate".*

In older child adoptions, where the child does remember the parent(s), positive phrases include *"to resume contact," "to see again."* These phrases are less loaded with drama. It is interesting to note that quite often adults who were adopted as older children are more interested in locating and meeting with siblings than birthparents.

"Telling" a child that he or she was adopted is important; however, "telling" implies a one-way communication flow. *"Sharing"* facts and feelings with one another, discussing adoption information with children sensitively at strategic points in their thought development must be a two-way listening and learning process. (See also EXPLAINING ADOPTION.)

therapy and therapists As increasing numbers of children with SPECIAL NEEDS are adopted, it is likely there will be a need for adopted children and their families to receive some ongoing assistance and, in some cases, therapy. In addition, some number of adopted persons who were adopted at birth or an early age will also need counseling, although the estimated percentages of adopted adults needing counseling is open to wide dispute.

Because therapists are susceptible to hearing and believing the same prejudices and myths as the layperson, it is crucial that adoptive parents and adopted persons identify a therapist who does not presume adoption is the sole reason or the pre-eminent reason for an adopted person to experience emotional difficulties. Nor should the therapist automatically presume the adoptive family is the primary cause of the child's problem.

It is also important that a therapist be knowledgeable and sensitive to the unique issues that adoption does have for the child and the parents. To say that adoption plays no role is often just as damaging as it is to say it is the sole reason for a child and parents to have difficulties.

According to Marian Sandmaier, author of *When Love is Not Enough,* therapists are particularly suspicious of adoptive parents who have adopted children with special needs, presuming that a healthy family would not wish to take on the "burden" of such a child. As a result, the therapist may instead presume that the adopting family is masochistic or has a desperate desire to be needed. Social workers strive mightily to screen out any individuals with such motives, and in fact most adoptive parents are motivated by a sincere love for children and a desire to share their love. Unless a therapist enters into a therapeutic relationship with a positive orientation toward the parents, time and energy will be wasted trying to find the hypothetical "causes" of the problems rather than focusing on the solutions.

It is also important to note that the family situation has greatly deteriorated by the time the family seeks out a counselor, and the family may be very discouraged. Often they have received little or no support from extended family members. Sandmaier says the family's urgent first need is support and validation that problems exist but there may well be a way to work them out.

In some cases, a therapist inexperienced with adoption may unfairly presume that the child's problems have been caused by the adoptive family when in fact, the child entered the family with problems that occurred before he or she ever met family members. The family may have extended heroic efforts to help the child and a blaming attitude will confuse them and will only exacerbate the problem. The parents need to be respected for being part of the solution, and not blamed for being the cause of the problem. It is also possible that the family is contributing to the child's problems, for example, overreacting to negative behavior that may be common to a child at a certain developmental stage.

How does a parent know if and when a child needs therapy? This is a difficult question to answer because much depends on the child's age, behavior and many other factors. There are, however, some basic guidelines to consider.

For example, if the child's overall academic performance has deteriorated, and teachers are expressing concern about the child, this is one indicator of a possible need for counseling. In addition, if the child's relationships with peers have changed, for example, the child no longer wishes to see friends or share activities with friends (or if the child has no friends), this is another indicator of a potential problem.

One of the best indicators of a child's healthy adjustment is to observe the spontaneity and frequency of a child's smile and laughter. If a child looks and acts depressed, a professional evaluation is recommended.

Finally, if the child has gained or lost a great deal of weight, the basis for weight change may be physical or psychological, and both possibilities should be explored.

As a result, the child should see a physician to rule out medical problems and subsequently see a qualified psychologist or social worker to determine any psychological problems. An ethical therapist will reassure parents if the child's behavior is essentially "normal."

If the school-age child is behaving in a secretive reclusive manner, in contrast to earlier behavior, or is hearing imaginary voices or hallucinating, the parents should seek professional help immediately. In addition, if the child is expressing suicidal thoughts, such ideas must be taken seriously.

Information on the birthparents' personality traits is a valuable source of information in understanding and accepting a child's development, and medical and psychological experts will request such information. (For example, was there a history of depression, emotional illness or other problems in the birthfamily.) *Note:* Just because a birthparent may have had such a problem does not necessarily mean the child has inherited a predisposition to mental illness.

An effective therapist can help family members work through the pain of separation and loss, for example, the loss of birthparents and foster parents faced by the child or the loss of fertility still felt by the adoptive family. The therapist might need to help the child overcome the anguish and confusion resulting from physical or sexual abuse or help the parents deal with their frustration at being unable to reach the goal of being perfect parents.

In addition, siblings who were already in the family will need to receive counseling as the jockeying for position occurs and the relative BIRTH ORDER among family members changes and evolves. Unfortunately, some counselors choose to exclude siblings and address only the adopted child or the adopted child and adoptive parents together, despite strong evidence that the bonds of siblings can be very intense.

Therapists Judith Schaffer and Christina Lindstrom have written on "Brief Solution-Focused Therapy," which they have used successfully with adoptive families seeking assistance. According to the authors, rather than concentrating on pathology, they instead perceive the family problem as ineffective behavior patterns among family members. The fact of adoption is accepted, and the family is encouraged to change their "interactive behavior." Say the authors, "As long as the family 'blames' the problem on the issue of adoption, they can feel guilty and stay stuck." As a result, Schaffer and Lindstrom attempt to empower families by assisting them with changes in behavior. For example, a newly-adopted seven-year-old child was acting in a very manipulative manner with his father. Rather than seeing this as disturbed behavior, the treatment team encouraged the father, a teacher, to "teach" the child how to be a son. (The child had been in many previous placements.)

Another important aspect of brief therapy sessions is to find exceptions to the problem—when negative behavior (such as bedwetting) does not occur, when a child is not hostile—to get away from the presumption that the behavior always happens and cannot be rectified.

Schaffer and Lindstrom believe that adoptive families are unusually responsive to brief solution-focused therapy. For other, more disturbed children, long-term treatment or even brief hospitalization may be necessary in order to help heal the wounds that have caused so much heartache for each of the family members. The main point being where the parents have comitted love, there is hope. (See also PSYCHIATRIC PROBLEMS OF ADOPTED PERSONS; SIBLINGS.)

Marian Sandmaier and Family Service of Burlington County, Mt. Holly, New Jersey, *When Love Is Not Enough: How Mental Health Professionals Can Help Special-Needs Adoptive Families* (Washington, D.C.: Child Welfare League of America, 1988).

Judith Schaffer and Christina Lindstrom, "Brief Solution-Focused Therapy with Adoptive Families," in *The Psychology of Adoption* (New York: Oxford University Press, 1990).

traditional adoption Anonymous or confidential adoption, the generally accepted practice of "classic adoption," wherein the identities of both the birthparents and the adoptive parents are unknown to each other. These are the types of adoptions that have been arranged, mostly by agencies, since around 1920 in the United States. Traditional adoptions are usually contrasted to so-called "open" or direct placements, although both types of adoptions have common elements.

Increasing numbers of traditional adoptions offer birthmothers broad choices, such as the religion of the adopting couple, whether the adopting parents are childless or already have children and other nonidentifying, specifying elements. Such choices are offered by most adoption agencies as well as many intermediaries who arrange adoptions. Such agencies also arrange a meeting between the birthmother and the prospective parents, which is on a first-name basis only. (If full names are exchanged, the adoption is open rather than traditional.) The majority of adoptions are traditional rather than open yet with choices provided so the birthmother has input to the choice of the family who will adopt the child.

Although a great deal of media attention has been focused on OPEN ADOPTION, proponents of traditional adoptions believe there is no apparent necessity for a change to open adoption. In fact, experts who support traditional adoptions believe there is insufficient evidence to support the idea that all or most adoptions should be open.

Wrote A. Dean Byrd, "This alleged acceptance of open adoption seems to be unsupported by anything other than the sparsest anecdotal data—data with virtually no sound theoretical rationale or scientific research to back it up."

Byrd believes that all members of the "adoption circle" can be negatively affected by open adoptions, which he believes cause damage that does not occur in traditional confidential adoptions.

Although it is generally believed and stated (by proponents of open adoption) that the birthmother benefits from openness, Byrd believes an open adoption allows birthparents to delay or try to avoid altogether the loss an adoption decision entails. In addition, "Ongoing contact may serve as a continuous reminder of the loss, or as a stimulus for the fantasy that relinquishing a child is not really a loss at all."

Byrd fears adoptive parents may not truly bond with a child if they must constantly confer with the birthmother or both birthparents. He worries that if the adoptive parents are "continually reminded that if the child is not really theirs," they will have difficulty bonding with the child, who, in turn, will suffer.

Finally, Byrd (and other experts) are concerned most about the effect on the child when a traditional adoption is ruled out altogether.

Describing a young adolescent in an identity conflict occurring at the time of increased birthmother contact, Byrd says the adopted adolescent went back and forth from the adoptive parents to the birthmother, and the child was very confused. According to Byrd, she stated, "I want to be like my adoptive mother, but my birth mother says I'm like her. I don't know what to do or who I am . . . My birth mother talks about lawsuits when things go wrong. Isn't there someone that I can sue?"

For a more detailed discussion of open adoption and open adoption versus traditional adoption, see OPEN ADOPTION. (See also CONFIDENTIALITY.)

A. Dean Byrd, "The Case for Confidential Adoption," *Public Welfare,* 62(Fall 1988): 20–23.

transracial adoption When this term is used, it generally refers to the adoption of black or biracial children by white adoptive families, although some individuals use the term to refer to any adoption across racial lines, including the most frequent transracial adoptions in the United States—adoptions of Asian children by white parents.

It is unknown how many transracial adoptions occur because the federal government stopped collecting such data in 1975; however, it is known that black and biracial children who are infants and older and who need adoptive families are considered to be children with SPECIAL NEEDS by many professionals in the adoption field.

Many social workers believe a family of the same race is the best place for a child to grow up; consequently, black children are usually placed with black families. But because black children usually wait longer than do white children for an adoptive family, some groups, including the NATIONAL COMMITTEE FOR ADOPTION, believe permanency, rather than racial matching, should be of paramount consideration.

According to the *Adoption Factbook,* published by the National Committee For Adoption, about 36,000 minority children are waiting for adoptive families, and many have remained in foster care for at least two years.

It should be noted that the INDIAN CHILD WELFARE ACT OF 1978 severely restricts transracial adoption of Native American children by imposing American Indian requirements rather than state requirements on the adoption of American Indians by non-Indians.

In addition, it should also be noted that people in the United States are not the only ones to whom racial background is significant. In some Asian cultures, a child of mixed race has extremely low status in the view of most other members of society, based solely on his racial background. Hopefully, such attitudes would not be evinced by such a broad segment of American society, although prejudice exists in the United States as well.

Background of Transracial Adoption
Once considered a liberal and positive act in the late 1960s and early 1970s, adoptions of black children by white parents apparently plummeted after the National Association of Black Social Workers issued a strong position against transracial adoption in 1972.

The National Association of Black Social Workers (NABSW) is evidently still very opposed to transracial adoptions. In an article published in the *Boston Globe*, Morris Jeff, president of the NABSW, stated his opposition, saying, "The family is the critical center of social force. We cannot build strong families by transferring our children to another racial or ethnic group."

The *Globe* reporter stated that being for or against transracial adoption did not appear to be related to the racial background of the person holding the opinion, in other words with blacks opposed and whites in favor of such family arrangements.

Many black foster children live with white foster parents, which would seem to defeat the purposes of the social workers who believe black children should be raised by blacks. Lawsuits have been filed by white foster parents wishing to adopt their black foster child and denied by the state social services department. A lawsuit in the state of Minnesota was fought and won by foster parents.

A Florida couple sought to adopt their biracial foster child and were told they could not adopt him because they were white. They joined forces with other foster parents who wished to adopt and sued the state on the grounds that their civil rights were being violated. That state agreed to do a HOME STUDY on the families and also conceded to pay the extensive legal fees the families had incurred. The families successfully adopted the children.

In cases involving divorced women who have subsequently married men of another race, lower courts have taken custody of the child away from the mother and granted custody to the father on the basis of race. Higher courts have almost always given the child back to the mother. Courts have decreed that race should not be a determining factor in deciding who shall have custody of children; for example, *Palmore v. Sidot* (1984) was a U.S. Supreme Court case that disallowed racial considerations. In this case, a white father tried to take custody of a child away from his ex-wife, who lived with her black boyfriend in a black neighborhood. The mother prevailed.

In another case, a judge at the Superior Court of Pennsylvania stated, "A court should declare the law. If the court frames its decree in consideration of convenience or discretion, it betrays the law . . . A court that yielded to considerations of convenience and discretion would not have declared that a black child may attend any public school; play at any public park; live in any neighborhood. The fundamental principle of our law is that all persons are created equal. A court's decree should always exemplify that principle."

Although this statement was made in a custody case between two parents, it could also be applied to transracial adoption.

Recruitment of Black Adoptive Parents
Some people have concluded that blacks are uninterested in formal adoptions or that they

adopt at a much lower rate than whites. Census Bureau data reveals this is not valid. (See ADOPTIVE PARENTS.) But blacks would have to dramatically increase their rate of adoption to "absorb" all the WAITING CHILDREN. It must also be noted that many blacks consider INFORMAL ADOPTION to be a satisfactory solution to the problem of a child needing a family.

The solution advanced by some social workers and agencies is to allow transracial adoption by Caucasians who are aware of and sensitive to black culture and live and work alongside blacks.

This answer is still unacceptable to many social workers, both black and white, and only court challenges can force transracial adoptions in some cases. In other cases, prospective adoptive parents who are white are never told about black or biracial children waiting for families. This is particularly true in the public agencies.

Some black social workers insist that recruitment of black adoptive parents is inadequate and that white social workers impose the standards used for whites on black prospective parents; consequently, many blacks are ineligible by virtue of age, income and other factors, despite the many waiting black children. Limiting criteria with respect to the age of adopting parents, children in the home already and other conditions are often applied to white adoptive parents because of a more limited number of infants and toddlers needing families. Critics argue there is no "baby shortage" of black infants and toddlers, thus age and income criteria for black prospective adoptive parents should be re-examined.

According to a 1987 article in *Ebony*, "because of obstacles Blacks face when contacting adoption agencies, many begin the adoption process, become exasperated and then just forget about the whole thing."

The author says, however, that even those who oppose transracial adoption believe a white adoptive home is better than a foster home or an institution. "But opponents vehemently stress that such placement should be a consideration *only* after every possible effort has been made to place the child in a same-race family."

Organizations such as ONE CHURCH, ONE CHILD, founded in 1981 by Rev. George Clements, a black Catholic priest, have been created to recruit black adoptive parents and have successfully recruited numerous, although not enough, black parents.

Arguments Against Transracial Adoption
Authors Owen Gill and Barbara Jackson have summarized key arguments against transracial adoption. The authors believe there are two primary categories of objections: "criticisms based on discrimination against the black community" and "criticisms based on the anticipated experiences of a black child in a white family."

The criticisms based on discrimination against blacks in general include such views as blacks supplying healthy children to childless white couples who can't find enough Caucasian infants to adopt. In addition, say the authors, critics believe "transracial adoption takes from the black community its most valuable resource which is its children."

Fears for children themselves include the idea that the child will feel different and unaccepted, that he will not be able to create and maintain relationships with grandparents and extended family members and that the child will be unable to relate to members of the black community.

Racial identity A strong criticism of transracial adoption is that a white family could not give a black child an appropriate sense of his or her racial identity. The argument is that the child will feel inferior and different and will have low self-esteem. Studies have not appeared to bear this view out.

Attorney James S. Bowen argues against transracial adoption. Says Bowen, "Given that racism continues to be pervasive in American society today, race considerations operate to impinge upon the Black child's self-concept during development. In view of this effect of racism, Black professionals most closely involved in society's welfare function of providing care to the displaced child strongly recommend that Black children are best reared in Black homes."

He also argues that allowing transracial adoptions would not free many children from foster care or institutional care because there is not a sufficient desire by whites to adopt blacks. (This same argument is often advanced to justify transracial adoption: Too many black children wait for adoptive families. Bowen believes they would continue to wait, even if transracial adoption were accepted by agencies.)

Bowen also believes that black values should be passed on to children, values such as "pride in the African heritage," "unity," "self-determination," "collective work and responsibility," "cooperative economics," "purpose," "creativity" and "faith."

Yet he concedes that if a black child is already living in a white home and bonding has already occurred, then it would probably be difficult to remove the child. In addition, if a white family is fostering a black child and wishes to adopt the child, the adoption should be allowed if no member of the child's extended family is interested in adopting and there are no appropriate nonrelative blacks who are interested in adopting the child.

Bowen's article included a proposed "Afro-American Child Welfare Act," presumably modeled on the Indian Child Welfare Act.

Supporters of transracial adoption point to studies that indicate black children placed in white homes are generally well-adjusted and happy.

In a test measuring racial identity, children in both traditional adoptive families (black children in black families) and transracial families were tested at age four and again at eight to determine if they felt a positive sense of their racial identity.

Researchers Joan F. Shireman and Penny R. Johnson used the "Clark Doll Test" to determine the level of racial identity in transracially adopted children.

The preschool transracially adopted children showed a marked positive identification as black: 71% of them identified as black compared to 53% of the traditionally adopted preschoolers. By age eight, the groups were virtually identical. Researchers concluded that racial identity was constant for the transracial group and a later development for the traditional group.

Because the majority of transracial adopters lived in primarily Caucasian neighborhoods, the researchers speculated whether or not racial identity would remain the same or change as the transracially adopted children grew older and into adolescence.

Longitudinal studies have provided the best vindication for transracial adoption. Rita Simon and Howard Altstein reported on their studies of transracially adopted children who have already reached adolescence, and the majority of the children appear to be doing very well. (More information is provided later in this essay.)

The researchers concluded, "The refusal to view transracial adoption as an option violates a basic tenet that the field of social work has been laboring to establish over the past several decades: to base the interventions of social workers on grounds that can be supported empirically."

A Ph.D. dissertation in 1988 by Carol Mecklenburg also apparently validates the success of transracial adoptions. In a study of 18 white families who adopted black children, Mecklenburg found the ego levels of adoptive parents and their adopted adolescent children were above comparison groups' ego levels.

Mecklenburg also speculated that perhaps families who adopt transracially have higher ego levels and more "congruent perceptions of themselves." She also found high ego developments in families in which the adolescents considered their parents flexible and "interpersonally connected."

Problems with Transracial Adoption
Even when Caucasian adoptive parents live in integrated neighborhoods and are well aware of racial issues, there are likely to be problems to face in the community and sometimes with the child's teacher.

A mother of Korean-born children was surprised to encounter prejudice against her black children that she had not encountered with her Korean children.

She wryly concluded that Asian children are positively stereotyped to be very bright and hard-working people, while too many Americans negatively stereotype blacks. (Unfortunately, sometimes expectations of the Korean child's performance can be unreasonably high; for example, some adoptive parents have reported that teachers expect all Asian children to excel in mathematics.)

Longitudinal Studies Researchers Rita Simon and Harold Altstein have extensively studied transracial adoption in longitudinal studies. At the last point of the study, the adopted children were mostly adolescents with an average age of 15 years, and if problems were going to show up, it's likely they would have already appeared or would appear in this tumultuous time.

The researchers compared transracially adopted children, birth children and white adopted children and reported on their findings in *Transracial Adoptees and Their Families: A Study of Identity and Commitment.*

They found no significant differences among the self-esteem of all categories of children. They also found strong familial ties felt by the "TRAs" (transracially adopted children).

In addition, they found little difference between the extended family relationships of adopted children and children born to the family. "Among the TRAs, 82 percent have at last one grandparent still alive, and 71 percent said they feel close to the grandparents. Among the children born into the family, 84 percent have grandparents who are still alive, and 53 percent felt close to them; and among the white adoptees, 87 percent have grandparents who are still alive, and 57 percent feel close to them. Forty-four percent of the TRAs, 50 percent of the children born into the families, and 38 percent of the white adoptees said that they visit or talk over the phone with their grandparents at least once a month . . . The TRAs do not sense that they are outsiders or that they are not accepted."

In addition, the majority of the transracially adopted children stated their intention is to not only complete high school but also attend college.

This is not to say that the researchers found the children were totally accepted by the outside world: 65% of the parents and 67% of the children reported they had experienced at least one racial incident, and the most prevalent incident was name-calling by other children (and also, unfortunately, by adults).

Wrote the researchers, "About 10 percent in both groups described incidents in which, in the opinion of the children and the parents, a teacher or a parent of a friend made insulting, racist remarks."

But few of the adolescents were affected, and a "temporary anger more than hurt, was their main reaction."

Preparing for Transracial Adoption
Black adoption worker Azizi Powell has offered her insights and advice to white parents adopting transracially.

Powell recommended preadoptive parents look inside themselves for any racism that may exist and ask themselves questions: "Do you make comments that indicate that you favor whites over nonwhites?" "Do you live in integrated neighborhoods?" "Do you interact with blacks and other people of color as equals?"

Powell also recommends that children who are biracial should be considered as black children rather than biracial, primarily because society at large perceives a biracial child as black.

The debate on transracial adoption is likely to continue as increasing numbers of black children enter the foster care system.

Melinda Beck with Elisa Williams, "Willing Families, Waiting Kids," *Newsweek,* September 12, 1988, 64.

James S. Bowen, "Cultural Convergences and Divergences: The Nexus Between Putative Afro-American Family Values and the Best Interests of the Child," *Journal of Family Law,* 26 (1987–88): 487–543.

Beth Brophy, "The Unhappy Politics of Interracial Adoption," *U.S. News & World Report,* November 13, 1989, 72–74.

Owen Gill and Barbara Jackson, *Adoption and Race: Black, Asian and Mixed Race Children in White Families* (London: Batsford Academic and Educational, 1983).

Joyce A. Ladner, *Mixed Families: Adopting Across Racial Boundaries* (New York: Anchor Press/Doubleday, 1977).

Walter Leavy, "Should Whites Adopt Black Children?" *Ebony,* September 1987, 76–82.

Jacqueline Macaulay and Steward Macaulay, "Adoption for Black Children: A Case Study of Expert Discretion," *Research in Law and Sociology,* 1(1978): 265–318.

Carol Elaine Mecklenburg, "Ego Development, Family Cohesion, and Adaptability in Families with Transracially Adopted Adolescents," Ph.D. diss, University of Minnesota, 1988.

National Committee For Adoption, *1989 Adoption Factbook,* (Washington, D.C.: National Committee For Adoption, 1989).

Shari O'Brien, "Race in Adoption Proceedings: The Pernicious Factor," *Tulsa Law Journal,* 21(1986): 485–498.

Azizi Powell, "Raise Your Child with Ethnic Pride," *OURS,* November/December 1988, 26–29.

Charles A. Radin, "Waiting for a Home: Opposition to Transracial Adoption Slows Black Placements," *Boston Globe,* November 30, 1989.

Judith Schaffer and Christina Lindstrom, *How to Raise an Adopted Child* (New York: Crown Publishers, 1989).

Joan F. Shireman and Penny R. Johnson, "A Longitudinal Study of Black Adoptions: Single Parent, Transracial, and Traditional," *Social Work,* 31(May–June 1986) 172–176.

Rita J. Simon and Howard Altstein, *Transracial Adoptees and Their Families: A Study of Identity and Commitment* (New York: Praeger, 1987).

Rita James Simon, *Transracial Adoption* (New York: Wiley, 1977).

Paul Stubbs, "Professionalism and the Adoption of Black Children," *British Journal of Social Work,* 17(1987): 473–492.

twins See SIBLINGS.

U

unadoptable Until the late 1970s, society considered older children (over age 10) and children with serious physical or emotional handicaps as "unadoptable," presuming no one would desire to adopt such a child. It was believed that most people prefer to adopt a healthy infant.

Today many social workers believe that the majority of children can successfully attain family membership, and some adoption experts claim no child is unadoptable.

It is difficult to find appropriate families for teenagers or children who have psychiatric problems, are abusive and exhibit other behavioral problems. Yet there are people who will volunteer to adopt children who are retarded and even children who have AIDS. As of this writing, there is a waiting list of people who wish to adopt children with DOWN SYNDROME or spina bifida. The challenge appears to be largely in identifying the right family for a specific child.

In some cases, a child may not wish to be adopted, and many states permit a child over a certain age (usually 14) to reject adoption as an option. The child may be used to the foster home or group home and unwilling to transfer her affections to an adoptive family.

It is important to understand that children who were once considered unadoptable may often require extensive therapy, and adoptive parents and social workers must not assume that love will conquer all barriers. (See also

ADOPTION ASSISTANCE PROGRAM; ADOPTION AND CHILD WELFARE ACT OF 1980; OLDER CHILD; PSYCHIATRIC PROBLEMS OF ADOPTED PERSONS; SPECIAL NEEDS.)

U.S. Immigration and Naturalization Service Federal agency under the U.S. Department of Justice that oversees all international adoptions; based in Washington, D.C. with regional offices nationwide. Outreach Program, which provides literature on international adoption, is based at 425 Eye St. NW, Washington, DC 20536.

updated home study Aspects of a home study that must be updated. Often when parents wish to adopt another child from an agency that has already studied them, approved them and placed a child with them, the updated home study need not be as comprehensive as the original home study. The social worker may request new physicals if six months or a year has passed since their last physical or may request other information.

The agency may not have placed a child with the couple yet, although they have been studied. If a child becomes available who appears would fit into this family setting but a year or more has elapsed, the agency may require an update, and additional fees may be required.

unwed parents The majority of birthparents who voluntarily choose adoption for their infants are unwed, and experts estimate 92% to 94% of all infants placed for adoption are born to single parents. The majority of these parents are over age 18. (See also BIRTHMOTHER; BIRTHFATHER; BIRTHPARENT; ILLEGITIMACY; MARRIED BIRTHPARENTS; MATURE WOMEN PLANNING ADOPTION; TEENAGE PREGNANCY.)

V

videotape The medium of videotape can be used very creatively, both in preparing children for an adoptive placement as well as in recruiting prospective adoptive parents. The videotape is a nonthreatening way for prospective adoptive parents to learn about a child, and a videotape of a family is a nonthreatening way for a child to learn about a particular family.

Television stations that offer "Wednesday's Child" or similar formats on waiting adoptable children with special needs will usually videotape the child and show the tape during a news program in an effort to recruit adoptive parents. This effort is geared toward the general public; however, individual agencies also create their own videotapes, showing them to families who might be suitable for particular children.

Said authors Glynne Gervais and Marilyn Panichi in *Mostly I Can Do More Things Than I Can't*, "A child can be seen in action and interacting. His personality, skills, and abilities are evident." If a child has a disability, it may be difficult to imagine the extent of the disability or how an individual child copes with a disability from reading about it in a written description. A videotape can show a family how the child looks, acts and feels.

Some agencies videotape prospective adoptive families in their own home and show the tapes to children, who, experts say, eagerly watch the tapes over and over, helping them a great deal with the preparation process.

Videotapes can also be used to help separated siblings keep in touch with each other or to help them prior to a planned reuniting of the siblings.

The primary disadvantage of videotape is that it is more costly and cumbersome than a photolisting book and requires more labor and training. (Panichi, however, has used videotapes to teach social workers how to videotape!)

Videotapes reveal far more than a photograph and a written description of a child. Say Gervais and Panichi, "Adoption has been described by some of our waiting children on videotapes in the following way:

'Adoption means love. Adoption means having a family to come home to for the holidays when I'm older. Adoption means not having to bounce like a basketball from home to home.' Words like these, spoken by a child, can have more impact than the slickest, most imaginatively planned media campaign.''

Mostly I Can Do More Things Than I Can't was published by the Illinois Department of Children and Family Services in 1987 and is available through Spaulding for Children at the National Resource Center for Special Needs Adoption, P.O. Box 337, Chelsea, MI 48118.

voluntary agency   See AGENCIES.

W

waiting children   The thousands of children with SPECIAL NEEDS who are in need of families to adopt them and wait for parents to be located or identified. (See also CAP BOOK.)

waiting lists   Rosters of couples or single people waiting for a home study or, more commonly, a roster of people already studied and selected and waiting for a child who will need them as parents.

Waiting lists vary greatly from agency to agency and exist primarily as a function of the imbalance between the numbers of infants in need of families and the much larger numbers of couples and single persons who are interested in adopting children, especially infants. (Waiting lists are much shorter for individuals interested in adopting older children or children with SPECIAL NEEDS.)

Some agencies require individuals to wait for at least a year before they may be studied while others will not accept applications after a certain number of applicants have registered and until they believe they will be able to do a home study and place a child with the applicant within a reasonable length of time.

Virtually all agencies maintain waiting lists of people who have been approved to adopt. Most agencies consider a group of approved families for the next child to be adopted. Many of these agencies also offer the birthmother the opportunity to choose the adopting family from a group of non-identifying resumes of previously-approved families.

Most prospective adoptive parents do not like the prospect of spending several years time on a waiting list, even if they understand the main reason for the wait to be an imbalance in numbers. Social workers believe that one good by-product of waiting lists is they may give applicants time that is often needed to seriously reflect on adoption and to work through any final infertility conflicts the family may have.

Parents interested in adopting a child with special needs usually are specifically matched to a child in terms of being able to deal with these special needs, and therefore, their wait may be very brief or very lengthy, depending on the type of child the family feels they can accept and also depending on the suitability of their family for the child.

waiting period   The time a family spends waiting to adopt a child, from the point of application to the time of placement.

Many families may state that they have waited years and years when they are actually considering the time from when they first thought about adopting a child until when the child came to them. Although numerous couples do wait years for their child, it is only reasonable to consider the waiting from the point in time when they actually took action to adopt the child by formally applying to an agency or retaining an attorney.

Studies have revealed that the most stressful time for adopting parents is that period spent in searching for an appropriate adoption agency or attorney and subsequently being accepted as a prospective parent. (See HOME STUDY.)

Although the waiting time after approval of the home study is also stressful, it is less anxiety-provoking than the time before approval because the family believes they will eventually be chosen for a child and they have done everything possible to make the adoption happen.

Wednesday's Child Media recruitment programs for children with special needs that occur on Wednesday, Tuesday, Thursday, etc.; also known as "Tuesday's Child, Thursday's Child," etc.

Photographs of waiting children in newspapers with descriptions of the child encourage interested prospective parents to write or call state or agency social workers. Television programs show VIDEOTAPES of a waiting child, providing numbers of social workers who can offer further information.

Waiting child recruitment programs are very effective tools to identify families for older children and other children with special needs. They are cumbersome for social workers, because many people who call are only mildly interested and unwilling to spend the time needed for classes and counseling; however, most social workers believe that even one potential prospect makes the program well worth the effort involved.

In addition, although families who contact the social worker may not be suitable for the particular Wednesday's Child of the week, they could be a very good family for another child needing a home.

Critics of Wednesday's Child programs charge that corporations could not engage in such "bait and switch" advertising and promotion. They also allege that often the child's problems are minimized in an attempt to effect an adoptive placement.

welfare Public assistance programs for indigent families.

Poor families with children may be eligible for Aid to Families with Dependent Children (AFDC), which is a monthly stipend paid through the state social services office. The amount depends on the number of children in the home, the state the family lives in, any support money coming from other sources and a variety of factors.

Families who are eligible for AFDC are also eligible for MEDICAID, which is a medical insurance program for welfare recipients, and should not be confused with Medicare, a medical insurance program for older Americans who are not on public assistance.

Some families are eligible for Medicaid only and receive no money payments.

All families who receive AFDC grants will also qualify to receive food stamps, a federally funded program to provide basic food needs to poor families.

Many teenagers and single birthmothers apply for and receive welfare benefits. These benefits may continue as long as the recipient remains indigent and his or her children are minors.

White House Task Force on Adoption
The Interagency Task Force on Adoption was formed under the Reagan administration in August 1987 to "identify barriers to adoption, propose appropriate solutions and suggest methods to promote adoption."

The task force contacted over 130 organizations and individuals, including public and private agency workers, adoptive parents, birthparents, adopted persons, attorneys, judges and others involved with adoptions. The final report of the group, *America's Waiting Children: A Report to the President from the Interagency Task Force on Adoption,* was issued on May 12, 1988.

The report focused on three major issues: studying the cases of children in foster care and the barriers preventing adoptable children from being adopted; increasing the number of adoptive parents and providing an opportunity to adopt to older people, single people and disabled people; promoting adoption as an option for women with crisis pregnancies.

The task force also recommended states consider implementing the following: involve citizen foster care review boards at the state or county level; provide specific and set guidelines on the time spent in attempts to reunite children with biological families; create greater accountability and supervision of social workers and attorneys who are responsible for foster children; improve computerized systems to track children in foster care; and schedule child welfare cases on court calendars in a timely manner. Many other recommendations were also made.

Presidential Task Force, *America's Waiting Children, Report to the President from the Interagency Task Force on Adoption,* Washington, DC, May 12, 1988.

working mothers Although the majority of mothers today are in the work force, many adoption agencies specify at least one parent must be willing to stay home with a newly-adopted child for some length of time, ranging from weeks to months. Such acquiescence is a condition of application that is pointed out to prospective adoptive parents.

Which parent stays home isn't always specified, but because of economic disparities, the wife is usually the individual selected. In the case of a single parent adoption, the time frame may be cut back or eliminated altogether, since the income of the single parent is what will support the child.

Parental leave policies vary from company to company and attempts to create a national parental leave policy for new parents of biological and adoptive parents have been made in recent years by members of Congress. If a company does not have a parental leave policy or if the time allowed for leave is shorter than the adoption agency requires, the adoptive parent may have to take a leave without pay or quit work altogether.

Some adoptive parents have found it ironic and unfair that one is expected to leave work at least temporarily and insist extra income is needed more than ever to support a child. They also say biological parents are not required to stay home with a child and believe such arbitrary judgements are unfair.

Others believe it is important for at least one parent to spend an intensive period with the child to facilitate bonding. This is true even when the child is an older child, although it is less likely a lengthy period at home would be required in the adoption of a school-age child.

When agencies request input from birthmothers on the type of adoptive parents they are seeking, most birthmothers have stated their preference for a mother who is not employed outside the home. Their attitude is if they had opted to parent the child, they would have been forced to work. They believe a full-time mother is a better situation than they could provide.

A similar attitude is evinced by birthmothers who prefer couples over single parents. (See also ADOPTIVE PARENTS; BIRTHMOTHER; PARENTAL LEAVE.)

wrongful adoption An adoption that should not have occurred or would not have occurred had all the relevant facts about the child been made available to the adoptive parents. Instead, information was deliberately misrepresented and/or withheld by the agency, and as a result, the adoptive parents were essentially defrauded.

The first reported successful case of wrongful adoption occurred in 1986 in *Burr v. Board of County Commissioners of Stark County in Ohio.*

The Burrs had adopted a 17-month-old boy in 1964. They had been told he was a healthy normal child born of an 18-year-old mother.

The child suffered numerous diseases and physical problems, and the Burrs opened the sealed adoption records with a court order in 1982. They sought this information because they believed the information might help them with the child's numerous physical problems.

They learned the child's birthmother was not 18 but was actually a 31-year-old inmate of a psychiatric institution, and the birthfather was probably another inmate. They also learned that psychological evaluations of the child indicated the child was subnormal intellectually and further evaluations were recommended. In addition, the social worker had not revealed that the child had been in two foster homes prior to his adoptive placement.

A jury awarded the Burrs $125,000 for medical and emotional damages. The decision was appealed to the Franklin County Court of Appeals of Ohio and later the Ohio Supreme Court, which both upheld the decision of the jury.

This case centered around misrepresentation of facts rather than omission of facts. Subsequent cases have centered on the basis of omission rather than commission; for example, six Texas couples sued the Texas Department of Human Services in a class action suit, alleging the state did not provide information on sexual and physical abuse suffered by the adopted children.

The case was dismissed in November 1988 by a federal judge on the grounds that adoptive parents have no constitutional rights to an adopted child's record. In addition, the judge held that the state would not be required to pay for psychiatric care for the children. At this writing, the case is on appeal.

Adoption agencies are not required to provide identifying information to adopting parents and in fact are precluded by most state laws from violating the birthparents' confidentiality; however, they are ethically bound to tell the truth about a child's medical and psychiatric status.

As a result, withholding information is not automatic grounds for a wrongful adoption suit. A California couple, however, was awarded $70,000 in 1988 from the state because a court decided the Orange County Department of Social Services knew a child was severely disturbed and did not tell the adoptive parents about it. In addition, the adoption was revoked. (Most adoptive parents are not seeking a revocation of the adoption but are seeking financial damages to cover psychological counseling for the child, extensive medical care or other needs.)

Claire Grandpre Combs, "Wrongful Adoption: Adoption Agency Held Liable for Fraudulent Representations," *Cincinnati Law Review*, 56(1987): 343–359.

John R. Maley, "Wrongful Adoption: Monetary Damages as a Superior Remedy to Annulment for Adoptive Parents Victimized by Fraud," *Indiana Law Review*, 20(1987): 709–734.

Michele Schiffer, "Fraud in the Adoption Setting," *Arizona Law Review*, 29(1987): 707–723.

Y

youths Minor children. In adoption, youths could be adolescent birthparents or adopted teenagers or children.

Z

zero population growth The concept, popularized by a group called Zero Population Growth (ZPG), that individuals should only reproduce themselves at the replacement rate; for example, a man and a woman should have no more than two children. The reason for this concern is the alleged overpopulation of our entire planet, which, zero population growth advocates believe, would be resolved if they and many others bore fewer children.

Others allege that poverty and hunger are primarily the result of an inequitable distribution of available resources, not overpopulation.

Zero population growth advocates may be actively involved in the group that formally promotes their philosophy, or they may be informal believers in this concept.

If many people were zero population growth advocates, then the alleged worldwide overpopulation problem would probably be resolved; however, many people in other countries believe in bearing many children or do not believe in using any family planning method, with the end result being they bear many children whether they planned the births or not.

Some proponents of zero population growth, because they may enjoy raising children very much, have opted to adopt children rather than to bear more children themselves. They reason that there are already children in the world needing homes, which they can provide.

Few adoption agencies in the U.S. will accept an application for a healthy nonminority infant from a family that continues to be fertile, as are many zero population growth advocates, and so such people often adopt older children or minority or handicapped infants, or children from other countries, again, reasoning that the children need families to belong to and loving parents.

Social workers are (or should be) careful to ensure the adopting family realizes they are adopting a child, not a social cause.

zygote adoption The transfer of a fertilized egg to a "gestational mother" who will carry the child to term and deliver and raise the child; also known as embryo adoption or adoptive pregnancy. Her husband is usually fertile and contributes his sperm. Comparisons are made between this process and artificial insemination of a woman by donor or purchased sperm. In some cases, donor sperm is also used, and the fetus will not be genetically related to either of its ultimate parents.

Subsequent custody suits over embryos as well as state laws against surrogate motherhood for profit will probably limit the number of females willing to donate their eggs as well as the number of women willing to be implanted; however, there are women with an altruistic goal of helping others who will donate their eggs and zygotes.

No legal adoption probably would be required in such an instance, since the "surrogate" mother will deliver the donated zygote and her name and her husband's name will appear on the birth certificate. Court challenges could theoretically overturn this current policy.

A key disadvantage mentioned by many critics of zygote adoption is that it appears likely money would change hands, especially between a donor mother and the gestational mother who carries the child. Thus, a variation of baby selling could occur.

If an intermediary is involved, as is likely, his fees could be exorbitant. Although baby selling is illegal, it is not clear what the status of embryo transfers are, and the whole philosophy of biomedical ethics is still evolving.

In addition, the problem of many infertile couples—the denial of infertility—is clearly a potential problem in zygote adoption, where the surrogate mother can pretend to herself and others that the child is genetically her own child.

Parents may choose not to tell the child at all of the genetic heritage, which could result in serious trauma if and when the child later learns he or she is not genetically related to the mother and/or father. It is also very difficult to obtain genetic nonidentifying (or identifying) information about the donor mother, since records are generally kept in strictest confidentiality.

Some sperm bank donors have given permission for their names to be released when the child is over 18, and such a policy or a policy to release nonidentifying information could be adapted by organizations that facilitate embryo adoptions; however, it appears unlikely.

Cynthia J. Bell, "Adoptive Pregnancy: Legal and Social Work Issues," *Child Welfare*, 65(September/October 1986): 421–435.

APPENDIXES

1. Birth Rates for Unmarried Women
2. State-by-State Domestic Adoption Rates in U.S.
3. State Social Services Offices
   Government Adoption Offices in Canada
4. Adoption Agencies
5. International Adoption Agencies
6. Adoption-Related Organizations
7. Adoptive Parent Groups
   Adoptive Parent Groups in Canada
8. Periodicals and Newspapers
9. Newsletters

1. BIRTH RATES FOR UNMARRIED WOMEN

Table 1. Numbers, Rates, and Ratios of Births to Unmarried Women, by Age of Mother and Race of Child: United States, 1988

Age of Mother	Number All Races	Number White	Number All Other Total	Number All Other Black	Rate All Races	Rate White	Rate All Other Total	Rate All Other Black	Ratio All Races	Ratio White	Ratio All Other Total	Ratio All Other Black
All ages	1,005,299	539,696	465,603	426,665	[1]38.6	[1]26.6	[1]81.8	[1]188.9	257.1	177.2	539.3	634.9
Under 15 years	9,907	3,522	6,385	6,111	—	—	—	—	935.7	864.7	980.0	988.5
15–19 years	312,499	168,641	143,858	133,419	36.8	24.8	85.9	98.3	653.3	534.6	883.2	911.8
15 years	22,456	10,105	12,351	11,702	⎫	⎫	⎫	⎫	877.0	785.2	969.8	982.2
16 years	44,101	22,535	21,566	20,168	26.5	17.1	64.1	74.1	799.7	693.4	952.1	969.0
17 years	69,580	37,861	31,719	29,429	⎭	⎭	⎭	⎭	725.8	615.3	923.9	946.1
18 years	85,659	47,577	38,082	35,100	52.7	36.4	120.3	136.1	642.3	529.1	876.6	906.9
19 years	90,703	50,563	40,140	37,020	⎭	⎭	⎭	⎭	538.7	426.2	807.3	845.4
20–24 years	350,905	186,598	164,307	151,308	56.7	38.3	124.3	138.2	328.7	231.9	625.1	686.8
25–29 years	196,365	105,218	91,147	82,825	48.1	33.8	94.6	99.2	158.5	104.1	398.9	493.9
30–34 years	94,874	51,596	43,278	38,724	31.7	22.9	57.9	58.7	118.1	78.0	304.5	413.0
35–39 years	34,408	20,109	14,299	12,358	14.9	11.5	25.4	25.3	127.7	92.3	276.2	379.8
40 years and over	6,341	4,012	2,329	1,920	[2]3.2	[2]2.6	[2]5.5	[2]5.3	155.5	125.1	267.8	370.4

[1]Rates computed by relating total births to unmarried mothers, regardless of age of mother, to unmarried women aged 15–44 years.
[2]Rates computed by relating births to unmarried mothers aged 40 years and over to unmarried women aged 40–44 years.

NOTE: For 42 States and the District of Columbia, marital status of mothers is reported on the birth certificate; for 8 States, mother's marital status is inferred; see Technical notes.

Table 2. Birth Rates for Unmarried Women by Age of Mother and Race of Child: United States, 1970–88

[Rates are live births to unmarried women per 1,000 unmarried women in specified group, estimated as of July 1]

Year and Race of Child	15–44 Years[1]	15–19 Years Total	15–17 Years	18–19 Years	20–24 Years	25–29 Years	30–34 Years	35–39 Years	40–44 Years[2]
All races									
Reported and/or inferred:[3]									
1988	38.6	36.8	26.5	52.7	56.7	48.1	31.7	14.9	3.2
1987	36.1	34.1	24.5	49.9	53.1	44.3	29.3	13.5	2.9
1986	34.3	32.6	22.9	48.9	49.7	42.0	26.9	12.2	2.7
1985	32.8	31.6	22.5	46.6	46.8	39.8	25.0	11.6	2.5
1984[4]	31.0	30.2	21.9	43.0	43.2	37.0	23.2	10.9	2.5
1983[4]	30.4	29.7	22.1	41.0	42.0	35.6	22.3	10.3	2.5
1982[4]	30.0	28.9	21.5	40.2	41.4	35.1	21.9	10.0	2.7
1981[4]	29.6	28.2	20.9	39.9	40.9	34.7	20.8	9.8	2.6
1980[4]	29.4	27.6	20.6	39.0	40.9	34.0	21.1	9.7	2.6
Estimated:[5]									
1980[4]	28.4	27.5	20.7	38.7	39.7	31.4	18.5	8.4	2.3
1979[4]	27.2	26.4	19.9	37.2	37.7	29.9	17.7	8.4	2.3
1978[4]	25.7	24.9	19.1	35.1	35.3	28.5	16.9	8.2	2.2
1977[4]	25.6	25.1	19.8	34.6	34.0	27.7	16.9	8.4	2.4
1976[4]	24.3	23.7	19.0	32.1	31.7	26.8	17.5	9.0	2.5
1975[4]	24.5	23.9	19.3	32.5	31.2	27.5	17.9	9.1	2.6
1974[4]	23.9	23.0	18.8	31.2	30.5	27.9	18.4	10.0	2.6
1973[4]	24.3	22.7	18.7	30.4	31.5	29.6	20.3	10.8	3.0
1972[4]	24.8	22.8	18.5	30.9	33.2	30.8	22.6	12.0	3.1
1971[6]	25.5	22.3	17.5	31.7	35.5	34.5	25.2	13.3	3.5
1970[6]	26.4	22.4	17.1	32.9	38.4	37.0	27.1	13.6	3.5
White									
Reported and/or inferred:[3]									
1988	26.6	24.8	17.1	36.4	38.3	33.8	22.9	11.5	2.6
1987	24.6	22.8	15.8	34.2	35.8	30.7	21.2	10.3	2.3
1986	23.2	21.5	14.6	33.2	33.5	29.2	19.2	9.3	2.1
1985	21.8	20.5	14.2	30.9	30.9	27.3	17.5	8.6	1.9

Appendix 313

1984[4]	20.1	19.0	13.5	27.6	27.8	24.5	16.1	8.0	1.9
1983[4]	19.3	18.5	13.5	26.1	26.4	22.9	15.3	7.5	1.9
1982[4]	18.8	17.7	12.9	25.1	25.7	22.2	14.7	7.1	2.0
1981[4]	18.2	17.1	12.4	24.6	24.9	21.6	13.6	6.9	1.8
1980[4]	17.6	16.2	11.8	23.6	24.4	20.7	13.6	6.8	1.8

Estimated:[5]

1980[4]	16.2	15.9	11.7	22.8	22.4	17.3	10.5	5.3	1.4
1979[4]	14.9	14.6	10.8	21.0	20.3	15.9	10.0	5.1	1.4
1978[4]	13.7	13.6	10.3	19.3	18.1	14.8	9.4	4.8	1.3
1977[4]	13.5	13.4	10.5	18.7	17.4	14.4	9.3	4.9	1.4
1976[4]	12.6	12.3	9.7	16.9	15.8	14.0	10.1	5.5	1.4
1975[4]	12.4	12.0	9.6	16.5	15.5	14.8	9.8	5.4	1.5
1974[4]	11.7	11.0	8.8	15.3	15.0	14.7	9.5	5.5	1.5
1973[4]	11.8	10.6	8.4	14.9	15.5	15.9	10.6	5.9	1.7
1972[4]	11.9	10.4	8.0	15.1	16.6	16.5	12.1	6.5	1.6
1971[6]	12.5	10.3	7.4	15.8	18.7	18.5	13.2	7.2	1.9
1970[6]	13.9	10.9	7.5	17.6	22.5	21.1	14.2	7.6	2.0

All other

Reported and/or inferred:[3]

1988	81.8	85.9	64.1	120.3	124.3	94.6	57.9	25.4	5.5
1987	78.3	81.6	61.3	114.1	116.6	89.2	54.2	23.9	5.4
1986	74.8	79.7	59.1	112.3	109.5	82.3	50.8	21.6	4.9
1985	73.2	79.4	59.1	109.9	105.7	77.9	48.8	21.4	4.7
1984[4]	71.4	78.3	59.3	106.1	101.3	75.8	45.0	20.5	4.7
1983[4]	72.3	78.3	60.2	104.6	101.1	77.3	44.7	20.1	4.9
1982[4]	73.9	79.2	60.7	107.0	102.1	78.9	44.4	20.0	5.4
1981[4]	75.4	79.2	60.3	109.0	104.5	80.1	45.6	19.7	5.7
1980[4]	77.2	81.7	63.1	111.6	106.6	79.1	46.9	19.2	5.6

Estimated:[5]

1980[4]	78.0	83.0	64.0	113.4	108.2	79.1	46.2	18.5	5.3
1979[4]	78.2	83.9	64.8	115.3	107.1	77.7	44.8	19.1	5.7
1978[4]	76.5	81.2	63.2	111.6	104.9	76.4	43.6	18.2	5.6
1977[4]	77.4	84.0	67.2	112.7	103.1	74.4	43.7	18.5	6.6
1976[4]	76.4	82.5	67.5	108.9	101.1	74.0	43.4	18.7	6.9
1975[4]	79.0	86.3	70.7	114.3	102.1	73.2	47.9	20.0	6.9
1974[4]	80.3	87.3	73.2	113.4	103.0	77.0	50.9	23.2	6.6
1973[4]	83.2	88.5	75.6	112.8	107.8	81.0	55.8	26.2	7.2
1972[4]	86.2	91.8	77.6	119.3	112.4	83.3	55.7	29.0	8.2
1971[6]	90.2	92.0	75.4	125.4	120.6	92.6	65.3	32.2	10.4
1970[6]	89.9	90.8	73.3	126.5	121.0	93.8	69.8	32.0	10.7

See footnotes at end of table.

Table 2. (continued)

Black[7]

Year and Race of Child	15–44 Years[1]	15–19 Years Total	15–17 Years	18–19 Years	20–24 Years	25–29 Years	30–34 Years	35–39 Years	40–44 Years[2]
Reported and/or inferred:[3]									
1988	88.9	98.3	74.1	136.1	138.2	99.2	58.7	25.3	5.3
1987	84.7	92.6	70.4	127.5	129.9	93.6	54.2	23.5	5.1
1986	80.9	89.9	67.4	125.0	121.4	86.7	51.1	21.6	4.7
1985	78.8	88.8	67.0	121.1	116.1	81.4	48.8	21.3	4.5
1984[4]	76.8	87.1	66.8	116.2	110.7	80.0	45.0	20.3	4.5
1983[4]	77.7	86.4	67.1	114.0	110.0	82.0	45.3	20.3	4.9
1982[4]	79.6	87.0	67.6	115.8	110.2	85.5	45.8	20.1	5.4
1981[4]	81.4	86.8	66.9	117.6	112.5	86.4	47.2	20.4	5.8
1980[4]	82.9	89.2	69.6	120.2	115.1	83.9	48.2	19.6	5.6
Estimated:[5]									
1980[4]	83.2	90.3	70.6	121.8	116.0	82.9	47.0	18.5	5.5
1979[4]	83.0	91.0	71.0	123.3	114.1	80.0	44.8	19.3	5.9
1978[4]	81.1	87.9	68.8	119.6	111.4	79.6	43.9	18.5	6.2
1977[4]	82.6	90.9	73.0	121.7	110.1	78.6	45.7	19.0	6.6
1976[4]	81.6	89.7	73.5	117.9	107.2	78.0	45.0	19.2	7.0
1975[4]	84.2	93.5	76.8	123.8	108.0	75.7	50.0	20.5	7.2
1974[4]	85.5	93.8	78.6	122.2	109.8	80.3	51.8	24.3	6.7
1973[4]	88.6	94.9	81.2	120.5	116.0	84.5	57.8	27.6	7.7
1972[4]	91.6	98.2	82.8	128.2	121.2	88.3	57.4	30.4	8.5
1971[6]	96.1	98.5	80.7	135.2	130.6	99.6	68.6	32.7	10.1
1970[6]	95.5	96.9	77.9	136.4	131.5	100.9	71.8	32.9	10.4

[1] Rates computed by relating total births to unmarried mothers, regardless of age of mother, to unmarried women aged 15–44 years.
[2] Rates computed by relating births to unmarried mothers aged 40 years and over to unmarried women aged 40–44 years.
[3] Data for States in which marital status was not reported have been inferred and included with data from the remaining States; see Technical notes.
[4] Based on 100 percent of births in selected States and on a 50-percent sample of births in all other States; see Technical notes.
[5] Births to unmarried women are estimated for the United States from data for registration areas in which marital status of mother was reported; see Technical notes.
[6] Based on a 50-percent sample of births.
[7] Included in All other.

2. STATE-BY-STATE ADOPTION RATES IN U.S.

Because there is a lag in the reporting of data to various state entities that are the primary sources which the National Committee for Adoption (NCFA) contacts to generate its statistics, a corresponding delay of NCFA reporting necessarily occurs. In respect to adoptions in the U.S. and particularly to unrelated adoptions, the changes from 1982 to 1986 were not statistically significant. It is not expected that the next reporting year will be significantly different from these numbers.

316 Appendix

Table 1. Related and Unrelated Domestic Adoptions and Foreign Adoptions: United States, 1986 National Committee For Adoption Survey

Geographic Division and State	(a) Related and Unrelated Domestic Adoptions	(b) Related Domestic Adoptions	(c) Unrelated Domestic Adoptions (Subtotal d+e+f)	(d) Unrelated Domestic Adoptions by Public Agencies	(e) Unrelated Domestic Adoptions by Private Agencies	(f) Unrelated Domestic Adoptions by Private Individuals	(g) Unrelated Domestic Adoptions of Infants (Included in c)	(h) Unrelated Domestic Adoptions of Children with Special Needs (Included in c)	(i) Foreign Adoptions (Not Included in a–h)
United States	104,088	52,931	51,157	20,064	15,063	16,040	24,589	13,568	10,019
New England	5,520	3,139	2,381	938	1,182	261	1,184	573	784
Maine	873	601	272	109	70	93	56	25	53
New Hampshire	512	346	166	62	43	61	49	50	54
Vermont	333	203	130	51	34	45	97	35	56
Massachusetts	2,334	1,176	1,158	411	747	0	560	307	383
Rhode Island	493	313	180	65	53	62	115	48	20
Connecticut	975	500	475	240	235	0	307	108	218
Middle Atlantic	12,949	5,882	7,067	3,084	1,802	2,181	2,851	1,707	2,085
New York	7,213	3,635	3,578	1,606	848	1,124	1,732	920	1,027
New Jersey	1,631	178	1,453	666	429	358	134	247	537
Pennsylvania	4,105	2,069	2,036	812	525	699	985	540	521
East North Central	17,218	6,873	10,345	3,598	3,770	2,987	5,079	2,891	1,705
Ohio	1,898	329	1,569	785	322	462	759	416	227
Indiana	3,791	2,296	1,495	1,058	235	202	275	489	94
Illinois	5,430	1,051	4,379	714	1,576	2,089	2,564	1,160	411
Michigan	4,115	2,074	2,041	725	1,316	0	988	541	618
Wisconsin	1,984	1,123	861	316	311	234	493	285	355
West North Central	9,229	5,896	3,333	1,240	1,384	709	1,411	873	1,441
Minnesota	2,100	1,500	600	290	285	25	260	215	771
Iowa	1,504	783	721	142	411	168	148	100	304
Missouri	2,660	1,755	905	501	174	230	438	262	164
North Dakota	484	311	173	1	172	0	49	64	34
South Dakota	482	247	235	75	113	47	114	49	39
Nebraska	1,009	801	208	35	102	71	164	53	83
Kansas	990	499	491	196	127	168	238	130	46

South Atlantic	21,033	12,515	8,518	3,546	2,216	2,756	4,235	2,292	978
Delaware	186	88	98	48	50	0	25	0	44
Maryland	1,400	647	753	231	277	245	364	200	331
District of Columbia	326	164	162	65	42	55	78	43	24
Virginia	2,348	1,541	807	448	241	118	120	223	224
West Virginia	1,254	982	272	100	40	132	135	120	46
North Carolina	3,535	2,515	1,020	568	322	130	494	270	67
South Carolina	1,569	930	639	255	165	219	532	169	27
Georgia	2,732	1,776	956	310	96	550	642	257	87
Florida	7,683	3,872	3,811	1,521	983	1,307	1,845	1,010	128
East South Central	7,046	4,532	2,514	909	612	993	1,307	676	276
Kentucky	1,040	646	394	182	67	145	279	169	85
Tennessee	2,058	1,249	809	221	262	326	392	214	90
Alabama	2,480	1,897	583	216	95	272	284	100	58
Mississippi	1,468	740	728	290	188	250	352	193	43
West South Central	14,572	7,639	6,933	2,734	1,796	2,403	3,291	1,291	406
Arkansas	1,541	777	764	305	197	262	370	202	31
Louisiana	1,683	1,188	495	165	135	195	174	278	57
Oklahoma	2,350	1,175	1,175	469	303	403	569	311	92
Texas	8,998	4,499	4,499	1,795	1,161	1,543	2,178	500	226
Mountain	7,220	3,554	3,666	1,555	893	1,218	1,607	795	680
Montana	652	329	323	129	83	111	156	86	75
Idaho	330	53	277	63	114	100	163	73	60
Wyoming	232	117	115	46	30	39	56	30	14
Colorado	2,036	1,267	769	275	300	194	326	250	273
New Mexico	979	177	802	595	119	88	97	7	55
Arizona	1,303	657	646	258	167	221	313	171	75
Utah	1,261	782	479	58	38	383	416	127	113
Nevada	427	172	255	131	42	82	80	51	15
Pacific	9,301	2,901	6,400	2,460	1,408	2,532	3,624	2,470	1,664
Washington	2,133	1,169	964	246	429	289	620	250	445
Oregon	1,161	125	1,036	295	446	295	697	300	290
California	5,069	1,093	3,976	1,751	423	1,802	2,070	1,808	714
Alaska	662	322	340	135	88	117	162	90	67
Hawaii	276	192	84	33	22	29	75	22	148

NOTES: (1) Categories a–h exclude 10,019 foreign-born children adopted from other countries in calendar 1986. (b) Categories a–h obtained by NCFA survey of State adoption experts listed in Appendix A, "Sources of Data Shown in Table 1". Category i obtained by NCFA from Immigration and Naturalization Service, and excludes 7 adoptees to Guam, 24 to Puerto Rico, and 2 to the Virgin Islands. (c) For methods of using data categories from reporting states to derive unreported data categories, see Appendix A.6, "Sources of data in table 1".

Table 2. Number and Percentage Distribution of Types of Unrelated Domestic Adoptions for Each State, Division, and the United States: 1986 National Committee for Adoption Survey

Geographic Division and State	Unrelated Domestic Adoptions Number	Percent	Unrelated Adoptions by Public Agencies	Unrelated Adoptions by Private Agencies	Unrelated Adoptions by Private Individuals
United States	51,157	100.0	39.2	29.4	31.4
New England	2,381	100.0	39.4	49.6	11.0
Maine	272	100.0	40.0	25.7	34.2
New Hampshire	166	100.0	37.3	25.9	36.7
Vermont	130	100.0	39.2	26.2	34.6
Massachusetts	1,158	100.0	35.5	64.5	0.0
Rhode Island	180	100.0	36.1	29.4	34.4
Connecticut	475	100.0	50.5	49.5	0.0
Middle Atlantic	7,067	100.0	43.6	25.5	30.9
New York	3,578	100.0	44.9	23.7	31.4
New Jersey	1,453	100.0	45.8	29.5	24.6
Pennsylvania	2,036	100.0	39.9	25.8	34.3
East North Central	10,345	100.0	34.8	36.4	28.9
Ohio	1,569	100.0	50.0	20.5	29.4
Indiana	1,495	100.0	70.8	15.7	13.5
Illinois	4,379	100.0	16.3	36.0	47.7
Michigan	2,041	100.0	35.5	64.5	0.0
Wisconsin	861	100.0	36.7	36.1	27.2
West North Central	3,333	100.0	37.2	41.5	21.3
Minnesota	600	100.0	48.3	47.5	4.2
Iowa	721	100.0	19.7	57.0	23.3
Missouri	905	100.0	55.4	19.2	25.4
North Dakota	173	100.0	0.6	99.4	0.0
South Dakota	235	100.0	31.9	48.1	20.0
Nebraska	208	100.0	16.8	49.0	34.1
Kansas	491	100.0	39.9	25.9	34.2

South Atlantic	8,518	100.0	41.6	26.0	32.4
Delaware	98	100.0	49.0	51.0	0.0
Maryland	753	100.0	30.7	36.8	32.5
District of Columbia	162	100.0	40.1	25.9	34.0
Virginia	807	100.0	55.5	29.9	14.6
West Virginia	272	100.0	36.8	14.7	48.5
North Carolina	1,020	100.0	55.7	31.6	12.7
South Carolina	639	100.0	39.9	25.8	34.3
Georgia	956	100.0	32.4	10.0	57.5
Florida	3,811	100.0	39.9	25.8	34.3
East South Central	2,514	100.0	36.2	24.3	39.5
Kentucky	394	100.0	46.2	17.0	36.8
Tennessee	809	100.0	27.3	32.4	40.3
Alabama	583	100.0	37.0	16.3	46.7
Mississippi	728	100.0	39.8	25.8	34.3
West South Central	6,933	100.0	39.4	25.9	34.7
Arkansas	764	100.0	39.9	25.8	34.3
Louisiana	495	100.0	33.3	27.3	39.4
Oklahoma	1,175	100.0	39.9	25.8	34.3
Texas	4,499	100.0	39.9	25.8	34.3
Mountain	3,666	100.0	42.4	24.4	33.2
Montana	323	100.0	39.9	25.7	34.4
Idaho	277	100.0	22.7	41.2	36.1
Wyoming	115	100.0	40.0	26.1	33.9
Colorado	769	100.0	35.8	39.0	25.2
New Mexico	802	100.0	74.2	14.8	11.0
Arizona	646	100.0	39.9	25.9	34.2
Utah	479	100.0	12.1	7.9	80.0
Nevada	255	100.0	51.4	16.5	32.2
Pacific	6,400	100.0	38.4	22.0	39.6
Washington	964	100.0	25.5	44.5	30.0
Oregon	1,036	100.0	28.5	43.1	28.5
California	3,976	100.0	44.0	10.6	45.3
Alaska	340	100.0	39.7	25.9	34.4
Hawaii	84	100.0	39.3	26.2	34.5

NOTES: Unrelated domestic adoptions category does not include foreign adoptions. Percentages may not add to 100.0 due to rounding.

Table 3. Special Needs Adoptions as a Percentage of Unrelated Domestic Adoptions and Percent Change for Each State, Division, and the United States: 1982 and 1986 National Committee For Adoption Survey

Geographic Division and State	Percentage 1982	Percentage 1986	Percent Increase + (or decrease −), in the Percentage 1982 to 1986
United States	27.6	26.5	(−4.0)
New England	31.5	24.1	(−23.5)
Maine	9.2	9.2	0.0
New Hampshire	27.8	30.1	+8.3
Vermont	16.3	26.9	+65.0
Massachusetts	41.9	26.5	(−36.8)
Rhode Island	39.1	26.7	(−31.7)
Connecticut	30.1	22.7	(−24.6)
Middle Atlantic	28.1	24.2	(−13.9)
New York	35.0	25.7	(−26.6)
New Jersey	14.7	17.0	+15.6
Pennsylvania	27.6	26.5	(−4.0)
East North Central	23.2	27.9	+20.3
Ohio	27.6	26.5	(−4.0)
Indiana	6.4	32.7	+410.9
Illinois	20.0	26.5	+32.5
Michigan	30.1	26.5	(−12.0)
Wisconsin	27.8	33.1	+19.1
West North Central	21.2	26.2	+23.6
Minnesota	9.1	35.8	+293.4
Iowa	27.6	13.9	(−49.6)
Missouri	27.6	29.0	+5.1
North Dakota	41.2	37.0	(−10.2)
South Dakota	11.4	20.9	+83.3
Nebraska	26.2	25.5	+2.7
Kansas	25.7	26.5	+3.1
South Atlantic	39.7	26.9	(−32.2)
Delaware	34.5	0.0	(−100.0)
Maryland	96.4	26.6	(−72.4)
District of Columbia	29.1	26.5	(−8.9)
Virginia	27.6	27.6	0.0
West Virginia	27.6	44.1	+59.8
North Carolina	27.6	26.5	(−4.0)
South Carolina	35.4	26.4	(−25.4)
Georgia	27.6	26.9	(−2.5)
Florida	43.4	26.5	(−38.9)
East South Central	32.2	26.9	(−16.5)
Kentucky	70.7	42.9	(−39.3)
Tennessee	26.2	26.5	+1.1
Alabama	17.6	17.2	(−2.3)
Mississippi	24.8	26.5	+6.9

Table 3. (*continued*)

Geographic Division and State	Percentage 1982	Percentage 1986	Percent Increase + (or decrease −), in the Percentage 1982 to 1986
West South Central	17.5	18.6	+6.3
Arkansas	26.1	26.4	+1.1
Louisiana	55.8	56.2	+0.7
Oklahoma	24.8	26.5	+6.9
Texas	9.7	11.1	+14.4
Mountain	18.8	21.7	+15.4
Montana	27.6	26.6	(−3.6)
Idaho	13.9	26.4	+89.9
Wyoming	27.7	26.1	(−5.8)
Colorado	27.7	32.5	+17.3
New Mexico	22.3	0.9	(−96.0)
Arizona	2.6	26.5	+919.2
Utah	3.5	26.5	+657.1
Nevada	50.7	20.0	(−60.6)
Pacific	37.3	38.6	+3.5
Washington	57.6	25.9	(−55.0)
Oregon	27.6	29.0	+5.1
California	35.2	45.5	+29.3
Alaska	27.8	26.5	(−4.7)
Hawaii	27.8	26.2	(−5.8)

NOTES: See note and sources on table 1. For 1986, see note and sources on table 1. For 1982 NCFA survey description, see National Committee For Adoption: *Adoption Factbook*. Washington, D.C. Nov. 1985.

Table 4. State Ranking of Numbers of Unrelated Domestic Adoptions, Infant Adoptions, Special Needs Adoptions, and Foreign Adoptions Based on the Top 10 States: 1986 National Committee for Adoption Survey

State Rank 1 = Highest Number	Unrelated Domestic Adoptions	Domestic Infant Adoptions	Domestic Special Needs Adoptions	Foreign Adoptions
1	Texas	Illinois	California	New York
2	Illinois	Texas	Illinois	Minnesota
3	California	California	Florida	California
4	Florida	Florida	New York	Michigan
5	New York	New York	Michigan	New Jersey
6	Michigan	Michigan	Pennsylvania	Pennsylvania
7	Pennsylvania	Pennsylvania	Texas	Washington
8	Ohio	Ohio	Indiana	Illinois
9	Indiana	Oregon	Ohio	Massachusetts
10	New Jersey	Washington	Oklahoma	Wisconsin

SOURCES: All data from the National Committee For Adoption's 1986 adoption survey, except that foreign adoptions data were ordered by NCFA from the Immigration and Naturalization Service, U.S. Department of Justice, Washington, D.C. calendar year 1986.

Table 5. Number of Domestic Infant Adoptions, Abortions, Live Births, and Nonmarital Live Births, and Ratios, for Each State, Division and the United States: 1986 National Committee For Adoption Survey, 1986 Live Births, and 1985 Abortions (Ratio per 1,000)

Geographic Division and State	Number				Ratios			
	Domestic Infant Adoptions	Abortions	Live Births	Nonmarital Live Births	Infant Adoptions per 1,000 Abortions	Infant Adoptions per 1,000 Live Births	Infant Adoptions per 1,000 Nonmarital Live Births	Abortions per 1,000 Live Births
United States	24,589	1,588,550	3,756,547	878,477	15.5	6.5	28.0	422.9
New England	1,184	85,350	181,227	33,764	13.9	6.5	35.1	471.0
Maine	56	4,960	16,709	3,171	11.3	3.4	17.7	296.8
New Hampshire	49	7,030	15,895	2,213	7.0	3.1	22.1	442.3
Vermont	97	3,430	8,139	1,359	28.3	11.9	71.4	421.4
Massachusetts	560	40,310	82,190	15,861	13.9	6.8	35.3	490.4
Rhode Island	115	7,770	13,444	2,656	14.8	8.6	43.3	578.0
Connecticut	307	21,850	44,850	8,504	14.1	6.8	36.1	487.2
Middle Atlantic	2,851	321,680	533,809	141,720	8.9	5.3	20.1	602.6
New York	1,732	195,120	264,027	77,535	8.9	6.6	22.3	739.0
New Jersey	134	69,190	108,812	24,887	1.9	1.2	5.4	635.9
Pennsylvania	985	57,370	160,970	39,298	17.2	6.1	25.1	356.4
East North Central	5,079	220,630	624,029	142,221	23.0	8.1	35.7	353.6
Ohio	759	57,360	158,026	36,917	13.2	4.8	20.6	363.0
Indiana	275	16,090	79,322	16,657	17.1	3.5	16.5	202.8
Illinois	2,564	64,960	176,717	47,843	39.5	14.5	53.6	367.6
Michigan	988	64,390	137,631	26,620	15.3	7.2	37.1	467.8
Wisconsin	493	17,830	72,333	14,184	27.7	6.8	34.8	246.5
West North Central	1,411	68,210	265,939	47,253	20.7	5.3	29.9	256.5
Minnesota	260	16,850	65,784	10,721	15.4	4.0	24.3	256.1
Iowa	148	9,930	38,771	5,825	14.9	3.8	25.4	256.1
Missouri	438	20,100	75,259	16,917	21.8	5.8	25.9	267.1
North Dakota	49	2,850	10,819	1,398	17.2	4.5	35.1	263.4
South Dakota	114	1,650	11,615	2,036	69.1	9.8	56.0	142.1
Nebraska	164	6,680	24,426	3,788	24.6	6.7	43.3	273.5
Kansas	238	10,150	39,265	6,568	23.4	6.1	36.2	258.5

Region/State							
South Atlantic	4,235	257,120	607,558	160,827	16.5	7.0	26.3	423.2
Delaware	25	4,590	9,718	2,621	5.4	2.6	9.5	472.3
Maryland	364	29,480	69,538	21,198	12.3	5.2	17.2	423.9
District of Columbia	78	23,910	10,045	5,800	3.3	7.8	13.4	2,380.3
Virginia	120	34,180	87,183	19,538	3.5	1.4	6.1	392.0
West Virginia	135	4,590	23,236	4,530	29.4	5.8	29.8	197.5
North Carolina	494	34,180	90,254	21,323	14.5	5.5	23.2	378.7
South Carolina	532	11,200	51,800	14,304	47.5	10.3	37.2	216.2
Georgia	642	38,340	98,183	26,701	16.7	6.5	24.0	390.5
Florida	1,845	76,650	167,601	44,812	24.1	11.0	41.2	457.3
East South Central	1,307	57,440	219,379	56,735	22.8	6.0	23.0	261.8
Kentucky	279	9,820	51,794	10,355	28.4	5.4	26.9	189.6
Tennessee	392	22,350	66,249	16,767	17.5	5.9	23.4	337.4
Alabama	284	19,380	59,465	15,385	14.7	4.8	18.5	325.9
Mississippi	352	5,890	41,871	14,228	59.8	8.4	24.7	140.7
West South Central	3,291	138,580	470,054	95,476	23.7	7.0	34.5	294.8
Arkansas	370	5,420	34,393	8,246	68.3	10.8	44.9	157.6
Louisiana	174	19,240	77,955	23,564	9.0	2.2	7.4	246.8
Oklahoma	569	13,100	50,640	9,426	43.4	11.2	60.4	258.7
Texas	2,178	100,820	307,066	54,240	21.6	7.1	40.2	328.3
Mountain	1,607	74,580	233,541	44,779	21.5	6.9	35.9	319.3
Montana	156	3,710	12,734	2,262	42.0	12.3	69.0	291.3
Idaho	163	2,660	16,448	1,949	61.3	9.9	83.6	161.7
Wyoming	56	1,070	8,633	1,202	52.3	6.5	46.6	123.9
Colorado	326	24,350	55,151	9,927	13.4	5.9	32.8	441.5
New Mexico	97	6,110	27,392	7,629	15.9	3.5	12.7	223.1
Arizona	313	22,330	60,874	15,598	14.0	5.1	20.1	366.8
Utah	416	4,440	36,412	3,575	93.7	11.4	116.4	121.9
Nevada	80	9,910	15,897	2,637	8.1	5.0	30.3	623.4
Pacific	3,624	364,960	621,011	155,702	9.9	5.8	23.3	587.7
Washington	620	30,990	69,440	13,745	20.0	8.9	45.1	446.3
Oregon	697	15,230	38,871	8,025	45.8	17.9	86.9	391.8
California	2,070	304,130	482,236	127,683	6.8	4.3	16.2	630.7
Alaska	162	3,450	12,167	2,531	47.0	13.3	64.0	283.6
Hawaii	75	11,160	18,297	3,718	6.7	4.1	20.2	609.9

SOURCES: Adoptions for 1986 from NCFA survey; see note and sources on table 1. 1986 live births and nonmarital live births from National Center for Health Statistics: "Advance Report of Final Natality Statistics, 1986" *Monthly Vital Statistics Report*. Vol. 37, No. 3, Supplement, July 12, 1988. 1985 abortion data from Stanley K. Henshaw and Jennifer Van Vort, "Abortion Services in the United States, Each State and Metropolitan Area, 1984–1985", the Alan Guttmacher Institute, New York, 1988. 1985 abortion data were used because 1986 data were not available at this printing.

Appendix

Table 6. Number of Foreign Adoptions, Percent Distribution, and 1985–1987 Percentage Change for Each State, Division, and the United States

Geographic Division and State	1985 Number	1985 Percent	1986 Number	1986 Percent	1987 Number	1987 Percent	Percent Increase + (or decrease −) 1985 to 1987
United States	9,261	100.0	9,909	100.0	10,068	100.0	+8.7
New England	689	7.3	726	7.4	872	8.6	+26.6
Maine	40	0.4	55	0.6	68	0.7	+70.0
New Hampshire	45	0.5	47	0.5	56	0.6	+24.4
Vermont	48	0.5	53	0.5	49	0.5	+2.1
Massachusetts	320	3.4	356	3.6	388	3.8	+21.3
Rhode Island	29	0.3	19	0.2	15	0.1	(−48.3)
Connecticut	207	2.2	196	2.0	296	2.9	+43.0
Middle Atlantic	2,048	22.2	2,067	20.9	2,147	21.4	+4.8
New York	1,017	11.1	1,052	10.7	1,080	10.8	+6.2
New Jersey	516	5.6	515	5.2	547	5.4	+6.0
Pennsylvania	515	5.5	500	5.0	520	5.2	+1.0
East North Central	1,450	15.6	1,724	17.5	1,863	18.5	+28.5
Ohio	217	2.3	234	2.4	253	2.5	+16.6
Indiana	99	1.1	91	0.9	97	1.0	(−2.0)
Illinois	308	3.3	396	4.0	428	4.2	+39.0
Michigan	529	5.7	626	6.4	779	7.8	+47.3
Wisconsin	297	3.2	377	3.8	306	3.0	+3.0
West North Central	1,292	14.0	1,453	14.8	1,290	12.9	(−0.2)
Minnesota	712	7.8	762	7.8	724	7.2	+1.7
Iowa	277	3.0	315	3.2	250	2.5	(−9.7)
Missouri	100	1.1	157	1.6	123	1.2	+23.0
North Dakota	40	0.4	37	0.4	24	0.2	(−40.0)
South Dakota	28	0.3	42	0.4	37	0.4	+32.1
Nebraska	86	0.9	87	0.9	86	0.9	0.0
Kansas	49	0.5	53	0.5	46	0.5	(−6.1)
South Atlantic	979	10.6	916	9.1	1,052	10.2	+7.5
Delaware	21	0.2	33	0.3	51	0.5	+142.9
Maryland	306	3.3	330	3.3	306	3.0	0.0

District of Columbia	30	0.3	14	0.1	32	0.3	+6.7
Virginia	230	2.5	199	2.0	237	2.3	+3.0
West Virginia	34	0.4	48	0.5	44	0.4	+29.4
North Carolina	43	0.5	54	0.5	64	0.6	+48.8
South Carolina	37	0.4	26	0.3	31	0.3	(−16.2)
Georgia	100	1.1	82	0.8	125	1.2	+25.0
Florida	178	1.9	130	1.3	162	1.6	(−9.0)
East South Central	241	2.6	260	2.6	273	2.7	+13.3
Kentucky	57	0.6	76	0.8	99	1.0	+73.7
Tennessee	81	0.9	88	0.9	100	1.0	+23.5
Alabama	65	0.7	62	0.6	34	0.3	(−47.7)
Mississippi	38	0.4	34	0.3	40	0.4	+5.3
West South Central	343	3.6	389	3.9	348	3.5	+1.5
Arkansas	21	0.2	27	0.3	28	0.3	+33.3
Louisiana	49	0.5	58	0.6	38	0.4	+22.4
Oklahoma	65	0.7	72	0.7	80	0.8	+23.1
Texas	208	2.2	232	2.3	202	2.0	+2.9
Mountain	639	7.0	696	7.0	634	6.2	(−0.8)
Montana	48	0.5	67	0.7	83	0.8	+72.9
Idaho	52	0.6	63	0.6	44	0.4	(−15.4)
Wyoming	15	0.2	15	0.2	17	0.2	+13.3
Colorado	266	2.9	280	2.8	218	2.2	(−18.1)
New Mexico	56	0.6	56	0.6	52	0.5	(−7.1)
Arizona	84	0.9	83	0.8	89	0.9	+6.0
Utah	102	1.1	120	1.2	116	1.1	+13.7
Nevada	16	0.2	12	0.1	15	0.1	(−6.3)
Pacific	1,580	17.1	1,678	17.0	1,589	15.7	+0.6
Washington	442	4.8	447	4.5	429	4.2	(−2.9)
Oregon	251	2.7	262	2.6	264	2.6	+5.2
California	639	7.0	744	7.6	700	7.0	+9.5
Alaska	58	0.6	75	0.8	74	0.7	+27.6
Hawaii	190	2.0	150	1.5	122	1.2	(−35.8)

NOTES: Percentages may not add to 100.0 due to rounding. Data are for fiscal years. Excluded from the totals are adoptees to Guam, Puerto Rico, and the Virgin Islands (7, 16, and 2 respectively in 1985; 6, 27, and 3 respectively in 1986; and 7, 21, and 1 respectively in 1987).

SOURCE: These data are based on special tabulations purchased from the Statistical Analysis Branch, Immigration and Naturalization Service (INS) by the National Committee For Adoption.

Table 7. Number and Percent of Foreign Adoptions in the U.S. According to Sex, Age, and Major Countries of Origin: Fiscal Years 1985, 1986, and 1987

Selected Characteristics	1985 Number	1985 Percent	1986 Number	1986 Percent	1987 Number	1987 Percent
Total	9,286	100.0	9,945	100.0	10,097	100.0
Sex						
Male	4,018	43.3	4,344	43.7	4,460	44.2
Female	5,268	56.7	5,601	56.3	5,637	55.8
Age						
Under 1 year	5,657	60.9	6,364	64.0	6,450	63.9
1–4 years	2,262	24.4	2,111	21.2	2,180	21.6
5–9 years	866	9.3	933	9.4	963	9.5
10 years or over	501	5.4	537	5.4	504	5.0
Major countries of origin ranked						
Korea	5,694	61.3	6,188	62.2	5,910	58.5
India	496	5.3	588	5.9	807	8.0
Colombia	622	6.7	550	5.5	724	7.2
Philippines	515	5.5	634	6.4	593	5.9

Guatemala	175	1.9	228	2.3	291	2.9
Chile	206	2.2	317	3.2	238	2.4
Mexico	137	1.5	143	1.4	178	1.8
Brazil	242	2.6	193	1.9	148	1.5
El Salvador	310	3.3	147	1.5	135	1.3
Honduras	181	1.9	135	1.4	114	1.1
All others	708	7.6	822	8.3	959	9.5
Major states of destination ranked						
New York	1,017	11.1	1,052	10.7	1,080	10.8
Michigan	529	5.7	626	6.4	779	7.8
Minnesota	712	7.8	762	7.8	724	7.2
California	639	7.0	744	7.6	700	7.0
New Jersey	516	5.6	515	5.2	547	5.4
Pennsylvania	515	5.5	500	5.0	520	5.2
Washington	442	4.8	447	4.5	429	4.2
Illinois	308	3.3	396	4.0	428	4.2
Massachusetts	320	3.4	356	3.6	388	3.8
Wisconsin	297	3.2	377	3.8	306	3.0
All others	4,242	42.6	4,723	41.4	4,821	41.4

NOTES: Total may not add to 100.0 due to rounding. Rankings are from highest to lowest based on 1987 data.

SOURCE: Compiled from data purchased by the National Committee For Adoption from the Statistical Analysis Branch, U.S. Immigration and Naturalization Service.

Table 8. Number of Unrelated Domestic Adoptions of Infants and as a Percentage of Unrelated Domestic Adoptions, 1986 Live Births, and 1986 Births to Unmarried Women for Each State, Division, and the United States: 1986 National Committee for Adoption Survey

Geographic Division and State	Unrelated Domestic Adoptions of Infants...	...as a Percentage of Unrelated Domestic Adoptions	...as a Percentage of 1986 Live U.S. Births[1]	...as a Percentage of 1986 Births to U.S. Unmarried Women[1]
United States	24,589	48.1	0.7	2.8
New England	1,184	49.7	0.7	3.5
Maine	56	20.6	0.3	1.8
New Hampshire	49	29.5	0.3	2.2
Vermont	97	74.6	1.2	7.1
Massachusetts	560	48.4	0.7	3.5
Rhode Island	115	63.9	0.9	4.3
Connecticut	307	64.6	0.7	3.6
Middle Atlantic	2,851	40.3	0.5	2.0
New York	1,732	48.4	0.7	2.2
New Jersey	134	9.2	0.1	0.5
Pennsylvania	985	48.4	0.6	2.5
East North Central	5,079	49.1	0.8	3.6
Ohio	759	48.4	0.5	2.1
Indiana	275	18.4	0.3	1.7
Illinois	2,564	58.6	1.5	5.4
Michigan	988	48.4	0.7	3.7
Wisconsin	493	57.3	0.7	3.5
West North Central	1,411	42.3	0.5	3.0
Minnesota	260	43.3	0.4	2.4
Iowa	148	20.5	0.4	2.5
Missouri	438	48.4	0.6	2.6
North Dakota	49	28.3	0.5	3.5
South Dakota	114	48.5	1.0	5.6
Nebraska	164	78.8	0.7	4.3
Kansas	238	48.5	0.6	3.6

Appendix 329

South Atlantic	4,235	49.7	2.6
Delaware	25	25.5	1.0
Maryland	364	48.3	1.7
District of Columbia	78	48.1	1.3
Virginia	120	14.9	0.6
West Virginia	135	49.6	3.0
North Carolina	494	48.4	2.3
South Carolina	532	83.3	3.7
Georgia	642	67.2	2.4
Florida	1,845	48.4	4.1
East South Central	1,307	52.0	2.3
Kentucky	279	70.8	2.7
Tennessee	392	48.5	2.3
Alabama	284	48.7	1.8
Mississippi	352	48.4	2.5
West South Central	3,291	47.5	3.4
Arkansas	370	48.4	4.5
Louisiana	174	35.2	0.7
Oklahoma	569	48.4	6.0
Texas	2,178	48.4	4.0
Mountain	1,607	43.8	3.6
Montana	156	48.3	6.9
Idaho	163	58.8	8.4
Wyoming	56	48.7	4.7
Colorado	326	42.4	3.3
New Mexico	97	12.1	1.3
Arizona	313	48.5	2.0
Utah	416	86.8	11.6
Nevada	80	31.4	3.0
Pacific	3,624	56.5	2.3
Washington	620	64.3	4.5
Oregon	697	67.3	8.7
California	2,070	52.1	1.6
Alaska	162	47.6	6.4
Hawaii	75	89.3	2.0

[1] Natality data on live births and births to unmarried women obtained from National Center for Health Statistics: "Advance Report of Final Natality Statistics, 1986," *Monthly Vital Statistics Report*, Vol. 37, No. 3, Supplement, July 12, 1988.

NOTE: Unrelated domestic adoptions of infants category does not include foreign adoptions.

3. STATE SOCIAL SERVICES OFFICES

ALABAMA

Dr. Jerry Milner
Alabama Department of Human Resources
64 N. Union St.
Montgomery, AL 36130
(205) 261-3409

ALASKA

Barbara McPhearson
Alaska Department of Health and Social Services
Pouch H-05
Juneau, AK 99811
(907) 465-3023

ARIZONA

Carol Lussier
Adoption Coordinator
P.O. Box 6123
Phoenix, AZ 85005
(602) 255-3981

ARKANSAS

Helen Beard
Permanency Planning Unit Manager
Division of Children and Family Services
Slot 808
P.O. Box 1437
Little Rock, AR 72203
(501) 682-8462

CALIFORNIA

James W. Brown
Chief, Adoptions Branch
California Department of Social Services
744 P St., M/S 19-69
Sacramento, CA 95814
(916) 445-3146

COLORADO

Barbara Kilmore
Colorado Department of Social Services
1575 Sherman St.
Denver, CO 80203
(303) 866-3209

CONNECTICUT

Jean Watson
Adoption Services Coordinator
Connecticut Department of Children and Youth Services
White Hall, Bldg. 2
Undercliff Rd.
Meriden, CT 06450
(203) 238-6640

DELAWARE

Carol King
1st State Executive Plaza
330 E. 30th St., 3d Floor
Wilmington, DE 19802
(302) 571-6419

DISTRICT OF COLUMBIA

Evelyn C. Andrews
District of Columbia Department of Human Services
500 1st St. NW, Room 8040
Washington, DC 20001
(202) 724-2093

FLORIDA

Gloria Walker
Florida Department of Health and Rehabilitative Services
1317 Winewood Blvd.
Tallahassee, FL 32399-0700
(904) 488-8000

GEORGIA

Forest Burson
Georgia Department of Human Resources
State Adoption Unit
878 Peachtree St. NE, Room 501
Atlanta, GA 30309-3917
(404) 894-3376

HAWAII

Beatrice Yuh
Hawaii Department of Human Services
Family and Children's Services
P.O. Box 339
Honolulu, HI 96809
(808) 548-7502

IDAHO

Shirley Wheatley
State Adoptions Coordinator
Department of Health and Welfare
Division of Family and Children's Services
450 W. State St.
Boise, ID 83720
(208) 334-5700 or
(208) 334-5697

ILLINOIS

Gary Morgan
Illinois Department of Children and Family Services
100 W. Randolph St., Suite 6-211
Chicago, IL 60601
(312) 917-6864

INDIANA

Dr. Ruth Lambert
Indiana Department of Public Welfare
Child Welfare and Social Services Division
141 South Meridian St., 6th Floor
Indianapolis, IN 46225
(317) 232-4448

IOWA

Margaret Corkery
Iowa Department of Human Services
Hoover State Office Building, 5th Floor
Des Moines, IA 50319
(515) 281-5358

KANSAS

Barbara Stodgell
Kansas Department of Social and Rehabilitative Services
300 SW Oakley
Topeka, KS 66606
(913) 296-4661

KENTUCKY

Sue Howard
Department for Social Services
275 E. Main St., 6th Floor
Frankfort, KY 40621
(502) 564-2136

LOUISIANA

Patsy Scott-Johnson
Adoption Program Manager
Louisiana Department of Health and Social Services
Division of Children, Youth and Family Services
Office of Community Services
P.O. Box 3318
Baton Rouge, LA 70821
(504) 342-9925

MAINE

Leanore Taylor
Maine Department of Human Services
State House
221 State St.
Augusta, ME 04333
(207) 289-3271

MASSACHUSETTS

Sheila Frankel
Massachusetts Department of Social Services
150 Causeway St.
Boston, MA 02114
(617) 727-0900, ext. 231

MICHIGAN

Richard Hoekstra
Michigan Department of Social Services
P.O. Box 30037
Lansing, MI 48909
(517) 373-3513

MINNESOTA

Robert DeNardo
Children's Services
Minnesota Department of Human Services
444 Lafayette Rd.
St. Paul, MN 55155-3831
(612) 296-5288

MISSISSIPPI

Mary Ann Everett
Mississippi Department of Public Welfare
P.O. Box 352
Jackson, MS 39205
(601) 354-0341

MISSOURI

Benita Weitzel
Missouri Division of Family Services
P.O. Box 88
Jefferson City, MO 65103
(314) 751-2427

MONTANA

Betty Bay
Department of Family Services
P.O. Box 8005
Helena, MT 59604
(406) 444-5900

NEBRASKA

Mary Dyer
Nebraska Department of Social Services
301 Centennial Mall
Lincoln, NE 68509
(402) 471-3121

NEVADA

Rota Rosaschi
Social Services
Nevada State Welfare Division
2527 N. Carson St.
Carson City, NV 89710
(702) 885-3023

NEW HAMPSHIRE

Glenna Law
New Hampshire Division for Children and Youth Services, Adoption Unit
6 Hazen Dr.
Concord, NH 03301
(603) 668-2330

NEW JERSEY

Mary Lou Sweeney
New Jersey Division of Youth and Family Service
1 S. Montgomery St., C.N. 717
Trenton, NJ 08626
(609) 633-3991

NEW MEXICO

Pat Shannon
Adoption Unit
New Mexico Human Services Department
P.O. Box 2348
PERA Building, Rm. 515
Santa Fe, NM 87504-2348
(505) 827-4109

NEW YORK

Peter Winkler
New York State Department of Social Services
40 N. Pearl St.
Albany, NY 12243
(518) 473-0855

NORTH CAROLINA

Robin Peacock
North Carolina Division of Social Services
325 N. Salisbury St.
Raleigh, NC 27611

NORTH DAKOTA

Linda Schell
North Dakota Department of Human Services
State Capitol Building
Bismarck, ND 58505
(701) 224-3580

OHIO

Kenneth E. Kotch
Ohio Department of Human Services
30 E. Broad St., 30th Floor
Columbus, OH 43266-0423
(614) 466-8520

OKLAHOMA

Jane Connor
Oklahoma Department of Human Services
P.O. Box 25352
Oklahoma City, OK 73125
(405) 521-2475

OREGON

Fred Stock
Oregon Department of Human Services
Children's Services Division
198 Commercial St. SE
Salem, OR 97310
(503) 378-4452

PENNSYLVANIA

Robert Gioffre
Pennsylvania Department of Public Welfare
Office of Children, Youth and Families
Health and Welfare Bldg. Annex
Box 2675
Harrisburg, PA 17105
(717) 787-7756

RHODE ISLAND

John Sinapi Jr.
Rhode Island Department of Children and Their Families
610 Mt. Pleasant Ave., Bldg. 5
Providence, RI 02908
(401) 457-4631

SOUTH CAROLINA

Mary Jo Morrison
Deputy for Adoption
Office of Children, Family, and Adult Services
South Carolina Department of Social Services
P.O. Box 1520
Columbia, SC 29202
(803) 734-5670

SOUTH DAKOTA

Patricia Stewart
South Dakota Department of Social Services
Child Protection Services
700 Governors Dr.
Pierre, SD 57501
(605) 773-3227

TENNESSEE

Joyce N. Harris
Tennessee Department of Human Services
400 Deaderick St.
Nashville, TN 37219
(615) 741-5935

TEXAS

Susan Klickman
Texas Department of Human Services
P.O. Box 2960
Austin, TX 78769
(512) 450-3302

UTAH

William Ward
Utah Department of Social Services
Division of Family Services
120 N. 200 West
Salt Lake City, UT 84103
(801) 538-4084

VERMONT

Cynthia Walcott
Vermont Department of Social & Rehabilitative Services

103 S. Main St.
Waterbury, VT 05676
(802) 241-2131

VIRGINIA

Brenda Kerr
Virginia Department of Social Services
8007 Discovery Dr.
Richmond, VA 23229-8699
(804) 662-9081

WASHINGTON

Patrick Weber
Washington Department of Social and Health Services, OB 41-C
Olympia, WA 98504
(206) 753-0965

WEST VIRGINIA

Family and Children Services
Bureau of Social Services

Department of Human Services
1900 Washington St.
Charleston, WV 25305
(304) 348-7980

WISCONSIN

Christopher Marceil
Wisconsin Department of Health and Social Services
P.O. Box 7851
Madison, WI 53707
(608) 266-0700

WYOMING

Patricia McDaniel
Division of Public Assistance and Social Services
Wyoming Department of Social Services
Hathaway Building, Room 319
Cheyenne, WY 82002
(307) 777-6789

GOVERNMENT ADOPTION OFFICES IN CANADA

Adoption Coordinator
Ministry of Social Services and Housing
Parliament Building
Victoria, British Columbia
V8W 3A2
(604) 387-3660

Program Supervisor, Adoption Services
Department of Social Services
9th Floor, Seventh Plaza
10030 107th St.
Edmonton, Alberta
T5J 3E4
(403) 422-0177

Program Manager, Adoption Services
Family Support Division
Department of Social Services
12th Floor
1929 Broad St.
Regina, Saskatchewan
S4P 3V6
(306) 787-5698

Adoption Coordinator
Department of Community Services
114 Garry St.
Winnepeg, Manitoba
R3C 1G1
(204) 945-6955

Adoption Coordinator
Ministry of Community and Social Services
2nd Floor, Ste. 209
700 Bay St.
Toronto, Ontario
M7A 1E9
(416) 327-4730

Director of Adoptions Internationale
3700 Rue Berri, 4e Etage
Montreal, Quebec
H2L 4G9
(514) 873-5226

Program Consultant, Adoption Services
Department of Health and Community Services
P.O. Box 5100
Fredrickton, New Brunswick
E3B 5G8
(506) 453-3830

Coordinator, Adoption Services
Department of Community Services
P.O. Box 696
Halifax, Nova Scotia
B3J 2T7
(902) 424-3205

Assistant Director of Child Welfare
Department of Social Services
3rd Floor
Confederation Building
P.O. Box 4750
St. Johns, Newfoundland
A1C 5T7
(709) 729-2667

Program Officer, Family and Children's Services
Government of the Northwest Territories
Yellowknife
Northwest Territory
X1A 2L9
(403) 920-8920

Placement and Support Services Supervisor
Department of Health and Human Resources
P.O. Box 2703
H-10, Ste. 201
Royal Banks Building
Whitehorse, Yukon Territory
Y1A 2C6
(403) 667-3002

4. ADOPTION AGENCIES

This listing, drawn from agencies accredited by the Council on Accreditation and/or members of the National Committee For Adoption, is only a sampling of the hundreds of adoption agencies nationwide. For a more complete listing, see *The Adoption Directory* by Ellen Paul, editor (New York: Gale Research Inc., 1989) and *CWLA's Guide to Adoption Agencies: A National Directory of Adoption Agencies and Adoption Resources* by Julia L. Posner (Washington, D.C., Child Welfare League of America, 1989).

ALABAMA

Children's Aid Society
3600 8th Ave. S, Suite 300
Birmingham, AL 35222

Lifeline Children's Services
2908 Pump House Rd.
Birmingham, AL 35243

ALASKA

Catholic Social Services
225 Cordova, Bldg. B
Anchorage, AK 99501

LDS Social Services
Alaska Mutual Bank Bldg.
4020 DeBarr St. #225A
Anchorage, AK 99508

ARIZONA

Aid for Adoption of Special Kids (AASK)
1611 E. Camelback, Suite 8
Phoenix, AZ 85016

Arizona Children's Home Association
2700 S. 8th Ave.
Tucson, AZ 85713

Catholic Family and Community Services
1825 W. Northern Ave.
Phoenix, AZ 85021

Family Service Agency
1530 E. Flower
Phoenix, AZ 85014

Jewish Family and Children's Services
2033 N. 7th St.
Phoenix, AZ 85006

LDS Social Services
235 S. El Dorado
Mesa, AZ 85202

LDS Social Services
P.O. Box 3544
Page, AZ 86040

LDS Social Services
P.O. Box 856
601 S. Main St.
Snowflake, AZ 85937

ARKANSAS

Bethany Christian Services
Prospect Bldg.
1501 N. University, Suite 564
Little Rock, AR 72207-5242

CALIFORNIA

Aid for Adoption of Special Kids (AASK)
3530 Grand Ave.
Oakland, CA 94610

Aid for Adoption of Special Kids (AASK)
National Office
450 Sansome #210
San Francisco, CA 94111

Bethany Christian Services
Unit #1
9556 Flower
Bellflower, CA 90706-5708

Catholic Community Services
349 Cedar St.
San Diego, CA 92101-3197

Children's Home Society of California
2727 W. 6th St.
Los Angeles, CA 90057

Holt International Children's Services
5230 Clark Ave., Suite 32
Lakewood, CA 90712

LDS Social Services
3000 Auburn Blvd., Suite 1
Sacramento, CA 95821

LDS Social Services
791 N. Pepper Ave.
Colton, CA 92324

LDS Social Services
3585 Maple St., Suite 256
Ventura, CA 93004

Vista del Mar
3200 Motor Ave.
Los Angeles, CA 90034

COLORADO

Bethany Christian Services
2140 S. Ivanhoe, Suite 106
Denver, CO 80222-5749

Denver Catholic Community Service
200 Josephine St.
Denver, CO 80206

Jewish Family and Children's Service of Colorado
300 S. Dahlia St., Suite 101
Denver, CO 80222

LDS Social Services
3263 Fraser St., Suite 3
Aurora, CO 80111

CONNECTICUT

The Casey Family Program
2710 North Ave., Suite 201
Bridgeport, CT 06604

Catholic Charities/Catholic Family Service
896 Asylum Ave.
Hartford, CT 06105

Child and Family Agency of Southeastern Connecticut
255 Hempstead St.
New London, CT 06320

Child and Family Services
1680 Albany Ave.
Hartford, CT 06105

Family and Children's Aid of Greater Norwalk
138 Main St.
Norwalk, CT 06851

Family Service Inc.
92 Vine St.
New Britain, CT 06052

DELAWARE

Catholic Social Services
1200 N. Broom St.
Wilmington, DE 19806-4297

Children's Bureau of Delaware
2005 Baynard Blvd.
Wilmington, DE 19802

DISTRICT OF COLUMBIA

Adoption Services Information Agency/ASIA
7720 Alaska Ave. NW
Washington, DC 20012

The Barker Foundation
4114 River Rd. NW
Washington, DC 20016

Family and Child Services of Washington, D.C.
929 L St. NW
Washington, DC 20001

FLORIDA

Catholic Community Services
9401 Biscayne Blvd.
Miami, FL 33138-2998

The Children's Home Society of Florida
3027 San Diego Rd.
P.O. Box 10097
Jacksonville, FL 32247-0097

Florida Baptist Children's Home
P.O. Box 8190
Lakeland, FL 33802

LDS Social Services
1020 N. Orlando Ave., Suite F
Winter Park, FL 32789

Shepherd Care Ministries Inc.
5935 Taft St., Suite B
Hollywood, FL 33021

Universal Aid for Children, Inc.
Box 610246
North Miami, FL 33161

GEORGIA

Bethany Christian Services
682 Mulberry
Macon, GA 31201-2622

Families First
P.O. Box 7948, Station C
Atlanta, GA 30357

Family Counseling Center
1914 Central Ave.
Augusta, GA 30904

Jewish Family Service
1605 Peachtree Rd. NE
Atlanta, GA 30309

The New Beginnings Adoption and Counseling Agency
3564 Forrest Rd.
Columbus, GA 31907

Parent and Child Development Services Inc.
21 E. Broad St.
Savannah, GA 31401

HAWAII

Child and Family Service
200 N. Vineyard Blvd. #20
Honolulu, HI 96817

Social Services of Honolulu
1500 S. Beretania St. #403
Honolulu, HI 96826

IDAHO

LDS Social Services
10740 Fairview, Suite 100
Boise, ID 83704

ILLINOIS

Bensenville Home Society
331 S. York Rd.
Bensenville, IL 60106

Bethany Christian Services
9730 S. Western St., Suite 203
Evergreen Park, IL 60642-2814

Catholic Social Services
P.O. Box 817
2900 W. Heading
Peoria, IL 61625

Chicago Child Care Society
5467 S. University Ave.
Chicago, IL 60615

Children's Home and Aid Society of Illinois
1122 N. Dearborn St.
Chicago, IL 60610

Counseling and Family Service
1821 N. Knoxville Ave.
Peoria, IL 61603

The Cradle Society
2049 Ridge Ave.
Evanston, IL 60204

Evangelical Child and Family Agency
1530 N. Main St.
Wheaton, IL 60187

Jewish Children's Bureau of Chicago
1 S. Franklin St.
Chicago, IL 60606

Lutheran Child and Family Services of Illinois
P.O. Box 78
River Forest, IL 60305

St. Mary's Services
717 W. Kirchoff Rd.
Arlington Heights, IL 60005-2358

INDIANA

Bethany Christian Services
9595 N. Whitley Dr., Suite 210
Indianapolis, IN 46240-1308

Childplace
2420 Highway 62
Jeffersonville, IN 47130

Children's Bureau of Indianapolis
615 N. Alabama St.
Indianapolis, IN 46204

Family and Children's Service
305 S. 3rd Ave.
Evansville, IN 47708

LDS Social Services
5151 W. 84th St.
Indianapolis, IN 46268

Lutheran Social Services
330 Madison St.
P.O. Box 11329
Fort Wayne, IN 46857-1329

IOWA

Bethany Christian Services
322 Central Ave. NW
P.O. Box 143
Orange City, IA 51041-1341

Catholic Council for Social Concern
818 5th Avenue
P.O. Box 723
Des Moines, IA 50309

Family Resources
115 W. 6th St.
P.O. Box 190
Davenport, IA 52805

Hillcrest Family Services
2005 Asbury Rd.
P.O. Box 1160
Dubuque, IA 52004-1160

Holt International Children's Services
2200 Abbott Dr.
Carter Lake, IA 51510

Lutheran Social Service of Iowa
3116 University Ave.
Des Moines, IA 50311

KANSAS

Gentle Shepherd Child Placement Services
  Inc.
P.O. Box 1172
Olathe, KS 66061

Heart of America Family Services
8047 Parallel Parkway
Kansas City, MO 66102

Kansas Children's Service League
P.O. Box 517
Wichita, KS 67201

LOUISIANA

Children's Bureau of
  New Orleans
The Maison Blanche Bldg.
921 Canal St., Suite 840
New Orleans, LA 70112

Jewish Children's Regional Service
5342 St. Charles Ave., Room 202
New Orleans, LA 70175-4998

LDS Social Services
2000 Old Spanish Trail
Pratt Center, Suite 115
Slidell, LA 70458

Volunteers of America
3900 N. Causeway, Suite 7200
Metairie, LA 70002-1737

MAINE

Community Counseling Center
622 Congress St.
P.O. Box 4016
Portland, ME 04101

St. Andre Home Inc.
283 Elm St.
Biddeford, ME 04005

Sweetser Children's Home
50 Moody St.
Saco, ME 04072

MARYLAND

Bethany Christian Services
1641 Route 3 N., #205
Crofton, MD 21114

Family and Children's Services of Central Maryland
204 W. Lanvale St.
Baltimore, MD 21217

Jewish Social Service Agency
6123 Montrose Rd.
Rockville, MD 20852

Jewish Family and Children's Services
5750 Park Heights Ave.
Baltimore, MD 21215

MASSACHUSETTS

Boston Children's Service Association
867 Boylston St.
Boston, MA 02116

Catholic Charities of the Diocese of Worcester
15 Ripley St.
Worcester, MA 01610

Children's Aid and Family Service
47 Holt St.
Fitchburg, MA 01420

New Bedford Child and Family Service
1061 Pleasant St.
New Bedford, MA 02740-6728

The New England Home for Little Wanderers
161 S. Huntington Ave.
Boston, MA 02130

MICHIGAN

Bethany Christian Services
901 Eastern Ave. NE
Grand Rapids, MI 49503

Child and Family Services of Michigan Inc.
2157 University Park Dr.
P.O. Box 348
Okemos, MI 48805

The Donald M. Whaley Children's Center
1201 N. Grand Traverse St.
Flint, MI 48503

Family and Child Service of Midland
116 Harold St.
Midland, MI 48640

LDS Social Services
37634 Enterprise Court
Farmington Hills, MI 48018

Methodist Children's Home Society
26645 W. Six Mile Rd.
Detroit, MI 48240

MINNESOTA

Bethany Christian Services
421 S. Main
Stillwater, MN 55082-5127

Children's Home Society of Minnesota
2230 Como Ave.
St. Paul, MN 55108

Jewish Family Service
1546 St. Clair Ave.
St. Paul, MN 55105

Lutheran Social Service of Minnesota
2414 Park Ave.
Minneapolis, MN 55404

MISSISSIPPI

Bethany Christian Services
Woodland Hills Office Bldg., Suite 545
3000 Old Canton Rd.
Jackson, MS 39216-4212

Mississippi Children's Home Society
P.O. Box 1078
Jackson, MS 39205

MISSOURI

Bethany Christian Services
7750 Clayton Rd.
St. Louis, MO 63117-1353

Children's Home Society of Missouri
9445 Litzsinger Rd.
St. Louis, MO 63144

LDS Social Services
517 W. Walnut
Independence, MO 64050

MONTANA

LDS Social Services
2001 Eleventh Ave.
Helena, MT 59601

NEBRASKA

Nebraska Children's Home Society
3549 Fontenelle Blvd.
Omaha, NE 68104

NEVADA

LDS Social Services
513 S. 9th St.
Las Vegas, NV 89101

NEW HAMPSHIRE

Child and Family Services of New Hampshire
P.O. Box 448
Manchester, NH 03105

LDS Social Services
131 Route 101A, Amherst Plaza, Suite 204
Amherst, NH 03031

NEW JERSEY

Bethany Christian Services
475 High Mountain Rd.
North Haledon, NJ 07508-2603

Catholic Charities
47 N. Clinton Ave.
P.O. Box 1423
Trenton, NJ 08607-1423

The Children's Home Society of New Jersey
929 Parkside Ave.
Trenton, NJ 08618

Holt International Children's Services
2490 Pennington Rd.
Trenton, NJ 08638

NEW MEXICO

Christian Placement Services
W. Star Route, Box 48
Portales, NM 88130

Family and Children's Services Inc.
1503 University Blvd., NE
Albuquerque, NM 87102

LDS Social Services
3811 Altrisco NW
Albuquerque, NM 87120

NEW YORK

Catholic Home Bureau
1011 First Ave.
New York, NY 10022

Child and Family Services
330 Delaware Ave.
Buffalo, NY 14202

The Children's Aid Society
105 E. 22nd St.
New York, NY 10010

Harlem-Dowling Children's Service
2090 Adam Clayton Powell, Jr. Blvd., 3rd Floor
New York, NY 10027

Hillside Children's Center
1183 Monroe Ave.
Rochester, NY 14620-1699

LDS Social Services
105 Main St., Suite H
Fishkill, NY 12524

Louise Wise Services
12 E. 94th St.
New York, NY 10028

Parsons Child and Family Center
845 Central Ave.
Albany, NY 12206

Spence-Chapin Services
6 E. 94th St.
New York, NY 10128

NORTH CAROLINA

Bethany Christian Services
25 Reed St.
P.O. Box 15569
Asheville, NC 28813-0569

The Children's Home Society of North Carolina
740 Chestnut St.
P.O. Box 14608
Greensboro, NC 27415-4608

Family Services
610 Coliseum Dr.
Winston-Salem, NC 27106

NORTH DAKOTA

The Village Family Service Center
P.O. Box 7398
Fargo, ND 58103-7398

OHIO

Beech Brook
3737 Lander Rd.
Pepper Pike, OH 44124

Bethany Christian Services
Walter L. Mitchell Bldg., Suite 340
1655 W. Market St.
Akron, OH 44313-7004

Catholic Service League of Summit County
640 N, Main St.
Akron, OH 44310

The Children's Home of Cincinnati
5051 Duck Creek Rd.
Cincinnati, OH 45227

Family Counseling and Crittendon Services
185 S. 5th St.
Columbus, OH 43215

Family Counseling Services of Central Stark County
618 2nd St. NW
Canton, OH 44703

Family Service Agency
535 Marmion Ave.
Youngstown, OH 44502

Gentle Care Adoption Services
243 E. Livingston
Columbus, OH 43215

Jewish Family Service
1710 Section Rd.
P.O. Box 37904
Cincinnati, OH 45222

LDS Social Services
4431 Marketing Place
Groveport, OH 43125

OKLAHOMA

Deaconess Home
5401 N. Portland
Oklahoma City, OK 73112

LDS Social Services
2017 S. Elm Place, #107
Broken Arrow, OK 74012

OREGON

The Boys and Girls Aid Society of Oregon
2301 N.W. Glisan St.
Portland, OR 97210

Catholic Services for Children
319 SW Washington St.
Portland, OR 97204

Holt International Children's Services
P.O. Box 2880
Eugene, OR 97402

LDS Social Services
3000 Market St. NE, Suite 268
Salem, OR 97301

PENNSYLVANIA

Catholic Charities of the Diocese of
  Harrisburg, PA
4800 Union Deposit Rd.
P.O. Box 3551
Harrisburg, PA 17105

Children and Youth Services of Delaware
  County
Front and Orange Sts.
Media, PA 19063

Children's Home of Pittsburgh
5618 Kentucky Ave.
Pittsburgh, PA 15232

Family and Children's Services of
  Lancaster
630 Janet Ave.
Lancaster, PA 17601

Family Adoption Center
Family Health Council
625 Stanwix St.
Pittsburgh, PA 15222

Family Services
United Way Bldg.
110 W. 10th St.
Erie, PA 16501

Jewish Family and Children's Service of
  Philadelphia
1610 Spruce St.
Philadelphia, PA 19103-6764

Women's Christian Alliance
1610–14 N. Broad St.
Philadelphia, PA 19121

RHODE ISLAND

Catholic Social Services
433 Elmwood Ave.
Providence, RI 02907

Children's Friend and Service
2 Richmond St.
Providence, RI 02903

Jewish Family Service
229 Waterman St.
Providence, RI 02906

SOUTH CAROLINA

Bethany Christian Services
300 University Ridge, Suite 114
Greenville, SC 29601-3645

SOUTH DAKOTA

LDS Social Services
2525 W. Main St., #310
Rapid City, SD 57702

TENNESSEE

Bethany Christian Services
4719 Brainerd Rd., Suite D
Chattanooga, TN 37411-3830

Child and Family Services of Knox County
114 Dameron Ave.
Knoxville, TN 37917

Family and Children's Service
201 23rd Ave. N
Nashville, TN 37203

Family and Children's Services of
  Chattanooga
300 E. 8th St.
Chattanooga, TN 37403

TEXAS

Children's Shelter of San Antonio
625 North Alamo
San Antonio, TX 78215

Family Counseling and Children's Services
3700 W. Waco Dr.
Waco, TX 76710

The Gladney Center
2300 Hemphill St.
Ft. Worth, TX 76110

Jewish Family Service
7800 Northaven Rd., Suite B
Dallas, TX 75230-3299

Los Ninos International Adoption Center
25231 Grogans Mill Rd., Suite 345
Woodlands, TX 77380

Smithlawn Home and Adoption Agency
Box 6451
Lubbock, TX 79413

UTAH

Children's Aid Society of Utah
652 26th St.
Ogden, UT 84401

LDS Social Services (main office)
50 E. North Temple, 7th Floor
Salt Lake City, UT 84150

VERMONT

Vermont Catholic Charities
351 North Ave.
Burlington, VT 05401

Vermont Children's Aid Society
79 Weaver St.
Winooski, VT 05404

VIRGINIA

Bethany Christian Services
246 Maple Ave. E, Suite 200
Vienna, VA 22180-4631

Jewish Family Service of Tidewater
7300 Newport Ave.
P.O. Box 9503
Norfolk, VA 23505

LDS Social Services
P.O. Box 638
8110 Virginia Pine Court
Chesterfield, VA 23832

WASHINGTON

Bethany Christian Services
103 East Holly, Suite 316
Bellingham, WA 98225-4718

Catholic Community Services/Seattle/King
  County
1715 E. Cherry St.
P.O. Box 22608
Seattle, WA 98122

Children's Home Society of Washington
3300 E. 65th St.
Seattle, WA 98115

WISCONSIN

Bethany Christian Services
W 255 N477 Grandview Blvd., Suite 207
Waukesha, WI 53188-1606

Catholic Social Services
3051 S. Lake Dr.
P.O. Box 2018
Milwaukee, WI 53201

Children's Service Society of Wisconsin
1212 S. 70th St.
West Allis, WI 53214

Lutheran Social Services
3200 W. Highland Blvd.
Milwaukee, WI 53208

Wisconsin Lutheran Child and Family
  Service
6800 N. 76th St.
P.O. Box 23980
Milwaukee, WI 53223

5. INTERNATIONAL ADOPTION AGENCIES

These are only a few of the many international adoption agencies in the United States. Some of these listed concentrate on intercountry adoptions while others arrange adoptions within the United States and abroad.

Adoption Services Information Agency (ASIA)
7720 Alaska Ave. NW
Washington, DC 20012

The Barker Foundation
4114 River Rd. NW
Washington, DC 20016

Bethany Christian Services
901 Eastern Ave. NE
Grand Rapids, MI 49503-1295

Children's Home Society of Minnesota
2230 Como Ave.
St. Paul, MN 55108

Dillon Children's Services
2525 E. 21st. St.
Tulsa, OK 74114

FCVN (Friends of Children of Various Nations)
600 Gilpin St.
Denver, CO 80218

Holt International Children's Services Inc.
P.O. Box 2880
Eugene, OR 97402

Los Ninos International Adoption Center
25231 Grogans Mill Rd.
Suite 345
Woodlands, TX 77380

Spence-Chapin Services
6 E. 94th St.
New York, NY 10028

Universal Aid for Children
8760 NE 2nd Ave.
Miami Shores, FL 33138

Welcome House
P.O. Box 836
Doylestown, PA 18901

6. ADOPTION-RELATED ORGANIZATIONS

Adoptees' Liberty Movement Association (ALMA)
P.O. Box 154
Washington Bridge Station
New York, NY 10033
(212) 581-1568

Adoption Defense Fund
1930 17th St. NW, Suite B
Washington, DC 20009
(202) 332-5728

Adoptive Families of America Inc. (AFA)
3333 Highway 100 N
Minneapolis, MN 55422
(612) 535-4829

Aid to Adoption of Special Kids America (AASK)
National Office
450 Sansome St., Suite 210
San Francisco, CA 94111
(415) 434-2275

American Adoption Congress
1000 Connecticut Ave. NW, Suite 9
Washington, DC 20036
(800) 274-OPEN

American Bar Association
750 N. Lake Shore Dr.
Chicago, IL 60611
(312) 988-5000

The American Fertility Society
2140 Eleventh Avenue S, Suite 200
Birmingham, AL 35205-2800
(205) 933-8494

American Public Welfare Association
810 First St. NE, Suite 500
Washington, DC 20002-4205
(202) 682-0100

The Association for Children and Adults with Learning Disabilities Inc. (ACLD)
4156 Library Rd.
Pittsburgh, PA 15234
(412) 341-1515

Association of Jewish Family & Children's Agencies
3084 State Highway 27, Suite 1
P.O. Box 248
Kendall Park, NJ 08824-0248
(800) 634-7346
(908) 821-0909

The CAP Book
700 Exchange St.
Rochester, NY 14608
(716) 232-5110

Catholic Charities USA
1319 F St. NW
Washington, DC 20004
(202) 639-8400

Center for Biomedical Ethics
3-110 Owre Hall, UMHC Box 33
Harvard St. at East River Rd.
Minneapolis, MN 55455
(612) 615-4917

Child Welfare League of America Inc.
440 First St. NW, Suite 310
Washington, DC 20001
(202) 638-2952

COAC Black Child Advocacy Program
875 Avenue of the Americas
New York, NY 10001

Concerned United Birthparents Inc.
2000 Walker St.
Des Moines, IA 50317
(515) 263-9588

Council on Accreditation of Services for Families and Children Inc.
520 Eighth Ave., Suite 2202B
New York, NY 10018
(212) 714-9399

Hastings Center
225 Elm Rd.
Briarcliff Manor, NY 10510
(914) 762-8500

Hispanic Adoption Program
New York Council on Adoptable Children
666 Broadway, Suite 820
New York, NY 10012
(212) 475-0222

Homes for Black Children
Sydney Duncan
2340 Calvert St.
Detroit, MI 48206
(313) 869-2316

Homes for Black Children
Cynthia Ann Owens
3131 E. 38th St.
Indianapolis, IN 46218
(317) 545-5281

Indian Adoptive Family Circle
New Mexico, DHS—Adoptions
P.O. Box 2349
Santa Fe, NM 87503-2348

Indian Child Adoption Network
611 12th Ave. S, Suite 300
Seattle, WA 98144

International Concerns Committee for Children
911 Cypress Dr.
Boulder, CO 80303

International Soundex Reunion Registry
P.O. Box 2312
Carson City, NV 89702-2312
(702) 882-7755

The National Adoption Center
1218 Chestnut St.
Philadelphia, PA 19107
(215) 925-0200

National Adoption Information Clearinghouse
1400 Eye St. NW, Suite 600
Washington, DC 20005
(202) 842-1919

National Association of Social Workers
7981 Eastern Ave.
Silver Spring, MD 20910
(301) 565-0333
(800) 565-0333
Publications catalog or ordering number:
 (800) 752-3590

National Center for Health Statistics
3700 East-West Highway, Room I-57
Hyattsville, MD 20872
(301) 436-8500

National Coalition to End Racism in America's Child Care System Inc.
22075 Koths
Taylor, Michigan 48180
(313) 295-0257

National Committee For Adoption
1930 17th St. NW
Washington, D.C. 20009-6207
(202) 328-1200

National Foster Parent Association Inc.
Information & Services Office
226 Kilts Dr.
Houston, TX 77024
(713) 467-1850

National Resource Center for Special Needs Adoption
P.O. Box 337
Chelsea, MI 48118
(313) 475-8693

The Native American Adoption Resource Exchange (NAARE)
200 Charles St.
Pittsburgh, PA 15238

North American Council on Adoptable Children (NACAC)
1821 University Ave., Suite N-498
St. Paul, MN 55104
(612) 644-3036

One Church, One Child
Patricia O'Neal-Williams
National Staff Director
1317 Winewood Blvd., Bldg. 8
Tallahassee, FL 32301
(904) 488-8251

National Association of Black Social
    Workers
Child Adoption Counseling and Referral
    Service
Leora Neal, Executive Director
271 W. 125th St., Rm. 414
New York, NY 10027
(212) 222-5200

National Black Child Development Institute
Carole Jones
1463 Rhode Island Ave. NW
Washington, DC 20005
(202) 387-1281

National Coalition of Hispanic Mental
    Health and Human Services Organization
1015 15th St. NW, Suite 402
Washington, DC 20005
(202) 638-0505

National Down's Syndrome Adoption
    Exchange
56 Midchester Ave.
White Plains, NY 10606
(914) 428-1236

National Urban League
Johanne C. Dixon
Adoption Resource and Advocacy Center
500 E. 62nd St.
New York, NY 10021
(212) 310-9239

Positive Adoption Attitudes in the Media
    (PAAM)
Box 15293
Chevy Chase, MD 20825
(202) 244-9092

Puerto Rican Association for Family
    Affairs Inc.
853 Broadway, 5th Floor
New York, NY 10003
(212) 673-7320

RESOLVE
5 Water St.
Arlington, MA 02174
(617) 643-2424

Up with Down Syndrome Foundation Inc.
9270 Hammocks Blvd., Suite 301
Miami, FL 33196
(305) 386-9115

7. ADOPTIVE PARENT GROUPS

ALABAMA

Val Rocco
Alabama Friends of Adoption
P.O. Box 131267
Birmingham, AL 35213

ARIZONA

Terri Lindenmeier
Arizona Getting International Families Together (A.G.I.F.T.)
16053 N. 47th Drive
Glendale, AZ 85306

ARKANSAS

Connie Foster
Miracles
1008 Barbara
Jacksonville, AR 72076

CALIFORNIA

Lansing Wood
FAIR
P.O. Box 51436
Palo Alto, CA 94303

Julie Neumiller
North Coast Adoptive Families
4146 Dry Creek Rd.
Healdsburg, CA 95448

Open Door Society of Los Angeles
12235 Silva Place
Cerritos, CA 90701

Yasha Souseoff
OURS Through Adoption
P.O. Box 85152-343
San Diego, CA 92138

COLORADO

Violet Pierce
Adoptive Families of Denver Inc.
6660 S. Race Circle W
Littleton, CO 80121

CONNECTICUT

Nancy Coughlin
The Adoption Connection
3 Hampden Circle
Simsbury, CT 06070

Adoption Connection
P.O. Box 188
Farmington, CT 06034

DELAWARE

Marilyn Cockrell
Adoptive Families with Information & Support
P.O. Box 7268
Wilmington, DE 19803

DISTRICT OF COLUMBIA

Michelle Hester
Barker Foundation International Parents Group
4114 River Rd. NW
Washington, DC 20016

FLORIDA

Dr. Kathie Erwin
Bay Area Adoptive Families
305 Orangewood Lane
Largo, FL 34640

Claudia Dreyer
Lifeline for Children Inc.
P.O. Box 17184
Plantation, FL 33318

Jan Lifshin
Parents Adoption Lifeline
4317 Willow Brook Circle
West Palm Beach, FL 33417

GEORGIA

Gail Pendergrast
Augusta Parent Adoption League (APAL)
P.O. Box 15354
Augusta, GA 30919-1354

Midge Hansell Miller
Korean Adoptive Parents' Support Group
4668 Wildginger Run
Lithonia, GA 30038

IDAHO

Beth McHugh
Adoptive Families of Southeastern Idaho
691 Ruth Ave.
Idaho Falls, ID 83401

ILLINOIS

Marietta Bear
All-Dopt
727 Ramona Place
Godfrey, IL 62035

Candace De Bois & Camille Grishaber
Illiana Adoptive Parents
6329 Streamwood Lane
Matteson, IL 60443

Ben Rhodes
Ours of Central Illinois
307 Victor
Normal, IL 61761

INDIANA

Jeanine Jones
Adoptive Parents Together Inc.
5320 Far Hill Rd.
Indianapolis, IN 46226

Sharon & Dave Trout
Tri-State Adoptive Families
520 South Alvord Blvd.
Evansville, IN 47714

IOWA

Karen Tucker
Central Iowa Adoptive Families
501 Skycrest Dr.
Ames, IA 50010

Chris Forcucci
Iowa City International Adoptive Families
RR2, Box 181
West Branch, IA 52358

Pro Adoption Coalition of Iowa
P.O. Box 1011
Cedar Rapids, IA 52406

KANSAS

Laura Hewitt
Holt Families of America
6708 Granada Rd.
Prairie Village, KS 66208

Stacy M. Barnes
OURS Through Adoption
c/o Humana Hospital/Education Dept.
10500 Quivira
Overland Park, KS 66215

KENTUCKY

Carolyn Brown
Parents & Adoptive Children of Kentucky (PACK)
47 Comer Dr.
Madisonville, KY 42431

LOUISIANA

Gerri Lattler
Korean-American Resource Exchange
8814 Bruin Dr.
Metairie, LA 70003

MAINE

Kitsie Claxton
Adoptive Families of Maine
129 Sunderland Dr.
Auburn, ME 04210

MARYLAND

Committee for Single Adoptive Parents
P.O. Box 15084
Chevy Chase, MD 20825

Carol Mowbray
F.A.C.E. Inc.
P.O. Box 28058
Baltimore, MD 21239

MASSACHUSETTS

Open Door Society of Massachusetts Inc.
867 Boylston St.
Boston, MA 02111

MICHIGAN

James & Maxine Berden
A.D.O.P.T.
6939 Shields Ct.
Saginaw, MI 48603

The Adoption Option
c/o Don Marengere
P.O. Box 7052
Huntington Woods, MI 48070-7052

Judy Drewyor
Adoption Resource Group
1101 Agate
Houghton, MI 49931

Patricia Brown
Greater Jackson Families for Adoption
6243 Mountie Way
Jackson, MI 49201

MINNESOTA

Adoption Option Committee
P.O. Box 24132
Edina, MN 55424

Roxanne W. Johnson
Heart & Seoul
10 Woodview Drive
Mankato, MN 56001

MISSISSIPPI

Mary Collins
Mississippi Council on Adoptable Children
P.O. Box 1184
Jackson, MS 39215

MISSOURI

Beckey Panagos
International Families
21 Richmond Court
St. Charles, MO 63303

Pat Krippner
Open Door Society of Missouri
6127 Waterman
St. Louis, MO 63112

MONTANA

Vern Barkell
Yellowstone International Adoptive
  Families
3433 Barley Circle
Billings, MT 59102

NEBRASKA

MaryLou Zgud
Kearney Area Adoption Association
P.O. Box 132
Kearney, NE 68848

NEW HAMPSHIRE

Betty & Gary Todd
Open Door Society of New Hampshire
40 Gerrish Dr.
Nottingham, NH 03290

NEW JERSEY

Beth Infuso/Janet Levin
Concerned Persons for Adoption
P.O. Box 179
Whippany, NJ 07981

Cynthia V. N. Peck
New Jersey Friends Through Adoption
161 Twin Brooks Trail
Chester, NJ 07930

Kathleen Becker
Rainbow Families
670 Oakley Place
Oradell, NJ 07649

Karen Rispoli
Stars of David-Central Jersey
337 Graham St.
Highland Park, NJ 08904

NEW MEXICO

Debra McElroy
Parents of International Adoption, Inc.
Box 91175
Albuquerque, NM 87199

NEW YORK

Adoptive Parents Committee Inc.
210 Fifth Ave.
New York, NY 10010

Catholic Adoptive Parents Association Inc.
Box 893
Harrison, NY 10528

Ermine Bennette
Latin America Parents Association—
New York
P.O. Box 339
Brooklyn, NY 11234

NORTH CAROLINA

Lauren S. Decker
South Piedmont Ours
Box 221946
Charlotte, NC 28222

Liz Grimes
Triad Adoptive Parent Support Group
133 Penny Rd.
High Point, NC 27260

NORTH DAKOTA

Jan Kearns
Minn-Kota Families Through Adoption
84 Meadowlark Lane
Fargo, ND 58102

OHIO

Colleen Roberts
Families United for Adoption
P.O. Box 82
Swanton, OH 43558

Sherrey Jacob
OURS of Greater Cincinnati
2101 St. James Ave.
Cincinnati, OH 45206

OKLAHOMA

SuDawn Peters
Families Adopting Children in Tulsa Area
47 N. Victor
Tulsa, OK 74110

OREGON

Northwest Adoptive Families Inc.
Box 25355
Portland, OR 97225-0355

PENNSYLVANIA

Pat Sexton
Open Door Society of Pennsylvania
1835 Troxell St.
Allentown, PA 18103

Amy Phillips
Parents' & Adopted Children's Organization, Mercer County
105 Wasser Rd.
Greenville, PA 16125

RHODE ISLAND

Susan Round
G.I.F.T. of R.I. Inc.
9 Shippee School House Rd.
Foster, RI 02825

SOUTH CAROLINA

Ellen Millard
District 1, SC Council on Adoptable Children
P.O. Box 5761
Greenville, SC 29606

Karen Kearse
Piedmont Adoptive Families
P.O. Box 754
Spartanburg, SC 29304-0754

SOUTH DAKOTA

Diane Almos
Families Through Adoption
218 18th Ave. S
Brookings, SD 57006

TENNESSEE

Eileen Douglass
Mid-South Families Through Adoption
1575 Goodbar
Memphis, TN 38104

Leo & Anita Bechard
OURS of Middle Tennessee
Kidd Rd., Box 55
Nolensville, TN 37135

Allen & Patty Morgan
Pappoos
6352 Bresslyn Rd.
Nashville, TN 37205

TEXAS

Bobbie T. Kerr
Council on Adoptable Children of Dallas
P.O. Box 141199
Dept. 366
Dallas, TX 75214

Mary Lou Mauldin
Council on Adoptable Children of
  Ft. Worth
2102 Carmel Ct.
Arlington, TX 76012

Clara Flores
COAC of Texas Inc.
Rt. 2, Box 177-F
Edinburg, TX 78539

UTAH

Margo Fugal
Hope of Utah
P.O. Box 1146
Provo, UT 84601

VERMONT

Judy LeMay
Vermont Families Through Adoption
16 Aspen Dr.
Essex Junction, VT 05452

VIRGINIA

COAC
708 Hadlow Drive
Springfield, VA 22152

Deidre L. Dubley
Families Through Adoption
360 Brittain Lane
Hampton, VA 23669

WASHINGTON

Lynn Thompson
Families Through Adoption of Washington
11323 SE 218th Place
Kent, WA 98031

WEST VIRGINIA

Linda Streets
Appalachian Families for Adoption
P.O. Box 2775
Charleston, WV 25330

WISCONSIN

Gerith Gier
Families Through Adoption
627 Bell Ave.
Sheboygan, WI 53081

Open Door Society-Milwaukee
3253 N. Hackett
Milwaukee, WI 53211

ADOPTIVE PARENT GROUPS IN CANADA

Adoptive Parents Association of British Columbia
#205-15463 104th Ave.
Surrey, British Columbia
V3R 1N9

Adoptive Parent Support Resources (this group covers adoption issues and options and provides a bimonthly publication with parent support group information for Canadians)
10950-159 St.
Edmonton, Alberta
T5P 3C1
(403) 483-9343

Canadopt
c/o Joan Cummings
RR #1
Ilderto, Ontario
N0M 2A0

Comox Valley Adoptive Parents Association
c/o Sheelagh Elmitt
Rural Route 5, Ste. 506
Comax, British Columbia
V9N 8B5

Latin American Adoptive Families in Canada (LAAF)
c/o Nancy Casserly
1463 Champlain Dr.
Peterborough, Ontario
K9L 1N3

Lower Mainland Adoptive Parents Association
Box 58175
Station L
Vancouver, British Columbia
V6P 6C5

The Open Door Society
1370 Bank St.
Ottawa, Ontario
K1H 7Y3

SNAP Group (Society of Special Needs Adoptive Parents)
403-11861 88th Ave.
Delta, British Columbia
V4C 3C6

8. PERIODICALS AND NEWSPAPERS

Adolescence
Libra Publishers Inc.
3089C Clairemont Dr., Suite 383
San Diego, CA 92117

American Behavioral Scientist
Sage Periodicals Press
2111 W. Hillcrest Dr.
Newbury Park, CA 91320

American Journal of Epidemiology
2007 E. Monument St.
Baltimore, MD 21205

The American Journal of Human Genetics
University of Chicago Press
5270 S. Woodlawn Ave.
Chicago, IL 60637

American Journal of Orthopsychiatry
American Orthopsychiatric Association
19 W. 44th St., Suite 1616
New York, NY 10036

American Journal of Psychiatry
American Psychiatric Association
1400 K St. NW
Washington, DC 20005

Archives of General Psychiatry
American Medical Association
535 N. Dearborn St.
Chicago, IL 60610

Arizona Law Review
University of Arizona
College of Law
Tucson, AZ 85721

Behavior Genetics
Plenum Publishing Co.
233 Spring St.
New York, NY 10013

The Boston Globe
Globe Newspaper Co.
135 Morrissey Blvd.
Boston, MA 02107

Brooklyn Law Review
Brooklyn Law School
250 Joralemon St.
Brooklyn, NY 11201

Child Abuse and Neglect
Pergamon Journals Inc.
Maxwell House
Fairview Park
Elmsford, NY 10523

Child and Adolescent Social Work
Human Sciences Press
72 Fifth Ave.
New York, NY 10011

Child Development
University of Chicago Press, Journals Div.
5720 S. Woodlawn Ave.
Chicago, IL 60637

Children and Youth Services Review
Pergamon Press Inc.
Maxwell House
Fairview Park
Elmsford, NY 10523

Child Psychiatry and Human Development
Human Sciences Press
72 Fifth Ave.
New York, NY 10011

Child Welfare
Child Welfare League of America Inc.
440 First St. NW, Suite 310
Washington, DC 20001

The Christian Science Monitor
The Christian Science Publishing Society
One Norway St.
Boston, MA 02115

Cincinnati Law Review
University of Cincinnati, College of Law
Cincinnati, OH 45221

Clearinghouse Review
National Clearinghouse for Legal Services
407 S. Dearborn, Suite 400
Chicago, IL 60605

Columbia Law Review
Columbia University
School of Law
435 W. 116th St.
New York, NY 10027

The Detroit News
615 Lafayette Blvd.
Detroit, MI 48231

Ebony
820 S. Michigan Ave.
Chicago, IL 60605

Family Law Quarterly
American Bar Association
1155 E. 60th St.
Chicago, IL 60637

Family Planning Perspectives
Alan Guttmacher Institute
111 Fifth Ave.
New York, NY 10003

Family Relations: Journal of Applied Family & Child Studies
National Council on Family Relations
1910 W. County Rd. B, Suite 147
St. Paul, MN 55113

Fertility and Sterility
American Fertility Society
2140 11th Ave. S, Suite 200
Birmingham, AL 35205-2800

Guidepost
American Association of Counseling and Development
5999 Stevenson Ave.
Alexandria, VA 22304

Illinois Bar Journal
Illinois State Bar Association
Illinois Bar Center
Springfield, IL 62701

International Journal of Behavioral Development

International Society for the Study of Behavioral Development
North-Holland Publishing Co.
Box 211
1000 AE Amsterdam
Netherlands

Journal of Abnormal Psychology
American Psychological Association
1200 17th St. NW
Washington, DC 20036

Journal of Child Psychology and Psychiatry
Pergamon Journals Inc.
Maxwell House
Fairview Park
Elmsford, NY 10523

Journal of Children in Contemporary Society
Haworth Press Inc.
28 E. 22 St.
New York, NY 10010

Journal of Criminal Law and Criminology
Northwestern University
357 E. Chicago Ave.
Chicago, IL 60611

Journal of Family Law
University of Louisville, School of Law
Louisville, KY 40292

The Journal of Family Practice
Appleton & Lange
25 Van Zant St.
P.O. Box 5630
East Norwalk, CT 06856

Journal of Genetic Psychology
Heldref Publications
4000 Albemarle St. NW
Washington, DC 20016

Journal of Jewish Communal Service
Conference of Jewish Communal Service
3084 State Hwy. 27, Suite 1
Kendall Park, NJ 08824-1657

Journal of Nervous and Mental Disease
Williams & Wilkins

428 E. Preston St.
Baltimore, MD 21202

The Journal of Pediatrics
The C. V. Mosby Co.
11830 Westline Industrial Dr.
St. Louis, MO 63146

*Journal of Personality and Social
Psychology*
American Psychological Association
1200 17th St. NW
Washington, DC 20036

Journal of Studies on Alcohol
Alcohol Research Documentation Inc.
Rutgers Center of Alcohol Studies
Smithers Hall, Busch Campus
P.O. Box 969
Piscataway, NJ 08855

*Journal of the American Academy of Child
and Adolescent Psychiatry*
Williams & Wilkins
428 E. Preston St.
Baltimore, MD 21202

Journal of the American Medical Association (JAMA)
535 N. Dearborn St.
Chicago, IL 60610

Kentucky Law Journal
University of Kentucky
College of Law
Lexington, KY 40506

Law, Medicine & Health Care
American Society of Law & Medicine
765 Commonwealth Ave., Suite 1634
Boston, MA 02215

Maryland Bar Journal
Maryland State Bar Association
905 Keyser Bldg.
Calvert and Redwood Sts.
Baltimore, MD 21202

*MCN, The American Journal of Maternal/
Child Nursing*
American Journal of Nursing Company
555 W. 57th St.
New York, NY 10019

Medical Aspects of Human Sexuality
Hospital Publications Inc.
500 Plaza Dr.
Secaucus, NJ 07094

Miami Herald
One Herald Plaza
Miami, FL 33132-1609

Minneapolis Star and Tribune
425 Portland Ave.
Minneapolis, MN 55488-0001

Nebraska Law Review
University of Nebraska, Lincoln
College of Law, Law Review
Lincoln, NE 68508

Neuroscience and Biobehavioral Review
Ankho International Inc.
Box 426
Fayetteville, NY 13066

New England Journal of Medicine
Massachusetts Medical Society
1440 Main St.
Waltham, MA 02154-1649

New Mexico Law Review
University of New Mexico, School of Law
1117 Stanford NE
Albuquerque, NM 87131

Oklahoma City University Law Review
Oklahoma City University
School of Law
2501 N. Blackwelder
Oklahoma City, OK 73106

The Orlando Sentinel
633 N. Orange Ave.
Orlando, FL 32801-1349

Psychiatry
Washington School of Psychiatry
1610 New Hampshire Ave.
Washington, DC 20007

Psychological Bulletin
American Psychological Association
1200 17th St. NW
Washington, DC 20036

Psychological Reports
Box 9229
Missoula, MT 59807-9229

Psychology Today
PT Partners
80 Fifth Ave.
New York, NY 10011

Public Welfare
American Public Welfare Association
1125 15th St. NW, Suite 300
Washington, DC 20005

Science
American Association for the Advancement of Science
1333 H St. NW
Washington, DC 20005

Science News
Science Service Inc.
1719 N St. NW
Washington, DC 20036

Scientific American
415 Madison Ave.
New York, NY 10017

Social Biology
Society for the Study of Social Biology
1180 Observatory Dr., Room 5440
Madison, WI 53706

Social Work
National Association of Social Workers
7981 Eastern Ave.
Silver Spring, MD 20910

Social Work Research & Abstracts
National Association of Social Workers
7981 Eastern Ave.
Silver Spring, MD 20910

Today's Christian Woman
Christianity Today Inc.
465 Gundersen Dr.
Carol Stream, IL 60188

Trial
Association of Trial Lawyers of America
1050 31st St. NW
Washington, DC 20007

Tulsa Law Journal
University of Tulsa, College of Law
3120 E. Fourth Place
Tulsa, OK 74104

University of Detroit Law Review
University of Detroit
School of Law
651 E. Jefferson Ave.
Detroit, MI 48226

The Wall Street Journal
200 Liberty St.
New York, NY 10281

Washburn Law Journal
Washburn University, School of Law
Topeka, KS 66621

Washington University Law Quarterly
Washington University, School of Law
St. Louis, MO 63130

Wisconsin Law Review
University of Wisconsin, Madison
Law School
975 Bascom Mall
Madison, WI 53706

Working Mother
230 Park Ave.
New York, NY 10169

9. NEWSLETTERS

This list represents only a few of the many newsletters written for and by adoptive parents, adopted adults, birthparents and others interested in adoption.

Add-Option
AASK America
450 Sansome St., Suite 210
San Francisco, CA 94111

Adoptalk
Adoptive Parents Committee Inc.
210 Fifth Ave.
New York, NY 10010

Adoptalk
North American Council on Adoptable
  Children (NACAC)
1821 University Ave., Suite N-498
St. Paul, MN 55104

Adopted Child
P.O. Box 9362
Moscow, ID 83843

Adoption Today
Concerned Persons for Adoption
51 Mandeville Ave.
Pequannock, NJ 07440

The ALMA Searchlight
Adoptees' Liberty Movement Association
P.O. Box 154
Washington Bridge Station
New York, NY 10033

The Children's Voice
National Coalition to End Racism in
  America's Child Care System
22075 Koths
Taylor, MI 48180

The Communique
Interracial Family Alliance
P.O. Box 16248
Houston, TX 77222

CUB Communicator
CUB Inc. (Concerned United Birthparents)
2000 Walker St.
Des Moines, IA 50317

The Decree
American Adoption Congress
1000 Connecticut Ave. NW, Suite 9
Washington, DC 20036

F.A.C.E. Facts
Families Adopting Children Everywhere
P.O. Box 28058, Northwood Station
Baltimore, MD 21239

FAIR
Families Adopting Inter-Racially
6267 W. Walbrook Dr.
San Jose, CA 95129

Hi Families
Holt International Families
P.O. Box 2880
Eugene, OR 97402

ICCC Newsletter
911 Cypress Dr.
Boulder, CO 80303

The Interracial Family Circle Newsletter
P.O. Box 53290
Washington, DC 20009

LAAF Quarterly
Latin American Adoptive Families (LAAF)
40 Upland Rd.
Duxbury, MA 02332

Legal Notes
National Committee For Adoption
1930 17th St. NW
Washington, DC 20009

MEMO
National Committee For Adoption
1930 17th St. NW
Washington, DC 20009

National Adoption Reports
National Committee For Adoption
1930 17th St. NW
Washington, DC 20009

The National Advocate
National Foster Parent Association Inc.
Information & Services Office
226 Kilts Dr.
Houston, TX 77024

Newsletter
Universal Aid for Children
8760 NE 2nd Ave.
Miami Shores, FL 33138

ODS News
Open Door Society
867 Boylston St., 6th Floor
Boston, MA 02116-2602

OURS, The Magazine of Adoptive Families
Adoptive Families of America
3333 Highway 100
Minneapolis, MN 55422

RESOLVE National Newsletter
RESOLVE Inc.
5 Water St.
Arlington, MA 02174

Roots & Wings
15 Nancy Terrace
Hackettstown, NJ 07840

The Roundtable
Journal of the National Resource Center for Special Needs Adoption
P.O. Box 337
Chelsea, MI 48118

Unmarried Parents Today
National Committee For Adoption
1930 17th St. NW
Washington, DC 20009

BIBLIOGRAPHY

Adamec, Christine. "Adopt a Boy," *OURS*, July/August 1988, 30–31.

———. *There ARE Babies to Adopt: A Resource Guide for Prospective Parents*. Lexington, Mass.: Mills & Sanderson, 1987.

———. "They Adopted From Afar," *Home Life*, January 1985.

———. "To Find a Child," *The Times Magazine*, May 2, 1983 (Army Times Publishing).

Adelberg, Robert Allen. "A Comparison Study of Searching and Non-Searching Adult Adoptees." Ed.D. diss., Boston University, 1986.

Altstein, Howard, and Simon, Rita J. *Intercountry Adoption: A Multinational Perspective*. New York: Praeger, 1991.

Andrews, Lori B. "Alternative Reproduction and the Law of Adoption," in *Adoption Law and Practice*. New York: Matthew Bender, 1988.

Atwater, Martha W. "A Modern-Day Solomon's Dilemma: What of the Unwed Father's Rights?", *University of Detroit Law Review*, 66(1989): 267–296.

Bachrach, Christine A., Ph.D.; Adams, Patricia F.; Sambrano, Soledad, Ph.D., and London, Kathryn A., Ph.D. "Adoption in the 1980's." *Advance Data from Vital and Health Statistics of the National Center for Health Statistics*, January 5, 1990. Government Printing Office.

Baran, A., Pannor, R., and Sorosky, A.D. *The Adoption Triangle*. Garden City, N.Y.: Anchor Press/Doubleday, 1984.

Barber, Dulan. *Unmarried Fathers*. London: Hutchinson of London, 1975.

Barth, Richard P. "Disruption in Older Child Adoptions," *Public Welfare*, 46(Winter 1988): 23–29.

———. "Educational Implications of Prenatally Drug Exposed Children," *Social Work in Education*, 13(1991): 130–136.

Barth, Richard P., and Berry, Marianne. *Adoption & Disruption: Rates, Risks, and Responses*. New York: Aldine De Gruyter, 1988.

Barth, Richard P.; Berry, Marianne; Yoskikami, Rogers; Goodfield, Regina K.; and Carson, Mary Lou. "Predicting Adoption Disruption," *Social Work*, (May–June 1988): 277–233.

Bassuk, Ellen, M.D., and Rubin, Lenore, Ph.D. "Homeless Children: A Neglected Population," *American Journal of Orthopsychiatry*, 57(April 1987): 279–285.

Beckerman, Adela. "Incarcerated Mothers and Their Children in Foster Care: The Dilemma of Visitation," *Child and Youth Services Review*, 11(1989): 175–183.

Berman, Michael D., "Unsealing Adoption Records." *Maryland Bar Journal*, 22(September/October 1989): 33–35.

Berry, Marianne, and Barth, Richard P. "A Study of Disrupted Adoptive Placements of Adolescents," *Child Welfare*, 69(May/June 1990): 209–225.

Blanton, Terril L., and Deschner, Jeanne. "Biological Mothers' Grief: The Postadoptive Experience in Open Versus Confidential Adoption," *Child Welfare*, 69(November–December 1990): 525–535.

Bohman, Michael, M.D. "Alcoholism and Crime: Studies of Adoptees," *Substance and Alcohol Actions/Misuse*, 4(1983): 137–147.

Bohman, Michael. *Adopted Children and Their Families*. Stockholm, Sweden: Proprius, 1970.

Brace, C. L. *The Best Method of Disposing of Our Pauper and Vagrant Children*. New York: Wynkoop, Hallenbeck & Thomas, 1859.

Brinich, Paul M., Ph.D. *Psychoanalytic and Psychodynamic Views of Adoption: A Bibliography*. revised September 21, 1989.

Brinich, Paul M., Ph.D., and Brinich, Evelin B., M.A. "Adoption and Adaptation," *The Journal of Nervous and Mental Disease*, 170:8(1982): 489–493.

Brodzinsky, Anne B. *The Mulberry Bird: Story of an Adoption*. Indianapolis: Perspectives Press, 1986.

Brodzinsky, David M., and Schecter, Marshall D., eds. *The Psychology of Adoption*. New York: Oxford University Press, 1990.

Bussiere, Alice, J. D. "Issues in Interstate Adoptions," in *Adoption of Children with Special Needs: Issues in Law and Policy*. Washington, D.C.: American Bar Association, 1985.

Buydens-Branchey, Laure, M.D.; Branchey, Marc H., M.D.; and Noumair, Debra, Ph.D. "Age of Alcoholism Onset," *Archives of General Psychiatry*, 46(March 1989): 225–230.

Cadoret, Remi J., M.D.; Cain, Colleen A.; and Grove, William M., M.S. "Development of Alcoholism in Adoptees Raised Apart from Alcoholic Biologic Relatives," *Archives of General Psychiatry*, 37(May 1980): 561–563.

Caplan, Lincoln. "An Open Adoption," Parts 1, 2, *The New Yorker*, May 21, 28, 1990, 73–95, 40–68.

Carlson, Richard R. "Transnational Adoption of Children," *Tulsa Law Journal*, 23(Spring 1988): 317–377.

Carney, Ann. *No More Here and There—Adopting the Older Child*. Chapel Hill: University of North Carolina Press, 1976.

Catholic Adoptive Parents Association. *Media Guidelines on Adoption Language*. Harrison, N.Y.: Catholic Adoptive Parents Association, 1988.

Chasnoff, Ira J., M.D.; Griffith, Dan R., Ph.D.; MacGregor, Scott, D.O.; Dirkes, Kathryn, B.M.E.; Burns, Kaytreen A., Ph.D. "Temporal Patterns of Cocaine Use in Pregnancy," *Journal of the American Medical Association*, 261(March 24/31, 1989), 1741–1744.

Cherian, Varghese I. "Birth Order and Academic Achievement of Children in Transkei," *Psychological Reports*, 66(1990): 19–24.

Chess, Stella, and Thomas, Alexander. *Know Your Child: An Authoritative Guide for Today's Parents*. New York: Basic Books. 1989.

Children's Home Society of California. *The Changing Picture of Adoption*. Los Angeles: Children's Home Society of California, 1984.

Child Welfare League of America. *Standards for Adoption Service*, rev. ed. Washington, D.C.: Child Welfare League of America, 1988.

Christenson, Larry. *The Wonderful Way That Babies Are Made*. Minneapolis: Bethany House, 1982.

Clark, E. Audrey, and Hanisee, Jeanette, "Intellectual and Adaptive Performance of Asian Children in Adoptive American Settings," *Development Psychology*, 18(1982): 595–599.

Clark, Natalie Loder. "New Wine in Old Skins: Using Paternity-Suit Settlements to Facilitate Surrogate Motherhood," *Journal of Family Law*, 25:3(1986–87): 483–527.

Cole, Elizabeth, and Donley, Kathryn. "History, Values, and Placement Policy Issues in Adoption," in *The Psychology of Adoption*. New York: Oxford University Press, 1990.

Coleman, Loren; Tilbor, Karen; Hornby, Helaine; and Boggis, Carol, eds. *Working with Older Adoptees: A Sourcebook of Innovative Models*. Portland: University of Southern Maine, Human Services Development Institute, 1988.

Combs, Claire Grandpre. "Wrongful Adoption: Adoption Agency Held Liable for Fraudulent Representations," *Cincinnati Law Review*, 56(1987): 343–359.

Committee on Adolescence. "Counseling the Adolescent about Pregnancy Options," *Pediatrics*, January 1989, 135–137.

Cook, Thomas F. "Transition to Parenthood: A Study of First-time Adoptive and Biological Parents." Ph.D. diss., University of Alabama, 1988.

Costin, Lela B.; Bell, Cynthia J.; and Downs, Susan W. *Child Welfare, Policies and Practice*. White Plains, N.Y.: Longman, 1991.

Crowe, Raymond R., M.D. "An Adoption Study of Antisocial Personality," *Archives of General Psychiatry*, 31(December 1974): 785–791.

Denney, Freddie Lee. "Characteristics Descriptive of Maltreated Children Whose Adoptions Disrupt (Texas)," M.S. thesis, University of Texas at Arlington, 1987.

Depp, Carole H. "Placing Siblings Together," *Children Today*, 12(March–April 1983): 14–19.

Deykin, Eva Y., Dr. P.H.; Patti, Patricia, M.S.; and Ryan, Jon, B.S. "Fathers of Adopted Children: A Study of the Impact of Child Surrender on Birthfathers," *American Journal of Orthopsychiatry*, 58(April 1988): 240–248.

Donley, Kathryn, M.S.W. "Sibling Attachments and Adoption." Unpublished, National Resource Center for Special Needs Adoption, Chelsea, Michigan.

Dorris, Michael. *The Broken Cord*. New York: Harper & Row, 1989.

Easson, William M. "Special Sexual Problems of the Adopted Adolescent," *Medical Aspects of Human Sexuality*, 28(July 1973): 92–103.

Eisenberg, Bart. "Road to Foreign Adoptions Gets Rockier," *The Christian Science Monitor*, February 28, 1990, 13.

Elster, Arthur B., and Lamb, Michael E. *Adolescent Fatherhood*. Hillsdale, N.J.: Lawrence Erlbaum 1986.

Engel, Fr. Paul. "Born Again Through Adoption," *Restoration* (September–October 1988).

Fahlberg, Vera, M.D., ed. *Residential Treatment: A Tapestry of Many Therapies*. Indianapolis: Perspectives Press, 1990.

Fales, Mary Jane. *Post-Legal Adoption Services Today*. Washington, D.C.: Child Welfare League of America, 1986.

Fanshel, David; Finch, Stephen J.; and Grundy, John F. "Foster Children in Life-Course Perspective: The Casey Family Program Experience," *Child Welfare,* 69(September–October 1989): 467–478.

Fein, Edith; Maluccio, Anthony N.; Hamilton, V. Jane; and Ward, Darryl E. "After Foster Care: Outcomes of Permanency Planning for Children," *Child Welfare* (November/December 1983).

Festinger, Trudy. *Necessary Risk: A Study of Adoptions and Disrupted Adoptive Placement.* Washington, DC: Child Welfare League of America, 1986.

Fisher, Florence. *The Search for Anna Fisher.* Greenwich, Conn.: Fawcett Crest, 1973.

Ford, Mary, M.S.W. "Challenges to the Child Welfare System: Medically Fragile Children and the Call for a Return to Orphanages." Paper presented at the 15th annual North American Council on Adoptable Children Training Conference, Arlington, Virginia, August 16–19, 1990.

Franklin, Robert R., M.D., and Brockman, Dorothy K. *In Pursuit of Fertility: A Consultation with a Specialist.* New York: Holt, Rinehart & Winston, 1990.

French, Anne Wiseman. "When Blood Isn't Thicker Than Water: The Inheritance Rights of Adopted-Out Children in New York," *Brooklyn Law Review,* 53(Winter 1988): 1007–1049.

Fulker, D. W.; DeFries, J. C.; and Plomin, Robert. "Genetic Influence on General Mental Ability Increases Between Infancy and Middle Childhood," *Nature,* 336(December 1988): 767–769.

Fullerton, Paul T. "Independent Adoption: The Inadequacies of State Law," *Washington University Law Quarterly,* 63(Winter 1985): 753–775.

Gabrielli, William F., Jr., and Mednick, Sarnoff A. "Genetic Correlates of Criminal Behavior," *American Behavioral Scientist,* 27(September–October 1983): 59–74.

Geissinger, Shirley. "Adoptive Parents' Attitudes Toward Birth Records," *Family Relations,* 33(October 1984): 579–584.

General Accounting Office. *Drug-Exposed Infants: A Generation at Risk.* GAO/HRD-90-138, June 1990.

General Accounting Office. *Foster Care: Incomplete Implementation of the Reforms and Unknown Effectiveness.* GAO/PEMD-89-17, August 1989.

Gill, Owen, and Jackson, Barbara. *Adoption and Race: Black, Asian and Mixed Race Children in White Families.* London: Batsford Academic and Educational, 1983.

Gilman, Lois. *The Adoption Resource Book.* New York: Harper & Row, 1987.

Gitlin, H. Joseph. *Adoptions: An Attorney's Guide to Helping Adoptive Parents.* Deerfield, Ill.: Callaghan, 1987.

Gittelsohn, John. "Film's Adoption Horror Tale Angers Koreans," *Boston Sunday Globe,* February 25, 1990.

Glenn, Norval D., and Hoppe, Sue Keir. "Only Children as Adults," *Journal of Family Issues,* September 1984.

Goettl, Kathryn. "Transition to Parenthood: A Comparison of Adoptive and Birth Parents." M.S.N. thesis, University of Wisconsin, Madison, 1989.

Gold, Rachel Benson. *Abortion and Women's Health: A Turning Point for America?* New York: Alan Guttmacher Institute, 1990.

Goldsmith, H. H. "Genetic Influences on Personality from Infancy to Adulthood," *Child Development,* 54(1983): 331–355.

Goldstein, J.; Freud, A.; and Solnit, Albert. *Beyond the Best Interests of the Child.* New York: Free Press, (1973, 1979).

Gonzalez, Eulalio Guadalupe. "Effects of Age at Placement and Length of Placement on Foreign and Domestic Adopted Children (Foreign Adoption)." Ph.D. diss., University of Akron, 1990.

Goodluck, Charlotte, M.S.W. "Mental Health Issues of Native American Transracial Adoptions," in *Adoption Resources for Professionals,* 194–208. Butler, Pa.: Mental Health Adoption Therapy Project, September 1986.

Grabe, Pamela V., ed. *Adoption Resources for Mental Health Professionals.* Butler, Pa.: Mental Health Adoption Therapy Project, September 1986.

Greene, Marcia Slacum. "Rebirth of Orphanages is Reviving Old Fears; In D.C., the Ghost of Junior Village Haunts Talk of New Orphanages," *Washington Post,* January 9, 1990.

Hallenbeck, Carol. *Our Child: Preparation for Parenting in Adoption,* instructor's guide. Wayne, Pa.: Our Child Press, 1988.

Hamilton, John. "The Unwed Father and the Right to Know of His Child's Existence," *Kentucky Law Journal,* 76(187–88): 949–1009.

Hardin, Mark, ed. *Foster Children in the Courts.* Boston: Butterworth Legal Publishers, 1983.

Hartfield, Bernadette W. "The Role of the Interstate Compact on the Placement of Children in Interstate Adoption," *Nebraska Law Review,* 68(1989): 292–329.

Holtan, Barbara, and Strassberger, Laurel, eds. *They Became Part of Us: The Experiences of Families Adopting Children Everywhere.* Baltimore: F.A.C.E., 1985.

Hollinger, Joan H., editor-in-chief. *Adoption Law and Practice.* New York: Matthew Bender, 1988.

Hollinger, Joan Heifetz. "Beyond the Best Interests of the Tribe: The Indian Child Welfare Act and the Adoption of Indian Children," *University of Detroit Law Review,* 66(1989): 450–501.

Hoopes, Janet L. *Prediction in Child Development: A Longitudinal Study of Adoptive and Nonadoptive Families.* Washington, D.C.: Child Welfare League of America, 1982.

Hormann, Elizabeth. *After the Adoption.* Old Tappan, N.J.: Revell, 1987.

Horn, Joseph M. "The Texas Adoption Project: Adopted Children and Their Intellectual Resemblance to Biological and Adoptive Parents," *Child Development,* 54(1983): 268–275.

Horowitz, Robert; Hardin, Mark; and Bulkley, Josephine. *The Rights of Foster Parents.* Washington, D.C.: American Bar Association, 1989.

Hostetter, Margaret K., M.D.; Iver, Sandra, R.N.; Bole, Kathryn, O.T.R.; and Johnson, Dana, M.D., Ph.D. "Unsuspected Infectious Diseases and Other Medical Diagnoses in the Evaluation of Internationally Adopted Children," *Pediatrics,* 83:4(April 1989): 559–564.

Hughes, Timothy. "Intestate Succession and Stepparent Adoptions: Should Inheritance Rights of an Adopted Child Be Determined by Blood or Law?" *Wisconsin Law Review,* 1988, 321.

Infausto, Felix. "Perspective on Adoption," *The Annals of the American Academy of Political and Social Science,* 383(May 1969): 1–12.

International Concerns Committee for Children. *Report on Foreign Adoption.* Boulder: International Concerns Committee for Children, 1989, 1990.

———. *Report on Foreign Adoption.* Boulder: International Concerns Committee for Children, 1990.

Jenks, Susan. "Drug Babies: An Ethical Quagmire for Doctors," *Medical World News,* February 12, 1990.

Jewett, Claudia. *Helping Children Cope with Separation and Loss*. Boston: Harvard Common Press, 1982.

Jewett, Claudia L. *Adopting the Older Child*. Boston: Harvard Common Press, 1978.

Johnston, Patricia Irwin. *An Adoptor's Advocate*. Indianapolis: Perspectives Press, 1984.

———. *Understanding: A Guide to Impaired Fertility for Family and Friends*. Indianapolis: Perspectives Press, 1983.

Kadushin, Alfred, and Martin, Judith A. *Child Welfare Services*. New York: Macmillan, 1988.

Katz, Linda. "An Overview of Current Clinical Issues in Separation and Placement," *Child and Adolescent Social Work,* 4:3,4(Fall, Winter 1987): 209–223.

Kauffman, Rosie Ann. "Reunion and Non-Reunion Searching Adult Adoptees: A Comparison of Identity, Physical Self and Family Self," Master's thesis, University of Texas at Arlington, 1987.

Kessler, Lynn Friedman. "The Measurement of Teachers' Attitudes Toward Adotped Children." Ph.D. diss., Fielding Institute, 1987.

Kim, Wun Jung, M.D., M.P.H.; Davenport, Charles, M.D.; Joseph, Jill, Ph.D.; Zrull, Joel, M.D.; and Woolford, Elizabeth, B.A. "Psychiatric Disorder and Juvenile Delinquency in Adopted Children and Adolescents," *Journal of the American Academy of Child and Adolescent Psychiatry,* 27(January 1988): 111–115.

Kirk, H. D. *Adoptive Kinship*. Port Angeles, Brentwood Bay B.C.: Ben-Simon, 1982.

Klagsbrun, Francine. "Debunking the 'Adopted Child' Syndrome," *Ms,* October 1986.

Kotsopoulos, Sotiris, M.D., Ph.D.; Cote, Andre, M.D.; Joseph, Llewelyn, M.D.; Pentland, Neomi, M.D.; Stavrakaki, Chryssoula, M.D.; Sheahan, Patrick, M.S.W.; and Oke, Louise, B.A. "Psychiatric Disorders in Adopted Children: A Controlled Study," *American Journal of Orthopsychiatry,* 58(October 1988): 608–612.

Kowal, Katherine A., Ph.D., and Schilling, Karen Maitland, Ph.D. "Adoption Through the Eyes of Adult Adoptees," *American Journal of Orthopsychiatry,* 55(July 1985): 354–362.

Kraft, Adrienne D., M.A.; Palombo, Joseph, M.A.; Mitchell, Dorena L., M.A.; Woods, Patricia K., M.A.; Schmidt, Anne W., M.A.; and Tucker, Nancy G., M.S.W. "Some Theoretical Considerations on Confidential Adoption," Parts 1, 2, 3 and 4. *Child and Adolescent Social Work,* 2, nos. 1, 2 and 3; 4, no. 1, 13–21, 69–82, 139–153, 13–14.

Krementz, Jill. *How It Feels to Be Adopted*. New York: Knopf, 1988.

Ladner, Joyce. *Mixed Families: Adopting Across Racial Boundaries*. Garden City, N.Y.: Anchor Press/Doubleday, 1977.

Laird, Joan, and Hartman, Ann, eds. *A Handbook of Child Welfare: Context, Knowledge, and Practice*. New York: Free Press, 1985.

Landers, Robert K. *Independent Adoptions. Quarterly's Edit,* 2, no. 22(1987).

Lasker, Judith N., and Borg, Susan. *In Search of Parenthood: Coping with Infertility and High Tech Conception*. Boston: Beacon Press, 1987.

Leavitt, David Keene. *Counseling Clients in Independent Adoptions*. Berkeley: California Continuing Education of the Bar, 1980.

Leavy, Walter. "Should Whites Adopt Black Children?" *Ebony,* September 1987.

Lehmann, Michelle L. "The Indian Child Welfare Act of 1978: Does it Apply to the Adoption of an Illegitimate Indian Child?" *Catholic University Law Review,* 38(1989): 511–541.

LeMay, Susan Kempf. "The Emergence of Wrongful Adoption as a Cause of Action," *Journal of Family Law,* 1988/89: 475–488.

LePere, Dorothy W., A.C.S.W.; Davis, Lloyd E., A.C.S.W.; Couve, Janus, A.C.S.W.; and McDonald, Mona, A.C.S.W. *Large Sibling Groups: Adoption Experiences.* Washington, D.C.: Child Welfare League of America, 1986.

Lewin, Tamar. "South Korea Slows Export of Babies for Adoption," *New York Times,* February 12, 1990, B1.

Leynes, Cynthia. "Keep or Adopt: A Study of Factors Influencing Pregnant Adolescents' Plans for Their Babies," *Child Psychiatry and Human Development,* 10 (Winter 1980): 105–112.

Lieberman, Florence, D.S.W.; Kenemore, Thomas K., Ph.D.; and Yost, Diane, M.S.W. *The Foster Care Dilemma.* New York: Human Sciences Press, 1987.

Lifton, Betty Jean. *Lost & Found: The Adoption Experience.* New York: Harper & Row, 1988.

Lindsay, Jeanne Warren. *Parents, Pregnant Teens and the Adoption Option: Help for Families.* Buena Park, Calif.: Morning Glory Press, 1989.

Lindsay, Jeanne, and Monserrat, Catherine. *Adoption Awareness: A Guide for Teachers, Counselors, Nurses and Caring Others.* Buena Park, Calif.: Morning Glory Press, 1989.

Littrell, Jill. "The Swedish Studies of the Adopted Children of Alcoholics," *Journal of Studies on Alcohol,* 49:6(1988): 491–498.

Loehlin, John C.; Horn, Joseph M.; and Willerman, Lee. "Modeling IQ Change: Evidence from the Texas Adoption Project," *Child Development,* 60(1989): 993–1004.

Loon, J. H. A. van. *Report on Intercountry Adoption.* Paper presented at Hague Conference on Private International Law Intercountry, The Hague, Netherlands, April 1990.

Lydens, Lois Adele. "A Longitudinal Study of Crosscultural Adoption: Identity Development Among Asian Adoptees at Adolescence and Early Development," Ph.D. diss., Northwestern University, 1988.

Maass, Peter. "Orphans: Korea's Disquieting Problem; National Embarrassment Over Letting Foreigners Take Children," *Washington Post,* December 14, 1989.

Macaulay, Jacqueline, and Macaulay, Stewart. "Adoption for Black Children: A Case Study of Expert Discretion," *Research in Law and Sociology,* 1(1978): 265–318.

Magid, Ken, and McKelvey, Carole A. *High Risk: Children Without a Conscience.* New York: Bantam, 1988.

Maley, John R. "Wrongful Adoption: Monetary Damages as a Superior Remedy to Annulment for Adoptive Parents Victimized by Fraud," *Indiana Law Review,* 20(1987): 709–734.

Marindin, Hope, ed. *The Handbook for Single Adoptive Parents.* Chevy Chase, MD.: Committee for Single Adoptive Parents, 1987.

Marquis, Kathlyn S., and Detweiler, Richard A. "Does Adopted Mean Different? An Attributional Analysis," *Journal of Personality and Social Psychology,* 48:4(1985): 1054–1066.

Mason, Mary M. *Miracle Seekers: An Anthology of Infertility.* Indianapolis: Perspectives Press, 1987.

Matthews, Anne Martin, and Matthews, Ralph. "Beyond the Mechanics of Infertility: Perspectives on the Social Psychology of Infertility and Involuntary Childlessness," *Family Relations,* 35(October 1986): 479–487.

Matthews, Robert Charles. "The Littlest Immigrants: The Immigration and Adoption of Foreign Orphans." Ph.D. diss., Virginia Polytechnic Institute and State University, 1986.

McCloud, Shari. "Seeing It Through" In *Adopting Children with Special Needs: A Sequel*. Washington D.C: North American Council on Adoptable Children, 1983.

McDermott, Virginia Anne, Ph.D. "Life Planning Services: Helping Older Placed Children with Their Identity," *Child and Adolescent Social Work*, 4:3, 4(Fall, Winter 1987): 245–263.

McLaughlin, Steven D.; Pearce, Susan E.; Manninen, Diane L.; and Winges, Linda D. "To Parent or Relinquish: Consequences for Adolescent Mothers," *Social Work*, 33(July–August 1988): 320–324.

McNamara, Joan, and McNamara, Bernard H., eds. *Adoption and the Sexually Abused Child*. Portland: University of Southern Maine, Human Services Development Institute, 1990.

McRoy, Ruth G.; Grotevant, Harold D.; and White, Kerry L. *Openness in Adoption: New Practices, New Issues*. New York: Praeger, 1988.

McRoy, Ruth G., and Zurcher, Louis Z., Jr. *Transracial and Inracial Adoptees: The Adolescent Years*. Springfield, Ill.: Thomas, 1983.

Mech, Edmund V. *Orientations of Pregnancy Counselors Toward Adoption*. Report for Department of Health and Human Services, Office of Population Affairs, 1984.

Mecklenburg, Carol Elaine. "Ego Development, Family Cohesion, and Adaptability in Families with Transracially Adopted Adolescents." Ph.D. diss., University of Minnesota, 1988.

Mednick, Sarnoff A., and Gabrielli, William F., Jr. "Genetic Influences in Criminal Convictions: Evidence from an Adoption Cohort," *Science* (May 25, 1984): 891–894.

Mednick, Sarnoff A.; Moffitt, Terrie E.; and Stack, Susan A., eds. *The Causes of Crime: New Biological Approaches*. Cambridge, England: Cambridge University Press, 1987.

Meezan, W.; Katz, S.; and Manoff-Russo, E. *Adoptions Without Agencies: A Study of Independent Adoptions*. New York: Child Welfare League of America, 1978.

Miall, Charlene E. "The Stigma of Adoptive Parent Status: Perceptions of Community Attitudes Toward Adoption and the Experience of Informal Social Sanctioning," *Family Relations*, 36(January 1987): 34–39.

Miles, Susan G. "Periodicals for Adoptive Families," *Serials Review* (Fall 1985): 21–29.

Misak, Margaret Klein. *Experience of Multiple Unwed Pregnancies: A Report from Selected Catholic Agencies*. Chicago: Catholic Charities of Chicago, 1982.

Moffitt, Terrie E. "Parental Mental Disorder and Offspring Criminal Behavior: An Adoption Study," *Psychiatry*, November 1987, 346–358.

Mosher, William D., Ph.D., "Use of Family Planning Services in the United States: 1982 and 1988," *Advance Data from Vital and Health Statistics of the National Center for Health Statistics*, no. 184, April 11, 1990.

Mosher, William D., Ph.D., and Pratt, William F., Ph.D. *Fecundity and Infertility in the United States, 1965–88*, National Center for Health Statistics, no. 192, December 4, 1990.

Moulden, Barbara Reid. "Characteristics of Families Who Adopt Children with Special Needs (Parenting, Traits)." Ph.D. diss., University of Texas at Austin, 1983.

Munsinger, Harry. "The Adopted Child's IQ: A Critical Review," *Psychological Bulletin*, 82(September 1975): 623–659.

National Committee For Adoption. "Adolescent Adoptees' 'Identity Formation' is Normal, Study Says," *National Adoption Reports* (March–April 1985), 6.

———. *Adoption Factbook*. Washington, D.C.: National Committee for Adoption, 1989.

———. *Adoption Factbook*. Washington, D.C.: National Committee for Adoption, 1985.

———. *Model Act for the Adoption of Children with Special Needs*. Washington, D.C.: National Committee For Adoption, 1982.

———. "Corporate Support for Adoption Grows," *National Adoption Reports* (May–June 1986), 2.

———. *Unmarried Parents Today,* July 13, 1989.

Nelson, Katherine A. *On the Frontier of Adoption: A Study of Special-Needs Adoptive Families*. New York: Child Welfare League of America, 1985.

Nichol, A. R., ed. *Longitudinal Studies in Child Psychology and Psychiatry*. New York: Wiley, 1985.

North American Council on Adoptable Children. *The Adoption Assistance and Child Welfare Act of 1980: The First Ten Years*. St. Paul, Minn.: NACAC, August 1990.

O'Brien, Robert, and Cohen, Sidney, M.D. *The Encyclopedia of Drug Abuse*. New York: Facts On File, 1984.

O'Brien, Shari. "Race in Adoption Proceedings: The Pernicious Factor," *Tulsa Law Journal,* 1986, 485–498.

Pannor, Reuben, and Baran, Annette. "Open Adoption a Standard Practice," *Child Welfare,* 63(May–June 1984): 245–250.

Pardes, Herbert, M.D.; Kaufmann, Charles A., M.D.; Pincus, Harold Alan, M.D.; and West, Anne. "Genetics and Psychiatry: Past Discoveries, Current Dilemmas, and Future Directions," *American Journal of Psychiatry,* 146(April 1989): 435–443.

Partridge, Susan; Hornby, Helaine; and McDonald, Thomas. *Learning from Adoption Disruption: Insights for Practice*. Portland, Me.: Human Services Development Institute, 1986.

———. *Legacies of Loss: Visions of Gain*. Washington, DC: Department of Health and Human Services, Office of Human Development Services, Administration for Children, Youth and Families, 1986.

Paul, Ellen. *The Adoption Directory*. New York: Gale, 1989.

Pendarvis, Leah Vorhes. "Anxiety Levels of Involuntarily Infertile Couples Choosing Adoption," Ph.D. diss., Ohio State University, 1985.

Pierce, William. "Survey of State Activity Regarding Surrogate Motherhood," *Family Law Reporter,* January 29, 1985.

———. "Taking Adoption Seriously," *Philanthropy,* May–June 1989, 9–10.

Plomin, Robert, and DeFries, J.C. "The Colorado Adoption Project," *Child Development,* 54(1983): 276–289.

Plomin, Robert; Loehlin, John C.; and DeFries, J C. "Genetic and Environmental Components of 'Environmental' Influences," *Developmental Psychology,* 21(1985): 391–402.

Podell, Richard J. "The Role of the Guardian Ad Litem: Advocating the Best Interests of the Child," *Trial,* April 1989, 31–34.

Posner, Julia L. *CWLA's Guide to Adoption Agencies: A National Driectory of Adoption Agencies and Adoption Resources*. Washington, D.C.: Child Welfare League of America, 1989.

Poston, Dudley L. Jr., and Cullen, Ruth. "Propensity of White Women in the United States to Adopt Children," *Social Biology,* Fall–Winter 1989.

Powers, Douglas, ed. *Adoption for Troubled Children: Prevention and Repair of Adoptive Failures Through Residential Treatment.* New York: Haworth Press, 1984.

Presidential Task Force. *A Report to the President from the Interagency Task Force on Adoption.* Washington, D.C., May 12, 1988.

Price, Susan B., and McElhinny, Jody. "Substantive Changes in Adoption and Relinquishment Law in Colorado," *Family Law Newsletter,* December 1987, 2183–2185.

Radin, Charles A. "Waiting for a Home: Opposition to Transracial Adoption Slows Black Placements," *Boston Globe,* November 30, 1989.

Raynor, Lois. *The Adopted Child Comes of Age.* London: George Allen & Unwin, 1980.

Register, Cheri. *"Are Those Kids Yours?": American Families with Children Adopted From Other Countries.* New York: Free Press, 1990.

Reid, Barbara Moulden. "Characteristics of Families Who Adopt Children with Special Needs," Ph.D. diss., University of Texas at Austin, 1983.

Resnick, Michael D. "Studying Adolescent Mothers' Decision Making About Adoption and Parenting," *Social Work,* January–February 1984, 5–10.

Rillera, Mary Jo, and Kaplan, Sharon. *Cooperative Adoption: A Handbook.* Westminster, Calif.: Triadoption, 1985.

Rosenberg, Jeffrey, "1988 Survey of State Laws on Access to Adoption Records," *The Family Law Reporter,* monograph no. 3, August 16, 1988.

Ross, Marlene. "The Educational Needs of Adoptive Parents." Ph.D. diss., American University, 1985.

Rutter, Michael. "Family and School Influences on Behavioural Development," *Journal of Child Psychology and Psychiatry,* 26:3(1985): 349–368.

Ryan, Angela Shen, M.S.W. "Intercountry Adoption and Policy Issues," *Journal of Children in Contemporary Society,* 14(Spring 1983): 49–60.

Sandmaier, Marian. *When Love is Not Enough: How Mental Health Professionals Can Help Special-Needs Adoptive Families.* Washington, D.C.: Child Welfare League of America, 1988.

Sapp, Susan Kubert. "Notice of Relinquishment: The Key to Protecting the Rights of Unwed Fathers and Adoptive Parents," *Nebraska Law Review,* vol. 67, 383–407.

Scarr, Sandra; Webber, Patricia L.; Weinberg, Richard A.; and Wittig, Michele A. "Personality Resemblance Among Adolescents and Their Parents in Biologically Related and Adoptive Families," *Journal of Personality and Social Psychology,* 40(1981): 885–898.

Scarr, Sandra, and Weinberg, Richard. "The Minnesota Adoption Studies: Genetic Differences and Malleability," *Child Development,* 54(1983): 260–267.

Schaffer, Judith, and Lindstrom, Christina. *How to Raise an Adopted Child.* New York: Crown, 1989.

Schecter, Marshall D. "Observations on Adopted Children," *Archives of General Psychiatry,* 3(July 1960): 21–32.

Schecter, Marshall D., M.D.; Carlson, Paul V., M.D.; Simmons, James Q., III, M.D.; and Work, Henry H., M.D. "Emotional Problems in the Adoptee," *Archives of General Psychiatry,* 10(February 1964): 109–118.

Schiffer, Michele. "Fraud in the Adoption Setting," *Arizona Law Review,* 29(1987): 707–723.

Seader, Mary Beth, M.S.W. "Pregnancy Counseling: Traditional and Experimental Practices." Paper written for the National Committee for Adoption, 1988.

Searles, John S. "The Role of Genetics in the Pathogenesis of Alcoholism," *Journal of Abnormal Psychology*, 97(May 1988): 153–167.

Segal, Ellen C., ed. *Adoption of Children with Special Needs: Issues in Law and Policy*. Washington, D.C.: American Bar Association, 1985.

Senior, Neil, M.D., and Himadi, Elaine, M.D. "Emotionally Disturbed, Adopted, Inpatient Adolescents." *Child Psychiatry and Human Development*, 15(Spring 1985): 189–197.

Sergeant, Georgia. "Alaska Tribe Wants Custody of Infant," *Trial*, 25(October 1989): 20–21.

Shireman, Joan F., and Johnson, Penny R. "A Longitudinal Study of Black Adoptions: Single Parent, Transracial, and Traditional," *Social Work*, 31(May–June 1986): 172–176.

Siegel, Stephanie E., Ph.D. *Parenting Your Adopted Child*. New York: Prentice Hall, 1989.

Silber, Kathleen, and Speedlin, Phylis. *Dear Birthmother: Thank You for Our Baby*. San Antonio: Corona, 1982.

Silverstein, Deborah N. "Identity Issues in the Jewish Adopted Adolescent," *Journal of Jewish Communal Service* (Summer 1985): 321–329.

Simon, Rita James. *Transracial Adoption*. New York: Wiley, 1977.

Simon, Rita J., and Altstein, Howard. *Transracial Adoptees and Their Families: A Study of Identity and Commitment*. New York: Praeger, 1987.

Singer, Leslie M.; Brodzinsky, David M.; Steir, Mary; and Waters, Everett. "Mother-Infant Attachment in Adoptive Families," *Child Development*, 56(1985): 1543–1551.

Slama, Jo Lynn. "Adoption and the Putative Father's Rights: Shoecraft V. Catholic Social Services Bureau," *Oklahoma City University Law Review*, 13(Spring 1988), 231–255.

Smith, Dorothy W., and Sherwen, Laurie Nehls. *Mothers and Their Adopted Children—The Bonding Process*. New York: Teresias Press, 1983.

Smith, Jerome, Ph.D., and Miroff, Franklin I. *You're Our Child: The Adoption Experience*. Lanham, Md.: Madison Books, 1987.

Smith, Robert R. *"Cox v. Whitten:* Limiting the Inheritance Rights of Adopted Adults—Arkansas Departs from a National Trend," *Arkansas Law Review*, 40(1987): 627–651.

Solnit, Albert J., M.D. "Child Placement Conflicts: New Approaches," *Child Abuse & Neglect*, 11(1987): 455–460.

Sørensen, Thorkild I. A.; Price, R. Arlen; Stunkard, Albert J.; and Schulsinger, Fini. "Genetics of Obesity in Adult Adoptees and Their Biological Siblings," *British Medical Journal*, 298(January 14, 1989): 87–90.

Sørensen, T. I.; Nielsen, G. G.; Andersen, P. K.; and Teasdale, T. W. "Genetic and Environmental Influences on Premature Death in Adult Adoptees," *New England Journal of Medicine*, 318(March 24, 1988): 727–732.

Spencer, Marietta. "The Terminology of Adoption," *Child Welfare*, 58(July/August 1979): 451–459.

Spencer, Marietta E. "Post-Legal Adoption Services: A Lifeling Commitment" in *Infertility and Adoption: A Guide for Social Work Practice*. New York: Haworth Press, 1988.

Sutter, William P. "It's Time to Be Fair—All Adopted Children Should Have Equal Rights," *Illinois Bar Journal*, December 1986, 224–227.

Teasdale, T. W., and Sørensen, T. I. A. "Educational Attainment and Social Class in Adoptees: Genetic and Environmental Contributions," *Journal of Biosocial Science,* 15(1983): 509–518.

Ternay, Marilyn R.; Wilborn, Bobbie; and Day, H. D. "Perceived Child-Parent Relationships and Child Adjustment in Families with Both Adopted and Natural Children," *Journal of Genetic Psychology,* 146:2(1985): 261–272.

Terpstra, Jake, M. S. W. "The Rich and Exacting Role of the Social Worker in Family Foster Care," *Child and Adolescent Social Work,* 4:nos. 3 and 4(Fall, Winter 1987).

Triseliotis, J. *In Search of Origins: The Experience of Adopted People.* London: Routledge and Kegan Paul, 1973.

U.S. Department of Health and Human Services. National Center for Health Statistics. "Advance Report of Final Natality Statistics, 1988," *Monthly Vital Statistics Report,* 39:4, supplement (August 15, 1990).

———. "Advance Report of Final Natality Statistics, 1987," *Monthly Vital Statistics Report, Final Data,* 38:3, supplement(June 29, 1989).

———. *Socioeconomic Differentials and Trends in the Timing of Births.* February 1981.

———. *Wanted and Unwanted Childbearing: United States, 1973–1982.* May 9, 1985.

U.S. Department of Health and Human Services. National Center on Child Abuse and Neglect. Office of Human Development Services, Administration for Children, Youth and Families, Children's Bureau. *Study Findings: Study of National Incidence and Prevalence of Child Abuse and Neglect: 1988.*

U.S. General Accounting Office, Report to the Chairman, Committee on Finance, U.S. Senate. *Drug-Exposed Infants: A Generation at Risk.* June 1990.

U.S. Congress. House Committee on Ways and Means. *Background Material and Data on Programs Within the Jurisdiction of the Committee on Ways and Means.* 101st Congress, 1st Session, March 15, 1989.

U.S. Congress. House Select Committee of Children, Youth, and Families. *No Place to Call Home: Discarded Children in America.* 101st Congress, 1st Session, November, 1989.

Valentine, Deborah, ed. *Infertility and Adoption: A Guide for Social Work Practice.* New York: Haworth Press, 1988.

Van Dusen, Katherine Teilmann; Mednick, Sarnoff A.; Gabrielli, William F., Jr.; and Hutchings, Barry. "Social Class and Crime in an Adoption Cohort," *The Journal of Criminal Law and Criminology* 74(Spring 1983): 249–269.

Wallisch, Natalie Haag. "Independent Adoption: Regulating the Middleman," *Washburn Law Journal,* vol. 24, 327–359.

Ward. Margaret, and Lewko, John H. "Problems Experienced by Adolescents Already in Families that Adopt Older Children," *Adolescence,* 23(Spring 1988): 221–228.

Weiss, Andrea. "Symptomology of Adopted and Nonadopted Adolescents in a Psychiatric Hospital," *Adolescence* (Winter 1985), 763–774.

Witmer, Helen L.; Herzog, Elizabeth; Weinstein, Eugene A.; and Sullivan, Mary E. *Independent Adoptions: A Follow-up Study.* New York: Sage Foundation, 1963.

Zeilinger, Richard. "The Need vs. the Right to Know," *Public Welfare,* 37(Summer 1979): 44–47.

INDEX

Bold face numbers indicate main headings

A

abandonment, **1–2**; abuse, 7; protective services, 235–236
abortion, **2–5**; confidentiality, 82; infant adoption, 160–161; open adoption, 213
Abramse, Allan F., 280–281
Abramson, Susan, 270
abuse, **5–10**; background information, 52; disruption, 100–101; protective services, 235–236; sexual abuse, 258–259; termination of parental rights, 289–290
academic progress, **10–11**; foster care, 128
Acquired Immune Deficiency Syndrome—*See AIDS*
acting out, 11; abuse, 7; self-esteem, 257
Adaptor's Advocate, An (Patricia Johnston), 163
Adelberg, Robert Allen, 253
adjustment, **11–13**; adolescent adopted persons, 13
adolescent adopted persons, **13–16**; divorce of adoptive parents, 103; siblings, 261
Adolescent Family Life Program, **16**; teenage parents, 282–283
adolescent parents: abuse, 8–9
adopted-away/adopted-in, **16**
Adopted Child Comes of Age, The (Lois Raynor), 27–28, 32–33
adoptee, 292–293
Adoptees' Liberty Movement Association (ALMA), xxvii, **17**, 275; open records, 219; search groups, 256
"adoptee" v. "adopted person," **16–17**
adoption, **17–18**
Adoption Assistance and Child Welfare Act (1980), xxviii–xxix, **18–19**; foster care, 127; parental rights, 227; permanency planning, 228; state laws, 183; termination of parental rights, 287
Adoption Assistance Program, **19–21**
Adoption Awareness: A Guide for Teachers, Counselors, Nurses and Caring Others (Jeanne Lindsay and Catherine Monserrat), 150
adoption circle, **21**
Adoption classes, 37, 111
Adoption Defense Fund, **21–22**
Adoption Factbook: birthmother, 63
Adoption Hall of Fame, **22**
Adoption Law and Practice (book): Adoption Assistance Program, 20–21
Adoption Listing Service: photolistings, 228
Adoption of Children Act (England, 1926), xviii
Adoption triad: attitudes about adoption, 47; loss, 185; terminology, 292
adoption triad, **22**
adoption triangle, **22**

Adoption Worker's Guide to Genetic Services (Julia B. Rauch and Nancy Rike), 52
Adoptive Families of America Inc. (AFA), **22–23**; advertising and promotion, 34; culture camps, 91; education of adoptive parents, 112
Adoptive parent groups (list): Canada, 354; United States, 349–353
Adoptive parents: AIDS, 41; case study, 78; terminology, 293; transracial adoption, 298–299
adoptive parents, **23–29**; abuse, 9–10
Adult adopted persons: open adoption, 215
adult adopted persons, **29–33**
adult adoptee, **29**
adults, adoption of, **29**
advertising and promotion, **33–35**; open adoption, 211; recruitment, 241
Agee, Mary Cunningham: birthmother, 63; mature women planning adoption, 190
agencies, **35–38**; designated adoption, 95–96; gender preference, 133; home study, 145–146; infant adoption, 161; international (list), 345; single adoptive parents, 264; sliding scale fees, 265; United States (list), 336–344; waiting lists, 304
AIDS, xxxii, **39–41**; abandonment, 1; drug abuse, 106, 109; foster care, 128; infant adoption, 162; medical problems of adopted children, 194
Aid to Families with Dependent Children (AFDC): Adoption Assistance Program, 20; Medicaid, 192; welfare, 305
Alabama: adoption agencies, 336; adoptive parent groups, 349; consent, 83; mutual consent registries, 199; notice, 207; open records, 217, 218; search and consent laws, 255; social services office, 330
Alan Guttmacher Institute: abortion, 3–4
Alaska: adoption agencies, 336; foster parent adoption, 131; gay and lesbian adoption, 132; notice, 207; open records, 217; sealed records, 252; social services office, 330
alcohol abuse and adopted persons, **41–44**; criminal behavior in adopted adults, 90
Ali, Shaista-Parveen: gay and lesbian adoption, 132–133
Alma Society Inc. v. Mellon, 218–219, 220
almshouses, **44–45**; history of adoption, xxii–xxv
Altstein, Howard, 70, 300–301
ambivalence, **45**
American Academy of Adoption Attorneys, The (AAAA), 45

American Adoption Congress (AAC), **45–46**; open records, 219; search groups, 256; support groups, 275
American Association for Protecting Children, 9; abuse, 5, 9
American Bar Association (ABA), **46**; Model State Adoption Act, 199
American Civil Liberties Union (ACLU), 125
American Fertility Society: bioethics, 54; fertility rates, 122–123
American Indians: fetal alcohol syndrome, 125; Indian Child Welfare Act of 1978, 158
American Public Welfare Association (APWA), **46–47**
Anderson, Kathryn, 76
Andujo, Estela, 143
Anstett, Richard, 230
Arizona: adoption agencies, 336; adoptive parent groups, 349; gay and lesbian adoption, 132; genetic data, 135; notice, 207; social services office, 330
Arkansas: adoption agencies, 336; adoptive parent groups, 349; insurance, 165; Interstate Compact on Adoption and Medical Assistance (ICAMA), 178; mutual consent registries, 199; notice, 207; open records, 218; search and consent laws, 255; social services office, 330
Association for Children and Adults with Learning Disabilities Inc. (ACLD), 184
Association of Jewish Family & Children's Agencies, **47**; Council on Accreditation of Services for Families and Children Inc., 88
at risk placement, **47**; foster care, 128–129; high risk placements, 143; immediate placements, 152–153; independent adoption, 156
attitudes about adoption, **47–49**; adolescent adopted persons, 14–15; AIDS, 40; birthgrandparent, 59; birthmother, 62–63; bonding and attachment, 72; gay and lesbian adoption, 132–133; teachers and adopted children, 279–280
attorneys, **49–50**; costs to adopt, 86; intermediary, 168
Atwater, Martha, 57
Augustus Caesar, xvii
Aumend, S. A. A., 253
autobiography, **50**
auxiliaries, **50**
AZT, 40

B

Baby Boom, xxix–xxx; fertility rates, 123; infertility, 162
Babylonians, ancient, xvii–xviii
baby selling, **50–51**; bioethics, 53; ethical issues, 115
baby shortage, **51–52**

373

374 Index

Bachrach, Christine, 27, 61–66
background information, **52**
Baran, Annette, 214–215
Barth, Richard P., 21; adoptive parents, 25; disruption, 100–101; drug abuse, 108; learning disabilities, 184
Bassuk, Ellen, 144
Beckerman, Adela, 288
Bentsen, Lloyd, 82
Berry, Barth, 99
Berry, Marianne, 99, 100
Best, Jessie, 164
Beyond the Best Interests of the Child (Goldstein, Freud and Solnit), xxx, 49
Bible, xvii, xviii
bibliography, **52–53**
Bibliography on Some Social and Psychological Aspects of Adoption, A (Paul Brinich), 53
Bigner, Jerry S., 8
bioethics, **53–54**
biographical information, **54–55**
biological parents, **55**
Biomedical Ethics Board, 54
biracial, **55**; special needs, 268
birth certificates, 152
birthday, **55**
birthfather, **55–59**; custody, 93; history of adoption, xxxi; open adoption, 210; putative father, 240; rights, 56–57; Supreme Court cases; 57–59; teenage parents, 284–285; terminology, 293
birthgrandparent, 59–60
birth kin, **60**
birthmother, **60–67**; abandonment, 1–2; hospitals' treatment of, 148–151; independent adoption, 155–156; loss, 185–186; open adoption, 210–216; poverty, 231; special needs, 267; terminology, 293
birth order, 67–68; birthmother, 62; siblings, 260; therapy and therapists, 296
birthparent, **68**; abandonment, 2; adoption, 17; agencies, 36; explaining adoption, 120; genetic predispositions, 136–139; married birthparents, 187; termination of parental rights, 286
birth rates for unmarried women (tables), 311–314
black adoptive parent recruitment program, **68–69**; recruitment, 241
black children: adolescent adopted persons, 15–16; agencies, 38; history of adoption, xxviii; One Church, One Child, 209; photolistings, 228–229; special needs, 268
Black Death, xix
black families, **69–70**; adoptive parents, 24
Blanchard, Amy, 254–255
Blanton, Terril, 213
blended families, **70**
Bliley, Thomas, 82
blood ties, 87
Blum, Kenneth, 42
boarder babies: abandonment, 1; drug abuse, 106
Bohman, Michael, 43; criminal behavior in adopted adults, 90; pregnancy after adoption, 232
bonding and attachment, **71–75**; cooperative adoption, 84

Bose, Jane, 64, 233
Boswell, John, xviii
Bowen, James S., 299–300
Brace, Charles Loring, xxiv–xxv, 78, 222–224
Brady, John, xxv
Braff, Anne, 119
Braxton, Earl, 208
breast-feeding an adopted infant, **75–77**
Brennan, Jack, 229
Brinich, Evelin, 30, 238–239
Brinich, Paul, 30, 52–53, 238–239
Brodzinsky, David M., 73, 119
Broken Cord, The (Michael Dorris), 125
Brown, Dirck W., 254–255
Burke, Andrew, xxv
Bush, Barbara, 140, 204
Bush, George, 114, 140
Bussiere, Alice, 178
Byrd, A. Dean, 213–214, 297

C

Caban v. Mohammed, 58
California: adoption agencies, 336–337; adoptive parent groups, 349; ethical issues, 115; gay and lesbian adoption, 132; genetic data, 135; maternity homes, 189; mutual consent registries, 199; open records, 218; search and consent laws, 255; social services office, 330
"Calling out," 77; National Adoption Week, 202
Calvin, Jamie, 140
Canada: adoptive parent groups, 354; social services offices (list), 334–335
CAP Book, **77**
Capron, Christiane, 166–167
Cardiff, Jeanette, 253
Care of Destitute, Neglected and Delinquent Children, The (Homer Folks), 44
Caribbean, 182
Carlson, Richard R., 169–170
Carstens, C.C., xxv–xxvi
case records, **77–78**
case study, 78
Catholic Adoptive Parents Association (CAPA), **78**
Catholic Charities USA, 88
Catholics, 243–244
Causes of Crime, The (ed. Samoff Mednick, Terrie E. Moffitt and Susan A. Stack), 88
Cerebral palsy, 96
Chasnoff, Ira, 105–106
Cherian, Varghese I., 210
Child labor laws, xxvii
Childless Veterans Assistance Act (1989), 82
Children Awaiting Adoptive Parents (CAAP), 228
Children Awaiting Placement (CAP), 34
Children's Aid Society of New York, 78
children's rights, **78–79**
Child Welfare League of America Inc., xxv–xxvi, 79; Council on Accreditation of Services for Families and Children Inc., 87, 88; mutual consent registries, 199; surrogate motherhood, 277
Cho, Baek-Sang, 180

"Chosen child," **79–80**; explaining adoption, 119
Church Home Society (Boston), 34
Citizenship: adoptive parents, 25
citizenship, **80**
Clark, Natalie Loder, 276
Clements, George H., 22, 68; One Church, One Child, 209; transracial adoption, 299
Cline, Foster, 74
Clinical Practice in Adoption, 254–255
Cloninger, C. Robert, 43, 88–89
Coccia, Carol, 203
Cocozzelli, Carmelo, 64–65
Colombia, 182
Colonial Orphan Asylum, xxviii
Colorado: adoption agencies, 337; adoptive parent groups, 349; designated adoption, 94–95; independent adoption, 154; inheritance, 164; Interstate Compact on Adoption and Medical Assistance (ICAMA), 178; mutual consent registries, 199; notice, 207; open records, 218; search and consent laws, 255; social services office, 330; termination of parental rights, 287
Colorado Adoption Project, 137
Committee for Mother and Child Rights, 56
Committee for Single Adoptive Parents, **80**, 263
Computers: interstate adoption, 178
computers, **80–81**
Concerned United Birthparents Inc. (CUB), **81**; open records, 219; search groups, 256
Confidentiality: history of adoption, xxvi–xxvii; open records, 220; research, 245; resume, 248; sealed records, 252
confidentiality, **81–82**
Congressional Coalition on Adoption, **82**
Connecticut: adoption agencies, 337; adoptive parent groups, 349; designated adoption, 94; independent adoption, 153; mutual consent registries, 199; notice, 207; open records, 218; parental leave, 225; search and consent laws, 255; social services office, 330; state laws, 183
Consent: interstate adoption, 178; notice, 207; revocation, 251
consent, **82–83**
"Consequences of the Adoption Decision, The" (Steven McLaughlin), 62
Constantine, xix
contract, **83**
Conway, Patricia, 162
Cook, Thomas, 26
Cooperative adoption: co-parenting, 84; open adoption, 210, 215
cooperative adoption, **83–84**
co-parenting, **84**
Coram, Thomas, xx
Corporate adoption benefits, 112–113
Corse, Sara J., 8
Costanzo, P., 137
Costin, Lela B., 225
Costs to adopt: agencies, 37; ethical issues, 116; independent adoption, 157
costs to adopt, **84–86**
Council of Adoptive Parents, 77

Index

Council on Accreditation of Services for Families and Children Inc., **87–88**
Counseling: agencies, 36; preadoptive counseling, 231–232; pregnancy counseling, 232–234
counseling, **88**
Court-mandated contracts, 83
court-mandated contracts, **86–87**
Courtney, Anna Marie, 63
Couve, Janus, 182
Covington, Sharon, 162
Cox, Susan, 180
Craig, Larry, 82
Criminal behavior in adopted adults: socioeconomic status, 266
criminal behavior in adopted adults, **88–91**
Crisis pregnancy: alcohol abuse and adopted persons, 41; mature women planning adoption, 190; physicians, 229–230; pregnancy counseling, 232; teenage parents, 281–282
crisis pregnancy, **91**
CSR Inc., 201
Cullen, Ruth, 25
Culture camps: Korean adopted children, 181
culture camps, **91**
culture shock, **91–93**
Curran, Mary Ann, 264
Custody: guardian ad litem, 142
custody, **93**

D

Dahlstrom, Cosette, 133–134
Davis, Lloyd, 182
Day, H.D., 100, 197–198
DeBolt, Dorothy, 22
DeBolt, Robert, 22
Delaware: adoption agencies, 337; adoptive parent groups, 349; designated adoption, 94; independent adoption, 153; Interstate Compact on Adoption and Medical Assistance (ICAMA), 178; notice, 207; religion, 188; social services office, 330; state laws, 183
delinquency, **93–94**
Denmark, 88
Denney, Freddie Lee, 100
Depp, Carole, 261
Deschner, Jeanne, 213
Designated adoption: advertising and promotion, 35; costs to adopt, 86; immediate placements, 153; independent adoption, 153; religion, 243; state laws, 183
designated adoption, **94–96**
Detweiler, Richard, 31
Developmental disabilities: learning disabilities, 183
developmental disabilities, **96–97**
Dewar, Diana, xx
Deykin, Eva Y., 56
diagnostic home, **97–98**
DiGiulio, Joan Ferry, 273
Direct placement: state laws, 183
direct placement, **98**
disabilities of adoptive parents, **98**
discipline, **98**
Disinformation, 173
Displaced Persons Act (1948), 168
disruption, **98–103**
Dissolution: disruption, 98–99
dissolution, **103**
District of Columbia: adoption agencies, 337; adoptive parent groups, 349; social services office, 330
divorce of adoptive parents, **103–104**
Dodd, Christopher, 105
Doe v. Roe, 59
Donley, Kathryn, 260
Dorris, Michael, 125
Down, Langdon, 104
Down syndrome, **104**
Drug abuse: foster care, 128; learning disabilities, 183–184; termination of parental rights, 288–289
drug abuse, **105–110**; abandonment, 1
Ducote, Richard, 289–290
Duke, Patty, 201
Duyme, Michel, 166–167

E

Easson, William, 13–14
Edna McConnell Clark Foundation, 6
Educational neglect, 206
Education of adoptive parents: adoptive parents, 24; disruption, 101
education of adoptive parents, **110–112**
Egan, Pauline, 15
Egypt, xvii
Emotional neglect, 205–206
Employment benefits: adoptive parents, 27; maternity leave, 189–190
employment benefits, **112–114**
Engel, Paul, 267
England, xix–xx
Entitlement: bonding and attachment, 71; confidentiality, 82; cooperative adoption, 84; designated adoption, 95; independent adoption, 156; naming, 200; open adoption, 212–213; relative adoptions, 242
entitlement, **114–115**
environment, **115**
ethical issues, **115–117**
etiquette, **117–118**
eugenics, **118**
Explaining adoption: grandparent adoptions, 141
explaining adoption, **118–121**

F

Fahlberg, Vera, 73–74, 246
Fairness for Adopting Families Act (1989), 82
Fales, Mary Jane, 231
family income, 5
Family Leave Benefits Act (1989), 82
Family Service America, 87, 88
family size, 5
family tree, 121
Fancett, Carrie, 272
fantasies of adopted children, **121–122**
Federal Disabilities Act (1984), 96
federal government, **122**
Feig, Laura, 109
Feigelman, William, 237
fertile adoptive parents, **122**
fertility rates, **122–123**
Festinger, Trudy, 61, 99
Fetal alcohol effect (FAE), 124
Fetal alcohol syndrome (FAS), **123–125**; criminal behavior in adopted adults, 90; drug abuse, 105; learning disabilities, 184
Films, 191–192
Finalization: judge, 179–180
finalization, **125**
Fisher, Florence, 17
Florida: adoption agencies, 337–338; adoptive parent groups, 349; black adoptive parent recruitment programs, 68–69; consent, 83; disabilities of adoptive parents, 98; employment benefits, 113; gay and lesbian adoption, 131–132; grandparent adoptions, 141; independent adoption, 154–155; insurance, 165; interstate adoption, 177–178; mutual consent registries, 199; open records, 218; search and consent laws, 255; social services office, 330; termination of parental rights, 287–288
Folks, Homer, xxiii–xxiv, 44
Ford, Gerald, 22
Ford, Kathleen, 281
Forever family: international adoption, 168
forever family, **125**
Forsythe, Peter, 6
Foster care: Adoption Assistance and Child Welfare Act of 1980, 18; federal government, 122; history of adoption, xxviii; homeless children, 144; infant adoption, 161; life book, 185; reunification, 249–250; sexual abuse, 258; special needs, 268; termination of parental rights, 287
foster care, **126–129**
Foster parent: adoptive parents, 24–25; disruption, 100–101
foster parent, **129–130**
Foster parent adoption: Adoption Assistance Program, 20; bonding and attachment, 73–74; open adoption, 215
foster parent adoption, **130–131**
foundations, **131**
France, xix
French, Anne Wiseman, 164–165

G

Gabrielli Jr., William F., 89
Galinsky, Ellen, 72–73
Gay and lesbian adoption: adults, adoption of, 29
gay and lesbian adoption, **131–133**
Geber, Gayle, 62
gender preference, **133–135**
Genetic data: background information, 52
genetic data, **135–136**
Genetic father, 293
genetic fingerprinting, **136**
Genetic mother, 293
genetic parents, **136**
Genetic predispositions: alcohol abuse and adopted persons, 42; psychiatric problems of adopted persons, 239; special needs, 267
genetic predispositions, **136–140**
Genetic testing, 118
George, Jody, 141

Georgia: adoptive parent groups, 349–350; consent, 83; disabilities of adoptive parents, 98; grandparent adoptions, 141; insurance, 165; Interstate Compact on Adoption and Medical Assistance (ICAMA), 178; mutual consent registries, 199; notice, 207; open records, 218; search and consent laws, 255; social services office, 331
Gerbner, George, 78, 191–192
Germany, xix
Gervais, Glynne, 303–304
Gill, Owen, 299
Gladney, Edna, xxvi, 110
Gladney Center, The, **110**
Glenn, Norval D., 209–210
Goettl, Kathryn, 26–27
Gonzalez, Eulalio, 173
Goodluck, Charlotte, 159
Grandparent: birthgrandparent, 59–60 grandparent, **140**
Grandparent adoptions: relative adoptions, 242
grandparent adoptions, **141**
grandparent rights, **141**
Great Depression, xxvi
Griffith, Dan, 105
Group homes: foster care, 126; orphanage, 221–222; residential treatment centers, 246
group homes, **141–142**
Grow, Lucille J., 61, 64
Guardian ad litem: gay and lesbian adoption, 132
guardian ad litem, **142**
Guatemala, 182
Gundersen, Luanne, 40
Guy, Rebecca, 238

H

Hage, Deborah, 21
Hall, G. Stanley, xxvii
Hallenbeck, Carol A., 111
Hammurabi, Code of, xvii
Handbook for Single Adoptive Parents, 80
Handel, Georg Friedrich, xx
Handicapped parents, 193
Handicaps, 267
Hardin, Mark, 19
hard to place children, **143**
Harris, Linda, 131–132
Harrison, Mary-Lynn, 73
Hartfield, Bernadette W., 177
Hartman, Ann, 97–98, 208
Hawaii: adoption agencies, 338; genetic data, 135; Interstate Compact on Adoption and Medical Assistance (ICAMA), 178; open records, 217; sealed records, 252; social services office, 331
Hebrews, ancient, xviii
Heiss, Elizabeth, 272
"Helpline," 23
Hepatitis B, 195
Hernandez, Donald, 23, 25
Herr, Kathleen, 62
Herzog, Elizabeth, 155
High risk placements: disruption, 101
high risk placements, **143**
Hindus, ancient, xvii
Hispanics/Latinos, **143**

History of adoption: birthmother, 65; open adoption, 211; transracial adoption, 298
history of adoption, xvii–xxxiii; almshouse, xxii–xxv; ancient times, xvii–xix; Europe, xix–xx; orphaned children, xxi–xxii; twentieth century, xxv–xxxii; United States, xx–xxxii
HIV (Human Immunodeficiency Virus), 39
Hogan, Patricia Turner, xxviii
Hollinger, Joan H., 199
Holmes Jr., R.B., 68, 209
Holt, Bertha, 181
Holt, Harry, 181
Holt International Children's Services, 180–181
Homeless children: abandonment, 2
homeless children, **143–145**
Homes for Black Children, 69
Home study: adoption, 17; adoptive parents, 25–26; adults, adoption of, 29; agencies, 37; autobiography, 50; baby selling, 50; case study, 78; costs to adopt, 84; education of adoptive parents, 110; grandparent adoptions, 141; independent adoption, 154; preadoptive counseling, 232; resume, 248; social workers, 265; terminology, 292, 293; updated home study, 303
home study, **145–148**
Hoopes, Janet, 13; identity, 152; siblings, 262; teachers and adopted children, 279–280
Hoover, Herbert, 46
Hoppe, Sue Keir, 209–210
Hormann, Elizabeth, 76
Horn, Joseph M., 167
Homby, Helaine, 99
hospitals' treatment of birthmothers, **148–151**
hotlines, **151**
How to Raise an Adopted Child (Judith Schaffer and Christina Lindstrom), 55, 140, 163
Human Immunodeficiency Virus—See HIV
Humphers v. First Interstate Bank, 219
Hunter, Anna, xxi
Hyperactivity, 97

I

Idaho: adoption agencies, 338; adoptive parent groups, 350; genetic data, 135; interstate adoption, 177; mutual consent registries, 199; open records, 218; search and consent laws, 255; social services office, 331
Identified adoption, 94–95, 243
identity, **152**
Ililonga, Sandi, 203–204
Illegitimacy: adoptive parents, 27; history of adoption, xxvi
illegitimacy, **152**; history of adoption, xxi
Illinois: adoption agencies, 338–339; adoptive parent groups, 350; consent, 83; mutual consent registries, 199; notice, 207; open records, 218; search and consent laws, 255; social services office, 331
immediate placements, **152–153**

Immigration and naturalization: international adoption, 169; orphan, 221; statistics, 271
immigration and naturalization, **153**
Immigration and Naturalization Service, U.S., **303**; birthmother, 66
income tax deductions, **153**
indenture, xxiv
Independent adoption: American Academy of Adoption Attorneys (AAAA), 45; attorneys, 49; baby selling, 50–51; costs to adopt, 85; designated adoption, 94–95, 96; direct placement, 98; home study, 145, 147; infertility, 163; intermediary, 168; international adoption, 171; interstate adoption, 177; religion, 243; resume, 248; state laws, 183; support groups, 274
independent adoption, **153–158**
India, **158**
Indiana: adoption agencies, 339; adoptive parent groups, 350; designated adoption, 95; mutual consent registries, 199; open records, 218; search and consent laws, 255; social services office, 331; termination of parental rights, 287
Indian Child Welfare Act (1978), xx, **158–160**; transracial adoption, 298
Indonesia, xvii
Infant adoption: adjustment, 12; background information, 52; bonding and attachment, 71; home study, 146; matching, 188; naming, 200; National Committee for Adoption, 204
infant adoption, **160–162**
Infertility: adoptive parents, 25; agencies, 36; loss, 186; National Committee for Adoption, 204; zygote adoption, 308
infertility, **162–163**
Informal adoption: simple adoption, 263; transracial adoption, 299
informal adoption, **163–164**
inheritance, **164–165**
In re Goldman, 187
Instruction on Respect for Human Life and Its Origin and on the Dignity of Procreation (Vatican publication), 54
Insurance: employment benefits, 113; ethical issues, 116; fertility rates, 123; military members and adoption, 196–197
insurance, **165–166**
Intelligence: environment, 115; genetic predispositions, 137–138; teachers and adopted children, 279
intelligence, **166–168**
Intermediary: costs to adopt, 85; independent adoption, 156–157; physicians, 230
intermediary, **168**
International adoption: baby selling, 50; birthmother, 66; bonding and attachment, 71; costs to adopt, 85–86; culture shock, 92–93; ethical issues, 116; etiquette, 117; explaining adoption, 120; gender preference, 133–134; home study, 146; infant adoption, 161; Korean adopted children, 180; Latin American adoptions, 182; medical history, 193; medical problems of adopted children, 194–196; National Committee for Adoption, 204; open adoption, 215–216; orphan, 221; physicians, 229; special needs, 268–269; state by state

adoption rates (tables), 324–327; table, 174–175
international adoption, **168–176**
International Concerns Committee for Children, 176; advertising and promotion, 34; India, 158; international adoption, 171, 172; Latin American adoptions, 182; single adoptive parents, 264; skin color, 265
International Soundex Reunion Registry (ISRR), **176–177**; search groups, 256
Interstate adoption: attorneys, 49; independent adoption, 157
interstate adoption, **177–178**
Interstate Compact on Adoption and Medical Assistance (ICAMA), **178–179**; American Public Welfare Association (APWA), 47; independent adoption, 157; interstate adoption, 177, 178
Interstate Compact on the Placement of Children, **179**; agencies, 35; American Public Welfare Association (APWA), 47; costs to adopt, 85
In the Best Interests of the Child, 93
Iowa: adoption agencies, 339; adoptive parent groups, 350; genetic data, 135; social services office, 331
Islamic cultures, xvii

J

Jackson, Barbara, 299
Jeff, Morris, 298
Jefferson, Thomas, xxi
Jeffreys, Alec, 136
Jewett, Claudia, 68, 256–257
Jewish adoption: adolescent adopted persons, 15; religion, 243; Stars of David, 270
Johnson, Penny R., 300
Johnston, Patricia: bonding and attachment, 72–73; entitlement, 114; infertility, 163
Jones, David P.H., 289
Jones, Kenneth, 124
Judge: adoption, 18; Adoption Assistance and Child Welfare Act of 1980, 19; finalization, 125
judge, **179–180**
Julius Caesar, xvii
Justinian, xix
Juvenile crime, 16

K

Kalmuss, Debra, 64
Kansas: adoption agencies, 339; adoptive parent groups, 350; employment benefits, 113; genetic data, 135; inheritance, 164; insurance, 165; Interstate Compact on Adoption and Medical Assistance (ICAMA), 178; open records, 217; sealed records, 252; social services office, 331
Kaplan, Sharon, 83
Katz, Michael B., xxii, xxvii
Katz, S., 155
Kauffman, Rosie Ann, 253
Kawashima, xxi
Keane, Noel, 275–276
Kellogg, Lori, 263
Kentucky: adoptive parent groups, 350; consent, 83; Interstate Compact on Adoption and Medical Assistance (ICAMA), 178; mutual consent registries, 199; open records, 218; search and consent laws, 255; social services office, 331
Kessler, Lynn Friedman, 278–279
Kim, Dong Soo, 133
King, Lula T., 70
Kirk, H. David, 49
Kirschner, David, 228, 237
Kirsh, Stephen, 45
Klein, Robert P., 73
Koran, xvii
Korean adopted children, **180–181**; culture camps, 91; gender preference, 133; international adoption, 168–169; naming, 200
Kowal, Katherine A., 31, 121–122, 254
Kraft, Adrienne, 215

L

Lakin, Drenda, 69, 246
La Leche League, 76–77
Lane, Francis, xxiv
Laning, Betty, 172, 176
Large families: adoptive parents, 28
large families, **181–182**
Large Sibling Groups: Adoption Experiences (booklet), 182
Latin American adoptions, **182**; adoptive parents, 23; culture camps, 91; international adoption, 171
Law of Adoption and Surrogate Parenting (Irving J. Sloan), 29
laws, state, **182–183**
Leake & Watts Children's Home (Yonkers, New York), 39, 40
learning disabilities, **183–184**
Legal father: birthfather, 56, 58
legal father, **184–185**
Legal issues: developmental disabilities, 97
Legal rights: birthfather, 56–57; birthgrandparent, 60; children's rights, 78–79; grandparent rights, 141; inheritance, 164–165; parental rights, 226–227
legitimation, xix
Lehr v. Robertson, 58
LePere, Dorothy, 103, 182
Levin, Carl, 218, 253
Levine, Katherine Gordy, 186
Lewko, John H., 198, 261
Leynes, Cynthia, 61
Lifebook: loss, 186–187; preparing a child for adoption, 234
lifebook, **185**
Lifton, Betty Jean, 254
Lindner, Elizabeth, 62, 64
Lindsay, Jeanne Warren, 60, 150–151
Lindstrom, Christina, 55; grandparent, 140; infertility, 163; therapy and therapists, 296
Liskov, Adele, 120
loss, **185–187**
Louisiana: adoption agencies, 339; adoptive parent groups, 350; consent, 83; genetic data, 135; inheritance, 164; insurance, 166; Interstate Compact on Adoption and Medical Assistance (ICAMA), 178; mutual consent registries, 199; open records, 218; search and consent laws, 255; social services office, 331
Lutheran Social Ministry System, 88
Lydens, Lois, 133, 172–173, 180–181

M

Maczka, Susan, 262
Maine: adoption agencies, 339–340; adoptive parent groups, 350; genetic data, 135; Interstate Compact on Adoption and Medical Assistance (ICAMA), 178; mutual consent registries, 199; open records, 218; parental leave, 225; search and consent laws, 255; social services office, 331
Malestic, Susan, 150
Manning, Anita, 288
Manoff-Russo, E., 155
Manu, Laws of, xvii
Marindin, Hope, 80
Marital status, 63
Marks, Leah Ruth, 288–289
Marquis, Kathlyn, 31
married birthparents, **187**
Maryland: adoption agencies, 340; adoptive parent groups, 350; grandparent adoptions, 141; mutual consent registries, 199; open records, 218; parental leave, 225; search and consent laws, 255
Massachusetts: adoption agencies, 340; adoptive parent groups, 351; almshouses, 44; designated adoption, 94; fertility rates, 123; gay and lesbian adoption, 132–133; history of adoption, xx–xxi; independent adoption, 153; Interstate Compact on Adoption and Medical Assistance (ICAMA), 178; mutual consent registries, 199; notice, 207; Open Door Society, 216; open records, 218; search and consent laws, 255; social services office, 331; state laws, 183
Massachusetts Adoption Resource Exchange (MARE): photolistings, 228
matching, **187–188**
Maternity homes: crisis pregnancy, 91; National Committee for Adoption, 204
maternity homes, **188–189**
Maternity leave: parental leave, 225
maternity leave, **189–190**
"Matrix of State Adoption Laws," 83, 98
Matthews, Robert Charles, 170
mature women planning adoption, **190–191**
McCauliff, C.M.A., xix
McCoy, Ruth G., 15–16
McDermott, Mark, 45
McDonald, Mona, 182
McDonald, Thomas, 99
McElhinny, Jody, 95
McGue, Matt, 167
McKenzie, Judith, 246
McLaughlin, Steven D., 62, 283
McNamara, Edward, 58
McNamara, Joan, 258–259
McRoy, Ruth G., 188, 278
Mech, Edmund, 232, 282–283
Mecklenburg, Carol, 300

Index

Media: advertising and promotion, 33–35; explaining adoption, 120; teenage parents, 284; Wednesday's Child, 305
media, **191–192**
Media Guidelines on Adoption Language (brochure), 78
Medicaid, **192**; abortion, 3; Adoption Assistance Program, 20; AIDS, 40; costs to adopt, 85; foster care, 128; independent adoption, 156; insurance, 165, 166; interstate adoption, 178; Interstate Compact on Adoption and Medical Assistance (ICAMA), 179; maternity homes, 189
Medical history: medical problems of adopted children, 194–196
medical history, **192–193**
Medically fragile: AIDS, 40; drug abuse, 106
medically fragile, **193–194**
medical problems of adopted children, **194–196**
Mednick, Sarnoff, 88–89
Meezan, William, 155
Menning, Barbara Eck, 247
Merrill, AnnaMarie, 176
Miall, Charlene E., 27, 48, 114
Michael H., and Victoria D., Appellants v. Gerald D., 58, 185
Michigan: adoption agencies, 340; adoptive parent groups, 351; almshouses, 44; designated adoption, 95; history of adoption, xxii; independent adoption, 153–154; mutual consent registries, 199; open records, 218; search and consent laws, 255; social services office, 332; state laws, 183; termination of parental rights, 288
military members and adoption, **196–197**
Miller, George, 18
Minnesota: adoption agencies, 340; adoptive parent groups, 351; consent, 83; designated adoption, 94; genetic data, 135; insurance, 166; Interstate Compact on Adoption and Medical Assistance (ICAMA), 178; mutual consent registries, 199; open records, 218; parental leave, 225; search and consent laws, 255; social services office, 332; state laws, 183
Miroff, Franklin I.: entitlement, 114; fantasies of adopted children, 121; hospitals' treatment of birthmother, 149; open records, 220; pregnancy counseling, 233
Misak, Margaret Klein, 62
Mississippi: adoption agencies, 340–341; adoptive parent groups, 351; inheritance, 164; Interstate Compact on Adoption and Medical Assistance (ICAMA), 178; notice, 207; social services office, 332
Missouri: adoption agencies, 341; adoptive parent groups, 351; foster care, 126; foster parent adoption, 131; Interstate Compact on Adoption and Medical Assistance (ICAMA), 178; search and consent laws, 255; social services office, 332
Mitchel, Leslie, 289
mixed families, **197–198**
Model State Adoption Act, **198–199**

Moffitt, Terrie E., 88, 90
Moncom, William, xxi
Mondale, Walter, 18
Monserrat, Catherine, 150–151
Montana: adoption agencies, 341; adoptive parent groups, 351; interstate adoption, 177; mutual consent registries, 199; open records, 218; search and consent laws, 255; social services office, 332; termination of parental rights, 287
Mooney, Sandra, 246
Moorman, Jeanne, 23, 25
Morgan, Gary T., 69
Morris, I.Z.T., 110
Morrison, Peter A., 280–281
Moses, xvii, xviii
Moses, Pamela, 58
Moses, Robert, 58
Mostly I Can Do More Things Than I Can't (Glynne Gervais and Marilyn Panichi), 303–304
multiethnic, **199**
Murphy, Solbritt, 7
Mutch, Patricia, 124
Mutual consent registries: ethical issues, 117; open records, 218–219; search, 252–253
mutual consent registries, **199–200**

N

naming, **200–201**
National Adoption Center, **201**; computers, 81; National Adoption Information Clearinghouse, 201–202; National Adoption Network, 202
National Adoption Information Clearinghouse, **201–202**; consent, 83; developmental disabilities, 96; disabilities of adoptive parents, 98; foster parent adoption, 131
National Adoption Network, **202**; National Adoption Center, 201
National Adoption Week, **202–203**; "calling out," 77; recruitment, 241
National Association of Black Social Workers (NABSW), xxviii; agencies, 38; black adoptive parent recruitment programs, 69; black families, 70; ethical issues, 116; transracial adoption, 298
National Association of Homes for Children (NAHC): Council on Accreditation of Services for Families and Children Inc., 88; group homes, 142
National Asssociation of Social Workers Inc. (NASW), **203**
National Center on Child Abuse and Neglect: abandonment, 1; sexual abuse, 258
National Coalition to End Racism in America's Child Care System Inc., **203–204**; special needs, 268
National Cocaine Hotline, 109
National Committee for Adoption (NCFA), xxx, **204–205**; Adoption Defense Fund, 21; Adoption Hall of Fame, 22; background information, 52; bioethics, 53; black families, 70; costs to adopt, 85; Council on Accreditation of Services for Families and Children Inc., 88; education of adoptive parents, 112; ethical issues, 115; history of adoption,

xxx; income tax deductions, 153; maternity homes, 189; mutual consent registries, 199; National Adoption Week, 203; pregnancy counseling, 233; sealed records, 252; statistics, 270–271; transracial adoption, 297
National Committee for Prevention of Child Abuse: abuse, 5
National Conference of Commissioners on Uniform State Laws (NCCUSL), 199
National Enquirer (newspaper), 77
National Foster Parent Association Inc., 128, 130
National Institute on Drug Abuse Drug Information Service, 109
National Organ Transplant Act (1984), 54
National Photo Listing of Children Waiting for Adoptive Parents—See CAP Book
Natural mother, 293–294
natural parents, **205**
Nebraska: adoption agencies, 341; adoptive parent groups, 351; Interstate Compact on Adoption and Medical Assistance (ICAMA), 178; mutual consent registries, 199; open records, 218; search and consent laws, 255; social services office, 332
Necessary Risk: A Study of Adoptions and Disrupted Adoptive Placements (Trudy Festinger), 99
Neglect: protective services, 235–236
neglect, **205–206**; abandonment, 1–2; abuse, 6–7
Nevada: adoption agencies, 341; Interstate Compact on Adoption and Medical Assistance (ICAMA), 178; mutual consent registries, 199; open records, 218; prostitution, 235; search and consent laws, 255; social services office, 332; surrogate motherhood, 275
New Hampshire: adoption agencies, 341; adoptive parent groups, 351; gay and lesbian adoption, 131; insurance, 166; Interstate Compact on Adoption and Medical Assistance (ICAMA), 178; mutual consent registries, 199; open records, 218; search and consent laws, 255; social services office, 332
New Jersey: adoption agencies, 341; adoptive parent groups, 351; foster parent adoption, 131; genetic data, 135; homeless children, 144; open records, 218; parental leave, 225–226; search and consent laws, 255; social services office, 332; termination of parental rights, 288
New Mexico: adoption agencies, 341; adoptive parent groups, 352; employment benefits, 113; insurance, 166; Interstate Compact on Adoption and Medical Assistance (ICAMA), 178; social services office, 332
Newsletters: list, 359–360
Newspapers: list, 355–358
New York City: history of adoption, xxii–xxiii; Orphan Train, 222
New York Foundling Hospital, xxv
New York Society for the Prevention of Cruelty to Animals, xxii
New York Society for the Prevention of Cruelty to Children, xxii

Index

New York State: adoption agencies, 341–342; adoptive parent groups, 352; almshouses, 44; consent, 83; genetic data, 135; independent adoption, 154; inheritance, 165; Interstate Compact on the Placement of Children, 179; mutual consent registries, 199; open records, 218; photolistings, 228; search and consent laws, 255; social services office, 332
Nicholson, Jack, 141
Nicola, Ray, 7
Nissen, Phyllis, 270
Noble, Ernest P., 42
Nonidentifying information: confidentiality, 82
nonidentifying information, **206**
No Place to Call Home: Discarded Children in America (Congressional report), 144
North American Council on Adoptable Children (NACAC), **206–207**; Adoption Assistance and Child Welfare Act of 1980, 18–19; education of adoptive parents, 112; National Adoption Week, 202
North Carolina: adoption agencies, 342; adoptive parent groups, 352; social services office, 332
North Dakota: adoption agencies, 342; adoptive parent groups, 352; designated adoption, 95; independent adoption, 153; mutual consent registries, 199; notice, 207; open records, 218; search and consent laws, 255; social services office, 333; state laws, 183
Norvell, Melissa, 238
Notice: revocation, 251
notice, **207**
Nursing Your Adopted Baby (Kathryn Anderson), 76
Nurturing Network, 63, 190
Nussbaum, Hedda, 9–10

O

Oberstar, James, 82
obesity, **207**
Octavian, xvii
Ohio: adoption agencies, 342; Adoption Assistance and Child Welfare Act of 1980, 19; adoptive parent groups, 352; gay and lesbian adoption, 131; genetic data, 135; history of adoption, xxiii; independent adoption, 154; mutual consent registries, 199; notice, 207; open records, 218; search and consent laws, 255; social services office, 333; termination of parental rights, 287
Oklahoma: adoption agencies, 342; adoptive parent groups, 352; inheritance, 164; Interstate Compact on Adoption and Medical Assistance (ICAMA), 178; social services office, 333; termination of parental rights, 287
Older child: academic progress, 10; adjustment, 12–13; background information, 52; life book, 185; naming, 200–201; special needs, 267–268; terminology, 294
older child, **207–209**
O'Neal-Williams, Patricia, 68–69, 209

One Church, One Child, **209**; black adoptive parent recruitment programs, 68–69
only child adoptive families, **209–210**
Open adoption: adult adopted persons, 30; agencies, 36; background information, 52; Concerned United Birthparents Inc., 81; confidentiality, 82; cooperative adoption, 83; co-parenting, 84; designated adoption, 95; entitlement, 114–115; ethical issues, 116–117; history of adoption, xxxi; homeless children, 144; hospitals' treatment of birthmother, 151; matching, 188; naming, 200; "openness," 217; open records, 219; relative adoptions, 242; research, 245; resume, 248; traditional adoption, 297
open adoption, **210–216**
Open Door Societies, 112, **216–217**
"Openness," 217
Open records: Adoptees' Liberty Movement Association (ALMA), 17; ethical issues, 117; mutual consent registries, 199; pathology and adoptive status, 228; search, 252; search groups, 256; support groups, 274
open records, **217–221**
Optional adopters, 122, 170
Oregon: adoption agencies, 342; adoptive parent groups, 352; gay and lesbian adoption, 132; genetic data, 135; mutual consent registries, 199; open records, 218; parental leave, 225; search and consent laws, 255; social services office, 333
Organizations: bioethics, 54; black adoptive parent recruitment programs, 69; bonding and attachment, 75; list, 346–348
Orkow, Bonnie, 7
orphan, 221
Orphanage: drug abuse, 107
orphanage, **221–222**
"Orphans of the living," 222
Orphan Train, **222–224**; history of adoption, xxiv–xxv; religion, 243
Orphan Train Heritage Society of America Inc. (OTHSA), xxv, 224
Orphan Voyage, 256
other studies, **237–240**
OURS, **224**; Adoptive Families of America Inc., 22
outdoor relief, xxii
Outreach: advertising and promotion, 35
outreach, 224

P

Pan American Indian Association (PAIA), 159
Panichi, Marilyn, 303–304
Pannor, Reuben, 214–215, 220, 276
parens patriae, **224–225**; history of adoption, xx
Parental leave: adoptive parents, 27; employment benefits, 113
parental leave, **225–226**
Parental rights: children's rights, 79; consent, 82–83
parental rights, **226–227**
Parent-Child Relations: An Introduction to Parenting (Jerry S. Bigner), 8
ParentFinders, 253

Parenting Your Adopted Child (Stephanie Siegel), 55, 140, 163
Parents, Pregnant Teens and the Adoption Option (Jeanne Warren Lindsay), 60
Parent's Guide to Intercountry Adoption (Betty Laning and Mary Taylor), 172
Partridge, Susan, 99
paterfamilias, xviii
pathology and adoptive status, **227–228**
Paton, Jean, 256
Patt, Emily C., 132
Patti, Patricia, 56
Pelton, Leroy H., 59–60, 61
Pendarvis, Leah Vorhes, 148
Pennsylvania: adoption agencies, 343; adoptive parent groups, 352; interstate adoption, 177–178; mutual consent registries, 199; open records, 218; parental leave, 225; religion, 188; search and consent laws, 255; social services office, 333; transracial adoption, 298
Periodicals: list, 355–358
Permanency planning: foster care, 127; "orphans of the living," 222; parental rights, 227
permanency planning, **228**
Peterson, Karen S., 288
Phips, William, xxi
Photolistings: CAP Book, 77; support groups, 274
photolistings, **228–229**
Physical neglect, 205
Physicians: intermediary, 168
physicians, **229–230**
Pirog-Good, Maureen, 284–285
placement, **230**
placement outcome, **231**
Podell, Richard, 142
Poor Law (England, 1601), xix
Positive Adoption Attitudes in Media (PAAM), 192
Positive reinforcement, 11
post-legal adoptive services, **231**
Post-Legal Adoptive Services Today (Mary Jane Fales), 231
Poston, Dudley L, Jr., 25
postplacement services, **231**
poverty, **231**
Powell, Azizi, 301
Prater, Gwendolyn, 70
preadoptive counseling, **231–232**
pregnancy after adoption, **232**
Pregnancy counseling: crisis pregnancy, 91
pregnancy counseling, **232–234**
Pregnancy Discrimination Act (1978), 189–190
Pregnancy Freedom of Choice Act (California), 189
prenatal care, **234**
"Prenatal Prediction of Child Abuse and Neglect: A Prospective Study" (Murphy, Orkow and Nicola), 7–8
preparing a child for adoption, **234–235**
preplacement visits, 235
Price, Susan, 95
Primogeniture, xix, xxi
Print media, 192
Pro-life advocates, 3–4, 54
prostitution, 235
protective services, **235–236**
Provisions for Accreditation, 87

380 Index

Psychiatric problems of adopted persons: adult adopted persons, 30–33; genetic predispositions, 137
psychiatric problems of adopted persons, **236–237**
Psychological parent: foster parent adoption, 131; Model State Adoption Act, 199
psychological parent, **240**
public assistance, **240**
Putative father, **240**; consent, 82
Putative father registries, 57

Q

Quillon v. Walcott, 57
Quincy, Josiah, xxiii

R

Race: adolescent adopted persons, 15–16; adoptive parents, 24; agencies, 37, 38; birthmother, 62; teenage parents, 283
race, **240–241**; abuse, 5; history of adoption, xxviii
Raffloer, Susan Marie, 30
rainbow families, **241**
Ramsay, Douglas, 73
rape, **241**
Rauch, Julia B., 52, 135
Raynor, Lois, 27–28, 32–33
"Real parents," **241**
"Recruiting and Preparing Adoptive Families for Black Children with Developmental Disabilities" (Gary T. Morgan and Drenda Lakin), 69
recruitment, **241–242**
Refugee Relief Act (1953), 169
Register, Cheri, 200
Reid, Barbara Moulden, 27, 269
Relative adoptions: grandparent adoptions, 141; open adoption, 216
relative adoptions, **242**
Religion: agencies, 35–36; matching, 187–188
religion, **242–244**; history of adoption, xxv
relinquishment, **244**
Report on Foreign Adoption, 68
Reproductive technologies: bioethics, 53–54; ethical issues, 115; eugenics, 118; infertility, 162; pregnancy after adoption, 232; surrogate motherhood, 275; zygote adoption, 308
reproductive technologies, **244–245**
research, **245**
Residential treatment centers: foster care, 126
residential treatment centers, **245–247**
Resnick, Michael D., 62–63, 64, 233, 283–284
RESOLVE Inc., **247–248**; ethical issues, 115; fertility rates, 123
Resume: agencies, 36; biographical information, 55
resume, **248–249**
Reunification: foster care, 128; termination of parental rights, 289
reunification, **249–250**
Reunion: terminology, 294
reunion, **250–251**
Reunion registry, 17

revocation, **251**
Rhode Island: adoption agencies, 343; adoptive parent groups, 352; inheritance, 164; Interstate Compact on Adoption and Medical Assistance (ICAMA), 178; parental leave, 225; religion, 188; social services office, 333
Rickarby, G.A., 15
Rights of Foster Parents, The, 130
Rike, Nancy, 52, 135
Rillera, Mary Jo, 83
Ritalin, 97
Rodriguez, Carolyne B., 103
Roe v. Wade: abortion, 2–4; bioethics, 54; history of adoption, xxix; infant adoption, 160–161
Roher, Daniela Rodda, 277
Roman Catholic church, 54—*See also* Catholics
Romans, ancient, xvii–xix
Rosenzweig-Smith, Janet, 250–251
Ross, Marlene, 111
Rubin, Lenore, 144
Russell, Cheryl, 123
Russell, William, xxi
Rutter, Michael, 71
Ryan, Jon, 56

S

Sachdev, Paul, 220–221, 251
Sandmaier, Marian, 258, 259, 295
Sapp, Susan, 57
Sau Fong-Siu, xxviii
Scarr, Sandra, 28, 167
Schaffer, Judith, 55, 108, 140, 163, 296
Schecter, Marshall, 30, 236–237
Schiffman, S., 137
Schilling, Karen Maitland, 31, 121–122, 254
Schmid, Kathleen, 8
Schneider, Heidi A., 219–220
Schreiber, Larry, 165
Schroeder, Patricia, 189
Schweiker, Richard S., 198
Seaburn, Brett A., 86–87
Seader, Mary Beth, 233–234
Sealed records: confidentiality, 81; ethical issues, 117; finalization, 125; naming, 200
sealed records, **252**
Search: Concerned United Birthparents Inc., 81; mutual consent registries, 199; open adoption, 211; support groups, 274
search, **252–255**
search and consent laws, **255–256**
Search groups: search, 252
search groups, **256**
Seidman, Matthew Sanford, 103
Self-esteem: sexual abuse, 258
self-esteem, **256–257**
Sexton, Patricia, 176
Sexual abuse: abuse, 6; teenage parents, 283
sexual abuse, **258–259**
Sexual identity: adolescent adopted persons, 13–14
Shaw, M., 129–130
Sherwen, Laurie, 71
Shireman, Joan F., 300
Shover, David, 87
Siblings: special needs, 267

siblings, **259–263**
Siegel, Stephanie, 55; grandparent, 140; infertility, 163; self-esteem, 257
Silber, Kathleen, 212–213
Silverstein, Deborah N., 15
Simon, Rita, 70, 300–301
simple adoption, **263**
Singer, Leslie M., 73, 119
single adoptive parents, **263–264**
Single Parents Adopting Children Everywhere (SPACE), **264–265**
Sisters of Charity of St. Vincent de Paul, xxv
Skeel, Harold, 167
Skin color: international adoption, 170
skin color, **265**
Skodak, Marie, 167
Sliding scale fees: costs to adopt, 85; ethical issues, 116; socioeconomic status, 266
sliding scale fees, **265**
Sloan, Irving J., 29
Smith, David, 124
Smith, Dorothy, 71
Smith, Eve Pearlman, 208
Smith, Jerome, 114, 121, 149, 220, 233
Sobczak, Judy, 14, 30–31
Sobol, Michael P., 253
Social services offices (list): Canada, 334–335; United States, 330–334
Social workers: acting out, 11; birthmother, 66; confidentiality, 81; disruption, 101; education of adoptive parents, 111; foster care, 128; home study, 146–147; hospitals' treatment of birthmother, 148–149; independent adoption, 155; infertility, 163; National Association of Social Workers Inc. (NASW), 203; open adoption, 215; preparing a child for adoption, 234; sexual abuse, 258
social workers, **265–266**; abuse, 5–7
Socioeconomic status: adoptive parents, 25; birthmother, 63–64; criminal behavior in adopted adults, 89; delinquency, 93–94; intelligence, 166–167; matching, 188; psychiatric problems of adopted persons, 238; teenage parents, 283
socioeconomic status, **266**
Sokoloff, Burton, 128
Sorensen, T.I.A., 28
Soule, Peggy, 77
South Carolina: adoption agencies, 343; adoptive parent groups, 352; genetic data, 135; Interstate Compact on Adoption and Medical Assistance (ICAMA), 178; mutual consent registries, 199; open records, 218; search and consent laws, 255; social services office, 333
South Dakota: adoption agencies, 343; adoptive parent groups, 352; Interstate Compact on Adoption and Medical Assistance (ICAMA), 178; mutual consent registries, 199; open records, 218; search and consent laws, 255; social services office, 333
Special needs: adjustment, 12; Adoption Assistance and Child Welfare Act of 1980, 18, 19; Adoption Assistance Program, 19–21; advertising and promotion, 33; agencies, 36–38; attorneys,

49–50; black families, 69–70; "Calling out," 77; case records, 78; computers, 81; costs to adopt, 85; developmental disabilities, 96; discipline, 98; education of adoptive parents, 111; federal government, 122; fertile adoptive parents, 122; forever family, 125; foundations, 131; Gladney Center, 110; hard to place children, 143; high risk placements, 143; home study, 145–146; identity, 152; income tax deductions, 153; infertility, 163; insurance, 166; interstate adoption, 178; large families, 182; medical problems of adopted children, 195–196; Model State Adoption Act, 198–199; National Adoption Center, 201; National Adoption Network, 202; National Adoption Week, 202; National Committee for Adoption, 204; North American Council on Adoptable Children, 206; older child, 207–208; "orphans of the living," 222; post-legal adoptive services, 231; prostitution, 235; psychiatric problems of adopted persons, 236; recruitment, 241; single adoptive parents, 264; social workers, 265; state by state adoption rates (table), 320–321; support groups, 274; termination of parental rights, 289; therapy and therapists, 294; transracial adoption, 297; waiting children, 304

special needs, **266–270**

"Special Sexual Problems of the Adopted Adolescent" (William Easson), 13–14

Spedlin, Phylis, 212–213

Spencer, Marietta, 227, 231

Spina bifida, 96

Stack, Susan A., 88

Stanley v. Illinois, xxxi, 57

Stars of David, **270**

State by state adoption rates (tables), 315–329

state social services department, **270**

statistics, **270–271**

Stein, Leslie, 13, 152, 262

Steinberg, Joel, 9–10

Steinberg, Lisa, 9

Steir, Mary, 73

Stepparents: grandparent rights, 141; inheritance, 164–165; relative adoptions, 242

stepparents, **272**

Stern, Elizabeth, 276

Stern, William, 276

Stilwell, Barbara, 121

Stone, Cathy Yvonne, 164

Subsidies: costs to adopt, 85; disruption, 101; socioeconomic status, 266

success rates, **273**

Sullivan, Mary E., 155

Support groups: adjustment, 13; auxiliaries, 50

support groups, **273–275**

Supreme Court, U.S., 57–59

surrender, **275**

Surrogate motherhood: bioethics, 53; ethical issues, 115

surrogate motherhood, **275–278**

Sweden, xviii

Syria, xvii

T

Targeted adoption: advertising and promotion, 35; designated adoption, 94; religion, 243

Tatara, Toshio, 126

Tax code, 130

Taylor, Linda, 196–197

Taylor, Mary, 172

Teachers and adopted children: academic progress, 11

teachers and adopted children, **278–280**

Teasdale, T.W., 28

Teenage parents: birthmother, 61

teenage parents, **280–286**

Teenagers: special needs, 267–268

Television, 191

Telling, 294

Tennessee: adoption agencies, 343; adoptive parent groups, 353; foster parent adoption, 131; mutual consent registries, 199; open records, 218; parental leave, 225; search and consent laws, 255; social services office, 333

Termination of parental rights: chart, 291; consent, 83; Model State Adoption Act, 198–199; relinquishment, 244; surrender, 275; terminology, 294

termination of parental rights, **286–290**; abandonment, 1

Terminology: attitudes about adoption, 48; explaining adoption, 119–120

terminology, **290**, **292–294**

Temay, Marilyn R., 100, 197–198

Texas: adoption agencies, 343–344; adoptive parent groups, 353; genetic data, 135; inheritance, 164; mutual consent registries, 199; open records, 218; search and consent laws, 255; social services office, 333

Therapy and therapists: disruption, 101–102; psychiatric problems of adopted persons, 239

therapy and therapists, **294–296**

Thomas, R. David, 114

Tourse, Phyllis, 40

Traditional adoption: ethical issues, 117

traditional adoption, **296–297**

Transracial adoption: black adoptive parent recruitment programs, 69; black families, 70; ethical issues, 115–116; explaining adoption, 120; Indian Child Welfare Act of 1978, 158–159; intelligence, 167; international adoption, 170; Korean adopted children, 181; National Coalition to End Racism in America's Child Care System Inc., 203; self-esteem, 257; special needs, 268

transracial adoption, **297–302**

Transracial and Inracial Adoptees: The Adolescent Years (Ruth G. McCoy and Louis Zurcher), 15–16

Triadoption Library Inc., 256

Trickett, Penelope K., 8

Triseliotis, J., 253

Tunisia, xvii

Twelve Tables, Laws of the, xviii

Twins, 261

U

Unadoptable: hard to place children, 143

unadoptable, **302–303**

Unwed mothers: abandonment, 1

unwed parents, **303**

updated home study, **303**

Up with Down Syndrome Foundation, 104

Utah: adoption agencies, 344; adoptive parent groups, 353; Interstate Compact on Adoption and Medical Assistance (ICAMA), 178; mutual consent registries, 199; open records, 218; search and consent laws, 255; social services office, 333

Utian, Wolf, 276

V

Valentine, Deborah, 162

Vanderbilt, Gloria, 216

Van Keppel, Margaret, 254–255

Vermont: adoption agencies, 344; adoptive parent groups, 353; inheritance, 164; mutual consent registries, 199; open records, 218; parental leave, 225; search and consent laws, 255; social services office, 333–334

Videotape: bonding and attachment, 71; photolistings, 228; support groups, 274

videotape, **303–304**

Vilardi, Emma May, 176

Virginia: adoption agencies, 344; adoptive parent groups, 353; history of adoption, xxi; social services office, 334

W

Waite, Linda J., 280–281

Waiting children: advertising and promotion, 33–34; black families, 69–70; "Calling out," 77; computers, 81; ethical issues, 116; fertile adoptive parents, 122; foster care, 129; National Adoption Center, 201; National Adoption Week, 202; North American Council on Adoptable Children, 206; support groups, 274; transracial adoption, 299

waiting children, **304**

Waiting lists: home study, 145, 148

waiting lists, **304**

Waiting period: agencies, 37

waiting period, **304–305**

Waldmann, Christopher, 74–75

Waner, Janet Susan, 251

Ward, Margaret, 28, 198, 260, 261

Washington: adoption agencies, 344; adoptive parent groups, 353; parental leave, 225; social services office, 334

Waters, Everett, 73

Watson, Kenneth, 212

Webber, Patricia L., 28

Webster v. Reproductive Services: abortion, 3

Wednesday's Child, **305**

Weinberg, Richard A., 28, 167

Weinstein, Eugene A., 155

Weiss, Andrea, 238

welfare, **305**

West Virginia: adoptive parent groups, 353; Interstate Compact on Adoption and Medical Assistance (ICAMA), 178; mutual consent registries, 199; notice,

207; open records, 218; search and consent laws, 255; social services office, 334
When Love Is Not Enough (Marian Sandmaier), 258, 295
Whitehead, Mary Beth, 53, 276
White House Task Force on Adoption, 305–306; gay and lesbian adoption, 131
Wilborn, Bobbie, 100, 197–198
Williams, Hank, 164
Williamson, Nancy, 133–134
Wilson, Mary Ellen, xxii
Winkler, Robin C., 254–255
Wisconsin: adoption agencies, 344; adoptive parent groups, 353; almshouses, 44; disabilities of adoptive parents, 98; genetic data, 135; Interstate Compact on Adoption and Medical Assistance (ICAMA), 178; mutual consent registries, 199; open records, 218; parental leave, 225; search and consent laws, 255; social services office, 334
Witmer, Helen L., 155
Wittig, Michele A., 28
Working mothers: adoptive parents, 27
working mothers, **306**
Wright, James, 144
Wrongful adoption: attorneys, 50; ethical issues, 117; genetic data, 135
wrongful adoption, **306–307**; abuse, 7
Wyoming: inheritance, 164; social services office, 334

Y

Yarrow, Leon J., 73
Yates, Douglas, xxiii
You're Our Child (Jerome Smith and Franklin Miroff), 114, 121, 220, 233
youths, **307**

Z

Zero population growth: fertile adoptive parents, 122
zero population growth, **307–308**
Zuravin, Susan J., 9
Zurcher Jr., Louis A., 15–16, 278
zygote adoption, **308**